From Idea
to Essay

SEVENTH EDITION

From Idea to Essay

◆

A RHETORIC, READER, AND HANDBOOK

Jo Ray McCuen
GLENDALE COMMUNITY COLLEGE

Anthony C. Winkler

ALLYN AND BACON

BOSTON   LONDON   TORONTO   SYDNEY   TOKYO   SINGAPORE

Editor: Eben Ludlow
Development Editor: Nancy Perry and Marlane Miriello
Production Supervisor: Jane O'Neill
Production Manager: Nick Sklitsis
Text and Cover Designer: Levavi & Levavi, Inc.
Art Director: Pat Smythe
Photo Researcher: Chris Migdol

Acknowledgments appear on pages 669–671, which constitute a continuation of the copyright page.

Library of Congress Cataloging-in-Publication Data

McCuen, Jo Ray, 1929–
    From idea to essay : a rhetoric, reader, and handbook / Jo Ray
  McCuen, Anthony C. Winkler. — 7th ed.
      p.   cm.
    Includes index.
    ISBN 0-02-379001-6
    1. English language—Rhetoric.   2. English language—Grammar—
  Handbooks, manuals, etc.   3. College readers.   4. Essays.
  I. Winkler, Anthony C.   II. Title.
  PE1408.394   1995
  808′.0427—dc20   94-25690
                            CIP

Printed in the United States of America
10 9 8 7 6 5 4 3 2   99 98 97 96

Preface

From Idea to Essay, seventh edition, is a systematic composition text/anthology that carefully leads the student through the complex process of essay writing. It is a book that virtually teaches by itself. Indeed, all chapters that teach writing follow exactly the same pedagogy and share the identical structure outlined below:

A. Reading for Ideas
   Story
   Poem

B. How to write (a narration, a description, etc.)
   Writing assignment
   Specific instructions
   Professional model
   Student model
   Alternate readings

C. Additional writing assignments

The short story or poem anthologized under the "Reading for Ideas" section introduces a literary theme that triggers a specific writing assignment. For example, in Unit 7, "Narration," the short story is "The Code" by Richard T. Gill, in which the writer narrates a poignant episode with his father that taught him a rueful lesson. This is followed by the poem "Richard Cory" about an inexplicable suicide. The writing assignment for this chapter, suggested by both the story and the poem, is "Narrate an incident or experience that taught you a lesson about life."

The "Specific Instructions" section in Unit 7 then gives students practical advice about how to prewrite on the assignment and how to do the actual writing. This advice is followed by two professional models: "It's Over, Debbie," in which an anonymous writer narrates a fateful (and troubling) decision made one sleepless night; and "Preserving the Species," in which a student recounts an experience that decided her on a career. The chapter ends with three alternate readings, several writing assignments as well as a photo writing assignment, in which students are asked to comment on the narrative theme of a photograph.

Within this structure, students are stimulated to write, instructed on how to proceed, and given realistic professional and amateur models with which they can gauge the success of their own efforts.

NEW TO THIS EDITION

- The most dramatic change in this edition is the increase in the number of readings. Previous editions featured two alternate readings after each chapter on writing. In this edition, that number has been increased to three, giving users a greater choice of rhetorical models. *From Idea To Essay,* seventh edition, now contains 36 essays, 9 stories, 9 poems, and 10 student essays, a range of material surely wide enough to offer something for everyone.

- This book continues to be divided into four parts: Part I, Fundamentals; Part II, Writing the Essay; Part III, The Research Paper; and Part IV, Revising the Essay, A Brief Handbook. We have restructured Part I, following suggestions made by longtime users. Many suggested that we move the previous editions' Unit 5, "Sentence Combining, Generating, and Judging" before the unit on the paragraph. "Sentence Combining, Generating, and Judging" is therefore now Unit 3. Unit 5 is now "Planning and Organizing the Essay," formerly Unit 3 in previous editions. To the unit on "Sentence Combining" we have also added additional exercises. In every unit on writing we still provide prewriting suggestions on how to do the writing assignment as well as ideas on how students may prewrite their way out of any beginning doldrums.

- To Unit 2 we have contributed additional material on the effects of audience on the writing process. Specifically, we now discuss the role of the instructor as the primary audience for classroom writing.

- To Unit 4, "The Paragraph," we have added a section on "Transitions Between Paragraphs," in which we discuss at length how a writer may gracefully move an idea between two paragraphs without breaking the train of thought. We have also added material on implied topic sentences to reflect more realistically the practice of paragraph writing today.

- To Unit 5 on "Planning and Organizing the Essay" we have added a discussion of so-called "Writer's Block," suggesting reasons for this condition and steps a writer can take to overcome it.

- In the new Unit 6, "Drafting, Revising, and Style," we walk students through three drafts of an actual student paper, showing the major and minor revisions a writer will typically make before submitting a final paper. The drafts are annotated in the margins explaining the changes the student made and the reasons for making them. Exercises at the end of the unit give students first drafts of papers to revise on their own and to practice what the chapter teaches.

- Twenty-one selections are new to this edition. All changes in the selections were made in response to classroom experience or to suggestions received from users.

- We have added material to the unit on "The Research Paper" explaining how to use the databases that have lately cropped up in libraries everywhere. We give students examples of the kinds of searches they can make on these systems to find material for use in their own papers.

- Annotated student essays still appear in every unit. These annotations are practical applications of the writing instruction found within the unit.

- The writing assignments have been revised to reflect the new emphasis in the text on the importance of audience and purpose in writing.

- This new edition still features "Photo Writing Assignments." This novel assignment will give students practice in the useful skill of writing about what they see, rather than only about what they have read.

- A comprehensive Instructor's Manual accompanies the text, offering advice and guidance for the instructor. The manual also contains sample syllabi, additional exercises, and comprehension quizzes that can be conveniently photocopied and used to ensure that students have read and understood the assigned readings and the answers to the questions found within the text.

Our thanks to our editor Eben Ludlow; development editors Nancy Perry and Marlane Miriello; the production supervisor, Jane O'Neill; and the art director, Pat Smythe. We would also like to thank the following reviewers of the seventh edition: Sandra A. Engel, Mohawk Valley Community College; Moselle Ford, Amarillo College; Elaine Hage, Forsyth Technical Community College; Kevin Hardy, Southeastern Louisiana University; Beverly Huttinger, Broward Community College; M. Jean Jones, Columbia State Community College; Helen W. Meadows, Danville Community College; and Ong Wooi-Chin, Long Beach Community College.

Anthony C. Winkler and Jo Ray McCuen

Contents

Unit 5:   Planning and Organizing the Essay   74

Unit 6:   Drafting, Revising, and Style   96

PART II: WRITING THE ESSAY 119

Unit 15: Argumentation   414

PART III: THE ESSAY EXAMINATION 461

Unit 16: Preparing for the Essay Examination   463

PART IV: THE RESEARCH PAPER   475

PART V: ENGLISH USAGE   567

From Idea to Essay

Fundamentals

The Writing Process

If you think that to write well you must be naturally gifted and numbered among a rare and blessed few, we will begin our book by telling you straightaway that you are wrong. Writing is typically hard work, even for the gifted. It usually involves toil and drudgery. Sometimes a writer is swept away by a torrent of sentences, but usually even finding the right word is a grind.

Writing, in fact, offers equal-opportunity harassment to all who regularly practice it. But the good news is that we do know something about how writers work, about what techniques are likely to give the best results, and about what you can do to write better. Even better is the news that if you apply yourself you can learn to write clear, readable prose.

We also know that writing is a process—a series of steps taken over time and directed toward the particular end of expressing on paper what the writer feels or thinks about a subject. And we know the steps in the process that give the best results. These are what this book will attempt to teach. You can learn them, and if you do, your writing will get better.

Yet students typically begin a course such as this one with serious misconceptions about the writing process, leading them to badly underrate their own talents. For example, when you get stuck on an assignment, you would be sorrily mistaken to interpret this as grim evidence that you cannot write. Getting stuck happens occasionally to all writers—from Shakespeare to Stephen King—and is a predictable part of the writing process.

Equally predictable is for the writing process to occur in three identifiable stages: prewriting, writing, and rewriting. These stages often overlap and even run together, but for the sake of discussion we will treat each as separate and distinct.

PREWRITING

The essay subject you have been assigned is second nature, and you already know everything under the sun about it. All you have to do is sit down, fingers floating above the keyboard, and the final copy will sparkle. Where are you? The answer is: in heaven.

On earth, however, you are likely to be assigned an essay on a subject you neither know nor care about. You won't know what to say, which side to take, or how you feel about it. This is exactly the moment for prewriting.

Prewriting refers to the preliminary steps writers take to acquaint themselves with their subjects before they begin to write. They read, interview experts, jot down main points, or simply think about the subject—before writing even a single word on it. During this stage you are groping toward a mastery of facts about the subject and also trying to decide which side you are on. If the assignment is on capital punishment, are you for or against it? If you are for it, why are you for it? If against, why? Do you think capital punishment is a deterrent, or are you repelled by the vengeful tit-for-tat ethic of its supporters?

Knowing the answers to these questions is important because most of us lie badly, whether with the tongue or the pen. We typically express ourselves better if we say or write what we truly believe. Prewriting gives us the chance not only to learn about the topic, but also to form personal opinions on it. These opinions, if honestly formed, are simply easier to express on paper than sham positions adopted to score a point. Writers who lament "I don't know what to say!" are really saying, "I don't know what I believe." Prewriting will help you find the stand or belief you need to write a worthwhile essay.

In Unit 5, "Planning and Organizing the Essay," we cover some specific tips to help your prewriting.

WRITING

Many students mistakenly think that they are bad writers because they write haltingly, with many stops and starts. But that is exactly how most writers work. They start, stop, pause, lunge forward another paragraph or two, halt, and retrace their steps before staggering ahead. They scratch out sentences, discard paragraphs, crumple up pages, and scribble in words.

We have testimony from many renowned writers to this effect, as well as evidence from numerous surviving manuscripts. We have the novelist Somerset Maugham's admission that he achieved an effect of ease in his writing style only "by strenuous effort." We have the Irish writer Oscar Wilde's remark made only half in jest that he spent the morning putting in a comma and the afternoon taking it out. Only the rare writer ever churns out publishable copy at first try. For ourselves, we never do.

The act of writing seldom proceeds in a straight line from start to effortless finish. A great deal of thinking and rethinking, of writing and rewriting, is involved in the process. If you find yourself similarly circling when you write rather than proceeding in a straight line, you are working very much like a professional writer.

REWRITING

In rewriting, the second stage of the writing process, the writer rereads and reworks the material to make it better. Nearly all writers rewrite. Some rewrite as they write, rereading and rewriting the material continually. Others rewrite in a separate step during which they pore over a first draft and systematically try to improve it. Still others do both—rewriting as they write as well as making a separate and distinct pass at the material.

It is during rewriting that word processors have proven themselves priceless. Before word processors, rewriting meant the drudgery of retyping or the expense of a secretarial service. Changing a single sentence sometimes entailed retyping an entire page or blotting it with unsightly correction fluid. With word processors, however, perfectionists can rewrite endlessly on the video screen. Once the writer thinks the text is perfect, the word processor handles the drudgery of printing.

Whether or not you rewrite with a word processor, rewriting usually includes one or all of the steps outlined below.

Revising

To revise is to make major changes in the work, to discard pages, move paragraphs, recast sentences. Most of the major restructuring of your essay will occur at this stage. However, it is also possible, as writers of every stripe can attest, to find some major defect in the work on your final reading and to have to make substantial changes at the last minute. Such oversights do occur in the revising stage, but they are happily infrequent.

Editing

The idea behind editing is simple: No writer is perfect on the first pass. A word that seemed brilliant by moonlight will seem stale in sunlight. A metaphor will be caught shamelessly huffing and puffing. All these corrections are made with editing. You search the manuscript and your brain for a better word, a stronger sentence, a more vivid and appropriate phrase, usually making judgments of style rather than of substance. It is here that you are also likely to spot and correct errors of grammar, punctuation, and form. Your manuscript at this stage should be nearly completed; editing merely applies the finishing touches.

Proofreading

The unsubmitted manuscript is never done—that is the proofreader's motto. There are always gnat-like errors to catch: misspelled words, incorrect punctuation, imperfect alignment, as, for example, a badly indented paragraph. The manuscript is almost finished; with proofreading you give it a last searching look.

You may find yourself editing, proofreading, and even revising either simultaneously or in a jumbled order. You may discover a major blunder in the text as you proofread and have to backtrack to a massive revision. But what you should certainly find yourself doing is reading the work, and repeatedly. Veteran writers are habitual rereaders of their own writing. It is only by poring over the text constantly that you will spot lumps in its style and phrasing, fissures in its content. Reading the work aloud is also a useful exercise for flushing out stilted passages. If a sentence or paragraph sticks in your mouth as you try to read it, chances are it will also choke your reader.

To give you a realistic sense of the writing and rewriting process, we have included student essays in Part II showing actual changes made by the writers during various stages of revision, editing, and proofreading. Examine the changes the writers made along with their marginal justifications for making them. You will no doubt recognize some of the kinds of problems you have had to deal with in writing your own essays.

Begin this course and book, then, with no illusions about the writing process. Rid yourself of the discouraging myths about effortless writing that might lead you to undervalue your own talents. There may be a few effortless writers on this planet, but we have never met one. For most of us, writing requires focus, concentration, and effort. It also offers the satisfaction that comes from putting down on paper exactly what you want to say, and the pleasure of discovering what you think about a subject.

Assembling a Portfolio

Artists of all kinds—painters, musicians, dancers, actors—gradually accumulate and carry with them a portfolio of their own work as evidence of their talent. Because writing, too, is an art, some college instructors encourage their students to create a portfolio of writing done during the course.

Creating a portfolio means gathering samples of your best work in a folder, to be reviewed and judged later. The idea is to give you practice at evaluating your own writing according to certain criteria such as sticking to the thesis, supplying supportive details, cutting deadwood, being coherent, writing emphatic paragraphs, and proofreading the final copy.

Even if your particular instructor does not require a formal portfolio, we recommend that you create one for your own use over the term of this course. Choosing your best work for a portfolio will sharpen your critical faculties and give you an editor's eye.

The portfolio will also preserve samples of your college writing for scrutiny long after you have left school. To the student grappling with the task of mastering a composition class, the idea of preserving work produced during these trying days may seem ludicrous. Trust us on this point, however. Long after you have passed the course and puddled into middle age, the day will come when you will regard your student essays in a more kindly light and wish you had saved them.

Writing Assignments

1. What prewriting activities do you do before you actually begin to write an essay? In a brief essay, describe these activities and how they contribute to your efforts at writing. If you never prewrite, write a justification of your writing habits.

2. Research the methods of writing and composing practiced by any well-known writer and describe them. Explain how they differ from your own.

3. Write a letter to a classmate in which you describe your own stages of writing. Assume that the classmate has been absent and does not know that writing is a process.

Elements of the Essay

Essay is a term not quite 400 years old. From the French *essai,* meaning "attempt," the word was coined by the sixteenth-century French writer Montaigne to name the new literary form he had just invented. Nowadays the word is used to refer to a variety of nonfiction prose whose common purpose is usually to express a writer's viewpoint or opinion on a topic.

The elements of the essay are divisible into two major parts: the *material* elements—the words, sentences, and paragraphs arranged by a writer on paper— and the *abstract* elements—the purpose, audience, and strategy that must enter into the writer's calculations and writing and which we will cover in this unit.

PURPOSE

Every essay has a purpose. This assertion seems simple enough, but it bristles with complications. The down-to-earth student might object that the purpose of writing any essay in freshman English is to pass the course. That, of course, may be a long-range purpose, but it is worthless as a means of helping you write your essay. What a writer should get from a well-conceived purpose is a guide for choosing words, sentences, and details. Purpose, in this sense, is the intent the writer has for writing the essay and the effects he or she hopes it will achieve.

Here is an example. Your assignment is to write about a childhood memory. Hundreds of memories churn about in your brain—so many you have no idea where to begin. Because it is a rainy day and you feel gloomy, you decide on a grim purpose: to recount the most miserable day of your entire childhood. With that one decision, you have narrowed the possibilities: You can block out all recollections of childhood merriment and zoom in on details and adjectives that depict how miserable you felt on that one day of gloom. With this clear purpose in mind, you know exactly what *not* to say, if not what to say.

It is the same if you are writing an essay whose purpose is to expose the sham and greed of Christmas. You know that you should blast the materialism of the season, not applaud it, that you should frown on Santa's spendthrift ways, not praise them. On the other hand, if you decided to write about Christmas as the most joyful season of the year, then you know to dust off the sugarplum metaphors and warmhearted images. If the purpose of your essay is to explain how to sail, you can forget about rowing or motoring. If your purpose is to amuse, you can try to be funny, and if to inform, to be informative.

Writers are often warned to stick to the point and stay on the track. Purpose gives you a point to stick to and a track to stay on. Conversely, beginning without a clear purpose almost always results in an essay that seems pointless and aimless. Here, for example, is the opening paragraph of an essay whose writer began with no clear sense of purpose.

> Christmas is a tradition many people celebrate throughout the world. The word *Christmas* comes from an early English phrase *Cristes Maesse* meaning "Mass of Christ." Christmas day is one of many holidays. The word *holiday* comes from the Anglo-Saxon word *holig daeg* or "holy day." However, many people lose sight of the fact that Christmas is a holy day. People are too busy with the artificial part of Christmas to remember the birth of Jesus.

If you detect a certain pointlessness to this paragraph, as if the writer were groping for direction, you would be right. Nothing is wrong with its diction or syntax. But lacking a purpose, the writing packs no punch. When we asked the student about this particular paragraph, she admitted that she had plunged into writing it without thinking about what she wanted to say.

What am I trying to say? What effect do I hope to achieve? What main point do I want to make? Begin your essay by asking and answering these questions honestly. Knowing at the very outset what you are trying to do in the essay will narrow your choices of language and details and help you to achieve a working focus.

In Unit 5 we cover various prewriting techniques that can help you find the purpose of your essay.

AUDIENCE

Many writers work by simply trying to write their clearest prose, without regard for whom it is intended. But in the long run this is a shortsighted tack. It is always preferable to tailor the work to a specific audience, especially if you know something about the readers for whom it is intended.

Tailoring your work does not mean giving the audience what you think it wants. Rather, it means presenting your work in a style and form appropriate to its readers. Much of this depends on common sense and a sensitivity to an audience's needs that any writer can cultivate. Indeed, as readers most of us can easily peg the audience for which a particular work was written. For example, what kind of audience do you think the writer meant the following paragraph for?

Ordinary life experiences that apparently involve manifestations of psi (i.e., telepathy, clairvoyance, precognition, or psychokinesis) can be of great psychological intensity and meaning, sometimes to the point of producing an experience of insight and spiritual blessedness at one extreme, or suffering, fear of going crazy, and maladaptive behavior at the other extreme. Psychological help may occasionally be required. In the past and, unfortunately, still too often in the present, such help was often irrelevant or worsened the client's state.

The passage is taken from the *Journal of the American Society for Psychical Research* and aimed at an audience of professional parapsychologists—students and researchers of the paranormal. Some telltale signs are its complex syntax (the opening sentence is 52 words long) and technical vocabulary (the writer assumes that the reader already knows the meanings of *telepathy, clairvoyance, precognition,* and *psychokinesis*). We infer the readers of the writing by assumptions the writer, Charles T. Tart, has obviously made about them.

The reverse must happen when we write. Now we should start by asking, who are my readers? What do they know about my subject? What am I trying to say to them, and how can I best say it? If you are writing for readers in a particular discipline, you might have to learn the jargon, the preferred habits of expression, and the ethic of the written word practiced in that particular field. As a student writer who must write for many courses, you would therefore be smart to read journals and articles from any discipline for which you must write essays.

The Instructor as Audience

For whom does the student write? The answer is, of course, for the audience assigned by the instructor. But how can that be, when only the instructor reads and marks the papers? And what adjustments for audience can students be expected to make when they are always writing for the same instructor?

In fact, the instructor in the classroom realistically reflects the working conditions of professional writers. This book, for example, although written for an audience of students, must first be approved by the publisher's editor, who will rate it. If the editor approves, the authors are paid (passed!). If the editor disapproves, the authors are told to rewrite the manuscript (flunked!). The procedure is eerily akin to the evaluations that take place in the classroom.

A dual audience is similarly found throughout the world of business. For example, you might be asked to write a sales brochure aimed at an audience of vendors, but the sales manager will have the final say over your copy. If you write a newsletter for your club, your work must pass muster with the president. Yet the editorial scrutiny of the sales manager or president should not undo your attempts to reach your principal audience—whether vendors or club readers.

Nor should you ignore the instructor as you address your audience. The writers of this book, for example, have editors whose preferences they know well (never to be revealed in these pages) and try to meet. Similarly, if you know that your instructor rigidly enforces the rule against split infinitives, you should naturally avoid using them in your writing. Instead of writing "to legally organize," which sticks the adverb "legally" between "to" and "organize," you should write "to organize legally." Likewise, if you know your instructor prefers formal constructions over contractions, you should choose "he should not have gone" over "he *shouldn't* have gone." Every writer who wishes to please will respect a reader's known preferences in such trivial matters.

STRATEGY

In the beginning is the idea; in the end is the essay. Strategy is the specific rhetorical pattern you use to organize the idea into the essay. There are nine such basic rhetorical patterns that can be used to write an essay, ranging from narration, in which the essay is organized to tell a story, to argumentation, in which the essay is organized to debate a point. These strategies exist to help you write better, more clearly, with sharpened focus and heightened emphasis. They do not exist for their own sake. And as you mature as a writer and gain self-confidence, you will naturally find yourself getting better at adapting these abstract strategies to your needs.

Most writing assignments will leave the organization up to you, and usually you will be able to choose one of the strategies, depending on the purpose you conceive for the essay. But sometimes an assignment not only specifies a topic, but also requires the use of a particular rhetorical pattern. For example, an assignment that asks you to compare/contrast your father with your mother dictates the rhetorical pattern of comparison/contrast. Similarly, the assignment asking you to write an essay defining "academic freedom" mandates the particular strategy of definition.

Other assignments, however, will typically allow you to organize the essay in any pattern or strategy you judge most effective for your particular purpose. For example, consider this assignment: "Write an essay about a favorite relative." Here you are free to choose your strategy. You could decide to tell a story about your mad aunt, organizing your essay by the strategy of narration. Or you could compare and contrast an aunt with an uncle, using the rhetorical strategy of comparison/contrast. On the other hand, you may choose to write about why your Uncle Hank became the black sheep of the family, organizing your essay by the strategy of causal analysis. Given the choice, you should always opt for the strategy that is most appropriate to your overall purpose, focus, and main idea.

Strategies of organization provide structure for both individual paragraphs and entire essays. For now we will briefly define each strategy and illustrate its structure and techniques in a single paragraph example.

Narration

To *narrate* means to tell a story. A paragraph or essay developed by narration therefore tells a story, sometimes from the personal point of view and sometimes from the third-person point of view. Narrative writing convinces the reader by using specific details, by following a clear and understandable sequence, and by recounting the story in terms readers may have experienced in their own lives. Here is an example of a paragraph developed by narration:

> Every morning I lay on the floor in the front parlour watching her door. The blind was pulled down to within an inch of the sash so that I could not be seen. When she came out on the doorstep my heart leaped. I ran to the hall, seized my books and followed her. I kept her brown figure always in my eye and, when we came near the point at which our ways diverged, I quickened my pace and passed her. This happened morning after morning. I had never spoken to her, except for a few casual words, and yet her name was like a summons to all my foolish blood.
>
> James Joyce, *Araby*

The details are specific and the sequence fast-paced and clear. Furthermore, the event recounted—young unrequited love—is one with which most readers can identify. Unit 7 teaches how to develop an entire essay by narration.

Description

If narration means to tell, *description* means to show. A paragraph or essay developed by description uses a dominant impression as a central theme to unify its descriptive details. In the following passage, the dominant impression of Braggioni is of an expensively dressed, grossly fat man. We have italicized specific words that support this impression.

> Braggioni catches her glance solidly as if he had been waiting for it, leans forward, *balancing his paunch* between his spread knees, and sings with tremendous emphasis, weighing his words. He has, the song relates, no father and no mother, nor even a friend to console him; lonely as a wave of the sea he comes and goes, lonely as a wave. His *mouth opens round* and yearns sideways, his *balloon cheeks* grow oily with the labor of song. He *bulges* marvelously in his *expensive garments*. Over his *lavender collar, crushed upon a purple necktie, held by a diamond hoop:* over his ammunition belt of *tooled leather worked in silver, buckled cruelly* around his *gasping middle:* over the *tops of his glossy yellow shoes Braggioni swells* with *ominous ripeness,* his mauve silk hose *stretched taut,* his ankles bound with the stout leather thongs of his shoes.
>
> Katherine Anne Porter, *Flowering Judas*

Without a dominant impression, a passage of description runs the risk of becoming overwhelmed by irrelevant details. Unit 8 teaches the use of a dominant impression in writing a descriptive essay.

Example

A paragraph or essay developed by *example* begins with a generalization, which it then supports with specific cases. The examples must be to the point, vivid, supportive of the generalization, and clearly connected to it by an introductory phrase such as "for example" or "for instance." Here is an example:

> Temperaments are so various that there may be even more than "nine and sixty ways" of writing books. Rousseau, for example, could not compose with pen in hand: but then Chateaubriand could not compose without. Wordsworth did it while walking, riding, or in bed; but Southey, only at his desk. Shakespeare, we are told, never blotted a line; Scott could toss first drafts unread to the printer; Trollope drilled himself, watch on desk, to produce two hundred and fifty words every quarter of an hour; Hilaire Belloc, so Desmond MacCarthy once told me, claimed to have written twenty thousand of them in a day; and in ten days Balzac could turn out sixty thousand.
>
> F. L. Lucas, *Style*

The generalization occurs in the first sentence, which also introduces the main idea the paragraph intends to document. Following the generalization are examples of various methods of composing used by nine different authors. The overuse of generalizations without supporting examples is a common failing of student writing. Unit 9 takes up the use of examples as a strategy in the writing of essays.

Definition

A *definition* says what something is and what it is not. A paragraph or essay developed by definition therefore focuses on specifying the characteristics of the subject—first by showing the general category it belongs to and then by distinguishing it from other items in the same category. Here is an example:

> Chemistry is that branch of science which has the task of investigating the materials out of which the universe is made. It is not concerned with the forms into which they may be fashioned. Such objects as chairs, tables, vases, bottles, or wires are of no significance in chemistry; but such substances as glass, wool, iron, sulfur, and clay, as the materials out of which they are made, are what it studies. Chemistry is concerned not only with the composition of such substances, but also with their inner structure.
>
> John Arrend Timm, *General Chemistry*

The writer first places chemistry in the category of science and then differentiates it from other scientific disciplines by the nature and content of its study. This definition is short and to the point. Definitions of more abstract and complex terms such as *love* and *justice,* on the other hand, can consume several paragraphs or entire essays. Unit 10 teaches the development of an essay by definition.

Comparison/Contrast

Comparison/contrast paragraphs or essays examine items for similarities and differences. The items are compared on certain specific bases, and the writer alternates from one to the other, indicating either similarities or differences through the use of appropriate phrases such as *on the other hand, likewise, similarly,* and *but.* In the following example, terms indicating comparison/contrast are in italics:

> The way in which culture affects language becomes clear by *comparing* how the English and Hopi languages refer to H_2O in its liquid state. English, like most other European languages, has only one word—"water"—and it pays no attention to what the substance is used for or its quantity. The Hopi of Arizona, *on the other hand,* use "pahe" to mean the large amounts of water present in natural lakes or rivers, and "keyi" for the small amounts in domestic jugs and canteens. English, *though,* makes other distinctions that Hopi does not. The speaker of English is careful to distinguish between a lake and a stream, between a waterfall and a geyser; *but* "pahe" makes no distinction among lakes, ponds, rivers, streams, waterfalls, and springs.
>
> Peter Farb, *Man at the Mercy of His Language*

The basis of this comparison/contrast between English and Hopi—the way these languages refer to water—is given early in the paragraph. Having announced his intention to compare and the basis of the comparison, the writer then catalogs the similarities and differences between the English and Hopi languages on this one item.

Two common weaknesses in essays based on comparison/contrast are (1) failure to fairly examine both items on the same basis, thus favoring one item over another, and (2) failure to use appropriate comparison/contrast expressions, thus disguising the intent of the paragraph or essay. Be alert to these pitfalls when writing your own comparison/contrast paragraphs and essays. Unit 11 discusses comparison/contrast as it applies to the development of an entire essay.

Process

Process refers to any "how-to-do-it" writing that gives step-by-step instructions. Generally considered to be the easiest strategy for developing a paragraph or an essay, a process might give instructions on how to bake a cake, how to true a bicycle wheel, how to use the library computer system, or how to play the recorder. The following example instructs the reader in how to sharpen a knife:

> The sharpening stone must be fixed in place on the table, so that it will not move around. You can do this by placing a piece of rubber inner tube or a thin piece of foam rubber under it. Or you can tack four strips of wood, if you have a rough worktable, to frame the stone and hold it in place. Put a generous puddle of oil in the stone—this will soon disappear into the surface of a new stone, and you will need to keep adding more oil. Press the knife blade flat against the stone in the

puddle of oil, using your index finger. Whichever way the cutting edge of the knife faces is the side of the blade that should get a little more pressure. Move the blade around three or four times in a narrow oval about the size of your fingernail, going *counterclockwise* when the sharp edge is facing right. Now turn the blade over in the same spot on the stone, press hard, and move it around the small oval *clockwise*, with more pressure on the cutting edge that faces left. Repeat the ovals, flipping the knife blade over six or seven times, and applying lighter pressure to the blade the last two times.

Florence H. Pettit, "How to Sharpen Your Knife,"
How to Make Whirligigs and Whimmy Diddles

Writing about a process is usually straightforward; it is considered so easy that many teachers will not allow the student to submit a process essay for a final exam. Other than the occasional muddling of the sequence, students generally have no trouble writing process paragraphs or essays. For further instruction on this strategy, see Unit 12.

Classification

To *classify* means to divide something and group its elements into major categories and types. For a classification to be useful it must be based on a single principle and be complete. For instance, say you had to write a paragraph or essay classifying students according to their year in college. If your classification included only freshmen, sophomores, and seniors, it would violate the requirement of completeness by omitting juniors. On the other hand, if your scheme included freshmen, sophomores, juniors, seniors, fraternity members, and nonfraternity members, it would no longer be based on a single principle. The first four categories refer to the student's year in college, whereas the fifth and sixth refer to membership or nonmembership in campus organizations.

Here is an example of a paragraph developed by classification:

A few words about the world's reaction to the concentration camps: the terrors committed in them were experienced as uncanny by most civilized persons. It came as a shock to their pride that supposedly civilized nations could stoop to such inhuman acts. The implication that modern man has such inadequate control over his cruelty was felt as a threat. Three different psychological mechanisms were most frequently used for dealing with the phenomenon of the concentration camp: (a) its applicability to man in general was denied by asserting (contrary to available evidence) that the acts of torture were committed by a small group of insane or perverted persons; (b) the truth of the reports were denied by ascribing them to deliberate propaganda. This method was favored by the German government which called all reports on terror in the camps horror propaganda (Greuelpropaganda); (c) the reports were believed, but the knowledge of the terror was repressed as soon as possible.

Bruno Bettelheim, *The Informed Heart*

The author first specifies the principle of the classifications—the psychological mechanisms used to deal with human cruelty. He then completes the classification by listing the mechanisms. Unit 13 teaches how to develop an entire essay by classification.

Causal Analysis

Causal analysis attempts to relate two events by asserting the occurrence of one event to be the reason for the occurrence of the other: A car engine blew up because it lacked oil. A woman slipped and fell because the pavement was slippery. A dog got rabies because it was bitten by a squirrel. Each of these statements asserts a causal relationship between two events.

Cause usually refers to an event in the past. First, the engine lacked oil, then it blew up; first, the pavement was slippery, then the woman fell; first, the dog was bitten, then it got rabies. *Effect,* on the other hand, usually refers to an event in the future. If a car engine is run without oil, it will blow up; if a well-used pavement is slippery, someone will probably fall; if a dog is bitten by a rabid squirrel, it will probably get rabies.

While cause relates two events by asserting one event as the *reason* for the other, effect relates two events by asserting one event as the *result* of another. If you write an essay giving as a reason for your father's bitterness his failure to fulfill his ambition to be a doctor, you are analyzing cause. If you write an essay analyzing what happens to a person who fails to fulfill a lifelong career ambition, you are analyzing effect. Both essays nevertheless would be considered examples of causal analysis.

Consider this paragraph, which analyzes why our age has no "giants":

> Why have giants vanished from our midst? One must never neglect the role of accident in history; and accident no doubt plays a part here. But too many accidents of the same sort cease to be wholly accidental. One must inquire further. Why should our age not only be without great men but even seem actively hostile to them? Surely one reason we have so few heroes now is precisely that we had so many a generation ago. Greatness is hard for common humanity to bear. As Emerson said, "Heroism means difficulty, postponement of praise, postponement of ease, introduction of the world into the private apartment, introduction of eternity into the hours measured by the sitting-room clock." A world of heroes keeps people from living their own private lives.
>
> Arthur M. Schlesinger, Jr., *The Decline of Heroes*

The following paragraph analyzes the effects of changes in the sun's nuclear balance:

> Inevitably, the solar nuclear balances will change. The hydrogen will be used up, converted into helium. The sun's core will start to burn helium in a struggle for life. The heat will increase, the sun will grow redder and swell, on the way to being a red giant star. As it expands it will bring biblical fire and brimstone to the inner

planets. Mercury, Venus will melt and drop into the expanding plasma; on earth, all life will be gone long before the oceans boil and vaporize and the rocks are smelted down.

Lennard Bickel, Our Sun: The Star We Live In

Student-written causal analyses sometimes suffer from *dogmatism*—an authoritative stating of opinion as fact without sufficient evidence. Cause and effect often have a complex and frail association, which you should assert with caution. For more on how to write a causal analysis, see Unit 14.

Argumentation

Argumentation, the final strategy for developing a paragraph or an essay, involves the persuasion of the reader to the writer's viewpoint. Such a paragraph or essay will often be a combination of the strategies discussed so far, simultaneously analyzing cause, describing, comparing/contrasting, and defining. Unlike a paragraph or essay developed by comparison/contrast, the argumentative paragraph or essay has no single strategy of development but is recognizable instead by its intent. Here, for example, is a paragraph that argues that the Bible is a human document:

> Can any rational person believe that the Bible is anything but a human document? We now know pretty well where the various books came from, and about when they were written. We know that they were written by human beings who had no knowledge of science, little knowledge of life, and were influenced by the barbarous morality of primitive times, and were grossly ignorant of most things that men know today. *For instance,* Genesis says that God made the earth, and he made the sun to light the day and the moon to light the night, and in one clause disposes of the stars by saying that "he made the stars also." This was plainly written by someone who had no conception of the stars. Man, by the aid of his telescope, has looked out into the heavens and found stars whose diameter is as great as the distance between the earth and the sun. We know that the universe is filled with stars and suns and planets and systems. Every new telescope looking further into the heavens only discovers more and more worlds and suns and systems in the endless reaches of space. The men who wrote Genesis believed, of course, that this tiny speck of mud that we call the earth was the center of the universe, the only world in space, and made for man, who was the only being worth considering. These men believed that the stars were only a little way above the earth, and were set in the firmament for man to look at, and for nothing else. Everyone today knows that this conception is not true.

> Description

> Example

> Causal analysis

Clarence Darrow, Why I Am an Agnostic

In presenting his argument, the writer resorts to a variety of strategies: he describes the men who wrote the Bible, gives an example of their ignorance, and analyzes the probable causes of it. An argument involves the complex formulation of ideas and facts; a paragraph or essay developed by argumentation therefore frequently employs more than one strategy.

BLENDING RHETORICAL PATTERNS

The rhetorical patterns are helpful guidelines for a beginning writer and should never be used to solely and rigidly dictate the final draft of your paragraph or essay. What you eventually write should depend on your purpose and audience, the main idea of your essay, and your particular gifts for expression. And you should never stifle any spontaneous and apt phrasing merely because it does not conform to a particular rhetorical pattern. To do so is to behave like Procrustes of Greek mythology, who cut off the legs of passersby to make them fit into his short bed.

Many paragraphs or essays do more or less conform to one strategy of development or another, but complex works will routinely blend several strategies. Here is an example:

Example

Contrast

Causal analysis

Example

We are a long, long way from understanding the complexities of individual motivation. We understand very imperfectly, *for example,* the inner pressures to excel which are present in some children and absent in others. We don't really know why, from earliest years, some individuals seem indomitable, while others are tossed about by events like the bird in a badminton game. Differences in energy and other physiological traits are partially responsible. Even more important may be the role of early experiences—relations with brothers and sisters, early successes and failures. We know, *for example,* that high standards may be a means of challenging and stimulating the child or, depending on the circumstances, a means of frightening and intimidating him.

John W. Gardner, *Excellence*

Essays are written with a dominant purpose conceived in the mind of the writer. But a translation of this dominant purpose onto the page generally requires many different kinds of paragraphs. It is a little like building a brick house. One uses not only brick, but also cement, lumber, sheetrock, tiles, and wire. Yet when the building is finished, it is indisputably a brick house, though constructed of many different kinds of material. Essays likewise have distinct and recognizable purposes. Some are intended primarily to describe; others set out to narrate; still others are written to analyze cause. Yet most are constructed of many different kinds of paragraphs.

For instance, a writer is attempting to explain why humans sleep. He is, to begin with, obliged to talk about the principal human states of mind: waking, sleeping, and dreaming. The paragraph that does this is developed by *division/classification.* But, he asks, what is sleep good for? He surveys the animal kingdom and finds that although some animals—sloths, armadillos, opossums, and bats—sleep between 19 and 20 hours a day, others, such as the shrew and the porpoise, sleep very little. He also mentions the case of humans who require only an hour or two of sleep daily. The paragraph that serves us this intriguing information has been developed by *example.* He then turns his attention to the kinds of sleep—dreaming and dreamless—and discusses the results of research into each, using a paragraph developed by *division/classification.* Finally, he concludes the discussion with a paragraph that speculates on some probable causes for the phenomenon of sleep. That paragraph is developed by *causal analysis*. Such a paragraph mix is quite typical of many essays written outside the classroom.

Practical Applications
of Rhetorical Strategies

Some students believe that what they are taught in English courses has little usefulness in the outside world. To dismiss this myth, we have selected some examples of real-world applications of the writing strategies discussed in this book. All examples were compiled from experiences either reported to the authors or lived by them.

1. You have applied for a job with a large multinational corporation and have gone successfully through a battery of screening tests. The candidates have been narrowed to a field of five. As a basis for final selection, the personnel psychologist has asked each applicant to write an essay about his or her greatest personal success. You sit down and try to think. Then you begin to write.
    Purpose: To persuade the personnel psychologist that you are the one for the job.
    Strategy: Narration.

2. You are a social worker responsible for supervising the living conditions in some state-supported nursing homes for the elderly. You find unsanitary living conditions at one nursing home and file a stop-payment order against it to cut off its state funding. Your supervisor asks you to explain the conditions at this nursing home in support of your action.
    Purpose: To convince the state to withdraw aid from this nursing home.
    Strategy: Description.

3. As a vocal member of your PTA group, you listen with horror as the school district officials propose curriculum changes that you are convinced will lower the standard of education. You are opposed to the changes because you have read of other districts in which such changes have not been beneficial. You meet with other parents who share your view and a committee is formed. You are asked to find examples of other districts where similar changes have produced no advantages.
    Purpose: To persuade the school district not to make the proposed changes in the curriculum.
    Strategy: Example.

4. You work as a textbook salesperson for a college publisher. A sociology book published by your company is being criticized by the professors using it because it lacks a section on "deviance." You report this to your editor, who fires back a memo asking you to find out exactly what the professors mean by "deviance."

Purpose: To acquaint the editor with the professors' complaint about the text.
Strategy: Definition.

5. You are employed in the accounting division of a major department store. An employee has made a suggestion for changing the method of reporting daily income. Your boss likes the idea but is uncertain that it would be enough of an improvement over the existing method to justify the change. You are asked to write a comparison of this new method with the existing one.
Purpose: To persuade the boss to adopt the new reporting method.
Strategy: Comparison/contrast.

6. Mad about creamy chocolate pudding, you have perfected the ideal recipe. Neither riches nor fame can tempt you to share it. Love, however, does. You sit down to write out the recipe for your beloved.
Purpose: To share your recipe for perfect chocolate pudding with a friend.
Strategy: Process.

7. You work in the counseling office of a major university where entering freshmen are required to take an English test. The university is planning new English classes for its freshmen, and you are assigned to write a report dividing and classifying the incoming freshmen according to their English placement scores.
Purpose: To gather data to help with curriculum planning.
Strategy: Classification.

8. Your firm specializes in the manufacture of household brushes. Sales of one particular item—a plastic brush designed as a bathroom grout cleaner—have slumped badly. Your boss assigns you to find out why.
Purpose: To find out why sales of this brush have fallen.
Strategy: Causal analysis.

9. You and eleven other jurors have listened for two weeks to a procession of witnesses. Finally, closeted with the other jury members, you begin the painstaking evaluation of evidence. Along with four other jurors, you become convinced of the defendant's guilt, but to your amazement and dismay, the remaining jurors have come to exactly the opposite view. Undecided himself, the foreman asks each group to prepare a written argument outlining its reasons for believing in the defendant's guilt or innocence. Your group assigns you to argue its viewpoint.
Purpose: To persuade your fellow jurors to vote in favor of a guilty verdict.
Strategy: Argument.

Consider the following essay questions taken from actual examinations given at various colleges and universities throughout the country. Implicit in every one is an essay that could be organized around one or a combination of the rhetorical modes.

From philosophy: Point to a place. Can you ever point to that same place again?

From physical science: Explain the implications of Heisenberg's Principle of Indeterminacy on experiments in physics.

From political science: What is MAD?

From chemistry: (1) Differentiate, first, between starch and glycogen and, second, between cellulose and starch. (2) High-compression automobile engines that operate at high temperatures are designed to oxidize hydrocarbons completely to carbon dioxide and water. In the process of attempting to completely oxidize the hydrocarbons, a non-carbon-containing pollutant is produced. What types of compounds are produced and why do high-compression engines favor the formation of these compounds?

From history: Explain the meaning of the Truman Doctrine.

From art history: Explain how the work of Joan Miró and Salvador Dali are both similar and different.

The first thing to notice is that essay questions in fields other than English do not usually specify the rhetorical mode you are expected to use in answering them. Often, essay questions in English classes specifically ask you, for example, to compare and contrast two entities, or to describe a process. But few essay exams in other disciplines are so obliging. What you must do, then, is decide on the best rhetorical mode to use in organizing your answer. Usually, the wording of the question will give you a hint.

The political science question ("What is MAD?"), for instance, is obviously asking for a definition. You must say what the acronym MAD stands for, what the term means, and where it comes from. The first part of the chemistry question, on the other hand, is asking for a comparison/contrast. You must answer by explaining how starch is different from glycogen, and cellulose from starch. Here is an excerpt from a student answer to this question:

Both starch and glycogen are disaccharides, but starch has a d-glycosidic bond that doesn't allow a great extent of H-bonding. Therefore starch is easier to break down than glycogen. Starch is found mainly in plants, whereas glycogen exists mainly in animals. Glycogen is the monomer unit of most fatty acids.

Although this is a technical answer, it is still easy to see that the student is systematically comparing and contrasting. She uses contrasting terms such as *but* and *whereas*. She says how starch and glycogen are similar and how they are different.

Sometimes, however, the rhetorical mode best suited to answer a question is not so clearly indicated in the question's wording. You must read the question carefully and decide what it is really asking. A question that asks you to explain something may be asking for an analysis of cause, a definition, or even a comparison/contrast. For example, the physical science question ("Explain the implications of Heisenberg's Principle of Indeterminacy on experiments in physics") is really asking for an analysis of effect, though its wording does not directly say so. To answer it, you would need to discuss how physics experiments have been affected by Heisenberg's principle. On the other hand, to answer the history question, you must write an extended definition of the Truman Doctrine; and to answer the last question, whose wording also asks for an explanation, you must compare and contrast the work of Joan Miró and Salvador Dali.

Many questions may also require you to answer in an essay that blends the rhetorical modes. For example, to answer the first question ("Point to a place. Can you ever point to that same place again?"), you must first define what is philosophically meant by "a place," and then argue whether or not it is possible to point to it again. Such an essay will be developed by two primary rhetorical modes—definition and argumentation.

Consider, as another example, the second chemistry question: "High-compression automobile engines that operate at high temperatures are designed to oxidize hydrocarbons completely to carbon dioxide and water. In the process of attempting to completely oxidize the hydrocarbons, a non-carbon-containing pollutant is produced. What types of compounds are produced and why do high-compression engines favor the formation of these compounds?" Your answer should consist of paragraphs that divide and classify—specifying the types of compounds produced—as well as paragraphs that analyze cause—saying why high-compression engines produce them. Professional writers routinely produce such blend essays. The main caution for the beginner is to use sufficiently strong transitions (sentences or even entire paragraphs) to make the leap from one rhetorical mode to the other. (See the section in Unit 4 on "Transitions between Paragraphs.")

In answering any essay question, your first aim should not be to answer in a recognizable rhetorical mode but, instead, to give exactly the kind of answer that is called for. Consider, for example, this question, taken from a philosophy quiz: "In a paragraph, explain what *virtue* meant to Aristotle and give three examples of it." The question is asking you to do two things: first, to define "virtue" as Aristotle understood the term and, second, to give three examples of it. Ordinarily, you might think that one or two examples of a term are enough to define it; but in this case you are specifically asked to give three, and that is what you must do. Here is how one student answered this question:

> Aristotle defined virtue as an action lying somewhere between the twin vices of excess and deficiency. In other words, virtue is temperance or the golden mean. Let us, for example, consider wartime circumstances. The man of virtue will not cower in fear of war, but neither will he rush unthinkingly into battle. When war is inevitable, the virtuous man will bravely fight in defense of his country. Attitude toward money provides another example. The miserly hoarder of gold is no more virtuous than the wasteful spender. Virtue lies somewhere in the middle—an attitude of generosity toward need. A third example may be drawn from the way one loses or keeps one's temper. The man who throws frequent temper tantrums is not virtuous, but neither is the one who shows no anger whatsoever, even in the face of unnecessary cruelty. Virtue again lies halfway between the two extremes—in the exercise of a cool head when faced with provocation but also in the display of righteous indignation when the circumstances demand it.

The rhetorical modes, in sum, can be used to solve any kind of writing problem. You may have to combine several modes in a single essay, or you may write a single essay in a dominant mode. The point to remember is that rhetorical modes are merely patterns for organizing and expressing your thoughts. Use them, and adapt them as necessary to clearly express your ideas on paper. Once you become a more experienced writer, you will probably discard the mechanical patterning behind them altogether while still heeding the principles of focus and organization that they teach.

THE CONTROLLING IDEA

No matter what strategy is used to develop it, every essay must be based on a *controlling idea*. Also called a *thesis,* the controlling idea is a summary statement of the essay's theme, in effect a declaration by the writer of what the essay intends to do—whether to argue, narrate, describe, or classify. The controlling idea is usually placed in the first paragraph, most often as its final sentence, early enough to serve both writer and reader. The writer is served by knowing what must be done, the reader by knowing what to expect. Here are three controlling ideas taken from different essays:

> The biggest piece of claptrap about the Press is that it deals almost exclusively, or even mainly, with news.
>
> > T. S. Matthews, "The Power of the Press"

> While I was still a boy, I came to the conclusion that there were three grades of thinking; and since I was later to claim thinking as my hobby, I came to an even stronger conclusion—namely, that I myself could not think at all.
> > William Golding, "Thinking as a Hobby"

> Although Boswell and Johnson belonged to the same literary club, were close friends, held the same views on the Monarchy and the English class system, there are significant differences in their literary opinions and preferences.
> > Student essay, "A Contrast of the Literary Opinions of Boswell and Johnson"

In the first essay, we expect the author to tell us why it is claptrap to say that the press deals with the news. We expect the second essay to catalog and explain the three grades of thinking; we expect the third to contrast the literary opinions and preferences of Boswell and Johnson.

To understand the relationship among these three elements of the essay—purpose, strategy, and controlling idea—consider three hypothetical approaches to an essay on farming.

Purpose: To explain the decline of agriculture as a college major.

Strategy: Write an *analysis of the causes* that have led to the decline of agricultural majors in college.

Controlling idea: Because of the growing cost of land, the low margin of profit for agricultural products, and the harshness of the farming life-style, today fewer students are choosing farming as a career.

Purpose: To give the reader a vivid picture of a day in a farmer's life.

Strategy: Write an essay *describing* life on the farm.

Controlling idea: The farmer's everyday world is made up of golden fields redolent with freshly mowed hay, ramshackle outbuildings used for storage, and the dimly lit lobbies of agricultural cooperatives.

Purpose: To illustrate to the reader the appeal of farming.

Strategy: Give two *examples* that illustrate the appeal of farm life.

Controlling idea: The hurly-burly excitement during the twin seasons of planting and harvesting best illustrate the perennial appeal of farm life to all generations.

Notice that in every case the chosen purpose dictates the best strategy and also influences the wording of the controlling idea. This sort of planning and shaping a writer will do during the prewriting phase and even while actually writing the work. Note that your calculations during prewriting should also take into account the audience of the essay. So, for example, if your audience is a writing instructor with an utterly urban soul, you might have to explain or even define farming habits and customs that an agrarian reader could be assumed to know. On the other hand, if your writing instructor hails from the farm, you can skip the basic definitions and explanations and adopt the manner of one writing to an insider. Either way, the essay will vary according to how much you think the instructor knows about life on the farm.

Writing Assignments

1. Write a paragraph specifying the conventions and expectations about writing that exist in your English class.

2. Explain in a paragraph any adaptations you might make in writing for different instructors.

3. Using any of the rhetorical modes, develop a paragraph on the topic of writing techniques.

4. Explain in a paragraph how a letter you write to a parent might differ from one you might write to a college dean.

5. Write a paragraph on the usefulness or irrelevance of a definite controlling idea to your particular writing habits.

The Sentence: Combining, Generating, Judging

The well-written essay has purpose, strategy, and a controlling idea. It uses supporting details effectively and consists of paragraphs that are unified and coherent. But aside from all this, a good essay—indeed, any good writing—has an even more basic characteristic: It is composed of effective sentences. If you cannot write a vigorous, expressive sentence, it is unlikely that you will write such an essay. Acquiring the skill to write effective sentences is part of the development of any writer.

Sentence combining can help you write better sentences and, consequently, better essays. It is defined as the grammatical and rhetorical technique of blending short sentences into a longer, more complex one. Studies continue to show that mastering sentence combining distinctly improves overall sentence variety and style, which is good news, indeed, because the techniques for combining sentences are surprisingly few and can be mastered quickly once you understand the fundamentals.

Before we begin, however, we should point out that this unit assumes a reader with a fundamental knowledge of grammar. Particularly, you need to know the difference between an independent and a dependent clause, which are the two elements that make up sentences. We shall review these briefly, but if you feel the need for a more in-depth review, you should find Part V of this book helpful.

As the term indicates, an *independent* clause is independent from the rest of the sentence because it can stand alone and make perfect sense. A *dependent* clause cannot stand alone but needs to be connected to an independent clause. Consider this sentence:

The level of poverty and squalor in large cities is appalling when one considers our country's wealth.

The sentence consists of one independent clause (in italics) and one dependent clause (in roman type). Notice how the first clause is a complete sentence by itself, able to stand alone and make perfect sense without having to be linked to any other words. The second clause, however, cannot stand alone and makes no sense unless it is linked to the first. Study the following sentences to understand the difference between independent and dependent clauses. In each case we have italicized the independent clause.

The mountains looked dark and gloomy because the sun had disappeared below the horizon.

Because he promised to run for office, *the town fathers seemed reassured.*

They believed in hell when they looked at all the damage caused by the earthquake.

After it was published in New York, *the book gained acceptance by the general public.*

Do not be confused by the fact that dependent clauses can also be used as nouns, adjectives, or adverbs in a sentence as indicated in the following examples:

That she is wealthy seems perfectly clear. (noun)

He always eats *as he was told to.* (adverb)

We all need parents *who are understanding.* (adjective)

SENTENCE COMBINING

The general theory behind sentence combining assumes a powerful sentence-making mechanism in the human brain. Everyone has a natural capacity to change the way sentences are combined by either adding words, deleting words, or submerging words.

In a sentence-combining drill, you are asked to combine two or more kernel sentences into a more complex one. A kernel sentence is the barest possible sentence, consisting only of a minimum subject and predicate. (For more on the subject and predicate of a sentence, see Unit 18, "Grammar Fundamentals.")

Here, for example, are three kernel sentences:

1. The sailor ate his breakfast.
2. The breakfast consisted of eggs.
3. The sunlight streamed through the porthole.

There is nothing grammatically wrong with these three sentences, for each is plainly understandable and correct. Nevertheless, an essay written entirely in such short sentences would seem childishly monotonous. One way to break the monotony and create a more mature style is to combine these simple sentences into a longer, more complex one:

While the sunlight streamed through the porthole, the sailor ate his breakfast of eggs.

or

As the sailor breakfasted on eggs, the sunlight streamed through the porthole.

Either sentence would seem a refreshing break in an essay written only in kernel sentences.

The aim of sentence combining, then, is to help you cultivate a writing style characterized by sentence variety. And one way to achieve sentence variety is to combine kernel sentences into longer ones. This combining is usually accomplished in one of three ways: by adding, deleting, or submerging.

Sentence Combining by Adding

The easiest way to combine sentences is to connect them unchanged by adding a comma and/or one of many connecting words such as *and, but, when, while, so, because, after,* and *as if.* Here are some examples:

ORIGINAL

1. They headed up the road.
2. They saw the sun set behind the slopes.
3. They felt afraid.

COMBINED

They headed up the road, they saw the sun set behind the slopes, and they felt afraid.

We have connected the first two sentences with a comma and the last with a comma and the connecting word *and.* This combination is possible only when the kernel sentences are brief; otherwise, a semicolon should be used:

ORIGINAL

1. He felt a sudden, sharp pain on the side of his head.
2. He turned just in time to see the enemy hiding behind a bush.
3. He aimed his rifle as steadily and carefully as he could.

COMBINED

He felt a sudden, sharp pain on the side of his head; he turned just in time to see the enemy hiding behind a bush; and he aimed his rifle as steadily and carefully as he could.

The substitution of a semicolon and the *and* for a period blends the sentences into a smoother passage.

ORIGINAL

1. She entered her office again.
2. A note from the landlord lay on the desk.

COMBINED

When she entered her office again, a note from the landlord lay on the desk.

The use of the word *when* subordinates the idea in the first sentence to the idea in the second, creating a third sentence whose logic is emphatic and clear. We now understand that the note was already on the desk *when* she walked in. Study the following examples:

ORIGINAL

1. At first the water in their thermos bottles was cold.
2. In less than an hour it had become as hot as tea.

COMBINED

At first the water in their thermos bottles was cold, but in less than an hour it had become as hot as tea.

The word *but* emphasizes contrast.

ORIGINAL

1. They stuck their heads together.
2. They were gossiping about us.

COMBINED

They stuck their heads together as if they were gossiping about us.
They stuck their heads together while they were gossiping about us.

or

They stuck their heads together because they were gossiping about us.

As you can see, the connecting word is enough to transform two short sentences into a longer one while emphasizing a relationship of contrast, condition, or cause and effect between the ideas.

Exercises in Sentence Combining by Adding

Write the following alphabetized entries as a single sentence, by adding either a comma or a connecting device.

1. a. Wit is often sharp and sarcastic.
   b. Humor is always soft and usually kind.
2. a. He studied artistic theory.
   b. He practiced mixing colors.
   c. He painted hundreds of canvases.
3. a. The Muslims of Mecca exclude women from religious festivities.
   b. They fear familiarity between women and their overlords.
4. a. Miracle plays were still performed on wagons in Shakespeare's day.
   b. Theaters had been built.
5. a. Some people are industrious in the sense that they work energetically for long periods of time.
   b. Others are lazy and idle.

Sentence Combining by Deleting

Sentences can also be combined by deleting repetitious words or phrases. Here are some examples:

ORIGINAL

1. Human beings are not machines.
2. Human beings are not robots.
3. Human beings are not stones without feelings.

COMBINED

Human beings are not machines, robots, or stones without feelings.

Deleting the repetitious phrase *human beings* creates a single sentence from three smaller ones.

ORIGINAL

1. The children were hungry.
2. The children were tired.
3. The children were disappointed.

COMBINED

The children were hungry, tired, and disappointed.

Sometimes you can combine ideas by deleting a repetitious word or phrase and substituting pronouns such as *who, which, that, whom, whose,* or *where:*

ORIGINAL

1. Among manufacturers serious legal problems are being caused by dissatisfied customers.
2. These customers are filing product liability suits.

COMBINED

Among manufacturers serious problems are being caused by dissatisfied customers who are filing product liability suits.

The pronoun *who* replaces the phrase *these customers,* creating a leaner sentence. Observe how pronouns serve as connections in the following sentences:

ORIGINAL

1. The pure individualist is an unhappy person.
2. The pure individualist has memories of selfish behavior that haunt her.

COMBINED

The pure individualist is an unhappy person whose memories of selfish behavior haunt her.

ORIGINAL

1. Newton's analysis of the light in a rainbow was a brilliant achievement.
2. Few people have matched this achievement.

COMBINED

Newton's analysis of the light in a rainbow was a brilliant achievement that few people have matched.

Exercises in Sentence Combining by Deleting

Combine the following alphabetized sentences by deleting words or using a pronoun to replace words.

1. a. The trouble between Israelis and Palestinians is a clash between two cultures.
   b. These cultures are fighting for supremacy in the Middle East.
2. a. Somehow she knew instinctively.
   b. She knew who had stolen her wallet.

3. a. He was a bold man.
   b. He wanted to find a new home.
   c. He wanted to lead a less structured life.
4. a. I want to find a man.
   b. I want to find a merry man.
   c. I want to find a wise man.
5. a. The quarrels of lovers are like summer storms.
   b. Summer storms make everything more beautiful once they have passed.

Sentence Combining by Submerging

Sentences may also be combined by submerging the parts of one sentence into another:

ORIGINAL

1. A letter had landed on Jack's desk.
2. The letter was from the Security Office.
3. The letter requested a report.
4. The report was to be about the deportation of aliens.

COMBINED

A letter from the Security Office requesting a report about the deportation of aliens landed on Jack's desk.

Sentence combining through submerging is like playing with a jigsaw puzzle: You try this piece, then that, and yet another until the parts fit snugly. Simply play with the ideas, lining them up and melding one into the other until the sentence means what you want it to without sounding choppy. Here are further examples:

ORIGINAL

1. The letter had an effect on Jack.
2. The effect was paralyzing.
3. The effect was paralyzing because Jack was responsible for all aliens.

COMBINED

The letter had a paralyzing effect on Jack because he was responsible for all aliens.

ORIGINAL

1. Jack was no miracle worker.
2. Jack adopted a typical obfuscating tactic.

3. Jack made a vague reply.
4. The reply said nothing.

COMBINED

Because Jack was no miracle worker, he adopted the typical obfuscating tactic of making a vague reply that said nothing.

Note that because numerous combinations are possible in using submersion as a technique for sentence combining, no exclusively right answer exists. For instance, the last cluster could just as well have been combined in this way:

Jack, not being a miracle worker, adopted a typical obfuscating tactic, which was to make a vague reply that said nothing.

The idea is to fuss with the sentence until you hit upon the wording that strikes your editorial sense as the most efficient and expressive.

ORIGINAL

1. The Dutch East India Company was chartered by the States-General of the Netherlands.
2. It was to expand trade.
3. It was to ensure close relations between the Dutch government and its colonial enterprises in Asia.

COMBINED

Chartered by the States-General of the Netherlands, the Dutch East India Company was intended to expand trade and to ensure close relations between the Dutch government and its colonial enterprises in Asia.

ORIGINAL

1. A hat provides considerable psychological security.
2. It protects the face.
3. It hides the face.
4. Curious onlookers cannot see the face.
5. These onlookers threaten one's privacy.

COMBINED

A hat provides psychological security by protecting the face and hiding it from curious onlookers who threaten one's privacy.

Exercises in Sentence Combining by Submerging

Combine the following alphabetized sentences using the technique of submerging. You do not need to use the exact words of the kernel sentences. Experiment until you find the wording that seems to yield the smoothest sentence.

1. a. She kept down her working crew.
   b. She handled her own correspondence.
   c. She browbeat a small corps of salespeople.
   d. She managed to make a very large profit.

2. a. As a reporter, Dickens had seen a good deal of Parliament.
   b. He had formed a contemptuous opinion of it.
   c. His opinion was never to change to the end of his life.

3. a. Firmness of purpose is one of the most necessary sinews of character.
   b. It is one of the best instruments of success.
   c. Without firmness of purpose, even a genius will waste effort in a maze of inconsistencies.

4. a. The American people were disturbed.
   b. The newspapers reported something.
   c. The Savings and Loan institutions had mishandled funds.
   d. Billions of dollars were lost.

5. a. One day we were walking by the seashore.
   b. She made an important revelation.
   c. It was a dark secret.
   d. She confided that she had terminal cancer.
   e. This revelation shook me to the core.

6. a. There was a little woman in the washhouse.
   b. This woman seemed deranged.
   c. She had a basket on her arm.
   d. The basket was filled with dripping clothes.
   e. A flood of angry, incoherent words poured out of her mouth.

7. a. Psychologists have drawn an important conclusion.
   b. The conclusion has to do with children who suffer from chronic disease.
   c. These children assume that the disease is a punishment.
   d. They often also assume that the treatment is more punishment.

8. a. There is today a push toward having test-tube babies.
   b. This reinforces the view that women's lives are unfulfilled unless they bear children.
   c. This view is all too prevalent in our society.
   d. The view also implies that women without children are worthless.

9. a. Argumentative writing pervades our society.
   b. We may not even recognize it as argumentative.

    c. Brochures come our way.

    d. Leaflets come our way.

    e. All of them urge us to vote for one candidate rather than another or for one cause rather than another.

10. a. Fame had little effect on Einstein as a person.

    b. However, he could not escape fame.

    c. He was always instantly recognizable in a crowd.

    d. He caused people to stop and stare wherever he was.

    e. These people would be overcome with a sudden air of solemnity.

    f. They realized that they were in the presence of a genius.

ANSWERS

Here are some sample answers. Many other possibilities exist.

1. She managed to make a very large profit by keeping down her working crew, handling her own correspondence, and browbeating a small corps of salespeople.

2. As a reporter, Dickens had seen a good deal of Parliament, forming a contemptuous opinion of it to the end of his life.

3. Firmness of purpose, without which even a genius will waste effort in a maze of inconsistencies, is one of the most necessary sinews of character as well as one of the best instruments of success.

4. The American people were disturbed when the newspapers reported that the Savings and Loan institutions had mishandled funds and had lost billions of dollars.

5. One day, while we were walking by the seashore, she revealed a dark secret—the important revelation that she had terminal cancer, a revelation that shook me to the core.

6. There was a little woman in the washhouse, a basket filled with dripping clothes on her arm, who seemed deranged as a flood of words poured out of her mouth.

7. Psychologists have drawn the important conclusion that children who suffer from chronic disease consider the disease—and sometimes also the treatment—a punishment.

8. Today's push toward having test-tube babies reinforces the view, all too prevalent in our society, that women's lives are unfulfilled or worthless unless they bear children.

9. Argumentative writing pervades our society, but we may not recognize it as such when brochures and leaflets come our way, all of them urging us to vote for one candidate rather than another or for one cause rather than another.

10. Although fame had little effect on Einstein as a person, he could not escape it, for he was always instantly recognizable in a crowd, causing people—

suddenly overcome with an air of solemnity—to stop and stare wherever he was as they realized that they were in the presence of a genius.

SENTENCE GENERATING

In a sentence-generating drill you are asked not merely to combine sentences but actually to expand them using your own ideas. The aim of this drill is to teach you how to use sentence combining to produce your own varied sentences. Consider this kernel sentence.

Mr. Jones lived in a mansion.

An expanded version might read as follows (the new portions are printed in italics):

Mr. Jones, *who made millions on the stock market,* lived in a mansion *in a secluded woods surrounded by vast green meadows.*

From expanding a single kernel sentence, you can move to expanding and combining several kernel sentences into a paragraph. Here, for example, are four kernel sentences followed by their expansion into a paragraph:

ORIGINAL

1. The hotel kitchen upset Nick and Nora.
2. It could ruin the simplest dish.
3. Today the corned beef looked terrible.
4. They decided to cook on a hot plate in their room.

EXPANDED

The hotel kitchen, with its inferior service, upset Nick and Nora. It could ruin the simplest dish, even an ungarnished poached egg. Today, the corned beef looked terrible, like a lump of altogether odious black grease. They decided to cook on a hot plate in their room, thus avoiding the kitchen's inevitable bungling of meat, vegetables, and baked goods.

Sentences can be generated by the following means: coordination, subordination, relative construction, participial construction, prepositional construction, appositive, or absolute construction. An example of each follows. The generated portion appears in italic letters.

Cassandra was a Greek prophetess, *and she was the daughter of Priam.*   Coordination

Although it is still solemn in tone, the Catholic requiem today reveals a more joyful attitude than it used to.   Subordination

Relative construction	The Samurai were Japanese feudal knights *who emerged during the twelfth-century wars between the Taira and Minamoto clans.*
Participial construction	Wagner's opera *Tristan and Isolde, based on Gottfried von Strassburg's version of the Arthurian legend,* represents the fullest musical and theatrical expression of German romanticism.
Prepositional construction	*Without the blessing of Luther,* the German peasants' cause would have ultimately met with defeat.
Appositive	It is precisely to keep infants and children from being battered—*to give them a temporary home, to feed and house them, and to provide some psychological counseling*—that halfway houses have been established in many major cities.
Absolute construction	*Dinner being served on a breezy patio,* we all dressed warmly.

Exercises

Add at least one clause or phrase to the sentences below. Try for variety by making your clauses or phrases modify different sentence elements.

MODEL

Original sentence	The formal gardens were turned into an enormous vegetable patch.
Transformation	The formal gardens, *which had been admired for their neoclassical symmetry,* were turned into an enormous vegetable patch.

1. a. The destroyers were skulking by the eastern cove.
   b. The rear admiral had taken over only two days before.
   c. Still, his task force should have wiped out the enemy.

2. a. Members of the postwar baby boom are now approaching middle age.
   b. They too are concerned about the effects of inflation and high interest rates.

3. a. It may seem profitless to worry about a nuclear holocaust.
   b. However, common sense dictates that we must confront the possibility honestly.

4. a. One of the odd things foreigners notice about Americans is their intolerance.
   b. This intolerance frequently extends to races, creeds, and role expectations.
   c. It often baffles foreigners, many of whom regard the American Constitution as enshrining just the opposite principles of tolerance and understanding.

5. a. Tennis is a sport for the millions.
   b. It offers players the rewards of vascular conditioning and exposure to the outdoors.
   c. Players have available to them many competitive leagues.

6. a. Most of us have felt that some physical trait makes us different from other people.

   b. These differences cause us to struggle in order to adjust.
   c. We must come to terms with them.

7. a. When a poor woman sees her neighbor working as a waitress even
      though the neighbor's husband has a job, she may become resentful.
   b. The waitress, of course, may feel guilty.
   c. That is why our government must provide a job for everyone who is able
      and willing to work.

8. a. Which is more important, knowledge or imagination?
   b. I consider the imagination more important than knowledge.
   c. It is only through the imagination that one can catch a glimpse of what
      can be.

9. a. Geoffrey was still far from his goal.
   b. He slowly approached the hillock, walking with difficulty.
   c. It was still bruisingly hot, and he longed to rest.
   d. Still, he pressed on.

10. a. To my anthropology professor teaching seemed to be a social calling.
    b. She loved the informal contacts with those she taught.
    c. She stayed in her office until late each afternoon, often the only person
       left.
    d. Her swivel chair allowed her to be comfortable in her enjoyment of the
       academic community.

ANSWERS

Here are some sample answers. Many other possibilities exist.

1. *To supply their starved, sick garrison,* the destroyers were skulking by the
   eastern cove, *dropping medical supplies and food overboard.* The rear
   admiral *commanding the flotilla* had taken over only two days before, *his
   force formed of worn-out units who longed to go home.* Still, his task force,
   with the advantages of radar, surprise, and superior firepower, should have
   wiped out the enemy.

2. Members of the postwar baby boom are now nearly middle-aged adults *who
   hope to find good jobs and to buy their own homes. Like their parents'
   generation,* they too worry about the effects of inflation and high interest
   rates, *which eat up savings accounts and cause businesses to go bankrupt.*

3. It may seem profitless to worry about a nuclear holocaust—*a third world
   war in which entire continents could be wiped out.* However, *after we study
   the historical trends of world powers and realize how simple it is to create
   nuclear power,* common sense dictates that the possibility must be confronted honestly.

4. One of the odd things foreigners notice about Americans—*whether Republi-
   cans, Democrats, urban dwellers, or country folks*—is their intolerance. This
   intolerance frequently extends to races, creeds, and role expectations,

carrying with it a willingness to shun and physically punish the ones perceived as different. It often baffles foreigners, many of whom regard the American Constitution, *with its emphasis on respect for individual freedoms,* as enshrining just the opposite principles of tolerance and understanding.

5. *Because it uses equipment that is comparatively inexpensive,* tennis, *once the tony entertainment of only the very wealthy,* is *today* a sport for the millions. It offers players, *who will range widely in ability, coordination, age, and overall fitness,* the rewards of vascular conditioning and exposure to the outdoors, *to say nothing of the enjoyment of healthy competitiveness.* Players have available to them many competitive leagues, *from the top professional leagues to the amateur contests sponsored by the United States Tennis Association, in which players of equal rank face each other in weekend matches.*

6. *At some point in our lives,* most of us have felt that some physical trait, *such as a big nose, bad skin, or bow legs,* makes us different from other people. *Whether real or imagined,* these differences cause us to struggle in order to adjust. *Both our pride and our common sense tell us that* we must come to terms with them *or succumb to an inferiority complex.*

7. When a poor woman, *struggling to keep her children clothed and fed on a paltry welfare check,* sees her neighbor working as a waitress even though the neighbor's husband has a steady job *as a mechanic at the local Chevrolet dealer,* she may become resentful. The waitress, of course, may feel guilty, *knowing that she has a job whereas her neighbor has not been able to find one.* That is why our government must *create an economy that is healthy enough* to provide a job for everyone who is able and willing to work.

8. Which is more important, knowledge *that tells you what is* or imagination *that tells you what could be?* I consider the imagination, *embracing as it does unheard music and unseen pictures,* more important than knowledge *that simply keeps track of what has already been sung or painted.* It is only through the imagination that one can catch a glimpse of what can be *as one dreams and reaches for the stars.*

9. Geoffrey was still far from his goal *when the sun began to drop near the rim of the distant mountains.* He slowly approached the hillock, walking with difficulty—*his bare feet cut and bleeding and his legs giving way to fatigue.* It was still bruisingly hot, *with not a breeze blowing,* and he longed to rest on *a cool grassy spot in the shade of a tree.* Still, he pressed on, *determined to reach the village before being engulfed by total darkness.*

10. To my anthropology professor teaching seemed to be a social calling *that allowed her to engage in pleasant conversation with present, as well as past, students who dropped by just to pass the time of day and listen to this scholarly woman talk.* She loved the informal moments with those she taught *as much or more than formal class lecture time.* She stayed in her

office until late each afternoon, *watching the shadows lengthen across the campus square,* often the only person left *in her wing of the Liberal Arts building.* Her swivel chair, *with a dark green pillow on its seat,* allowed her to *lean back, hands clasped behind her head, and* be comfortable in her enjoyment of the academic community.

JUDGING THE SENTENCE

Because any given passage can be written any number of different ways, all writers are faced with nearly endless possibilities of expression. Consequently, it is not enough merely to combine kernel sentences into longer ones: the combination itself must be more effective than the originals. Consider, for instance, the complex but tone-deaf sentence below. It can hardly be called an improvement over a succession of kernel sentences.

> The little red house in the ugly, run-down neighborhood that had suffered through numerous attacks of violence by hideous bands of hoodlums who were poor and uneducated was finally burned down.

The ultimate aim of sentence combining is to produce more readable sentences, not merely more complex ones. To do so requires that you develop an ear for judging the best possible version of several sentences created through either sentence combining or sentence generating. In judging the various versions of sentences, you should attend to the following criteria:

1. Clarity (Which version is the clearest?)
2. Economy (Which version is the most economical?)
3. Emphasis (Which version is the most emphatic?)
4. Stylistic sophistication (Which version sounds the best?)

Obviously, an ear for these qualities comes only with time and practice. But it is a useful exercise nevertheless to read through the following sentences and try to see why one version is preferable to the other. Even if you cannot put into words the reason for your choice, you might be able intuitively to tell which sentence is better. And when you can accurately and consistently make this kind of choice, you will be well on the way to being able to choose which of your own sentences are stronger and should be used, and which are weaker and should be cut.

Exercises

Choose from each group of two sentences below the one you find more effective, and be prepared to explain why.

MODEL

    a. Swiss watchmakers are trained by an apprentice system and they work under an accomplished master for years before they are allowed to work independently.

    b. Trained by an apprentice system, Swiss watchmakers work under an accomplished master for years before they are allowed to work independently.

ANSWER

The second version (b) is more emphatic, because it subordinates a participial phrase to the base sentence rather than having two base sentences joined by coordination. In this case, the information provided in the base sentence is the more important.

1. a. Groping helplessly in the dark, she was trying to turn on the light.
   b. She was, groping helplessly in the dark, trying to turn on the light.

2. a. While they were clothed in colorful uniforms, the three army captains signed the papers from headquarters.
   b. Clothed in colorful uniforms, the three army captains signed the papers from headquarters.

3. a. After a seizure, the grand mal victim will often lie stretched out, his body shivering, and his eyes are half open, and his voice is unable to utter a word.
   b. After a seizure, the grand mal victim will often lie stretched out, his body shivering, his eyes half open, and his voice unable to utter a word.

4. a. *Ecumenism* is a term applied to the movement aimed at unifying rather than separating the churches of the world.
   b. *Ecumenism* is a term applied to the movement aimed at unifying rather than to separate the churches of the world.

5. a. Drinking with publishers for hours was a habit developed by the aging novelist, who was suffering from a deep depression that came from having lost popularity with her reading audience.
   b. Suffering from a deep depression caused by a loss of popularity with her reading audience, the aging novelist developed the habit of spending hours drinking with publishers.

6. a. In more robust days than these, a hundred years or so ago, there were many heartily sadistic sports to enjoy.
   b. A hundred years or so ago, there were many heartily sadistic sports to enjoy, in more robust days than these.

7. a. Whispers are not restricted to the bearing of bad news, and there are men who smell injustice however softly it walks.
   b. There are men who smell injustice however softly it walks, and whispers are not restricted to the bearing of bad news.

8. a. Being a bully he had only one object, to humiliate his enemies and cowing them also.
   b. Being a bully he had only one object, to humiliate and cow his enemies.
9. a. Following the tragedy recriminations were exchanged and blame assigned randomly.
   b. Recriminations were exchanged and blame randomly assigned in the aftermath of the tragedy.
10. a. Most women have internalized Freud's messages of inferiority, and, in attempting to adjust, defer to men.
    b. Attempting to adjust, most women have internalized Freud's messages of inferiority and defer to men generally.

The Paragraph

Paragraph comes from the Middle Latin word *paragraphus,* meaning a sign that designates a separate part. Without question, the human brain prefers to view the whole as a collection of parts—a prejudice that has decisively affected the shape of written communication. Words are grouped into phrases, phrases into clauses, and clauses into sentences. Sentences are melded into paragraphs, paragraphs into sections, and sections into chapters. Such are the constituent parts of a book, which may or may not itself be cleaved into separate volumes.

USES OF THE PARAGRAPH

The aim of paragraphing is to signal the introduction of a new idea, the amplification of some significant aspect of an old one, or the transition from one idea to another. In effect, the paragraph is the means by which ideas may be packaged on the page according to their importance. The reader does not have to ferret through a jumble of words for the significant points but is guided to them by the familiar paragraph indentation.

Paragraphs That Signal a New Idea

Consider the following two paragraphs, on the subject of how much a hometown can change in 30 years:

> Sights have changed: there is a new precision about street and home, a clearing away of chicken yards, cow barns, pigeon-crested cupolas, weed lots and coulees, the dim and secret adult-free rendezvous of boys. An intricate metal "jungle gym"

is a common backyard sight, the back swing uncommon. There are wide expanses of clear windows designed to let in the parlor light, fewer ornamental windows of colored glass designed to keep it out. Attic and screen porch are slowly vanishing and lovely shades of pastel are painted upon the new houses, tints that once would have embarrassed farmer and merchant alike.

Sounds have changed: I heard not once the clopping of a horse's hoof, nor the mourn of a coyote. I heard instead the shriek of brakes, the heavy throbbing of the once-a-day Braniff airliner into Minot, the shattering sirens born of war, the honk of a diesel locomotive which surely cannot call to faraway places the heart of a wakeful boy like the old steam whistle in the night. You can walk down the streets of my town now and hear from open windows the intimate voices of the Washington commentators in casual converse on the great affairs of state; but you cannot hear on Sunday morning the singing in Norwegian of the Lutheran hymns; the old-country accents grow fainter in the speech of my Velva neighbors.

Eric Sevareid, This Is Eric Sevareid

The first paragraph deals with changes in sights; the second, with changes in sounds. The catalog of changes is partitioned into two paragraphs and dealt with separately. It is a little as if the writer had said to the reader, "Listen, I'm going to tell you how the sights of my hometown have changed." And when he has done with that topic, he nudges the reader once again and says, "And now I'll tell you how the sounds of my hometown have changed."

The division into two paragraphs here is natural and logical. A reader has the opportunity to savor the one sort of change before being treated to the other. Moreover, the writing has an intensity and concentration that would have been badly diluted had both kinds of changes been merely jumbled together in a single block of print.

Paragraphs That Amplify an Old Idea

Writers often come to a point at which specific illustrations must be given, exceptions noted, and amplifications made. Each such turn in the writing cries out for a separate paragraph. The following is an example of such a shift:

About 900 B.C., another Asiatic people, known today as Etruscans, arrived via the sea on the western coast of central Italy in the vicinity of Rome. Etruscan origins and language, however, remain as irritatingly unknown today as do the Sumerian. But Roman legends, supported by Greek rumors, depict the Etruscans as descendants of the Hittites who had fled their disintegrating empire in the twelfth century B.C. in the aftermath of the fall of Troy.

Cruel, clever, and sexy, the Etruscans killed off the natives, invented gladiatorial games, drained the marshes, plied the seas with commerce, traversed the heartland of Europe with goods, and founded a religion built on fornication, death, and hellfire. The senior trinity of their gods consisted of a holy father, a virgin mother, and an immaculately begotten daughter. In Etruscan theology, the dead went first to purgatory for judgment, where, if found guilty, their souls were damned to various degrees of torment, the ultimate punishment being eternal hellfire. In the thirteenth century A.D., these concepts seeped into Christianity via the *Divina Commedia* of Dante, who was steeped in Etruscan mythology.

Max I. Dimont, Those Indestructible Jews

The first paragraph simply introduces the Etruscans in a general way and puzzles over their obscure origins. The second paragraph amplifies on the Etruscan character. In this way the writer has separated the general from the specific, a tactic that gives focus to the writing and spares the reader from having to make any dizzying leap of logic.

Paragraphs That Signal a Transition

Often a writer needs to carefully bridge the gap between the ideas contained in one paragraph and those expounded in another. And where the shift in the line of thought between two paragraphs is sudden and complicated, a transition paragraph may be used to help the reader along. Here is an example:

First topic

Indeed, instead of seeing evolution as a smooth process, many of today's life scientists and archaeologists are studying the "theory of catastrophes" to explain "gaps" and "jumps" in the multiple branches of the evolutionary record. Others are studying small changes that may have been amplified through feedback into sudden structural transformations. Heated controversies divide the scientific community over every one of these issues.

Transition

But such controversies are dwarfed by a single history-changing fact.

Second topic

One day in 1953 at Cambridge in England a young biologist, James Watson, was sitting in the Eagle pub when his colleague, Francis Crick, ran excitedly in and announced to "everyone within hearing distance that we had found the secret of life." They had. Watson and Crick had unraveled the structure of DNA.

Alvin Toffler, The Third Wave

The author writes about two principal topics: the attitude of life scientists and archaeologists toward evolution; the discovery of the basic building block of life, DNA. But the two topics are sufficiently different to require a major transition before the leap between them can be made. That is the purpose of the brief transition paragraph—to nudge the reader along from one topic to the next. By such devices do writers move their discussions between dissimilar topics without leaving the reader behind.

THE SHAPE OF THE PARAGRAPH

Paragraphs usually consist of three parts: a topic sentence, supporting details, and a summary sentence. The topic sentence presents the topic or main idea of the paragraph, which the supporting details develop and the summary sentence recaps.

The order of these three elements distinguishes the form of a paragraph and the placement of the topic sentence that typically determines its shape.

Topic Sentence at the Beginning

Often, but not always, a paragraph begins with its topic sentence and ends with a summary sentence. Between the two are usually crammed supporting details. The paragraph that conforms to this arrangement may be conceptualized as having a shape like the one sketched below:

```
┌─────────────────────────────┐
│      TOPIC SENTENCE          │
└─┐                         ┌─┘
  │    Supporting           │
  │    details              │
┌─┘                         └─┐
│   RESTATEMENT OF             │
│   TOPIC SENTENCE             │
└─────────────────────────────┘
```

This odd-looking shape—something like an overstuffed sandwich—reminds us that paragraphs typically begin and end with generalizations, between which are crammed more specific and supportive assertions. Here is such a paragraph:

> *By a strange perversity in the cosmic plan, the biologically good die young.* Species are not destroyed for their shortcomings but for their achievements. The tribes that slumber in the graveyards of the past were not the most simple and undistinguished of their day, but the most complicated and conspicuous. The magnificent sharks of the Devonian period passed with the passing of the period, but certain contemporaneous genera of primitive shellfish are still on earth. Similarly, the lizards of the Mesozoic era have long outlived the dinosaurs who were immeasurably their biologic betters. Illustrations such as these could be endlessly increased. The price of distinction is death.
>
> John Hodgdon Bradley, "Is Man an Absurdity?"
> *Harper's Magazine,* October 1936

(Margin notes: Topic sentence; Supporting details; Summary sentence)

The topic sentence of this paragraph, with which it begins, is the main idea that "the biologically good die young." Supporting details and examples are then supplied in sentences 2 through 5, and the final sentence rephrases the main idea and slightly extends it. A paragraph organized in this way is said to move from the general to the particular.

The primary advantage of this arrangement is that it is conventional and expected, and paragraphs that use it are therefore easy to read. We get the main idea of the paragraph immediately; the details follow later. Some reading programs capitalize on the popularity of this order by teaching a method of skimming that consists of glancing at the opening sentences of paragraphs. Most of the time the reader who does that will get the gist of what the paragraph is trying to say—assuming that its topic sentence does indeed come first.

Other paragraphs routinely begin with a topic sentence but omit the final summary of the generalization. If the topic sentence has been adequately developed and the point of the paragraph is quite clear, a final summarizing sentence is neither required nor desirable. The writer's aim, after all, is to make a point, not to abide by some ideal paragraph shape. Here is a paragraph that begins with a topic sentence but omits a final summarizing sentence:

Topic sentence

It by no means follows that computers will in the immediate future exhibit human creativity, subtlety, sensitivity, or wisdom. A classic and probably apocryphal illustration is in the field of machine translation of human languages: a language—say, English—is input and the text is output in another language—say, Chinese. After the completion of an advanced translation program, so the story goes, a delegation which included a U.S. senator was proudly taken through a demonstration of the computer system. The senator was asked to produce an English phrase for translation and promptly suggested, "Out of sight, out of mind." The machine dutifully whirred and winked and generated a piece of paper on which were printed a few Chinese characters. But the senator could not read Chinese. So, to complete the test, the program was run in reverse, the Chinese characters input and an English phrase output. The visitors crowded around the new piece of paper, which to their initial puzzlement read, "Invisible idiot."

Carl Sagan, *The Dragons of Eden*

In this particular paragraph, a final summarizing sentence would have all but ruined the impact of the punch line.

Topic Sentence at the End

Some paragraphs are constructed in quite the opposite way, to proceed from the particular to the general, from supporting details to the main idea. Such paragraphs may be conceptualized as having the following visual shape:

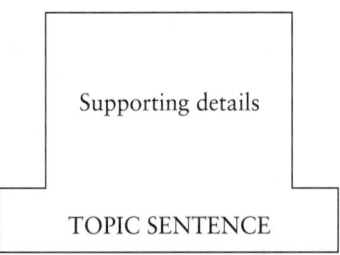

Here is a paragraph to illustrate this organization:

Supporting details

When we watch a person walk away from us, his image shrinks in size. But since we know for a fact that he is not shrinking, we make an unconscious correcting and "see" him as retaining his full stature. Past experience tells us what his true stature is with respect to our own. Any sane and dependable expectation of the future requires that he have the same stature when we next encounter him. *Our perception is thus a prediction; it embraces the past and the future as well as the present.*

> Warren J. Wittreich, *Visual Perception and Personality*

Topic sentence

The paragraph opens with an example of how a person appears to shrink in size as he or she walks away from us. The fact is then explained by the topic sentence, which generalizes about perception.

The chief advantage of this arrangement is that it makes a topic sentence seem especially emphatic, somewhat like a delayed punch line. On the other hand, because this arrangement is unconventional, paragraphs conforming to it are hard to follow and difficult to scan.

There is nothing particularly mystifying about why this is so: in our daily communicating, we simply are more accustomed to getting the big idea first and the details later. Reversing this expected order makes a paragraph more difficult to read at a glance. Paragraphs conforming to this odd shape are therefore used by writers to provide a mild change of pace. The other kind of paragraph, where the topic sentence comes first and the supporting details later, is by far the more common of the two.

Topic Sentence in the Middle

It would be a mistake to infer from this discussion that paragraphs rigidly conform to one or the other of these two shapes. Writing is such a creative enterprise that considerable variation in paragraphs is to be expected. There is, for instance, the paragraph that has its topic sentence somewhere in the middle. Here is one such example:

As long as women were brought up and educated very differently from men and as long as their whole mode of life was different, it was safe and suitable to uphold the traditional beliefs as to certain mental sex differences. But as the differentiation in the education of the two sexes lessened so have the actual differences in their abilities and interest. *Today the survival of some of these stereotypes is a psychological strait jacket for both sexes.* Witness the fact that some 40 per cent of women undergraduates have confessed (the proportion was confirmed in two studies on widely separated college campuses) that they have occasionally "played dumb" on dates; that is, concealed some academic honor, pretended ignorance of a subject, "threw games," played down certain skills in obedience to the unwritten law that the man must be superior in those particular areas. If he *were* superior, the stratagem would not be necessary. "It embarrassed me that my 'steady' in high school," recalled a college junior in an interview, "got worse marks than I. A boy should naturally do better in school. I would never tell him my marks and would often ask him to help me with my homework." Confront the belief "a boy should naturally do better in school" with the fact that the marks of high school girls are

Topic sentence

generally somewhat superior to those of boys, probably because girls study more conscientiously. Could a surer recipe for trouble be invented?

Mirra Komarovsky, "The Bright Girl's Dilemma,"
Women in the Modern World

Such paragraphs are often found buried somewhere in the middle of an essay where the argument is the thickest. A transition sentence or two, a little preamble, and the topic sentence of the paragraph is forced to take a seat somewhere in the middle pews. What is important, however, is not where the topic sentence is actually placed, but how adequately it has been developed and proved.

The advantage of placing the topic sentence in the middle of a paragraph is that the writer then has a chance to link its main point with the preceding discussion. Paragraphs are usually not written in isolation, but more often as the smaller unit of some larger structure—such as a memo or essay. Knitting together separate paragraphs to express the thesis of an essay requires the skillful use of transitions as well as a variation in where and how successive topic sentences are presented.

In sum, although the topic sentence will typically occur at the beginning of a paragraph, sometimes it will also be found crouching in the middle or bringing up the rear. The essay written so that every topic sentence dutifully comes at the beginning of every paragraph would soon seem tiresome and mechanical. And because tiresome writers are only grudgingly read and mechanical arguments only rarely persuade, you would be smart to write paragraphs whose topic sentences vary not only in wording but also in placement.

Topic Sentence Developed over Two Paragraphs

Sometimes a topic sentence is too complex to be developed in a single paragraph. In the following example, a single topic sentence, "There are many types of poetical obscurity," is developed in two paragraphs:

There are many types of poetical obscurity. There is the obscurity that results from the poet's being mad. This is rare. Madness in poets is as uncommon as madness in dogs. A discouraging number of reputable poets are sane beyond recall. There is also the obscurity that is the result of the poet's wishing to appear mad, even if only a little mad. This is rather common and rather dreadful. I know of nothing more distasteful than the work of a poet who has taken leave of his reason deliberately, as a commuter might of his wife.

Then there is the unintentional obscurity or muddiness that comes from the inability of some writers to express even a simple idea without stirring up the bottom. And there is the obscurity that results when a fairly large thought is crammed into a three- or four-foot line. The function of poetry is to concentrate; but sometimes over-concentration occurs, and there is no more comfort in such a poem than there is in the subway at the peak hour.

E. B. White, "Types of Poetical Obscurity"

Developing an idea over two or more paragraphs gives a writer the advantage of a leisurely pace that allows supporting details and informative or humorous asides to be woven into the argument. An idea can be treated at greater length than would otherwise be possible, and many instances, facts, and details cited in its support. The more leisurely pace of development may also help the reader follow a writer's complex argument.

Topic Sentence Implied

Finally, not all paragraphs are written with explicit topic sentences. Indeed, many paragraphs have topic sentences that are not stated, but only implied. Here is an example:

> The little crowd of mourners—all men and boys, no women—threaded their way across the market-place between the piles of pomegranates and the taxis and the camels, wailing a short chant over and over again. What really appeals to the flies is that the corpses here are never put into coffins, they are merely wrapped in a piece of rag and carried on a rough wooden bier on the shoulders of four friends. When the friends get to the burying-ground, they hack an oblong hole a foot or two deep, dump the body in it and fling over it a little of the dried-up, lumpy earth, which is like broken brick. No gravestone, no name, no identifying mark of any kind. The burying-ground is merely a huge waste of hummocky earth, like a derelict building-lot. After a month or two no one can even be certain where his own relatives are buried.
>
> George Orwell, "Marrakech"

The topic sentence implied in this paragraph may be variously paraphrased, but clearly the writer intends to tell us that the funerals he observed in Marrakech were dreary and horrible. Notice that the impact of the paragraph is not necessarily heightened by making this topic sentence explicit. Compare, for example, this doctored paragraph with the topic sentence added:

> *Funerals in Marrakech are dreary and horrible affairs.* The little crowd of mourners—all men and boys, no women—threaded their way across the market-place between the piles of pomegranates and the taxis and the camels, wailing a short chant over and over again. What really appeals to the flies is that the corpses here are never put into coffins, they are merely wrapped in a piece of rag and carried on a rough wooden bier on the shoulders of four friends. When the friends get to the burying-ground, they hack an oblong hole a foot or two deep, dump the body in it and fling over it a little of the dried-up, lumpy earth, which is like broken brick. No gravestone, no name, no identifying mark of any kind. The burying-ground is merely a huge waste of hummocky earth, like a derelict building-lot. After a month or two no one can even be certain where his own relatives are buried.

Orwell's details are already so vivid and gripping that the addition of an explicit topic sentence has little or no effect on the paragraph. Indeed, if anything, the explicit topic sentence seems to detract rather than add to the strength of the writing.

Implied topic sentences are most commonly found in the middle of an essay, where they add to a theme already stated. Here is an example:

> Neurotic, self-loathing, arrogant, and vociferous, Kepler was drubbed with tiresome regularity by his classmates. He fared little better once out in the world, where he tried but failed to become a Lutheran minister. He sought solicitude in marriage, but his wife, he said with the bleak objectivity of a born observer, was "simple of mind and fat of body. . . . stupid, sulking, lonely, melancholy." Kepler tried to make a living casting horoscopes, but was seldom paid; he spent much of his time trekking from one court to another to plead for his fee, drawing titters from the flunkies when he appeared, in his baggy, food-stained suit, tripping over himself with apologies and explanations, getting nowhere. His lifetime earnings could not have purchased the star-globe in Tycho's library.
>
> Timothy Ferris, *Coming of Age in the Milky Way*

The paragraph is about the life of Johannes Kepler, one of the giants of astronomy who, in collaboration with Tycho Brahe, an observational astronomer of the sixteenth century, contributed immensely to our knowledge of the universe. Implied in this paragraph is the topic sentence, "Kepler was the most unlikely of men to be a world-class astronomer," or something to that effect, echoing a theme that occurred earlier in the essay.

The implied topic sentence, a subtle touch common in the essays of professionals, is seldom encouraged in student paragraphs. Why? The simple answer is that writing with an implied topic sentence can quickly lure the unpracticed writer into a muddle. Usage over time reduces this likelihood, but paragraphs with implied topic sentences are simply harder to keep focused. For the beginner, the safest course is to pen paragraphs whose topic sentences make the writer's aim and meaning explicit.

CHARACTERISTICS OF THE PARAGRAPH

Paragraphs vary widely in shape, style, length, and complexity, but all good paragraphs share the characteristics of *unity, coherence,* and *completeness.*

Unity

Good paragraphs do not beat about the bush; they approach the subject directly, moving toward the main point of the topic sentence without distraction. This straightforward progression in a paragraph is called *unity.* To be unified, a paragraph must stick to its main point and never stray from it. It must avoid irrelevancies of every kind and never wander or drift from its primary focus. If the topic sentence of the paragraph promises a discussion of cows, then the supporting details will be about cows and nothing else.

The following are examples of two paragraphs that lack unity. Notice the irrelevant information, set in italics, that destroys the unity of the paragraphs. Then read the paragraphs without the italicized sentences and notice how markedly the writing improves:

The deadly routine of my studies and work turned the past year into unbearable boredom. Each day proceeded with unerring predictability, from sunrise to sunset. If I were to use a symbol to reflect my life this past year, it would be one gigantic yawn—so dull was the schedule by which I was tyrannized. *Of course, there were always a few bright accidents that invaded the boredom, but they were rare.* Every morning at 7:00 A.M. the alarm dragged me out of bed so that I could race to school in time to answer Prof. Huber's Western Civilization roll call at 8:07 A.M. For the next 50 minutes I listened to the prof drone through his battered and stained lecture notes on the meaning of *civitas,* the First Triumvirate, or the Barbarian Invasion. I took plenty of notes so that I could quote verbatim on the next test. Then I moved on to the next class, Introduction to Psychology, where the instructor always got hung up on "standard deviations," "chi square," and "correlation" because those were his graduate work specialties. Then I moved on to the next class, and the next—all equally numbing to my senses.

At 1:00 P.M. it was time to report to my job as cashier of the Arco self-service gas station, located one block from where I live. *I should probably mention that I live in Bakersfield, a town whose reputation is cruelly maligned. I have found that most people think of Bakersfield as the garbage dump of creation. "How can you stand to live in that ugly place?" they often ask. "Nothing but Okies, fog, and cow dung there," they insist. But I'm defensive of my hometown, so I stick up for it.* Anyway, at the Arco station, I sat in a cage, like a monkey at the zoo, collecting money through a barred window from citizens whose lives must have been duller than mine, judging by the way their feet dragged and their faces drooped. "That will be $8.50. Thank you ma'am." "That will be $9.00. Thank you, sir." "No, you will have to work the pump yourself. This is self-service." I repeated myself over and over again—endlessly until I felt that my voice was floating out in the air somewhere, separate from my body. Sometimes I almost wished for a robbery to inject a moment of excitement into my life. *My friend Jimmy Davenport, who works for a posh liquor store, was held up once, and the robbers handcuffed him in the men's toilet, along with the manager of the store and two customers. He told me that he was never so scared in his life as when he looked down the barrel of that big black pistol one of the robbers stuck in his face.* But for me the most exciting event of the job was when I opened my sandwich bag to see if I was having salami or cream cheese.

Every writer occasionally succumbs to distractions and strays from the topic sentence, but most of the time this mistake is caught and corrected during revision. Staying with your main point sometimes even requires you mercilessly to discard compelling but irrelevant details.

There is, moreover, this ancient rule of thumb that might help you to achieve unity: Each new sentence of a paragraph should begin with old information and end by adding something new. Consider, as an example, the practice of this rule in the following paragraph:

> Mathematicians discovered that there were various series of numbers, each one smaller than the one before, which, if added together, come to a total that equals pi exactly. The only trouble is that *the series of numbers* goes on and on and on and on and never comes to an end. *This means if you add up* the first eight numbers of the series you come close to pi; if you add up the first 16 you come closer; if you add up the first 32 you come still closer and so on—but you never get it exactly. *What's more, the numbers are* mathematically complicated and it takes time to work out exactly what each *successive number* is.
>
> Isaac Asimov, "Mathematicians Look for a Piece of Pi"

Admittedly, no one writes paragraphs by deliberately stitching together old and new information in successive sentences. But all writers do this unconsciously, as they focus their attention on the business of advancing the topic. In the paragraph above, we have italicized those phrases that hark back to old information. The rest of the respective sentences add something new. Observe this rule in your own writing, and your paragraphs are likely to be capably unified.

Coherence

A well-written paragraph has coherence: its sentences are not only clear, logical, and grammatically correct, but also arranged so that the reader easily understands the flow of thoughts and the relationships among them. Perhaps the best way to achieve coherence is to think of your paragraph as a single unit rather than a succession of sentences. The focal point of the unit is the topic sentence, which all other sentences of the paragraph should coherently work to support.

We occasionally receive paragraphs like this:

> In the past year it's been through times of extreme highs and lows in my emotional outlook on life. The trend of any life seems to follow this general pattern. Some of the high moments were meeting new people that turned out to be much more than mere acquaintances, having the newly met person turn into a friend a person could know for the rest of their life. Also meeting and going out with a few special girls, which in our relationship between each other bloomed into a kind of affection for ourselves. Then, too, I gave top performances in the area of athletics, track and field, and also in baseball were most gratifying.

This paragraph is incoherent because of two principal defects: First, its topic sentence is muddled; second, it is occasionally ungrammatical. To revise this or any other paragraph, we suggest that you follow this process.

SUGGESTION 1:   *Check the topic sentence.* If your topic sentence is vague or otherwise muddled, your paragraph will most likely follow suit. "In the past year it's been through times of extreme highs and lows in my emotional outlook on life" is a fuzzy sentence that does not suggest a pattern of development for the paragraph as a topic sentence should ideally do.

We asked the student to tell us what exactly he meant and he replied: "The last year of my life was a rough one with many ups and downs." We suggested that he set this down as a revisable beginning. He wrote:

The last year of my life was a rough one with many ups and downs.

This revised topic sentence is clearer and gives a better sense of what is to come: examples that demonstrate how rough the year has been. But it still struck us as overly broad, requiring the writer to cram too many details into a single paragraph, perhaps tempting him to a recital of generalities. When we pointed out this objection to the student, he mulled over his wording and decided to rewrite the sentence to deal with the worst "down" he had coped with over the past year—his unsettled relationships with girls. He came up with this revision:

Over the past year I have been involved in a series of disappointing relationships with girls.

For his supporting details, the student made a list of his disappointing relationships in the order of their occurrence:

I met Maria in May. She started dating my best friend in June.

In July I went to the beach and met Sarah. Two weeks later she moved out of state.

In August, Heather, a girl I work with, asked me out on a date. She didn't show up.

In September my girlfriend from back home wrote me a "Dear John" letter. She had decided to marry someone she knew from grammar school.

Last month I asked Autumn, a girl I have classes with, to go with me to a football game. She said yes then changed her mind at the last minute. I saw her at the game with another guy.

These details, woven into the prose with the odd transition, were all the student needed to finish the paragraph. Moreover, the list suggested a neat chronological order for the examples. Here is the final draft of the paragraph:

Over the past year I have been involved in a series of disappointing relationships with girls. I met Maria in May. She started dating my best friend in June. In July I went to the beach and met Sarah. Two weeks later she moved out of state. In August, Heather, a girl I work with, asked me out on a date. She didn't show up. It got even worse after that. In September my girlfriend from back home wrote me a "Dear John" letter saying that she had decided to marry someone she knew from grammar school. Worst of all was what happened last month when I asked Autumn, a girl I have classes with, to go with me to a football game. At first she said yes. Then she changed her mind at the last minute. I saw her at the game with another guy.

The paragraph is now coherent, crammed with specifics, readable, and interesting.

A paragraph may also be incoherent because of grammatical lapses. The following suggestions and examples will help you recognize and correct the most common kinds of errors.

SUGGESTION 2: *Avoid mixed constructions.* Sentences have built-in predictable patterns and structures. When we hear the beginning of a good sentence, we can almost always reasonably anticipate its ending. For example, when we hear a sentence that begins "If you don't play the lottery," we might anticipate it to end, "you can't expect to win." But we never expect a sentence that begins "If you don't play the lottery" to end with "winning is hopeless." And if we came upon a construction that began with one clear pattern, then unpredictably veered off into another, we would most likely be confused. The previous sentence, for example, ended much as you might expect it to from the way it began. But consider how you would react if we had written it this way: "And if we came upon a construction that began with one pattern, then unpredictably veered off into another, confusing our sense of anticipation is what such a sentence would do." Such a sentence can be understood, but not as quickly and as easily as the sentence whose ending follows the pattern predicted by its beginning. Sentences that begin with one structural pattern but inexplicably end in another are called mixed constructions.

Here are several examples of mixed constructions along with their revisions:

Mixed	By bowing to the pressure of special interests is a sure way for a politician to lose respect.
Improved	Bowing to the pressure of special interests is a sure way for a politician to lose the respect of voters.

or

A politician who bows to the pressure of special interests is sure to lose voters' respect.

Mixed	Whereas parents insist on stifling their children's independence, they encourage rebellion.
Improved	When parents insist on stifling their children's independence, they encourage rebellion.
Mixed	Because the writer's style is difficult makes readers avoid her work.
Improved	Because the writer's style is difficult, readers avoid her work.

Avoiding or editing out all mixed constructions from your paragraphs will immediately improve their coherence.

SUGGESTION 3: *Use pronouns that refer only to identifiable antecedents.** Here is an example of incoherence resulting from poor pronoun reference:

> Everybody today wants psychological advice so that *they* will tell *them* what to do. But *that's* a way of avoiding *your* problems and losing *one's* sense of responsibility, *which* is the only healthy way to survive.

A careless and inconsistent use of pronouns jumbles the ideas. The passage simply does not stick together properly. To whom do *they* and *them* refer? What does *that's* stand for? Why is there a sudden shift from *everybody* to *your* and yet another shift to *one's*? Finally, *which* seems to refer to "responsibility," creating further confusion. Now observe the revision:

> Everybody today wants psychological advice from a counselor who will tell him or her what to do. But relying on counseling is a way of avoiding problems and losing one's sense of responsibility; without responsibility a happy life is impossible.

SUGGESTION 4: *Use similar grammatical structures to achieve balance in a sentence.* This is called *parallelism.*** The use of parallelism could improve the following sentence:

> Walking a beat, riding patrol cars, and the work of an undercover agent are all dangerous aspects of police work.

Walking and *riding* are similar in form, but "the work of an undercover agent" breaks the pattern. The following is an improvement:

> Walking a beat, riding patrol cars, and doing undercover work are all dangerous aspects of police work.

SUGGESTION 5: *Use transition words to help the reader move easily through your writing.* Transition words identify the logical connection between two parts of a sentence. They help the reader to move smoothly from one idea to another. For example:

She searched and searched for her purse. She could not find it.	Too abrupt
She searched and searched for her purse, *but* she could not find it.	Improved
Romance may express itself in a variety of ways. A man may send a woman a dozen long-stemmed roses. A husband may plan and cook a gourmet meal.	Too abrupt
Romance may express itself in a variety of ways. *For example*, a man may send a woman a dozen long-stemmed roses. *Or, as a romantic gesture*, a husband may plan and cook a gourmet meal.	Improved

---

*For an explanation of antecedent, see page 580.
**For a fuller explanation of parallelism, see page 610.

When choosing a transition word, be certain of the type of signal you wish to send the reader—addition, contrast, specification, or conclusion (see kinds of conjunctions, p. 583).

SUGGESTION 6: *Repeat key words to attract and hold your reader's attention.* Notice the effective repetition of the word *dance* in the following excerpt from Hans Christian Andersen's *The Red Shoes:*

> The shoes would not let her do what she liked: when she wanted to go to the right, they *danced* to the left. When she wanted to *dance* up the room, the shoes *danced* down the room, and then down the stairs, through the streets and out of the town gate. Away she *danced,* and away she had to *dance,* right into the dark forest. Something shone up above the trees and she thought it was the moon, for it was a face, but it was the old soldier with the red beard. He nodded and said, "See what pretty *dancing* shoes!"
>
> This frightened her terribly and she wanted to throw off the red shoes, but they stuck fast. She tore off her stockings, but the shoes had grown fast to her feet. So off she *danced,* and off she had to *dance,* over fields and meadows, in rain and sunshine, by day and by night, but at night it was fearful.

The repetition of the word *dance* holds the reader's attention and reinforces the point of the fairy tale—that the red shoes were magical.

Completeness

A paragraph is incomplete if it fails to adequately support or document its topic sentence. There are no rules governing the length of an adequately developed paragraph. The topic sentence must guide you. The topic sentence "A pig is ugly" could probably be supported in 100 words; on the other hand, "Poverty is ugly" might require at least 300 words. The more restricted and narrow the topic sentence, the shorter the paragraph required. Your first concern should be to support your topic sentence with an array of specific details.

Here are two examples. First, notice how skimpy and unsatisfying this paragraph is, consisting as it does merely of one or two supporting generalizations:

> The defensive backfielders of football are disciplined men. They are tenacious and controlled. They must be tough and defend aggressively.

This paragraph is woefully empty. Sentences 2 and 3 simply parrot the content of sentence 1 without adding any detail, substantiation, examples, or proof. Here is an example of a well-developed paragraph on the same topic:

> *In the defensive backfield the aggression gets buried under more and more inhibition and discipline.* These men are like long-distance runners: They are loners, but they are nowhere near as hungry for glory as are the wide receivers. In place of the vanity and fantasies of the wide receivers, the defensive backs

experience depression and rage. They have traits that can be found in offensive linemen, wide receivers, and linebackers. They are tenacious. They must learn zone and man-on-man pass-defense patterns that require incredible self-discipline in the furor of battle. They must not be led by their natural inclination, which is to follow receivers out of their zone before the quarterback releases the ball on a pass play. They must execute patterns precisely. To counter running plays, however, they must move up fast and, though lighter and weaker than the running backs they are trying to stop, hit very hard. So they need controlled and timed brutality and anger.

Arnold J. Mandell, "In Pro Football They Play Best Who Play
What They Are," Saturday Review/World, 5 October 1974

To write effective, complete paragraphs, you need an eye for details; you also need to know the difference between a generalization and a specific detail. A generalization is a broad statement that is relatively abstract and lacking in facts. A specific detail, on the other hand, names names, delivers definite opinion, and contains particulars. Consider, for example, this paragraph:

At the turn of the century, many diseases shortened human life. People did not live very long; what life they had was miserable. If disease did not kill them, poor hygiene did. Most people died from causes that no longer kill. Many were unhappy from the premature mortality around them. Families could not rely on younger members to outlast their parents. However, through improvements in medicine and public hygiene, we now live many years longer.

If you think the writer has said anything in this paragraph, you are mistaken. The writer has simply repeated the topic sentence in a string of generalizations. We need more details. What diseases killed people? How was medicine improved? What improvements were made in public hygiene? How much longer do people now live? A writer does not need to be a genius to amass these sorts of details—solid library research is all that is needed. Consider this paragraph as it was actually written:

At the turn of this century, infectious diseases were the primary health menace to this nation. Acute respiratory conditions such as pneumonia and influenza were the major killers. Tuberculosis, too, drained the nation's vitality. Gastrointestinal infections decimated the child population. A great era of environmental control helped change all this. Water and milk supplies were made safe. Engineers constructed systems to handle and treat perilous human wastes and to render them safe. Food sanitation and personal hygiene became a way of life. Continual labors of public health workers diminished death rates of mothers and their infants. Countless children were vaccinated. Tuberculosis was brought under control. True, new environmental hazards replaced the old. But people survived to suffer them. In 1900, the average person in the United States rarely eked out fifty years of life. Some twenty years have since been added to this life expectancy.

Benjamin A. Kogan, Health: Man in a Changing Environment

By the time we read the final sentence, we are convinced simply because of the writer's generous use of details.

To give you a better idea of the difference between generalizing and being specific, we have doctored this student paragraph to show how the same idea, expressed as a generalization, can be immeasurably improved if it is packed with details. The italicized sentences we added are the more specific:

> When I was a very young boy I was active athletically. *When I was between the ages of 9 and 13, I enjoyed baseball, participated in cross-country, played forward on a soccer team, and took tennis lessons.* But as I got older, I stopped being active. *But when I turned 14, I found that I disliked baseball, that cross-country racing made me weary, that soccer was boring, and that tennis took too much effort.* I quit all my sports and became a couch potato. *I quit every program and began spending my days and evenings watching television or lounging around idly.* Soon I began to have a weight problem and found that I was tiring easily and had no energy. *Soon I ballooned from a svelte 120 lbs. to a flabby 160 lbs. and found that I panted after walking up a few steps and could hardly make it around the block on my bicycle without gasping.* I soon returned to my sports and now find that I look and feel much better. *At 16 I returned to baseball, cross-country racing, soccer, and tennis, and now am down to 132 lbs., with a muscular physique, and wind so good that I sometimes bicycle for the sheer joy of it.*

Exactly what kind of supporting details you should use in your paragraphs will vary with your subject, but as a general rule it is always better to write in specifics than in generalities. This means that if you are writing an essay about the ill effects of cigarette smoking, you should learn enough about your subject to be able to name not only the harmful gases given off by cigarettes but also the specific diseases they cause. Any writer who pens a sentence such as "Cigarette smoke contains a variety of dangerous gases, including carbon monoxide, formaldehyde, and hydrogen cyanide" will inevitably sound more competent than the one who merely writes, "Cigarette smoke contains many dangerous gases." And the difference between the first writer, who sounds competent, and the second, who sounds vague, is neither style, nor grammar, nor any of the other indefinables of writing that students are constantly urged to absorb. It is only that the first writer is more specific than the second. Nothing more.

JOURNALISTIC PARAGRAPHS

If you have ever read a newspaper or magazine, this discussion on completeness might strike you as odd, because popular writing often traffics in the very sort of skimpy paragraph we preach against. Indeed, as we have already said, paragraphs do come in a variety of shapes and sizes. A particularly specialized kind of paragraph has evolved from journalistic writing. Often, this sort of paragraph is no more than a sentence or two long, is entirely devoid of supporting detail, and is intended to present no more than the bare bones of a case. This journalistic paragraph is designed to be gulped down at a glance by a reader crowded in a bus or squashed between commuters in a subway. Here is an example, taken from a newspaper:

> There is no joy in "Wrigleyville." The lights will go on.
> Ivy-walled Wrigley Field, host to 72 summers of daytime baseball, may be lighted up for night games this season, the Chicago City Council decided Thursday night after years of debate pitting tradition against progress.
> Baseball purists and residents of "Wrigleyville," a North Side neighborhood around the ballpark, for years have supported a city law banning night games.
> "Turn on the Lights," *Atlanta Constitution,* 26 February 1988

Paragraphs of this shape, skimpiness, and size, however suitable for newspaper readers, are not recommended for student essays. Newspaper writers are intent on supplying the bare facts to readers who are themselves too harried and rushed to want more. Student writers, on the other hand, are beset by different pressures and expectations. Teachers expect students to write fully developed paragraphs just as newspaper readers expect reporters to serve up only the bare bones of a story. If you are writing for the student newspaper, use the journalistic paragraph. But if you are writing an essay for an English class, use the more familiar, better-developed paragraph that allows you to assert a generalization and then completely support it.

Transitions Between Paragraphs

An essay consists of ideas united around a central thesis and expressed in separate paragraphs. And it is the responsibility of the careful writer to link these separate paragraphs with their individual freight of ideas into a seamless train of thought. Among the several common techniques used to link paragraphs are repetition, transitional words and phrases, transitional questions, and bridging sentences.

Repetition

Successive paragraphs may be linked by repeating in their initial sentences some word or phrase that is common and equally important to both. Here is an example:

> I have experienced *loneliness* many times in my life, but until recently I lived my *loneliness* without being aware of it. In the past I tried to overcome my sense of isolation by plunging into work projects and entering into social activities. By keeping busy and by committing myself to interesting and challenging work, I never had to face, in any direct or open way, the nature of my existence as an isolated and solitary individual.
> I first began to awaken to the meaning of *loneliness,* to feel *loneliness* in the center of my consciousness, one terrible day when my wife and I were confronted with the necessity of making a decision. . . .
> Clark E. Moustakas, "The Terror and Love in Loneliness"

Repetition of the word *loneliness* in the initial sentences serves to link the paragraphs.

The same effect may be achieved through the repetition of a similar or identical opening phrase, as in this example:

> *I want a wife* who will not bother me with rambling complaints about a wife's duties. But I want a wife who will listen to me when I feel the need to explain a rather difficult point I have come across in my course of studies. And I want a wife who will type my papers for me when I have written them.
>
> *I want a wife* who will take care of the details of my social life. When my wife and I are invited out by my friends, I want a wife who will take care of the babysitting arrangements. . . .
>
> Judy Syfer, "I Want a Wife"

This sort of linkage is so strong that overuse of it may cause your paragraphs to seem clumsily yoked. Of course, that may be exactly the effect you are after—as Syfer is—for emphasis.

Transitional Words and Phrases

The language is rich in ready-made phrases that writers routinely use to link paragraphs. Here is an example:

> In every cultivated language there are two great classes of words which, taken together, comprise the whole vocabulary. First, there are those words with which we become acquainted in ordinary conversation, which we learn, that is to say, from the members of our own family and from our familiar associates, and which we should know and use even if we could not read or write. They concern the common things of life, and are the stock in trade of all who speak the language. Such words may be called "popular," since they belong to the people at large and are not the exclusive possession of a limited class.
>
> *On the other hand,* our language includes a multitude of words which are comparatively seldom used in ordinary conversation. Their meanings are known to every educated person, but there is little occasion to employ them at home or in the market-place. . . .
>
> J. B. Greenough and G. L. Kittredge, "Learned Words and Popular Words"

The italicized phrase, *on the other hand,* links the two paragraphs, the first of which discusses popular words, the second, learned words.

Depending on the flow of thought in the writing, you can choose from among a nearly inexhaustible stock of ready-made phrases to link your paragraphs. These include *the fact is, furthermore, moreover, in contrast to, first . . . second . . . third, in short, in sum, then,* and so on. These phrases are not simply polite mannerisms; rather, they serve a useful function of making a passage easier to read by stitching together ideas that may not automatically follow.

Transition Question

Opening a paragraph with a transition question is one way to link it and its ideas to the preceding one. Here is an example:

> There are three kinds of book owners. The first has all the standard sets and best-sellers—unread, untouched. (This deluded individual owns wood pulp and ink, not books.) The second has a great many books—a few of them read through, most them dipped into, but all of them as clean and shiny as the day they were bought. (This person would probably like to make books his own, but is restrained by a false respect for their physical appearance.) The third has a few books or many—every one of them dogeared and dilapidated, shaken and loosened by continual use, marked and scribbled in from front to back. (This man owns books.)
>
> *Is it false respect, you may ask, to preserve intact and unblemished a beautifully printed book, an elegantly bound edition?* Of course not. I'd no more scribble all over a first edition of *Paradise Lost* than I'd give my baby a set of crayons and an original Rembrandt.
>
> Mortimer Adler, "How To Mark a Book"

The writer of this particular paragraph directs his question to the reader, which adds a folksy and informal touch to the writing. But it is not necessary for a transition question to be so bluntly addressed to the reader; it is only necessary for the question to briefly recap what went before while pointing toward what is to come next.

Bridging Sentence

Some paragraph transitions consist of an initial bridging sentence that both sums up what went before and anticipates what is to come after. Here are two examples of it, describing the execution of Mary, Queen of Scots:

> Briefly, solemnly, and sternly they delivered their awful message. They informed her that they had received a commission under the great seal to see her executed, and she was told that she must prepare to suffer on the following morning.
>
> *She was dreadfully agitated.* For a moment she refused to believe them. Then, as the truth forced itself upon her, tossing her head in disdain and struggling to control herself, she called her physician and began to speak to him of money that was owed to her in France. At last it seems that she broke down altogether, and they left her with fear either that she would destroy herself in the night, or that she would refuse to come to the scaffold, and that it might be necessary to drag her there by violence.
>
> *The end had come.* She had long professed to expect it, but the clearest expectation is not certainty. The scene for which she had affected to prepare she was to encounter in its dread reality, and all her busy schemes, her dreams of vengeance, her visions of a revolution, with herself ascending out of the convulsion

and seating herself on her rival's throne—all were gone. She had played deep, and the dice had gone against her.

James Anthony Froude, "The Execution of Queen"

Bridging sentences are widely used in modern journalism and are especially favored by many popular magazines such as *Time*.

Paragraphs without Transitions

Do paragraphs always need some formal transition between them? The answer is no. Sometimes the continuity of theme is sufficiently strong between two paragraphs to require no formal transition. Essentially, you must use your common sense. If the new paragraph introduces an entirely new idea or a significantly different wrinkle to an old one, you may need a transition. On the other hand, if the second paragraph merely continues to add details to what has already been said in the first, no transition may be necessary.

Here is an example of two paragraphs that require no transition. The common theme between them—fishing at the end of the day—provides a focus strong enough to eliminate the need for any transition.

> Occasionally, after my hoeing was done for the day, I joined some impatient companion who had been fishing on the pond since morning, as silent and motionless as a duck or a floating leaf, and, after practising various kinds of philosophy, had concluded commonly, by the time I arrived, that he belonged to the ancient sect of Coenobites. There was one older man, an excellent fisher and skilled in all kinds of woodcraft, who was pleased to look upon my house as a building erected for the convenience of fishermen; and I was equally pleased when he sat in my doorway to arrange his lines. Once in a while we sat together on the pond, he at one end of the boat, and I at the other; but not many words passed between us, for he had grown deaf in his later years, but he occasionally hummed a psalm, which harmonized well enough with my philosophy. Our intercourse was thus altogether one of unbroken harmony, far more pleasing to remember than if it had been carried on by speech. When, as was commonly the case, I had none to commune with, I used to raise the echoes by striking with a paddle on the side of my boat, filling the surrounding woods with circling and dilating sound, stirring them up as the keeper of a menagerie his wild beasts, until I elicited a growl from every wooded vale and hillside.
>
> In warm evenings I frequently sat in the boat playing the flute, and saw the perch, which I seem to have charmed, hovering around me, and the moon travelling over the ribbed bottom, which was strewed with the wrecks of the forest. Formerly I had come to this pond adventurously, from time to time, in dark summer nights, with a companion, and, making a fire close to the water's edge, which we thought attracted the fishes, we caught pouts with a bunch of worms strung on a thread, and when we had done, far in the night, threw the burning brands high into the air like skyrockets, which, coming down into the pond, were

quenched with a loud hissing, and we were suddenly groping in total darkness. Through this, whistling a tune, we took our way to the haunts of men again.

Henry David Thoreau, "Evening Hours at the Pond"

Using Varied Paragraph Transitions

All writers eventually develop signature traits in their styles—and one could be a fondness for, say, the bridging sentence transition. But to overuse the same kind of paragraph transition is to risk benumbing your reader. The ideal is to use a variety of paragraph transitions as this excerpt does (transitions are in italics):

> Let us, *for example,* examine the case of a man I will call Victor Clauson. He is a junior executive with a promising future, a wife who loves him, and two healthy children. Nevertheless he is anxious and unhappy. He is bored with his job, which he believes saps his initiative and destroys his integrity; he is also dissatisfied with his wife, and convinced he never loved her. Feeling like a slave to his company, his wife, and his children, Clauson realizes that he has lost control over the conduct of his life.
>
> *Is this man "sick"?* And if so, what can be done about it? At least half a dozen alternatives are open to him. He could throw himself into his present work or change jobs or have an affair or get a divorce. Or he could develop a psychosomatic symptom such as headaches and consult a doctor. Or, as still another alternative, he could seek out a psychotherapist. Which of these alternatives is the *right* one for him? The answer is not easy.
>
> *For in fact,* hard work, an affair, a divorce, a new job may all "help" him; and so may psychotherapy. But "treatment" cannot change his external, social situation; only he can do that. What psychoanalysis (and some other therapies) *can* offer him is a better knowledge of himself, which may enable him to make *new choices* in the conduct of his life.
>
> *Is Clauson "mentally sick"?* If we so label him, what then is he to be cured of? Unhappiness? Indecision? The consequences of earlier unwise decisions?
>
> *These are problems in living, not diseases.* And by and large it is such problems that are brought to the psychiatrist's office. To ameliorate them he offers not treatment or cure but psychological counseling. To be of any avail this process requires a consenting, cooperative client. There is, indeed, no way to "help" an individual who does not want to be a psychiatric patient. When treatment is *imposed* on a person, inevitably he sees it as serving not his own best interests, but the interests of those who brought him to the psychiatrist (and who often pay him).
>
> Thomas S. Szasz, M.D., "What Psychiatry Can and Cannot Do"

Using a variety of transitional devices, ranging from a transitional phrase to questions to a bridging sentence, this writer produces paragraphs that cover his theme in bright and sprightly sequence.

Beginning and Ending Paragraphs

Journalistic and transition paragraphs are two specialized variations on the paragraph format and consequently somewhat different in structure from the usual workhorse paragraph found in the thick of an essay. Other paragraphs likely to vary in structure and form are those that open or close an essay.

Beginning Paragraphs

Beginning paragraphs that lack snap are frequently, and avoidably, the result of the writer's timidity. But the beginning of your essay is no time to hesitate or hedge. It is here that you must make your stand and take the plunge. For example, one student, writing an argument against wearing mortarboards for graduation, used this humdrum beginning:

> In this essay I should like to argue that although mortarboards are part of the traditional regalia worn at college graduations, these caps are uncomfortable and the convention of wearing them should be discarded.

Although clear and to the point, this opening has no zest, no spirit, no magnetic draw. Yet the writer was passionate in her convictions against mortarboards. After encouragement to speak out, the student revised the opening as follows:

> In fifteenth-century France, a mortarboard was part of the common dress code for university students. They wore it to distinguish themselves from the aristocracy, who wore velvet caps, and the clergy, whose caps were of wool. But these distinctions being entirely meaningless today, it is senseless to burden students with the discomfort of having to march down an aisle and across a platform, mortarboard teetering, to receive a diploma. Surely a gown is enough formal attire for the occasion.

The revision provides intriguing and interesting information on the origins of the mortarboard. Indeed, the origins of a subject can often provide interesting sidelights that might engage a reader's interest. Following are some examples of opening strategies to consider.

BEGIN WITH AN ANECDOTE.   From an essay probing the effect of humor on physical health:

> The story is told that the aging Ethel Barrymore, famous Hollywood actress, was in her dressing room when a studio usher knocked at the door to tell her that two women who claimed to have gone to school with her were outside.
> "What shall I do?" asked the usher.
> "Wheel them in!" replied the indomitable Ethel.

To be able to laugh at oneself is the cornerstone of mental health, which in turn affects one's physical health. Modern scientific research attests to the fact that a sense of humor has healing qualities.

—from a student essay

BEGIN WITH A MEMORABLE PERSONAL EXPERIENCE.   From an essay on marriage and the family:

I shall never forget the minister's opening words at my close friend's marriage ceremony last year. When the bride and groom had clasped hands and were standing in front of him, the minister addressed the couple with these words: "Yolanda and Felix, has it ever occurred to you that your love is absurd? In fact, your marriage is absurd." Of course, an embarrassed hush fell over the entire audience as they mulled over this unusual question, but in actuality the minister was calling attention to a profound truth—that it is rather amazing for a young man and woman to choose each other as lifelong marriage partners out of a whole society. Why that particular man? Why this particular young woman? In essence, every successful marriage is absurd in the sense that, viewed logically, it seems fraught with impossibilities. This essay will analyze the economic, social, and psychological characteristics that help create a solid marriage partnership.

—from a student essay

BEGIN WITH A QUESTION.   From an essay defining poverty:

You ask me what is poverty? Listen to me. Here I am, dirty, smelly, and with no "proper" underwear on and with the stench of my rotting teeth near you. I will tell you. Listen to me. Listen without pity. I cannot use your pity. Listen with understanding. Put yourself in my dirty, worn-out, ill-fitting shoes, and hear me.

—from Jo Goodwin Parker, "What Is Poverty?"

BEGIN WITH A THOUGHT-PROVOKING QUOTATION.   From an essay on our obsession with numbers:

"The very hairs of your head," says *Matthew 10:30,* "are all numbered." There is little reason to doubt it. Increasingly, everything tends to get numbered one way or another, everything that can be counted, measured, averaged, estimated or quantified. Intelligence is gauged by a quotient, the humidity by a ratio, the pollen by its count, and the trends of birth, death, marriage and divorce by rates. In this epoch of runaway demographics, society is as often described and analyzed with statistics as with words. Politics seems more and more a game played with percentages turned up by pollsters, and economics a learned babble of ciphers and indexes that few people can translate and apparently nobody can control. Modern civilization, in sum, has begun to resemble an interminable arithmetic class in which, as Carl Sandburg put it, "numbers fly like pigeons in and out of your head."

—from Frank Trippett, "Getting Dizzy by the Numbers"

BEGIN WITH AN IRONIC OBSERVATION. From an essay on foreign influences on American culture:

There can be no question about the average American's Americanism or his desire to preserve this precious heritage at all costs. Nevertheless, some insidious foreign ideas have already wormed their way into his civilization without his realizing what was going on. Thus dawn finds the unsuspecting patriot garbed in pajamas, a garment of East Indian origin; and lying on a bed built on a pattern which originated in either Persia or Asia Minor. He is muffled to the ears in un-American materials; cotton, first domesticated in India; linen, domesticated in the Near East; wool from an animal native to Asia Minor; or silk whose uses were first discovered by the Chinese. All these substances have been transformed into cloth by a method invented in Southwestern Asia. If the weather is cold enough he may even be sleeping under an eiderdown quilt invented in Scandinavia.

—from Ralph Linton, "The 100% American"

BEGIN BY ANSWERING THE QUESTION POSED BY YOUR TITLE. From an essay on the future of marriage entitled "Does Marriage Have a Future?":

The answer to this question is an unequivocal yes. The future of marriage is, I believe, as assured as any human social form can be. There are, in fact, few human relationships with a more assured future. For men and women will continue to want intimacy, they will continue to want the thousand and one ways in which men and women share and reassure one another. They will continue to want to celebrate their mutuality, to experience the mystic unity that once led the church to consider marriage a sacrament. They will therefore, as far into the future as we can project, continue to commit themselves to each other. There is hardly any probability that such commitments will disappear and that all relationships between them will become merely casual or transient. The commitment may not take the form we know today, although that, too, has a future. But some form of commitment there will be. It may change its name; people may say they are "pair-bound" rather than married, but there will be such "paired" men and women bound to each other in one way or another. Still, I do not see the traditional form of marriage retaining its monopolistic sway. I see, rather, a future of marital options.

—from Jessie Bernard, "Does Marriage Have a Future?"

BEGIN WITH A SURPRISING STATEMENT. From an essay arguing for the superiority of women over men:

Physically and psychically women are by far the superiors of men. The old chestnut about women being more emotional than men has been forever destroyed by the facts of two great wars. Women under blockade, heavy bombardment, concentration camp confinement, and similar rigors withstand them vastly more successfully than men. The psychiatric casualties of civilian populations under such conditions are mostly masculine, and there are more men in our mental hospitals than there are women. The steady hand at the helm is the hand that has had the practice at rocking the cradle. Because of their greater size and weight men are physically more powerful than women—which is not the same thing as saying that they are stronger. A man of the same size and weight as a woman of comparable background and occupational status would probably not be any more powerful than a woman. As far as constitutional strength is concerned women are stronger than men. Many diseases from which men suffer can be shown to be largely influenced by their relation to the male Y-chromosome. From fertilization on more males die than females. Deaths from almost all causes are more frequent in males at all ages. Though women are more frequently ill than men, they recover from illness more easily and more frequently than men.

—from Ashley Montagu, "Women as the Superiors of Men"

BEGIN IN THE MIDDLE OF THINGS BY SKETCHING A SCENE.   From an essay on methods of teaching freshman composition:

"Will spelling count?" In my first year of teaching freshman composition I had a little act I performed whenever a student asked that inevitable question. Frowning, taking my pipe out of my mouth, and hesitating, I would try to look like a man coming down from some higher mental plane. Then, with what I hoped sounded like a mixture of confidence and disdain, I would answer, "No. Of course it won't."

—from Jack Connor, "Will Spelling Count?"

BEGIN WITH A STATISTIC.   From an essay on drug use in American society:

If you pick twenty adults at random, the odds are that fifteen of them drink moderately, two are problem drinkers and one is a desperate alcoholic. Two who use alcohol are also using marijuana, a couple are taking tranquilizers on doctors' orders and one or two have been popping barbiturates to relieve insomnia and are perilously close to addiction. Three or four have taken amphetamines to stay awake or to lose weight and nearly all of them drink caffeine, another stimulant. Ten or twelve of this group of twenty continue to smoke tobacco even after the medical hazards of that habit have been amply documented. One has probably taken acid or mescaline. The children of some have sniffed glue or carbon tet for kicks (thereby risking brain and liver damage), more smoke pot and some have had an LSD trip. The drug culture, as the newspapers call it, doesn't just belong to the kids; everyone's in it together.

—from Joel Fort, M.D., "The Drug Explosion"

Ending Paragraphs

Take leave of your audience with an emphatic exit. Do not timidly shrink or fade, as does this conclusion:

And so, the reasons I have just cited are why animal experimentation is wrong.

No writer can expect to inspire a reader with such a drooping conclusion. Here is an improved version:

Researchers defend their work on animals scientifically on the basis of the similarities between animals and people, but then they defend this same work morally on the basis of their differences. Well now, they cannot have it both ways. Besides, the differences are not so clear-cut. Some animals have a more highly developed intelligence than some human beings. Ponder this question: If we were to be discovered by some more intelligent creatures in the universe, would they have the right to experiment on us?

Your ending paragraph should restate your thesis, summarize your major points, or emphasize your position. This being your last chance to make an impact, you should make this paragraph as emphatic as possible. Now is no time to bring up new topics or unrelated thoughts. And always remember the adage that "it is better to leave your reader before your reader leaves you."

There are as many ways to end a paragraph as to begin one. Here are some suggestions and examples for climactic endings.

END WITH A POINTED QUESTION.   From an essay arguing that although eccentrics and social misfits may be a burden to their families and a nuisance to the public, usually they are not mentally ill, and hospitalizing them may do more harm than good:

> We regard the rich and influential psychiatric patient as a self-governing, responsible client—free to decide whether or not to be a patient. But we look upon the poor and the aged patient as a ward of the state—too ignorant or too "mentally sick" to know what is best for him. The paternalistic psychiatrist, as an agent of the family or the state, assumes "responsibility" for him, defines him as a "patient" against his will, and subjects him to "treatment" deemed best for him, with or without his consent. Do we really need more of this kind of psychiatry?
>
> —from Thomas S. Szasz, M.D., "What Psychiatry Can and Cannot Do"

END WITH AN INCISIVE SUMMARY.   From an essay listing the causes of why the Japanese are acquiring more global competence than are Americans:

> In sum, the Japanese spend eleven million dollars a year on study abroad for their students, as opposed to our four million dollars; the Japanese introduce foreign languages into their elementary school curriculum whereas we usually wait until high school; and the Japanese reveal an enormous curiosity about successful countries and their way of doing things. We had better start improving our own global competence by imitating the Japanese attitude or we shall quickly decline into a third-class nation.
>
> —from a student essay

END WITH A PERCEPTIVE OBSERVATION.   From an essay defining "migraine headache":

> Migraine headache affects not only the head, but the entire body. It includes overpowering fatigue, cyclical vomiting, strokelike aphasia, temporary blindness, painful sensitivity to light, clumsy bodily motions, and a crippling inability to

make even routine decisions. What is surprising to any who have ever suffered this debilitating malady is that no one ever dies of migraine.

—from a student essay

END WITH AN ALLUSION.   From an essay describing the lonely-hearts personals columns in various urban magazines.

> That, of course, may be mere sentimentalism. Whatever works. Loneliness is the Great Satan. Jane Austen, who knew everything about courtship, would have understood the personals columns perfectly. Her novel *Emma,* in fact, begins, "Emma Woodhouse, handsome, happy, clever, and rich, with a comfortable home and happy disposition." The line might go right into the *New York Review of Books.*
>
> —from Lance Morrow, "Advertisements for Oneself"

The key to writing clever beginning paragraphs and emphatic closing ones is, as you might suspect, effort and rewriting. Seldom does a zippy opening or a climactic closing drop into a writer's lap. Most of the time, after the essay is written, the writer will discover from rereading and rewriting the material a way to make the opening better. Similarly, strong endings are usually mined, not casually found. It is through repeated digging into the material, through successive efforts at rewriting, that the writer will most likely unearth a gem suitable for the beginning or ending.

The Relationship between Beginning and Ending

No pat relationship exists between the beginning and the ending of an essay that may be expressed in a formula. But there is a geometric shape that more or less applies to the essay, and it is a circle. Typically, essays hark back to their beginnings in their endings. The final paragraph may decisively evoke the essay's opening, or may only vaguely hint at it. Or, for that matter, the ending may atypically make no mention at all of the beginning.

Nevertheless, it is true that many essays will circle back to their beginnings in their endings. And many will do so imagistically, by alluding in the final paragraph to an image that occurred in the essay's opening. Here is an example of an essay that does so almost precisely:

THE BEGINNING

> While I was still a boy, I came to the conclusion that there were three grades of thinking; and since I was later to claim thinking as my hobby, I came to an even stranger conclusion—namely, that I myself could not think at all.
>
> I must have been an unsatisfactory child for grownups to deal with. I remember how incomprehensible they appeared to me at first, but not, of course, how I appeared to them. It was the headmaster of my grammar school who first brought the subject of thinking before me—though neither in the way, nor with the result he intended. He had some statuettes in his study. They stood on a high cupboard

behind his desk. One was a lady wearing nothing but a bath towel. She seemed frozen in an eternal panic lest the bath towel slip down any farther, and since she had no arms, she was in an unfortunate position to pull the towel up again. Next to her, crouched the statuette of a leopard, ready to spring down at the top drawer of a filing cabinet labeled A—AH. My innocence interpreted this as the victim's last, despairing cry. Beyond the leopard was a naked, muscular gentleman, who sat, looking down, with his chin on his fist and his elbow on his knee. He seemed utterly miserable.

THE ENDING

If I were to go back to the headmaster's study and find the dusty statuettes still there, I would arrange them differently. I would dust Venus and put her aside, for I have come to love her and know her for the fair thing she is. But I would put the Thinker, sunk in his desperate thought, where there were shadows before him—and at his back, I would put the leopard, crouched and ready to spring.

—from William Golding, "Thinking as a Hobby"

The opening paragraphs of this classic essay uses statuettes to represent and classify thinking into three distinct types, an image to which the ending also pointedly returns. This is a nearly perfect example of a final paragraph achieving closure by repeating an image with which the essay opened.

Many essays also use their conclusions to hark back to their openings, but few do so as neatly. Here is another example, in which a final paragraph hints at the opening, but only indirectly:

THE BEGINNING

As I approached the age of 82, I was confronted by a savage rejection of everything decent I had stood for. In the 1988 election, President Reagan announced that anyone who was a liberal—he used the phrase "the L word" as if it were fatally contaminated—was outside the mainstream of American life and intimated that the liberal's patriotism was suspect. Vice President Bush, seeking our highest office, went a lot farther by shouting that anyone who did not wish to recite the Pledge of Allegiance daily was probably false to the honored traditions of our nation; and his running mate, Senator Quayle, declared: "Michael Dukakis is a member of the American Civil Liberties Union, while George Bush is a member of the National Rifle Association," as if that made the former a loathsome traitor and the latter a great patriot. I found all this denigration of liberals personally offensive.

THE ENDING

When I have been dead 10 years and a family comes to tend the flowers on the grave next to mine, and they talk about the latest pitiful inequity plaguing their town, they will hear a rattling from my grave and can properly say: "That's Jim again. His knee is still jerking."

—from James Michener, "We Can Create a Decent Society"

Opening the essay by describing the disrepute into which liberals had fallen during the Reagan years, the author proceeds to identify himself unashamedly only as a knee-jerk liberal. The playful image of his knee still jerking in the grave nicely rounds off the discussion.

This tendency for essays to be circular in form, to end with a backward glance at their beginnings, can provide a crude gauge of whether or not you have strayed from the point. If your ending is wildly different from your beginning, you should make sure the essay delivered just what the thesis promised and did not unwittingly wander off into alien territory.

Exercises

1. Identify the topic sentence in each of the following paragraphs and state whether the material moves from the particular to the general or from the general to the particular.

   a. Everyone who makes money in the mechanical city uses the money that he makes there to escape, as far and as frequently as he can, from the inferno that is the source of his wealth. As soon as he can afford it, he moves his home out from within the city-limits into suburbia; he takes his holidays in what is still left of genuinely rural country; and, when he retires, he withdraws to die on the French Riviera or in Southern California or at Montreux or Vevey. This is not surprising, considering that the mechanized city is as repulsively ugly as the mass-produced manufactures that it pours out. It is, however, a spiritual misfortune for a worker to be alienated emotionally from the place in which he has done his work, has earned his living, and has made his mark, for good or for evil, on the history of the human race.

      Arnold Toynbee, *Cities on the Move*

   b. If you enjoy working out the strategy of games, tic-tac-toe or poker or chess; if you are interested in the frog who jumped up three feet and fell back two in getting out of a well, or in the fly buzzing between the noses of two approaching cyclists, or in the farmer who left land to his three sons; if you have been captivated by codes and ciphers or are interested in crossword puzzles; if you like to fool around with numbers; if music appeals to you by the sense of form which it expresses—then you will enjoy logic. You ought to be warned, perhaps. Those who take up logic get glassy-eyed and absentminded. They join a fanatical cult. But they have a good time. Theirs is one of the most durable, absorbing and inexpensive of pleasures. Logic is fun.

      Roger W. Holmes, *The Rhyme of Reason*

   c. Computers, it is often said, manipulate symbols. They don't deal with numbers directly, but with symbols that can represent not only numbers but also words and pictures. Inside the circuits of the digital computer these symbols exist in electrical form, and there are just two basic symbols—a high voltage and a low voltage. Clearly, this is a marvelous kind of symbolism for a machine; the circuits don't have to distinguish between nine different shades of gray but only between black and white, or, in electrical terms, between high and low voltages.

Tracy Kidder, The Soul of a New Machine

d. There is a queer stillness and a curious peaceful repose about the Etruscan places I have been to, quite different from the weirdness of Celtic places, the slightly repellent feeling of Rome and the old campagna, and the rather horrible feeling of the great pyramid places in Mexico, Teotihuacan and Cholula, and Mitla in the south; or the amiably idolatrous Buddha places in Ceylon. There is a stillness and a softness in these great grassy mounds with their ancient stone girdles, and down the central walk there lingers still a kind of homeliness and happiness. True, it was a still and sunny afternoon in April, and larks rose from the soft grass of the tombs. But there was a stillness and a soothingness in all the air, in that sunken place, and a feeling that it was good for one's soul to be there.

D. H. Lawrence, Etruscan Places

2. Identify the pattern of development used in the following paragraphs.

a. The "human condition" may be defined as a measure of the extent to which the potential for living is realized under the limitations of the inborn genes and of the environment of the Earth. Full potential means adequate food, shelter, clothing, education, and health care, plus useful and creative work and leisure for every normal baby born. The slums of Calcutta or Rio, the ghettos of the West, represent a potential close to zero.

Stuart Chase, Two Cheers for Technology

b. I have said that a scientific answer must be practical as well as sensible. This really rules out at once the panaceas which also tend to run the argument into a blind alley at this stage; the panaceas which say summarily "Get rid of them." Naturally, it does not seem to me to be sensible to get rid of scientists; but in any case, it plainly is not practical. And whatever we do with our own scientists, it very plainly is not practical to get rid of the scientists of rival nations; because if there existed the conditions for agreement among nations on this far-reaching scheme, then the conditions for war would already have disappeared. If there existed the conditions for international agreement, say to suspend all scientific research, or to abandon warlike research, or in any other way to forgo science as an instrument of nationalism—if such agreements could be reached, then they would already have disappeared. So, however we might sigh for Samuel Butler's panacea in Erewhon, simply to give up all machines, there is no point in talking about it. I believe it would be a disaster for mankind like the coming of the Dark Ages. But there is no point in arguing this. It just is not practical, nationally or internationally.

Jacob Bronowski, Science, the Destroyer or Creator

c. Lenin, with whom I had a long conversation in Moscow in 1920, was, superficially, very unlike Gladstone, and yet, allowing for the difference of time and place and creed, the two men had much in common. To begin with the differences: Lenin was cruel, which Gladstone was not; Lenin had no respect for tradition, whereas Gladstone had a great deal; Lenin considered all means legitimate for securing the victory of his party, whereas for Gladstone politics was a game with certain rules that must be observed. All these differences, to my mind, are to the advantage of Gladstone, and accordingly Gladstone on the whole had beneficent effects, while Lenin's effects were disastrous. In spite of all these dissimilarities, however, the points of resemblance were quite as profound. Lenin supposed himself to be an atheist, but in this he was mistaken. He thought that the world was governed by the dialectic, whose instrument he was; just as much as Gladstone, he conceived of himself as the human agent of a superhuman Power. His ruthlessness and unscrupulousness were only as to means, not as to ends; he would not have been willing to purchase personal power at the expense of apostasy. Both men derived their personal force from this unshakable conviction of their own rectitude. Both men, in support of their respective faiths, ventured into realms in which, from ignorance, they could only cover themselves with ridicule— Gladstone in Biblical criticism, Lenin in philosophy.

—Bertrand Russell, Unpopular Essays

Writing Assignments

1. Write a paragraph in which you give examples of some common superstitions in modern life.

2. Define *infatuation* in one paragraph.

3. Write a paragraph comparing or contrasting the process of writing an essay with that of writing a personal letter.

4. In a paragraph, classify the kinds of housing that students at your campus occupy.

5. In a paragraph, state the probable reasons for the popularity of newspaper advice columns.

6. Narrate a love-at-first-sight episode in a single paragraph.

7. In one paragraph, state the effects of a failing grade in your major course.

8. In a single paragraph, argue for or against the pass/fail system of grading.

9. Write a single paragraph outlining the steps involved in any process with which you are familiar.

10. In a paragraph, describe any jogger you have ever observed.

Planning and Organizing the Essay

Let us begin by admitting that planning and organizing do not come naturally to everybody. Some of us are happy to plunge right into whatever we are doing and improvise as we go along. Others are more comfortable planning the minute details of every task before taking even the first step. This same immense variation exists among writers, perhaps even more acutely, given the wide variations in their temperaments and working habits.

That said, we still think the beginning writer is better off writing from an organized plan than from pure inspiration. Most of the time the beginner is groping for content as well as for form—for what to say as well as how to say it—and a plan can help with finding both. Student writers frequently work under a classroom deadline, and even a roughly sketched outline can ease the pressure when the clock is ticking and the page stubbornly resists being filled up.

The kind of planning and organizing we have in mind, which this unit covers, includes finding a topic and prewriting on it, devising a controlling idea or thesis for that topic, and making a rough sketch or formal outline of your essay.

FINDING A TOPIC

Our primary suggestion for finding a topic is that you write about what you know. Common sense tells us that it is surely easier to write about a subject we intimately know than to tackle one about which we know nothing. With the known subject it is easier to find appropriate details, to understand what to emphasize and what to skip, and to summarize your position in a thesis.

But if you cannot write about what you know, the next best approach is to know about what you write. Before you pen a single word, read about the topic and consult campus experts on it for their opinions. Go to the library and browse through magazines and books. Interview professors and others who have experience with your topic. For example, if you are writing a paper about the problems of the handicapped, you might interview handicapped students for a real-world glimpse into the difficulties they face daily. Similarly, if you were doing an essay on law enforcement, you could enliven it by including the views of a criminology professor or by interviewing and quoting someone who is or has been a police officer. Most people are happy to share their views with student writers. Begin the actual writing only when you know the topic well enough to hold and defend an intelligent opinion about it.

All this advice, of course, assumes that you have the choice of a topic as well as the time to do this thinking and planning. However, if your instructor gives you a definite writing assignment—for example, to write an essay contrasting the poetry of Robert Frost with the poetry of John Donne—you plainly have no choice. Similarly, if you are writing an essay in class for a test, you obviously cannot jog to the library and look up the facts.

But let us say that you have been given a fairly general assignment such as to write a classification essay about a force, a group, a system, a ritual, or an emotion. The assignment is due in a week. How do you proceed to narrow this general assignment into a suitable topic?

PREWRITING ACTIVITIES

First, you do the necessary reading and research. You gather your facts. You stake out the territory you intend to write about and explore it thoroughly. Then you begin the prewriting.

Prewriting refers to all the preliminary steps a writer might take in preparing to write. It includes randomly thinking about the topic, systematically gathering information about it, and sketching out a possible structure for the essay. Even those not temperamentally inclined to prewrite can benefit from at least thinking about the topic before committing pen to paper. Professional writers often spend more time on prewriting than on actual writing.

The several aims of prewriting can all be reduced to a single overall goal: to equip you to write a better essay. Part of the prewriting quest is to find an opinion or point of view to which you feel particularly committed. Dig and search until you find a vein of ore that makes you scream "Eureka!" Writing about that will invest your words with the energy and voice you need to make your point.

Making that discovery, however, may require you to engage in one or more of the following prewriting activities.

Freewriting

Freewriting means writing freely and creatively on the assignment. Your goal is to put down every random idea, notion, thought, or opinion that pops into your head about the general subject. First you write down the assignment, word for word, on the top of the paper. Then you begin the freewriting. If you get stuck, write "I'm stuck" and keep going. Here's an example of freewriting on a typical assignment:

Write a classification essay about a force, a group, a system, a ritual, or an emotion.

What is a force? What is a system? Do I want to write about a force, a system, a group, or an emotion? What emotion? Rituals, rituals, what are rituals? I picture religious robes and candles burning in various church nooks and crannies, I hear voices chanting in unison, responding to the priest. I like the word ritual, though. Hmmmm. What group? I'm stuck. I'm stuck. Name some emotions? I don't want to write about groups. Rituals? What rituals? Who has rituals? There's the ritual of the lecture, of grading, of classroom interaction. I feel stuck. Keep writing! Keep writing! It will come. Ritualistic hand washing. Lady Macbeth washed her hands constantly, trying to get the blood of her victims off. It would not come off. Definitely neurotic. Closer to home, more ordinary ritual: Every time my father walks past the kitchen sink, he tightens the faucet and wipes it off with a dishcloth. Or every time my Grandma goes to the supermarket, she drives a mile out of her way to drive past the office where my Uncle Howard used to work, before he died of a heart attack 23 years ago. Or my brother dust-busting out his new car every time he gets home. He's honoring his sense of ownership, the work and discipline it took to save enough money to buy himself a new Mustang. These rituals give meaning, in an odd sort of way.

After a fruitful session of freewriting, your focus is likely to be narrower than before, even if only in a negative sense. You may decide, for example, that you absolutely do not want to classify a group or an emotion. Fine and good; that is progress. You have narrowed your options and at least know what you do not want to write about.

But usually freewriting reveals a predisposition, a slight leaning toward one topic over all others. Follow that hunch in another freewriting session.

Religious rituals. We have many in our church. The services are loaded with rituals. The sacraments are rituals. The relationship between priest and laic is governed by rituals. The behavior of the congregation is governed by rituals.

Now you have a better idea of what you want to do—you want to focus your essay on the rituals of your church. One way to do this is to ask yourself a question about one of the items on the list. The answer to this question, if complete enough, can be the controlling idea of your essay.

For example, you might ask this question about the sacramental rituals mentioned above: "What kinds of sacramental rituals does my church use?" Your answer might be as follows:

The seven sacraments of the Greek Orthodox Church are Holy Baptism, Holy Chrism, Holy Communion, Holy Confession, Holy Marriage, Holy Unction, and Holy Orders.

And that can be the controlling idea or thesis of an essay classifying the sacramental rituals practiced by your church.

In freewriting, remember to suspend all hesitations, doubts, and fears, and simply allow your creative energies to surge. You scribble and jot until you uncover a leaning toward a particular topic. Then you freewrite further on the narrowed topic until you hit upon a particular part of it that strikes you as usable. You ask yourself a question about that particular part, give yourself a detailed answer, and end up with a tentative controlling idea or thesis for your essay.

Talking

Talking about the assigned subject with yourself, or better yet with a willing friend, can help you find a suitable topic. We do not mean the sort of rambling talk that might be carried on over a cup of coffee or a soda pop. What we have in mind is purposeful talk, where you or your friend asks pointed questions aimed at ferreting out particular subtopics you might find appealing in your chosen subject.

Here is an example of the sort of conversation you might hold with yourself or a friend:

The assignment is to classify a group, a ritual, an emotion, or a force into its major types. Which would you like to work on?

I don't know. Maybe the force. Or maybe the ritual.

Let's try ritual. What kinds of rituals do you think you could write about?

Dating rituals, maybe. Holiday rituals. Say, rituals at Christmas and Thanksgiving. Maybe rituals involved in becoming a member of a fraternity.

Do you feel comfortable writing about any of those rituals?

Yeah, I suppose so.

But you're not enthusiastic?

Not particularly. Seems sort of dull and boring.

What do you particularly like? What hobbies or outside activities do you really like to do that you might classify into types?

Well, I like my training in Ki. Ki is a martial arts discipline.

Does it have types you could write about?

Of course, it does! I could write about the levels of Ki that can be mastered by the initiate.

What are these levels?

There're four in all. Kyung ki (lightness), Hung ki (heaviness), Chul ki (hardness), and Ma ki (numbness).

So there you are.

If this example strikes you as a little too pat, remember that we are interested in imparting a principle, not in causing numbness (Ma ki) with drawn-out dialogue. Our point is that talking systematically to yourself or a friend about the subject can reveal overlooked subtopics that you might be keen to write your essay about. All of us are likely to write with more enthusiasm and sparkle about a topic we like than about one we think stuffy. It is possible to write well about a stuffy topic, but it is a difficult feat for even the most disciplined writer.

Clustering

Clustering is freewriting done in the style of a doodle. It is simply the diagrammatic representation of possible subtopics that you might include in your essay. It is also a method of narrowing a broad subject into a manageable topic. Here is how clustering works: You begin by drawing a rectangle in the middle of the page and filling it in with your subject. Let us say you are assigned to write an essay on hypocrisy. Your basic diagram will look like this:

```
┌──────────────────┐
│                  │
│     hypocrisy    │
│                  │
└──────────────────┘
```

Then you add smaller boxes attached to the main rectangle by spokes. In each smaller box you write who, what, when, where, and why—scribbling below each box some tentative answers and ideas. The resulting diagram might look like this:

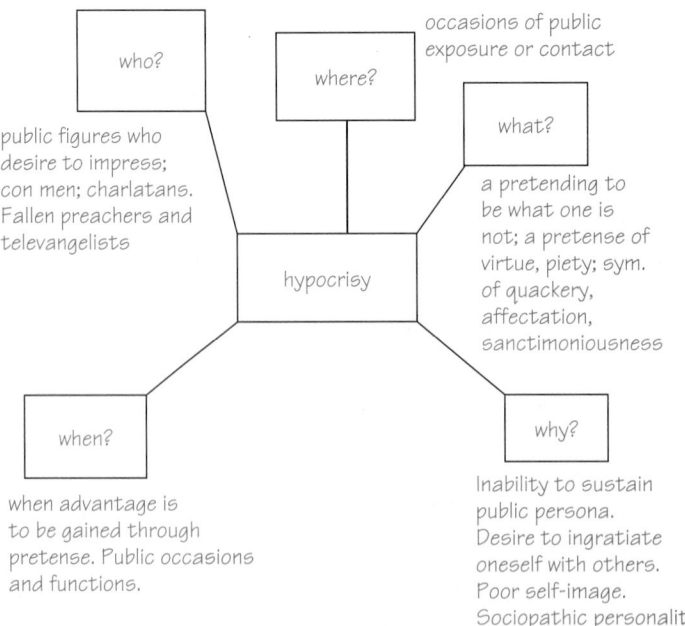

Conscientiously answer the questions in the satellite boxes—providing appropriate facts, figures, examples, anecdotes, and testimonials—and you will have the bare-bones details necessary for writing your essay. You can also use a cluster to plan an essay on a narrowed subject that you have decided to treat with a particular strategy. For example, let us say that you decide to write an essay on hypocrisy, using the strategy of definition. (For more on definition, see Unit 10.) You can then develop a cluster showing the lexical meaning of "hypocrisy" as well as other obvious subtopics you might also cover. Here is an example:

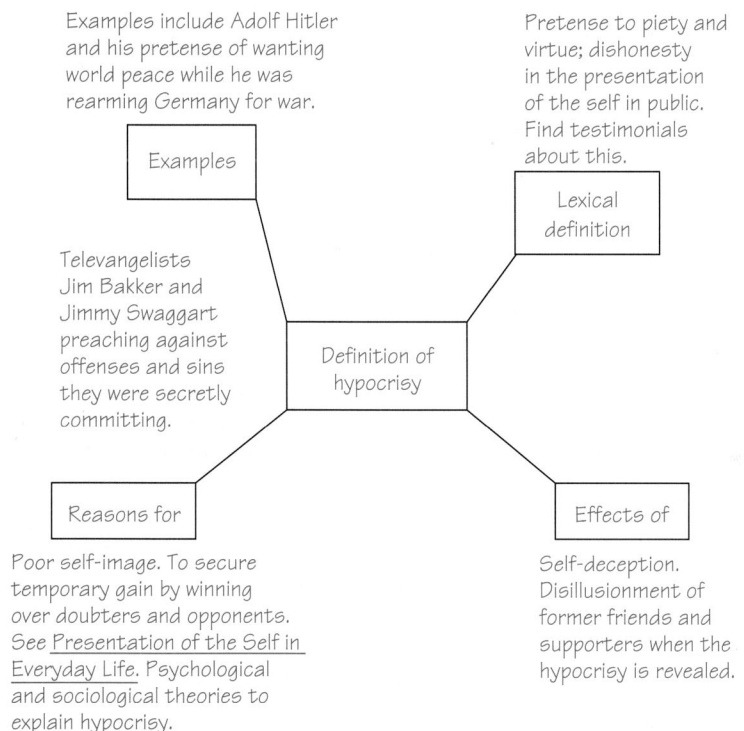

Whether you find your narrowed topic through freewriting, talking, or clustering, be sure to observe the central principle with which this section opened: to always write about what you know, or at least to know about what you write. Imagination is a wonderful faculty, but in expository writing there simply is no substitute for the familiarity and details suggested by actual contact with a topic.

WRITER'S BLOCK

Writer's block is a supposed condition in which afflicted writers are said to be unable to freely express their opinions on paper. In movies, the scenario usually features a rumpled writer hunched over a desk, straining vainly to write, while clumps of discarded manuscript on the floor testify to the futility of the effort. We say it is a "supposed condition" because we think writer's block is misnamed.

In fact, writers are seldom blocked from saying what they believe and desperately want to say; they are more typically blocked when they try to say what they do not want to say or when they have nothing to say. What passes for writer's block is usually nothing more than writer's emptiness.

We are speaking, of course, of expository prose where writers try to express themselves factually on a topic, not fiction writing, which is altogether another kettle of fish. But with expository prose, there are several common reasons for so-called writer's block.

Psychological Reasons

Naturally, we cannot tailor a textbook to address every psychological cause of writer's block, but as teachers we know that the most common cause is a professed hatred of writing, often brought about by a bad experience with a past instructor or a mistaken idea of one's own talent.

We have no solution to the first cause except to say that all of us occasionally encounter an instructor with whom we are not compatible, but to hate writing on that account is as irrational as hating honey because you detest one bee. As for the belief that you are a naturally rotten writer, we also know that students often underestimate their ability to write because they do not understand the writing process. When they find themselves writing slowly and falteringly, they take that as proof of their ineptness as writers. Yet it is perfectly normal for a writer to work hours on an essay and produce only one good page.

The good writer is not one who dashes off 50 pages at one sitting and never makes a mistake. That creature is mainly a figment of scriptwriters' imagination and only rarely exists in real life. Indeed, testimony from notable writers down through the ages tells us that writing is a chore, a labor; that it is slow and agonizing work; that it involves repeated rewriting, stopping and starting again. If this is the way you work, you are not a bad writer but merely a typical one.

Physical Reasons

Among the physical factors that can contribute to writer's block are the use of poor equipment or the choice of an inappropriate site for composing.

Writing with a pen or a typewriter can be sheer labor compared to writing with a word processor. Some writers who are eruptive composers can find themselves frustrated if they are forced to gush through the capillary of a pen. The solution to this particular problem is to get and use a word processor. Nearly everyone's writing is improved by the use of a word processor, which allows multiple revisions on the screen without the grind of retyping. Some modern college libraries even make word processors available for a low rental fee, an investment we heartily recommend to those students who cannot afford their own machines.

As for finding an appropriate site for writing, the best place is not always a quiet alcove overlooking a peaceful vista with birds dutifully chirping in the background. Some writers do indeed favor such an Edenic setting, but others prefer the clamor of a bus station. If you find yourself utterly unproductive as you wait for inspiration to strike in a quiet library, maybe you should try writing in front of the blaring television while your roommate practices a trumpet solo. You know where you do your best writing, and you should try to stick with that particular setting.

The Internal Editor

Finally, there is the problem of the internal editor who sometimes bedevils our best efforts at writing.

Within each of us, the theory goes, is an internal editor who sits in silent judgment of our every sentence. This editor consists of every grammatical lesson we ever learned, every red-inked comment we ever received on the margins of our papers. It is the collected teachings of all we think we know about writing. And sometimes—because of stress, the pressure of a deadline, or some other reason—this internal editor becomes so severe and judgmental a critic that we simply cannot produce a single line that we like. When that happens, every word we put down on paper seems so ridiculous that we develop a block.

The solution often recommended to shut up a faultfinding internal editor is simply to sit down and write. Or, do as the writer William Stafford recommends: Whenever you feel blocked, simply lower your standards. Write without looking back; put everything down exactly as it occurs to you. Later, you can always go back and sift through and edit what you have written. But for now, just write with abandon and a complete suspension of judgment. Often, this tactic is effective in silencing a too severe internal editor.

But the technique that works for us no matter what the cause of the so-called block is a simple and effective one: rereading our work. When we get stuck or think ourselves on the wrong track, we return to the first word and reread what we have written, editing as we do. Sooner or later we find where we took a wrong turn or made a misstep. If we do not find it on the first rereading pass, we reread the work again, changing words and sentences here and there. And if necessary, we reread it again. Nothing is better for writing than rereading, and all conscientious writers incessantly and repeatedly reread every page they have written until they are satisfied. This technique works; it is tedious but miraculously effective for us. Try it next time you feel blocked while writing an essay.

FINDING THE THESIS

The thesis is not simply a statement saying what you are going to do. More than that, it is a formal summary of your essay's topic and is usually best worded to have an argumentative edge and to commit your essay to a specific rhetorical strategy.

The usefulness of the thesis lies in its limiting effect on a writer's efforts. As writers, all of us know how utterly vast the blank page can be, especially when we are groping toward our initial topic and have only a vague idea of what we want to write. It is then that a well-worded thesis can help point us in one direction and provide us with a useful limit for our thinking and writing.

The Too-Narrow or Too-Broad Thesis

Many mishaps can occur to a sentence as it journeys from the writer's brain, where it hatched as an idea for a topic, onto the page, where it becomes a thesis. Two errors are particularly common: the overly narrow or overly broad thesis.

A thesis that is overly narrow usually leaves the writer scrambling for something to say, causing the wordiness known affectionately as "padding." Here is an example of what we mean by an overly narrow thesis:

> Hundreds of northside commuters have to drive their cars south to the city every weekday morning.

The test of an overly narrow thesis is whether or not it leaves the writer anything of significance to argue or assert. So hundreds of northside commuters drive south to work everyday? And hundreds more drive north, and possibly another few hundred drive east and west. So what? We are left to fill in the blanks around a dead-end utterance. Here is a much improved version:

> Hundreds of northside commuters have to drive their cars south to the city every weekday morning because public transportation is not available from the suburbs of Atlanta.

Now we have room for argument. We can show how we are squandering precious energy through the folly of encouraging the lone commuter; we can point out how the northern suburbs of Atlanta, and the city itself, will eventually suffer economically and culturally from the lack of public transportation.

The overly broad thesis, in contrast, does not choke off argument with its littleness; instead, it rather overwhelms the writer with its bigness. Here is an example:

> This paper will explain the reasons why wars are fought.

Utterly impossible. A book may take a stab at such an enormous topic; a 500-word essay would be a pinprick. Worse yet, the effort at writing a small essay on a big topic can easily seduce a writer into penning generalities.

The simplest way of gauging whether or not your topic—as summarized in your thesis—is too big for your essay is to check the library reference sources on it. A topic such as the causes of war is likely to generate scores of references, which ought to warn you that you may be biting off more than you can chew. Remember that a

500-word essay can, at best, only nibble on a topic. Use your common sense. For example, the student who initially attempted to write an essay about war changed the thesis to how his father felt about serving in Vietnam—a topic that is certainly more manageable in a short essay.

As you frame your thesis, bear in mind that its overriding purpose is to help you focus on a specific topic. For example, if you were assigned an essay on "the outdoors," you could end up chasing a nearly limitless number of subtopics and tacks before you actually decided on any particular one. On the other hand, penning this thesis beforehand gives the essay a definite direction and also establishes a humorous voice as well as an argumentative purpose for it:

> Of all the currently popular outdoor sports, hiking should be shunned as the one most likely to cause sciatica and oxygen poisoning and to predispose ordinary people to despise their usual habitats.

Refining the Thesis

We do not wish to leave you with the impression that the thesis will always occur to you before you start to write the essay or that it will always automatically emerge from your prewriting efforts. Sometimes it will and sometimes it will not. Writers generally have a vague idea of what they want to write before they actually begin writing. But sometimes writing about a topic is the only way to discover how you really feel about it and what particular opinions you truly hold. The ideal, however, is to have a preliminary thesis that gives you a firm idea of what you want to say.

Let us say, for example, that you are asked to write about your activities of the past year. How do you discover and refine the thesis for an essay on such a topic?

First, begin by asking yourself some questions about the past year: "What did I mainly do during the past year?" "How did I feel most of the time?" "Did I learn anything different or was I stuck in a rut?" "Have I suffered constant upheavals, or have I led a calm existence?" "Has my family approved of me or not?" After playing with these questions and others, you hit on the following crudely worded ideas:

1. Most of the time I have been hassled with money worries.
2. Basically, it's been deadly dull which I can't stand, making me so bored day in and day out.
3. The last year spent learning frugality.
4. Major upheavals have caused me to sink or swim as I met various Waterloos.
5. Why have I felt so guilty all year?
6. The first six months were misery. The second six months were ecstasy.

To find the topic, we began with a question. Our thesis should implicitly answer the underlying question that led to it. And the answer to that underlying question will, in turn, logically suggest the best development for your essay.

Consider the following revisions:

1. Meeting my monthly expenses on a budget of $300 has kept me anxious and depressed all year.
(The word *hassled* has been refined to "anxious and depressed." "Money worries" have been more specifically identified as "monthly expenses." The phrase "on a budget of $300" helps explain the writer's anxiety and worry. The underlying question: meeting what monthly expenses has kept me anxious and depressed? Develop by *examples*.)

2. Because of the deadly routine of my studies and work, the past year has been unbearably boring.
(Incoherence is the main problem with the original version, its words not adding up to a comprehensible thought. The reader gets the general meaning but has to guess where the essay is leading. The underlying question behind the more pointed and purposeful revision: Why has the past year been so boring? Develop by *causal analysis*.)

3. Over the last year I have learned the meaning of frugality.
(The original version is a sentence fragment. Through rewording, we have turned the fragment into a complete sentence. The underlying question: what have I learned about the meaning of frugality over the past year? Develop by *definition* or *narration*.)

4. Major upheavals required difficult decisions from me this past year.
(The original version misuses a figure of speech. Waterloo was a famous battlefield; one cannot sink or swim in it. Figures of speech tend to blur meaning and should be avoided in the wording of a controlling idea. The underlying question: what major upheavals required difficult decisions? Develop by *narration* or *examples*.)

5. Because of several serious errors in judgment, I felt guilt-ridden most of last year.
(Our new version simply turns a question into an answer, thereby giving better direction to the content of the essay. The underlying question: why have I felt guilty all year? Develop by *causal analysis*.)

6. In contrast to my misery during the first six months of the year, I spent the second six months in a glorious, ecstatic mood.
(The original version suggests two unrelated controlling ideas that tend to tug the reader in separate directions. Blended together in a single thesis, these two statements now answer the underlying question: how did my first six months contrast with the second? Develop by *comparison/contrast*.)

From this discussion, we can propose six guidelines for writing good controlling ideas. Your controlling idea should

1. predict the content of your essay as specifically as possible without wasting words

2. be clear and coherent

3. be stated in one complete sentence

4. not be obscured by figures of speech

5. be a statement, not a question

6. move toward a single point, not diverge into two or more ideas.

The Informal Outline

You know your topic. You have read a great deal about it. You have a controlling idea expressed as a thesis. Now what do you do? Make a plan.

The plan does not need to be formal and complicated (although if your instructor requires a formal outline, that is what you will have to do). It may, instead, be an informal sketch of the essay, of what you intend to say in it, of what sequence of points you mean to cover.

Here is an example. The student is writing an essay contrasting two friends. Her outline is informal, intended not for submission to the instructor, but for her own use. To the left of her entries, she has noted the successive points on which her contrast will be based:

Controlling idea: My two closest friends, John
and Mark, are nearly exact
opposites in their handling of money.

Attitude toward money: I. John has contempt for money.
Mark has reverence for money.

Willingness to spend money: II. John spends without hesitation.
Mark comparison shops.

Items to be bought: III. John buys what he wants.
Mark buys what he can afford.

If you wish to abandon altogether the numbering system used in outlines, you can simply make a *jot list* of your essay. This is a list on which you jot down your main points with perhaps a note or two about what details to include under each as support. Jot lists are personal creations that are never submitted to an instructor and may consequently be as neat, messy, or scribbled over as you like, just so long as they help you plan better. Here is an example of a jot list a student did for an essay recounting the effects of a stroke:

Controlling idea: A stroke affects the
victim, the victim's family, and the long-range
plans of the victim and the family.

Effects of a Stroke:
Physical effects on the victim
Impairment of physical functions. Slurred
speech. Memory lapses.

Effects on the family
    Loss of former living standard. Decline in
    income. Increased care and attention must
    be given to the victim.

Effects on long-range plans
    College plans must be changed. Vacation plans
    must be postponed.

Another informal outline is a diagrammatic one such as the example that follows, which resembles a computer programmer's chart. Every rectangle represents a single paragraph, and the arrows the linkage between them. In each rectangle the student scribbled down the main points she intended to cover. You can also use a separate index card for each major entry, giving you the flexibility to add or discard entries as the need arises without having to redo the entire outline.

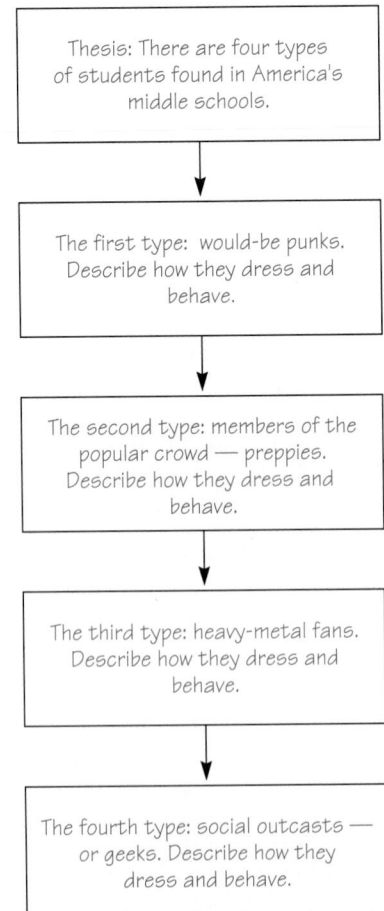

Thesis: There are four types of students found in America's middle schools.

The first type: would-be punks. Describe how they dress and behave.

The second type: members of the popular crowd — preppies. Describe how they dress and behave.

The third type: heavy-metal fans. Describe how they dress and behave.

The fourth type: social outcasts — or geeks. Describe how they dress and behave.

Informal outlines are especially handy for mapping out in-class writing assignments. But to be useful they must record at least the main points of your essay in the proper order. It also helps to write your thesis at the top of the page to keep your attention unwaveringly focused on the main point of the essay.

THE FORMAL OUTLINE

The formal outline is known, loved, and hated by legions of admirers and detractors. For plotting the development of an essay down to the last word it has no rival. Many instructors regard the formal outline and its attendant discipline as an indispensable prewriting activity for any major writing assignment.

The formal outline subdivides the controlling idea of the essay into smaller ideas, which are then developed in separate paragraphs. The currently accepted form of outlining uses Roman numerals, capital letters, and Arabic numerals to order ideas according to their importance. Consider this sample outline:

Controlling idea

   I. Main idea
     A. Subidea
     B. Subidea
       1. Subdivision of subidea
       2. Subdivision of subidea
  II. Main idea
     A. Subidea
     B. Subidea
       1. Subdivision of subidea
       2. Subdivision of subidea

A typical outline keeps subdividing larger ideas into smaller ones. This, of course, means that every subdivided idea must have at least two subcategories, because it is impossible to divide anything into fewer than two parts.

This example is known as a three-level outline, because it has three levels of entries designated by a roman numeral, a capital letter, and an arabic numeral. Longer papers use the more complex four-level outline, whose shell is sketched out below:

Controlling idea

   I. Main idea
     A. Subidea
       1. Division of a subidea
         a. Minor idea
     B. Subidea
       1. Division of a subidea
         a. Minor idea

II. Main idea
   A. Subidea
      1. Division of a subidea
         a. Minor idea
   B. Subidea
      1. Division of subidea
         a. Minor idea

Here is a four-level outline of an essay on the process of movie script writing. *Controlling idea:* Because so many tastes have to be satisfied, movie script writing tends to be a drawn-out process involving criticisms from many sources and nearly endless revisions.

I. Movie scripts must satisfy many tastes.
   A. The producer has to be satisfied with the script.
      1. The producer often requests criticism of a script from advisers.
         a. Scriptwriters occasionally field criticisms from producer's secretaries.
         b. Scriptwriters must also please the producer's spouse.
      2. The producer must get a script that satisfies the financial backers.
         a. Scriptwriters must cope with criticisms from investors.
         b. Scriptwriters must even field criticisms from the investor's accountant.
   B. The director has to be satisfied with the script.
      1. The director often has input from film technicians.
         a. Scriptwriters must deal with the director's advisers, whose concerns are technical rather than dramatic.
         b. Scriptwriters must resist technicians' encroachment on the script's story line.
      2. The director must determine if the script can be made within the available budget.
         a. Scriptwriters often revise dramatic sequences to save expense.
         b. Scriptwriters often rewrite because of the limitations of a special effects department.
II. Movie scripts are consequently subject to nearly endless revisions.
   A. The procedure for rewriting is often spelled out in the script-writing contract.
      1. The primary rewriter is the creator of the script.
         a. Contracts often financially penalize the creator of the script who refuses further rewriting.
         b. Contracts give producers the discretion to bring in a rewriter in the event of a dispute with the script creator.
      2. Rewriting disputes are referred to arbitration.
         a. Arbitrators must often judge which writer's or rewriter's contribution deserves a screen credit.

    b. Arbitrators must decide which writer is entitled to residuals from
      the film.
   B. The producer and director often work as rewriters.
    1. Script rewriting is nontechnical work that can usually be done by
      anyone.
     a. Producers often contribute scenes.
     b. Directors often suggest scene changes.
    2. Script rewriting may even occur during filming.
     a. Actors and actresses will deliberately change lines during a scene.
     b. Actors and actresses will spontaneously misspeak a line that will
      be used.

Writing from such a sophisticated outline entails only a fleshing out of the entries
and the insertion of appropriate examples and details. The rule of thumb for the
inclusion or omission of entries in an outline can be stated simply: Use the outline to
frame out the paragraphs of your essay; include as entries those ideas that separately
or in combination with another can be developed into a paragraph.

The Sentence Outline or the Topic Outline

You can write either a *sentence outline* or a *topic outline*. All entries in a sentence
outline are full sentences, whereas the entries in a topic outline consist of single
words or phrases. The following excerpts illustrate the difference.

TOPIC OUTLINE

Controlling idea: Two primary problems confronting adolescents are extreme
dependence on family and the search for personal identity.

  I. Extreme dependence on family
   A. Financial
   B. Emotional
  II. Search for personal identity
   A. Between childhood and adulthood
   B. Difficulty of finding self in today's world
   C. Blurred social standards
   D. No official rites of passage to adulthood

SENTENCE OUTLINE

Controlling idea: Two primary problems confronting adolescents are extreme
dependence on family and the search for personal identity.

  I. Adolescents are extremely dependent on their families.
   A. Because jobs for the young don't pay well, adolescents have to depend
    on parents for financial support.

    B. Because parents have always provided emotional stability, adolescents feel lost without parental support.

II. Adolescents are perplexed by their search for an identity in a changing world.
    A. They are torn between acting as children and acting as adults.
    B. It is difficult for adolescents to form ideals or goals when their world is in an upheaval.
    C. Blurred social standards cause frustration and consequent insecurity in adolescents.
    D. Without official rites of passage to adulthood, adolescents in American society must establish their own rites to account for their emerging identities.

The advantage of the topic outline is that it is brief, giving an instant overview of the entire essay. A sentence outline, on the other hand, provides a complete and detailed plan of the essay. Here is the rule of thumb: Use topic outlines for simple subjects; use sentence outlines for complex subjects.

USE OF THE OUTLINE

The outline is a map of what you will cover in the essay. It should tell you whether you are developing your controlling idea logically and should indicate the supporting points you need. The most important function of the outline, however, is to prevent the essay from dwelling on some topics while failing to develop others. It is easy for a writer working without an outline to drift from the central focus of the controlling idea and stray to irrelevant topics. Here is an example of just such an error. The writer was working without an outline:

> Because of its practical uses as well as its psychological effects, my backpack is my most valuable possession. It is difficult to describe, but it resembles a chair that one places on one's hips and piles with things like sleeping bag, canteen, pots, underwear, and mosquito poison.
>
> My backpack gives me a sense of independence because it represents perseverance and self-reliance as I climb trail after trail. I know, when I set out on a trail, that for the next three or four days, my backpack and I will be challenged by the mountain, as were the old mountaineers of our country. So I fill it carefully and methodically with all the equipment I will need—from food to clothing.
>
> Campfire time is the nicest part about camping, but sitting around the campfire I sometimes wish I had a transistor radio, which is what I thought I was getting when I got my backpack.
>
> It's been a tradition in our family to go backpacking every summer, so each member of my family has his own backpack and each of us has to carry his own load up the mountain trails. As we climb, we sing, watch the beautiful scenery, and occasionally munch on some food. My favorite climb is Mt. Whitney, although

once I had a terrible case of altitude sickness when I reached the top. I hope that never happens again because I really suffered.

I wish I had a Kelty backpack because it is the best. Mine is just a plain orange nylon polyester backpack of some minor brand, but it will do until I can afford the Kelty. My dad surprised me with the backpack on my last birthday. I had expected a transistor radio, but instead I received the backpack, which pleased me enormously. I plan to use it frequently.

Here is a sketchy outline of this effort, made after the essay was written:

Controlling idea: Because of its practical uses as well as its psychological effects, my backpack is my most valuable possession.

    I. My backpack gives me a sense of independence.
       A. It represents perseverance.
       B. I feel like a mountaineer with it.

   II. Campfire time is the nicest part about camping.
       A. Sometimes I wish I had a transistor radio.
       B. I got a backpack instead.

  III. It's a tradition in our family to camp.
       A. We have a good time climbing and singing.
       B. I got sick at Mt. Whitney, my favorite climbing spot.

  IV. I wish I had a Kelty backpack.
       A. Mine is just a plain orange polyester backpack.
       B. I had expected a transistor radio.

This outline would have alerted any veteran writer to trouble looming ahead. Its main entries are not parallel, meaning they are not similarly phrased. (For more on parallelism, see page 610 of the *Handbook* and page 55 of Unit 4.) *Parallelism* in an outline is more than a nicety of form; it is also a technique for focusing an essay on a succession of related topics. As it stands now, this outline lacks a central focus, which means its subtopics neither support nor develop the controlling idea, "Because of its practical uses as well as its psychological effects, my backpack is my most valuable possession." No doubt as the writer composed the essay, she became caught up in writing about her fond memories of campfires and her family's camping tradition, forgetting that neither topic adds to the discussion of the practical or psychological uses of her backpack, which is her controlling idea. Although such an oversight is easily made during the heat of composing, it would have been quickly spotted in an outline.

Even if you are not temperamentally inclined to write from a prepared outline, the example demonstrates that making an outline of the finished essay can spotlight any major errors you made during the writing. If you do work from a prepared outline, add and delete topics in its entries depending on whether they fit in with your controlling idea. Make your entries parallel to ensure a common focus to your topics. After discussions with her peer editing group, the student prepared this revised outline:

Controlling idea: Because of its practical uses as well as its psychological effects, my backpack is my most valuable possession.

 I. My backpack is sturdy and well made.
    A. It is made of nylon polyester.
    B. It resembles a chair.
 II. My backpack came from my father.
    A. It was a surprise birthday present.
    B. Backpacking is a family tradition.
 III. My backpack has practical uses.
    A. It serves as a portable restaurant.
    B. I can use it as a folding motel.
 IV. My backpack has important psychological effects.
    A. It gives me a feeling of strength and self-reliance.
    B. It gives me a feeling of independence.

Purpose   To acquaint the reader with why the backpack is your most valuable possession.

Strategy   Analysis of why you value your backpack: *causal analysis*.

This revised outline is distinctly different from and better than the earlier one. First, its main entries are parallel, each beginning with the identical initial phrasing, "My backpack." Second, key words from the controlling idea are repeated in some of the main entries, thus establishing continuity between the thesis and the outlined topics. The third entry, for example, deals with the "practical uses" of the backpack, and the fourth details its "psychological effects," both of which are mentioned in the thesis, or controlling idea. Notice also that at the bottom of the outline the writer specified both a purpose and a strategy for the essay. Neither is, strictly speaking, part of the outline; the writer is merely making a note to herself. Here is the revised essay that resulted from this outline:

Made of bright orange waterproof nylon polyester tied to a light aluminum frame, my backpack resembles a chair that I tie to my back and pile high with camping necessities. Because of its practical uses as well as its psychological effects, my backpack is my most valuable possession.

My dad surprised me with this pack on my eighteenth birthday. I had expected a transistor radio, but instead I received the backpack, which pleased me enormously because backpacking is a tradition in our family and everyone except me had his own personal backpack.

I value my backpack for its practical uses. It is really a portable restaurant capable of carrying sixty pounds of food tucked away in its various compartments. When properly filled, my backpack will feed me for ten days in comfort and style. Whenever I get to a particularly beautiful spot, after climbing for two or three hours, I can simply set down my pack, open the food compartment, spread out a picnic of dried and canned foods, and dine on a meal washed down with the tang of a mountain stream. Out in the crisp blue mountain air, the fare tastes better than that of a four-star Michelin bistro. Once the sun has disappeared and night has fallen, I can check in without a reservation, for my backpack is also a folding motel. It contains all I need: insect repellent, a propane lantern, a sleeping bag, and a portable tent. The rains can pour and the winds can howl, but I remain immune to the elements and to the mountain.

I value my backpack also because of its psychological effect on me. When I am carrying it on my back, slowly inching up the mountains, one steady step at a time, I feel strong and self-reliant. In liberating me from restaurants, motels, and grocery stores, my backpack helps me overcome the timidity in myself, making me feel independent and free. Sometimes I imagine myself an early American mountaineer—tough, strong, and weatherbeaten. I don't have to rely on expensive tourist traps because my backpack supplies everything I will need during the time that I will be camping out. For both its practical uses and its psychological effects, my backpack is truly my most valuable possession.

The outline for the improved essay indicates that the practical uses of the backpack and its psychological effects are roughly equal in importance, and this equality is reflected in the wording of the controlling idea: "Because of its practical uses as well as its psychological effects, my backpack is my most valuable possession." The writer has therefore attempted to give approximately equal time and space to both aspects of her subject. Having written the essay, she can then check to be sure that both ideas have been emphasized in the essay according to their importance in the outline. If she discovers that she has written five paragraphs on the practical uses of the backpack but dismissed its psychological effects in one skimpy sentence, she knows that the essay is obviously lopsided and needs to be rewritten.

Not all outlines reflect a symmetrical and equal development of all subideas. The outline on the problems of adolescent youth, for example, lists two points that need to be developed under the first subidea, "Adolescents are extremely dependent on their families," and four points under the second subidea, "Adolescents are perplexed by their search for an identity in a changing world." Common sense tells us that more space is required to develop four points under one subidea than two points under another. If, however, the subidea with the greater number of points ends up being only a skimpy paragraph, the writer has probably muddled the train of thought and produced a lopsided essay.

Exercises

1. Break down the following controlling ideas into their logical major divisions:
   a. The major strokes in tennis can be grouped into five types: the service, the topspin shot, the chop, the full volley, and the overhead smash.
   b. Secretion of digestive juices in the stomach, constriction of the circulatory system, and an elevated heartbeat are some of the effects of smoking.

   c. Migraine headaches are accompanied by vascular pain, nausea, and an extreme sensitivity to all sensory stimuli.

   d. Making reservations for guests; providing directions to restaurants, theaters, and meeting venues; and troubleshooting complaints are the major responsibilities of a hotel concierge.

2. Rewrite the following thesis statements to correct any major errors:

   a. Financial debt can result in a make-or-break situation for the affected family.

   b. Ancient art and literature suggest that homosexuality has been around a long time, and it is just becoming fashionable to come out of the closet in America.

   c. The concept of an unmarried woman choosing to have a baby and raise it herself.

   d. What makes Type A personalities tick?

   e. Some people care more than others about having to be in school, knowing, however, the value of education must be in life a paramount asset.

3. Rewrite the following outlines, correcting any defects:

   a. *Controlling idea:* A manual portable typewriter is less expensive, less distracting, and more convenient than an electric portable.

      I. The manual portable typewriter is less expensive than an electric portable.
        A. The manual typewriter has no motor or electrical wiring.
        B. The electric typewriter has an expensive motor, drive chain, and electrical grounding system.

      II. The manual portable typewriter is less distracting than an electric portable.
        A. The manual typewriter makes only the noise of its keys striking against the platen.
        B. The motor of an electric typewriter makes a constant whirring noise.

      III. The electric portable with cartridge ribbons is troublesome to use.
        A. The cartridge ribbon feature makes a big job out of correcting a simple mistake.
        B. The cartridge ribbons are more expensive than ordinary ribbons.

      IV. The manual portable is more convenient than an electric portable.
        A. The manual is lighter, smaller, and requires no electrical outlet.
        B. The electric typewriter is heavier, bulkier, and requires an electrical outlet.

   b. *Controlling idea:* The art of reading faster requires a student to read actively, avoid regressions, and be flexible in adjusting the reading pace for material of varying difficulty.

      I. Active reading is necessary to increase reading speed.
        A. Active reading requires a preview of the passage.
        B. Active reading is emotional reading.

II. Regressions must be avoided.
   A. Regression or rereading of material shows a lack of confidence.
   B. Regression can be minimized by reading at a higher speed than usual.

III. Some books are more fun to read than others.
   A. Detective stories are the most fun of all.
   B. Material that is slightly racy is also fun to read.

IV. Reading pace must be adjusted for the particular material.
   A. Shakespeare and poetry cannot be speed-read.
   B. Technical material also requires a slower pace.

6

Drafting, Revising, and Style

Drafting, the attempt at actually writing the essay, usually begins after the research and reading have all been done and almost always after a thesis has been devised. If we seem cautious in our qualifiers, it is because writers are so wildly individualistic in their methods that absolute pronouncements are risky. While most writers will not begin the draft without a definite thesis, other fearless souls like to venture out onto the wide open page with neither thesis nor outline to guide them. For such brave explorers, the draft is a voyage of discovery—of what they think about the topic, of what they intend to say. We cannot recommend this method for beginners, however; the safer procedure is to map out the terrain with a thesis and to plot out the possible course of the essay with an outline.

Whatever your particular method, drafting is the time to practice compositional eccentricities. If you like writing with a background din, put on some hard rock and turn up the stereo. If you prefer peace and quiet, get thee to a nunnery or a graveyard. Choose the place to write that is ideal *for you*, a method of writing that works *for you*, and the writing instrument that *you prefer,* whether quill pen or laptop computer.

How many drafts should you write? The ideal answer is, as many as you need to perfect your paper. But because this is not an ideal world for harried students who must write many papers for several classes, we recommend a minimum of three drafts. The first draft should simply get something down on paper. Revise this for macro errors and you end up with the second draft. After editing and proofreading this second draft, you type up or print out the final draft for submission.

TIPS ON DRAFTING

Although writers and their methods are infinitely varied, there are still some time-tested practices that can help anyone write a better draft.

Keep Your Audience in Mind

Write down on a note card or sheet of paper a statement of what you are writing, for whom, and for what effect. For example, if you are writing a paper aimed at persuading a landlubber audience of the joys of sailing, you might jot down the following: "500-word essay on sailing aimed at novices to convince them to take up the sport." This may strike you as kindergarten advice, but we firmly believe that no writer ever went broke remembering the overall aims of an assignment.

Keep Your Purpose in Mind

You may begin with one purpose and have every intention of keeping it, but during the drafting discover a better and more energetic aim for your essay. If so, go with the energy. Creativity is exactly what drafting is meant to bring out. Remember, your aim is to produce revisable copy, not flawless pages. Whatever you come up with during the first draft will be revised during the second. You are a sculptor trying to find a stone to chisel. Your first draft will be the raw stone. You will do the chiseling during revising and editing.

Organize Your Main Points

An easy way to make a rough outline of your essay is to write down your main points on separate index cards. You may also jot down supporting details on each card. Shuffle the cards to reflect the order of presentation of your points. Experiment with rearranging the cards until you are satisfied that you have the best and most emphatic sequence. Then begin the writing.

Include Ample Specific Details

If you pack details behind your points, your paragraphs will seem solid and substantial. If you do not, they will seem like this one—vague and empty:

> Thinking back into the history of music, one can still hear the peaceful melodies of Bach and Beethoven—sounds to soothe the soul, not torment the mind. As words were added to the music, song developed and warmed our hearts. From the 1960s

and 1970s came songs of love and despair, tunes to portray fun in the sun, and choruses of rhyme and reason. Each of these songs either contained deep sentiment or meaning or simply provided easy listening or a light beat to dance to. Again there were songs to provide thought and fun and to ease the mind. Then came the 1980s.

The problem with this paragraph—from an actual student essay—is not its language, which is conventional and easy to read, nor its style, which is fairly clean. It is emptiness of content. What love songs of the 1960s and 1970s does the writer mean? With a little effort, he could have named some—"Little Green Apples" by Bobby Russell, "Michelle" by the Beatles, "The First Time Ever I Saw Your Face" by Roberta Flack—and sounded impressively authoritative. That is what you must try hard to do in your draft.

Write in Any Sequence You Prefer

We are tediously linear writers. We begin with the first word and slog a path doggedly through to the last. But that is not necessarily the best way for all writers to work. You may, as you begin your draft, have the words for a brilliant ending paragraph come tumbling into your head. In that case, write the last paragraph first. Do what works best for you.

Be Patient

We hardly exaggerate when we say that for a writer to breeze through a first draft without repeatedly stopping and starting is rare. Do not delude yourself, as some do, into believing that the faltering progress of your draft marks you as an inept writer. If anything, it signals that your working habits are normal and healthy. So be patient. Writing is always rough going at first. Dorothy Canfield Fisher, a seasoned writer, compared starting to write with a baseball pitcher warming up his arm. Keep on writing and your prose, like a pitcher's curve ball, is bound to get better.

Use a Word Processor

If possible, do your drafting on a word processor. The magic of the word processor is that it allows an unlimited number of corrections without the attendant fatigue of retyping. With a typewriter, you are faced with the tediousness of sometimes having to retype an entire page because you made one or two minor changes to a single sentence. But with a word processor corrections are made on a screen—with miraculous ease—and all the drudgery of printing is done by the computer. Most word processors also have built-in spelling checkers that scan your text at electronic speed and suggest corrections. Some even have programs that correct grammar. Using a word processor will make a slow writer faster and almost any writer better.

Be warned, however, that you should not rely solely on spelling or grammar checkers to keep your text clean. No spell checker can tell you whether you have misused "their" for "there." No grammar checker can match the human eye in sensitivity to lapses of style.

If you are lucky enough to write your draft with a word processor, we recommend two tricks that we practice ourselves in our own writing.

The first is to edit not only on the screen, but also on the actual printed page. When you are nearly satisfied with your text, print it out and edit it with a pencil or pen. In doing so you not only get a lifelike view of your text that a mere screen equivalent simply cannot match, you also preserve your original in case you later decide to restore some or all of it.

The second technique is to create a file for saving large erasures or deletions. Many word processors save the last change in a buffer and allow you to reinstate it with a few keystrokes, but the material is typically lost when you turn off the machine. If you create a file and save your erasures, you can reinstate this text if you decide later that it isn't so bad after all. You might also store the separate drafts for later comparison.

THE FIRST DRAFT

Taking the plunge is basically the whole idea of the first draft: to commit yourself on paper to some specific topic or theme. The only failsafe way to do this is to start writing, no matter how falteringly or awkwardly—just begin. How much you know about your topic, how deeply you believe in it, will become apparent once you actually begin the draft. If you find yourself scrounging to come up with something to write, chances are you either chose the wrong topic or you need to read more about it. On the other hand, if you find yourself straining to use pompous language, you probably do not truly believe in your own topic and are trying to fake your way through it. The solution is to continue writing and revising until you find out how you really feel about the topic.

The text you produce in drafting will be clumsy, scrawled over, and perhaps occasionally incoherent. Good; that is exactly how a first draft should look and read. You are fumbling for a way through the topic and for a grip on how you really feel about it. This process of self-discovery should cause tentativeness.

To give you a realistic idea of the successive steps involved in producing a paper, we will follow an actual student paper through three stages: a *draft*, a *revision*, and a final editing for *style*. The assignment was to write a paper that answered the question, "Who Am I?" A student named Alfredo Silva agreed to let us peer over his shoulder during the entire process.

Following is Alfredo's draft, annotated by the marginal comments of his instructor.

STUDENT ESSAY

First Draft   Alfredo Silva

Who Am I?

Try for a more captivating opening that answers the question

My professional goal is to be a history teacher and help children of Mexican decent to 1
become successful. In my fantasies I see Nobel Prize-winning immunologists with
surnames such as Gomez or Castillo. I also see brown-skinned, brown-eyed senators,
Supreme Court justices, university presidents, journalists, and CEOs of conglomerates.
                                                   leaders-women as well as men-
These persons, whom I have taught, would be dedicating their lives to improving our
                                                                          They
country's morality, customs, political system, philosophy, and education. These leaders
would in turn set strong examples for all of the young people to follow. In the society of
my vision, racial violence, high school dropouts, teenage pregnancies, and drug abuse
have vanished.

Don't shift key words

(d)
                                              vision
Although I know that my aspiration cannot be realized overnight, I am firmly convinced 2
             bedrock
that education is the basis of any significant social change. Knowledge of what went
                                                                       ref
wrong is the most powerful start for righting what is wrong. To cause change we must
join forces. As a unit we can accomplish more than we can as individuals. We can
         e   talents, shore up each other's weaknesses,
compliment each other's weaknesses and therefore be strong as a whole. Through
                                guard   *Hispanic*
cooperation we as a people can defend ourselves against losing our identity or our culture,
while still promoting an American way of life. This country has a lot to offer all of its
citizens, including Hispanics. In turn, Hispanics can contribute to maintaining a reputation
for the United States as a great place to call home. I have thought of other careers, even
          because - - - -
contemplating law, accounting, and nursing. Yet, I have settled on being a history teacher.

Too vague. Replace with more specific motivation that you feel.

The Hispanic community needs history teachers. Our children need to know that the 3
pain and suffering of my ancestors was in the pursuit of liberties that we would not
otherwise have. They need to know the immeasurable courage of people like Patrick
Henry, who cried out, "Give me liberty or give me death!" They need to know about
people who believed so much in this country that they were willing to die for it so that
future freedom would be guaranteed to anyone wanting it enough.

4   ~~Personally, I consider myself~~ *I am also* a romantic extrovert. I come from a family of seven siblings,

emotional
so relationships ~~have always been easy for~~ *are familiar to* me. I was taught always to be open and honest

with my feelings. As I was growing up, I found that this honesty and straightforwardness

were not always appreciated. I turned to writing poems in an effort to express myself in

certain
subtle ways. Eventually I began using poetry to sort out the confusion I felt after events

in my life began to affect me greatly. For me writing in verse is a ~~very~~ spiritual experience.

In my poems I ask many questions that I did not know I had. Sometimes an inspiring

then
thought will enter my mind, or a striking image will appeal to my emotions. I will be bound

to my desk for hours, trying to figure out exactly how I feel and how to express the feeling.

5   Although I am continually struggling to find out who I am, I think the answer may lie

in the pages of my tattered notebooks in which I unburden my heart and my mind. An

important aspect of a happy life is peace of mind, which can be found in communication.

Poetry is my clue to the mystery of who I am, for it is through it that I communicate my

wants and needs.

Here you need to provide further explanation. Were you hurt? Did people turn on you?

Provide an example

Avoid this fatuous word

What questions?

Try to clinch your ending. Give it some punch.

REVISING THE FIRST DRAFT

Ideally, you should begin the drafting well enough ahead of your paper's deadline to allow yourself the break of a day or two before doing the revision. This respite will give you a fresh eye and allow you to see weaknesses that you might otherwise miss. Naturally, this is not always practicable advice, especially if you have a pressing deadline, but experience teaches that the writer's eye is keener, and the judgment clearer, after a break.

It is the macro elements of the essay—especially the paragraph—that your focus should be on during the revision. Later, you can worry about grammar, spelling, and punctuation; for now, your aim should be the repair of any major structural flaws in the larger parts of the essay. We recommend the following checklist:

1. Check your opening paragraph.
2. Check your sequence of points.
3. Check for adequate examples and details.
4. Check paragraph transitions.

Check Your Opening Paragraph

You probably wrote the opening paragraph before you were fully warmed up and the words really flowing, and for that reason it is here that you are likely to find wooden passages. Check to see if the style and tone of the opening paragraph fit in with the rest of the paper. For example, here is an opening paragraph that begins in typically wooden fashion:

> The concept of an unmarried woman choosing to have a baby and raise it by herself has become increasingly prevalent. There is much publicity on celebrities having children out of wedlock. In the last several years this concept has wrongly been made to be a glamorous and stylish way of life. An unmarried woman who purposely has a child out of wedlock is selfish, immature, and clearly not able to make a rational decision on her own.

Realizing that she had written this before she had found her "voice" for the essay (see "Put a Personal Voice in the Writing" on page 110), the writer made these revisions:

> Today it has become almost common for an unmarried woman to choose to have and raise a baby alone. With much publicity, many celebrities have had children out of wedlock, their example making single motherhood seem a glamorous and stylish way of life. My own feeling is that an unmarried woman who purposely has a child out of wedlock is selfish, immature, and clearly not able to make a rational decision on her own.

This is a brisker and more direct opening.

You should also revise your paragraph, if necessary, to give it a more grabby opening. See Unit 4 for some suggestions about how to pep up your opening paragraph.

Check Your Sequence of Points

One easy way to do this, as we suggested in Unit 5, is to make an after-the-fact rough outline of the essay. You are looking to make sure that you covered your major points in the order announced in the thesis. For example, the above opening paragraph charges the unmarried mother with being "selfish, immature, and clearly not able to make a rational decision on her own." If the last of these points—the alleged irrationality of the unwed mother—is covered first, something is badly amiss.

Check for Adequate Examples and Details

Check your paragraph for completeness (for a discussion of completeness, see page 56 of Unit 4). Sometimes an anecdote or extended example is all that is needed to beef up an otherwise empty paragraph. Here is an example from the essay against unwed mothers:

Although many women feel that intentionally having a child out of wedlock has become acceptable, they clearly do not have any sense of logic. The woman is only thinking of herself and therefore basing her decisions on very selfish reasons. They are evading the real issues for having a child. A child is something created by a man and a woman who want to show their love for each other, and for a baby. The unwed mother cannot see the future, only the present she feels she needs to have a child for reasons such as she is getting older, or is not seriously involved with a man now or in the immediate future.

Its other problems aside, this paragraph needs the bite of an example. When a peer editing group pointed this out to the writer, she made the following revision:

Although many women feel that intentionally having a child out of wedlock has become acceptable, they clearly do not have any sense of logic. These women only think of themselves and therefore base their decisions on very selfish reasons. My sister, for example, had a baby 14 years ago for a man she knew only briefly and has never kept up with. Now the child is asking questions about her father, and my sister has no answers for her. She cannot tell her daughter that she deliberately used the man only to get pregnant and without telling him of her intentions. She cannot admit that she does not know where he is because she didn't care for him then or now. If she tells the truth, she will be setting a terrible moral example. Meanwhile, my niece is asking more and more questions every day.

The poignant example makes this a much more effective paragraph.

Check Paragraph Transitions

During the heat of composition, writers often forget to carefully link up paragraphs. You may find that you need to add a bridging sentence or transitional phrase (see pages 59–62 of Unit 4 for examples).

ACHIEVING STYLE

"Have something to say, and say it as clearly as you can. That is the only secret of style." So wrote Matthew Arnold (1822–1888), the English poet and critic. Indeed, it is hard to imagine a more crucial component of style than clarity. And it is impossible to imagine how witless and muddled writing can be stylish.

Here is an example of what we mean by muddled writing:

Cloverdale College's planning efforts have made a serious attempt to stress the city's key barometer as being the future direction of its youth, seeking primarily to diffuse the painful alienation by struggling to build cooperation among diverse groups with efforts like its multicultural curriculum having developed subject matter that encourages students in becoming acquainted with cultural diversity and to appreciate it.

This paragraph is murky because its sentence is too long and overburdened. More sentences, and simpler ones, are needed. Here is a possible rewrite:

> In studying the future, Cloverdale College has tried to use its students as the key barometer for all planning efforts. It has particularly focused on the painful alienation felt by individual cultural groups on campus, such as Armenians, Koreans, or Hispanics. And it has developed multicultural classes whose course content builds cooperation among diverse cultural groups by teaching students to appreciate the advantages of cultural diversity.

The key to writing clearly—and consequently with a dab of style—is to unravel tangled sentences and reduce them to shorter and more straightforward units. And the cause of muddled writing is usually a combination of three factors: The writer does not understand the subject, believes that language should reflect an imagined self-importance, or simply does not know how to edit.

Whatever the cause, however, some basic principles of editing can help transform muddled writing into clear prose.

Simplify Your Grammar

The first principle of clarity is to write sentences that clearly say who is doing what in the subject and what is being done in the predicate (for more on subject and predicate, see pages 569–570). Examine the following sentence:

> A lack of agreement on the part of the Honors Program Committee prevented the determination of whether an additional amount of money was needed for student recruitment endeavors by the Honors Society.

This sentence is not only long, but also unclear in the relationship between its subject and predicate. The actor, the Honors Program Committee, skulks behind an abstract noun—*lack of agreement*—while the contemplated action—spending extra money—crouches behind a passive verb. The rewrite should specify exactly who did what and what was done:

> The Honors Program Committee could not agree on whether it should spend more money to recruit students for the Honors Society.

It is now plain who acted and what the actor did:

Subject	*Verb*
Committee	could (not) agree
It	should spend

Express Action in Verbs Rather Than Nouns

Noun constructions tend to make actions seem as if they were impersonal objects rather than freely made choices and have consequently found favor in the writing of education committees and government panels. Verbs, on the other hand, add directness, briskness, and accountability—which is why they have fallen into disfavor in the prose of collective bodies.

Consider, for example, this sentence, which could have sprung from the pages of any committee report: "There will be a freezing of all funds." By whom?, you might ask. Is this freezing an act of God or the work of human hands? It is impossible to tell. In expressing the action as a noun, the writer has to name no responsible actor. Here is a rewrite that expresses the action in a verb, ascribes it to a specific actor, and results in a more direct sentence: "The president will freeze all funds." Here are other examples along with suggested rewrites:

There was an instant dissemination of information on the part of the officers to the troops.	Noun construction
The officers instantly disseminated the information to the troops.	Rewrite
The making of payments by the grandfather to his son was a requirement imposed by the courts.	Noun construction
The courts required the grandfather to make payments to his son.	Rewrite

Student writers will sometimes use such constructions to fudge any opinion they feel tentative or insecure about bluntly expressing. Instead of writing, "This poet writes an annoyingly abstract line that, even after it is deciphered, often seems empty and pointless," they will say, "The abstractness of this poet and her work has sometimes been noted." Strictly as a matter of style, however, the bluntness of the first sentence is always preferable to the fuzziness of the second.

Avoid the Passive Voice

English has two voices: the active and the passive. In the active voice, actor and action are clearly linked through a straightforward verb: "Jim smashed Susie's pumpkin with a hammer." In the passive voice, on the other hand, the actor is often disguised by the construction of the verb and may even altogether disappear. "Susie's pumpkin was smashed with a hammer." The culprit of this deed, Jim, lurks unnamed in the passive verb.

Most of the time you are better off writing in the active voice. Your prose will be cleaner, more direct, and vastly easier to read than if you did otherwise. On the other hand, in some rare instances the passive voice is justified, especially when an action is more significant than its actor. Here is an example:

In 1993 *four federal agents* were shot by the Branch Davidians when the Bureau of Alcohol, Tobacco, and Firearms made its raid to confiscate illegal firearms.

That four federal agents were shot is more important than who shot them, justifying use of the passive voice.

Of the two voices, the active is the more vigorous and definitely the one you should ordinarily use. Instead of writing, "More space is needed in the parking lot to accommodate the massive number of commuting students," it is better to write, "The massive number of commuting students need more space in the parking lot."

Be Brief and to the Point

A sentence may be grammatical but still graceless, as is this one:

> During this same time period Elizabeth Murray Smith insisted on having a "prenuptial agreement," a legal document, with her husband, written so that her husband could not acquire all her wealth after they were married.

The writer uses unnecessary words in the original. Trimmed down, the sentence loses no meaning, yet is considerably clearer:

> During this same period Elizabeth Murray Smith insisted on a prenuptial agreement to prevent her husband from acquiring all of her wealth after they were married.

For the sake of brevity, you should use as few words as possible while not stating what is already obvious to the reader from the context. You should also not overburden your sentences with too many parenthetical asides, as this writer does:

> Douglass was, of course, unaware that ultimately war would be the result of that awakening of the South, but from the days of the Wilmot Proviso, *past the terrible disappointment of the passage of the vile, abominable Fugitive Slave Act, the foulest component of the loathsome Compromise of 1850,* through to his abandonment in 1856 of what was left of the Liberty Party, *the Radical Abolitionist party of Gerrit Smith, in favor of the rising Republican Party,* Douglass was exhilarated by the thought that men of goodwill like Gerrit Smith—*and Frederick Douglass*— would somehow persuade legislators to use the law to end slavery.
>
> William S. McFeely, *Frederick Douglass*

If we eliminate the parenthetical information, we are left with a more straightforward and readable sentence:

> Douglass was, of course, unaware that ultimately war would be the result of that awakening of the South, but from the days of the Wilmot Proviso through to his abandonment in 1856 of what was left of the Liberty Party, Douglass was exhilarated by the thought that men of goodwill like Gerrit Smith would somehow persuade legislators to use the law to end slavery.

Many have the mistaken idea that fatter sentences are more dazzling to a reader than leaner and plainer ones. But that belief is a myth. All writing improves on a diet high on directness and low on redundancy, triteness, and grandiosity.

REDUNDANCY.   Redundancy refers to the use of unnecessarily repetitious language. One common redundancy in the English language is the overuse of *word pairs*, such as "true and accurate," "long and hard," "willing and able," "hope and trust," or "basic and fundamental." These deadwood pairs, which roll effortlessly off the pen out of sheer habit, only glut the sentence. Instead of writing, "We hope and trust to remain healthy," simply write, "We hope to remain healthy." In other words, choose only one of the pairs.

A second redundancy occurs through the use of *words whose meaning is already implicit in an earlier word,* for example, writing that "a table is round in shape" when "round" obviously implies shape. Other redundancies of this kind are "few in number" (few already implies number), "red in color" (red is always a color), and "future hopes" (hope always involves the future).

TRITENESS.   Triteness is the use of stale expressions and prepackaged phrases. Sometimes the prudent use of colloquial phrases can add an endearing and democratic tone to writing. But most of the time prepackaged phrases and expressions such as "worth her weight in gold," "as clear as day," and "the burning question" are merely annoying. If you cannot think of an original metaphor, better to write down what you have to say plainly without using any of these lame phrases. Instead of writing, "the order was *clear as the living day,*" merely write "the order was clear."

The following commonly used prepackaged phrases, for example, can and should be turned into a single word:

in this day and age	today
owing to the fact that	because
despite the fact that	although
if it should happen that	if
on the occasion of	when
in anticipation of	before
subsequent to	after
concerning the matter	about
it is necessary that	must

GRANDIOSITY.   Grandiosity is an annoying fondness for big words over common ones. In prose, plainer is usually better; and in college papers especially, reams of which the harried instructor must read, a simpler style is always greeted with reward and gratitude. Moreover, the common word is usually the more effective. Listen to this passage from a student college application:

As I apply to your college, I am cognizant of the fact that doing so is in response to my ancient reveries of attaining an education in an environment completely supportive of my educational objectives and a campus affording me the best in learning environments.

Pity the screening committee that must wade through this stilted passage. It is not likely to be impressed. How much more convincing and human to have sounded plain and simple, as this student did:

> Since I was a child I have dreamed of attending Mount Sinai College, where my father earned his degree in American history. I have always loved your campus for its rustic beauty, and I especially value the emphasis your program places on personal instruction. I am convinced that I will get a first-rate education at your college.

Grandiosity can be avoided if you say what you have to say in plain and simple English. Doing so will mean using a plain but precise diction. Here are some examples of pompous terms to avoid, along with their more common synonyms:

termination	end
facilitate	help
ascertain	find out
endeavor	try
inception	beginning, start
envisage	see
transpire	happen
incisive	biting
conflagrant	burning
traverse	cross

Our personal bugbear, which we think deserves special mention, is the use of "utilize" when "use" is meant. Utilize your common sense; use "use" if you mean "use."

Vary Your Sentences

Variety is the spice of style. Passages that monotonously begin with the same word or use the same sentence type and length are stultifying to read. Yet with elementary sentence combining, even a droning passage can be made to sparkle. Here is an example:

> There are two basic personality descriptions that can be used to describe people of all walks of life. There is, for example, the type A personality who is described as aggressive and driven. There is also the type B personality who is described as laid back and optimistic. There are profound differences between the two types of personalities that scientists are just beginning to find out.

Notice that all the sentences of this paragraph unremittingly open on the same word, *there*, which creates a monotonous effect. After the student worked through the sentence combining chapter, she rewrote the passage this way:

People of all walks of life can be classified into two basic personality types. The type A personality is described as a person who is aggressive and driven. In sharp contrast is the type B personality, who is habitually laid back and optimistic. Between the two types of personalities exist profound differences science is just beginning to discover.

We think it generally lazy to begin two sentences in a row on the same word, unless it is being deliberately done for emphasis, and inexcusable to begin three in a row with the same opening.

Edit Awkward Language

Some mishaps of style are caused by awkwardness of language and phrasing. And most can easily be remedied with simple editing. Here, for example, is an awkwardness that editing would easily have remedied:

> His victories at Fort Henry and Donelson demonstrated to Sherman that if the Union put its mind to it, it could achieve success.
>
> John F. Marszalek, from *Sherman: A Soldier's Passion for Order*

In this sentence two *it*s with different meanings are awkwardly kissing. Simple rewriting entirely removes this inelegance:

> His victories at Fort Henry and Donelson demonstrated to Sherman that a determined Union could achieve success.

or

> His victories at Fort Henry and Donelson demonstrated to Sherman that if the Union made up its mind, it could achieve success.

Another common source of awkwardness is the overuse of the same preposition in a single sentence. Here is an example:

> The Christmas dinner was filled *with* chatter *with* all the relatives *with* children.

or

> He was thinking *of* resigning his job *of* which he was very proud because *of* the cuts in the budget.

Only a pittance of rewriting is required to remove this awkwardness:

> The Christmas dinner was filled *with* the chattering of the relatives and their children.
> Although proud of his job, he was contemplating resigning over budget cuts.

Finally, there is the awkwardness of unintentional internal rhymes, which can make even a somber passage seem ridiculously flippant. Here is a sentence that is often quoted as a classic example of this miscue:

> Hence no force however great can stretch a cord however fine into an horizontal line which is accurately straight: there will always be a bending downwards.
>
> William Whewell, Elementary Treatise on Mechanics

Here "great" rhymes with "straight" and "fine" with "line." One possible rewrite is to eliminate the rhyming words in favor of unrhymed synonyms:

> Hence no force however powerful can stretch a cord however thin into an horizontal line which is accurately straight: there will always be a bending downwards.

Put a Personal Voice in the Writing

Every writer begins a new assignment by groping to find just the right voice for the piece. This problem of finding the right voice is especially acute for the student writer with no particular sense of commitment to the topic and no feeling one way or another about it. Here is an example of what we mean:

> Financial debt is a dangerous situation. It is like the spider's web that holds the struggling fly. The victim of debt can be overcome by his creditors like the merciless spider devouring his prey. Debt is caused by many circumstances which include unemployment, lack of effective budgeting, and mismanagement of credit.

The problem with this paragraph is not grammatical but rhetorical: It has no definite voice, no personality, and might have been penned by an unfeeling robot. We infer that the writer does not care about the topic, is bored with it, but is dutifully cobbling together some sentences in hopes of fulfilling the assignment.

Here, on the other hand, is an opening paragraph with a personal voice. In it the writer clearly knows who she is and what she believes and quite plainly intends to tell us:

> Do blondes have more fun? Perhaps, if being stereotyped as bubbly, cheap, and stupid can be considered fun. However, most of the time these accusations and idiotic beliefs are as shallow as the people practicing them.

The voice behind this paragraph is indignant, aroused, and opinionated—someone who is clearly sick to death of the stereotypes of the dumb blonde. And the snap in the writing mainly comes from the writer's impassioned commitment to her viewpoint.

How do you project a personal voice in your writing? You do so by writing about topics and subjects that deeply interest you. If the assigned topic seems hopelessly humdrum, probe different approaches to it until you find one that is appealing. For example, the paragraph about blondes was on the assigned topic of "stereotypes." The writer, who is blonde, decided to tackle the annoying stereotypes to which she herself had been repeatedly subjected. Once she had her topic, her anger bubbled into the writing and created the indignant voice she successfully projected. There is no chicken-or-egg mystery about this. Writers always write better when they have something to say; and writers are more likely to have something to say when they care about the topic.

If you think that the best way to write your essay is to play it safe and straddle the fence, you are wrong. The best essays always take a clearly defined stand that commits the writer to a definite, often argumentative, point of view. Once committed to saying something definite, writers usually find that the emotional commitment also gives them the voice needed to write a crisp and opinionated essay.

Following is Alfredo's revision of the first draft, including the comments of his instructor.

STUDENT ESSAY

Second Draft   Alfredo Silva

Who Am I?

1   I have a dream: I would like to become the Bard of my community. In the Middle Ages, bards and troubadors related the history of their people through poetry and song. In some past life I may have been a bard because the longing to be one keeps rolling over me in a familiar wave. I am a Mexican Don Quixote--filled with idealism for the future of my people. In my fantasies I see Nobel Prize-winning immunologists with surnames such as Gomez or Castillo. I also see brown-skinned, brown-eyed senators, Supreme Court justices, university presidents, journalists, and CEOs of conglom*e*rates. These ~~persons~~ *leaders*--women as well as men ~~would be~~ *are* dedicating their lives to improving our country's morality, customs, political system, philosophy, and education. ~~These leaders would in turn~~ *They* set strong examples for all the young people to follow. In the society of my vision, racial violence, high school dropouts, teenage pregnancy, and drug abuse have vanished.

2   While I know that my dream cannot be realized overnight, I am firmly convinced that education is the bedrock ~~and cornerstone~~ of any significant social change. Knowledge of what went wrong is the ~~most powerful~~ *necessary* start*ing point* for righting what is wrong. To cause change we Hispanics must join forces because as a unit we can accomplish more than we can as individuals. We can complement each other's talents, shore up each other's weaknesses, and therefore be strong as a whole. Through cooperation we ~~as a people~~ can guard against losing our Hispanic identity or our culture while still promoting an American way of life. This country has *rich treasures* ~~a lot~~ to offer all of its citizens, including Hispanics. In turn, Hispanics can

Lovely beginning-- much more captivating than the original

redundant logic

help foster the
~~contribute to maintaining a~~ reputation *of* for the United States as a great place to call home.

I have thought of other careers, even contemplating law, accounting, and nursing. Yet, I have settled on being a history teacher because in that profession I can best reveal to my

life, liberty, and the pursuit of happiness for all.
people what sacrifices Americans made in order to ensure ~~the pursuit of liberty for everyone.~~

Be more direct. / Sp

I have a dark side to my personality.
~~In my self observation, my darkest side stares me in the face.~~ I am competitive to an   3
almost destructive point. For instance, I play tennis, soccer, and basketball for recreation and to release tension. I vent much of my frustration through sweat and even through blood. Of course, I am careful not to hurt anyone but myself. As an athlete I am my worst enemy as much as I am my best friend. In fact, on the court and on the field I am often

Be specific about this transformation.
brutal competitor
transformed into a ~~different kind of person.~~ I believe that through this physical ~~catharsis~~ *metamorphosis* I
Consequently I often
can more easily deal with the tedium and toil of everyday life. ~~That leads me to the problem~~
conduct
~~of finding~~ myself apologizing for ~~conduct that is, what we say,~~ unsportsmanlike, Some may
say that a sport is only a game, but to me sports teach many of life's necessary lessons--
that getting ahead requires a competitive edge, that team work is often an excellent
shortcut to success, and that we control our own destinies.

I am also a romantic extrovert. I come from a family of seven siblings, where emotional   4
relationships were familiar staples of my family life. I was taught always to be open and
But
honest with my feelings. ~~As~~ I was growing up, I found that this openness and honesty
were not always appreciated. Quite often they were either misinterpreted or rejected. For
mad
instance, in my early teen years I once told a girl on whom I had a ~~powerful~~ crush, "~~Like,~~
Hey, I'd like to spend the rest of my life with you." Well, she was so repulsed that she
never spoke to me again, and to this day the sight of this girl fills me with embarrassment.
boldly informed
On another occasion I ~~told~~ a teacher that I had difficulty concentrating in his class because
it was so boring. The result? I was promptly ushered to the front of the class, where I was

redundant
forced to answer questions even though I never raised my hand ~~once.~~ Gradually I turned
to writing poems in an effort to express myself in subtle ways. Eventually I began using
's
poetry to sort out the confusion I felt after certain events in my life, such as my father
's   death
~~having a serious~~ stroke and my close friend ~~dying in a car accident,~~ tore me apart inside.
For me writing poetry is a spiritual experience. In my poems I ask many questions that I

did not know I had, such as "What purpose does education have for me?" "Why do people lie?" "When will I die?" Sometimes an inspiring thought will enter my mind, or a striking image will appeal to my emotions. I will then be bound to my desk for hours, trying to figure out exactly how I feel and how to express the feeling in a poem. Although I am continually struggling to find out who I am, I think the answer may lie in the pages of my tattered poetry notebooks in which I unburden my heart and my mind. An important aspect of a happy life is peace of mind, which can be found in communication. Poetry is my clue to the mystery of who I am, for it is through it that I communicate my wants and needs.

5   In a sense I am an ordinary person, but my love for the Hispanic people energizes me and makes me want to be an inspiration to others. I am convinced that an ordinary person can become an extraordinary person when he gives unselfishly and with passion.

Find an ending that clinches the essay. Make it brief; sometimes less is more.

I am an ordinary man, but I have extraordinary dreams.

EDITING THE SECOND DRAFT

Now is the time to check your grammar and punctuation. If you have any questions, you can refer to the grammar section at the end of this book. Now is likewise the time to check spelling, verify facts, ensure that both sentences and paragraphs are coherent. You should also *proofread* the paper for any typing miscues.

Pay particular attention to these common micro errors:

1. Check subject–verb agreements.
2. Check pronoun antecedents. Watch for errors such as "The garden *implements* were so carefully concealed that no one could find *it*."
3. Check for comma splices and the misuse of fragments.
4. Check for use of the wrong word, for example, "*Their* are many bargains to be found in the thrift shop."
5. Check for faulty diction and overuse of grand words.

When you are finished with this mechanical overhaul of spelling, grammar, logic, and rhetoric, give the whole paper a final critical reading to make sure that it hangs together and is both logical and convincing.

Following is the final draft of Alfredo's paper.

STUDENT ESSAY

Final Draft   Alfredo Silva

Who Am I?

1   I have a dream: I would like to become the Bard of my community. In the Middle
Ages, bards and troubadours related the history of their people through poetry and song.
In some past life I may have been a bard because the longing to be one keeps rolling
over me in a familiar wave. I am a Mexican Don Quixote—filled with idealism for the
future of my people. In my fantasies I see Nobel Prize-winning immunologists with
surnames such as Gomez or Castillo. I also see brown-skinned, brown-eyed senators,
Supreme Court justices, university presidents, journalists, and CEOs of conglomerates.
These leaders—women as well as men—are dedicating their lives to improving our
country's morality, customs, political system, philosophy, and education. They set
strong examples for all the young people to follow. In the society of my vision,
racial violence, high school dropouts, teenage pregnancy, and drug abuse have
vanished.

2   While I know that my dream cannot be realized overnight, I am firmly convinced that
education is the bedrock of any significant social change. Knowledge of what went
wrong is the necessary starting point for righting what is wrong. To cause change we
Hispanics must join forces because as a unit we can accomplish more than we can as
individuals. We can complement each other's talents, shore up each other's
weaknesses, and therefore be strong as a whole. Through cooperation we can guard
against losing our Hispanic identity or our culture, while still promoting an American
way of life. This country has rich treasures to offer all of its citizens, including
Hispanics. In turn, Hispanics can help foster the reputation of the United States as a
great place to call home. I have thought of other careers, even contemplating law,
accounting, and nursing. Yet, I have settled on being a history teacher because in that
profession I can best reveal to my people what sacrifices Americans made in order to
ensure life, liberty, and the pursuit of happiness for all.

3   I have a dark side to my personality. I am competitive to an almost destructive point.
For instance, I play tennis, soccer, and basketball for recreation and to release tension. I

vent much of my frustration through sweat and even through blood. Of course, I am careful not to hurt anyone but myself. As an athlete I am my worst enemy as much as I am my best friend. In fact, on the court and on the field I am often transformed into a brutal competitor. I believe that through this physical metamorphosis I can more easily deal with the tedium and toil of everyday life. Consequently I often find myself apologizing for unsportsmanlike conduct. Some may say that a sport is only a game, but to me sports teach many of life's necessary lessons—that getting ahead requires a competitive edge, that team work is often an excellent shortcut to success, and that we control our own destinies.

I am also a romantic extrovert. I come from a family of seven siblings, where emotional relationships were familiar staples of my family life. I was taught always to be open and honest with my feelings. But as I was growing up, I found that this openness and honesty were not always appreciated. Quite often they were either misinterpreted or rejected. For instance, in my early teen years I once told a girl on whom I had a mad crush, "Hey, I'd like to spend the rest of my life with you." Well, she was so repulsed that she never spoke to me again, and to this day the sight of this girl fills me with embarrassment. On another occasion I boldly informed a teacher that I had difficulty concentrating in his class because it was so boring. The result? I was promptly ushered to the front of the class, where I was forced to answer questions even though I never raised my hand. Gradually I turned to writing poems in an effort to express myself in subtle ways. Eventually I began using poetry to sort out the confusion I felt after certain events in my life, such as my father's stroke and my close friend's death, tore me apart inside. For me writing poetry is a spiritual experience. In my poems I ask many questions that I did not know I had, such as "What purpose does education have for me?" "Why do people lie?" "When will I die?" Sometimes an inspiring thought will enter my mind, or a striking image will appeal to my emotions. I will then be bound to my desk for hours, trying to figure out exactly how I feel and how to express the feeling in a poem. Although I am continually struggling to find out who I am, I think the answer may lie in the pages of my tattered poetry notebooks in which I unburden my heart and my mind. An important aspect of a happy life is peace of mind, which can be found in communication. Poetry is my clue to the mystery of who I am, for

it is through it that I communicate my wants and needs.

5   I am an ordinary man, but I have extraordinary dreams.

Exercises

1. Revise the following passage from a student essay.

   There were two things I learned in Karate before I learned to fight. The first thing was respect. I was told that I must salute to the Korean, United States, and our martial arts flag before entering or leaving the training hall. To acknowledge my teachers and elders such as black belts, I must also bow to them. When ever asked a question my reply of yes sir or no sir is expected of me given in a confident tone. There examples of respect are symbolic to every day life. We must respect each other countries to live a peaceful life. When we are kind and acknowledge people, there becomes a friendly atmosphere.

   The second thing I learned was defensive movements. How to block a punch or a kick. How to escape being held. A few basic blocks such as low and high blocks. I was not very happy because I wanted to learn how to kick like in the movies and all I was taught was respect and defensive hand movements. Each lesson became more advanced and the escape movements became natural movements for me. By the time I learned my requirements I realized Karate was for humble people that wanted to protect themselves if bothered.

   Confidence in all aspects of life was gained after most advanced martial artist have trained for several years. After receiving the next belt, breaking bricks or several boards or winning a trophy in a tournament bring an unbeatable attitude. After people accomplish difficult feats, they tend to be able to overcome their fears and obstacles in life. After training in Karate, they learn that they are winners.

2. Rewrite the following sentences in more direct grammar. Make sure the actor is stated as a subject and the action as a verb.
   a. His expectation was to attract young Americans to the martial art of Tae Qwan Do.
   b. The instructor's rebuttal to the accusation was of importance to him.
   c. There was deep anger among the employees over the loss of a pay raise.
   d. Indefinite continuance of financial support for the choral group cannot be guaranteed as long as the hospital sees no great need for such entertainment.
   e. Although methods of corroborating the validity of English prerequisites have been improved, acceptance as useful by the Academic Affairs Committee of any present prerequisite is not possible.

3. Change the passive voice into active only where necessary; otherwise, leave the sentence as is.
   a. Many verses have been written by people who believe they are poets but who are merely rhymesters.

   b. Until after the election, derogatory remarks about the Democratic ticket were continually made by Professor Smith.

   c. A mock earthquake, including evacuating people from the Tower Building, creating a command post, establishing a triage area, and organizing a system of transportation was planned by the Safety Committee.

   d. During the medieval period man was no longer viewed as a superb creature, capable of Promethean achievements; rather, he was viewed as a pitiful being, tarnished by original sin and in need of moral redemption.

   e. The ability of women to make right executive decisions under stress has generally been underestimated by society.

4. Get rid of redundancy in the following sentences.

   a. In this day and age families should limit themselves to two children in order not to overcrowd the various different countries of Planet Earth.

   b. By taking ballet dancing lessons, I have achieved a greater self-confidence in myself.

   c. All of our cities' bureaucratic agencies that provide and offer services, such as law enforcement, fire prevention, sewage disposal, or library service, cannot continue to grow, develop, and expand without higher local taxes.

   d. All of Eloise Martin's hopes and desires were based on her belief that human beings are basically and fundamentally able to set goals they can reach through dedication and by applying themselves.

   e. Suddenly the computer graft turned red in color and become ugly in appearance.

5. Replace the trite, prepackaged expressions in the following sentences.

   a. For years Gillespie thought he was sitting in the catbird seat, but in the end he went to jail for illegal drug trafficking, trapped in his own compromised cleverness.

   b. Yes, Pete McClure should be appointed Senior Vice-President of Marketing because throughout 20 years of time he has paid his dues to Brendon and Company by years of backbreaking work, selling to small businesses and private merchants at a time when our product was not popular.

   c. What I despise about my boss is that he simply rides roughshod over his employees in order to get the almighty dollar.

   d. Anyone who continues to buy Johnson and Smith stocks is just fishing in troubled waters.

   e. Most of the crowd attending the town meeting simply had their own axe to grind or their own beds to feather, and they were not the least concerned about whether the proposed housing development was good or bad for the neighborhood.

6. Recast the following sentences to get rid of grandiose diction.

   a. Various tennis coaches called to ascertain how much equipment could be appropriated on lease from the university and then transmitted to the tournament leaders.

   b. Dear Mr. Webster: I am in receipt of your letter of March 10, which endeavors to explain your absence at the last townhouse Executive Committee meeting.

c. Surely it is incumbent upon education to facilitate the understanding by students of how to envisage life in all of its richness, its profundity, and its mystery.

d. Prior to my arrival at Harvard, I had conceived of a campus that would be socially harsh, frigid, and filled with discordant factors, whose only compensation would be all of the knowledge I would acquire.

e. Her visage was smiling in reverie as she reclined in the grass, reading a tome of Amy Lowell's poems.

Writing the Essay

Narration

READING FOR IDEAS

Some things are better, and more dramatically, left unsaid than expressed in writing, especially in a narrative. In this moving tale, for example, the writer leaves volumes unsaid about his motives and thoughts during a climactic religious exchange with his dying father. At the end of the story he also implies what he might have said to comfort his stricken father, but failed to say. Nevertheless, the narrator ends by learning a rueful lesson about the selfishness and the narrowness of a self-imposed code of conduct. Allow the story to trigger some memories of your own and ask yourself the following questions: Has an experience ever taught me a lesson about life? What have I learned from a memorable experience?

The Code
RICHARD T. GILL

Richard Thomas Gill (b. 1927) was born on Long Island, in New York, and received his Ph.D. at Harvard University. A former assistant professor of economics at Harvard, Gill has presented a fifteen-part series on public television titled "Economics and the Public Interest." He has been the principal bass of New York's Metropolitan Opera since 1973 and is an occasional contributor of stories to the New Yorker *and* Atlantic Monthly. *Gill is the author of several books, among them* Economic Development: Past and Present *(1963) and* Economics and the Public Interest *(second edition 1972).*

1   I remember, almost to the hour, when I first began to question my religion. I don't mean that my ideas changed radically just at that time. I was only twelve, and I continued to go to church faithfully and to say something that could pass for prayers each night before I went to sleep. But I never again felt quite the same. For the first time in my life, it had occurred to me that when I grew up I might actually leave the Methodist faith.

2   It all happened just a few days after my brother died. He was five years old, and his illness was so brief and his death so unexpected that my whole family was almost crazed with grief. My three aunts, each of whom lived within a few blocks of our house, and my mother were all firm believers in religion, and they turned in unison, and without reservation, to this last support. For about a week, a kind of religious frenzy seized our household. We would all sit in the living room—my mother, my aunts, my two sisters, and I, and sometimes Mr. Dodds, the Methodist minister, too—saying prayers in low voices, comforting one another, staying together for hours at a time, until someone remembered that we had not had dinner or that it was time for my sisters and me to be in bed.

3   I was quite swept up by the mood that had come over the house. When I went to bed, I would say the most elaborate, intricate prayers. In the past, when I had finished my "Now I lay me down to sleep," I would bless individually all the members of my immediate family and then my aunts, and let it go at that. Now, however, I felt that I had to bless everyone in the world whose name I could remember. I would go through all my friends at school, including the teachers, the principal, and the janitor, and then through the names of people I had heard my mother and father mention, some of whom I had never even met. I did not quite know what to do about my brother, whom I wanted to pray for more than for anyone else. I hesitated to take his name out of its regular order, for fear I would be committed to believing that he had really died. But then I *knew* that he had died, so at the end of my prayers, having just barely mentioned his name as I went along, I would start blessing him over and over again, until I finally fell asleep.

4   The only one of us who was unmoved by this religious fervor was my father. Oddly enough, considering what a close family we were and how strongly my mother and aunts felt about religion, my father had never shown the least interest in it. In fact, I do not think that he had *ever* gone to church. Partly for this reason, partly because he was a rather brusque, impatient man, I always felt that he was something of a stranger in our home. He spent a great deal of time with us children, but through it all he seemed curiously unapproachable. I think we all felt constrained when he played with us and relieved when, at last, we were left to ourselves.

5   At the time of my brother's death, he was more of a stranger than ever. Except for one occasion, he took no part in the almost constant gatherings of the family in the living room. He was not going to his office that week—we lived in a small town outside Boston—and he was always around the house, but no one ever seemed to know exactly where. One of my aunts—Sarah, my mother's eldest sister—felt very definitely that my father should not be left to himself, and she was continually saying to me, "Jack, go upstairs and see if you can find him and talk to him." I remember going timidly along the hallway on the second floor and peeking into the bedrooms, not knowing what I should say if I found him and half afraid that he would scold me for going around looking into other people's rooms. One afternoon, not finding him in any of the bedrooms, I went up

into the attic, where we had a sort of playroom. I remember discovering him there by the window. He was sitting absolutely motionless in an old wicker chair, an empty pipe in his hands, staring out fixedly over the treetops. I stood in the doorway for several minutes before he was aware of me. He turned as if to say something, but then, looking at me or just above my head—I was not sure which—he seemed to lose himself in his thoughts. Finally, he gave me a strangely awkward salute with his right hand and turned again to the window.

About the only times my father was with the rest of us were when we had meals or 6
when, in the days immediately following the funeral, we all went out to the cemetery, taking fresh flowers or wreaths. But even at the cemetery he always stood slightly apart—a tall, lonely figure. Once, when we were at the grave and I was nearest him, he reached over and squeezed me around the shoulders. It made me feel almost embarrassed as though he were breaking through some inviolable barrier between us. He must have felt as I did, because he at once removed his arm and looked away, as though he had never actually embraced me at all.

It was the one occasion when my father was sitting in the living room with us that 7
started me to wondering about my religion. We had just returned from the cemetery— two carloads of us. It was three or four days after the funeral and just at the time when, the shock having worn off, we were all experiencing our first clear realization of what had happened. Even I, young as I was, sensed that there was a new air of desolation in our home.

For a long time, we all sat there in silence. Then my aunts, their eyes moist, began 8
talking about my brother, and soon my mother joined in. They started off softly, telling of little things he had done in the days before his illness. Then they fell silent and dried their eyes, and then quickly remembered some other incident and began speaking again. Slowly the emotion mounted, and before long the words were flooding out. "God will take care of him!" my Aunt Sarah cried, almost ecstatically. "Oh, yes, He will! He will!" Presently, they were all talking in chorus—saying that my brother was happy at last and that they would all be with him again one day.

I believed what they were saying and I could barely hold back my tears. But swept up 9
as I was, I had the feeling that they should not be talking that way while my father was there. The feeling was one that I did not understand at all at the moment. It was just that when I looked over to the corner where he was sitting and saw the deep, rigid lines of his face, saw him sitting there silently, all alone, I felt guilty. I wanted everyone to stop for a while—at least until he had gone upstairs. But there was no stopping the torrent once it had started.

"Oh, he was too perfect to live!" Aunt Agnes, my mother's youngest sister, cried. "He 10
was never a bad boy. I've never seen a boy like that. I mean he was never even naughty. He was just too perfect."

"Oh, yes. Oh, yes," my mother sighed.

"It's true," Aunt Sarah said. "Even when he was a baby, he never really cried. There was never a baby like him. He was a saint."

"He *was* a saint!" Aunt Agnes cried. "That's why he was taken from us!"

"He was a perfect baby," my mother said.

"He was taken from us," Aunt Agnes went on, "because he was too perfect to live."

11   All through this conversation, my father's expression had been growing more and more tense. At last, while Aunt Agnes was speaking, he rose from his chair. His face was very pale, and his eyes flashed almost feverishly. "Don't talk like that, Agnes!" he exclaimed, with a strange violence that was not anger but something much deeper. "I won't have you talking like that any more. I don't want anybody talking like that!" His whole body seemed to tremble. I had never seen him so worked up before. "Of course he was a bad boy at times!" he cried. "Every boy's bad once in a while. What do you have to change him for? Why don't you leave him as he was?"

12   "But he was such a perfect baby," Aunt Sarah said.

"He *wasn't* perfect!" my father almost shouted, clenching his fist. "He was no more perfect than Jack here or Betty or Ellen. He was just an ordinary little boy. He wasn't perfect. And he wasn't a saint. He was just a little boy, and I won't have you making him over into something he wasn't!"

13   He looked as though he were going to go on talking like this, but just then he closed his eyes and ran his hand up over his forehead and through his hair. When he spoke again, his voice was subdued. "I just wish you wouldn't talk that way," he said. "That's all I mean." And then, after standing there silently for a minute, he left the living room and walked upstairs.

14   I sat watching the doorway through which he had gone. Suddenly, I had no feeling for what my mother and my aunts had been saying. It was all a mist, a dream. Out of the many words that had been spoken that day, it was those few sentences of my father's that explained to me how I felt about my brother. I wanted to be with my father to tell him so.

15   I went upstairs and found him once again in the playroom in the attic. As before, he was silent and staring out the window when I entered, and we sat without speaking for what seemed to me like half an hour or more. But I felt that he knew why I was there, and I was not uncomfortable with him.

16   Finally, he turned to me and shook his head. "I don't know what I can tell you, Jack," he said, raising his hands and letting them drop into his lap. "That's the worst part of it. There's just nothing I can say that will make it any better."

17   Though I only half understood him then, I see now that he was telling me of a drawback—that he had no refuge, no comfort, no support. He was telling me that you were all alone if you took the path that he had taken. Listening to him, I did not care about the drawback. I had begun to see what a noble thing it was for a man to bear the full loss of someone he had loved.

II

18   By the time I was thirteen or fourteen I was so thoroughly committed to my father's way of thinking that I considered it a great weakness in a man to believe in religion. I wanted to grow up to face life as he did—truthfully, without comfort, without support.

19   My attitude was never one of rebellion. Despite the early regimen of Sunday school and church that my mother had encouraged, she was wonderfully gentle with me, particularly when I began to express my doubts. She would come into my room each

night after the light was out and ask me to say my prayers. Determined to be honest with her, I would explain that I could not say them sincerely, and therefore should not say them at all. "Now, Jack," she would reply, very quietly and calmly, "you mustn't talk like that. You'll really feel much better if you say them." I could tell from the tone of her voice that she was hurt, but she never tried to force me in any way. Indeed, it might have been easier for me if she *had* tried to oppose my decision strenuously. As it was, I felt so bad at having wounded her that I was continually trying to make things up—running errands, surprising her by doing the dishes when she went out shopping—behaving, in short, in the most conscientious, considerate fashion. But all this never brought me any closer to her religion. On the contrary, it only served to free me for my decision *not* to believe. And for that decision, as I say, my father was responsible.

Part of his influence, I suppose, was in his physical quality. Even at that time—when he was in his late forties and in only moderately good health—he was a most impressive figure. He was tall and heavychested, with leathery, rough-cast features and with an easy, relaxed rhythm in his walk. He had been an athlete in his youth, and, needless to say, I was enormously proud of his various feats and told about them, with due exaggeration, all over our neighborhood. Still, the physical thing had relatively little to do with the matter. My father, by that time, regarded athletes and athletics with contempt. Now and again, he would take me into the back yard to fool around with boxing gloves, but when it came to something serious, such as my going out for football in high school, he invariably put his foot down. "It takes too much time," he would tell me. "You ought to be thinking of college and your studies. It's nonsense what they make of sports nowadays!" I always wanted to remind him of *his* school days, but I knew it was no use. He had often told me what an unforgivable waste of time he considered his youth to have been. 20

Thus, although the physical thing was there, it was very much in the background—little more, really, than the simple assumption that a man ought to know how to take care of himself. The real bond between us was spiritual, in the sense that courage, as opposed to strength, is spiritual. It was this intangible quality of courage that I wanted desperately to possess and that, it seemed to me, captured everything that was essential about my father. 21

We never talked of this quality directly. The nearest we came to it was on certain occasions during the early part of the Second World War, just before I went off to college. We would sit in the living room listening to a speech by Winston Churchill, and my father would suddenly clap his fist against his palm. "My God!" he would exclaim, fairly beaming with admiration. "That man's got the heart of a tiger!" And I would listen to the rest of the speech, thrilling to every word, and then, thinking of my father, really, I would say aloud that, of all men in the world, the one I would most like to be was Churchill. 22

Nor did we often talk about religion. Yet our religion—our rejection of religion—was the deepest statement of the bond between us. My father, perhaps out of deference to my mother and my sisters and aunts, always put his own case very mildly. "It's certainly a great philosophy," he would say of Christianity. "No one could question that. But for the rest . . ." Here he would throw up his hands and cock his head to one side, as if to say that he had tried, but simply could not manage the hurdle of divinity. This view, however mildly it may have been expressed, became mine with absolute clarity and certainty. I 23 concluded that religion was a refuge, without the least foundation in fact. More than that, I positively objected to those—I should say those *men,* for to me it was a peculiarly masculine matter—who turned to religion for support. As I saw it, a man ought to face life as it really is, on his own two feet, without a crutch, as my father did. That was the heart of the matter. By the time I left home for college, I was so deeply committed to this view that I would have considered it a disloyalty to him, to myself, to the code we had lived by, to alter my position in the least.

24   I did not see much of my father during the next four years or so. I was home during the summer vacation after my freshman year, but then, in the middle of the next year, I went into the Army. I was shipped to the Far East for the tail end of the war, and was in Japan at the start of the Occupation. I saw my father only once or twice during my entire training period, and, naturally, during the time I was overseas I did not see him at all.

25   While I was away, his health failed badly. In 1940, before I went off to college, he had taken a job at a defense plant. The plant was only forty miles from our home, but he was working on the night shift, and commuting was extremely complicated and tiresome. And, of course, he was always willing to overexert himself out of a sense of pride. The result was that late in 1942 he had a heart attack. He came through it quite well, but he made no effort to cut down on his work and, as a consequence, suffered a second, and more serious, attack, two years later. From that time on, he was almost completely bedridden.

26   I was on my way overseas at the time of the second attack, and I learned of it in a letter from my mother. I think she was trying to spare me, or perhaps it was simply that I could not imagine so robust a man as my father being seriously ill. In any event, I had only the haziest notion of what his real condition was, so when, many months later, I finally did realize what had been going on, I was terribly surprised and shaken. One day, some time after my arrival at an American Army post in Japan, I was called to the orderly room and told that my father was critically ill and that I was to be sent home immediately. Within forty-eight hours, I was standing in the early-morning light outside my father's bedroom, with my mother and sisters at my side. They had told me, as gently as they could, that he was not very well, that he had had another attack. But it was impossible to shield me then. I no sooner stepped into the room and saw him than I realized that he would not live more than a day or two longer.

27   From that moment on, I did not want to leave him for a second. Even that night, during the periods when he was sleeping and I was of no help being there, I could not get myself to go out of the room for more than a few minutes. A practical nurse had come to sit up with him, but since I was at the bedside, she finally spent the night in the hallway. I was really quite tired, and late that night my mother and my aunts begged me to go to my room and rest for a while, but I barely heard them. I was sure he would wake up soon, and when he did, I wanted to be there to talk to him.

28   We did talk a great deal that first day and night. It was difficult for both of us. Every once in a while, my father would shift position in the bed, and I would catch a glimpse of his wasted body. It was a knife in my heart. Even worse were the times when he would reach out for my hand, his eyes misted, and begin to tell me how he felt about me. I tried to look at him, but in the end I always looked down. And, knowing that he was dying, and feeling desperately guilty, I would keep repeating to myself that he knew how I felt, that he would understand why I looked away.

There was another thing, too. While we talked that day, I had a vague feeling that my   29
father was on the verge of making some sort of confession to me. It was, as I say, only
the vaguest impression, and I thought very little about it. The next morning, however, I
began to sense what was in the air. Apparently, Mr. Dodds, the minister, whom I barely
knew, had been coming to the house lately to talk to my father. My father had not said
anything about this, and I learned it only indirectly, from something my mother said to
my eldest sister at the breakfast table. At the moment, I brushed the matter aside. I told
myself it was natural that Mother would want my father to see the minister at the last.
Nevertheless, the very mention of the minister's name caused something to tighten inside
me.

Later that day, the matter was further complicated. After lunch, I finally did go to my   30
room for a nap, and when I returned to my father's room, I found him and my mother
talking about Mr. Dodds. The conversation ended almost as soon as I entered, but I was
left with the distinct impression that they were expecting the minister to pay a visit that
day, whether very shortly or at suppertime or later in the evening, I could not tell. I did
not ask. In fact, I made a great effort not to think of the matter at all.

Then, early that evening, my father spoke to me. I knew before he said a word that the   31
minister was coming. My mother had straightened up the bedroom, and fluffed up my
father's pillows so that he was half sitting in the bed. No one had told me anything, but
I was sure what the preparations meant. "I guess you probably know," my father said to
me when we were alone, "we're having a visitor tonight. It's—ah—Mr. Dodds. You
know, the minister from your mother's church."

I nodded, half shrugging, as if I saw nothing the least unusual in the news. "He's come   32
here before once or twice," my father said. "Have I mentioned that? I can't remember if
I've mentioned that."

"Yes, I know. I think Mother said something, or perhaps you did. I don't remember."

"I just thought I'd let you know. You see, your mother wanted me to talk to him.
I—I've talked to him more for her sake than anything else."

"Sure. I can understand that."

"I think it makes her feel a little better. I think—" Here he broke off, seeming   33
dissatisfied with what he was saying. His eyes turned to the ceiling, and he shook his head
slightly, as if to erase the memory of his words. He studied the ceiling for a long time
before he spoke again. "I don't mean it was all your mother exactly," he said. "Well,
what I mean is he's really quite an interesting man. I think you'd probably like him a good
deal."

"I know Mother has always liked him," I replied. "From what I gather most people
seem to like him very much."

"Well, he's that sort," my father went on, with quickening interest. "I mean, he isn't
what you'd imagine at all. To tell the truth, I wish you'd talk to him a little. I wish you'd
talk things over with him right from scratch." My father was looking directly at me now,
his eyes flashing.

"I'd be happy to talk with him sometime," I said. "As I say, everybody seems to think
very well of him."

"Well, I wish you would. You see, when you're lying here day after day, you get to   34
thinking about things. I mean, it's good to have someone to talk to." He paused for a

moment. "Tell me," he said, "have you ever . . . have you ever wondered if there wasn't some truth in it? Have you ever thought about it that way at all?"

35 I made a faint gesture with my hand. "Of course, it's always possible to wonder," I replied. "I don't suppose you can ever be completely certain one way or the other."

"I know, I know," he said, almost impatiently. "But have you ever felt—well, all in a sort of flash—that it *was* true? I mean, have you ever had that feeling?"

36 He was half raised up from the pillow now, his eyes staring into me with a feverish concentration. Suddenly, I could not look at him any longer. I lowered my head.

"I don't mean permanently or anything like that," he went on. "But just for a few seconds. The feeling that you've been wrong all along. Have you had that feeling— ever?"

37 I could not look up. I could not move. I felt that every muscle in my body had suddenly frozen. Finally, after what seemed an eternity, I heard him sink back into the pillows. When I glanced up a moment later, he was lying there silent, his eyes closed, his lips parted, conveying somehow the image of the death that awaited him.

38 Presently, my mother came to the door. She called me into the hall to tell me that Mr. Dodds had arrived. I said that I thought my father had fallen asleep but that I would go back and see.

It was strangely disheartening to me to discover that he was awake. He was sitting there, his eyes open, staring grimly into the gathering shadows of the evening.

"Mr. Dodds is downstairs," I said matter-of-factly. "Mother wanted to know if you felt up to seeing him tonight."

39 For a moment, I thought he had not heard me; he gave no sign of recognition whatever. I went to the foot of the bed and repeated myself. He nodded, not answering the question but simply indicating that he had heard me. At length, he shook his head. "Tell your mother I'm a little tired tonight," he said. "Perhaps—well, perhaps some other time."

"I could ask him to come back later, if you'd like."

"No, no, don't bother. I—I could probably use the rest."

I waited a few seconds. "Are you sure?" I asked. "I'm certain he could come back in an hour or so."

40 Then, suddenly, my father was looking at me. I shall never forget his face at that moment and the expression burning in his eyes. He was pleading with me to speak. And all I could say was that I would be happy to ask Mr. Dodds to come back later, if he wanted it that way. It was not enough. I knew, instinctively, at that moment that it was not enough. But I could not say anything more.

41 As quickly as it had come, the burning flickered and went out. He sank back into the pillows again. "No, you can tell him I won't be needing him tonight," he said, without interest. "Tell him not to bother waiting around." Then he turned on his side, away from me, and said no more.

42 So my father did not see Mr. Dodds that night. Nor did he ever see him again. Shortly after midnight, just after my mother and sisters had gone to bed, he died. I was at his side then, but I could not have said exactly when it occurred. He must have gone off in his sleep, painlessly, while I sat there awake beside him.

In the days that followed, our family was together almost constantly. Curiously   43
enough, I did not think much about my father just then. For some reason, I felt the
strongest sense of responsibility toward the family. I found myself making the arrangements for the funeral, protecting Mother from the stream of people who came to the
house, speaking words of consolation to my sisters and even to my aunts. I was never
alone except at night, when a kind of oblivion seized me almost as soon as my head
touched the pillow. My sleep was dreamless, numb.

Then, two weeks after the funeral, I left for Fort Devens, where I was to be discharged   44
from the Army. I had been there three days when I was told that my terminal leave would
begin immediately and that I was free to return home. I had half expected that when I was
at the Fort, separated from the family, something would break inside me. But still no
emotion came. I thought of my father often during that time, but, search as I would, I
could find no sign of feeling.

Then, when I had boarded the train for home, it happened. Suddenly, for no reason   45
whatever, I was thinking of the expression on my father's face that last night in the
bedroom. I saw him as he lay there pleading with me to speak. And I knew then what he
had wanted me to say to him—that it was really all right with me, that it wouldn't change
anything between us if he gave way. And then I was thinking of myself and what I had
said and what I had *not* said. Not a word to help! Not a word!

I wanted to beg his forgiveness. I wanted to cry out aloud to him. But I was in a   46
crowded train, sitting with three elderly women just returning from a shopping tour. I
turned my face to the window. There, silent, unnoticed, I thought of what I might have
said.

Vocabulary

unison (2)   constrained (4)   intangible (21)
brusque (4)   inviolable (6)   deference (23)

Questions on Meaning and Technique

1. What was the author's childhood faith? How old was he when he thought he
   might give it up?
2. Why, after the death of his brother, did the narrator feel he had to bless
   everyone, even people whose names he had heard mentioned but whom he
   really didn't know?
3. What was the value of religion to the narrator's mother and aunts? Where is
   this stated?
4. What did the past athletic prowess of the father have to do with the code
   that developed between him and the narrator? How was the code related to
   "masculinity"?
5. What "intangible quality" drew the author to his father?
6. Examine paragraphs 24 and 26 and identify at least two devices the author
   uses to move the story along.

7. In paragraph 40, the narrator says of his father, "He was pleading with me to speak," and that he, the narrator, knew that his answer "was not enough." What did the narrator's father want him to say? Why didn't the narrator say it?

8. What does "The Code" have to say about role-playing and about rigid beliefs in "masculinity"?

9. How would you characterize the father's deathbed behavior? Was he courageous? Cowardly?

10. What is the significance of the final scene and the three elderly women in the train?

READING FOR IDEAS

Behind every poem is a character whose world view it may describe, a narrator who may be part of its plot, or a speaker who merely exists to give the poem a voice. Ask yourself who the voice behind this poem is, and to what class and sex he or she probably belongs. Notice the implicit social differences that exist between the speaker and the subject of the poem, Richard Cory. Why does the speaker find Cory's suicide so mystifying? Ask yourself, further, whether Cory's suicide, reported by a member of his own privileged class, would seem as shocking.

Richard Cory
EDWIN ARLINGTON ROBINSON

Edwin Arlington Robinson (1869–1935) was regarded during his lifetime as the greatest U.S. poet. He was born in Head Tide, Maine, and educated at Harvard University. His many volumes of verse include The Children of the Night *(1897),* The Man Who Died Twice *(1924; Pulitzer Prize), and* Tristram *(1928; Pulitzer Prize). Robinson, who never married, lived a life of quiet reclusiveness, spending many of his summers at the MacDowell Colony for artists and writers (in New Hampshire).*

1   Whenever Richard Cory went down town,
     We people on the pavement looked at him:
     He was a gentleman from sole to crown,
     Clean favored, and imperially slim.

2   And he was always quietly arrayed,
     And he was always human when he talked;
     But still he fluttered pulses when he said,
     "Good-morning," and he glittered when he walked.

3   And he was rich—yes, richer than a king—
     And admirably schooled in every grace:

In fine, we thought that he was everything
To make us wish that we were in his place.

So on we worked, and waited for the light.   4
And went without the meat, and cursed the bread;
And Richard Cory, one calm summer night,
Went home and put a bullet through his head.

Questions on Meaning and Technique

1. From whose viewpoint is this poem narrated? What rhetorical advantages does this viewpoint afford the writer?

2. Why was Richard Cory the envy of those who saw him? Enumerate his enviable characteristics.

3. What is the meaning of, "But still he fluttered pulses when he said, "Good-morning . . .""

4. Aside from the narrative form, what other rhetorical mode is evident in this poem?

5. What do we know about the "we" who narrate this poem? Why is it important that we have some information about them?

How to Write a Narration

Narration tells what happened. A storyteller who begins with "Once upon a time . . ." is introducing the first step in what will probably become a bending, tortuous progression of happenings. Narration, in its widest sense, includes history, biography, personal experience, travel, and fiction—in short, any writing that recounts the events of a story in a dramatic and climactic order.

Writing Assignment

Narrate an incident or experience that taught you a lesson about life. Re-create it on paper exactly as you remember it. Keep the events in the order in which they occurred. At the end of the narrative, say what the incident or experience taught you.

Specific Instructions

PREWRITING ON THE ASSIGNMENT.   The key word in this assignment is *lesson*. Your experience must not be merely gripping or tellable; it must also have taught you something, and you should be able to say what. Note, for example, that in the student model essay, the writer tells us in her final paragraph that watching the veterinarian deliver the dead pronghorn bison baby determined her choice of career. From that day on, she decided to study animal science and become a veterinarian.

Begin your prewriting by outlining the most memorable experience or adventure you have ever had. If you have had more than one such experience—most of us have—choose the one that stirs you most. If necessary and you cannot quite decide on any particular experience, talk out the assignment with a friend or the instructor.

Decide next on what lesson the experience taught you and formulate that in a sentence or two. This lesson, properly worded as preamble or conclusion to your story, could become the theme for your narrative. But do not be too mechanical about it. Often it is more effective to let a conclusion unfold naturally from the story rather than to begin by slugging the reader hard over the head with it.

The details for writing this assignment will come from memory, which tends to be fragmentary and fleeting, so you might also jot these down as you relive the experience in preparing to write about it. Often, in reliving an experience we are hit with occasional images and flashes of description; scribble these down also. Later, as you actually do the writing, you can incorporate these bursts of inspiration into the prose.

NARRATIVE WRITING MUST HAVE A CONSISTENT POINT OF VIEW. *Point of view* refers to the vantage point from which a story is told. A story is always told by someone from some point of view. The most elemental point of view for any writer is the first-person narrator. In its simplest application, this point of view may be the writer telling the story as an "I" who lived or saw it. In more complex application, the "I" telling the story is innocent of its full implications. This narrator has a limited vision and grasp and, indeed, functions in the story as a character manipulated by the author. For example, this narrator from Poe's "The Cask of Amontillado" is mad but does not know it:

> The thousand injuries of Fortunato I had borne as best I could, but when he ventured upon insult, I vowed revenge. You, who so well know the nature of my soul, will not suppose, however, that I gave utterance to a threat. At *length* I would be avenged; this was a point definitely settled—but the very definitiveness with which it was resolved precluded the idea of risk. . . .
>
> Edgar Allan Poe, *The Cask of Amontillado*

We learn the extent of his madness later when we see the dementedly cruel revenge he takes on Fortunato, whom he lures into a vault, gets drunk, shackles to a wall, and entombs behind mortar and stone.

Probably the most commonly used point of view today is the omniscient narrator. This person sees all, hears all, and reports all, moving across time and place at will. Characters are referred to as "he" or "she," and their actions, motives, and thoughts are related by this invisible but omniscient agent. Few student narratives, except for those written in creative writing classes, use the omniscient point of view, because most student narrative assignments ask for the recounting of a personal experience, requiring the use of the "I" perspective.

In using the first-person point of view, you must decide early who you are in the story, take on the voice of your assumed character, and remain faithful to it throughout the telling. For instance, if you are relating an incident from the point of view of a young boy, the language of the story should reflect his youthfulness. It would seem incongruous if, having indicated to the reader that the story is to be told from a boy's point of view, you then make him sound like an elderly college professor.

Writers resort to a variety of techniques and devices to make their prose reflect the character they have assumed as the narrator. The most common technique is playacting: the writer simply pretends to be the person narrating the story and tries to write the way that person would write.

This passage is taken from a story narrated from the point of view of an uneducated slave. Notice how the language is wrenched to reflect his character:

> A long time ago, in times gone by, in slavery times, there was a man named Cue. I want you to think about him. I've got a reason.
>
>   He got born like the cotton in the boll or the rabbit in the pea patch. There wasn't any fine doings when he got born, but his mammy was glad to save him. Yes. He didn't get born in the Big House, or the overseer's house, or any place where the bearing was easy or the work light. No, Lord. He came out of his mammy in a field hand's cabin one sharp winter, and about the first thing he remembered was his mammy's face and the taste of a piece of bacon rind and the light and shine of the pitch-pine fire up the chimney. Well, now, he got born and there he was.
>
>   Stephen Vincent Benét, *Freedom's a Hard-Bought Thing*

Whatever character you choose to hide behind—innocent young boy, lonely middle-aged man, or wise old woman—you must remain with him or her throughout your narrative. Don't be one character in one paragraph, only to shift suddenly to another in the next. Such an abrupt change makes the point of view choppy and inconsistent. Here is an example of the sort of shift to avoid:

> Jessica and I hated all grownups. We'd climb onto my parents' four-story apartment roof, and you can bet that we were up to no good. Gosh, sometimes we'd spit down on old lady Gunther 'cause she was such a grouch about us playing on her lawn. I find it rather nostalgic to reflect on those budding days of my youth, when life was free and easy and each day was the dawn of a new adventure.

Notice the sudden shift from mischievous child to reflective adult in line 4.

THE NARRATION MUST HAVE A THEME. Unlike most assignments, the narrative generally uses a theme in place of a thesis. A theme is the central or dominant topic of a work that functions like a thesis but is usually implied rather than stated. A thesis, on the other hand, is a clear statement of a writer's commitment to a certain tack. The theme of a narration is basically its main point. Often this theme is subtle and unstated but still present as a unifying chord throughout the story. For example, "The Code" tells the story of a code of atheism between a young man and his father that eventually became a barrier between them. That a rigidly held belief can have a chilling effect on human intimacy is a theme of this story, even though the author does not proclaim it outright. We are left, instead, to infer this theme from the narrative. Similarly, the implicit theme of the poem "Richard Cory" is that things are often not what they seem, but again the poet does not directly say so. Instead, Richard Cory in all his resplendence is shown from the viewpoint of a poor, admiring townsman, and we are left to wonder why a man seemingly so blessed would commit suicide.

Similarly, your own narration must have a theme or it will strike your reader as pointless. To write a narrative with a central theme, it helps to imagine a reader on the other end of your story asking, "So what?" All of us have at one time or another been forced to sit through self-indulgent stories that ramble on between trivial episodes without seeming to make a central point. We are tempted to blurt, "So what?" and if the teller has no answer, to walk away in a huff. As a narrator, you are under a similar obligation to make your narration meaningful, to give it some central theme or topic that justifies its reading. Begin your narrative by asking yourself the impudent, "So what?" And be sure that by the end of your narrative you have answered that question.

PACE YOUR NARRATION TO FOCUS ON IMPORTANT SCENES.　Every reader of fiction has encountered passages that read like this:

> The first time I saw her she was chasing a schnauzer in the park. Her hair was wind-blown and wild as she dodged pedestrians and bicyclists and ran screaming after the runaway schnauzer. Her calico frock billowed in furls as she tried to run in floppy leather-thonged sandals. She was as lissome and lovely as ever a woman could be. *I didn't see her for three weeks after that.* Then one Tuesday morning, as I was taking a postdigestive jog along the elm-lined footpath, I saw her again.

Three sentences are devoted to a description of the encounter between the narrator and the girl in the park; then three weeks are dismissed in a single, brief sentence. Obviously, life was not suspended during those three weeks, but because that intervening period is unimportant to the narrative, it is quickly passed over.

This is an example of pacing, an important and commonsense principle of narrative writing. Unimportant time, events, and scenes are dismissed as the narrative focuses on and develops in detail only what is important to its theme. For example, in "The Code" the author glosses over his enlistment in the army during wartime in this brief paragraph:

> I did not see much of my father during the next four years or so. I was home during the summer vacation after my freshman year, but then, in the middle of the next year, I went into the Army. I was shipped to the Far East for the tail end of the war, and was in Japan at the start of the Occupation. I saw my father only once or twice during my entire training period, and, naturally, during the time I was overseas I did not see him at all.
>
> Richard Gill, "The Code"

Four years go up in the puff of a single sentence because nothing significant to the theme of the story occurred during that particular stretch of time. If the writer had catalogued his various army adventures here instead of skipping over them as he did, he would only have diluted the drive of his narrative and ruined the upcoming climactic deathbed scene.

Common sense must guide you in selecting scenes and events to be developed in your own narration, but the ultimate underlying principle is the relevance of the material to your theme.

USE VIVID DETAILS TO DESCRIBE PEOPLE AND PLACES IN YOUR NARRATIVE.   People and places are the lifeblood of your narration. Make them real and distinct through the use of forceful details (see Unit 8, "Description"). Here, for example, is how one author describes his main character, a young prodigy by the name of Wallace. Notice the wealth of specific details that the author uses:

> As a matter of fact, one look at Wallace should have been enough to tell the teachers what sort of genius he was. At fourteen, he was somewhat shorter than he should have been and a good deal stouter. His face was round, owlish and dirty. He had big, dark eyes, and his black hair, which hardly ever got cut, was arranged on his head as the four winds wanted it. He had been outfitted with attractive and fairly expensive clothes, but he changed from one suit to another only when his parents came to call on him and ordered him to get out of what he had on.
>
> Richard Rovere, "Wallace"

Detailed dialogue is another technique that narration uses to infuse life in a character. In "The Code," dialogue reveals the father as a man who will not tolerate emotional, irrational beliefs. For example, when the aunts go into hysterics over the death of the author's younger brother, calling him "a perfect baby," "a saint," "too perfect to live," the father angrily reacts:

> His face was very pale, and his eyes flashed almost feverishly. "Don't talk like that, Agnes!" he exclaimed, with a strange violence that was not anger but something much deeper. "I won't have you talking like that any more. I don't want anybody talking like that!" His whole body seemed to tremble. I had never seen him so worked up before. "Of course he was a bad boy at times!" he cried. "Every boy's bad once in a while. What do you have to change him for? Why don't you leave him as he was?"
>
> Richard Gill, "The Code"

A vivid narrative requires careful observation of people and their environment, and the inclusion of details that contribute most efficiently to a clear, vigorous, and interesting story.

READING FOR IDEAS

One of the hallmarks of a good narrative is how quickly and easily it sets the contexts of time, place, character, and action for the story to follow. This one tells us all we need to know by the end of the first paragraph and does so nearly effortlessly. What troubled many readers, however, was the writer's unemotional tone. Did the narrator dispatch Debbie because of compassion or exhaustion? Do you think the narrator was a man or a woman? What do you think of the mother's reaction? What is your opinion of what the resident did?

PROFESSIONAL MODEL

It's Over, Debbie

ANONYMOUS

When the essay reprinted below appeared in the January 8, 1988, issue of the Journal of the American Medical Association, *it instantly drew heated reactions from readers. Was the author an actual resident recounting an actual experience? If so, who was the girl, and was the resident within legal and ethical boundaries? So far the* Journal *has refused to disclose the identity of the author, citing the constitutional amendment that guarantees freedom of the press. If we pass over the editorial quarreling associated with this narrative, we are still faced with its core question: At what point is life no longer worth preserving, and who has a right to decide when a life is no longer worth living?*

1   The call came in the middle of the night. As a gynecology resident rotating through a large, private hospital, I had come to detest telephone calls, because invariably I would be up for several hours and would not feel good the next day. However, duty called, so I answered the phone. A nurse informed me that a patient was having difficulty getting rest, could I please see her. She was on 3 North. That was the gynecologic-oncology unit, not my usual duty station. As I trudged along, bumping sleepily against walls and corners and not believing I was up again, I tried to imagine what I might find at the end of my walk. Maybe an elderly woman with an anxiety reaction, or perhaps something particularly horrible.

2   I grabbed the chart from the nurses' station on my way to the patient's room, and the nurse gave me some hurried details: a 20-year-old girl named Debbie was dying of ovarian cancer. She was having unrelenting vomiting apparently as the result of an alcohol drip administered for sedation. Hmmm, I thought. Very sad. As I approached the room I could hear loud, labored breathing. I entered and saw an emaciated, dark-haired woman who appeared much older than 20. She was receiving nasal oxygen, had an IV, and was sitting in bed suffering from what was obviously severe air hunger. The chart noted her weight at 80 pounds. A second woman, also dark-haired but of middle age, stood at her right, holding her hand. Both looked up as I entered. The room seemed filled

with the patient's desperate effort to survive. Her eyes were hollow, and she had suprasternal[1] and intercostal[2] retractions with her rapid inspirations.[3] She had not eaten or slept in two days. She had not responded to chemotherapy and was being given supportive care only. It was a gallows scene, a cruel mockery of her youth and unfulfilled potential. Her only words to me were, "Let's get this over with."

I retreated with my thoughts to the nurses' station. The patient was tired and needed rest. I could not give her health, but I could give her rest. I asked the nurse to draw 20 mg of morphine sulfate into a syringe. Enough, I thought, to do the job. I took the syringe into the room and told the two women I was going to give Debbie something that would let her rest and to say good-bye. Debbie looked at the syringe, then laid her head on the pillow with her eyes open, watching what was left of the world. I injected the morphine intravenously and watched to see if my calculations on its effects would be correct. Within seconds her breathing slowed to a normal rate, her eyes closed, and her features softened as she seemed restful at last. The older woman stroked the hair of the now-sleeping patient. I waited for the inevitable next effect of depressing the respiratory drive. With clocklike certainty, within four minutes the breathing rate slowed even more, then became irregular, then ceased. The dark-haired woman stood erect and seemed relieved.

3

It's over, Debbie.

4

Vocabulary

gynecology (1)	ovarian (2)	retraction (2)
resident (1)	unrelenting (2)	chemotherapy (2)
rotating (1)	sedation (2)	syringe (3)
gynecologic-oncology (1)	emaciated (2)	intravenously (3)

Questions on Meaning and Technique

1. How does the narrator respond to the call in the middle of the night? How does his or her response affect the central idea of the narrative?

2. Did the actual patient live up to the resident's imagination of what might be found on 3 North? Why or why not?

3. What figurative image does the narrator use to describe the patient's condition? How effective do you consider the image?

4. What is the importance of the "second woman," mentioned in paragraph 2?

5. What main message did you receive from the narrative? Do you agree with the message? Why or why not?

6. How effective is the ending of the essay? Explain your answer.

---

[1]Above the breastbone (to which the ribs are attached)
[2]Between the ribs
[3]Breathing in

7. Although no one knows who actually wrote this article, it is widely presumed to have been written by an intern. How does the narrator manage to convey a sense of medical expertise in the writing?

STUDENT ESSAY

First Draft   Gabrielle Scheidig

Preserving the Species

The original opening was trite. The replacement grabs the reader's attention more quickly.

The heartbeat of life is not hypothesis or theory, but personal experience

~~Life is filled with experiences, from the moment a baby opens its eyes, to the moment they close forever. In every day life a person reads books, sees films, or, unfortunately, is involved in accidents.~~ Experience**s** rule**s** endlessly in everyone's life. I have had many unforgettable experiences~~in my life~~, yet, there is one that shall never lose its intensity in my mind. This experience ~~helped me decide to~~ *was crucial in helping me decide to* pursue animal science as a career in order to ~~strive to help~~ *ensure* species survival, *especially among endangered animals*   1

elimination of wordiness

clarifies which zoo

Saturdays were zoo days for me. This meant that every Saturday I drove to the *city* zoo bright and early in the morning, either to give tours, to help with youth workshops, or to assist a keeper. Today was keeper day.   2

clarifies the circumstances of the narrative

My assignment was the pronghorn bison string. *to whom I was assigned this Saturday,* I had assisted ~~that~~ *the* particular keeper, (on many occasions before,) so the work was routine for me. Little did I suspect how that day was not going to turn out to be routine at all.   3

After I had cleaned and fed the Arabian oryx, located in the corral neighboring that of the pronghorn, I took a brief break. The keeper was in her office phoning the *zoo's* veterinarian to express concern for a young pronghorn due to give birth any time. Once off the phone, the keeper explained that she was concerned because the pregnant pronghorn was   4

makes for better pacing by adding details

restless and highly nervous. She was battering herself against her stall walls, *My heart started to beat faster; I felt scared.* I began to count time until the veterinarian arrived. All of us would feel better once this

Doctor is more natural.

experienced animal ~~physician~~ *doctor* could assess the situation and offer his expertise. In the meantime, the keeper asked me to feed some infant pronghorns in a stall right next to the pregnant animal and simultaneously to keep an eye on her so she would not harm

Specific image adds drama.

herself. As I was feeding the infants, I could hear the female moaning and ~~hitting~~ the *crashing violently against*

Insert A

walls of her stall~~with loud crashes.~~ I peeked through the stall boards to check her. She

had several scratches on her shoulders, and little chunks of her hair were missing *from her coat* here

and there. As she suddenly flung herself into a sharp turn, I noticed a tiny leg jutting out

of her birth canal. ~~Excitedly~~ *Anxiously* I dashed off to inform the keeper. She was greeting the   *Anxiously is more accurate.*

veterinarian, who gave me a quick smile and then followed me back to the stall.

5   I felt deep admiration for this man, who seemed so naturally to mix compassion with

professional confidence. Gently, yet firmly, he checked the female, who by now seemed

~~beside herself.~~ *in a furor of pain* His decisive judgment was given quickly: "Let's get her down and pull   *more specific*

out the baby." He told us that the baby was causing a problem in the womb and was

thus hampering the delivery. "The longer we let her hit the walls, the greater the chance

of a dead baby," he said. At the zoo, when an infant dies, it is like a murder. Every   *Addition creates some foreshadowing.*

animal is in the zoo to help preserve its species. *I felt this duty of species preservation being imposed on me that moment.* The vet worked rapidly, making every

motion count. Before I knew it, he had the female down and on a tarp in the driveway

outside the stall. ~~Since~~ *W*e did not have enough time to transport her to the medical   *Avoids repeating "since."*

center; the driveway would have to be sufficient. ~~Since~~ Only three of us were present--the

vet, the keeper, and I--we had to divide the necessary duties. *and* The keeper was to run for

supplies; I was to keep the female's head off the ground while holding an I.V. and

monitoring her breathing; and the veterinarian was to deliver the baby. How deftly the   *Addition slows down the narrative to focus on the moment.*

vet accomplished his assignment. *Insert B* But the baby was twisted into an abnormal position,

making delivery impossible. Patiently and tirelessly the veterinarian worked away,

turning and twisting this way and that.

6   All three of us ~~participants~~ felt the intensity of the moment *in which we were participating*. Sweat trickled down my

forehead and *onto* my cheeks. The female pronghorn had been subdued and lay there looking   *smoother sentence*

quiet and peaceful. Her nostrils ~~expanded~~ *widened* and ~~constricted~~ *narrowed* rhythmically. The vet had

(Insert A)
Over and over again, she would fling herself forward
or sideways as if attacking an invisible demon.

(Insert B)
With the agility of a seasoned obstetrician, he reached into
the pronghorn's birth canal and tried to deliver the baby.

finally pushed the tiny leg back into the birth canal and now proceeded to untwist the

I was filled with agonizing apprehension.

baby.∧Would the delivery be successful? After what seemed a nerve-wracking eternity,

It lay there like a wet stuffed animal.

the baby pronghorn slipped onto the driveway with a gush of fluid.∧It was dead. "Birth

without life," the veterinarian muttered. He showed little emotion. He was a scientist,

after all; but I sensed hurt in his ironic pronouncement. I could not bear to look at the tiny

With immense pluck she had survived a traumatic incident.

thing. Rather, I kept my eyes on the mother.∧The baby was slipped into a bag and loaded

onto the zoo truck, to be transported to the health center for investigative research. The

three of us, who had taken part in one of nature's significant moments, placed the mother

gently into her stall so she could rest. She would be fine; the veterinarian had helped her

done his best

and saved her from unnecessary suffering. He had ~~performed nobly~~ even though he could

not save the baby this time. *Insert C*

> This experience helped me decide what to study in college. I wanted to study animal   7
>
> science so that I could some day assist in the preservation of animal species, as the
>
> veterinarian had done that memorable Saturday.

This experience was a turning point in my life. For the first time ever I felt an exultation about the lifework I would choose. I would study animal science so that I could dedicate myself to the preservation of animal species, as the veterinarian had done that memorable Saturday.

(*Insert C*)

Next time would be better. There would always be a next time — the opportunity to help preserve a species.

Addition creates more suspense, better pacing.

Simile adds vividness.

Addition explains why it was better to look at the mother.

"Done his best" is less fanciful.

Addition introduces a note of hope.

The original conclusion was lackluster. The substitute is a better clincher.

STUDENT ESSAY

Final Draft   Gabrielle Scheidig

Preserving the Species

1   The heartbeat of life is not hypothesis or theory, but personal experience. Experience

rules endlessly in everyone's life. I have had many unforgettable experiences; yet, there

is one that shall never lose its intensity in my mind. This experience was crucial in

helping me decide to pursue animal science as a career in order to ensure species

survival, especially among endangered animals.

Saturdays were zoo days for me. This meant that every Saturday I drove to the city   2
zoo bright and early in the morning, either to give tours, to help with youth workshops,
or to assist a keeper. Today was keeper day.

My assignment was the pronghorn bison string. On many occasions before, I had   3
assisted the particular keeper to whom I was assigned this Saturday, so the work was
routine for me. Little did I suspect how that day was not going to turn out to be routine
at all.

After I had cleaned and fed the Arabian oryx, located in the corral neighboring that   4
of the pronghorn, I took a brief break. The keeper was in her office phoning the zoo's
veterinarian to express concern for a young pronghorn due to give birth any time. Once
off the phone, the keeper explained that she was concerned because the pregnant
pronghorn was restless and highly nervous. She was battering herself against her stall
walls. My heart started to beat faster; I felt scared. I began to count time until the veterinarian arrived. All of us would feel better once this experienced animal doctor could
assess the situation and offer his expertise. In the meantime, the keeper asked me to
feed some infant pronghorns in a stall right next to the pregnant animal and simultaneously to keep an eye on her so she would not harm herself. As I was feeding the infants, I could hear the female moaning and crashing violently against the walls of her
stall. Over and over again, she would fling herself forward or sideways as if attacking
an invisible demon. I peeked through the stall boards to check her. She had several
scratches on her shoulders, and little chunks of hair were missing from her coat here
and there. As she suddenly flung herself into a sharp turn, I noticed a tiny leg jutting
out of her birth canal. Anxiously I dashed off to inform the keeper. She was greeting the
veterinarian, who gave me a quick smile and then followed me back to the stall.

I felt deep admiration for this man, who seemed so naturally to mix compassion with   5
professional confidence. Gently, yet firmly, he checked the female, who by now seemed
in a furor of pain. His decisive judgment was given quickly: "Let's get her down and
pull out the baby." He told us that the baby was causing a problem in the womb and
was thus hampering the delivery. "The longer we let her hit the walls, the greater the
chance of a dead baby," he said. At the zoo, when an infant dies, it is like a murder.

Every animal is in the zoo to help preserve its species. I felt this duty of species preservation being imposed on me that moment. The vet worked rapidly, making every motion count. Before I knew it, he had the female down and on a tarp in the driveway outside the stall. We did not have enough time to transport her to the medical center; the driveway would have to be sufficient. Only three of us were present—the vet, the keeper, and I—and we had to divide the necessary duties. The keeper was to run for supplies; I was to keep the female's head off the ground while holding an I.V. and monitoring her breathing; and the veterinarian was to deliver the baby. How deftly the vet accomplished his assignment! With the agility of a seasoned obstetrician, he reached into the pronghorn's birth canal and tried to deliver the baby. But the baby was twisted into an abnormal position, making delivery impossible. Patiently and tirelessly the veterinarian worked away, turning and twisting this way and that.

6   All three of us felt the intensity of the moment in which we were participating. Sweat trickled down my forehead and onto my cheeks. The female pronghorn had been subdued and lay there looking quiet and peaceful. Her nostrils widened and narrowed rhythmically. The vet had finally pushed the tiny leg back into the birth canal and now proceeded to untwist the baby. I was filled with agonizing apprehension. Would the delivery be successful? After what seemed a nerve-wracking eternity, the baby pronghorn slipped onto the driveway with a gush of fluid. It lay there like a wet stuffed animal. It was dead. "Birth without life," the veterinarian muttered. He showed little emotion. He was a scientist, after all; but I sensed hurt in his ironic pronouncement. I could not bear to look at the tiny thing. Rather, I kept my eyes on the mother. With immense pluck she had survived a traumatic incident. The baby was slipped into a bag and loaded onto the zoo truck, to be transported to the health center for investigative research. The three of us, who had taken part in one of nature's significant moments, placed the mother gently into her stall so she could rest. She would be fine; the veterinarian had helped her and saved her from unnecessary suffering. He had done his best even though he could not save the baby this time. Next time would be better. There would always be a next time—the opportunity to help preserve a species.

7   This experience was a turning point in my life. For the first time ever I felt an exultation about the lifework I would choose. I would study animal science so that I

could dedicate myself to the preservation of animal species, as the veterinarian had
done that memorable Saturday.

READING FOR IDEAS

As you read this excerpt from a personal diary that was posthumously discovered
and published some 30 years after it was written, there are some basic
considerations to remember. First, its writer probably had no conscious intent of
publication and consequently framed her thoughts spontaneously and with little
regard to an audience. Second, a diary being always a first-person narrative, we
have to infer the mind and character of its author from her own reporting. It is
useful to bear in mind that at the time of writing this, the author was not only
injured and isolated by an avalanche, but also pregnant. Her aim was personal
survival as well as the delivery and survival of her unborn child. What picture of
the author do you get from these diary entries? How do you rate her skill at
coping? What do you find most remarkable about her tale? How does the author
seem to react to her ordeal?

ALTERNATE READING

Marooned in Alaska
MARTHA MARTIN

*We do not know the identity of this remarkable diarist. What we do know is that the
manuscript was discovered and published by a Macmillan editor some 30 years after
it was written. At the time of its writing, Martha Martin, a pseudonym, was the
pregnant wife of an Alaskan gold prospector and cut off from her husband by an
avalanche that also broke her arm. Stranded in a prospector's cabin for the winter,
she devised a makeshift splint for her arm, killed an otter with an axe, cured its skin
to make a blanket for her baby, delivered the baby unaided after two days of labor,
and was finally picked up by a fishing party of Indians. The baby, whom she named
Donnas, died shortly after the author was reunited with her husband.*

WINTER, 1920s

I killed a sea otter today. I actually did kill a sea otter. I killed him with the ax, dragged   1
him home, and skinned him. I took his liver out, and ate part of it. I'm going to eat the
rest of it, and his heart, too. His liver was quite large, bigger than a deer's, and it had
more lobes to it. It was a very good liver, and I enjoyed it.

Most of today was devoted to the sea otter; getting the hide off was a real task. It's a   2 lovely skin, the softest, silkiest, thickest fur I have ever seen. I am going to make a robe for my baby out of the beautiful fur. My darling child may be born in a lowly cabin, but she shall be wrapped in one of the earth's most costly furs.

3   It was such a splendid piece of luck. Lucky in more ways than one. The otter might have killed me, although I have never heard of such a thing.

4   This morning I went to the woods to gather a load of limbs. As I was coming home with them, I saw the tide was nearly out, and I thought I'd walk over to the bar and take a look at the boat . . . I was going along, swinging the ax in my left hand, managing the crutch with the right hand, . . . not thinking of anything in particular, when right beside me I heard a bark. It was like a dog bark; not a bow-wow bark, more of a yip. I looked around and saw a huge creature reared up on its haunches. I saw its white teeth.

5   Without thinking, I swung the ax at the side of its head, saw it hit, felt the jar in my arm, heard the thud. As I swung the ax, I turned and tried to run. I was so terrified the thing would nab me from behind that I could hardly move. I glanced over my shoulder to see how close it was. It hadn't budged from where it dropped . . .

6   I got down on my knees and examined it from one end to the other. First off, I noticed the lovely fur. I took off my glove and ran my fingers through the nice silky coat. I decided right then I would have the skin. I saw it as a baby blanket . . .

7   It is very much against the law to kill a sea otter. Right now I don't care a rap for law. I'd like to have a picture of a game warden who could arrest me now. I am safe enough from the law, and I think I always will be. Under the circumstances I doubt if any judge would send me to jail for what I have done . . .

8   I dragged my kill home, and was a long time doing so. I'll bet the creature weighed a hundred pounds. I worked and worked, rested, pulled, and dragged, rested some more, and by and by I reached the cabin with my prize . . .

9   I decided to skin it exactly the way the men do a deer. I have watched them many times, but I never helped or paid much attention. I didn't know very much about skinning a fur-bearing animal when I went to work on that creature. How I wished I had an Indian squaw to instruct and help me . . .

10   The head was a mess, so I just cut the skin at the neck line and let the head fur go. I chopped off the feet and threw them in the stove. After I got the legs and sides skinned, I turned the otter on his belly and worked the skin off his back down to the tail. I had more trouble with that tail than I did with all the rest of the animal, I wanted it for a neckpiece, and I tried to get the bony tail out without slitting the skin. It can't be done . . .

11   My hands got awful cold examining the innards, rather smelly, too. I had let the fire go down, and there wasn't enough hot water for me to scrub properly. I made up the fire, washed a little, and then sat down to rest and gloat over my wonderful sea-otter fur . . .

I woke up in the night, and felt rested, so I got up, lit the carbide lamp, and sat here writing all about my sea otter.

I had planned to work on my otter skin today, but when I looked out this morning I saw Old Nick was flaunting a plume [a sign that a cold wind was coming up] . . . I put all my energy into gathering wood and left the skin alone . . .

12

Goodness, I have lots of work to do before I am ready for my little darling. I must get the fur finished for her. I am determined my child shall have a priceless gift . . .

13

I've begun scraping off the fat from my otter skin, and it's about half done. I have learned a few things about scraping skins: they scrape better when they are stretched tight over the end of a block of wood, and the fat comes off easier when it is cold. Another thing, when a skin looks scraped, it still has lots of fat on it. I know I'll have to go over the whole hide at least twice . . .

14

At last I have finished scraping the otter skin. It is all very nicely done, and not one single hole did I cut in it . . . I am going to scrub it well in lots of warm soapy water . . .

15

Goodness me, I have more chores than a farmer . . .

16

Hurray! My otter skin is nailed to the door. It's the biggest thing—much bigger than I thought it was. It nearly covers the whole door . . .

17

The wind still howls, swirls, and rages. It's awful cold, maybe ten below. All the peaks look like volcanoes with their great trailing plumes . . . I brought in some more wood today, but I didn't stay out long. It was too cold and windy . . .

18

While I was out in the cold, my breasts ached. They drew up and the nipples stuck out firm, and they ached. When I came in I examined them, and found they were swelling and have water in them, not milk, but clear water. Soon my child will be here, and I am not yet ready to receive her. So much to do and so little time . . .

19

I have decided to burn the floor. I'll cut the part I have already taken up, now, and save the rest for reserve. There are seven sills, all logs ten to twelve inches through, under the floor, which is nailed to them. If I can dig around them, saw them in two, pry them out, and cut them into blocks, they'll make a lot of fine wood. They are yellow cedar, and so is the puncheon . . .

20

The otter skin is a disappointment. It's as hard as a board, and I'm just sick about it. I might make it into a Robinson Crusoe umbrella, but it can never become an infant's robe in its present stiff state. I remember reading or hearing that the Eskimoes chew skins to make them soft. It would take a lot of chewing to make this big skin soft. I just can't chew it, and I won't even try.

21

22   The fur is lovely, and it smells clean. I put my face in it, and it's the softest thing I've ever touched. I do wish the skin wasn't so stiff. There must be some way I can fix it. Baby must have one present.

23   If we were home she would have many gifts—a ring, a silver cup with her name on it, a necklace, a silver spoon, a baby book, dresses with lace and ribbons, fine soft knitted things. Even in this northland she would have gifts if anyone knew we were here . . .

24   I believe I have found a way to soften the otter skin. I doubled over a corner of it, and it didn't break as I thought it might, so I folded it some more. No breaks. I kept on folding and creasing it, and now it is no longer board-like; but it's still a very long way from being as soft as I want it to be.

25   I washed a few clothes today. I want clean things for the coming of my child. Surely she will be here soon. I am getting things ready to receive her, and I have done a lot of sewing. Tomorrow I will bathe and make myself presentable for a newborn child . . .

26   I made a birth cloth today from one of Don's union suits. It is all wool and should serve nicely to wrap a newborn child in . . .

27   I plan to use string raveled from a flour sack to tie the cord. I boiled a piece to make sure it is clean . . .

28   I've worked again on the fur, and I'm pleased with the result. I used a different system—pulled it back and forth around the bunk pole. I admire the fur more and more, and I want so much to get it soft enough to use for my baby . . .

29   The milk case is pretty well filled with baby things. Don's shaving soap is in one of the pockets. Shaving soap should be good for baby. It seems right to bathe my child with her father's shaving soap . . .

30   Only a few more days now until I will have a child in my arms.

31   I have been working and working at the otter skin, and I am making progress . . . A dozen times a day I pick it up, rub a part of it between my hands, brush it, hold it to my face, hold it at arm's length to admire it . . .

32   The wind has died away. It is very much warmer, and a haze covers the sky. I went wood gathering and was delighted with my outing. I saw twenty-six deer, and I brought some boughs for the ones who will pay me a friendly call . . . Two ravens came to eat the otter. I wonder how they knew it was there . . . Maybe they smelled it. My thrush never comes back, and I liked it so much. Those mean old jays—I really shouldn't feed them a crumb . . .

33   I baked bread, lots of it, far more than I need for myself. The deers are fond of bread, and I thought I'd have an extra amount on hand. Five of them came today to bum a

handout, and I didn't disappoint them. I think all of them have been here several times before, but I can be sure of only one—Sammy with the mark on his throat. He is the tamest of the lot, and knows me. He even eats out of my hand . . .

I pounded up my cast and put it on the floor with the gravel. It was quite hard, much harder than I thought. If I had fallen, the cast would have given my arm good protection. Now that my arm is well, I haven't worn the cast for weeks. I don't use my crutch any more, either, but I'm not disposing of it yet . . .   34

I always think of the child as a girl. What if it's a boy? Oh, it couldn't be . . .   35

This awful deep snow and hard cold is going to kill off much of our wild life. Poor creatures, what a pity they can't all be like bears and sleep the winter through. But then, what would I do without my friendly bums to come around and ask for bread and lick their chops at me?   36

Since the baby came down to live in the lower part of my abdomen, I have been constipated, and I don't like it. I think it's the cause of my swollen ankles. I had absolutely nothing here to correct it, so I looked around to see what the wilderness might provide, and hit on the idea of eating seaweed. Certainly it can be called roughage . . . I went along the beach and gathered a mess . . . I picked it over well, washed it thoroughly, and ate quite a lot—ate it raw. It wasn't too awful, but I certainly don't like the stuff. It was very effective, almost more effective than I desired it to be. I was busy all day with the honey bucket . . .   37

The otter skin is getting to be as soft as I want it to be. I have invented another way to soften it. I made a small mallet and gently pound the folded fur over a block of wood . . .   38

The fur is finished, and it's exactly as I wished it to be. I am very proud of it. So soft and warm—such a lovely thing. I shall wrap my baby in it when she goes for her outings, and we will walk pridefully along the beach . . .   39

Snow seals every crack, so I only burn a little wood when there is no wind, and open the door for air.   40

I have bathed and washed my head. My hair has grown about three inches and is as curly as can be.[1] I like short hair because it's so easy to wash and dry. I think I may keep it short and never again be bothered with hairpins . . .   41

My body is heavy, and my movements are slow and not too definite. I am becoming clumsy and awkward. I don't like it. Maybe I should sit down and just twiddle my thumbs until Baby comes. I do hope she comes before I use up all this water and burn all my wood . . .   42

---

[1]Martha had treated her scalp wounds with bacon grease, but mice nibbled at the grease while she slept and she cut her hair to the roots.

43   I brought a few branches and put a bouquet of cedar and hemlock boughs on my windowsill and placed the finest of Don's ore specimens on either side of it. The window has a nice look, as though a man and a woman lived here . . .

44   There was a little show of blood, and when I saw it I remembered my mother saying it was a sure sign that the child would be born soon . . .

45   I have never seen a child born. I always felt inadequate to help and was too modest to want to be a spectator. I have never seen anything born—not even a cat . . . I am no longer afraid, yet I do wish someone were with me to help me take care of the child . . .
    [Martha's child was born after two days of labor, during which she cooked, cared for herself and wrote recollections of life with her husband to try "to order my thoughts, be calm, and not bother my head about all I don't know." Again, she found herself able to cope alone, to deliver the child, to rest, to tie the cord, cut it, and then deliver the afterbirth. And the next day she went on with her narrative.]

46   My darling little girl-child, after such a long and troublesome waiting I now have you in my arms. I am alone no more. I have my baby.

47   I went outside for a short walk on the beach today. It's the first time I've been out since the baby came. The tide was nearly low, and there were dozens of deer on the beach, maybe forty or fifty, maybe as many as a hundred . . . Poor things, they are starving . . . I just can't let all the deer starve. I can cut a little brush, maybe enough to keep some of them alive . . .

48   Several of them followed me back to the cabin and begged for food. I fed them a little, and promised more. I promised to bake lots of bread and make a feast . . . It will be the christening feast for the baptism of Donnas. I'll invite the deer to come share our joy and gladness and our food . . .

49   Yesterday was lovely. A beautiful late winter day with a bright sun and a warm southerly breeze. It was a perfect christening day . . . When the deer saw me go for a little walk and heard me call to them, they came, and all went well.

50   Donnas was dressed in all her finery and wrapped in the otter robe, only her little face showing deep down in the fur . . .

51   "Donnas Martin, I baptize thee in the name of the Father, and of the Son, and of the Holy Ghost. Amen."

52   I dipped the tips of my fingers in the water and signed my child with the sign of the cross. Then I threw more bread morsels to our guests, whose attention had begun to wander . . .

53   I held my baby close, wrapped well in her fur robe, loved her and talked to her. It's wondrous good to talk. It's been so long since I've talked to anyone . . . I told her all about us.

"I'm the queen," I told her, "and you are the little princess. The cabin is our palace.   *54*
None are here to dare dispute our word."

I told her the deer are our helpers and our friends, our subjects and our comfort, and   *55*
they will give us food and clothing according to our needs. I told her of the birds, the little
ptarmigan, the geese, ducks, grouse, and the kindly owl; the prankish ravens and the
lordly eagle. Told her of the fishes, the clams, and the mussels. Told her of the mink and
the otter, and the great brown bear with his funny, furry cub. Told her of the forest and
of the things it will give us; of roots, stems, leaves, and berries, and the fun of gathering
them; of the majestic mountain uprising behind us with a vein of gold-bearing ore coming
straight from its heart. Told her that all these things were ours to have and to rule over
and care for . . .

This afternoon I went out and cut brush for the deer. I left baby alone in the cabin,   *56*
explaining that it was my duty as reigning queen to provide for my subjects. I told her
famine was now on our land and I must go cut brush . . .

When deer are hungry, they behave differently than when well fed. When a deer is   *57*
feeling good, he will look up for his food, at least some of the time; but when he is weak
with hunger he looks down all the time. There's lots of browse within reach if they would
only stretch their necks to get it, but they act stupid, and don't seem to know anything
about the food within their reach. Perhaps they are too weak to stretch up: maybe they
get dizzy looking up . . .

Half an hour before dark seven gray arctic geese came in and settled on the beach   *58*
almost in front of the cabin. They are either sick or exhausted, or maybe they're tame
geese. I went out to look at them, being careful not to frighten them away. I was ready to
duck back into the cabin at the first sign of alarm. They didn't seem alarmed, and I went
quite close to them. I then gave them food, and they paid no attention to me. Why should
wild geese act so? Has something happened to me since my baby came?

This is the last piece of usable paper. But that doesn't matter, for I no longer have such   *59*
need to write. I have no problems to ponder through . . . I am not lonely any more; I have
my baby for company . . .
Soon someone will come and find us here . . .
Maybe the Indians will come to their fish camp . . .

The Indians have come, good, good Indians. Shy, fat, smelly, friendly, kindhearted   *60*
Indians.

Early this morning Donnas and I were out on the beach, she getting the benefit of the   *61*
warm spring sun, and I putting the finishing touches on the bottom of my overturned
dinghy. I looked up from my work and saw two Indian canoes near the far side of the Arm.

I rushed to the cabin, grabbed my gun, and fired call shots. I shouted and waved. The   *62* canoes turned and started toward my shore.

63   Hurriedly I made up the fire and set coffee water to boil. I brought out my baby's best clothes and got her into them in a jiffy. I ran outside and waved, saw I had time, rushed back and prettied myself up.

64   The cabin was already clean, and there were fresh blueberry blossoms on the windowsill and on the table. I shook out the otter skin to fluff the fur, wrapped Donnas in it, and went to the water's edge. There we awaited our guests.

65   Both canoes grounded at about the same time, and right in front of me. For a little while we just looked at each other. I was all trembly, and it was hard to behave with dignity. After what seemed a rather long time, I did manage to say, "Good morning."

66   "Hello." A breathing space, then another "Hello."
"I'm glad to see you." That came a little easier.
"You bet," was the reply, and following a pause, "By golly."
There was a consultation in Siwash.
"Not dead?"
"No, not dead."

67   So the conversation went on until I had told my story. No one made a move to get out of the canoes, and it occurred to me they might be waiting politely for an invitation. I hastened to extend one, ending with, "And come see my baby." I held her out toward them.

68   They piled out, nineteen of them. They didn't seem to see the baby, or me either. All eyes were on the otter skin. There was much Siwash talk, then the spokesman fingered the fur. "Against law. You go jail."

69   They all laughed.
"Where you get otter?"

70   I pointed to the spot on the beach where I had killed the animal, then I acted out the part. That seemed to loosen my tongue, and I talked a streak. The Indians laughed and laughed. They came and fingered the fur, stroked it, looked at the underside.

71   Then an old squaw said, "Pret-ty good." Splendid words of praise . . .

72   I knew these poor people needed all the fish they could catch, and I hated to ask them to take time out to do anything for me, yet I thought I had been here long enough, so I asked to be taken to Big Sleeve.

73   "You bet," was the quick answer. But the west wind was blowing, and it would increase until sundown. It would be better to go in the morning . . .

74   I was glad for a little more time in my cabin. I almost didn't want to leave at all, I was so mixed up. . . .

Vocabulary

puncheon (20)

Questions on Meaning and Technique

1. What does the opening paragraph with its episode about killing the otter immediately tell you about the writer?

2. Given the unstated fact that the author's situation was desperate—she was injured, pregnant, and marooned in an isolated cabin during a severe winter—what is most remarkable about the tone of her diary?

3. Some feminist editors have responded enthusiastically to this diary. What elements of the author's outlook do you think would appeal especially to feminists?

4. What step-by-step process does the author unwittingly recount in her diary?

5. What earmarks of a diary characterize the writing of this piece?

6. What do you think the author is giving up by being reunited with her husband and civilization?

7. The author confesses at the end of the excerpt to almost not wanting "to leave at all, I was so mixed up. . . ." Why do you think she felt that way?

8. The diary was written in the 1920s and published in 1952. What, if any, characteristics of the writing style can you point to that identifies it as a period piece?

9. What does it add to your reading of this excerpt to learn that Donnas died shortly after the family was reunited?

Writing Assignments

1. Write a narration about any outdoors experience.

2. Write a narration about an incident or action that you later regretted.

READING FOR IDEAS

This selection is a ghost story from another culture told by a former British Colonial administrator to whom the incident occurred. The Gilbert Islands, where the story is set, are a small archipelago in the central Pacific named after their British discoverer, Captain Thomas Gilbert. The Gilbertese, as does every culture, have their own sacred myths to explain life and death, and whether or not these paint a preposterous picture depends largely on the beholder's point of view. At the outset of the story, Grimble is clearly a debunking disbeliever, until matters take an inexplicable turn. Ask yourself whether our own myths about death and the hereafter are any more or less logical than the beliefs of the Gilbertese. Do you believe Grimble's story? Why? What do you think he saw on the beach, if not a migrating ghost?

ALTERNATE READING

The Limping Man of Makin-Meang
Sir Arthur Grimble

Sir Arthur Grimble (1888–1956) was born in Hong Kong and educated at Cambridge University. Joining the British Colonial Service in 1914, he was posted to the Gilbert and Ellice Islands where he served in various roles as an administrator before being transferred to St. Vincent in the Caribbean. During his tenure in the Gilbert Islands, Sir Arthur became a fluent scholar of Gilbertese and one of the only white men initiated into the islanders' societies. In 1948 he retired from the Colonial Service and began a second career as a broadcaster and raconteur for the BBC. His talks on his Colonial Service adventures were later collected and published in A Pattern of Islands *(1952), from which this excerpt was taken.*

1   It is clearly up to a District Officer to be listening and learning all the time. But there is a mortal difference of spirit between genuine research and prying. The danger is, the genuine thing can deteriorate by such subtle and unconscious stages into mere over-curiosity that a *bona-fide* student may find himself poised on the very brink of fiddling before he wakes up to the horrid change that has gone on inside him. That was what happened to me on Makin-Meang.

2   Perhaps the eeriness of the island's reputation for ghosts, added to the odd taciturnity of its villagers, had something to do with my ineptitude. But I base no defence on that. The District Officer's job is to find ways through to his people, not to leave them groping for ways through to himself.

3   I had heard of the ghosts of Makin-Meang before I got there. The people of Tarawa and Maiana and Abaiang were full of tales about them. They told me that the whole Gilbertese race, for over thirty generations by their count (it was sixty or so by mine), had looked on that most northerly island of the group as their halfway house between the lands of the living and the dead.

4   The story went that, when anyone died, his shade must first travel up the line of islands to Makin-Meang. Going ashore there on a southern beach, it must tread the length of the land to a sand-spit at the northern tip called the Place of Dread. This was not an actual place-name, but simply a term of fearful reference to the locality—for there sat Nakaa, the Watcher at the Gate, waiting to strangle all dead folk in his terrible net. The ghost had no hope of winning through to paradise except by way of the Gate, and no skill or cunning of its own could save it from the Net. Only the anxious family rituals, done over its dead body, could avail for that; and even these might fail if any outsider were to break in upon their course.

The reasonableness or not of these beliefs is of no concern. It was the age and   5
intensity of them that weighed on Makin-Meang. Every yard of the island was loaded with
the terrors and hopes that sixty generations of the living, and the dying, and the
long-dead, from end to end of the Gilbert group, had focused upon it. The impress of
man's thought was as heavy as footfalls on its paths. I wondered if that was why those
silent villagers always seemed to be listening inside their ears for some sound I could
never hear.

They were courteous and gentle, but they would not talk to me about the place where   6
Nakaa sat; they did not even try to change the subject when I raised it; they simply
dropped their eyes and removed themselves into abysses of reserve. It was not from them
but from my orderly, a Tarawa man, that I learned how best to avoid the horror of
meeting a ghost face to face. He lived in such open fear of doing so himself that the
Native Magistrate had let him know out of pity.

He told me that the shades of all the folk who died on the other fifteen islands found   7
their way to Nakaa by the road above the western beach, whereas only those of local
people used the eastern path. There were therefore many more chances of meeting
ghosts on the west side than on the east. Not that it mattered greatly which way you
chose going north, because you were travelling with the stream anyhow, and the only
thing you had to remember was never, never to look behind you. But coming back
against the northbound traffic, you must take no road save the eastern one. You could
find out in advance when that was safe or not by asking if any local death was expected
the day you planned to use it.

When I had finished my routine work on the island, I naturally wanted to see the Place   8
of Dread, so I called the Native Magistrate along one morning and asked him to find me
a guide.

I have never seen a face change and darken as swiftly as his did at my simple request.   9
He stood dumb for a while with downcast eyes; then, still looking at the ground, 'Do not
go to that place,' he exclaimed, and again, on a higher note, passionately, 'Do not go!'
The edge on his voice made it seem almost as if he had said, 'I order you not to go.'

'But why?' I said irritably. 'What's all this nonsense about Nakaa's place? What's all   10
the mystery? Shall I offend anyone by going?'

'Nobody will be offended,' he replied, 'but do not go. The place is perilous.'   11

'But why perilous for me, a Man of Matang?'[1]   12

His only reply was to wrap himself away in a cloak of silence. So I tried another line: 13
'You're a member of a Christian church. You surely can't believe still that souls go that
way to Heaven or Hell. Or do you?'

He lifted his eyes to mine, crossing himself. 'Not Christian souls,' he whispered, 'but   14
pagan ones . . . to Hell . . . they still walk the island . . . and Nakaa stays there . . . and
there is fear . . .' His voice trailed off into mumbles; I got no more out of him.

I should of course have made up my mind in all decency then to find the place for   15
myself. The island is a straight, lagoonless ribbon, and I could not possibly have missed its

---

[1]The Gilbertese believed that fair-skinned Europeans were their ancestral relatives from the mythical and
paradisical land of Matang. Hence Grimble refers to himself, and was referred to by the Gilbertese, as "a Man of
Matang."

tapering northern end. But I was cussed: 'Please find a village constable who isn't afraid to be my guide,' I said, 'and send him to me here.'

16 He looked at me mutely, spread his hands in a hopeless little gesture, and left. The constable, a giant of a man with bushy eyebrows and a grimly smileless face, appeared within the next half-hour. He said before we started that, as I was a stranger, I must take the western path going northward, just as the ghosts of strangers did, and that I must be careful not to look back.

17 'And if I do look back?' I said.

18 'If you look back and see a ghost,' he replied, 'you will be dead within a year,' and marched off ahead of me without another word.

19 I followed him in silence, eyes front, for perhaps half an hour, when he stepped suddenly into the coconut forest on our right. 'Come in among the trees,' he called without turning his head: 'This is my land. There is a thing you must carry to Nakaa.'

20 The thing was a seed-coconut. It appeared that every stranger, on his first visit to the Place of Dread, must bring with him a sprouting nut to plant in Nakaa's grove. I thought well of the idea until he told me I must carry it myself. It had an enormous sprout. I am inclined to believe he chose that particular one with deliberate malice, seeing that the only correct way to carry it (or so he said) was upright in my cupped hands with elbows well in against my ribs. I felt a complete ass sweating meekly behind him in that ridiculous attitude for the next five or six miles with my aspidistra-like trophy fluttering in the wind.

21 I planted the nut at his order where the trees petered out in a sandy desolation at the island's tip. When it was done to his liking, he just walked away into the forest.

22 'Here!' I called. 'Where are you going now?'

23 'I will wait here,' he replied. 'There in the north is the place you seek,' and was lost among the trees.

24 There was nothing in that empty waste to distinguish it from fifty other such promontories in the Gilbert group. It was merely a blazing acre or two of coral rock shaken by bellowing surf and strident with the shrieks of swarming sea-birds. I walked to the point where the meeting tide-rips boiled. It was from there that happy ghosts, the Net of Nakaa passed, fared forth across the sea to be gathered at last with their fathers. I knew that in that very flash of time, from somewhere down the chain of islands, the thoughts of dying folk might be winging their way in wistfulness and fear to the spot where I was standing. But somehow, my mind only played with the idea. There was no sense of reality. The place itself put me utterly out of tune with the old beliefs. Perhaps it was the noise. Death is so quiet, and there was nothing in Nakaa's domain but that din of birds and shattered waters and the trade wind's diapason booming in my ears.

25 Nevertheless, the brazen heat of rocks and sand that drove me out at last did have its importance, because it gave me the thirst that led to what followed. I went straight back to my guide among the trees and asked him in all innocence to pick me a drinking nut.

26 He sprang back as if I had struck him: 'I cannot do that,' he almost barked, 'I cannot do that. These trees are Nakaa's.' Fear oozed out of him, almost as tangible as sweat.

27 I could not press him to violate his belief; nor had I learned yet to scale a forty-foot tree for myself; so I had to sit down there in Nakaa's grove to a sickeningly dry lunch of bully-beef and biscuit. I remember muttering to myself, 'This is how the old devil strangles foreign ghosts, anyhow,' as I gulped the stuff down.

It was past two o'clock when we started for home down the eastern path. My friend   28
told me that his proper place going south was in the rear, and dropped forty paces
behind. Perhaps he just wanted to keep out of my sight as well as the sound of my voice;
anyway, it was I who led the way against the traffic-stream of local ghosts.

After ten minutes' walking, with thirst at concert pitch, I stopped and croaked back at   29
him (he would not come near), 'Are we out of Nakaa's grove yet?'

Not yet, he shouted back, there was still a mile or more of it. It was then that an   30
unpleasant little worm within me turned. I made up my mind to disregard his scruples and
ask anyone we met, anywhere, to pick me a nut. And there, in the midst of that peevish
thought was suddenly a man coming along the track to help me.

Across the arc of a curving beach, I saw him appear round a point. I could follow every   31
yard of his course as he came nearer. My eyes never left him, because my intent was
pinned on his getting me that drink. He walked with a strong limp (I thought that might
make it hard for him to climb a tree). He was a stocky, grizzled man of about fifty, clad
rather ceremoniously in a fine mat belted about his middle (a poor kit for climbing,
commented my mind). As he came up on my left, I noticed that his left cheek was scored
by a scar from jawbone to temple, and that his limp came from a twisted left foot and
ankle. I can see the man still in memory.

But the question is—did he see me? He totally ignored the greeting I gave him. He did   32
not even turn his eyes towards me. He went by as if I didn't exist. If anyone was a ghost
on that pathway, I was—for him. He left me standing with one futile hand flapping in the
air to stay him. I watched his dogged back receding towards my on-coming guide. I was
shocked speechless. It was so grossly unlike the infallible courtesy of the islanders.

He was just about to pass the constable when I found voice again: 'Ask that chief to   33
stop,' I called back, 'he may need some help from us.' It had struck me he might be a
lunatic at large: possibly harmless, but we ought to make sure of that. But the din of the
surf may have smothered my voice, for the constable didn't seem to hear. He passed the
newcomer twenty yards from where I stood, without a sign of recognition.

I ran back to him. 'Who is that man?' I asked.   34

He stopped in his tracks, gazing at my pointed finger. 'How?' he murmured hesitantly,   35
using the Gilbertese equivalent for, 'Say it again.'

I said it again, sharply, still pointing. As we stood dumbly looking at each other, I saw   36
swift beads of sweat—big, fat ones—start out of his forehead and lose themselves in his
eyebrows.

Then it was as if something suddenly collapsed inside him. It was horrible. 'I am afraid   37
in this place!' he screamed high in his head, like a woman, and, without another word, he
bolted out on the beach with an arm guarding his eyes. He disappeared at a run round
the point, and I didn't see him again until I got back to my quarters.

But there he was when I arrived, on the verandah with the Native Magistrate. I saw the   38
two of them absorbed in talk, the constable violently gesturing now and then as I
approached the house. But they stepped apart as soon as they heard my footsteps, and
stood gravely collected when I entered, waiting for me to speak.

I plunged head-first into my petulant story. The sum of it was that the constable had   39
witnessed the discourtesy of the man with the limp, and was now trying his silly best to
shield him from censure. It might be very loyal, but did he take me for a fish-headed

fool? To pretend he hadn't seen the fellow . . . well . . . really! And so on. I was very young.

40 The Native Magistrate waited with calm good manners for me to run down, and then asked what the man was like.

41 I told him of the twisted foot, and the belted mat, and the scar.

42 He turned to exchange nods with the constable: 'That was indeed Na Biria,' he murmured, and they nodded at each other again.

43 'Na Biria?' I echoed. 'Is he a lunatic?'

44 He dropped his eyelids, meaning, 'No.'

45 'Then bring him to me this evening.'

46 He looked me straight in the eyes: 'I cannot do that.'

47 'Cannot? What word is this . . . cannot? Is everybody here dotty today? Why cannot you bring him?'

48 'He is dead,' said the Magistrate, and added as I stood dumb, 'He died this afternoon, soon before three o'clock.'

49 They were both so remote; the whole place was so secretive; my mind was as fagged as my body; everything in that moment conspired to weaken its resistance against the improbable. Perhaps I was being bluffed; I don't know; but I suddenly had the picture of Na Biria in the article of death projecting his dying thought, with sixty generations of fear behind it, along that path through Nakaa's grove to the Place of Dread beyond. Had I received the impact of his thought as it passed my way? Or if not, what was it I had seen?

50 I knew it was not only thirst that made my mouth so dry, and that angered me. 'If he only died at three, he is not yet buried, and I can see his body,' I exclaimed.

51 'His body lies in the village,' replied the Magistrate.

52 'And I can see it?' I insisted.

53 He paused a long time before bowing his head in assent. But brusquely then the constable interrupted: 'No! The Man of Matang is a stranger! They are straightening the way of the dead. No stranger must break in . . . No! . . . No!'

54 The Magistrate silenced him with a gesture. 'I am a Christian,' he said solemnly to me: 'I will take you. Let us go at once.'

55 I followed him out of the house.

56 We heard the mourners wailing from a hundred yards off. I saw a dozen of them flogging the purlieus of the open-sided house with staves, to frighten away strange ghosts. I went near enough to see people sitting with raised arms at the head and feet of a body. But I halted outside the circle of beaters. It was finding them so earnestly at work that brought me back to the decencies. These folk believed utterly in what they were doing. For them, the dead man's whole eternity depended on their ritual. For them, the intrusion of me, a stranger, would send him to certain strangulation in Nakaa's net. What earthly or heaven-born right had I, for a moment's peevishness, to condemn them for the rest of their days to that hideous conviction? I suddenly felt as small as I was. I could go no farther. I turned away from the house. The Native Magistrate followed me in silence.

Vocabulary

bona-fide (1)	strident (24)	censure (39)
taciturnity (2)	diapason (24)	brusquely (53)
ineptitude (2)	infallible (32)	purlieus (56)
aspidistra-like (20)	petulant (39)	

Questions on Meaning and Technique

1. What is the point of this story and where is it stated? What advantage does a writer gain by putting the main point there?

2. What is the writer's attitude toward what he did? How does this attitude endear him to the reader?

3. What explanation of the cause of the islanders' superstitions does the author advance in paragraph 5? How does this explanation strike you?

4. Why did the author wish to visit the Place of Dread? What does this odd curiosity tell you about him?

5. The author writes in paragraph 15, "But I was cussed." What does he mean by this?

6. As evidenced in paragraph 27, what attitude does the author hold toward the superstitions about Nakaa?

7. Implicit in the author's story is a relationship that existed between the English and the Gilbertese. How would you characterize this relationship? What is your evidence for this characterization?

8. What explanation does the author offer for the man he thinks he saw on the beach? How reasonable does this explanation seem to you?

9. In his closing paragraph, the author writes: "I suddenly felt as small as I was." With that statement, what recognition about his own behavior do you think he came to?

Writing Assignments

1. Write a narrative essay about any experience with sickness or death.

2. In an essay, reconstruct the Grimble episode, giving a plausible explanation for what you think really happened.

READING FOR IDEAS

This brief vignette by a practicing surgeon gives us a glimpse into the seething frustration and anger of a terminal patient. Selzer does not tell us anything about the man except that he is a double amputee who never receives visitors and is disliked by his nurses because he is troublesome. Ask yourself why the patient persists in his inexplicable and disruptive habit. Try to consider his actions from the viewpoint of nurses and attendants and from the man himself.

ALTERNATE READING

The Discus Thrower
RICHARD SELZER

Richard Selzer, M.D. (b. 1928), has been a practicing surgeon at Yale University since 1960. Born in Troy, New York, and educated at Albany Medical School, he is also an acclaimed essayist and short story writer whose collections include Rituals of Surgery *(1974),* Mortal Lessons *(1974), and* Letters to a Young Doctor *(1982).*

1   I spy on my patients. Ought not a doctor to observe his patients by any means and from any stance, that he might the more fully assemble evidence? So I stand in the doorways of hospital rooms and gaze. Oh, it is not all that furtive an act. Those in bed need only look up to discover me. But they never do.

2   From the doorway of Room 542 the man in the bed seems deeply tanned. Blue eyes and close-cropped white hair give him the appearance of vigor and good health. But I know that his skin is not brown from the sun. It is rusted, rather, in the last stage of containing the vile repose within. And the blue eyes are frosted, looking inward like the windows of a snowbound cottage. This man is blind. This man is also legless—the right leg missing from midthigh down, the left from just below the knee. It gives him the look of a bonsai, roots and branches pruned into the dwarfed facsimile of a great tree.

3   Propped on pillows, he cups his right thigh in both hands. Now and then he shakes his head as though acknowledging the intensity of his suffering. In all of this he makes no sound. Is he mute as well as blind?

4   The room in which he dwells is empty of all possessions—no get-well cards, small, private caches of food, day-old flowers, slippers, all the usual kickshaws of the sickroom. There is only the bed, a chair, a nightstand, and a tray on wheels that can be swung across his lap for meals.

5   "What time is it?" he asks.

6   "Three o'clock."

7   "Morning or afternoon?"

8   "Afternoon."

9   He is silent. There is nothing else he wants to know.

10   "How are you?" I say.

11   "Who is it?" he asks.

12   "It's the doctor. How do you feel?"

13   He does not answer right away.

14   "Feel?" he says.

"I hope you feel better," I say.   15

I press the button at the side of the bed.   16

"Down you go," I say.   17

"Yes, down," he says.   18

He falls back upon the bed awkwardly. His stumps, unweighted by legs and feet, rise   19
in the air, presenting themselves. I unwrap the bandages from the stumps, and begin to
cut away the black scabs and the dead, glazed fat with scissors and forceps. A shard of
white bone comes loose. I pick it away. I wash the wounds with disinfectant and redress
the stumps. All this while, he does not speak. What is he thinking behind those lids that
do not blink? Is he remembering a time when he was whole? Does he dream of feet? Of
when his body was not a rotting log?

He lies solid and inert. In spite of everything, he remains impressive, as though he   20
were a sailor standing athwart a slanting deck.

"Anything more I can do for you?" I ask.   21

For a long moment he is silent.   22

"Yes," he says at last and without the least irony. "You can bring me a pair of shoes."   23

In the corridor, the head nurse is waiting for me.   24

"We have to do something about him," she says. "Every morning he orders   25
scrambled eggs for breakfast, and, instead of eating them, he picks up the plate and
throws it against the wall."

"Throws his plate?"   26

"Nasty. That's what he is. No wonder his family doesn't come to visit. They probably   27
can't stand him any more than we can."

She is waiting for me to do something.   28

"Well?"   29

"We'll see," I say.   30

The next morning I am waiting in the corridor when the kitchen delivers his breakfast.   31
I watch the aide place the tray on the stand and swing it across his lap. She presses the
button to raise the head of the bed. Then she leaves.

In time the man reaches to find the rim of the tray, then on to find the dome of the   32
covered dish. He lifts off the cover and places it on the stand. He fingers across the plate
until he probes the eggs. He lifts the plate in both hands, sets it on the palm of his right
hand, centers it, balances it. He hefts it up and down slightly, getting the feel of it.
Abruptly, he draws back his right arm as far as he can.

There is the crack of the plate breaking against the wall at the foot of his bed and the   33
small wet sound of the scrambled eggs dropping to the floor.

And then he laughs. It is a sound you have never heard. It is something new under the   34
sun. It could cure cancer.

Out in the corridor, the eyes of the head nurse narrow.   35

"Laughed, did he?"   36

She writes something down on her clipboard.   37

A second aide arrives, brings a second breakfast tray, puts it on the nightstand, out of   38
his reach. She looks over at me shaking her head and making her mouth go. I see that we
are to be accomplices.

39 "I've got to feed you," she says to the man.

40 "Oh, no you don't," the man says.

41 "Oh, yes I do," the aide says, "after the way you just did. Nurse says so."

42 "Get me my shoes," the man says.

43 "Here's oatmeal," the aide says. "Open." And she touches the spoon to his lower lip.

44 "I ordered scrambled eggs," says the man.

45 "That's right," the aide says.

46 I step forward.

47 "Is there anything I can do?" I say.

48 "Who are you?" the man asks.

49 In the evening I go once more to that ward to make my rounds. The head nurse reports to me that Room 542 is deceased. She has discovered this quite by accident, she says. No, there had been no sound. Nothing. It's a blessing, she says.

50 I go into his room, a spy looking for secrets. He is still there in his bed. His face is relaxed, grave, dignified. After a while, I turn to leave. My gaze sweeps the wall at the foot of the bed, and I see the place where it has been repeatedly washed, where the wall looks very clean and very white.

Vocabulary

    repose (2)
    facsimile (2)
    kickshaws (4)

Questions on Meaning and Technique

1. What symbolism do you think might be behind the patient ordering the same egg dish every day, in spite of not eating it?

2. Selzer says that he "spies" on his patients. Do you think this word is appropriate for what he reportedly does? Why do you think he does it?

3. Writing about the patient in Room 542, Selzer describes his eyes as "looking inward like the windows of a snowbound cottage." What figure of speech is this? Why is it appropriate here?

4. How would you characterize the title of this piece?

5. What do we learn about the patient from the brief dialogue between him and his doctor?

6. In his final paragraph, Selzer writes, "I go into his room, a spy looking for secrets." What secrets do you think he is looking for?

7. How would you sum up the main point of this narrative?

Writing Assignments

1. Write a narrative on the theme of frustration.

2. Narrate any encounter with a physician.

Photo Writing Assignment

White boy and black boy shaking hands. Michael Coers © 1975 *The Courier-Journal.* Reprinted with permission.

Using your imagination, narrate a plausible story detailing the events that might have led up to the moment depicted in this photograph. Pace your narration properly by passing over unimportant events while stressing important ones. Try to make the characters come to life through vivid details.

Additional Writing Assignments

1. Narrate any incident from your life in which you were forced by a role to suppress your true feelings. Describe the effect this suppression had on you.

2. Tell a ghost story or a story of some occult or unexplainable experience you have had.

3. Narrate a family conflict that illustrates how you feel about your mother and/or your father.

4. Narrate an incident that revealed to you the true nature or character of an aunt, uncle, or cousin.

5. Narrate the story of the day when "everything went wrong" and how you responded to the challenge.

6. Narrate a story about an accident or mishap that you either witnessed or experienced yourself.

7. Narrate a love story or experience.

8. Robert Southey once said, "Curses are like young chickens, they always come home to roost." Narrate an experience from your life that explains or illustrates this observation.

9. Tell the story of the most thrilling and exciting day of your life.

10. Narrate a story about an experience with a very young child.

Description

"The Lament" is the story of a poor Russian cabdriver overwhelmed by the grief of losing his only son. Read the story for a dominant impression—a central theme that unifies the descriptive details. Observe carefully the accumulation of details and how they fit into the narrative. What does the story tell you about grief, about society, and about human capacity for suffering? What is the conflict in the story? How is it finally resolved? What feelings does the story arouse in you?

The Lament
ANTON CHEKHOV

Anton Pavlovich Chekhov (1860–1904), the son of a grocer and grandson of a serf, was a Russian physician whose stories and plays won him international acclaim during his lifetime. Among his theatrical masterpieces are The Seagull *(1898),* Uncle Vanya *(1899),* The Three Sisters *(1901), and* The Cherry Orchard *(1904). His stories are collected in* At Twilight *(1887) and* Stories *(1888).*

It is twilight. A thick wet snow is twirling around the newly lighted street lamps, and lying in soft thin layers on roofs, on horses' backs, on people's shoulders and hats. The cabdriver Iona Potapov is quite white, and looks like a phantom; he is bent double as far as a human body can bend double; he is seated on his box; he never makes a move. If a whole snowdrift fell on him, it seems as if he would not find it necessary to shake it off. His little horse is also quite white, and remains motionless; its immobility, its angularity, and its straight wooden-looking legs, even close by, give it the appearance of a gingerbread horse worth a *kopek*. It is, no doubt, plunged in deep thought. If you were

1

163

snatched from the plow, from your usual gray surroundings, and were thrown into this slough full of monstrous lights, unceasing noise, and hurrying people, you too would find it difficult not to think.

2   Iona and his little horse have not moved from their place for a long while. They left their yard before dinner, and up to now, not a fare. The evening mist is descending over the town, the white lights of the lamps replacing brighter rays, and the hubbub of the street getting louder. "Cabby for Viborg way!" suddenly hears Iona, "Cabby!"

3   Iona jumps, and through his now-covered eyelashes sees an officer in a greatcoat, with his hood over his head.

"Viborg way!" the officer repeats. "Are you asleep, eh? Viborg way!"

4   With a nod of assent Iona picks up the reins, in consequence of which layers of snow slip off the horse's back and neck. The officer seats himself in the sleigh, the cabdriver smacks his lips to encourage his horse, stretches out his neck like a swan, sits up, and, more from habit than necessity, brandishes his whip. The little horse also stretches its neck, bends its wooden-looking legs, and makes a move undecidedly.

5   "What are you doing, werewolf!" is the exclamation Iona hears from the dark mass moving to and fro, as soon as they have started.

"Where the devil are you going? To the r-r-right!"

"You do not know how to drive. Keep to the right!" calls the officer angrily.

6   A coachman from a private carriage swears at him; a passerby, who has run across the road and rubbed his shoulder against the horse's nose, looks at him furiously as he sweeps the snow from his sleeve. Iona shifts about on his seat as if he were on needles, moves his elbows as if he were trying to keep his equilibrium, and gapes about like someone suffocating, who does not understand why and wherefore he is there.

7   "What scoundrels they all are!" jokes the officer; "one would think they had all entered into an agreement to jostle you or fall under your horse."

Iona looks round at the officer, and moves his lips. He evidently wants to say something, but the only sound that issues is a snuffle.

"What?" asks the officer.

8   Iona twists his mouth into a smile, and with an effort says hoarsely:

"My son, *barin,* died this week."

"Hm! What did he die of?"

Iona turns with his whole body toward his fare, and says:

"And who knows! They say high fever. He was three days in the hospital, and then died. . . . God's will be done."

"Turn round! The devil!" sounds from the darkness. "Have you popped off, old doggie, eh? Use your eyes!"

"Go on, go on," says the officer, "otherwise we shall not get there by tomorrow. Hurry up a bit!"

9   The cabdriver again stretches his neck, sits up, and, with a bad grace, brandishes his whip. Several times again he turns to look at his fare, but the latter has closed his eyes, and apparently is not disposed to listen. Having deposited the officer in the Viborg, he stops by the tavern, doubles himself up on his seat, and again remains motionless, while the snow once more begins to cover him and his horse. An hour, and

another. . . . Then, along the footpath, with a squeak of galoshes, and quarreling, come three young men, two of them tall and lanky, the third one short and humpbacked.

"Cabby, the Police Bridge!" in a cracked voice calls the humpback. "The three of us for two *griveniks!*"

Iona picks up his reins, and smacks his lips. Two *griveniks* is not a fair price, but he 10
does not mind whether it is a *rouble* or five *kopeks*—to him it is all the same now, so long as they are fares. The young men, jostling each other and using bad language, approach the sleigh, and all three at once try to get onto the seat; then begins a discussion as to which two shall sit and who shall be the one to stand. After wrangling, abusing each other, and much petulance, it is at last decided that the humpback shall stand, as he is the smallest.

"Now then, hurry up!" says the humpback in a twanging voice, as he takes his place 11
and breathes on Iona's neck. "Old furry! Here, mate, what a cap you have! There is not a worse one to be found in all Petersburg! . . ."

"He-he!—he-he!" giggles Iona. "Such a . . ."

"Now you, 'such a,' hurry up, are you going the whole way at this pace? Are you? . . . Do you want it in the neck?"

"My head feels like bursting," says one of the lanky ones. "Last night at the Donkmasovs, Vaska and I drank the whole of four bottles of cognac."

"I don't understand what you lie for," says the other lanky one angrily; "you lie like a 12
brute."

"God strike me, it's the truth!"

"It's as much the truth as that a louse coughs!"

"He, he," grins Iona, "what gay young gentlemen!"

"Pshaw, go to the devil!" says the humpback indignantly.

"Are you going to get on or not, you old pest? Is that the way to drive? Use the whip a bit! Go on, devil, go on, give it to him well!"

Iona feels at his back the little man wriggling, and the tremble in his voice. He listens 13
to the insults hurled at him, sees the people, and little by little the feeling of loneliness leaves him. The humpback goes on swearing until he gets mixed up in some elaborate six-foot oath, or chokes with coughing. The lankies begin to talk about a certain Nadejda Petrovna. Iona looks round at them several times; he waits for a temporary silence, then, turning round again, he murmurs;

"My son . . . died this week."

"We must all die," sighs the humpback, wiping his lips after an attack of coughing. 14
"Now, hurry up, hurry up! Gentlemen, I really cannot go any farther like this! When will he get us there?"

"Well, just you stimulate him a little in the neck!"

"You old pest, do you hear, I'll bone your neck for you! If one treated the like of you with ceremony one would have to go on foot! Do you hear, old serpent Gorinytch! Or do you not care a spit?"

Iona hears rather than feels the blows they deal him. 15

"He, he," he laughs. "They are gay young gentlemen, God bless 'em!"

"Cabby, are you married?" asks a lanky one.

"I? He, he, gay young gentlemen? Now I have only a wife and the moist ground. . . .
He, ho, ho . . . that is to say, the grave. My son has died, and I am alive. . . . A wonderful
thing, death mistook the door . . . instead of coming to me, it went to my son. . . ."

16   Iona turns round to tell them how his son died, but at this moment, the humpback,
giving a little sigh, announces, "Thank God, we have at last reached our destination,"
and Iona watches them disappear through the dark entrance. Once more he is alone, and
again surrounded by silence. . . . His grief, which has abated for a short while, returns
and rends his heart with greater force. With an anxious and hurried look, he searches
among the crowds passing on either side of the street to find whether there may be just
one person who will listen to him. But the crowds hurry by without noticing him or his
trouble. Yet it is such an immense, illimitable grief. Should his heart break and the grief
pour out, it would flow over the whole earth, so it seems, and yet no one sees it. It has
managed to conceal itself in such an insignificant shell that no one can see it even by day
and with a light.

17   Iona sees a hall porter with some sacking, and decides to talk to him.

"Friend, what sort of time is it?" he asks.

"Past nine. What are you standing here for? Move on."

18   Iona moves on a few steps, doubles himself up, and abandons himself to his grief. He
sees it is useless to turn to people for help. In less than five minutes he straightens
himself, holds up his head as if he felt some sharp pain, and gives a tug at the reins; he
can bear it no longer. "The stables," he thinks, and the little horse, as if it understood,
starts off at a trot.

19   About an hour and a half later Iona is seated by a large dirty stove. Around the stove,
on the floor, on the benches, people are snoring; the air is thick and suffocatingly hot.
Iona looks at the sleepers, scratches himself, and regrets having returned so early.

20   "I have not even earned my fodder," he thinks. "That's what's my trouble. A man who
knows his job, who has had enough to eat, and his horse too, can always sleep peacefully."

21   A young cabdriver in one of the corners half gets up, grunts sleepily, and stretches
toward a bucket of water.

"Do you want a drink?" Iona asks him.

"Don't I want a drink!"

"That's so? Your good health! But listen, mate—you know, my son is dead. . . . Did
you hear? This week, in the hospital. . . . It's a long story."

22   Iona looks to see what effect his words have, but sees none—the young man has
hidden his face and is fast asleep again. The old man sighs, and scratches his head. Just
as much as the young one wants to drink, the old man wants to talk. It will soon be a
week since his son died, and he has not been able to speak about it properly to anyone.
One must tell it slowly and carefully; how his son fell ill, how he suffered, what he said
before he died, how he died. One must describe every detail of the funeral, and the
journey to the hospital to fetch the dead son's clothes. His daughter Anissia has remained
in the village—one must talk about her too. Is it nothing he has to tell? Surely the listener
would gasp and sigh, and sympathize with him? It is better, too, to talk to women;
although they are stupid, two words are enough to make them sob.

23   "I'll go and look after my horse," thinks Iona, "there's always time to sleep. No fear
of that!"

He puts on his coat, and goes to the stables to his horse; he thinks of the corn, the   24
hay, the weather. When he is alone, he dares not think of his son; he can speak about
him to anyone, but to think of him, and picture him to himself, is unbearably painful.

"Are you tucking in?" Iona asks his horse, looking at its bright eyes; "go on, tuck in,   25
though we've not earned our corn, we can eat hay. Yes! I am too old to drive—my son
could have, not I. He was a first-rate cabdriver. If only he had lived!"

Iona is silent for a moment, then continues: 26

"That's how it is, my old horse. There's no more Kuzina Ionitch. He has left us to live,
and he went off pop. Now let's say, you had a foal, you were the foal's mother, and suddenly,
let's say, that foal went and left you to live after him. It would be sad, wouldn't it?"

The little horse munches, listens, and breathes over its master's hand. . . . Iona's   27
feelings are too much for him, and he tells the little horse the whole story.

Vocabulary

angularity (1)	brandishes (4)
slough (1)	petulance (10)

Questions on Meaning and Technique

1. How does the title "The Lament" relate to the content of this story?
2. The death of a loved one is not the only loss probed in the story. What other sorrows are examined?
3. What is Iona's overwhelming desire throughout the story? Why does he have this desire?
4. What do all of Iona's passengers have in common?
5. In what paragraph does Iona think about the exact steps he should take in expressing his grief?
6. Examine paragraph 1, and point out some details suggesting that the story will involve some kind of grief, sadness, or loss.
7. What details create the dominant impression of a father grieving for his son? Point to specific paragraphs.
8. What is the conflict of the story? How is it resolved?

READING FOR IDEAS

The language of poetry is often powerfully evocative. Here, for example, with a
stark economy of words, a poet evokes a vivid scene of grief, showing us a weeping
husband leaving a hospital with his wife's coat on a mild December day. The scene
merely hints of personal sorrow and loss suffered on a lovely winter day, effectively
leaving the rest to our imagination. Ask yourself what assumptions the poet makes
about the man. Are her assumptions reasonable?

Coats

JANE KENYON

Jane Kenyon (b. 1947), American poet, was born in Michigan and educated at the University of Michigan. Her work has been published in such magazines as the New Yorker *and* New Republic, *and collected in* From Room to Room *(1978) and* The Little Boat *(1986). In 1981 she was a fellow of the National Endowment for the Arts.*

1   I saw him leaving the hospital
     with a woman's coat over his arm.
     Clearly she would not need it.
     The sunglasses he wore could not
     conceal his wet face, his bafflement.

2   As if in mockery the day was fair,
     and the air mild for December. All the same
     he had zipped his own coat and tied
     the hood under his chin, preparing
     for irremediable cold.

Vocabulary

irremediable

Questions on Meaning and Technique

1. The poet does not personalize the man by telling us, for example, anything about his particular age and looks. Why? What does this omission add to the poem?
2. Why was it "mockery" that "the day was fair"? From whose point of view is this line meant?
3. What symbolic meaning does the poem seem to impute to "coats"?
4. What do you think is meant by "irremediable cold"? What kind of cold is this?
5. What ironic implication about the protection afforded by coats does the poem make?

HOW TO WRITE A DESCRIPTION

A description is a word picture. It is the attempt to use words to depict some person, place, feeling, animal, event, or thing. It may be as exotic as a description of a faraway palace or as ordinary as a poster describing a lost dog. And for all the almost infinite variety that writers occasionally try to describe, there are still some basic techniques that work in nearly all descriptions.

A vivid description supports a dominant impression with specific details. The dominant impression of a description is its central and unifying theme. In *The Godfather,* for instance, Mario Puzo bases his descriptions of all Don Corleone's sons on the dominant impression of their resemblance to Cupid. This impression is introduced in the description of Sonny and then applied to all the other sons:

> Sonny Corleone was tall for a first generation American of Italian parentage, almost six feet, and his crop of bushy, curly hair made him look even taller. *His face was that of a gross Cupid, the features even but the bow-shaped lips thickly sensual, the dimpled cleft chin in some curious way obscene.*

With slightly varying details, this dominant impression accommodates a description of the Don's second son, Frederico Corleone:

> He was short and burly, not handsome but with the same Cupid head of the family, the curly helmet of hair over the round face and the sensual bow-shaped lips. Only, in Fred, these lips were not sensual but granite!ike.

A contrast to this dominant impression is provided in the description of Michael Corleone, the third son:

> Michael Corleone was the youngest son of the Don and the only child who had refused the great man's direction. He did not have the heavy, Cupid-shaped face of the other children, and his jet black hair was straight rather than curly. His skin was clear olive-brown that would have been called beautiful in a girl. He was handsome in a delicate way.

Writing Assignment

Describe as vividly as you can a person, a place, or an event. Begin by picking a subject that strikes you with force. If possible, accumulate details and impressions by observing your subject up close. Next, find the dominant impression created by the person, place, or event, and state it in one sentence. The dominant impression of a place might be "Ben's cafe is a dingy hole in the wall." Of a person, it might be "Alicia has a delicate beauty." Of an event, it might be "The wedding was nerve-wracking." Support your dominant impression with details, omitting anything irrelevant that might break the unity of the impression. Develop the dominant impression and selected supporting details into a well-shaped essay.

Specific Instructions

PREWRITING ON THE ASSIGNMENT.   What should you write about? The assignment is open-ended enough to give you a real choice among the allowable categories of a person, place, or event. For some lucky few there will be no hesitation; they will immediately know what they want to do or say. Even so, they will probably need to outline and flesh out their ideas. On the other hand, if you are numbered among those who truly have no ideas of what to describe or even where to begin, prewriting is one way to discover a possible topic.

One way to begin is to make a list with three headings: person, place, or event. You can be as carefree, haphazard, or organized as you like as you make your list. Under each heading jot down, in any order that they occur to you, candidates for your description. For example, under the heading "person" you might list memorable friends, lovers, relatives, or acquaintances. Under "place" you might jot down your hometown, favorite hiking trail, vacation spot, or swimming beach. Do the same under "event" until you have exhausted your ideas.

Once the list is complete, review the individual entries and decide which one fires you with a spark of enthusiasm. Hardened writers who depend on assignments for their bread and butter often have to write about boring topics and do so as enduringly as possible. But there is no good reason why you should burden yourself with a boring topic. As you pore over the entries under the three headings, sooner or later one or the other is bound to give you a rush or a zing. That is the one you should write about.

ESTABLISH THE DOMINANT IMPRESSION. Before beginning to write, you should establish the dominant impression of whatever you wish to describe. The dominant impression in a description is the equivalent of the controlling idea in other types of essays. If you decide to describe a place, visit the place and spend some time observing it. The details observed will often suggest a suitable dominant impression. Once chosen, this dominant impression in turn will influence your selection of details.

For example, suppose you decide to write a description of your local airport lobby. You visit the airport and observe the following details:

1. A man's hat falls off as he races down the hall to catch his plane.

2. A sailor passionately kissing a woman suddenly looks at his watch and abruptly heads toward the escalator.

3. A little girl shrieks as an elderly woman—probably her grandmother—jerks her out of the arms of her mother to rush along toward Gate 31.

4. A fat executive takes a last hurried drag from his cigar before huffing and puffing his way to the ticket counter.

5. People of all sizes, ages, and races scramble across the lobby, bumping into one another and then resuming their frantic journeys.

6. A well-manicured woman sits casually on a bench reading *Cosmopolitan* and looking bored.

7. Two uniformed porters belly-laugh over a joke during a lull in foot traffic.

Most of these details suggest a dominant impression of the airport as a place where people are *rushed*. You formulate the following controlling idea, which includes this dominant impression: "At certain hours the International Airport lobby is a thoroughfare for people who are *rushed*."

The function of the dominant impression at this stage of the essay is to provide a standard for judging the relevance of details. Details that support the dominant impression are relevant; those that contradict it are irrelevant. Details 1 through 5, for instance, can be included because they support this dominant impression, but details 6 and 7 must be omitted because they contradict it. The dominant impression, therefore, acts as a pattern that unifies the description, preventing your essay from being mercilessly pulled in two or three different directions by irrelevant details.

FOCUS THE DOMINANT IMPRESSION.   Like the controlling idea, the dominant impression must have a focus. The following dominant impressions lack focus:

Toward evening the meadow becomes eerie in its forsaken barrenness as the magpies chatter happily.	Unfocused
Toward evening the meadow becomes eerie in its forsaken barrenness as the wind howls and groans.	Better
(Happily chattering magpies destroy the idea of "forsaken barrenness.")	
A translucent fragility was the outstanding feature of this husky old lady.	Unfocused
A translucent fragility gave beauty to the face of this aristocratic old lady.	Better
("Husky" ruins the impression of fragility.)	

SELECT SPECIFIC AND SENSORY DETAILS.   A good dominant impression attracts details the way a whirlpool sucks water toward its center. You must not only avoid irrelevant details that obscure the dominant impression of your description, but also select details that are specific and appeal to the senses.

Lack of *specific details* is the biggest mistake in student descriptions. The overwhelming tendency is to fill the page with mushy generalizations—for example:

One could tell at a look that Chaim Sachar was poor and slovenly. He was always hungry, and as a result he would wander about with a hungry attitude. His continual poverty caused him to become stingy to the point where he would collect garbage to use as fuel for his stove, and he cooked poor meals.

The description never comes to life because the supporting evidence is so vague. Contrast the above with another account:

Two small eyes, starved and frightened, peered from beneath his dishevelled eyebrows; the red rims about his eyes were reminiscent of the time when he would wash down a dish of fried liver and hard-boiled eggs with a pint of vodka every morning after prayer. Now, all day long, he wandered through the marketplace, inhaling butcher-shop odors and those from restaurants, sniffing like a dog, and occasionally napping on porters' carts. With the refuse he had collected in a basket, he fed his kitchen stove at night; then, rolling the sleeves over his hairy arms, he would grate turnips on a grater.

Isaac Bashevis Singer, "The Old Man"

Now the portrait leaps at you, punctuated by specific details, including "dishevelled eyebrows," "red rims about his eyes," and "hairy arms." The first description seems to present a shadowy figure in a darkened room, whereas the second reveals that same figure after the lights have been turned on.

Remember, too, that you can appeal to your reader through all the *senses*. You can make a reader see, taste, smell, touch, and hear what you are describing:

The winter was difficult. There was no coal, and since several tiles were missing from the stove, the apartment was filled with thick black smoke each time the old man made a fire. A crust of blue ice and snow covered the window panes by November, making the rooms constantly dark or dusky. Overnight, the water on his night table froze in the pot. No matter how many clothes he piled over him in bed, he never felt warm; his feet remained stiff, and as soon as he began to doze, the entire pile of clothes would fall off, and he would have to climb out naked to make his bed once more. There was no kerosene; even matches were at a premium. Although he recited chapter upon chapter of the Psalms, he could not fall asleep. The wind, freely roaming about the rooms, banged the doors; even the mice left. When he hung up his shirt to dry, it would grow brittle and break, like glass.

Isaac Bashevis Singer, "The Old Man"

The passage uses details that appeal to the reader's senses:

Visual	"crust of *blue ice* and snow covered the window panes"
Auditory	"the wind, freely roaming about the room, *banged* the door"
Tactile	"No matter how many clothes he piled over him in bed, he never *felt warm*."

USE FIGURES OF SPEECH. To add vividness to a description, a writer often uses colorful words and expressions along with figures of speech, most commonly, similes and metaphors. A simile is a figure of speech that draws an explicit comparison between two items; one thing is openly declared to be "like" another. For example, in his poem "The Love Song of J. Alfred Prufrock," T. S. Eliot in a famous simile openly likens the evening to an etherized patient:

Let us go then, you and I,
When the evening is spread out against the sky
Like a patient etherized upon a table . . .

The metaphor also draws a comparison, but an implicit one without the use of a linking "like" between the compared items. Here, for example, Shakespeare implicitly compares aging to a tree in autumn:

That time of year thou mayst in me behold
When yellow leaves, or none, or few do hang
Upon those boughs which shake against the cold,
Bare ruined choirs where late the sweet birds sang.

Had the bard said, "That time of year thou mayst in me behold / When I am *like* a tree whose yellow leaves, or none, or few do hang . . ." the figure would have been a simile.

Writers frequently mix these figures of speech in a single passage, depending on what and for whom they are writing. Here, for example, a writer describes a woman, using a combination of two similes and a metaphor:

> She was a little woman, with brown, dull hair very elaborately arranged, and she had prominent blue eyes behind invisible pince-nez. Her face was long, *like a sheep's;* but she gave no impression of foolishness, rather of extreme alertness; *she had the quick movements of a bird.* The most remarkable thing about her was her voice, high, metallic, and without inflection; it fell on the ear with a hard monotony, irritating to the nerves *like the pitiless clamour of the pneumatic drill.*
>
> W. Somerset Maugham, "Rain"

A caution: avoid the obvious, trite figures of speech, such as "busy as a bee," "white as a sheet," "big as a bear." Worn and ineffective, such figures hit readers in the face *like a truck,* and could possibly render them *dead as a doornail.* If you use figures of speech, make them *as fresh as a daisy.* Get the idea?

READING FOR IDEAS

While giving us a poetic description of the canyon country in southern Utah and Arizona, the author also warns that to plunder nature is to destroy its beauty and thus deprive the next generation of nature's inspiring and liberating powers. To understand this description fully, you must be tuned to the author's view that the kind of awesome, rugged wilderness he knew well has a spiritual aspect that goes beyond cliffs, chasms, rivers, or trees. In fact, he tells us that no human being—painter or writer—can hope to capture the reality of this landscape; it must be experienced. As you read, ask yourself where, if any place, you have looked at a view and felt completely free and spiritually uplifted. You may need to review mentally the most remarkable walks or travels you have taken. On those excursions, did you ever come across a sight that lifted you above the workaday world to a realm of awesome beauty that you still remember with delight? In retrospect, how did you respond to the sight? Did you feel breathless, awed, afraid, lonely? Or did some other feeling overwhelm you? List the dominant impression of the sight and then list the details that support the dominant impression.

PROFESSIONAL MODEL

Come On In
EDWARD ABBEY

Edward Abbey (b. 1927) is a writer who specializes in books and articles about the American West, especially the vast and deserted mountain areas that dominate New Mexico, Utah, Arizona, and Colorado. Born in Pennsylvania but a graduate of the University of New Mexico, Abbey spent many years as a park ranger and forest fire lookout in remote areas of the wilderness, where he discovered that solitude lent him strength and serenity through the awesome and beautiful aspects of nature. His writing often reflects a deep fear of civilization's brutal, damaging assault on nature, especially the isolated desert spots. Among his works are a novel, The Monkey Wrench Gang *(1975), and several collections of essays or journal entries:* Desert Solitaire: A Season in the Wilderness *(1968),* The Journal Home: Some Words in Defense of the American West *(1977),* Abbey's Road *(1979),* Down the River *(1982), and* Beyond the Wall *(1984).*

1   The canyon country of southern Utah and northern Arizona—the Colorado Plateau—is something special. Something strange, marvelous, full of wonders. As far as I know there is no other region on earth much like it, or even remotely like it. Nowhere else have we had this lucky combination of vast sedimentary rock formations exposed to a desert climate, a great plateau carved by major rivers—the Green, the San Juan, the Colorado—into such a surreal land of form and color. Add a few volcanoes, the standing necks of which can still be seen, and cinder cones and lava flows, and at least four separate laccolithic mountain ranges nicely distributed about the region, and more hills, holes, humps and hollows, reefs, folds, salt domes, swells and grabens, buttes, benches and mesas, synclines, monoclines, and anticlines than you can ever hope to see and explore in one lifetime, and you begin to arrive at an approximate picture of the plateau's surface appearance.

2   An approximate beginning. A picture framed by sky and time in the world of natural appearances. Despite the best efforts of a small army of writers, painters, photographers, scientists, explorers, Indians, cowboys, and wilderness guides, the landscape of the Colorado Plateau lies still beyond the reach of reasonable words. Or unreasonable representation. This is a landscape that has to be seen to be believed, and even then, confronted directly by the senses, it strains credulity.

3   Comprehensible, yes. Perhaps nowhere is the basic structure of the earth's surface so clearly, because so nakedly, revealed. And yet—when all we know about it is said and measured and tabulated, there remains something in the soul of the place, the spirit of the whole, that cannot be fully assimilated by the human imagination.

4   My terminology is far from exact; certainly not scientific. Words like "soul" and "spirit" make vague substitutes for a hard effort toward understanding. But I can offer no better. The land here is like a great book or a great symphony; it invites approaches toward comprehension on many levels, from all directions.

The geologic approach is certainly primary and fundamental, underlying the attitude 5
and outlook that best support all others, including the insights of poetry and the wisdom
of religion. Just as the earth itself forms the indispensable ground for the only kind of life
we know, providing the sole sustenance of our minds and bodies, so does empirical truth
constitute the foundation of higher truths. (If there is such a thing as higher truth.) It
seems to me that Keats was wrong when he asked, rhetorically, "Do not all charms fly
. . . at the mere touch of cold philosophy?" The word "philosophy" standing, in his day,
for what we now call "physical science." But Keats was wrong, I say, because there is
more charm in one "mere" fact, confirmed by test and observation, linked to other facts
through coherent theory into a rational system, than in a whole brainful of fancy and
fantasy. I see more poetry in a chunk of quartzite than in a make-believe wood nymph,
more beauty in the revelations of a verifiable intellectual construction than in whole misty
empires of obsolete mythology.

The moral I labor toward is that a landscape as splendid as that of the Colorado 6
Plateau can best be understood and given human significance by poets who have their
feet planted in concrete—concrete data—and by scientists whose heads and hearts have
not lost the capacity for wonder. Any good poet, in our age at least, must begin with the
scientific view of the world; and any scientist worth listening to must be something of a
poet, must possess the ability to communicate to the rest of us his sense of love and
wonder at what his work discovers.

The canyon country does not always inspire love. To many it appears barren, hostile, 7
repellent—a fearsome land of rock and heat, sand dunes and quicksand, cactus,
thornbush, scorpion, rattlesnake, and agoraphobic distances. To those who see our land
in that manner, the best reply is, yes, you are right, it is a dangerous and terrible place.
Enter at your own risk. Carry water. Avoid the noonday sun. Try to ignore the vultures.
Pray frequently.

For a few others the canyon country is worth only what they can dig out of it and haul 8
away—to the mills, to the power plants, to the bank.

For more and more of those who now live here, however, the great plateau and its 9
canyon wilderness is a treasure best enjoyed through the body and spirit, *in situ*[1] as the
archeologists say, not through commercial plunder. It is a regional, national and
international treasure too valuable to be sacrificed for temporary gain, too rare to be
withheld from our children. For us the wilderness and human emptiness of this land is not
a source of fear but the greatest of its attractions. We would guard and defend and save
it as a place for all who wish to rediscover the nearly lost pleasures of adventure,
adventure not only in the physical sense, but also mental, spiritual, moral, aesthetic and
intellectual adventure. A place for the free.

Here you may yet find the elemental freedom to breathe deep of unpoisoned air, to 10
experiment with solitude and stillness, to gaze through a hundred miles of untrammeled
atmosphere, across redrock canyons, beyond blue mesas, toward the snow-covered
peaks of the most distant mountains—to make the discovery of the self in its proud
sufficiency which is not isolation but an irreplaceable part of the mystery of the whole.

Come on in. The earth, like the sun, like the air, belongs to everyone—and to no one. 11

---

[1]From Latin: "In the original state."

Vocabulary

sedimentary (1)	mesas (1)	empirical (5)
plateau (1)	synclines (1)	coherent (5)
laccolithic (1)	monoclines (1)	verifiable (5)
grabens (1)	anticlines (1)	obsolete (5)
buttes (1)	credulity (2)	agoraphobic (7)

Questions on Meaning and Technique

1. What is the dominant impression in the author's description of the Colorado Plateau? State this impression in one sentence, using no more than three key words.

2. Could you live in the area that Abbey describes so graphically? What might the average person miss if he or she had to stay for long periods of time in an area like the Colorado Plateau?

3. How would you characterize the author's language? To what kind of audience does it appeal? Pay particular attention to imagery, diction, and tone.

4. What connection does the author make between empiricism and the scene he describes? If you are unsure about the definition of empiricism, look up the term in a dictionary.

5. What place do poetry and science have in giving significance to this landscape? Could other disciplines add significance? Explain your answers.

6. Do you agree with the author that "any good poet, in our age at least, must begin with the scientific view of the world"? Support or deny the author's contention by supplying your own view on the role of the poet in our age.

7. Besides giving us a description of the sublimely rugged Colorado Plateau, what other purpose does the author have? Where is this purpose most clearly stated? Do you agree with the author? Why or why not?

8. How effective is the final paragraph of the essay? Replace it with a paragraph of your creation and see if it changes the essay substantially.

STUDENT ESSAY

First Draft   Chip McClendan

Parting
~~When Love Departs~~

original title too mushy

The editing gets rid of mixed or incongruous imagery.

The key turns imperceptibly in the lock. The hinges scream with indignation as if, awakened from their silent slumber, their resentment could be aired ~~by the~~ ~~tired moan~~ *in harsh jangle* of metal on metal. The sun ~~blasts~~ *streaks* into the murky den, ~~piercing~~ *blinding* my eyes like ~~razors on soft~~ *a camera flash*   1

~~flesh.~~ Silhouetted in the doorway she stands. The sunlight through her cascading tresses
forms a soft   *This backdrop of golden light stands in sharp contrast to the darkened look on*
~~appears as a~~ halo. ~~Shafts of light burst forth all around her.~~ *her face. Somehow she presents*
                                   an image of beauty filtered through sadness.

2   *To* ~~Through~~ my alcohol-soaked vision she appears like an angel to a lost shepherd. I hide
                                                              Budweiser
my feelings behind a blank stare, pretending to sip casually from the ~~beer~~ can I hold in

my hand. I buy time that way. ~~T~~ime before those inevitable first words must be spoken.
                     ritualistic   *conversation*
She speaks first, offering me a polite ~~traditional~~ greeting. But we both know that ~~words~~
  is
~~are~~ not the real reason behind her visit. She has come to pick up her curling iron, her
                                                                        personal
nightgown, and a few old Van Morrison albums. She has come to gather the remnants of

her life with me. By this time, words have been lost in the tempest of emotions we are
                              forced air of indifference
both feeling. I wave her through with an ~~indifferent air~~. "You know where they are," I

say. She does. This apartment, after all, had been her home too.

3   The phone lies off its hook on a mahogany lamp table nearby, buzzing incessantly, like

the ringing in one's ears after a loud rock concert. I don't bother to hang it up. I hear her

rummaging in the back room. "So the good old days are gone," I think. "No more kite
                                                      on the bank of a
flying in the park, her dark hair billowing in the wind like reeds ~~by a~~ slow-moving river
                                                          tender
and her body taut like a clockspring, ~~filled with energy~~" The ~~frigid~~ ice on my heart begins
                     tender
to melt with the heat of ~~worn~~ memories. There would be no more lazy evenings spent
                                       flaring up, then
together in front of a cozy fire, occasional sparks, ~~bursting forth~~ to land and glow warmly
                   soft
in the darkness, casting ~~orange~~ light shadows along her angular jawbone. No longer
                                                   gazing intently
would I see her almond-shaped, jade ~~green~~ eyes ~~staring blankly~~ into the fire's depths,

drawn by the passion with which the fire burns. The most important part of my life was

walking out the door.
                entering from the hallway,
4   When she appears again, I see the box of her belongings in her arms. Odds and ends
                                                     Insert A
jut out like refugees on an overcrowded fishing boat. She places the box on a chair and
                                                   Irish fisherman's
then walks over to where I am standing. Wearing an oversized sweater, she looks like a

ten-year-old tomboy on the school playground. But this is not a child; this is a mature

woman who embodies the eternal contradictions of her sex: she is sensitive yet strong;

Insert A
I notice a dog-eared novel by Jane Austen, a lace-trimmed satin pillow with
"Mother" embroidered on it, a bright pink T-shirt—and, of course, the curling iron,
the nightgown, and the records.

[Margin notes:]

The revision creates a more focused dominant impression.

The changes here improve diction to make the description more vivid or specific.

misplaced modifier corrected

improved wording

perspective added

details added to make description more vivid

aggressive yet patient. She extends her hand and offers me the brass door key she is

holding. Her beautiful face is dark with pent-up emotions. Wrapping her outstretched

fingers around the key, I ask her to keep it. "You might need it again some day," I say.

She answers me with a faint nod and a doleful smile. Then she turns away silently, lifts

the box off the chair, and leaves.

(Insert B)

I stare silently at the closed door, tearing apart inside. Hanging up the phone, I think   5

of all kinds of apologies I should have made.

The revised ending creates more drama by featuring a seemingly irrelevant action.

(Insert B)

I stare silently at the door she has just closed behind her. I am being torn apart.
Then my feet move mechanically toward the lamp table and I hang up the telephone.

STUDENT ESSAY

Final Draft   Chip McClendan

Parting

1   The key turns imperceptibly in the lock. The hinges scream with indignation as if,

awakened from their silent slumber, their resentment could be aired in the harsh jangle

of metal on metal. The sun streaks into the murky den, blinding my eyes like a camera

flash. Silhouetted in the doorway she stands. The sunlight through her cascading

tresses forms a soft halo. This backdrop of golden light stands in sharp contrast to the

darkened look on her face. Somehow, she presents an image of beauty filtered through

sadness.

2   To my alcohol-soaked vision she appears like an angel to a lost shepherd. I hide my

feelings behind a blank stare, pretending to sip casually from the Budweiser can I hold

in my hand. I buy time that way—time before those inevitable first words must be

spoken. She speaks first, offering me a polite ritualistic greeting. But we both know

that conversation is not the real reason behind her visit. She has come to pick up her

curling iron, her nightgown, and a few old Van Morrison albums. She has come to

gather the personal remnants of her life with me. By this time, words have been lost in the tempest of emotions we are both feeling. I wave her through with a forced air of indifference. "You know where they are," I say. She does. This apartment, after all, had been her home too.

The phone lies off its hook on a mahogany lamp table nearby, buzzing incessantly, 3 like the ringing in one's ears after a loud rock concert. I don't bother to hang it up. I hear her rummaging in the back room. "So the good old days are gone," I think. "No more kite flying in the park, her dark hair billowing in the wind like reeds on the bank of a slow-moving river and her body taut with energy like a clockspring." The ice on my heart begins to melt with the heat of tender memories. There would be no more lazy evenings spent together in front of a cozy fire, occasional sparks flaring up, then bursting forth to land and glow warmly in the darkness, casting soft light shadows along her angular jawbone. No longer would I see her almond-shaped, jade eyes gazing intently into the fire's depths, drawn by the passion with which the fire burns. The most important part of my life was walking out the door.

When she appears again, entering from the hallway, I see the box of her belongings 4 in her arms. Odds and ends jut out like refugees on an overcrowded fishing boat. I notice a dog-eared paperback novel by Jane Austen, a lace-trimmed satin pillow with "Mother" embroidered on it, a bright pink T-shirt—and, of course, the curling iron, the nightgown, and the records. She places the box on a chair and then walks over to where I am standing. Wearing an oversized Irish fisherman's sweater, she looks like a ten-year-old tomboy on the school playground. But this is not a child; this is a mature woman who embodies the eternal contradictions of her sex: she is sensitive yet strong; aggressive yet patient. She extends her hand and offers me the brass door key she is holding. Her beautiful face is dark with pent-up emotions. Wrapping her outstretched fingers around the key, I ask her to keep it. "You might need it again some day," I say. She answers me with a faint nod and a doleful smile. Then she turns away silently, lifts the box off the chair, and leaves.

I stare silently at the door she has just softly closed behind her. Inside I am being 5 torn apart. Then my feet move mechanically toward the lamp table and I hang up the telephone.

READING FOR IDEAS

The excerpt that follows is a journalistic summary of the life of Richard Wagner (1813–1883), who is revered as one of the great composers of all time. Written by an admitted admirer, this brief biography takes an altogether different tack than you might expect, and confesses freely, catalogues even, Wagner's cruelty and pettiness. Notice the careful adherence of the essay to the dominant impression of Wagner as a "monster of conceit." The intriguing conclusion of the essay raises a question: Is the author morally right in his view that possessing musical genius exempted Wagner from observing ordinary decency and kindness in his personal relationships?

ALTERNATE READING

The Monster

DEEMS TAYLOR

Deems Joseph Taylor (1885–1966) was an American composer, critic, editor, translator, and writer. Taylor was music editor for Encylopaedia Britannica *and the composer of the operas* The King's Henchmen *and* Peter Ibbetson, *both of which were performed by New York's Metropolitan Opera company. Between 1936 and 1943 Taylor was host for the New York Philharmonic Sunday radio broadcasts, later turning these talks into the book* Of Men and Music, *from which this selection comes.*

1   He was an undersized little man, with a head too big for his body—a sickly little man. His nerves were bad. He had skin trouble. It was agony for him to wear anything next to his skin coarser than silk. And he had delusions of grandeur.

2   He was a monster of conceit. Never for one minute did he look at the world or at people, except in relation to himself. He was not only the most important person in the world, to himself; in his own eyes he was the only person who existed. He believed himself to be one of the greatest dramatists in the world, one of the greatest thinkers, and one of the greatest composers. To hear him talk, he was Shakespeare, and Beethoven, and Plato, rolled into one. And you would have had no difficulty in hearing him talk. He was one of the most exhausting conversationalists that ever lived. An evening with him was an evening spent in listening to monologue. Sometimes he was brilliant; sometimes he was maddeningly tiresome. But whether he was being brilliant or dull, he had one sole topic of conversation: himself. What *he* thought and what *he* did.

3   He had a mania for being in the right. The slightest hint of disagreement, from anyone, on the most trivial point, was enough to set him off on a harangue that might last for hours, in which he proved himself right in so many ways, and with such exhausting volubility, that in the end his hearer, stunned and deafened, would agree with him, for the sake of peace.

It never occurred to him that he and his doing were not of the most intense and   4
fascinating interest to anyone with whom he came in contact. He had theories about
almost any subject under the sun, including vegetarianism, the drama, politics, and music;
and in support of these theories he wrote pamphlets, letters, books . . . thousands upon
thousands of words, hundreds and hundreds of pages. He not only wrote these things,
and published them—usually at somebody else's expense—but he would sit and read
them aloud, for hours, to his friends and his family.

He wrote operas; and no sooner did he have the synopsis of a story, but he would   5
invite—or rather summon—a crowd of his friends to his house and read it aloud to them.
Not for criticism. For applause. When the complete poem was written, the friends had to
come again, and hear *that* read aloud. Then he would publish the poem, sometimes
years before the music that went with it was written. He played the piano like a
composer, in the worst sense of what that implies, and he would sit down at the piano
before parties that included some of the finest pianists of his time, and play for them, by
the hour, his own music, needless to say. He had a composer's voice. And he would
invite eminent vocalists to his house, and sing them his operas, taking all the parts.

He had the emotional stability of a six-year-old child. When he felt out of sorts, he   6
would rave and stamp, or sink into suicidal gloom and talk darkly of going to the East to
end his days as a Buddhist monk. Ten minutes later, when something pleased him, he
would rush out of doors and run around the garden, or jump up and down on the sofa,
or stand on his head. He could be grief-stricken over the death of a pet dog, and he could
be callous and heartless to a degree that would have made a Roman emperor shudder.

He was almost innocent of any sense of responsibility. Not only did he seem incapable   7
of supporting himself, but it never occurred to him that he was under any obligation to do
so. He was convinced that the world owed him a living. In support of this belief, he
borrowed money from everybody who was good for a loan—men, women, friends, or
strangers. He wrote begging letters by the score, sometimes groveling without shame, at
others loftily offering his intended benefactor the privilege of contributing to his support,
and being mortally offended if the recipient declined the honor. I have found no record of
his ever paying or repaying money to anyone who did not have a legal claim upon it.

What money he could lay his hands on he spent like an Indian rajah. The mere   8
prospect of a performance of one of his operas was enough to set him to running up bills
amounting to ten times the amount of his prospective royalties. On an income that would
reduce a more scrupulous man to doing his own laundry, he would keep two servants.
Without enough money in his pocket to pay his rent, he would have the walls and ceiling
of his study lined with pink silk. No one will ever know—certainly he never knew—how
much money he owed. We do know that his greatest benefactor gave him $6,000 to pay
the most pressing of his debts in one city, and a year later had to give him $16,000 to
enable him to live in another city without being thrown into jail for debt.

He was equally unscrupulous in other ways. An endless procession of women   9
marched through his life. His first wife spent twenty years enduring and forgiving his
infidelities. His second wife had been the wife of his most devoted friend and admirer,
from whom he stole her. And even while he was trying to persuade her to leave her first
husband he was writing to a friend to inquire whether he could suggest some wealthy
woman—any wealthy woman—whom he could marry for her money.

10   He was completely selfish in his other personal relationships. His liking for his friends was measured solely by the completeness of their devotion to him, or by their usefulness to him, whether financial or artistic. The minute they failed him—even by so much as refusing a dinner invitation—or began to lessen in usefulness, he cast them off without a second thought. At the end of his life he had exactly one friend left whom he had known even in middle age.

11   He had a genius for making enemies. He would insult a man who disagreed with him about the weather. He would pull endless wires in order to meet some man who admired his work, and was able and anxious to be of use to him—and would proceed to make a mortal enemy of him with some idiotic and wholly uncalled-for exhibition of arrogance and bad manners. A character in one of his operas was a caricature of one of the most powerful music critics of his day. Not content with burlesquing him, he invited the critic to his house and read him the libretto aloud in front of his friends.

12   The name of this monster was Richard Wagner. Everything that I have said about him you can find on record—in newspapers, in police reports, in the testimony of people who knew him, in his own letters, between the lines of his autobiography. And the curious thing about this record is that it doesn't matter in the least.

13   Because this undersized, sickly, disagreeable, fascinating little man was right all the time. The joke was on us. He *was* one of the most stupendous musical geniuses that, up to now, the world has ever seen. The world did owe him a living. People couldn't know those things at the time, I suppose; and yet to us, who know his music, it does seem as though they should have known. What if he did talk about himself all the time? If he had talked about himself for twenty-four hours *every* day for the span of his life he would not have uttered half the number of words that other men have spoken and written about him since his death.

14   When you consider what he wrote—thirteen operas and music dramas, eleven of them still holding the stage, eight of them unquestionably worth ranking among the world's great musico-dramatic masterpieces—when you listen to what he wrote, the debts and heartaches that people had to endure from him don't *seem* much of a price. Eduard Hanslick, the critic whom he caricatured in *Die Meistersinger* and who hated him ever after, now lives only because he was caricatured in *Die Meistersinger.* The women whose hearts he broke are long since dead; and the man who could never love anyone but himself has made them deathless atonement, I think, with *Tristan und Isolde.* Think of the luxury with which for a time, at least, fate rewarded Napoleon, the man who ruined France and looted Europe; and then perhaps you will agree that a few thousand dollars' worth of debts were not too heavy a price to pay for the *Ring* trilogy.

15   What if he was faithless to his friends and to his wives? He had one mistress to whom he was faithful to the day of his death: Music. Not for a single moment did he ever compromise with what he believed, with what he dreamed. There is not a line of his music that could have been conceived by a little mind. Even when he is dull, or downright bad, he is dull in the grand manner. There is greatness about his worst mistakes. Listening to his music, one does not forgive him for what he may or may not have been. It is not a matter of forgiveness. It is a matter of being dumb with wonder that his poor brain and body didn't burst under the torment of the demon of creative energy that lived inside him, struggling, clawing, scratching to be released; tearing, shrieking at him to write the music

that was in him. The miracle is that what he did in the little space of seventy years could have been done at all, even by a great genius. Is it any wonder that he had no time to be a man?

Vocabulary

synopsis (5)	burlesquing (11)
rajah (8)	libretto (11)
scrupulous (8)	

Questions on Meaning and Technique

1. In one brief sentence, what is the dominant impression of Richard Wagner, as portrayed in this essay? Where is it first stated?
2. How does the author go about supporting this dominant impression? Give two or three examples from the text.
3. Do you agree with the author's view that Richard Wagner had a perfect right to be the monster he was? In other words, do geniuses have privileges that ordinary people do not have? Support your answer with reasons.
4. Of all the monstrosities committed by Wagner, which offended you most? Why?
5. What does the author mean when he says (paragraph 13), "The world did owe him a living"?
6. In paragraph 7, why does the author use the word *innocent* rather than *void* or *free from*?
7. In what paragraph does the author lend credibility to the facts offered in this essay?

Writing Assignments

1. Write a description of anyone you have known whom you consider a "monster."
2. In an essay, describe someone whom you consider a saint.

READING FOR IDEAS

During the Battle of Gettysburg—fought between July 1 and 3, 1863—a division of Confederate soldiers under the command of George E. Pickett charged the heavily fortified center of the Union forces. The resulting carnage exacted a disastrous toll on the Confederates, forcing their retreat across the Potomac River on July 4, 1863, and marking a turning point in the war. Haley was a Union foot soldier in the 17th Maine Regiment on that day, and he recorded his observations of the doomed charge in a series of notebooks that eventually comprised his published journal.

Bear in mind, as you read, that Haley's version of events is a narrow eyewitness account of the fighting as seen through the eyes of a grunt. Ask yourself how Haley is characterized by his own remarks and observations.

ALTERNATE READING

Pickett's Charge at the Battle of Gettysburg
PRIVATE JOHN W. HALEY, 17TH MAINE REGIMENT

John W. Haley (1840–1921) served in the 17th Maine Regiment from August 7, 1862, to the day it was mustered out, June 10, 1865. He participated in many of the most notable Civil War battles from the Battle of the Wilderness to Auburn and Kelly Ford. After the war he worked in various odd jobs as a night watchman and newspaper reporter before settling down as a librarian in Maine. He was a gifted amateur artist and historian and designated a study room in his library especially for women, a gesture far ahead of his time. In 1919 he published his journal, boasting that he personally transcribed by hand its 440,000 words without a blot.

JULY 3RD.

1   We turned out early. Hunger had such a grip on us that it dragged us forth. Most had not eaten in thirty-six hours and felt we could devour a horse or a mule, provided it hadn't been too long defunct. The teams with rations didn't arrive until 9 o'clock. After filling up, we had orders to take position in rear of the 6th Corps, somewhat to the right of where we were engaged yesterday. During the forenoon there was nothing but an occasional crack of the pickets' rifles, and we rested on our arms.

2   Shortly after noon there were signs of activity in the Confederate lines. Artillery was being massed on Seminary Ridge and the same was true of infantry, although the woods concealed them. About 1 o'clock the Rebel cannon opened on us, and ours were soon replying. For two hours there was probably the greatest artillery duel ever fought on this planet. The air seethed with old iron. Death and destruction were everywhere. Men and horses mangled and bleeding; trees, rocks, and fences ripped and torn. Shells, solid shot, and spherical case shot screamed, hissed, and rattled in every direction. Men hugged the ground and sought safety behind hillocks, boulders, ledges, stone walls, bags of grain—anything that could give or suggest shelter from this storm of death.

3   We hardly knew what it meant, but some of our generals did, and preparations were made accordingly. General Hunt, chief of artillery, ordered our gunners to cease firing in order to cool the guns. No sooner was this done than the Rebels, supposing they had silenced us, began to come out of the woods and form in line of battle.

4   As soon as all was ready, the column commenced the march. Our guns opened on them with solid shot and shells as soon as they were within range. This had no effect except to huddle them closer. As they drew nearer, our guns increased the havoc in their ranks. Solid shot and shell, then grape, cannister, and spherical case ploughed through their lines and

rattled in their midst, sweeping them by the hundreds from the field. But on they pressed, bravely and firmly, closing up on the colors as gap after gap opened in their ranks.

A 32-pounder on Round Top fired down the line obliquely and took out as many as   5
twenty files. Even this didn't arrest their progress. Just before the charge, while the air was reeking with death, General Hancock,[1] whose front Longstreet[2] was covering, rode slowly from right to left of his line and encouraged his men to hold.

At this time the Confederates had reached the Emmettsburg road and, having two   6
fences to climb, all suggestion of alignment was lost. They were now little other than a mob, but they came on and on. They were determined to come in spite of grape, cannister, and bullets. Our division and many others hastened to the scene to take part in the closing act of this drama.

On they pushed, delivering a withering fire. But our fire was equally destructive, and   7
they soon presented a bloody and desperate appearance. No troops could resist the awful attack to which they were exposed. It was a sheet of fire, backed by a wall of steel. They couldn't reach the wall and *live*.

The Confederates were now treated to a heavy flank fire, and this seemed to take all   8
the gimp out of them. Many fled in confusion to the rear, pursued by the troops of Hay's division. Hundreds, aye thousands, threw down their arms and came in as prisoners where they had vainly sought to come as victors. Most of those on the left of the Rebel column remained—dead, wounded, or prisoner. The Union troops, by a simultaneous attack, now closed in on them, capturing all who did not seek safety in flight. Many threw themselves on the ground to escape the merciless storm of missiles hurled at them; others held up their hands in token of surrender. "He that outlives this day, and comes safe home,/ Will stand a tiptoe when this day is named."[3]

By 4 o'clock the repulse was complete, the victory won. Thousands who two hours   9
before were in the flush of manhood now lay dead, dying, or prisoners. The Confederates staked all and lost.

No one can describe the scenes of this day. We who were participants were in such a   10
maddening whirl that we can give but little that is intelligible. Babel was perfect order compared to the confusion of these two hours of bloody encounter. Then all was still, the carnival of death was done, and we took a breathing spell.

At the close of the charge General Hancock fell, severely wounded. He sent word to   11
General Meade of the repulse and advised an immediate pursuit, but nothing was done.

This was Lee's third attempt to pierce our lines. July 1st on our right, July 2nd on our   12
left, and today our center. On each of these days success seemed to perch on the Rebel banners at first, but was wrested from them. It is certain that General Lee regards this action as a crisis in the affairs of the Confederacy. He would never have made this charge, putting his best troops into the venture, had he not felt certain of success. His feelings as he saw his troops mowed down must have been quite indescribable.

His admirers claim that Lee is very humane. This may be so, but he witnessed the   13
slaughter of his men from the cupola of the seminary and, from the very first, it must

---

[1]Winfield Scott Hancock (1824–1886), Union General.
[2]James Longstreet (1821–1904), Confederate General.
[3]From Shakespeare's *King Henry V,* Act 4, Scene 3, li 40.

have been plain to him that if any of his men reached the Union line, they could never hold it for an instant. Lee's troops learned the folly of attempting to charge across over a mile of open country against an army quite as large as their own, more or less protected by embankments, stone walls, and boulders, and with a superabundance of artillery.

14 As soon as this charge ended, silence settled over the scene. A painful silence, broken only by the sigh or groan of some poor mangled victim. Where but a few moments before the smoke of battle, the cannon's roar, the rattle of musketry, the groan, the cheer, the prayer, the curse had filled the air, there was now profound stillness as though the very elements were appalled and stood mute. A fitting climax to this dreadful struggle, the details of which are indeed sickening. "O stay not to recount the tale./ 'Twas bloody, and 'tis past./ The fairest cheek might well grow pale,/ To hear it to the last." How many firesides in the North and South are plunged today into deepest sorrow? Just a few short hours, and thousands are torn and mangled, better dead than living.

15 I imagine from my own feelings that every one of these cherished the hope that *he* would come out all right, or at least alive, and prayed that this might be the last struggle. It *was* the last for many of them.

16 About dark our division was sent out on picket in the field in front. It has never been my lot to see and experience such things as on this occasion. The dead lay everywhere, and although not a half day has passed since they died, the stench is so great that we can neither eat, drink, nor sleep. Decomposition commences as soon as life is extinct. As we cannot sleep, we pass the time bringing in the wounded and caring for them. The dead are frightfully smashed, which is not to be wondered at when we consider how they crowded up onto our guns, a mass of humanity, only to be hurled back an undistinguish-able pile of mutilated flesh, rolling and writhing in death.

17 No tongue can depict the carnage, and I cannot make it seem real: men's heads blown off or split open; horrible gashes cut; some split from the top of the head to the extremities, as butchers split beef. Some of the Rebels are very bitter toward us although we do all in our power to alleviate their sufferings, even exposing ourselves to danger to do so. One of our officers crawled on his hands and knees to give a wounded Rebel a drink, and came near paying for it with his life when another Rebel, near the wounded man, fired at him.

18 It pains me to state that some of our own men taunt these wounded with their lack of success and engage in political arguments, apparently forgetting how incongruous that business is. This custom is by no means monopolized on our side. It is to be deprecated, however, as it in no wise softens the asperities of war and helps keep alive sectional hate. The men who indulge in this kind of lingo soon learn that the characters and sentiments of their opponents haven't changed with their condition, and though the Rebels acknowledge our kindness in caring for them, they still claim that they are *right* in their attempt to destroy this government.

19 Among the wounded is a little, flaxen-haired boy from North Carolina who is only fourteen years old, giving credence to the report that the Confeds rob the cradle and the grave. To keep the ranks full, they take old men beyond the military age and young ones who haven't reached it, and hustle them to the front.

Vocabulary

defunct (1)	mangled (2)	havoc (4)
obliquely (5)	repulse (9)	carnage (17)
incongruous (18)	deprecated (18)	asperities (18)

Questions on Meaning and Technique

1. What does the tone of the opening paragraph tell us immediately about Haley?
2. What are some of the earmarks of style and editing that identify this excerpt as a reconstructed diary rewritten much later after the event?
3. What is Haley's attitude toward the Confederate wounded?
4. What do you think the author hoped to accomplish in the two quotations of poetry? What is your opinion of the effectiveness of these quotations?
5. How do you suppose Haley's account of the battle differs from what we would expect in an eyewitness report by a modern footsoldier?
6. In his description Haley uses the present tense from paragraph 15 on. What does the use of this tense add to his description?
7. In his account in paragraph 14 of the aftermath of the charge, what other rhetorical strategy does the author use to intensify his description?
8. What specific details does Haley use in paragraph 2 that add credence to his eyewitness account?
9. What is history's opinion of Pickett's charge at Gettysburg?

Writing Assignments

1. Write an essay describing the kind of man you imagine Haley to be—based on his diary excerpt.
2. Using your imagination, describe a Civil War battlefield after a ferocious battle.

READING FOR IDEAS

The title of this excerpt, "The Odors of Homecoming," prepares us for an extravagant description of the smells of the poet's home, and to a certain extent we are not disappointed. Neruda, however, is too original a writer to focus only on the aromas of his home. He treats us to a spectrum of its sights as well, while reserving his richest language for a loving catalog of long familiar smells. This is no sparse journalistic piece that can be breezed through in a blink. Instead, it cries out for a slow and careful reading that savors to the full the richness of the poet's imagery.

ALTERNATE READING

The Odors of Homecoming

Pablo Neruda

Pablo Neruda (1904–1973), Chilean poet and Nobel Prize winner, born in Parral, Chile, is ranked among the greatest modern poets writing in Spanish. An ardent Communist, he was elected to the Chilean senate in 1945 but was forced to flee his country in 1948 because of deadly political turmoil. He returned in 1952 and resumed his political activity until shortly before his death. Neruda published many books of poetry, among them Twenty Love Poems and One Song of Despair *(1924),* Elementary Odes *(1954), and* Toward the Splendid City *(1971). He was awarded the Nobel Prize in literature in 1971.*

1   My house nestles among many trees. After a long absence, I like to lose myself in hidden nooks to savor my homecoming. Mysterious, fragrant thickets have appeared that are new to me. The poplar I planted in the back of the garden, so slim it could barely be seen, is now an adult tree. Its bark is patterned with wrinkles of wisdom that rise toward the sky to express themselves in a constant tremor of new leaves in the treetop.

2   The chestnut trees were the last to recognize me. When I arrived, their naked, dry branches, towering and unseeing, seemed imperious and hostile, though the pervading spring of Chile was germinating amid their trunks. Every day I went to call on them, for I understood that they demanded my homage, and in the cold of morning stood motionless beneath the leafless branches, until one day a timid green bud, high overhead, came out to look at me, and others followed. So my reappearance was communicated to the wary, hidden leaves of the tallest chestnut tree, which now greets me with condescension, tolerating my return.

3   In the trees the birds renew their age-old trills, as if nothing ever happened beneath the leaves.

4   A pervasive odor of winter and years lingers in the library. Of all places, this was the most suffused with absence.

5   There is something of mortality about the smell of musty books; it assaults the nostrils and strikes the rugged terrain of the soul, because it is the odor of oblivion, of buried memory.

6   Standing beside the weathered window, staring at the blue and white Andean sky, I sense that behind my back the aroma of spring is pitting its strength against the books. They resist being rooted out of their long neglect, and still exude signs of oblivion. Spring enters every room, clad in a new dress and the odor of honeysuckle.

7   The books have been unruly in my absence. None is missing, but none is in its place. Beside an austere volume of Bacon, a rare seventeenth-century edition, I find Salgari's *The Captain of Yucatan,* and in spite of everything, they've got along rather well together. On the other hand, as I pick up a solitary Byron, its cover drops off like the dark wing of an albatross. Laboriously, I stitch spine and cover, but not before a puff of cold Romanticism clouds my eyes.

The shells are the most silent occupants of my house. They endured the years of the   8
ocean, solidifying their silence. Now, to those years have been added time and dust. Their
cold, glinting mother-of-pearl, their concentric Gothic ellipses, their open valves, remind
me of distant coasts, long-ago events. This incomparable lance of rosy light is the
Rostellaria, which the Cuban malacologist Carlos de la Torre, a magus of the deep, once
conferred upon me like an underseas decoration. And here, slightly more faded and
dusty, is the black "olive" of the California seas, and, of the same provenance, the oyster
of red spines and the oyster of black pearls. We almost drowned in that treasure-laden
sea.

There are new occupants, books and objects liberated from boxes long sealed. The   9
pine boxes come from France. The boards smell of sunny noon in the Midi, and as I pry
them open, they creak and sing, and the golden light falls on the red bindings of Victor
Hugo. *Les Misérables,* in an early edition, arrives to crowd the walls of my house with its
multitude of heartrending lives.

Then, from a large box resembling a coffin, comes the sweet face of a woman, firm   10
wooden breasts that once cleaved the wind, hands saturated with music and brine. It is
the figure of a woman, a figurehead. I baptize her María Celeste, because she has all the
mystery of a lost ship. I discovered her radiant beauty in a Paris *bric-à-brac,* buried
beneath used hardware, disfigured by neglect, hidden beneath the sepulchral rags and
tatters of the slums. Now, aloft, she sails again, alive and new. Every morning her cheeks
will be covered by mysterious dew or saltwater tears.

All at once the roses are in bloom. Once I was an enemy of the rose, of its   11
interminable literary associations, of its arrogance. But as I watched them grow, having
endured the winter with nothing to wear and nothing to cover their heads, and then as
snowy breasts or glowing fires peered from among hard and thorny stems, little by little
I was filled with tenderness, with admiration for their ox-like health, for the daring, secret
wave of perfume and light they implacably extract from the black earth at just the right
moment, as if duty were a miracle, as if they thrived on precise maneuvers in harsh
weather. And now roses grow everywhere, with a moving solemnity I share—remote,
both they and I, from pomp and frivolity, each absorbed in creating its individual flash of
lightning.

Now every wave of air bears a soft, trembling movement, a flowery palpitation that   12
pierces the heart. Forgotten names, forgotten springs, hands that touched briefly,
haughty eyes of yellow stone, tresses lost in time: youth, insistently throbbing with
memories and ecstatic aromas.

It is the perfume of the honeysuckle, the first kisses of spring.   13

Vocabulary

imperious (2)	pervading (2)	homage (2)
pervasive (4)	suffused (4)	exude (6)
concentric (8)	ellipses (8)	malacologist (8)
magus (8)	provenance (8)	saturated (10)
sepulchral (10)	interminable (11)	implacably (11)
palpitation (12)		

Questions on Meaning and Technique

1. The author writes in paragraph 2 that "the chestnut trees were the last to recognize me." What literary technique is he using here?

2. What characteristics of the author's style identify his poetic background?

3. What is "Romanticism" in the sense that the author means in paragraph 7? What do you think he means by "cold Romanticism"?

4. What is *Les Misérables*, mentioned in paragraph 9? What is the meaning of the allusion to "its multitude of heartrending lives"?

5. What can you deduce about the poet's reading habits from the books and authors he alludes to as belonging to his library?

6. In paragraph 11, the author mentions the "interminable literary associations" of the rose. What are some of these associations?

7. In paragraph 4, the author writes: "A pervasive odor of winter and years lingers in the library. Of all places, this was the most suffused with absence." What does this passage indirectly say about Neruda?

Writing Assignments

1. In an essay, describe the odors of your home.

2. Write a description of your favorite childhood haunt.

Additional Writing Assignments

1. Using "dingy" as your dominant impression, write a description of an imaginary place. Support the impression with details.

2. Describe your conception of how the ideal modern man or woman should look.

3. Go to your local supermarket, notebook in hand. Observe the scene around you and reduce it to a single dominant impression. Write down the dominant impression and some details that support it. From these notes, develop a descriptive essay.

4. Describe your favorite nature spot or scene.

5. Describe your closest friend. Begin with a dominant impression and develop details to support it.

6. Write a description of the worshipers in a church, chapel, synagogue, or temple.

7. Develop a descriptive essay comparing your boyfriend or girlfriend to a flower, animal, or object.

8. Write a description of a seaside resort you have visited.

9. Write a description of your favorite pet, living or dead.

10. Describe the smells of the house or apartment where you spent your childhood.

11. Write a description of any country scene during autumn.

Photo Writing Assignment

Cellist Vedran Smalovic plays a requiem in Heroes Cemetery in Sarajevo. Tom Stoddart, Katz
Pictures

Write an essay describing the scene in this photograph. You might try to answer
these questions: What is the dominant impression of the picture? What prompted
the musician to bring his cello to a graveyard? What are some of the sensory details that appeal to you? Make your description vivid by using figurative language
when appropriate.

Example

Read the excerpt "We're Poor," which is as self-contained and climactic as any short story. Notice the accumulation of small representative details throughout that finally lead the narrator to the numbing conclusion at the end of the narrative. After reading the narrative, ask yourself what pattern the details of your life over the past year suggest. What kind of year has it been? What has been its main theme? Try to answer these questions in a single sentence that could serve as the controlling idea for an essay.

We're Poor
FLOYD DELL

Floyd Dell (1887–1969), advocate of pacifist and liberal causes, was a prolific novelist, playwright, and short story writer. He wrote ten novels, six books of nonfiction, several plays, and an autobiography, Homecoming *(1933), from which this excerpt comes. The following excerpt poignantly recounts a child's discovery that his family is poor.*

1   That fall, before it was discovered that the soles of both my shoes were worn clear through, I still went to Sunday school. And one time the Sunday-school superintendent made a speech to all the classes. He said that these were hard times, and that many poor children weren't getting enough to eat. It was the first that I had heard about it. He asked everybody to bring some food for the poor children next Sunday. I felt very sorry for the poor children.

Also, little envelopes were distributed to all the classes. Each little boy and girl was to   2
bring money for the poor, next Sunday. The pretty Sunday-school teacher explained that
we were to write our names, or have our parents write them, up in the left-hand corner
of the little envelopes. . . . I told my mother all about it when I came home. And my
mother gave me, the next Sunday, a small bag of potatoes to carry to Sunday school. I
supposed the poor children's mothers would make potato soup out of them. . . . Potato
soup was good. My father, who was quite a joker, would always say, as if he were
surprised, "Ah! I see we have some nourishing potato soup today!" It was so good that
we had it every day. My father was at home all day long and every day, now; and I liked
that, even if he was grumpy as he sat reading Grant's *Memoirs*. I had my parents all to
myself, too; the others were away. My oldest brother was in Quincy, and memory does
not reveal where the others were: perhaps with relatives in the country.

Taking my small bag of potatoes to Sunday school, I looked round for the poor   3
children; I was disappointed not to see them. I had heard about poor children in stories.
But I was told just to put my contribution with the others on the big table in the side room.

I had brought with me the little yellow envelope, with some money in it for the poor   4
children. My mother had put the money in it and sealed it up. She wouldn't tell me how
much money she had put in it, but it felt like several dimes. Only she wouldn't let me write
my name on the envelope. I had learned to write my name, and I was proud of being able
to do it. But my mother said firmly, no, I must not write my name on the envelope; she
didn't tell me why. On the way to Sunday school I had pressed the envelope against the
coins until I could tell what they were; they weren't dimes but pennies.

When I handed in my envelope, my Sunday-school teacher noticed that my name   5
wasn't on it, and she gave me a pencil; I could write my own name, she said. So I did. But
I was confused because my mother had said not to; and when I came home, I confessed
what I had done. She looked distressed. "I told you not to!" she said. But she didn't
explain why. . . .

I didn't go back to school that fall. My mother said it was because I was sick. I did have   6
a cold the week that school opened; I had been playing in the gutters and had got my feet
wet, because there were holes in my shoes. My father cut insoles out of cardboard, and
I wore those in my shoes. As long as I had to stay in the house anyway, they were all
right.

I stayed cooped up in the house, without any companionship. We didn't take a Sunday   7
paper any more, but the Barry *Adage* came every week in the mails; and though I did not
read small print, I could see the Santa Clauses and holly wreaths in the advertisements.

There was a calendar in the kitchen. The red days were Sundays and holidays; and   8
that red 25 was Christmas. (It was on a Monday, and the two red figures would come
right together in 1893; but this represents research in the World Almanac, not memory.)
I knew when Sunday was, because I could look out of the window and see the neighbors'
children, all dressed up, going to Sunday school. I knew just when Christmas was going
to be.

But there was something queer! My father and mother didn't say a word about   9
Christmas. And once, when I spoke of it, there was a strange, embarrassed silence; so I
didn't say anything more about it. But I wondered, and was troubled. Why didn't they say

anything about it? Was what I had said I wanted (memory refuses to supply that detail) too expensive?

10 I wasn't arrogant and talkative now. I was silent and frightened. What was the matter? Why didn't my father and mother say anything about Christmas? As the day approached, my chest grew tighter with anxiety.

11 Now it was the day before Christmas. I couldn't be mistaken. But not a word about it from my father and mother. I waited in painful bewilderment all day. I had supper with them, and was allowed to sit up for an hour. I was waiting for them to say something. "It's time for you to go to bed," my mother said gently. I had to say something.

12 "This is Christmas Eve, isn't it?" I asked, as if I didn't know.

13 My father and mother looked at one another. Then my mother looked away. Her face was pale and stony. My father cleared his throat, and his face took on a joking look. He pretended he hadn't known it was Christmas Eve, because he hadn't been reading the papers. He said he would go downtown and find out.

14 My mother got up and walked out of the room. I didn't want my father to have to keep on being funny about it, so I got up and went to bed. I went by myself without having a light. I undressed in the dark and crawled into bed.

15 I was numb. As if I had been hit by something. It was hard to breathe. I ached all through. I was stunned—with finding out the truth.

16 My body knew before my mind quite did. In a minute, when I could think, my mind would know. And as the pain in my body ebbed, the pain in my mind began. I knew. I couldn't put it into words yet. But I knew why I had taken only a little bag of potatoes to Sunday school that fall. I knew why there had been only pennies in my little yellow envelope. I knew why I hadn't gone to school that fall—why I hadn't any new shoes—why we had been living on potato soup all winter. All these things, and others, many others, fitted themselves together in my mind, and meant something.

17 Then the words came into my mind and I whispered them into the darkness:

18 "We're poor!"

That was it. I was one of those poor children I had been sorry for, when I heard about them in Sunday school. My mother hadn't told me. My father was out of work, and we hadn't any money. That was why there wasn't going to be any Christmas at our house.

19 Then I remembered something that made me squirm with shame—a boast. (Memory will not yield this up. Had I said to some Nice little boy, "I'm going to be President of the United States"? Or to a Nice little girl: "I'll marry you when I grow up"? It was some boast as horribly shameful to remember.)

20 "We're poor." There in bed in the dark, I whispered it over and over to myself. I was making myself get used to it. (Or—just torturing myself, as one presses the tongue against a sore tooth? No, memory says not like that—but to keep myself from ever being such a fool again: suffering now, to keep this awful thing from ever happening again. Memory is clear on that; it was more like pulling the tooth, to get it over with—never mind the pain, this will be the end!)

21 It wasn't so bad, now that I knew. I just hadn't known! I had thought all sorts of foolish things: that I was going to Ann Arbor—going to be a lawyer—going to make speeches in the Square, going to be President. Now I knew better.

22 I had wanted (something) for Christmas. I didn't want it, now. I didn't want anything.

I lay there in the dark, feeling the cold emotion of renunciation. (The tendrils of desire   23
unfold their clasp on the outer world of objects, withdraw, shrivel up. Wishes shrivel up,
turn black, die. It is like that.)

It hurt. But nothing would ever hurt again. I would never let myself want anything   24
again.

I lay there stretched out straight and stiff in the dark, my fists clenched hard upon   25
Nothing. . . .

In the morning it had been like a nightmare that is not clearly remembered—that one   26
wishes to forget. Though I hadn't hung up any stocking, there was one hanging at the
foot of my bed. A bag of popcorn, and a lead pencil, for me. They had done the best they
could, now they realized I knew about Christmas. But they needn't have thought they had
to. I didn't want anything.

Questions on Meaning and Technique

1. How would you characterize the style of this excerpt? Why do you think the author chose to write it in this style?

2. How old was the author at the time of his discovery that his family was poor? How typical of that age does he seem in the narrative?

3. What effects of poverty did the author's family suffer from that are typical of all poor people? What effects of poverty do you regard as the worst?

4. In spite of her own family's need, the author relates that his mother made contributions of food and money to the poor. What does this gesture say about her?

5. Psychologists say that small children think in very concrete terms. What passages of this excerpt seem to confirm this view?

6. In paragraphs 9 and 10, how does the author dramatize his mounting sense of suspicion and foreboding about his family's true condition?

7. What effect do you think the discovery about the poverty of his family likely had on the author's later development? What effect do you think such a discovery is likely to have on any child?

8. The author says that his body knew the truth before his mind did. Is this plausible? Why or why not?

READING FOR IDEAS

Poetry has evolved far from the days when it mainly rhapsodized about birds frolicking in the skies and the beauties of nature. This poem, in sharp contrast to that tradition, is strictly urban and uses as its speaker a desperately hungry man. Notice that the poem uses only one punctuation mark—at the very end. Be careful to follow its syntax. Ask yourself what important point the author is making about poverty and crime.

Late Rising

JACQUES PREVERT

Jacques Prevert (1900–1977) was among the most popular French poets of his day. His poetry, which ranges from satirical to gloomy, was collected and sung in nightclub performances long before they were published as literary works. His published work includes Paroles (1946), Spectacle (1951), *and* To Paint the Portrait of a Bird (1970).

1 Terrible
 is the soft sound of a hardboiled egg
 cracking on a zinc counter
 and terrible is that sound

5 when it moves in the memory
 of a man who is hungry
 Terrible also is the head of a man
 the head of a man hungry
 when he looks at six o'clock in the morning

10 in a smart shop window and sees
 a head the color of dust
 But it is not his head he sees
 in the window of 'Chez Potin'
 he doesn't give a damn

15 for the head of a man
 he doesn't think at all
 he dreams
 imagining another head
 calf's-head for instance

20 with vinegar sauce
 head of anything edible
 and slowly he moves his jaws
 slowly slowly
 grinds his teeth for the world

25 stands him on his head
 without giving him any comeback
 so he counts on his fingers one two three
 one two three
 that makes three days he has been empty

and it's stupid to go on saying it can't   30
go on It can't go on because
it does
Three days
three nights

without eating   35
and behind those windows
pâté de foie gras wine preserves
dead fish protected by their boxes
boxes in turn protected by windows

these in turn watched by the police   40
police protected in turn by fear
How many guards for six sardines . . .
Then he comes to the lunch counter
coffee-with-cream buttered toast

and he begins to flounder   45
and in the middle of his head
blizzard of words
muddle of words
sardines fed

hardboiled eggs coffee-with-cream   50
coffee black rum food
coffee-with-cream
coffee-with-cream
coffee crime black blood

A respectable man in his own neighborhood   55
had his throat cut in broad daylight
the dastardly assassin stole from him
two bits that is to say
exactly the price of a black coffee

two slices of buttered toast   60
and a nickel left to tip the waiter
Terrible
is the soft sound of a hardboiled egg
cracking on a zinc counter

and terrible is that sound when it moves   65
in the memory

of a man who is hungry.   67

(Translated by Selden Rodman)

Questions on Meaning and Technique

1. What, according to the poem, is the effect of hunger on a person?

2. The author uses no sentences in this poem. What is the poem's basic unit of syntax?

3. What common rhetorical technique does the poem use to stress the desperateness of the hungry man?

4. What unorthodox use does the author make of capitalizations in this poem? Comment on the effectiveness of this technique.

5. Whom does the speaker blame for his hunger and misery? Whom do you think an actual sufferer would blame?

6. How would you characterize the mood of the speaker?

7. What does the speaker order in the restaurant? What implication does the poem make about where he got the money to buy this inadequate food?

8. What point does this poem make on the cause of crime? What is your attitude toward this alleged cause?

9. Between lines 44 and 54, what technique does the author use to characterize the thinking of the hungry man at the lunch counter?

HOW TO WRITE WITH EXAMPLES

An example is an illustration that unmistakably clarifies and enforces the point you are making. During the Middle Ages, most sermons ended with an *exemplum,* a little story that illustrated some important religious truth. Knowing that these stories would awaken dozing audiences and instill them with zeal or fear, the church priests told vivid tales about the evils of money and the dangers of disobedience. The example is still favored in prose writing as a means of proving a point or explaining an idea.

Writing Assignment

Write an essay that uses at least three extended examples to support the thesis that poverty exists in your neighborhood, town, or state.

Specific Instructions

PREWRITING ON THE ASSIGNMENT. The assignment calls for an essay that develops three extended examples of poverty in your neighborhood, town, or state. By "extended example" we mean an example developed in some detail and extended over the course of several sentences or paragraphs. The following example is not extended:

"Women's language" shows up in all levels of English. For example, women are encouraged to make far more precise discriminations in naming colors than men do. Words like "mauve," "beige," "ecru," "aquamarine," "lavender," and so on, are unremarkable in a woman's vocabulary, but largely absent from that of most men.

Robin Lakoff, "Women's Language"

Here, on the other hand, is a legitimate extended example:

Years ago some people accused of serious crimes pleaded "insanity." Today they are often charged with it. Instead of receiving a brief jail sentence, a defendant may be branded "insane" and incarcerated *for life* in a psychiatric institution.

This is what happened, for example, to a filling-station operator I will call Joe Skulski. When he was told to move his business to make way for a new shopping center, he stubbornly resisted eviction. Finally the police were summoned. Joe greeted them with a warning shot in the air. He was taken into custody and denied bail, because the police considered his protest peculiar and thought he must be crazy. The district attorney requested a pretrial psychiatric examination of the accused. Mr. Skulski was examined, pronounced mentally unfit to stand trial, and confined in the state hospital for the criminally insane. Through it all, he pleaded for the right to be tried for his offense. Now in the mental hospital he will spend years of fruitless effort to prove that he is sane enough to stand trial. If convicted, his prison sentence would have been shorter than the term he has already served in the hospital.

Thomas S. Szasz, M.D., "What Psychiatry Can and Cannot Do"

Because the topic is already specified in the wording of the assignment, the aim of your prewriting efforts should be to find the area of poverty in your neighborhood, town, or state you wish to cover and to amass specific details that you can include in your examples. If you are like most of us, you will find poverty just around the corner. As a prewriting activity, we suggest you take a drive to the affected area and look it over for yourself. Try to group your impressions under three principal signs of poverty: perhaps the ruined state of the houses, the neglected condition of the streets, the unkempt appearance of the residents. Or you may prefer, instead, to illustrate poverty in your town by writing about three symptoms of it—perhaps homelessness, high unemployment, or skyrocketing crime rates.

Personal observation usually provides the most vivid details for examples, but you may be among the lucky few to live in a neighborhood and adjoining town that is entirely free of poverty. If that is the case, you will have to resort to library research to find information about poverty in your state (unfortunately, no state is entirely free of poverty). Newspapers and regional magazines can usually provide you with all the facts and information you need. Again, remember to look for material that can be used in three extended examples.

USE EXAMPLES THAT ARE RELEVANT.   An example has failed if it does not help your reader to see the general truth of what you are saying. The following example misses the point:

Read Aloud

As the Bible says, there is a right time for everything—even for being born and for dying. For example, the other day I failed my social science test. The day before had been beastly hot—90 degrees in the shade—and I just didn't feel like studying, so I stretched out on the couch, fanning myself and watching TV. I guess it was my time to die intellectually because when the exam was handed back, it was decorated with a big fat F.

The example used is too trivial to illustrate such a somber philosophic truth. The biblical reference deserves a more significant example. On the other hand, the following passage uses an example that is exactly to the point:

Some people will do the strangest things to gain fame. For example, there are those who go in for various kinds of marathons, dancing or kissing or blowing bubble gum for days at a time, to get their names in the paper or in a record book of some kind. Then there are people who sit on flagpoles or who perch on the ledges of skyscrapers for a week or more, apparently enjoying the attention they receive from the crowd below. There are people who hope to be remembered by someone because they ate the most cream pies or because they collected the most bottle tops. And there are even people who seek public notice by way of setting a record for the number of articles of clothing they can put on at one time or the number they can take off. Of course, there are a few mentally twisted individuals who seek fame at the expense of other people's property or even lives, but fortunately the great majority of people satisfy their urge to be remembered in ways that produce little more damage than tired lips or a bad case of indigestion.

Sheila Y. Graham, *Writingcraft*

Topic

These examples do a good job of illustrating the idea that "Some people will do the strangest things to gain fame."

USE DETAILS TO MAKE YOUR EXAMPLE VIVID. The reader should be able to visualize the actual circumstances described in your example. Many examples are ineffective because they are vague rather than vivid. Consider the vague and consequently boring example in this passage:

There is no control over memory. Sometimes one remembers the most trivial details. For example, I remember trivial things about my father, about pieces of furniture in our house, and about insignificant places that I once visited. I even remember a particular shopping spree that took place a long time ago.

Now observe how the same ideas come to life through the use of detailed examples:

Read Aloud

There is no control over memory. Soon you find yourself being vague about an event which seemed so important at the time that you thought you'd never forget it. Or unable to recall the face of someone who you could have sworn was there forever. On the other hand, trivial and meaningless memories may stay with you for life. I can still shut my eyes and see Victoria grinding coffee on the pantry steps, the glass bookcase and the books in it, my father's pipe rack, the leaves of the sandbox tree, the wallpaper of the bedroom in some shabby hotel, the hairdresser in Antibes. It's in this way that I remember buying the pink Milanese-silk underclothes, the assistant who sold them to me, and coming into Bond Street holding the parcel.

Jean Rhys, The New Yorker, 26 April 1976

Vividness is the basic difference between the first and second passages. The first passage lacks details whereas the second bristles with them.

WHEN NECESSARY, ESTABLISH A CLEAR CONNECTION BETWEEN YOUR EXAMPLE AND THE POINT YOU ARE MAKING.   This advice is particularly important when you begin an essay or a paragraph with an illustration. Consider the following:

A 13-year-old girl has had one leg amputated, but three times a week she is put through the humiliation of being forced to change into gym shorts. Says the teacher, "Those are the rules and there's no reason you can't keep score while the other girls play."

A high-school teacher accidently bumps into the upraised hand of a girl who wants to ask a question. The teacher cries out that the girl is trying to strike her and that if it happens again she'll call the police.

A first-grade teacher forces a boy to sit all day in a wastepaper basket as punishment for being noisy. When an assistant principal orders the boy's release after 2½ hours, it is some minutes before he can stand up straight. He can barely limp to his seat.

Without a connecting comment, these examples are puzzling. The reader wonders what they are intended to illustrate. The sequel makes clear the connection between the examples and the point they illustrate:

These are all documented cases of teacher ineptitude, insensitivity or brutishness. While the overwhelming majority of America's teachers are professionally competent and sensitive to children's needs, there are enough who are unfit to cause concern among both parents and school administrators.

Bernard Bard, "Unfeeling Teachers?"
Ladies Home Journal, March 1976

Connective expressions commonly used to introduce an example are for example, to illustrate, for instance, and a case in point is. Frequently, however, writers will omit a formal connective in introducing their examples provided the context makes clear what is being illustrated:

People who sneer at "fancy theories" and prefer to rely on common sense and everyday experience are often in fact the victims of extremely vague and sweeping hypotheses. This morning's newspaper contains a letter from a young person in Pennsylvania who was once "one of a group of teenage pot smokers. Then a girl in the crowd got pregnant. Her baby was premature and deformed and needed two operations." The newspaper's adviser to the teenage lovelorn printed that letter approvingly, as evidence that the price of smoking marijuana is high.

Paul Heyne and Thomas Johnson,
Toward Economic Understanding

This passage clearly illustrates what is meant by "victims of . . . vague and sweeping hypotheses." No connective phrase is necessary; the connection is established by the context.

READING FOR IDEAS

In this excerpt from *Down and Out in Paris and London* (1933), British writer George Orwell gives examples of the humiliations and sufferings he endured during his days of destitution in Paris. Orwell groups his examples under four discoveries that one learns when one is suddenly poor, and is exacting and detailed in recounting bitter instances of them. Which do you think would be worse—the humiliations or physical sufferings of poverty? What implications does the lethargy Orwell attributes to hunger have for the poor and programs aimed at helping them? The editors estimate that, reckoned in the buying power of today's currency, Orwell was attempting to live on the equivalent of $6 per day.

PROFESSIONAL MODEL

Poverty

GEORGE ORWELL

George Orwell, a pseudonym used by Eric Arthur Blair (1903–1950), was a British novelist and essayist, perhaps best known for his futuristic novel 1984 *(1949). Born in India, Orwell attended Eton and served with the Indian imperial police in Burma, an experience recounted in* Burmese Days *(1934). His works include* Down and Out in Paris and London *(1933),* Animal Farm *(1946), and the volume of essays* Shooting an Elephant *(1950).*

1   It is altogether curious, your first contact with poverty. You have thought so much about poverty—it is the thing you have feared all your life, the thing you knew would happen to you sooner or later; and it is all so utterly and prosaically different. You thought it would be quite simple; it is extraordinarily complicated. You thought it would be terrible; it is merely squalid and boring. It is the peculiar *lowness* of poverty that you discover first; the shifts that it puts you to, the complicated meanness, the crustwiping.

2   You discover, for instance, the secrecy attaching to poverty. At a sudden stroke you have been reduced to an income of six francs a day. But of course you dare not admit it—you have got to pretend that you are living quite as usual. From the start it tangles you in a net of lies, and even with the lies you can hardly manage it. You stop sending clothes

to the laundry, and the laundress catches you in the street and asks you why; you mumble something, and she, thinking you are sending the clothes elsewhere, is your enemy for life. The tobacconist keeps asking why you have cut down your smoking. There are letters you want to answer, and cannot, because stamps are too expensive. And then there are your meals—meals are the worst difficulty of all. Every day at meal-times you go out, ostensibly to a restaurant, and loaf an hour in the Luxembourg Gardens, watching the pigeons. Afterwards you smuggle your food home in your pockets. Your food is bread and margarine, or bread and wine, and even the nature of the food is governed by lies. You have to buy rye bread instead of household bread, because rye loaves, though dearer, are round and can be smuggled in your pockets. This wastes you a franc a day. Sometimes, to keep up appearances, you have to spend sixty centimes on a drink, and go correspondingly short of food. Your linen gets filthy, and you run out of soap and razor-blades. Your hair wants cutting, and you try to cut it yourself, with such fearful results that you have to go to the barber after all, and spend the equivalent of a day's food. All day you are telling lies, and expensive lies.

You discover the extreme precariousness of your six francs a day. Mean disasters happen and rob you of food. You have spent your last eighty centimes on half a litre of milk, and are boiling it over the spirit lamp. While it boils a bug runs down your forearm; you give the bug a flick with your nail, and it falls plop! straight in the milk. There is nothing for it but to throw the milk away and go foodless.   3

You go to the baker's to buy a pound of bread, and you wait while the girls cut a pound for another customer. She is clumsy, and cuts more than a pound. "*Pardon, monsieur,*" she says, "I suppose you don't mind paying two sous extra?" Bread is a franc a pound, and you have exactly a franc. When you think that you too might be asked to pay two sous extra, would have to confess that you could not, you bolt in panic. It is hours before you dare venture into a baker's shop again.   4

You go to the greengrocer's to spend a franc on a kilogram of potatoes. But one of the pieces that make up the franc is a Belgian piece, and the shopman refuses it. You slink out of the shop, and can never go there again.   5

You have strayed into a respectable quarter, and you see a prosperous friend coming. To avoid him you dodge into the nearest café. Once in the café you must buy something, so you spend your last fifty centimes on a glass of black coffee with a dead fly in it. One could multiply these disasters by the hundred. They are part of the process of being hard up.   6

You discover what it is like to be hungry. With bread and margarine in your belly, you go out and look into the shop windows. Everywhere there is food insulting you in huge, wasteful piles; whole dead pigs, baskets of hot loaves, great yellow blocks of butter, strings of sausages, mountains of potatoes, vast Gruyère cheeses like grindstones. A snivelling self-pity comes over you at the sight of so much food. You plan to grab a loaf and run, swallowing it before they catch you; and you refrain, from pure funk.   7

You discover the boredom which is inseparable from poverty; the times when you have nothing to do and, being underfed, can interest yourself in nothing. For half a day at a time you lie on your bed, feeling like the *jeune squelette** in Baudelaire's poem. Only   8

---

*"The young (female) skeleton." The poem referred to is No. 94 of Baudelaire's *Fleurs du mal.*

food could rouse you. You discover that a man who has gone even a week on bread and margarine is not a man any longer, only a belly with a few accessory organs.

9   This—one could describe it further, but it is all in the same style—is life on six francs a day. Thousands of people in Paris live it—struggling artists and students, prostitutes when their luck is sour, out of work people of all kinds. It is the suburbs, as it were, of poverty.

Vocabulary

prosaically (1)
squalid (1)
ostensibly (2)
precariousness (3)

Questions on Meaning and Technique

1. What, according to Orwell, was so utterly different about poverty from the way he thought it would be?
2. Throughout the piece the author uses "you" rather than "I" in describing his encounter with poverty. What do you think he's trying to accomplish?
3. What four principal discoveries did Orwell make about poverty? What examples does he use to explain them?
4. At the beginning of the second paragraph, Orwell introduces his examples with "for instance." How does he introduce his later examples?
5. Orwell calls life on six francs a day "the suburbs of poverty." What does the phrase imply about the poverty he experienced and described?

STUDENT ESSAY

First Draft   Tom Meade

Poverty in Atlanta

Insert A   the

This anecdote makes a good introduction by focusing on a specific example of poverty.

People living in plush surroundings of North Atlanta may be fully isolated from the real   1

world of grinding poverty ~~in their great city. Poverty is undoubtedly visible in most~~

Insert A

Jan Trimble, aged 50, lived in a local mental hospital during most of her adult life. Because she was not deemed dangerous to herself and others, she was forced to move to the streets two years ago when funding cuts were made at her institution. She now exists by foraging through dumpsters for food, and she finds shelter from the biting cold at night under stacks of cardboard boxes. All of her worldly goods are contained in a grimy brown shopping bag.

Insert B

~~third world countries, but it~~ has sifted its way into this booming city of opportunity--

Atlanta. One chilling ~~fact that is~~ *thought* almost incomprehensible to most Atlantans is ~~the~~

that some people actually have no home, no place to live.

~~thought of someone's not having a home.~~

What a degrading condition!

2   ~~There are an~~ estimated five to ten thousand homeless people *survive* in Atlanta. Many of
         A

them are also plagued by other personal problems, such as alcohol, drugs, mental

illness, divorce, or job loss--problems for which state agencies *take little or no* ~~need to take more~~

responsibility *and do not begin to solve* ~~in solving.~~

The revision connects the introduction with the rest of the paper.

No new papagraph is needed. This passage simply clarifies the thesis.

3   Working as a security guard in Atlanta, I am regularly exposed to the reality of

poverty in various communities. The picture of old people hunched over picking up tin

cans on the sidewalks is permanently etched in my memory. On blustery days, I have

crossed paths with these people and have felt compassion as I ~~see~~ *have seen* their torn coats,

their dirty shirts, their floppy old hats, and their dilapidated shoes worn without socks.

I have instinctively drawn back from their toothless faces and reeking breath because

the sight *and smell* was unpleasant--certainly not to be compared with *the well-heeled look and pleasant scent of* my family members or

friends. Striking up a conversation with some of these poverty-stricken individuals is

difficult ~~at times.~~ They stutter and mumble. And even when one can distinguish

individual words, the meaning *of their sentences* is untranslatable gibberish. However, they make it very

clear when they are begging for money.

consistent tense

Details support contrast.

Editing improves logic.

4   ⌐ Move entire ¶ to end.
    ⌐One encouraging note in all this is ~~the fact~~ that there is a growing interest in helping

the poor of Atlanta. For example, at a south-side elementary school gymnasium,

Atlanta City Councilman Jabari Simama recently urged old-guard Black leaders to share

their new-found economic gains with the poor. "Our real threat," he said, "is our failure

up until now to extend opportunities to poor people." Moreover, House Speaker Tom

Murphy's plan to seek five to ten million dollars in government funds for homeless

shelters reassures us that *perhaps* something will be done soon ~~for~~ *on behalf of* the thousands for whom

Moving this paragraph to the end of the essay allows it to offer readers some hope. The last sentence is a strong ending.

Perhaps adds caution and avoids repetition of for.

Insert B

as experienced by Jan Trimble. While newspaper and television have graphically
portrayed the poverty in third-world countries such as Ethiopia and Bangladesh,
they have not made equally visible the poverty that

shelters do not exist. Although these funds will not be available ~~for eight months, the~~ [*tomorrow or even next month,*] ~~fact they are envisioned~~ [*envisioning them*] is a move in the right direction. Unfortunately, ~~no one can deny the fact that~~ far too many corpse bags will be filled before the project is completed. Death ~~is~~ [*will continue to be*] a common, everyday occurrence (for the poor,)

[margin: better emphasis]

Many of us remember reading or seeing news coverage about the pitiful demise of Nicholas Paul Burke, the twenty-three-month-old son of Mike and Anne Burke. He died at a shelter for the homeless in a fire so intense that it drove away all would-be rescuers. Nicholas died from a condition no medical examiner lists as a cause of death-- homelessness. Nicholas received a ~~brief~~ [*paltry*] funeral, paid for by a public who ~~felt guilty,~~ [*wanted to expiate its general guilt for having neglected the helpless*] but much too often bodies like ~~his~~ [*this child's*] go unclaimed and unidentified. Faces remain nameless. Graves go unmarked.

[margin: smoother text, more specificity about public guilt]

~~One~~ [*An*] irony that strikes ~~me~~ [*one with force*] is the juxtaposition of poverty and wealth. [*in Atlanta*] The grounds of Georgia State University ~~in Atlanta is~~ [*are*] a good example. Here the ~~well-heeled~~ [*prosperous members of the*] middle class congregate habitually for picnics preceding football games. They spread out their delicious food on tables--fried chicken, barbequed meatballs, multiple salads of potato, beans, and macaroni. They laugh and joke as they fill their stomachs with these delicacies, washing them down with Coca-Cola or beer. Then they wrap up the leftovers, packing them into coolers or baskets, and head for their nice new cars that will take them to the game just blocks away. On the way they pass the Baptist church, where a line of shabby-looking, disheveled men ~~have gathered~~ [*has formed*] to wait for a bowl of soup and a piece of bread. This group of indigents stands in sharp contrast to the group on their way to the football game. The poor are silent; their eyes are hollow; their expression is haggard. The affluent are laughing; their eyes sparkle with joie de vivre; their expression is self-satisfied. While the football ~~lovers~~ [*fans*] had overindulged on picnic food, these poor men had been standing around for hours, [*hungrily*] waiting for soup and bread.

[margin: An avoids repeating one.]

[margin: Well-heeled has already been used two paragraphs earlier.]

[margin: Lines don't "gather."]

[margin: Underline foreign words.]

The holidays are a time when the poor of Atlanta receive public attention. ~~Cries for coats,~~ [*Urgent appeals for clothes*] food, and money are issued from pulpits, [*over*] the radio, and [*through*] street ~~solicitors.~~ [*solicitations*] Christmas meals are donated in churches and rescue missions. But one wonders if the donors who give away ~~extra~~ [*superfluous*] coats, canned goods, and loose cash really understand

[margin: better parallelism]

5

6

7

what it means to be poor all year long and to live daily without the basic sustenance taken for granted by the rest of society.

8   ~~It~~ It is clearly/evident that/Atlanta has a current crisis of/poverty. Ignoring the crisis will not make it disappear. In fact, poverty, which is one of life's most degrading problems, is a growing/issue. Quoting from a recent /motion picture, /"The needs of the many /outweigh the /needs of the few."

delete

With the new ending in place, this paragraph becomes surplus.

STUDENT ESSAY

Final Draft   Tom Meade

Poverty in Atlanta

Jan Trimble, aged 50, lived in a local mental hospital during most of her adult life. Because she was not deemed dangerous to herself and others, she was forced to move to the streets two years ago when funding cuts were made at her institution. She now exists by foraging through dumpsters for food, and she finds shelter from the biting cold at night under stacks of cardboard boxes. All of her worldly goods are contained in a grimy brown shopping bag.   1

People living in the plush surroundings of North Atlanta may be fully isolated from the real world of grinding poverty as experienced by Jan Trimble. Although newspapers and television have graphically portrayed the poverty in third-world countries such as Ethiopia and Bangladesh, they have not made equally visible the poverty that has sifted its way into this booming city of opportunity—Atlanta. One chilling thought almost incomprehensible to most Atlantans is that some people actually have no home, no place to live. What a degrading condition! An estimated five to ten thousand homeless people survive in Atlanta. Many of them are also plagued by other personal problems, such as alcohol, drugs, mental illness, divorce, or job loss—problems for which state agencies take little or no responsibility and do not begin to solve.   2

Working as a security guard in Atlanta, I am regularly exposed to the reality of poverty in various communities. The picture of old people hunched over, picking up tin cans on the sidewalks, is permanently etched in my memory. On blustery days, I have crossed paths with these people and have felt compassion as I have seen their torn coats, their dirty shirts, their floppy old hats, and their dilapidated shoes worn without   3 socks. I have instinctively drawn back from their toothless faces and reeking breath because the sight and smell were unpleasant—certainly not to be compared with the well-heeled look and pleasant scent of my family members or friends. Striking up a conversation with some of these poverty-stricken individuals is difficult. They stutter and mumble. And even when one can distinguish individual words, the meaning of their sentences is untranslatable gibberish. However, they make it very clear when they are begging for money.

4   Many of us remember reading or seeing news coverage about the pitiful demise of Nicholas Paul Burke, the twenty-three-month-old son of Mike and Anne Burke. He died at a shelter for the homeless in a fire so intense that it drove away all would-be rescuers. Nicholas died from a condition no medical examiner lists as a cause of death—homelessness. Nicholas received a paltry funeral, paid for by the public who wanted to expiate its general guilt for having neglected the helpless, but much too often bodies like this child's go unclaimed and unidentified. Faces remain nameless. Graves go unmarked.

5   An irony that strikes one with force is the juxtaposition of poverty and wealth in Atlanta. The grounds of Georgia State University are a good example. Here prosperous members of the middle class congregate habitually for picnics preceding football games. They spread out their delicious food on tables—fried chicken, barbequed meatballs, multiple salads of potato, beans, and macaroni. They laugh and joke as they fill their stomachs with these delicacies, washing them down with Coca-Cola or beer. Then they wrap up the leftovers, packing them into coolers or baskets, and head for their nice new cars that will take them to the game just blocks away. On the way they pass the Baptist church, where a line of shabby-looking, disheveled men has formed to wait for a bowl of soup and a piece of bread. This group of indigents stands in sharp contrast to the group on their way to the football game. The poor are silent; their eyes are hollow; their expression is haggard. The affluent are laughing; their eyes sparkle with joie de vivre; their expression is self-satisfied. While the football fans had overindulged on picnic food, these poor men had been standing around for hours, hungrily waiting for soup and bread.

6   The holidays are a time when the poor of Atlanta receive public attention. Urgent appeals for clothes, food, and money are issued from pulpits, over the radio, and

through street solicitation. Christmas meals are donated in churches and rescue missions. But one wonders if the donors who give away superfluous coats, canned goods, and loose cash really understand what it means to be poor all year long and to live daily without the basic sustenance taken for granted by the rest of society.

One encouraging note in all this is that there is a growing interest in helping the poor of Atlanta. For example, at a south-side elementary school gymnasium, Atlanta City Councilman Jabari Simama recently urged old-guard Black leaders to share their new-found economic gains with the poor. "Our real threat," he said, "is our failure up until now to extend opportunities to poor people." Moreover, House Speaker Tom Murphy's plan to seek five to ten million dollars in government funds for homeless shelters reassures us that perhaps something will be done soon on behalf of the thousands for whom shelters do not exist. Although these funds will not be available tomorrow or even next month, envisioning them is a move in the right direction. Unfortunately, far too many corpse bags will be filled before the project is completed. For the poor, death will continue to be a common, everyday occurrence.

7

Reading for Ideas

The following selection, first published by the *New Yorker* in 1939, is typical of the humor that made Thurber a beloved American writer. Thurber assumes, as did most people of his generation, that the male was the principal aggressor during courtship, with the female being merely the passive and often fickle object. With the changing roles between men and women and the emergence of feminism, is this assumption still true today? What stereotypes does Thurber seem to assume and perpetuate in this article? How do you think an audience of feminists might react to its underlying assumptions?

ALTERNATE READING

Courtship Through the Ages
James Thurber

James Thurber (1894–1961), American humorist, cartoonist, and social commentator, was a staffer on the New Yorker *from 1927 to 1933 and afterwards a principal contributor to that magazine. Thurber's work, though humorous, also contains psychological insight. His main books are* My Life and Hard Times *(1933),* Fables for Our Time *(1940), and* The Thurber Carnival *(1945).*

1   Surely nothing in the astonishing scheme of life can have nonplussed Nature so much as the fact that none of the females of any of the species she created really cared very much for the male, as such. For the past ten million years Nature has been busily inventing ways to make the male attractive to the female, but the whole business of courtship, from the marine annelids up to man, still lumbers heavily along, like a complicated musical comedy. I have been reading the sad and absorbing story in Volume 6 (Cole to Dama) of the *Encyclopaedia Britannica.* In this volume you can learn all about cricket, cotton, costume designing, crocodiles, crown jewels, and Coleridge, but none of these subjects is so interesting as the Courtship of Animals, which recounts the sorrowful lengths to which all males must go to arouse the interest of a lady.

2   We all know, I think, that Nature gave man whiskers and a mustache with the quaint idea in mind that these would prove attractive to the female. We all know that, far from attracting her, whiskers and mustaches only made her nervous and gloomy, so that man had to go in for somersaults, tilting with lances, and performing feats of parlor magic to win her attention; he also had to bring her candy, flowers, and the furs of animals. It is common knowledge that in spite of all these ''love displays'' the male is constantly being turned down, insulted, or thrown out of the house. It is rather comforting, then, to discover that the peacock, for all his gorgeous plumage, does not have a particularly easy time in courtship; none of the males in the world do. The first peahen, it turned out, was only faintly stirred by her suitor's beautiful train. She would often go quietly to sleep while he was whisking it around. The *Britannica* tells us that the peacock actually had to learn a certain little trick to wake her up and revive her interest: he had to learn to vibrate his quills so as to make a rustling sound. In ancient times man himself, observing the ways of the peacock, probably tried vibrating his whiskers to make a rustling sound; if so, it didn't get him anywhere. He had to go in for something else; so, among other things, he went in for gifts. It is not unlikely that he got this idea from certain flies and birds who were making no headway at all with rustling sounds.

3   One of the flies of the family Empidae, who had tried everything, finally hit on something pretty special. He contrived to make a glistening transparent balloon which was even larger than himself. Into this he would put sweetmeats and tidbits and he would carry the whole elaborate envelope through the air to the lady of his choice. This amused her for a time, but she finally got bored with it. She demanded silly little colorful presents, something that you couldn't eat but that would look nice around the house. So the male Empis had to go around gathering flower petals and pieces of bright paper to put into his balloon. On a courtship flight a male Empis cuts quite a figure now, but he can hardly be said to be happy. He never knows how soon the female will demand heavier presents, such as Roman coins and gold collar buttons. It seems probable that one day the courtship of the Empidae will fall down, as man's occasionally does, of its own weight.

4   The bowerbird is another creature that spends so much time courting the female that he never gets any work done. If all the male bowerbirds became nervous wrecks within

the next ten or fifteen years, it would not surprise me. The female bowerbird insists that a playground be built for her with a specially constructed bower at the entrance. This bower is much more elaborate than an ordinary nest and is harder to build; it costs a lot more, too. The female will not come to the playground until the male has filled it up with a great many gifts: silvery leaves, red leaves, rose petals, shells, beads, berries, bones, dice, buttons, cigar bands, Christmas seals, and the Lord knows what else. When the female finally condescends to visit the playground, she is in a coy and silly mood and has to be chased in and out of the bower and up and down the playground before she will quit giggling and stand still long enough even to shake hands. The male bird is, of course, pretty well done in before the chase starts, because he has worn himself out hunting for eyeglass lenses and begonia blossoms. I imagine that many a bowerbird, after chasing a female for two or three hours, says the hell with it and goes home to bed. Next day, of course, he telephones someone else and the same trying ritual is gone through again. A male bowerbird is as exhausted as a night-club habitué before he is out of his twenties.

The male fiddler crab has a somewhat easier time, but it can hardly be said that he is 5 sitting pretty. He has one enormously large and powerful claw, usually brilliantly colored, and you might suppose that all he had to do was reach out and grab some passing cutie. The very earliest fiddler crabs may have tried this, but, if so, they got slapped for their pains. A female crab will not tolerate any caveman stuff; she never has and she doesn't intend to start now. To attract a female, a fiddler crab has to stand on tiptoe and brandish his claw in the air. If any female in the neighborhood is interested—and you'd be surprised how many are not—she comes over and engages him in light badinage, for which he is not in the mood. As many as a hundred females may pass the time of day with him and go on about their business. By nightfall of an average courting day, a fiddler crab who has been standing on tiptoe for eight or ten hours waving a heavy claw in the air is in pretty sad shape. As in the case of all males of all species, however, he gets out of bed next morning, dashes some water on his face, and tries again.

The next time you encounter a male web-spinning spider, stop and reflect that he is 6 too busy worrying about his love life to have any desire to bite you. Male web-spinning spiders have a tougher life than any other males in the animal kingdom. This is because the female web-spinning spiders have very poor eyesight. If a male lands on a female's web, she kills him before he has time to lay down his cane and gloves, mistaking him for a fly or a bumblebee who has tumbled into her trap. Before the species figured out what to do about this, millions of males were murdered by ladies they called on. It is the nature of spiders to perform a little dance in front of the female, but before a male spinner could get near enough for the female to see who he was and what he was up to, she would lash out at him with a flat-iron or a pair of garden shears. One night, nobody knows when, a very bright male spinner lay awake worrying about calling on a lady who had been killing suitors right and left. It came to him that this business of dancing as a love display wasn't getting anybody anywhere except the grave. He decided to go in for web-twitching, or strand-vibrating. The next day he tried it on one of the near-sighted girls. Instead of dropping in on her suddenly, he stayed outside the web and began monkeying with one of its strands. He twitched it up and down and in and out with such a lilting rhythm that the female was charmed. The serenade worked beautifully; the female let him live. The

Britannica's spider-watchers, however, report that this system is not always successful. Once in a while, even now, a female will fire three bullets into a suitor or run him through with a kitchen knife. She keeps threatening him from the moment he strikes the first low notes on the outside strings, but usually by the time he has got up to the high notes played around the center of the web, he is going to town and she spares his life.

7 Even the butterfly, as handsome a fellow as he is, can't always win a mate merely by fluttering around and showing off. Many butterflies have to have scent scales on their wings. Hepialus carries a powder puff in a perfumed pouch. He throws perfume at the ladies when they pass. The male tree cricket, Oecanthus, goes Hepialus one better by carrying a bottle of wine with him and giving drinks to such doxies as he has designs on. One of the male snails throws darts to entertain the girls. So it goes, through the long list of animals, from the bristle worm and his rudimentary dance steps to man and his gift of diamonds and sapphires. The golden-eye drake raises a jet of water with his feet as he flies over a lake; Hepialus has his powder puff, Oecanthus his wine bottle, man his etchings. It is a bright and melancholy story, the age-old desire of the male for the female, the age-old desire of the female to be amused and entertained. Of all the creatures on earth, the only males who could be figured as putting any irony into their courtship are the grebes and certain other diving birds. Every now and then a courting grebe slips quietly down to the bottom of a lake and then, with a mighty ''Whoosh!,'' pops out suddenly a few feet from his girl friend, splashing water all over her. She seems to be persuaded that this is a purely loving display, but I like to think that the grebe always has a faint hope of drowning her or scaring her to death.

8 I will close this investigation into the mournful burdens of the male with the *Britannica's* story about a certain Argus pheasant. It appears that the Argus displays himself in front of a female who stands perfectly still without moving a feather. . . . The male Argus the *Britannica* tells about was confined in a cage with a female of another species, a female who kept moving around, emptying ashtrays and fussing with lampshades all the time the male was showing off his talents. Finally, in disgust, he stalked away and began displaying in front of his water trough. He reminds me of a certain male (Homo sapiens) of my acquaintance who one night after dinner asked his wife to put down her detective magazine so that he could read her a poem of which he was very fond. She sat quietly enough until he was well into the middle of the thing, intoning with great ardor and intensity. Then suddenly there came a sharp, disconcerting *slap!* It turned out that all during the male's display, the female had been intent on a circling mosquito and had finally trapped it between the palms of her hands. The male in this case did not stalk away and display in front of a water trough; he went over to Tim's and had a flock of drinks and recited the poem to the fellas. I am sure they all told bitter stories of their own about how their displays had been interrupted by females. I am also sure that they all ended up singing ''Honey, Honey, Bless Your Heart.''

Vocabulary

annelids (1)   doxies (7)
habitué (4)   intoning (8)
badinage (5)

Questions on Meaning and Technique

1. What is the controlling idea of the essay? Where is it stated?

2. Which of the examples cited is most closely allied to the human situation? What does the example reveal?

3. What does the courting grebe of paragraph 7 signify?

4. According to the essay, what is the only successful technique in courting the female? What is not enough?

5. What is ironic about the essay? How does Thurber achieve this irony?

6. Thurber's essay is a mixture of slang and scholarly language. What are some examples of both extremes? What is the effect of this mixture?

7. How does the title relate to the essay?

8. Can you think of instances in nature that would demonstrate a point of view opposite to that expressed by Thurber?

9. Does the *Encyclopaedia Britannica* really contain a section on the courtship of animals, or is this a fictional account?

10. What are the conventional courtesies men offer women today? How do they differ from courtesies of, say, the Renaissance?

Writing Assignments

1. Write an essay giving examples of some of the stranger dates you have had.

2. The traditional courtesies between men and women are changing for the better (or the worse). Develop that thesis with appropriate examples.

READING FOR IDEAS

This essay by a master mariner and writer gives examples of the way ships' captains typically react to departures and landfalls—two important events in a sailor's life. Conrad is better known as a superb novelist than an essayist, but his account is lovingly embellished with the rich details of personal observation. Ask yourself what psychological as well as nautical reasons a modern reader might use to account for the behavior of these maritime captains.

ALTERNATE READING

Landfalls and Departures
JOSEPH CONRAD

Joseph Conrad (1857–1924), a Polish-born English writer (his Polish name was Józef Teodor Konrad Walecz Korzeniowski), published his first novel, Almayer's

Folly, in 1895 at the age of 38. Conrad went to sea as a 17-year-old boy and became a master mariner and British citizen in 1884. He is regarded as one of the greatest stylists of the English language, his adopted tongue, and his works are characterized by rich symbolism and lush prose. They include, among many others, The Nigger of the Narcissus *(1897),* Lord Jim *(1900), and* Nostromo *(1904). A recurring theme of Conrad's work is the conflict that results when primitive cultures encounter modern civilization.*

And shippes by the brinke comen and gon,
And in swich forme endure a day or two.
The Frankeleyns Tale

I

1 Landfall and Departure mark the rhythmical swing of a seaman's life and of a ship's career. From land to land is the most concise definition of a ship's earthly fate. A "Departure" is not what a vain people of landsmen may think. The term "Landfall" is more easily understood; you fall in with the land, and it is a matter of a quick eye and of a clear atmosphere. The Departure is not the ship's going away from her port any more than the Landfall can be looked upon as the synonym of arrival. But there is this difference in the Departure: that the term does not imply so much a sea event as a definite act entailing a process—the precise observation of certain landmarks by means of the compass card.

2 Your Landfall, be it a peculiarly shaped mountain, a rocky headland, or a stretch of sand-dunes, you meet at first with a single glance. Further recognition will follow in due course; but essentially a Landfall, good or bad, is made and done with at the first cry of "Land ho!" The Departure is distinctly a ceremony of navigation. A ship may have left her port some time before; she may have been at sea, in the fullest sense of the phrase, for days; but, for all that, as long as the coast she was about to leave remained in sight, a southern-going ship of yesterday had not in the sailor's sense begun the enterprise of a passage.

3 The taking of Departure, if not the last sight of the land, is, perhaps, the last professional recognition of the land on the part of a sailor. It is the technical, as distinguished from the sentimental, "good-by." Henceforth he has done with the coast astern of his ship. It is a matter personal to the man. It is not the ship that takes her Departure; the seaman takes his Departure by means of cross-bearings which fix the place of the first tiny pencil-cross on the white expanse of the track-chart, where the ship's position at noon shall be marked by just such another tiny pencil-cross for every day of her passage. And there may be sixty, eighty, any number of these crosses on the ship's track from land to land. The greatest number in my experience was a hundred and thirty of such crosses from the pilot station at the Sand Heads in the Bay of Bengal to the Scilly's light. A bad passage. . . .

4 A Departure, the last professional sight of land, is always good, or at least good enough. For even if the weather is thick, it does not matter much to a ship having all the open sea before her bows. A Landfall may be good or bad. You encompass the earth

with one particular spot of it in your eye. In all the devious tracings the course of a sailing-ship leaves upon the white paper of a chart she is always aiming for that one little spot—maybe a small island in the ocean, a single headland upon the long coast of a continent, a light-house on a bluff, or simply the peaked form of a mountain like an ant heap afloat upon the waters. But if you have sighted it on the expected bearing, then that Landfall is good. Fogs, snowstorms, gales thick with clouds and rain—those are the enemies of good Landfalls.

II

Some commanders of ships take their Departure from the home coast sadly, in a spirit   5
of grief and discontent. They have a wife, children perhaps, some affection at any rate, or perhaps only some pet vice; that must be left behind for a year or more. I remember only one man who walked his deck with a springy step, and gave the first course of the passage in an elated voice. But he, as I learned afterwards, was leaving nothing behind him, except a welter of debts and threats of legal proceedings.

On the other hand, I have known many captains who, directly their ship had left the   6
narrow waters of the Channel, would disappear from the sight of their ship's company altogether for some three days or more. They would take a long dive, as it were, into their state-room, only to emerge a few days afterwards with a more or less serene brow. Those were the men easy to get on with. Besides, such a complete retirement seemed to imply a satisfactory amount of trust in their officers, and to be trusted displeases no seaman worthy of the name.

On my first voyage, as chief mate with good Captain Mac W_____ I remember that   7
I felt quite flattered, and went blithely about my duties, myself a commander for all practical purposes. Still, whatever the greatness of my illusion, the fact remained that the real commander was there, backing up my self-confidence, though invisible to my eyes behind a maple-wood veneered cabin-door with a white china handle.

That is the time, after your Departure is taken, when the spirit of your commander   8
communes with you in a muffled voice, as if from the sanctum sanctorum of a temple; because, call her a temple or a "hell afloat"—as some ships have been called—the captain's state-room is surely the august place in every vessel.

The good Mac W_____ would not even come out to his meals, and fed solitarily in his   9
holy of holies from a tray covered with a white napkin. Our steward used to bend an ironic glance at the perfectly empty plates he was bringing out from there. This grief for his home, which overcomes so many married seamen, did not deprive Captain Mac W_____ of his legitimate appetite. In fact, the steward would almost invariably come up to me, sitting in the captain's chair at the head of the table, to say in a grave murmur, "The captain asks for one more slice of meat and two potatoes." We, his officers, could hear him moving about in his berth, or lightly snoring, or fetching deep sighs, or splashing and blowing in his bathroom; and we made our reports to him through the keyhole, as it were. It was the crowning achievement of his amiable character that the answers we got were given in a quite mild and friendly tone. Some commanders in their periods of seclusion are constantly grumpy, and seem to resent the mere sound of your voice as an injury and an insult.

10   But a grumpy recluse cannot worry his subordinates, whereas the man in whom the sense of duty is strong (or, perhaps, only the sense of self-importance), and who persists in airing on deck his moroseness all day—and perhaps half the night—becomes a grievous infliction. He walks the poop darting gloomy glances as though he wished to poison the sea, and snaps your head off savagely whenever you happen to blunder within ear-shot. And these vagaries are the harder to bear patiently, as becomes a man and an officer, because no sailor is really good-tempered during the first few days of a voyage. There are regrets, memories, the instinctive longing for the departed idleness, the instinctive hate of all work. Besides, things have a knack of going wrong at the start, especially in the matter of irritating trifles. And there is the abiding thought of a whole year of more or less hard life before one, because there was hardly a southern-going voyage in the yesterday of the sea which meant anything less than a twelve-month. Yes; it needed a few days after the taking of your departure for a ship's company to shake down into their places, and for the soothing deep-water ship routine to establish its beneficent sway.

11   It is a great doctor for sore hearts and sore heads, too, your ship's routine, which I have seen soothe—at least for a time—the most turbulent of spirits. There is health in it, and peace, and satisfaction of the accomplished round; for each day of the ship's life seems to close a circle within the wide ring of the sea horizon. It borrows a certain dignity of sameness from the majestic monotony of the sea. He who loves the sea loves also the ship's routine.

12   Nowhere else than upon the sea do the days, weeks, and months fall away quicker into the past. They seem to be left astern as easily as the light air-bubbles in the swirls of the ship's wake, and vanish into a great silence in which your ship moves on with a sort of magical effect. They pass away, the days, the weeks, the months. Nothing but a gale can disturb the orderly life of the ship; and the spell of unshaken monotony that seems to have fallen upon the very voices of her men is broken only by the near prospect of a Landfall.

13   Then is the spirit of the ship's commander stirred strongly again. But it is not moved to seek seclusion and to remain, hidden and inert, shut up in a small cabin with the solace of a good bodily appetite. When about to make the land, the spirit of the ship's commander is tormented by an unconquerable restlessness. It seems unable to abide for many seconds together in the holy of holies of the captain's state-room; it will go out on deck and gaze ahead, through straining eyes, as the appointed moment comes nearer. It is kept vigorously upon the stretch of excessive vigilance. Meantime, the body of the ship's commander is being enfeebled by want of appetite; at least, such is my experience, though "enfeebled" is perhaps not exactly the word. I might say, rather, that it is spiritualized by a disregard for food, sleep, and all the ordinary comforts, such as they are, of sea life. In one or two cases I have known that detachment from the grosser needs of existence to remain regrettably incomplete in the matter of drink.

14   But these two cases were, properly speaking, pathological cases, and the only two in all my sea experience. In one of these two instances of a craving for stimulants, developed from sheer anxiety, I cannot assert that the man's seaman-like qualities were impaired in the least. It was a very anxious case, too, the land being made suddenly, close-to, on a wrong bearing, in thick weather, and during a fresh on-shore gale. Going

below to speak to him soon after, I was unlucky enough to catch my captain in the very act of hasty cork-drawing. The sight, I may say, gave me an awful scare. I was well aware of the morbidly sensitive nature of the man. Fortunately, I managed to draw back unseen, and taking care to stamp heavily with my sea-boots at the foot of the cabin stairs, I made my second entry. But for this unexpected glimpse, no act of his during the next twenty-four hours could have given me the slightest suspicion that all was not well with his nerve.

III

Quite another case, and having nothing to do with drink, was that of poor Captain B_____. He used to suffer from sick headaches, in his young days, every time he was approaching a coast. Well over fifty years of age when I knew him, short, stout, dignified, perhaps a little pompous, he was a man of a singularly well-informed mind, the least sailor-like in outward aspect, but certainly one of the best seamen whom it has been my good luck to serve under. He was a Plymouth man, I think, the son of a country doctor, and both his elder boys were studying medicine. He commanded a big London ship, fairly well known in her day. I thought no end of him, and that is why I remember with a peculiar satisfaction the last words he spoke to me on board his ship after an eighteen months' voyage. It was in the dock in Dundee, where we had brought a full cargo of jute from Calcutta. We had been paid off that morning, and I had come on board to take my sea chest away and to say good-by. In his slightly lofty but courteous way he inquired what were my plans. I replied that I intended leaving for London by the afternoon train, and thought of going up for examination to get my master's certificate. I had just enough service for that. He commended me for not wasting my time, with such an evident interest in my case that I was quite surprised; then, rising from his chair, he said: 15

"Have you a ship in view after you have passed?"   16

I answered that I had nothing whatever in view.   17

He shook hands with me and pronounced the memorable words: 18

"If you happen to be in want of employment, remember that as long as I have a ship you have a ship, too."   19

In the way of compliment there is nothing to beat this from a ship's captain to his second mate at the end of a voyage, when the work is over and the subordinate is done with. And there is a pathos in that memory, for the poor fellow never went to sea again after all. He was already ailing when we passed St. Helena; was laid up for a time when we were off the Western Islands, but got out of bed to make his Landfall. He managed to keep up on deck as far as the Downs, where, giving his orders in an exhausted voice, he anchored for a few hours to send a wire to his wife and take aboard a North Sea pilot to help him sail the ship up the east coast. He had not felt equal to the task by himself, for it is the sort of thing that keeps a deep-water man on his feet pretty well night and day.   20

When we arrived in Dundee, Mrs. B_____ was already there, waiting to take him home. We travelled up to London by the same train; but by the time I had managed to get through with my examination the ship had sailed on her next voyage without him, and, instead of joining her again, I went by request to see my old commander in his home. This is the only one of my captains I have ever visited in that way. He was out of bed by   21 then, "quite convalescent," as he declared, making a few tottering steps to meet me at the sitting-room door. Evidently he was reluctant to take his final cross-bearings of this earth for a Departure on the only voyage to an unknown destination a sailor ever undertakes. And it was all very nice—the large, sunny room; his deep easy-chair in a bow window, with pillows and a footstool; the quiet, watchful care of the elderly, gentle woman who had borne him five children, and had not, perhaps, lived with him more than five full years out of the thirty or so of their married life. There was also another woman there in a plain black dress, quite grey-haired, sitting very erect on her chair with some sewing, from which she snatched side-glances in his direction, and uttering not a single word during all the time of my call. Even when, in due course, I carried over to her a cup of tea, she only nodded at me silently, with the faintest ghost of a smile, on her tight-set lips. I imagine she must have been a maiden sister of Mrs. B._____ come to help nurse her brother-in-law. His youngest boy, a late-comer, a great cricketer it seemed, twelve years old or thereabouts, chattered enthusiastically of the exploits of W. G. Grace. And I remember his eldest son, too, a newly-fledged doctor, who took me out to smoke in the garden, and, shaking his head with professional gravity, but with genuine concern, muttered: "Yes, but he doesn't get back his appetite. I don't like that—I don't like that at all." The last sight of Captain B_____ I had was as he nodded his head to me out of the bow window when I turned round to close the front gate.

22   It was a distinct and complete impression, something that I don't know whether to call a Landfall or a Departure. Certainly he gazed at times very fixedly before him with the Landfall's vigilant look, this sea-captain seated incongruously in a deep-back chair. He had not then talked to me of employment, of ships, of being ready to take another command; but he had discoursed of his early days, in the abundant but thin flow of a wilful invalid's talk. The women looked worried, but sat still, and I learned more of him in that interview than in the whole eighteen months we had sailed together. It appeared he had "served his time" in the copper-ore trade, the famous copper-ore trade of old days between Swansea and the Chilean coast, coal out and ore in, deep-loaded both ways, as if in wanton defiance of the great Cape Horn seas—a work, this, for staunch ships, and a great school of staunchness for West-Country seamen. A whole fleet of copper-bottomed barques, as strong in rib and planking, as well-found in gear, as ever was sent upon the seas, manned by hardy crews and commanded by young masters, was engaged in that now long-defunct trade. "That was the school I was trained in," he said to me almost boastfully, lying back among his pillows with a rug over his legs. And it was in that trade that he obtained his first command at a very early age. It was then that he mentioned to me how, as a young commander, he was always ill for a few days before making land after a long voyage. But this sort of sickness used to pass off with the first sight of a familiar landmark. Afterwards, he added, as he grew older, all that nervousness wore off completely; and I observed his weary eyes gaze steadily ahead, as if there had been nothing between him and the straight line of sea and sky, where whatever a seaman is looking for is first bound to appear. But I have also seen his eyes rest fondly upon the faces in the room, upon the pictures on the wall, upon all the familiar objects of that home, whose abiding and clear image must have flashed often on his memory in times of stress and anxiety at sea. Was he looking out for a strange Landfall, or taking with an untroubled mind the bearings for his last Departure?

It is hard to say, for in that voyage from which no man returns Landfall and Departure   23
are instantaneous, merging together into one moment of supreme and final attention.
Certainly I do not remember any sign of faltering in the set expression of his wasted face,
no hint of the nervous anxiety of a young commander about to make land on an
uncharted shore. He had had too much experience of Departures and Landfalls! And had
he not "served his time" in the famous copper-ore trade out of Bristol Channel, the work
of the staunchest ships afloat, and the school of staunch seamen?

Vocabulary

synonym (1)   moroseness (10)
entailing (1)   vagaries (10)
encompass (4)   beneficent (10)
blithely (7)   turbulent (11)
communes (8)   solace (13)
sanctum sanctorum (8)   incongruously (22)
august (8)   discoursed (22)

Questions on Meaning and Technique

1. What is the author's definition of a departure, and how does this meaning
   differ from the way a landsman might use the term?

2. Why is a departure always good to a seaman and sailing ship, but a landfall
   either good or bad?

3. Conrad is writing about mariners of the turn of the century when many ships
   were still sailing vessels. What significant differences do you think exist
   between sailors nowadays and during Conrad's day?

4. How do you think the mystique of seagoing, of which Conrad writes, was
   affected by the move from sailing ships to modern powered vessels?

5. With what or whom does paragraph 8 implicitly liken the commander of a
   ship? Is this comparison justified?

6. In covering landfalls and departures, what other rhetorical mode does
   Conrad follow?

7. What is the overall organizing principle behind this essay?

8. Conrad gives examples both of good-natured captains and grumpy ones.
   What is significantly different about his treatment of each type? What does
   this indirectly say about the kind of captains Conrad sailed under?

9. What, by implication, is Conrad's attitude toward the sea and seagoing?

10. Conrad's writing style is notably rich and occasionally roundabout. How, for
    example, might this sentence be more directly worded: "In one or two cases
    I have known that detachment from the grosser needs of existence to remain
    regrettably incomplete in the matter of drink"?

Writing Assignments

1. Develop by examples an essay on the rituals involved with beginning and ending a new semester or quarter at school.

2. The nautical names of things often differ from their land-based equivalents—for example, the front of a ship is known as its "bow." Develop an essay on this theme, giving examples of these differences.

READING FOR IDEAS

This article is an informative catalog of eponyms—objects or events named after real people—and shows us how some famous eponyms were formed. As you read try to think of other examples of eponyms the writer does not mention. Notice how the writer organizes his examples in a clear and orderly sequence.

ALTERNATE READING

The Word as Person: Eponyms

DON FARRANT

Don Farrant (b. 1912), a business writer and historian, lives in St. Simons Island, Georgia.

1   When the Fourth Earl of Sandwich was hungry, he would ask his valet to prepare an easy-to-eat snack, instructing him to take two pieces of bread and put a slice of meat between them. The servant did as told and it was a turning point in culinary history. The earl, who lived from 1718–1792, had no way of knowing he was immortalizing himself . . . with the sandwich.

2   Our language contains many terms that were once the names of actual persons. These are eponymous words, from the noun *eponym:* "One whose name is so prominently connected with anything as to be a figurative designation for it."

3   Nellie Melba, an Australian soprano (1861–1931), also gave her name to a well-known food item. She disliked thick cuttings of bread, common at the time, considering them coarse and inelegant, and made a practice of preparing thin slices, toasted until crisp. Poor Madame Melba—little did she know she'd be better remembered by future generations for Melba toast than for her operatic achievements.

4   The long history of wearing apparel gives us some fascinating eponyms. The cardigan sweater, for example, got its name from James T. Brudenell (1797–1868), Seventh Earl of Cardigan and a British general who gained fame in the Crimean War.

5   The rich and handsome earl showed public spirit by sitting faithfully in Parliament for many years and through lengthy army service. It was he who led the famous Charge of

the Light Brigade at the Battle of Balaklava in 1854. Overall, his popularity was diminished by a quarrelsome nature and his tendency to brag about his battlefield exploits. But alas, he is remembered less for that famous charge than for his fondness for a collarless jacket opening down the front, known as the cardigan sweater.

It was Amelia Bloomer, an American feminist, who decided young ladies should wear   6
a costume consisting of a short skirt and loose trousers gathered at the ankles. This was dubbed a *bloomer*—and a variation, used for sports and gathered at the knee, became known as *bloomers*. Outmoded today, Amelia's creation was important enough to become a part of the language.

Or take the Duke of Wellington, who defeated Napoleon at Waterloo. His place   7
in history is, of course, assured, but the Iron Duke gave a lesser-known contribution: the Wellington boot, loose at the top with a front portion which came up above the knee.

Transportation, too, has stirred up some interesting eponyms over the years. Back in   8
the 19th Century, George M. Pullman (1831–1897) didn't think railroad cars provided enough comfort on long trips. He introduced a special car with sleeping quarters for passengers. His name will be forever associated with the Pullman car.

Henry Peter Brougham (1778–1868) was a British political leader and supporter of   9
humanitarian causes. As a member of the House of Lords, Brougham (pronounced *broom*) fought consistently for liberal policies and urged abolition of the slave trade. He was energetic and witty, but at times a bit eccentric. In the 1830s, after he was raised to the peerage and became Lord Chancellor of England, a special, four-wheel closed carriage, the Brougham, was designed for him. Later, its popularity spread to the Continent and America.

In the arena of personal appearance, the pompadour hairstyle came to us from the   10
Marquise de Pompadour (properly, Jeanne Antoinette Poisson, 1721–1764). A close associate of Louis XV of France, the marquise set a trend by working up a style of dressing her hair high over the forehead.

Inventors have done much to enrich our language with name-inspired nouns. It was a   11
Frenchman, Louis Braille (1809–1852), who developed a system of printing in which alphabetical characters are represented by raised dots. Braille is still used the world over—all due to the dedication of a teacher who wanted to give sightless people a better chance to communicate.

Generations of chemistry students have used the invention of Robert W. Bunsen   12
(1811–1899). The German professor devised a distinctive type of gas burner for laboratory work—the Bunsen burner.

Back in the late 18th Century, a Scottish inventor named John Loudon McAdam   13
(1756–1836) conducted road-making experiments in England. When he was general surveyor of the Bristol Turnpike Trust, he came up with a new system calling for an impervious surface over dry soil, utilizing proper drainage, a slight camber, and a compact layer of small stones. Nowadays, *macadam* is a general term for pavements or road surfaces made up of layers of crushed stone or gravel.

Three related words—galvanic, galvanized, and galvanometer—are eponyms all,   14
stemming from Luigi Galvani (1737–1798), an Italian physiologist. He was a pioneer in electrophysiology and certainly a man ahead of his time. He was constantly applying electrodes to various objects, attempting to trace the path of electrical impulses.

15   Probably Galvani's most significant discovery was the electrical nature of nerve action. In textbooks today, *galvanic* means having the effect of an electric shock. *Galvanize* means either to stimulate to action or to coat iron or steel with zinc to guard against corrosion. A *galvanometer* is a device for detecting an electric current.

16   Sometimes eponyms reflect the contributor's own unattractive traits. Such is the case with Captain Charles Boycott (1832–1897), a land agent in Ireland in the 1880s, who collected rents in such a tyrannical, unbending way that he infuriated his tenants.

17   When Boycott's process servers, carrying eviction papers, were attacked by a mob, he decided to send out infantry to collect the rents. Things got worse: laborers refused to work for the man, and he was refused accommodations while traveling. Frequently, he did not receive letters intended for him. Out of all this came the term *boycott*—a refusal to engage in relations with a person or firm in order to bring about a change in terms or a settlement of some sort.

18   When the 12th Earl of Derby originated a horse race for three-year-olds in 1779, little did he know he was starting a tradition. Called first "Derby's race at Epsom," it soon became an annual event; Derby Day is still one of the biggest sporting occasions of the year in Britain, taking place every June. In the U.S., the most heralded horse race is the Kentucky Derby, held each May at Churchill Downs. Both these events have large purses and attract crowds of more than 100,000.

19   In the world of medicine, Dr. Franz Anton Mesmer, a German physician (1734–1815), developed a deep rapport with his patients and may have used a form of hypnotism to treat them. In 1767, he joined the faculty of Vienna's Advanced Medical Center. As a physician he had many theories and although some were unsubstantiated, such as that of "magnetic body fluids," he was surely a leader in promoting close doctor-patient relationships. Mesmerism is still associated with casting a spell; it was, in fact, an early term for hypnotism.

20   Sailors can tell you what a Plimsoll mark is—but not many others can. It's the line on the side of a ship's hull that indicates the amount of cargo it can safely carry. It was named for Samuel Plimsoll (1824–1898), a 19th-Century English reformer. Due to his insistence, Parliament passed the Merchant Shipping Act (1876), fixing compulsory limits of cargo under various ocean conditions and providing for the line on the hull. Prior to this law, vessels sometimes would be lost at sea due to overloading.

21   Anyone who has changed a light bulb knows the word *watt*—a unit of electrical power. It stems from James Watt, a Scottish engineer (1736–1819), who designed the engine which first made steam power feasible. Other devices are credited to this mechanical genius, who also did research in chemistry and metallurgy.

22   A waterproof outer garment made of rubber-coated fabric is known in many circles as a *mackintosh*—but whence the name? It derives from one Charles Macintosh (1766–1843), a British chemist and inventor who made significant contributions to chemical technology, including a procedure for producing lead and aluminum acetates. Macintosh, who tired of getting soaked every time he went out in the rain, came up with what is today his most famous invention—the raincoat which bears his name.

23   Then there's the Morse code, an orderly arrangement of dots and dashes which has played a vital role in communication history. Most of us know that the inventor of the

telegraph, Samuel F.B. Morse, also gave his name to the code he devised. To his credit, Morse was an artist as well as a technician, and is today recognized as one of the best of the early American portrait painters.

New words come about in strange ways, giving fame, even immortality, to people   24
who, in many cases, would rather be remembered for other things. Whether they like it or not, eponymous words are a sort of memorial—a lasting tribute to those who contributed to life, and often improved it.

Vocabulary

culinary (1)
camber (13)
feasible (21)

Questions on Meaning and Technique

1. What other rhetorical strategy is obviously at work in this article?
2. What underlying logic implicitly links the author's first two examples?
3. For what kind of audience do you think this article was written? What evidence from the text can you cite to support your conclusion?
4. The author uses no transition in paragraph 6, yet weighs in with a bridging sentence at the beginning of paragraph 11. What rhetorical explanation can you give for this difference?
5. At the end of paragraph 2, the author includes a quotation defining *eponym*. What would a student writer be required to do differently with such a quotation?
6. Why does the writer, for the most part, simply cite his examples without an introductory phrase or word?
7. All the examples mentioned by the author are from long ago. What modern examples of eponyms can you think of?

Writing Assignments

1. Write an essay, developed by examples, on nicknames.
2. Write an essay citing at least three examples of other eponymous words not mentioned in this article.

Additional Writing Assignments

Illustrate the following with appropriate *examples:*

1. Getting sick in America can bankrupt even the well-off person.
2. Not all old people are fuddy-duddy, conservative, or timid.

3. All that glitters is not gold.

4. On the whole, movies nowadays are too gory.

5. Americans are too moralistic in their politics.

6. Many doctors emerge from medical school with an inflated and egotistic opinion of themselves and their profession.

7. Growth for its own sake is not always good, whether for institutions or businesses.

8. Some television shows are vulgar and tasteless.

9. Participation in sports is not for everyone, nor should it be.

10. Gun control can make (does not make) a difference.

Photo Writing Assignment

Big Duck Store. Harvey A. Weber.

The photograph is an example of striking, grotesque advertising. Write an essay on outlandish advertising using other examples from your own observation. Make sure that each example illustrates the characteristic you are clarifying.

Definition

READING FOR IDEAS

"Arrangement in Black and White" is a story about prejudice. As you listen to the main character in the story reveal her attitude toward blacks, ask yourself, "What is prejudice? How is it acquired? How can it be stopped?" From your own experience, what are some examples of prejudice? Be prepared to give a one-sentence definition of the word *prejudice*.

Arrangement in Black and White
DOROTHY PARKER

Dorothy Parker (1893–1967) was an American poet and short story writer. She gained a reputation as a wit while serving as drama critic for Vanity Fair *(1916–1917) and book reviewer for the* New Yorker *(1927). Her first volume of poetry, which brought her instant fame, was* Enough Rope *(1926). It was followed by such volumes as* Death and Taxes *(1931) and* Not So Deep as a Well *(1936). Her short stories, which were usually satirical attacks on the ways and customs of her time, were collected and published in 1942.*

1   The woman with the pink velvet poppies twined round the assisted gold of her hair traversed the crowded room at an interesting gait combining a skip with a sidle, and clutched the lean arm of her host.

2   "Now I got you!" she said. "Now you can't get away!"
       "Why, hello," said her host. "Well. How are you?"

"Oh, I'm finely," she said. "Just simply finely. Listen. I want you to do me the most terrible favor. Will you? Will you please? Pretty please?"

"What is it?" said her host.   3

"Listen," she said. "I want to meet Walter Williams. Honestly, I'm just simply crazy about that man. Oh, when he sings! When he sings those spirituals! Well, I said to Burton, 'It's a good thing for you Walter Williams is colored,' I said, 'or you'd have lots of reason to be jealous.' I'd really love to meet him. I'd like to tell him I've heard him sing. Will you be an angel and introduce me to him?"

"Why, certainly," said her host. "I thought you'd met him. The party's for him. Where   4
is he, anyway?"

"He's over there by the bookcase," she said. "Let's wait till those people get through   5
talking to him. Well, I think you're simply marvelous, giving this perfectly marvelous party for him, and having him meet all these white people, and all. Isn't he terribly grateful?"

"I hope not," said her host.   6

"I think it's really terribly nice," she said. "I do. I don't see why on earth it isn't perfectly all right to meet colored people. I haven't any feeling at all about it—not one single bit. Burton—oh, he's just the other way. Well, you know, he comes from Virginia, and you know how they are."

"Did he come tonight?" said her host.   7

"No, he couldn't," she said. "I'm a regular grass widow tonight. I told him when I left, 'There's no telling what I'll do,' I said. He was just so tired out, he couldn't move. Isn't it a shame?"

"Ah," said her host.   8

"Wait till I tell him I met Walter Williams!" she said. "He'll just about die. Oh, we have more arguments about colored people. I talk to him like I don't know what, I get so excited. 'Oh, don't be so silly,' I say. But I must say for Burton, he's heaps broader-minded than lots of these Southerners. He's really awfully fond of colored people. Well, he says himself, he wouldn't have white servants. And you know, he had this old colored nurse, this regular old nigger mammy, and he just simply loves her. Why, every time he goes home, he goes out in the kitchen to see her. He does, really, to this day. All he says is, he says he hasn't got a word to say against colored people as long as they keep their place. He's always doing things for them—giving them clothes and I don't know what all. The only thing he says, he says he wouldn't sit down at the table with one for a million dollars. 'Oh,' I say to him, 'you make me sick, talking like that.' I'm just terrible to him. Aren't I terrible?"

"Oh, no, no, no," said her host. "No, no."   9

"I am," she said. "I know I am. Poor Burton! Now, me, I don't feel that way at all. I haven't the slightest feeling about colored people. Why, I'm just crazy about some of them. They're just like children—just as easygoing, and always singing and laughing and everything. Aren't they the happiest things you ever saw in your life? Honestly, it makes me laugh just to hear them. Oh, I like them. I really do. Well, now, listen, I have this colored laundress, I've had her for years, and I'm devoted to her. She's a real character. And I want to tell you, I think of her as my friend. That's the way I think of her. As I say to Burton, 'Well, for Heaven's sakes, we're all human beings!' Aren't we?"

10   "Yes," said her host. "Yes, indeed."

"Now this Walter Williams," she said. "I think a man like that's a real artist. I do. I think he deserves an awful lot of credit. Goodness, I'm so crazy about music or anything, I don't care *what* color he is. I honestly think if a person's an artist, nobody ought to have any feeling at all about meeting them. That's absolutely what I say to Burton. Don't you think I'm right?"

11   "Yes," said her host. "Oh, yes."

"That's the way I feel," she said. "I just can't understand people being narrow-minded. Why, I absolutely think it's a privilege to meet a man like Walter Williams. Yes, I do. I haven't any feeling at all. Well, my goodness, the good Lord made him, just the same as He did any of us. Didn't He?"

12   "Surely," said her host. "Yes, indeed."

"That's what I say," she said. "Oh, I get so furious when people are narrow-minded about colored people. It's just all I can do not to say something. Of course, I do admit when you get a bad colored man, they're simply terrible. But as I say to Burton, there are some bad white people, too, in this world. Aren't there?"

13   "I guess there are," said her host.

"Why, I'd really be glad to have a man like Walter Williams come to my house and sing for us some time!" she said. "Of course, I couldn't ask him on account of Burton, but I wouldn't have any feeling about it at all. Oh, can't he sing! Isn't it marvelous, the way they all have music in them? It just seems to be right *in* them. Come on, let's go on over and talk to him. Listen, what shall I do when I'm introduced? Ought I to shake hands? Or what?"

14   "Why, do whatever you want," said her host.

"I guess maybe I'd better," she said. "I wouldn't for the world have him think I had any feeling. I think I'd better shake hands, just the way I would with anybody else. That's just exactly what I'll do."

15   They reached the tall young Negro, standing by the bookcase. The host performed introductions; the Negro bowed.

16   "How do you do?" he said.

The woman with the pink velvet poppies extended her hand at the length of her arm and held it so for all the world to see, until the Negro took it, shook it, and gave it back to her.

17   "Oh, how do you do, Mr. Williams," she said. "Well, how do you do. I've just been saying, I've enjoyed your singing so awfully much. I've been to your concerts, and we have you on the phonograph and everything. Oh, I just enjoy it!"

18   She spoke with great distinctness, moving her lips meticulously, as if in parlance with the deaf.

19   "I'm so glad," he said.

"I'm just simply crazy about that 'Water Boy' thing you sing," she said. "Honestly, I can't get it out of my head. I have my husband nearly crazy, the way I go around humming it all the time. Oh, he looks just as black as the ace of—Well. Tell me, where on earth do you ever get all those songs of yours? How do you ever get hold of them?"

20   "Why," he said, "there are so many different—"

21   "I should think you'd love singing them," she said. "It must be more fun. All those darling old spirituals—oh, I just love them! Well, what are you doing, now? Are you still keeping up your singing? Why don't you have another concert, some time?"

"I'm having one the sixteenth of this month," he said.   22

"Well, I'll be there," she said. "I'll be there, if I possibly can. You can count on me. Goodness, here comes a whole raft of people to talk to you. You're just a regular guest of honor! Oh, who's that girl in white? I've seen her some place."

"That's Katherine Burke," said her host.   23

"Good Heavens," she said, "is that Katherine Burke? Why, she looks entirely different off the stage. I thought she was much better-looking. I had no idea she was so terribly dark. Why, she looks almost like—Oh, I think she's a wonderful actress! Don't you think she's a wonderful actress, Mr. Williams? Oh, I think she's marvelous. Don't you?"

"Yes, I do," he said.   24

"Oh, I do, too," she said. "Just wonderful. Well, goodness, we must give someone else a chance to talk to the guest of honor. Now, don't forget, Mr. Williams, I'm going to be at that concert if I possibly can. I'll be there applauding like everything. And if I can't come, I'm going to tell everybody I know to go, anyway. Don't you forget!"

"I won't," he said, "Thank you so much."   25

The host took her arm and piloted her into the next room.

"Oh, my dear," she said. "I nearly died! Honestly, I give you my word, I nearly passed away. Did you hear that terrible break I made? I was just going to say Katherine Burke looked almost like a nigger. I just caught myself in time. Oh, do you think he noticed?"

"I don't believe so," said her host.   26

"Well, thank goodness," she said, "because I wouldn't have embarrassed him for anything. Why, he's awfully nice. Just as nice as he can be. Nice manners, and everything. You know, so many colored people, you give them an inch, and they walk all over you. But he doesn't try any of that. Well, he's got more sense, I suppose. He's really nice. Don't you think so?"

"Yes," said her host.   27

"I liked him," she said. "I haven't any feeling at all because he's a colored man. I felt just as natural as I would with anybody. Talked to him as naturally, and everything. But honestly, I could hardly keep a straight face. I kept thinking of Burton. Oh, wait till I tell Burton I called him 'Mister'!"

Vocabulary

sidle (1)

Questions on Meaning and Technique

1. What kind of person is the main character of this story? How would you describe her to someone who has not read the story?

2. The woman insists blatantly that she has no racial prejudice. "I haven't any feeling at all," she repeatedly says. What evidence have you that she is wrong? Refer to specific passages in the story.

3. What are examples of the way the woman stereotypes blacks?

4. What is Burton's attitude toward blacks? Does it differ from the woman's?

5. What is the attitude of the host toward the woman? What is his role in the story?

READING FOR IDEAS

Conflicting sharply with the outward simplicity of its rhyming stanzas, this poem recounts a painful childhood memory of racial hate. Ask yourself, as you read, how young children such as this bigoted Baltimorean come to absorb such loathsome attitudes so early. What kind of adult do you think this young Baltimorean bigot promises to be? And what effect do you think this ugly encounter had on the speaker?

Incident

COUNTEE CULLEN

Countee Cullen (1903–1946) was born in New York City and educated at New York University and Harvard. He was a major member of the 1920s black literary explosion known as the Harlem Renaissance. His work includes Color *(1925),* Copper Sun *(1927), and* The Ballad of the Brown Girl *(1927).*

1   Once riding in old Baltimore,
           Heart-filled, head-filled with glee,
       I saw a Baltimorean
           Keep looking straight at me.

2   Now I was eight and very small,
           And he was no whit bigger,
       And so I smiled, but he poked out
           His tongue and called me, "Nigger."

3   I saw the whole of Baltimore
           From May until December:
       Of all the things that happened there
           That's all that I remember.

Questions on Meaning and Technique

1. What is the theme of this poem? State it in one complete sentence.

2. Why do you think the little boy from Baltimore called the speaker a "Nigger"? Comment on the social implications.

3. How does the title "Incident" stress the poem's theme?

4. In stanza 2, what contrast adds a sad irony to the poem?

5. How do we know that the speaker was not prepared to encounter prejudice?

6. What would your reaction be if you witnessed the incident described in the poem?

How to Write a Definition

Definition is the method of development used whenever it is necessary to clarify the meaning of any "fuzzy" or controversial word or term. In the course of an essay or a conversation, we often use words or expressions whose meanings are perfectly obvious to us but less so to our readers or listeners. Sometimes the problem lies with the word we have used—it may be either abstract or otherwise unclear, perhaps having many different meanings. Such, for instance, is no doubt the case with the word *love*. No matter how dictionaries strain to give a single meaning to this word, their cause is a lost one. Men and women who have been blissfully in love will think the word means happiness second only to paradise. But for many others—husbands who have been cuckolded, wives who have been betrayed, lovers who have been jilted—the word will carry a bitter sting. The meanings that many words have are similarly conditioned by our experience, making it necessary to define them in oral or written communication.

The *semantic triangle* is often used to explain why some words have murky meanings and others do not. Semanticists say that words evoke two responses from us. First, we may be clearly or dimly aware of the dictionary meaning of a word, which semanticists call its *referent*, and which is also known as its *denotation*. For instance, the word *grapefruit* has as its referent the particular tangy citrus fruit that we all know by that name. Little disagreement is possible in this case. One may show a picture of a grapefruit, or even produce an example of the fruit itself to settle an argument over what the word means. Where the referent of a word is an object or a thing, such as *grapefruit, textbook, pencil,* or *fountain pen,* the possibility of its meaning being misunderstood is lessened. "What do you mean by *paperclip?*" the puzzled Martian asks. You simply produce the thing and show it to the creature. Words that have visible referents are said to be *concrete;* words with nonvisible referents are said to be *abstract. Paperclip* is therefore a concrete word; *love* is an abstract word.

There is a second response that words evoke from us—known to semanticists as the *reference,* also known as its *connotation*—and here we are on unsteady ground. For the references of words are those feelings and emotions they arouse in us, and these are inseparable from our experiences with the words. Here we are entirely at the mercy of personal experiences. The jilted bridegroom will likely express the bitterest feelings about the word *love;* ask him what it means and he will probably rant on about "a sham, a charade, an illusion." On the other side, the contented husband of some 25 years will carry on about "sharing golden moments, reading the Sunday papers over coffee, bucking each other up in times of trouble" and that sort of thing. No matter how these two pore over a dictionary, they're hardly likely to reconcile their differing references about *love*. And because *love* is an abstract word with no visible referent, misunderstandings about its meaning are inevitable. It is precisely for such words that definitions are necessary.

The references of words are also affected by political or public experiences. During the years preceding the Second World War, for instance, Hitler repeatedly justified his designs on other countries by citing Germany's need for *Lebensraum*— territory for political and economic expansion. Eventually, this word came to signify *German imperialism* to the allies—something entirely different from what it meant to the Germans. Similarly, in the 1960s the phrase *law and order* was widely bandied about. To some it meant racial repression; to others, it signified opposition to public disorder. By 1968, when candidate Richard Nixon used the phrase in his

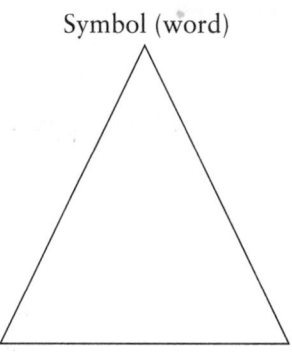

Symbol (word)

Reference (connotation)

thoughts, prejudices,
experiences associated
with the word

Referent (denotation)

what the word stands for,
the dictionary meaning

The Semantic Triangle

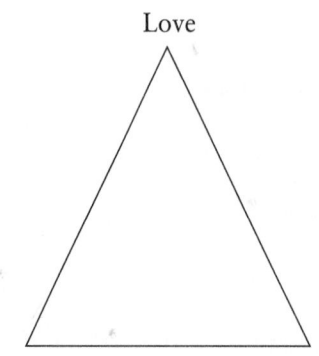

Love

Reference
(connotation)

sharing, giving,
supporting

Referent
(denotation)

deep and tender
feeling of
affection

Semantic triangle on *love*
from contented husband's
point of view

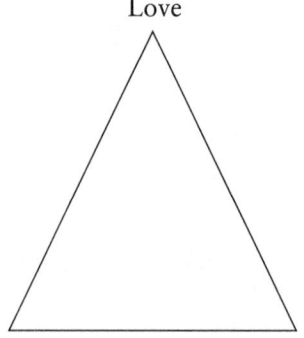

Love

Reference
(connotation)

sham, illusion,
charade

Referent
(denotation)

deep and tender
feeling of
affection

Semantic triangle on *love*
from jilted lover's point
of view

nomination acceptance speech, he was obliged to add:

> And to those who say that law and order is the code word for racism, here is a reply: Our goal is justice—justice for every American. If we are to have respect for law in America, we must have laws that deserve respect. Just as we cannot have progress without order, we cannot have order without progress.
>
> Richard Nixon, *Nomination Acceptance Speech,* 8 August 1968

This addition was necessary because the reference underlying this phrase had been so muddied that the phrase had become a polarizing catchword. Something similar seems to be happening today with the word *abortion.* The word has provoked so many vastly differing references in the minds of those who support and those who oppose abortion that it can no longer be said to have a single, clearcut meaning.

Writing Assignment

The story and poem depict dramatic instances of prejudice. Using them as your initial context, define *prejudice* in an essay. First, look up the referent of the word in a dictionary. Choose the definition that most closely corresponds to your own idea of the word's meaning. Then begin your essay by writing, "Prejudice is . . . ," stating and then expanding your definition.

[handwritten margin note: IN CLASS POSSIBILITY.]

Specific Instructions

PREWRITING ON THE ASSIGNMENT. *Prejudice* is one of those abstract words whose connotative meaning is difficult to pinpoint. On the surface, we know that it is a noun form of the verb "prejudge," which means to jump to conclusions about someone or something before we have the facts. But to enliven your essay, you need to move beyond denotative meaning and analyze the poisonous connotations of this word. One focus of your prewriting efforts, then, should be to gather historical, anecdotal, and testimonial accounts of prejudice and its ill effects.

Unless you live in an ideal world and are someone rare, you yourself have most likely either felt or inflicted prejudice. Perhaps your girlfriend's father became prejudiced against you because he thought you were too short, too fat, too foreign, too boring, or whatever. Or your boyfriend's mother might have rejected you for similar prejudicial reasons. These incidents, incorporated as extended examples in your essay, can shed light on the meaning of prejudice. Notice, for example, how chance encounters with prejudice are recounted in the sample student essay.

As for inflicting prejudice, even the saints among us have occasionally been guilty of that. Narrating these incidents of prejudice in ourselves can be painful but enlightening. You may have been prejudiced at some time in your life, for example, against fraternity members, business majors, football players, Girl Scouts, or army chaplains. Making notes about these occurrences and incorporating them into the essay as examples can add some zest to your definition.

Note, however, that in a formal essay you should not simply pack your definition with such personal anecdotes. You also need to research and find historical instances of prejudice to include in your essay (see Unit 17, The Research Paper, for suggestions about how to do this). Unhappily, American history is a warehouse swollen with innumerable cases of personal, institutional, and corporate prejudice. The Native Americans, for example, were widely regarded by westward-bound pioneers as chronic beggars who spent a good deal of their day sponging food from the wagon trains crossing the prairie. The pioneers did not understand that Native American tradition viewed food sharing as a sign of peace and friendship. Yet this entry from a pioneer woman's diary shows the prejudice that greeted this custom:

> The bucks with their bows and arrows, beaded buckskin garments and feather head gears were much in evidence and though these prairie redmen were generally friendly they were insistent beggars, often following us for miles and at mealtime disgustingly stood around and solicited food. They seldom molested us, however, but it was a case of the Indian, as well as the poor, "Ye always have with ye."
>
> Catherine Haun, "A Woman's Trip Across the Plains in 1849," manuscript diary

This sort of example, cited in the essay with appropriate commentary, can be an enlightening inclusion in your definition of prejudice.

USE THE ETYMOLOGY OF A WORD TO CLARIFY ITS MEANING. The etymology of a word or phrase provides information about its origins and earliest meanings. The dictionary is a rich source of etymologies, which are usually given in brackets after the entries. From Webster's *New World Dictionary,* second college edition, we learn that the word *boycott* was derived form Captain C. C. Boycott, a land agent in Ireland whose neighbors banded together against him; that *poet* comes from the Greek word *poietes,* meaning "one who makes"; that *prejudice* is the English equivalent of the Latin word *praejudicium,* which itself is a blend of *prae,* meaning "before," and *judicium,* meaning "judgment." The etymology usually gives a thumbnail history of the word or phrase that can throw light on its meaning. It is therefore often a good beginning point for a defining essay. Here, for example, is how one writer uses etymology to help define *botulism:*

> There are life-forms which, in the course of evolution, have developed poisons designed to kill, or to prevent themselves from being eaten. Venoms are produced by a variety of animals from jellyfish to reptiles. Plants develop a variety of poisonous substances designed to taste bad to an animal that nibbles and to kill if the animal persists.
>
> Pride of place, however, must be taken by the product of a bacterium which is to be found everywhere and which harms no one—ordinarily. It is *Clostridium botulinum. Clostridium* is Latin for "little spindle," which describes its shape, and *botulinum* is from the Latin word *botulus,* which means "sausage," where it has sometimes been detected.
>
> Isaac Asimov, "World's Most Deadly Poison . . . The Botulin Spore"
> *Science Digest,* January 1972

This etymology tells us not only what the spore looks like, but also where it has been found.

Even if a word or term has an unknown origin, sometimes a discussion of its probable beginnings can give a useful glimpse into its background. Here, for example, a writer speculates on where the baseball term *bullpen* came from:

> No one, much less the pitcher out there, knows quite why a bullpen is called as it is. One of the accepted theories is that the term is derived from the many Bull Durham tobacco signboards erected out beyond the outfield fences at the turn of the century. In 1909 the tobacco company put up 150 of these signs in baseball parks, the advertisements dominated by a large peaceful-looking domestic bull. Local merchants would pay up to $50 if a batter could hit the bull on the fly. Relief pitchers warmed up under or behind the sign, in an area many authorities believe began to be called the "bullpen."
>
> Others suspect the word is lifted from the prison term for the detention area where defendants waited until they stood trial, an accurate enough description of the life cycle of a relief pitcher. Yet another theory suggests that the bullpen was originally the area where fans were herded behind ropes, where they had to wait until an inning was over before being seated.
>
> George Plimpton, "The Lore of the Bullpen"

Obviously, not all words have fascinating etymologies. The recently minted, for instance, will seem as though they were spontaneously generated out of nothing as flies were once thought to be. Most such words are Americanisms. The etymologies of such words, for instance, as *hooker, blurb* (which was an arbitrary coinage), *milksop,* or *fall guy* are not especially useful. *Horse opera* seemed to have come from nowhere, and it is not especially enlightening to learn that *fiscal* comes from the Latin word *fiscus,* meaning "a basket of rushes, public chest." Yet where the etymology of a word tells something about its meaning, writers often use this information as a starting point for their definitions.

GIVE EXAMPLES, STATE FUNCTIONS, AND SHOW EFFECTS OF THE DEFINED TERM.   An adequate definition of a term requires more than a summary of its exact meaning. Often, it is necessary to expand on the lexical definition by giving examples, stating functions, and showing the effects of the defined term. Here, for instance, is a rather peppy paragraph from a student essay that attempts to define love by giving an extended example of its effects:

> Love is the pitter-patter of the heart, butterflies in the tummy, the invisible symphonies that swallows dance to on silken twilit evenings; but most of all, it is a sudden, urgent lunacy. As an example, I offer the night I met Julie. I had saved for months to go to dinner at Chez François. I had the meal all planned. Appetizer: oysters sauteed in olive oil. Main course: lobster steamed in wine with herb sauce. Vegetable: eggplant stuffed with mushrooms. Wine: a white Macon, which I was just about to select when I met Julie—the cocktail waitress. I took one look in her eyes and my appetite went down the tube. I know that's slang and that I should write something more elegant, but I actually felt my appetite dropping from my belly down to my toes—as if it fell down a tube—and, with a little imagination, I

thought I even saw it roll out on the carpet and scurry away like a routed mouse. The rest of the night I just kept ordering one drink after another so that Julie would come around and I could talk to her. I ate part of a lobster feeler and then abandoned the carcass to the vultures; the eggplant stayed on the plate as if some lobotomized hen had laid it there by mistake. I never touched a mushroom. All I did was drink, chat with Julie, make a desperate and inaudible moan to myself, and get roaringly drunk. $54.89 later and I ended up eating a McDonald's hamburger. That's love, brother, that's love.

A more sober example can be found in an essay by the late Scottish-born scholar Gilbert Highet, who set out to define *kitsch*. First, Mr. Highet tells us that the word *kitsch* is of Russian origin, that it "means vulgar showoff, and it is applied to anything that took a lot of trouble to make and is quite hideous." Then he proceeds to make this clearer by giving examples of kitsch:

> Of course, it is found in all the arts; think of Milan Cathedral, or the statues in Westminster Abbey, or Liszt's settings of Schubert songs. There is a lot of it in the United States—for instance, the architecture of Miami, Florida, and Forest Lawn Cemetery in Los Angeles. Many of Hollywood's most ambitious historical films are superb kitsch. Most Tin Pan Alley love songs were perfect 100 per cent kitsch.
>
> Gilbert Highet, *Kitsch*

The rest of the essay simply goes on to catalog one example after another of kitsch in literature.

Another dimension may be added to a definition by an analysis of the function of a term. For example, the sewing machine may be defined as a mechanism that allows a tailor or a seamstress to stitch cloth together automatically. This definition may then be extended by stating specific functions, as follows:

> There are over 2,000 varieties of modern sewing machines designed for stitching processes in the great sewing industries making up clothing, boots and shoes, corsets, hats, hosiery, etc. There are machines especially designed for sewing regular or fancy shank buttons on shoes; for sewing sweat leathers into stiff felt, soft felt or straw hats; for trimming scalloping and over-edging lace curtains; for sewing silk initials, monograms or floral designs upon material at one operation. There is a seven needle machine for making seven parallel rows of fine double chain stitching simultaneously. This machine is fitted with seven needles and seven loopers, and its capacity is 20,000 stitches per minute.
>
> *Encyclopaedia Britannica*

CLARIFY THE DEFINITION BY STATING WHAT THE TERM IS NOT. To explain what a thing is, it is often convenient also to say what it is not. By this kind of indirection, a writer can make clear what is meant by a certain term. Here, for example, are two paragraphs taken from the essay "The Sophisticated Man" by Marya Mannes. She has already defined the sophisticated man as one who has acquired certain "perceptions, tastes, and attitudes." She then proceeds to these two paragraphs. The first sketches the sophisticated man in action; the second presents his opposite as a contrast:

> Would you recognize this kind of man if you saw him across the room? I think so. He's the one with an attractive woman; conservatively dressed, but easy in his clothes. His hair is trimmed close to his head, but not too close. His hands are well-groomed, but not manicured. He does not laugh loudly or often. He is looking directly at the woman he speaks to, but he is not missing the other attractive women as they enter; a flick of the eye does it. For in all ways this man is not obvious. He would no more appear to examine a woman from the ankles up than he would move his head as he read or form the words with his lips. His senses are trained and his reflexes quick. And how did they get that way? From experience, from observation, and from deduction. He puts two and two together without adding on his fingers. He is educated in life.
>
> Now what about that fellow over there—the one in the light-grey suit and the crew cut? He is telling a long story rather loudly to a girl who would rather not be hearing it. He is not, of course, aware of this, since he is not only a little tight but unaccustomed to watching the reactions of women. He will look down the front of her dress but not see the glaze in her eyes. He has not been educated in observation. He is, according to the dictionary, unsophisticated in that he is natural and simple and lacking in experience.
>
> Marya Mannes, "The Sophisticated Man"

By knowing what the sophisticated man is not, we have a better idea of what he is.

In defining a migraine headache, one person noted that a migraine "is a headache so powerful that it can cause temporary blindness, terrible vomiting spells, over-powering fatigue, mental confusion, and acute sensitivity to any light or noise. While under the influence of a bad migraine, the victim may actually wish he or she could die because the pain is so devastating." So far the writer has defined a migraine headache by stating what it is. But then she sums up her definition by stating what a migraine is not: "In brief, a migraine is not your common variety of dull headache that can be cured with two aspirins or a cup of coffee." By providing a negative definition, the writer ensures that the reader understands the severity of migraine headaches.

AMPLIFY THE DEFINITION UNTIL THE MEANING IS CLEAR.   The kind of amplification that a writer should give depends, of course, on the term being defined. The only hard-and-fast rule is that one should give as much detail as necessary to make clear what a term or word means. Writers resort to a variety of guises to accomplish this. Here, for example, a writer is defining high blood pressure. First, he says clearly what it is; then he proceeds to detail its consequences on the human body:

> High blood pressure, or hypertension, is exactly what it says, a condition in which the blood is being pumped through the vast network of arteries with unusually high force. It's difficult to say at what point the blood pressure rises from "normal" to "high," as measured by the column of mercury on the doctor's

sphygmomanometer or blood pressure recorder. But generally physicians classify a person as hypertensive if his diastolic pressure—the smaller of the two-number pressure readings—is 95 millimeters of mercury or higher.

Everyone experiences temporary increases in blood pressure. Emotions can push up pressure for short periods, for instance. Indeed, a patient's apprehension about a blood pressure reading can raise his pressure a bit, which is why doctors usually insist on taking three readings in a two-week period before making a firm diagnosis of hypertension.

As late as the 1920's physicians didn't think high blood pressure was a threat to health. In fact, it was deemed a natural and necessary attempt by the body to keep sufficient blood flowing through arteries that were beginning to harden and narrow from age or disease.

In the last few years, however, researchers have developed hard evidence that high blood pressure, if left unchecked for a few years, sharply increases the risk of a heart attack, heart failure or a stroke leading to disability and/or death. Epidemiological studies such as the Framingham study, for instance, show the rate of heart attack among men whose diastolic pressure was 105 or higher was more than twice that of men with pressures of less than 95 and three and a half times that of men with pressures of less than 85 millimeters of mercury.

Jerry Bishop, I Think I'm Having a Heart Attack

USE OTHER RHETORICAL PATTERNS TO EXPAND ON YOUR DEFINITION. Where necessary or appropriate, writers will often add to their definitions by elaborating in successive paragraphs on various features, functions, and characteristics of a term. The paragraphs that follow may seem to be developed according to various methods—some may seem primarily descriptive, some essentially an analysis of effect. But each is working toward the ultimate goal of the writer—to define a medieval *tournament* and explain its place in the life of a knight:

Originating in France and referred to by others as "French combat" (*conflictus Gallicus*), tournaments started without rules or lists as an agreed-upon clash of opposing units. Though justified as training exercises, the impulse was the love of fighting. Becoming more regulated and mannered, they took two forms; jousts by individuals, and melees by groups of up to forty on a side, either *à plaisance* with blunted weapons or *à outrance* with no restraints, in which case participants might be severely wounded and not infrequently killed. Tournaments proliferated as the noble's primary occupation dwindled. Under the extended rule of monarchy, he had less need to protect his own fief, while a class of professional ministers was gradually taking his place around the crown. The less he had to do, the more energy he spent in tournaments artificially reenacting his role.

A tournament might last as long as a week and on great occasions two. Opening day was spent matching and seeding the players, followed by days set apart for jousts, for melees, for a rest day before the final tourney, all interspersed with feasting and parties. These occasions were the great sporting events of the time, attracting crowds of bourgeois spectators from rich merchants to common artisans, mountebanks, food vendors, prostitutes, and pickpockets. About a hundred knights usually participated, each accompanied by two mounted squires, an armorer, and six servants in livery. The knight had of course to equip himself with painted and gilded armor and crested helmet costing from 25 to 50 livres, with a war-horse costing from 25 to 100 livres in addition to his traveling palfrey, and with banners and trappings and fine clothes. Though the expense could easily bankrupt him, he might also come away richer, for the loser in combat had to pay a ransom and the winner was awarded his opponent's horse and armor, which he could sell back to him or to anyone. Gain was not recognized by chivalry, but it was present at tournaments.

Because of their extravagance, violence, and vainglory, tournaments were continually being denounced by popes and kings, from whom they drained money. In vain. When the Dominicans denounced them as a pagan circus, no one listened. When the formidable St. Bernard thundered that anyone killed in a tournament would go to Hell, he spoke for once to deaf ears. Death in a tournament was officially considered the sin of suicide by the Church, besides jeopardizing family and tenantry without cause, but even threats of excommunication had no effect. Although St. Louis condemned tournaments and Philip the Fair prohibited them during his wars, nothing could stop them permanently or dim the enthusiasm for them.

With brilliantly dressed spectators in the stands, flags and ribbons fluttering, the music of trumpets, the parade of combatants making their draped horses prance and champ on golden bridles, the glitter of harness and shields, the throwing of ladies' scarves and sleeves to their favorites, the bow of the heralds to the presiding prince who proclaimed the rules, the cry of poursuivants announcing their champions, the tournament was the peak of nobility's pride and delight in its own valor and beauty.

Barbara W. Tuchman, A Distant Mirror: The Calamitous 14th Century

It follows from all we have said in this section that the defining essay should give more than just a lexical meaning of a word, phrase, or term. Anyone can look in a dictionary and see the starkest, bare-bones summation of a referent. The essay that defines should give considerably more. It should show not only the mummified meaning of a term to be found in any dictionary, but also the living word as it exists in the mind of the individual writer.

READING FOR IDEAS

This excerpt comes from a speech given by Allport at the Claremont Colleges in 1952. Notice the lively oral style complete with short sentences and occasional slang. As you read, consider the differences between what Spinoza calls "love" prejudice, a positive bias in favor of someone or something, and "hate" prejudice, a negative bias against someone or something. In what ways are the two alike? What do you think are the obligations of a country that prides itself on democratic principles to suppress ethnic prejudice among its citizens? Do you regard prejudice as an unalterable fact of life or the results of ignorance? What are your own prejudices?

PROFESSIONAL MODEL

The Nature of Prejudice
GORDON ALLPORT

Gordon Allport (1897–1967) was an American psychologist born in Montezuma,
Indiana, and educated at Harvard. Allport was a president of the American
Psychological Association and a prolific author of books, among them The Psychol-
ogy of Radio *(1935),* Personality: A Psychological Interpretation *(1937),* The Nature of
Prejudice *(1954), and* Pattern and Growth in Personality *(1961).*

1   Before I attempt to define prejudice, let us have in mind four instances that I think we all would agree involve prejudice.

2   The first is the case of the Cambridge University student, who said, "I despise all Americans. But," he added, a bit puzzled, "I've never met one that I didn't like."

3   The second is the case of another Englishman, who said to an American, "I think you're awfully unfair in your treatment of Negroes. How *do* Americans feel about Negroes?" The American replied, "Well, I suppose some Americans feel about Negroes just the way you feel about the Irish." The Englishman said, "Oh, come now! The Negroes are human beings!"

4   Then there's the incident that occasionally takes place in various parts of the world (in the West Indies, for example, I'm told). When an American walks down the street the natives conspicuously hold their noses till the American goes by. The case of odor is always interesting. Odor gets mixed up with prejudice because odor has great associative power. We know that some Chinese deplore the odor of Americans. Some white people think Negroes have a distinctive smell and vice versa. An intrepid psychologist recently did an experiment; it went as follows. He brought to a gymnasium an equal number of white and colored students and had them take shower baths. When they were nice and clean he had them exercise vigorously for fifteen minutes. Then he put them in different rooms, and he put a clean white sheet over each one. Then he brought his judges in, and each went to the sheeted figures and sniffed. They were to say, "white" or "black," guessing at the identity of the subject. The experiment seemed to prove that when we are sweaty we all smell bad in the same way. It's good to have experimental demonstration of the fact.

5   The fourth example I'd like to bring before you is a piece of writing that I quote. Please ask yourselves, who, in your judgment, wrote it. It's a passage about the Jews.

> The synagogue is worse than a brothel. It's a den of scoundrels. It's a criminal assembly of Jews, a place of meeting for the assassins of Christ, a den of thieves, a house of ill-fame, a dwelling of iniquity. Whatever name more horrible to be found, it could never be worse than the synagogue deserves.
>
> I would say the same things about their souls. Debauchery and drunkenness have brought them to the level of lusty goat and pig. They know only one thing: to satisfy their stomachs and get drunk, kill, and beat each other up. Why should we salute

them? We should have not even the slightest converse with them. They are lustful, rapacious, greedy, perfidious robbers.

Now who wrote that? Perhaps you say Hitler, or Goebbels, or one of our local 6 anti-Semites? No, it was written by Saint John Chrysostom, in the fourth century A.D. Saint John Chrysostom, as you know, gave us the first liturgy in the Christian church still used in the Orthodox churches today. From it all services of the Holy Communion derive. Episcopalians will recognize him also as the author of that exalted prayer that closes the offices of both matin and evensong in the *Book of Common Prayer.** I include this incident to show how complex the problem is. Religious people are by no means necessarily free from prejudice. In this regard be patient even with our saints.

What do these four instances have in common? You notice that all of them indicate 7 that somebody is "down" on somebody else—a feeling of rejection, or hostility. But also, in all these four instances, there is indication that the person is not "up" on his subject—not really informed about Americans, Irish, Jews, or bodily odors.

So I would offer, first a slang definition of prejudice: *Prejudice is being down on* 8 *somebody you're not up on.* If you dislike slang, let me offer the same thought in the style of St. Thomas Aquinas. Thomists have defined prejudice as *thinking ill of others without sufficient warrant.*

You notice that both definitions, as well as the examples I gave, specify two ingredients 9 of prejudice. First there is some sort of faulty generalization in thinking about a group. I'll call this the process of *categorization.* Then there is the negative, rejective, or hostile ingredient, a *feeling* tone. "Being down on something" is the hostile ingredient; "that you're not up on" is the categorization ingredient; "Thinking ill of others" is the hostile ingredient; "without sufficient warrant" is the faulty categorization.

Parenthetically I should say that of course there is such a thing as *positive* prejudice. 10 We can be just as prejudiced *in* favor of as we are against. We can be biased in favor of our children, our neighborhood or our college. Spinoza makes the distinction neatly. He says that *love prejudice* is "thinking well of others, through love, more than is right." *Hate prejudice,* he says, is "thinking ill of others, through hate, more than is right."

Vocabulary

associative (4)	iniquity (5)	perfidious (5)	liturgy (6)
deplore (4)	rapacious (5)	anti-Semites (6)	matin (6)

Questions on Meaning and Technique

1. How does the author begin his essay? What is his purpose?
2. Why does the author think that odor often gets mixed up in prejudice?
3. The author refers to an experimental demonstration that proves that odor is not associated with race. What other firmly held beliefs have been negated by experimental demonstrations?

---

*The book of services and prayers used in the Church of England.

4. Why does the author end paragraph 6 by saying, "In this regard be patient even with our saints"?

5. What is the author's slang definition of *prejudice?* What is his more literary definition?

6. What is a present-day example of the process of categorization?

7. What is "positive prejudice"? What examples does the author supply?

8. Who is Spinoza? Look him up in your dictionary.

9. In your opinion, what are the pitfalls resulting from both negative and positive prejudice?

10. What is your own definition of *prejudice?* What are some of your prejudices? How do you deal with them? What prejudices in others bother you most?

STUDENT ESSAY

First Draft   Cole Ollinger

titled supplied

Prejudice: Child of Ignorance

(Insert A)

The added introduction, paraphrasing Shakespeare, gives the title a literary flavor and is less trite.

The American Heritage Dictionary defines prejudice as "the state or act of holding   1

unreasonable preconceived judgments or convictions." The word ~~itself~~ is rooted in the

closely

Latin "praejudicium," ~~loosely~~ translated as "previous judgment," an origin that remains

relevant to the current popular meaning.

For instance,

transition added

Prejudice is often confused with simple preference. ʌ Gentlemen may prefer blonds to   2

Or,   may

brunettes without ~~accurately~~ being accused of showing prejudice. ʌ A person ~~usually~~

certain

chooses a ~~favorite~~ style of clothing or flavor of ice cream without prejudice. These are

merely

~~simply~~ matters of taste.

for instance,   convinced a driver   model

transitional clause added

(Insert B) If experience has ~~guided someone~~ to purchase one ~~brand~~ of car instead of another,   3

experience

sexist pronoun avoided

then this person is not showing prejudice because ~~his knowledge~~ is applicable. I owned

Ford   kept breaking down;

an American ~~car~~ that ~~performed inconsistently~~ so now I own a dependable Japanese

(Insert A)

Prejudice by any other name would still be the
lowest form of thinking. It squints when it looks
and lies when it talks. It restrains civilization
with the manacles of cruel barbarism.

(Insert B)

Prejudice is often confused with reasoned choice.

Honda
~~model.~~ In this instance, I am not prejudiced~~.~~ ⟨Insert C⟩ My father, on the other hand, buys

irrationally
American cars strictly out of patriotic chauvinism, ~~innately~~ distrusting Japanese,

German, French, or any other foreign cars; ~~thus,~~ he exhibits prejudice when shopping

for automobiles.

In short, an unfavorable   is not prejudicial, but
4   ~~If a disfavorable~~ opinion or decision ~~is~~ based on ~~a study of~~ facts ~~then no prejudice~~
when it is based on pure bias, it is prejudicial.
~~exists. For example,~~ a bank that refuses a loan to someone with a poor credit rating ~~has~~
years of
not acted with prejudice~~.~~; ⟨Insert D⟩

5   Prejudice is a common occurrence that can ~~severely~~ damage ~~a particular group of~~

people.
No
6   ¶ Recently, at a party I attended, I was the ~~focal point~~ of a relatively harmless yet
victim
annoying kind of prejudice. A group of guests had gathered in a corner to discuss books

recently read. I expressed my admiration for Walker Percy's novels; then someone else

brought up the Beat Generation writers, such as Allen Ginsberg and Jack Kerouac. The

conversation became animated as everyone either praised or condemned the Beat

because
writers. But for some reason, my comments were ignored. The group felt that ~~since~~ I

liked Walker Percy, I couldn't possibly understand the literature of the Beat Generation.

In actuality, I am quite familiar with this group of writers, and the ignorant conclusions

of the other people at the party showed prejudice. ⟨Insert E⟩ The Romans' cruel attitude toward
this
the early Christians is an example of ~~another, much more~~ brutal kind of prejudice.

Jupiter and other
7   At a time when most Romans still worshipped mythological gods, the Christian faith
forbidden
was ~~considered taboo.~~ In their bitter scorn of Christianity, the Romans unmercifully
stoning, crucifying, and
tortured helpless Christians, forcing them to hide in caves and catacombs even though

they were doing nothing wrong.

⟨Insert C⟩
against American cars; I simply made a choice
based on sound reasoning.

⟨Insert D⟩
however, a bank that refuses to give someone a loan
just because that person looks poor is being prejudiced.

⟨Insert E⟩
While my experience was inconsequential and
hurt only me, prejudice can result in enormous
cruelty with global consequences. For instance,

sentence needed
completion

w/more accurate

Revision makes
paragraph more
coherent and
emphatic.

no ¶ needed

new paragraph
with transitional
sentence needed

no ¶ needed

details added

In our own century, Adolf Hitler carried out a campaign of atrocities against ~~the~~   8

Jews. Propagating the lie that Jews belonged to an inferior race, Hitler ordered them

starved, gassed, or executed. Six million people, including defenseless women and

children, died as a result of this dictator's infamous prejudice.

> *Original version is too inclusive.*

Americans have ~~been equally guilty~~ _not been free_ of prejudice. To this day, blacks are still the   9

frequent victims of _groundless_ suspicion and derision that originated over two hundred years ago.

Initially, blacks were socially and economically suppressed as slaves. Then, after finally

being given their freedom as a result of the Civil War, they were continually terrorized

by white supremacist groups like the Ku Klux Klan. Ironically, even the American

government played a role in this prejudice--clear into the 1960s--by denying blacks the

right to vote. Insensitive whites _today_ continue to label blacks as "niggers" or "coons." And

in the 1988 Super Bowl game, the fact that the Washington quarterback, Doug Williams,

was a black became a burning issue, albeit one that was completely irrelevant to the

player's ability to gain a victory for his team.

> *Repetition of key word prejudice helps coherence.*
>
> *clarifies the kind of prejudice*

Other minority groups have encountered ~~similar difficulties~~ _prejudice_ in our country. Americans   10

have ~~always~~ _often_ treated immigrants with hostility. ~~Again,~~ in recent history, ~~these~~ _certain immigrant_ groups

were given nicknames that obviously manifested prejudice _against their national origins_. Italians were called "dagos"

or "wops." Chinese were called "chinks." Japanese were called "japs." All Irishmen

were considered hopeless drunks; people from Oklahoma were thought of as stupid and

> *avoids needless repetition of and in same sentence*

dirty; ~~and~~ Mexicans were reputed to be lazy and undependable. An even subtler and far

more damaging prejudice than this childish name calling was the harm done by

companies and individuals who, without the slightest reason, flatly refused to hire

immigrants simply because they were not American born.

In the job market, women have been victims of prejudice. For many years our culture   11

dictated that a woman's place was in the home; hence, women were seldom given the

> *avoids specificity and prunes deadwood*

chance to prove their abilities _in prestigious professions_. Men ~~in general~~ were thought to be more capable of suc-

~~cessful performance~~ in the corporate world. Salary figures emphasized this point as men

~~standardly~~ _usually_ earned more money than women in the same job. This is a textbook example

of prejudice. With great effort and much litigation, American women have significantly

improved their situation in recent years, but cases of sexual prejudice linger on.

12　Women in other parts of the world ~~have not been so fortunate.~~ *continue to be held back by prejudice* In the Arabic
countries, *for example,* women are still rarely permitted to speak in public and must cover their
heads and faces with a <u>chador</u> in order to prevent them~~selves~~ from ~~tempting~~ *seducing* strange
men. These women are certainly not evil temptresses, but because of a centuries-old
tradition, they are treated as if showing their faces were a~~s~~ indecorous~~, as showing~~
~~their breasts.~~

more accurate

13　Prejudice occurs so often that everyone has, in some form or another, felt its effects.
Recently, I have felt the sting of prejudice from blacks. I am white, but I like to play
basketball in a predominantly black section of town. Frequently my black teammates
will not pass me the ball because of my color and because they consider me a stranger.
I have also felt the prejudice ~~against~~ *leveled at* people who are excessively tall. Because of my
height, other basketball players insist that I play close to the basket instead of playing
guard, which is my natural position. Even the playground is filled with prejudice.

w/more honest

14　Another area of prejudice is product manufacture. Anyone who is taller than six feet
feels the prejudice of stores who never sell beds that are long enough to keep a tall
person's feet from dangling off the end of the mattress. People who are left-handed also
feel victimized by manufacturer prejudice because they rarely can find golf clubs, school
desks, guitars, or other items to suit their left-handedness.

15　Prejudice exists everywhere and ranges from petty social exclusion ~~of a person~~ to
violent persecution ~~of an entire race.~~ Whenever people make decisions based on
preconceived ideas--whether on the sidewalk or in the boardroom--they act with
prejudice.

prunes deadwood, making the conclusion more concise

STUDENT ESSAY

Final Draft　　　　　　　　　　　　　　　　　　　　　　　　　Cole Ollinger

Prejudice: Child of Ignorance

Prejudice by any other name would still be the lowest form of thinking. It squints when　　1
it looks and lies when it talks. It restrains civilization with the manacles of cruel
barbarism. *The American Heritage Dictionary* defines *prejudice* as "the state or act of

holding unreasonable preconceived judgments or convictions." The word is rooted in the Latin "praejudicium," closely translated as "previous judgment," an origin that remains relevant to the current popular meaning.

2   Prejudice is often confused with simple preference. For instance, gentlemen may prefer blonds to brunettes without being accused of showing prejudice. Or, a person may choose a certain style of clothing or flavor of ice cream without prejudice. These are merely matters of taste.

3   Prejudice is often confused with reasoned choice. If, for instance, experience has convinced a driver to purchase one model of car instead of another, then this person is not showing prejudice because experience is applicable. I owned an American Ford that kept breaking down; so now I own a dependable Japanese Honda. In this instance, I am not prejudiced against American cars; I simply made a choice based on sound reasoning. My father, on the other hand, buys American cars strictly out of patriotic chauvinism, irrationally distrusting Japanese, German, French, or any other foreign cars; he exhibits prejudice when shopping for automobiles. A bank that refuses a loan to someone with years of bad credit ratings has not acted with prejudice; however, a bank that refuses to give someone a loan just because that person looks poor is being prejudiced. In short, an unfavorable opinion or decision based on facts is not prejudicial, but when it is based on pure bias, it is prejudicial.

4   Prejudice is a common occurrence that can damage people. Recently, at a party I attended, I was the victim of a relatively harmless yet annoying kind of prejudice. A group of guests had gathered in a corner to discuss books recently read. I expressed my admiration for Walker Percy's novels; then someone else brought up the Beat Generation writers, such as Allen Ginsberg and Jack Kerouac. The conversation became animated as everyone either praised or condemned the Beat writers. But for some reason, my comments were ignored. The group felt that because I liked Walker Percy, I couldn't possibly understand the literature of the Beat Generation. In actuality, I am quite familiar with this group of writers, and the ignorant conclusions of the other people at the party showed prejudice.

5   While my experience was inconsequential and hurt only me, prejudice can result in enormous cruelty with global consequences. For instance, the Romans' cruel attitude

toward the early Christians is an example of this brutal kind of prejudice. At a time when most Romans still worshipped Jupiter and other mythological gods, the Christian faith was forbidden. In their bitter scorn of Christianity, the Romans unmercifully tortured helpless Christians, stoning, crucifying, and forcing them to hide in caves and catacombs even though they were doing nothing wrong.

In our own century, Adolf Hitler carried out a campaign of atrocities against Jews.   6
Propagating the lie that Jews belonged to an inferior race, Hitler ordered them starved, gassed, or executed. Six million people, including defenseless women and children, died as a result of this dictator's infamous prejudice.

Americans have not been free of prejudice. To this day, blacks are still the frequent   7
victims of groundless suspicion and derision that originated over two hundred years ago. Initially, blacks were socially and economically suppressed as slaves. Then, after finally being given their freedom as a result of the Civil War, they were continually terrorized by white supremacist groups like the Ku Klux Klan. Ironically, even the American government played a role in this prejudice—clear into the 1960s—by denying blacks the right to vote. Insensitive whites today continue to label blacks as "niggers" or "coons." And in the 1988 Super Bowl game, the fact that the Washington quarterback, Doug Williams, was a black became a burning issue, albeit one that was completely irrelevant to the player's ability to gain a victory for his team.

Other minority groups have encountered prejudice in our country. Americans have   8
often treated immigrants with hostility. In recent history, certain immigrant groups were given nicknames that obviously manifested prejudice against their national origins. Italians were called "dagos" or "wops." Chinese were called "chinks." Japanese were called "japs." All Irishmen were considered hopeless drunks; people from Oklahoma were thought of as stupid and dirty; Mexicans were reputed to be lazy and undependable. An even subtler and far more damaging prejudice than this childish name calling was the harm done by companies and individuals who, without the slightest reason, flatly refused to hire immigrants simply because they were not American-born.

In the job market, women have been victims of prejudice. For many years our culture   9
dictated that a woman's place was in the home; hence, women were seldom given the

chance to prove their abilities in prestigious professions. Men were thought to be more capable of success in the corporate world. Salary figures emphasized this point as men usually earned more money than women in the same job. This is a textbook example of prejudice. With great effort and much litigation, American women have significantly improved their situation in recent years, but cases of sexual prejudice linger on.

10   Women in other parts of the world continue to be held back by prejudice. In the Arabic countries, for example, women are still rarely permitted to speak in public and must cover their heads and faces with a *chador* in order to prevent them from seducing strange men. These women are certainly not evil temptresses, but because of a centuries-old tradition, they are treated as if showing their faces were indecorous.

11   Prejudice occurs so often that everyone has, in some form or another, felt its effects. Recently, I have felt the sting of prejudice from blacks. I am white, but I like to play basketball in a predominantly black section of town. Frequently my black teammates will not pass me the ball because of my color and because they consider me a stranger. I have also felt the prejudice leveled at people who are excessively tall. Because of my height, other basketball players insist that I play close to the basket instead of playing guard, which is my natural position. Even the playground is filled with prejudice.

12   Another area of prejudice is product manufacture. Anyone who is taller than six feet feels the prejudice of stores who never sell beds that are long enough to keep a tall person's feet from dangling off the end of the mattress. People who are left-handed also feel victimized by manufacturer prejudice because they rarely can find golf clubs, school desks, guitars, or other items to suit their left-handedness.

13   Prejudice exists everywhere and ranges from petty social exclusion to violent persecution. Whenever people make decisions based on preconceived ideas—whether on the sidewalk or in the boardroom—they act with prejudice.

READING FOR IDEAS

The author of this moving essay was stricken with a degenerative disease at age 29 and has been coping with its fateful progression every since. In this emotional essay, she calls herself a "cripple" and writes unflinchingly about herself, her disease, and its effects on her. It is a measure of our present squeamishness about the physically stricken that "cripple" has virtually evolved into a taboo, used only coarsely as an insult. Yet, insists the author, it is the word that fits her best. What do you think of the euphemisms that have lately trickled into our vocabulary as descriptions of the handicapped? Do you agree with the author that it is less demeaning to a disabled person to be called a "cripple" than some polite euphemism such as "physically challenged"?

ALTERNATE READING

A Life Defined by Losses and Delights

Nancy Mairs

Nancy Mairs, writer, was born in Long Beach, California, in 1943. She attended Wheaton College (A.B. in English Literature, 1964) and the University of Arizona (Ph.D. in English, 1972). Between 1966 and 1972 she was a technical editor for the Smithsonian Astrophysical Laboratory, MIT Press, and the Harvard Law School. In 1972 she was diagnosed as having multiple sclerosis. She is the author of a poetry collection, In All the Rooms of the Yellow House *(1984, winner of the Western States Book Award), and of* Plaintext *(1986).*

I am a cripple. I choose this word to name me. I choose from among several   1
possibilities, the most common of which are "handicapped" or "disabled." I made the choice a number of years ago, unaware of my motives for doing so. People—crippled or not—wince at the word "cripple," as they do not at "handicapped" or "disabled." Perhaps I want them to wince. I want them to see me as a tough customer, one to whom the fates/gods/viruses have not been kind, but who can face the truth of her existence squarely. As a cripple, I swagger.

"Cripple" seems to me a clean word, straightforward and precise. As a lover of words,   2
I like the accuracy with which it describes by condition: I have lost the full use of my limbs. "Disabled," by contrast, suggests any incapacity, physical or mental. And I certainly don't like "handicapped," which implies that I have deliberately been put at a disadvantage, by whom I can't imagine, in order to equalize chances in the great race of life. These words seem to me to be moving away from my condition, to be widening the gap between word and reality. Most remote is the recently coined euphemism "differently abled," which strikes me as pure verbal garbage designed, by its ability to describe anyone, to describe no one.

I haven't always been crippled, a fact for which I am grateful. To be whole of limb is,   3
I know from experience, infinitely more pleasant and useful than to be crippled; and if that knowledge leaves me open to bitterness at my loss, the physical soundness I once enjoyed (though I did not enjoy it half enough) is well worth the occasional stab of regret.

When I was 28 I started to trip and drop things. What at first seemed my natural   4
clumsiness soon became too pronounced to shrug off. I consulted a neurologist, who told

me that I had a brain tumor. About a year and a half later I developed a blurred spot in one eye. I had, at last, the episodes requisite for a diagnosis: multiple sclerosis. I have never been sorry for the doctor's initial misdiagnosis, however. For almost a week, until the negative results of the tests were in, I thought that I was going to die right away. Every day for the past nearly 10 years, then, has been a kind of gift. I accept all gifts.

5   Multiple sclerosis is a chronic degenerative disease of the central nervous system; during its course, which is unpredictable and uncontrollable, one may lose vision, hearing, speech, and ability to walk, control of bladder and/or bowels, strength in any or all extremities, sensitivity to touch, vibration, and/or pain, potency, coordination of movements—the list of possibilities is lengthy and, yes, horrifying. One may also lose one's sense of humor. That's the easiest to lose and the hardest to survive without.

6   In the past 10 years, I have sustained some of these losses; my disease has been slowly progressive. My left leg is now so weak that I walk with the aid of a brace and a cane. I no longer have much use of my left hand. Now my right side is weakening as well. Overall, though, I've been lucky so far; the terrain left me has been ample enough to continue many activities that absorb me: writing, teaching, raising children and plants and snakes, reading, speaking publicly about MS and depression, even playing bridge with people honorable enough to let me scatter cards without sneaking a peek.

7   Lest I begin to sound like Pollyanna, however, let me say that I don't like having MS. I hate it. My life holds realities—harsh ones, some of them—that no right-minded human being ought to accept without grumbling: One of them is fatigue. I know of no one with MS who does not complain of bone-weariness; I wake up in the morning feeling the way most people do at the end of a bad day, and I take it from there.

8   I am lucky that my predilections were already solitary, sedentary, and bookish. I am a superb, if messy, cook. I play a fiendish game of Scrabble. I like to sit on my front steps with my husband as we make sure that the sun gets down once more behind the sharp childish scrawl of the Tucson Mountains.

9   This lively plenty has its bleak complement, of course, in all the things I can no longer do. I will never run, except in dreams, and I can no longer pick up babies, play piano, braid my hair. I am immobilized by acute attacks of depression, which may or may not be related to MS.

10   These two elements, the plenty and the privation, are never pure, nor are the delight and wretchedness that accompany them. The most important struts in the framework of my existence, of course, are my husband and children. Dismayingly few marriages survive the MS test, and why should they? Most 22- and 19-year-olds, like George and me, can vow in clear conscience, after a childhood of chicken pox and summer colds, to keep one another in sickness and in health so long as they both shall live. Not many are equipped for the dismay, the extra work, the boredom that a degenerative disease can insinuate into a relationship. Children experience similar stresses when faced with a crippled parent, and they are more helpless, since parents and children can't usually get divorced. Deprived of legal divorce, the child can at least deny the mother's disability, even her existence, forgetting to tell her about recitals and PTA meetings, never inviting friends to the house. Many do.

But I've been limping along for 10 years now, and so far George and the children are   11
still at my left elbow, holding tight. Anne and Matthew vacuum floors and dust furniture
and rake up dog droppings with just enough grumbling so I know that they don't have
brain fever. And far from hiding me, they're forever welcoming gaggles of friends while
I'm wandering through the house in Anne's filmy pink baby doll pajamas. And they all
yell at me, laugh at some of my jokes, in short, treat me as an ordinary human being. I
think they like me. Unless they're faking. . . .

Faking. There's the rub. Tugging at the fringes of my consciousness always is the   12
terror that people are kind to me only because I'm a cripple. My mother almost shattered
me once, with that instinct mothers have for striking blows along the fault-lines of their
children's hearts, by telling me, in an attack on my selfishness, "We all have to make
allowances for you, of course, because of the way you are." She was awfully angry but at
the time I felt my worst fear, suddenly realized. I could bear being called selfish: I am. But
I couldn't bear the corroboration that those around me were doing what I'd always
suspected them of doing, professing fondness while silently putting up with me because
of the way I am. A cripple. I've been a little cracked ever since.

Along with this fear comes a relentless pressure to please. Part of the pressure arises   13
from social expectations. In our society, anyone who deviates from the norm had better
find some way to compensate. Like fat people, who are expected to be jolly, cripples
must bear their lot meekly and cheerfully. A grumpy cripple isn't playing by the rules.
And much of the pressure is self-generated. Early on I vowed that, if I had to have MS, by
God I was going to do it well. This is a class act, ladies and gentlemen.

Because I hate being crippled, I sometimes hate myself for being a cripple. Over the years   14
I have come to expect—even accept—attacks of violent self-loathing. Physical imperfection,
even freed of moral disapprobation, still defies and violates the ideal, especially for women,
whose confinement in their bodies as objects of desire is far from over. Today's ideal woman,
who lives on the glossy pages of dozens of magazines, seems to be between the ages of 18
and 25; her hair has body, her underarms are dry; she has a career but is still a fabulous cook,
especially of meals that take less than 20 minutes to prepare; she jogs, swims, plays tennis,
sails, but does not bowl. Though usually white and often blonde, she may be black, Hispanic,
Asian, or Native American, so long as she is unusually sleek. She may be old, provided she
is selling a laxative or is Lauren Bacall. But she is never a cripple.

At my age, however, I don't spend much time thinking about my appearance. The   15
burning egocentricity of adolescence, which assures one that all the world is looking all
the time, has passed; I'm also too old to believe in the accuracy of self-image. The
self-loathing I feel is neither physically nor intellectually substantial. What I hate is not me
but a disease.

I am not a disease.   16

And a disease is not—at least not single-handedly—going to determine who I am.   17

I learned that one never finishes adjusting to MS. One does not, after all, finish   18
adjusting to life, and MS is simply a fact of my life—not my favorite fact, of course—but
as ordinary as my nose and my yellow Mazda station wagon. It may at any time get
worse, but no amount of worry can prepare me for a new loss. My life is a lesson in
losses. I learn one at a time.

19   The absence of a cure often makes MS patients bitter toward their doctors. Doctors are, after all, the priests of modern society whose business is to heal. Doctors too think of themselves as healers, and for this reason many have trouble dealing with MS patients, whose disease in its intransigence defeats their aims and mocks their skills. Too few doctors, it is true, treat their patients as whole human beings, but the reverse is also true. I have always tried to be gentle with my doctors, who often have more at stake in terms of ego than I do. I may be frustrated by the incurability of my disease, but I am not diminished by it, and they are.

20   This gentleness is part of the reason I'm not sorry to be a cripple. I didn't have it before. It has opened my life enormously.

21   If a cure were found, would I take it? In a minute. I may be a cripple, but I'm only occasionally a loony and never a saint. Anyway, in my brand of theology God doesn't give bonus points for a limp.

Vocabulary

euphemism (2)	complement (9)	corroboration (12)
predilections (8)	privation (10)	egocentricity (15)
sedentary (8)	insinuate (10)	intransigence (19)

Questions on Meaning and Technique

1. This essay is anthologized in the chapter on definition. What definition may it be said to attempt?

2. Why do euphemisms seem to widen the gap between word and reality?

3. Why do you think the word *cripple* has fallen into polite disuse? What connotations does this word hold for you?

4. By what mode is paragraph 4 developed?

5. What kind of paragraphs does the author mainly use? In what kind of publication do you think this originally appeared?

6. How would you characterize the tone of this essay? What can you infer about the author from her tone?

7. What do you think about the author's assertion that the confinement of women "in their bodies as objects of desire is far from over"? Do you agree or disagree with her on this point? Justify your answer.

8. What is the attitude of the author toward her doctors?

Writing Assignments

1. Write an extended definition of the word *euphemism*.

2. Write an essay defining AIDS.

READING FOR IDEAS

Definitions do not have to be dour and dull, as this one shows. Nor do we have to know the name of a verbal error to make it. Whether or not we know the proper name of the mispronunciation defined in this piece, most of us have occasionally committed a spoonerism. Donald not only defines *spoonerism* for us, he also treats us to a brief but hilarious biography of Spooner himself. As you read, ask yourself how understatement contributes to the humor of this article. What rhetorical strategy does the author heavily rely on to advance the definition?

ALTERNATE READING

Will Someone Please Hiccup My Pat?

WILLIAM SPOONER DONALD

William Spooner Donald (b. 1910) was a career British navy officer between 1924 and 1949 and has been a freelance writer since leaving the service. A nephew of the famous Reverend William Archibald Spooner, from whose transpositions of initial syllables the term spoonerism *was derived, Donald has written screenplays, plays, and memoirs, among them* Hong Kong Cocktail *(play, 1951),* Pickled Salts *(play, 1951),* Stand by for Action *(memoir, 1956), and* Hanky Panky in the Highlands *(play, 1968).*

One afternoon nearly a hundred years ago the October wind gusted merrily down   1
Oxford's High Street. Hatless and helpless, a white-haired clergyman with pink cherubic features uttered his plaintive cry for aid. As an athletic youngster chased the spinning topper, other bystanders smiled delightedly—they had just heard at first hand the latest "Spoonerism."

My revered relative William Archibald Spooner was born in 1844, the son of a   2
Staffordshire county court judge. As a young man, he was handicapped by a poor physique, a stammer, and weak eyesight; at first, his only possible claim to future fame lay in the fact that he was an albino, with very pale blue eyes and white hair tinged slightly yellow.

But nature compensated the weakling by blessing him with a brilliant intellect. By   3
1868 he had been appointed a lecturer at New College, Oxford. Just then he would have been a caricaturist's dream with his freakish looks, nervous manner, and peculiar mental kink that caused him—in his own words—to "make occasional felicities in verbal diction."

Victorian Oxford was a little world of its own where life drifted gently by; a world   4
where splendid intellectuals lived in their ivory towers of Latin, Euclid, and Philosophy; a world where it was always a sunny summer afternoon in a countryside, where Spooner admitted he loved to "pedal gently round on a well-boiled icicle."

5   As the years passed, Spooner grew, probably without himself being aware of the fact, into a "character." A hard worker himself, he detested idleness and is on record as having rent some lazybones with the gem, "You have hissed all my mystery lessons, and completely tasted two whole worms."

6   With his kindly outlook on life, it was almost natural for him to take holy orders; he was ordained a deacon in 1872 and a priest in 1875. His unique idiosyncrasy never caused any serious trouble and merely made him more popular. On one occasion, in New College chapel in 1879, he announced smilingly that the next hymn would be "Number one seven five—Kinkering Kongs their Titles Take." Other congregations were treated to such jewels as ". . . Our Lord, we know, is a shoving Leopard . . ." and ". . . All of us have in our hearts a half-warmed fish to lead a better life. . . ."

7   Spooner often preached in the little village churches around Oxford and once delivered an eloquent address on the subject of Aristotle. No doubt the sermon contained some surprising information for his rustic congregation. For after Spooner had left the pulpit, an idea seemed to occur to him, and he hopped back up the steps again.

8   "Excuse me, dear brethren," he announced brightly, "I just want to say that in my sermon whenever I mentioned Aristotle, I should have said Saint Paul."

9   By 1885 the word "Spoonerism" was in colloquial use in Oxford circles, and a few years later, in general use all over England. If the dividing line between truth and myth is often only a hairsbreadth, does it really matter? One story that has been told concerns an optician's shop in London. Spooner is reputed to have entered and asked to see a "signifying glass." The optician registered polite bewilderment.

10   "Just an ordinary signifying glass," repeated Spooner, perhaps surprised at the man's obtuseness.

11   "I'm afraid we haven't one in stock, but I'll make inquiries right away, sir," said the shopkeeper, playing for time.

12   "Oh, don't bother, it doesn't magnify, it doesn't magnify," said Spooner airily, and walked out.

13   Fortunately for Spooner, he made the right choice when he met his wife-to-be. He was thirty-four years old when he married Frances Goodwin in 1878. The marriage was a happy one, and they had one son and four daughters. Mrs. Spooner was a tall, good-looking girl, and on one occasion the family went on a short holiday in Switzerland. The "genial Dean," as he was then called, took a keen interest in geology, and in no time at all he had mastered much information and many technical definitions on the subject of glaciers.

14   One day at lunchtime the younger folk were worried because their parents had not returned from a long walk. When Spooner finally appeared with his wife, his explanation was: "We strolled up a long valley, and when we turned a corner we found ourselves completely surrounded by erotic blacks."

15   He was, of course, referring to "erratic blocks," or large boulders left around after the passage of a glacier.

16   In 1903 Spooner was appointed Warden of New College, the highest possible post for a Fellow. One day walking across the quadrangle, he met a certain Mr. Casson, who had just been elected a Fellow of New College.

17   "Do come to dinner tonight," said Spooner, "we are welcoming our new Fellow, Mr. Casson."

18   "But, my dear Warden, I *am* Casson," was the surprised reply.

"Never mind, never mind, come along all the same," said Spooner tactfully. 19

On another occasion in later years when his eyesight was really very bad, Spooner 20
found himself seated next to a most elegant lady at dinner. In a casual moment the latter
put her lily-white hand onto the polished table, and Spooner, in an even more casual
manner, pronged her hand with his fork, remarking genially, "My bread, I think."

In 1924 Spooner retired as Warden. He had established an astonishing record of 21
continuous residence at New College for sixty-two years first as undergraduate, then as
Fellow, then Dean, and finally as Warden. His death in 1930, at the age of eighty-six,
was a blushing crow to collectors of those odd linguistic transpositions known by then
throughout the English-speaking world as Spoonerisms.

Vocabulary

plaintive (1)
caricaturist (3)
idiosyncrasy (6)
colloquial (9)
obtuseness (10)

Questions on Meaning and Technique

1. What does the title have to do with the definition in this essay?
2. What is the main technique used by the author in defining *spoonerism?*
3. Why does the author put quotation marks around "character" in paragraph 5? What does "character" mean, used in this sense?
4. Where does the author finally tell us what a *spoonerism* is? Why does he wait so long?
5. What sort of treatment do you think Spooner's odd mental kink might have received, say, in a modern business environment? Do you think it would have been treated with equal geniality and tolerance?
6. What is the point of paragraph 4, and why was making it necessary?
7. What part do you think Oxford played in the coinage of the term *spoonerism?*

Writing Assignments

1. Write a definition of the word *pun*, giving several examples of it.
2. Define *sarcasm* and *irony* in an essay, making a distinction between them.

READING FOR IDEAS

Few words are as incendiary as the word *nigger*, an early form of which was first
used—as this article tells us—in the manifest of a Dutch slave ship that dropped
anchor at Jamestown, Virginia, in 1619. What dismays this writer is the adoption of

the term by black performers, especially rappers, who defiantly use it to refer to themselves. As you read this article, ask yourself whether the conflict is merely one of lexical definition or one that exists between cultures and generations in the black community.

ALTERNATE READING

The Power of a Word
Leonard Pitts, Jr.

Leonard Pitts, Jr., is the pop music critic for the Miami Herald. *He is the author of several books on the pop music scene, among them* Papa Joe's Boys *(1983) and* Reach Out: The Diana Ross Story *(1983).*

1   I write today about a word.

2   Nigger.

3   Go ahead, try it out. Roll it around in your mind. Test it out on your ear. *Listen* to it.

4   Nigger.

5   I've always hated the sound of it—the harsh grinding of those two consonants hitting each other like pieces of an ice floe.

6   I've always hated the fact of it, too. It is a low, mean word that demeans both the user and the person he or she uses it against.

7   And yet . . .

8   As an American alive in the waning days of the 20th century, I can't escape that word.

9   It comes not just from the expected places—not just from boobs in bedsheets with dunce caps on their heads or dirt-dumb, Confederate flag-waving bozos from Birmingham to Boston.

10   No, I hear it more, hear it louder, hear it uttered with a perverse and unfathomable pride, in music. It seeps from the CD player, drips out of the radio, booms forth from the car next to mine at the stoplight.

11   Virtually every rapper who values his macho strut uses it. Ice-T flies it like a banner: "Straight-Up Nigga" goes the song title. N.W.A flaunts it as a given name: The acronym stands for Niggaz With Attitude. Ice Cube, KRS-One and other rap tough guys use it interchangeably to mean "friend," "brother," "homeboy" or "African-American man."

12   Yes, there are isolated islands of self-respect, where rappers risk their cool to save their dignity. Public Enemy declared in '91, "I don't wanna be called 'Yo, Niga.'" But it was like spitting into the wind.

13   Two summers ago I spoke to a group of young journalism students. Three black kids, sitting together, challenged my contention that rap was wrong to popularize the word "nigger." They asked me what was wrong with it.

14   I was shocked. They truly didn't know.

I know the counterarguments, most of them so lame they ought to be on crutches.   15
The most popular one holds that constant use will demystify the word, rob it of its hateful, hurtful sting.

Comedian Paul Mooney subscribes to that theory. He recently sent out a pamphlet   16
advertising his new album, "Race."

It was designed so that when you opened it, the word assaulted you: "NIGGER" in   17
big, fat type. The word was repeated, growing a little smaller each time until at the bottom of the page, it had become infinitesimal.

It was a powerful piece of graphic art. It was also a lie. Because contrary to popular   18
belief, "nigger" does not diminish with use.

It was in late August 1619 that the history of the African-American people began, as   19
a Dutch ship dropped anchor at Jamestown, Va. The ship's manifest listed among its cargo 20 "Negars"—indentured servants.

That was 374 years ago. Since then, the word has been in constant, nonstop   20
use—snarled by the overseer, spat by the factory boss, whispered by the intellectual, chanted by the lynch mob and yes, bantered with fraternal good cheer by blacks among blacks.

Can anyone argue that all that use has diminished the word? Can anyone say that it   21
has lost its sting?

Noted thinker Axl Rose once defended his use of "nigger" by claiming that the word   22
doesn't necessarily connote black people but any contemptible human being, no matter the race. Interesting theory. Since we're now in the business of giving new meaning to ancient terms, why stop with "nigger"? Let's declare that "moronic" means wonderful and "jerk" means man. And then let's agree that Rose is the most moronic jerk to come along in years.

Funny, it didn't sound like a compliment, did it?   23

The strange thing about all this is that once, not too long ago, the movers and shakers   24
of black pop culture rose up, almost as if on cue, and rejected the word "nigger."

Much of that revolved around comedian Richard Pryor, whose 1974 break-through   25
album was called "That Nigger's Crazy." But in the late '70s, Mr. Pryor publicly renounced the word, which had long been a staple of his humor. He explained his reasons in an Ebony magazine profile and also in a comedy routine in which he recounted his visit to a thriving African city. He told of walking on streets teeming with Africans, streets on which no matter where he turned, he saw faces and skin tones that mirrored his own. In a moment of stunning, revelatory power, Mr. Pryor said, he began to understand something of what a white man feels walking down a street in America. "I suddenly realized, I didn't see any niggers."

The rest of the black entertainment community soon followed Mr. Pryor's lead;   26
indeed, the rest of black America followed them all. It became less acceptable to use the ugly word—even in jest, even in private. "Nigger" went up on that high shelf where we, African-Americans, stored all the other artifacts of our degradation and self-hatred. It went up there next to all the old slanders about foulness and inferiority, up there behind the creams that claimed to bleach your complexion white and right in front of the scalp-scalding preparations that were supposed to give you "good" hair.

27   It stayed there for years and pretty much gathered dust. Until about 1987 or so, when the gangsta rappers came along, pulled it down, polished it up and made it new again. They've worn it proudly since then: a perverse badge of ignorant cool.

28   I'm reminded of a song written in 1900 by author and civil rights pioneer James Weldon Johnson. Its proper title is "Lift Ev'ry Voice and Sing," but it is probably better known as "The Negro National Anthem." It says, in part:

29   "Stony the road we trod, bitter the chastening rod, felt in the days when hope, unborn had died. Yet with a steady beat, have not our weary feet, come to the place for which our fathers died."

30   And I'm forced to wonder. Is *this* the place for which our fathers died? This place in which African-Americans degrade and malign themselves with an ugly old word whose only proper place is the dustbin of history? Because if this *is* that place, and if those lies are indeed truth, if that word is all that we are or can be, then let's not stop here, let's set the whole record straight. Pull out the history books, and let's do some wholesale revision.

31   Frederick Douglass, pioneering abolitionist. Nigger.

32   George Washington Carver, brilliant scientist. Nigger.

33   Rosa Parks, mother of the civil rights movement. Nigger.

34   Emmett Till, 14-year-old lynch victim. Nigger.

35   Maya Angelou, poet. Nigger.

36   Dr. Martin Luther King Jr., martyred civil rights leader. Nigger.

37   Seven years ago, I wrote a poem for Black History Month. One passage goes:

38   "Who am I?

39   I am a mammy.

40   I am a coon, a spade, a jungle bunny, a jig-a-boo, a darky, a beast . . . a shiftless, good for nothing nigger.

41   At least, that's what I was told.

42   God help me, that's what I sometimes
Believed."

43   God help us all. Because some of us still do.

Vocabulary

demeans (6)	infinitesimal (17)	artifacts (26)
perverse (10)	indentured (19)	degradation (26)
acronym (11)	renounced (25)	malign (30)

Questions on Meaning and Technique

1. What device does the author use for emphasis that is not commonly available to the student writer of essays?

2. Why was the author so shocked to find out that some young black students did not know the hateful meanings associated with the word *nigger*? What hopeful sign might be read in this ignorance?

(*Continued on page 260.*)

Photo Writing Assignment

Three girls talking to a police officer. © Leonard Freed/Magnum Photos, Inc.

Write an essay defining *authority* as you imagine it is perceived by these children. Is the police officer threatening, mean, and fearsome; or, is he benevolent and friendly? Pay particular attention to the officer's body language and to the little girls' reaction.

3. What is your opinion of the theory that repeated use of a crude word will demystify it and diminish its significance?

4. How would you characterize the author's introduction to Axl Rose in paragraph 22?

5. According to the author, comedian Richard Pryor reportedly claimed that when he was in Africa he "began to understand what a white man feels walking down a street in America." What feeling do you think Pryor meant? What opposite feeling might a black person in America routinely experience?

6. Pitts writes in paragraph 27: "Until about 1987 or so, when the gangsta rappers came along. . . ." How do you explain his use of the word *gangsta?*

7. What implicit definition does the author propose for the word *nigger?* How does this definition differ, if it does, from the one seemingly intended by the rappers?

8. In his final paragraph, of what does Pitts implicitly accuse those who flaunt the use of the word? Do you agree with his charge?

9. The author invites the reader to say the word out loud, to really listen to it. When you do, how does using it make you feel? Why?

Writing Assignments

1. Write a definition of the word *nigger* as you think it is meant by the rappers. If necessary, cite some lines from rap music to support your definition.

2. A burning issue in the South lately has been the incorporation of the Confederate emblem in many state flags. Write an essay defining what the Confederate flag symbolizes to you.

Additional Writing Assignments

Beginning with a lexical definition and extending the definition into a full essay, define one of the following terms. Be sure your essay answers the question, "What is it?"

1. alienation	2. respectability
3. fanaticism	4. good manners
5. marital fidelity	6. happiness
7. virtue	8. hypocrisy
9. TB	10. mercy
11. evil	12. no-fault insurance

Comparison/Contrast

READING FOR IDEAS

In "Chaste Clarissa" a self-indulgent, promiscuous male meets a beautiful married woman whom he wants to seduce. The setting for this story is Holly Cove, a fictional resort island off the coast of New England, where well-established families vacation in a leisurely social setting. The residents of Holly Cove know each other well and gossip about events and people associated with their little island. The conflict of the story resides in the clash between Clarissa and Baxter, two characters with completely different ambitions and images of self. The difference between the two is important in creating the tension of the narrative plot. As you read this story, try to compare and contrast the personalities of Baxter and Clarissa by focusing on specific traits that belong to each. Also try to understand the contrasting backgrounds that motivate their behaviors.

The Chaste Clarissa
JOHN CHEEVER

John Cheever (1912–1982) was an American writer of fiction. Born in Quincy, Massachusetts, from middle-class parents, Cheever began his writing career at seventeen by publishing a series of sketches titled "Expelled" in the New Republic. He received growing recognition for his short stories satirizing the upper middle class with their pretenses and problems. His best stories were published in the New Yorker. Most often his stories center on the choices people make to avoid the lack of adventure or ecstasy attending standard suburban life. Cheever's characters tend to bury their marital woes and boredom in fantasies. Among Cheever's short story collections are the following: The Way Some People Live *(1943),* The Enormous Radio *(1953),* The Housebreaker of Shady Hill *(1958), and* The World of Apples *(1972). In 1978, all of his short stories were collected in one volume,* The Stories of John Cheever. *Cheever has also written several novels, among them* The Wapshot Chronicle *(1957),* The Wapshot Scandal *(1964),* Bullet Park *(1969), and* O What a Paradise It Seems *(1982).*

1   The evening boat for Vineyard Haven was loading freight. In a little while, the warning whistle would separate the sheep from the goats—that's the way Baxter thought of it—the islanders from the tourists wandering through the streets of Woods Hole. His car, like all the others ticketed for the ferry, was parked near the wharf. He sat on the front bumper, smoking. The noise and movement of the small port seemed to signify that the spring had ended and that the shores of West Chop, across the Sound, were the shores of summer, but the implications of the hour and the voyage made no impression on Baxter at all. The delay bored and irritated him. When someone called his name, he got to his feet with relief.

2   It was old Mrs. Ryan. She called to him from a dusty station wagon, and he went over to speak to her. "I knew it," she said. "I knew that I'd see someone here from Holly Cove. I had that feeling in my bones. We've been traveling since nine this morning. We had trouble with the brakes outside Worcester. Now I'm wondering if Mrs. Talbot will have cleaned the house. She wanted seventy-five dollars for opening it last summer and I told her I wouldn't pay her that again, and I wouldn't be surprised if she's thrown all my letters away. Oh, I hate to have a journey end in a dirty house, but if worse comes to worst, we can clean it ourselves. Can't we, Clarissa?" she asked, turning to a young woman who sat beside her on the front seat. "Oh, excuse me, Baxter!" she exclaimed. "You haven't met Clarissa, have you? This is Bob's wife, Clarissa Ryan."

3   Baxter's first thought was that a girl like that shouldn't have to ride in a dusty station wagon; she should have done much better. She was young. He guessed that she was about twenty-five. Red-headed, deep-breasted, slender, and indolent, she seemed to belong to a different species from old Mrs. Ryan and her large-boned, forthright daughters. " 'The Cape Cod girls, they have no combs. They comb their hair with codfish bones,' " he said to himself but Clarissa's hair was well groomed. Her bare arms were perfectly white. Woods Hole and the activity on the wharf seemed to bore her and she was not interested in Mrs. Ryan's insular gossip. She lighted a cigarette.

4   At a pause in the old lady's monologue, Baxter spoke to her daughter-in-law. "When is Bob coming down, Mrs. Ryan?" he asked.

5   "He isn't coming at all," the beautiful Clarissa said. "He's in France. He's—"

6   "He's gone there for the government," old Mrs. Ryan interrupted, as if her daughter-in-law could not be entrusted with this simple explanation. "He's working on this terribly interesting project. He won't be back until autumn. I'm going abroad myself. I'm leaving Clarissa alone. Of course," she added forcefully, "I expect that she will *love* the island. Everyone does. I expect that she will be kept very busy. I expect that she—"

7   The warning signal from the ferry cut her off. Baxter said goodbye. One by one, the cars drove aboard, and the boat started to cross the shoal water from the mainland to the

resort. Baxter drank a beer in the cabin and watched Clarissa and old Mrs. Ryan, who were sitting on deck. Since he had never seen Clarissa before, he supposed that Bob Ryan must have married her during the past winter. He did not understand how this beauty had ended up with the Ryans. They were a family of passionate amateur geologists and bird-watchers. "We're all terribly keen about birds and rocks," they said when they were introduced to strangers. Their cottage was a couple of miles from any other and had, as Mrs. Ryan often said, "been thrown together out of a barn in 1922." They sailed, hiked, swam in the surf, and organized expeditions to Cuttyhunk and Tarpaulin Cove. They were people who emphasized *corpore sano** unduly, Baxter thought, and they shouldn't leave Clarissa alone in the cottage. The wind had blown a strand of her flame-colored hair across her cheek. Her long legs were crossed. As the ferry entered the harbor, she stood up and made her way down the deck against the light salt wind, and Baxter, who had returned to the island indifferently, felt that the summer had begun.

Baxter knew that in trying to get some information about Clarissa Ryan he had to be careful. He was accepted in Holly Cove because he had summered there all his life. He could be pleasant and he was a good-looking man, but his two divorces, his promiscuity, his stinginess, and his Latin complexion had left with his neighbors a vague feeling that he was unsavory. He learned that Clarissa had married Bob Ryan in November and that she was from Chicago. He heard people say that she was beautiful and stupid. That was all he did find out about her.   8

He looked for Clarissa on the tennis courts and the beaches. He didn't see her. He went several times to the beach nearest the Ryans' cottage. She wasn't there. When he had been on the island only a short time, he received from Mrs. Ryan, in the mail, an invitation to tea. It was an invitation that he would not ordinarily have accepted, but he drove eagerly that afternoon over to the Ryans' cottage. He was late. The cars of most of his friends and neighbors were parked in Mrs. Ryan's field. Their voices drifted out of the open windows into the garden, where Mrs. Ryan's climbing roses were in bloom. "Welcome aboard!" Mrs. Ryan shouted when he crossed the porch.   9

"This is my farewell party. I'm going to Norway." She led him into a crowded room.   10

Clarissa sat behind the teacups. Against the wall at her back was a glass cabinet that held the Ryan's geological specimens. Her arms were bare. Baxter watched them while she poured his tea. "Hot? . . . Cold? Lemon? . . . Cream?" seemed to be all she had to say, but her red hair and her white arms dominated that end of the room. Baxter ate a sandwich. He hung around the table.   11

"Have you ever been to the island before, Clarissa?" he asked.   12

"Yes."   13

"Do you swim at the beach at Holly Cove?"   14

"It's too far away."   15

"When your mother-in-law leaves," Baxter said, "you must let me drive you there in the mornings. I go down at eleven."   16

*Healthy body.

17   "Well, thank you." Clarissa lowered her green eyes. She seemed uncomfortable, and the thought that she might be susceptible crossed Baxter's mind exuberantly. "Well, thank you," she repeated, "but I have a car of my own and—well, I don't know, I don't—"

18   "What are you two talking about?" Mrs. Ryan asked, coming between them and smiling wildly in an effort to conceal some of the force of her interference. "I know it isn't geology," she went on, "and I know that it isn't birds, and I know that it can't be books or music, because those are all things that Clarissa doesn't like, aren't they, Clarissa? Come with me, Baxter," and she led him to the other side of the room and talked to him about sheep raising. When the conversation had ended, the party itself was nearly over. Clarissa's chair was empty. She was not in the room. Stopping at the door to thank Mrs. Ryan and say goodbye, Baxter said that he hoped she wasn't leaving for Europe immediately.

19   "Oh, but I am," Mrs. Ryan said. "I'm going to the mainland on the six-o'clock boat and sailing from Boston at noon tomorrow."

20   At half past ten the next morning, Baxter drove up to the Ryans' cottage. Mrs. Talbot, the local woman who helped the Ryans with their housework, answered the door. She said that young Mrs. Ryan was home, and let him in. Clarissa came downstairs. She looked more beautiful than ever, although she seemed put out at finding him there. She accepted his invitation to go swimming, but she accepted it unenthusiastically. "Oh, all right," she said.

21   When she came downstairs again, she had on a bathrobe over her bathing suit, and a broad-brimmed hat. On the drive to Holly Cove, he asked about her plans for the summer. She was noncommittal. She seemed preoccupied and unwilling to talk. They parked the car and walked side by side over the dunes to the beach, where she lay in the sand with her eyes closed. A few of Baxter's friends and neighbors stopped to pass the time, but they didn't stop for long, Baxter noticed. Clarissa's unresponsiveness made it difficult to talk. He didn't care.

22   He went swimming. Clarissa remained on the sand, bundled in her wrap. When he came out of the water, he lay down near her. He watched his neighbors and their children. The weather had been fair. The women were tanned. They were all married women and, unlike Clarissa, women with children, but the rigors of marriage and childbirth had left them all pretty, agile, and contented. While he was admiring them, Clarissa stood up and took off her bathrobe.

23   Here was something else, and it took his breath away. Some of the inescapable power of her beauty lay in the whiteness of her skin, some of it in the fact that, unlike the other women, who were at ease in bathing suits, Clarissa seemed humiliated and ashamed to find herself wearing so little. She walked down toward the water as if she were naked. When she first felt the water, she stopped short, for, again unlike the others, who were sporting around the pier like seals, Clarissa didn't like the cold. Then, caught for a second between nakedness and the cold, Clarissa waded in and swam a few feet. She came out of the water, hastily wrapped herself in the robe, and lay down in the sand. Then she spoke, for the first time that morning—for the first time in Baxter's experience—with warmth and feeling.

"You know, those stones on the point have grown a lot since I was here last," she   24
said.

"What?" Baxter said.   25

"Those stones on the point," Clarissa said. "They've grown a lot."   26

"Stones don't grow," Baxter said.   27

"Oh yes they do," Clarissa said. "Didn't you know that? Stones grow. There's a stone   28
in Mother's rose garden that's grown a foot in the last few years."

"I didn't know that stones grew," Baxter said.   29

"Well, they do," Clarissa said. She yawned; she shut her eyes. She seemed to fall   30
asleep. When she opened her eyes again, she asked Baxter the time.

"Twelve o'clock," he said.   31

"I have to go home," she said. "I'm expecting guests."   32

Baxter could not contest this. He drove her home. She was unresponsive on the ride,   33
and when he asked her if he could drive her to the beach again, she said no. It was a hot,
fair day and most of the doors on the island stood open, but when Clarissa said goodbye
to Baxter, she closed the door in his face.

Baxter got Clarissa's mail and newspapers from the post office the next day, but when   34
he called with them at the cottage, Mrs. Talbot said that Mrs. Ryan was busy. He went
that week to two large parties that she might have attended, but she was not at either. On
Saturday night, he went to a barn dance, and late in the evening—they were dancing
"Lady of the Lake"—he noticed Clarissa, sitting against the wall.

She was a striking wallflower. She was much more beautiful than any other woman   35
there, but her beauty seemed to have intimidated the men. Baxter dropped out of the
dance when he could and went to her. She was sitting on a packing case. It was the first
thing she complained about. "There isn't even anything to sit on," she said.

"Don't you want to dance?" Baxter asked.   36

"Oh, I love to dance," she said. "I could dance all night, but I don't think *that's*   37
dancing." She winced at the music of the fiddle and the piano. "I came with the Hortons.
They just told me there was going to be a dance. They didn't tell me it was going to be
this kind of a dance. I don't like all that skipping and hopping."

"Have your guests left?" Baxter asked.   38

"What guests?" Clarissa said.   39

"You told me you were expecting guests on Tuesday. When we were at the beach."   40

"I didn't say they were coming on Tuesday, did I?" Clarissa asked. "They're coming   41
tomorrow."

"Can't I take you home?" Baxter asked.   42

"All right."   43

He brought the car around to the barn and turned on the radio. She got in and   44
slammed the door with spirit. He raced the car over the back roads, and when he brought
it up to the Ryans' cottage, he turned off the lights. He watched her hands. She folded
them on her purse. "Well, thank you very much," she said. "I was having an awful time
and you saved my life. I just don't understand this place, I guess. I've always had plenty of
partners, but I sat on that hard box for nearly an hour and nobody even spoke to me. You
saved my life."

"You're lovely, Clarissa," Baxter said.   45

46   "Well," Clarissa said, and she sighed. "That's just my outward self. Nobody knows the real me."

47   That was it, Baxter thought, and if he could only adjust his flattery to what she believed herself to be her scruples would dissolve. Did she think of herself as an actress, he wondered, a Channel swimmer, an heiress? The intimations of susceptibility that came from her in the summer night were so powerful, so heady, that they convinced Baxter that here was a woman whose chastity hung by a thread.

48   "I think I know the real you," Baxter said.

49   "Oh no you don't," Clarissa said. "Nobody does."

50   The radio played some lovelorn music from a Boston hotel. By the calendar, it was still early in the summer, but it seemed, from the stillness and the hugeness of the dark trees, to be much later. Baxter put his arms around Clarissa and planted a kiss on her lips.

51   She pushed him away violently and reached for the door. "Oh, now you've spoiled everything," she said as she got out of the car. "Now you've spoiled everything. I know what you've been thinking. I know you've been thinking it all along." She slammed the door and spoke to him across the window. "Well, you needn't come around here any more, Baxter," she said. "My girl friends are coming down from New York tomorrow on the morning plane and I'll be too busy to see you for the rest of the summer. Good night."

52   Baxter was aware that he had only himself to blame; he had moved too quickly. He knew better. He went to bed feeling angry and sad, and slept poorly. He was depressed when he woke, and his depression was deepened by the noise of a sea rain, blowing in from the northeast. He lay in bed listening to the rain and the surf. The storm would metamorphose the island. The beaches would be empty. Drawers would stick. Suddenly he got out of bed, went to the telephone, called the airport. The New York plane had been unable to land, they told him, and no more planes were expected that day. The storm seemed to be playing directly into his hands. At noon, he drove in to the village and bought a Sunday paper and a box of candy. The candy was for Clarissa, but he was in no hurry to give it to her.

53   She would have stocked the icebox, put out the towels, and planned the picnic, but now the arrival of her friends had been postponed, and the lively day that she had anticipated had turned out to be rainy and idle. There were ways, of course, for her to overcome her disappointment, but on the evidence of the barn dance he felt that she was lost without her husband or her mother-in-law, and that there were few, if any, people on the island who would pay her a chance call or ask her over for a drink. It was likely that she would spend the day listening to the radio and the rain and that by the end of it she would be ready to welcome anyone, including Baxter. But as long as the forces of loneliness and idleness were working on his side, it was shrewder, Baxter knew, to wait. It would be best to come just before dark, and he waited until then. He drove to the Ryans' with his box of candy. The windows were lighted. Clarissa opened the door.

54   "I wanted to welcome your friends to the island," Baxter said. "I—"

55   "They didn't come," Clarissa said. "The plane couldn't land. They went back to New York. They telephoned me. I had planned such a nice visit. Now everything's changed."

56   "I'm sorry, Clarissa," Baxter said. "I've brought you a present."

"Oh!" She took the box of candy. "What a beautiful box! What a lovely present! 57
What—" Her face and her voice were, for a minute, ingenuous and yielding, and then he
saw the force of resistance transform them. "You shouldn't have done it," she said.

"May I come in?" Baxter asked.   58

"Well, I don't know," she said. "You can't come in if you're just going to sit around."   59

"We could play cards," Baxter said.   60

"I don't know how," she said.   61

"I'll teach you," Baxter said.   62

"No," she said. "No, Baxter, you'll have to go. You just don't understand the kind of   63
woman I am. I spent all day writing a letter to Bob. I wrote and told him that you kissed
me last night. I can't let you come in." She closed the door.

From the look on Clarissa's face when he gave her the box of candy, Baxter judged   64
that she liked to get presents. An inexpensive gold bracelet or even a bunch of flowers
might do it, he knew, but Baxter was an extremely stingy man, and while he saw the
usefulness of a present, he could not bring himself to buy one. He decided to wait.

The storm blew all Monday and Tuesday. It cleared on Tuesday night, and by   65
Wednesday afternoon the tennis courts were dry and Baxter played. He played until
late. Then, when he had bathed and changed his clothes, he stopped at a cocktail
party to pick up a drink. Here one of his neighbors, a married woman with four
children, sat down beside him and began a general discussion of the nature of married
love.

It was a conversation, with its glances and innuendoes, that Baxter had been through   66
many times, and he knew roughly what it promised. His neighbor was one of the pretty
mothers that Baxter had admired on the beach. Her hair was brown. Her arms were thin
and tanned. Her teeth were sound. But while he appeared to be deeply concerned with
her opinions on love, the white image of Clarissa loomed up in his mind, and he broke
off the conversation and left the party. He drove to the Ryans'.

From a distance, the cottage looked shut. The house and the garden were perfectly   67
still. He knocked and then rang. Clarissa spoke to him from an upstairs window.

"Oh, hello, Baxter," she said.   68

"I've come to say goodbye, Clarissa," Baxter said. He couldn't think of anything   69
better.

"Oh, dear," Clarissa said. "Well, wait just a minute. I'll be down."   70

"I'm going away, Clarissa," Baxter said when she opened the door. "I've come to say   71
goodbye."

"Where are you going?"   72

"I don't know." He said this sadly.   73

"Well, come in, then," she said hesitantly. "Come in for a minute. This is the last time   74
that I'll see you, I guess, isn't it? Please excuse the way the place looks. Mr. Talbot got sick
on Monday and Mrs. Talbot had to take him to the hospital on the mainland, and I
haven't had anybody to help me. I've been all alone."

He followed her into the living room and sat down. She was more beautiful than ever.   75
She talked about the problems that had been presented by Mrs. Talbot's departure. The
fire in the stove that heated the water had died. There was a mouse in the kitchen. The
bathtub wouldn't drain. She hadn't been able to get the car started.

76   In the quiet house, Baxter heard the sound of a leaky water tap and a clock pendulum. The sheet of glass that protected the Ryans' geological specimens reflected the fading sky outside the window. The cottage was near the water, and he could hear the surf. He noted these details dispassionately and for what they were worth. When Clarissa finished her remarks about Mrs. Talbot, he waited a full minute before he spoke.

77   "The sun is in your hair," he said.

78   "What?"

79   "The sun is in your hair. It's a beautiful color."

80   "Well, it isn't as pretty as it used to be," she said. "Hair like mine gets dark. But I'm not going to dye it. I don't think that women should dye their hair."

81   "You're so intelligent," he murmured.

82   "You don't mean that?"

83   "Mean what?"

84   "Mean that I'm intelligent."

85   "Oh, but I do," he said. "You're intelligent. You're beautiful. I'll never forget that night I met you at the boat. I hadn't wanted to come to the island. I'd made plans to go out West."

86   "I can't be intelligent," Clarissa said miserably. "I must be stupid. Mother Ryan says that I'm stupid, and Bob says that I'm stupid, and even Mrs. Talbot says that I'm stupid, and—" She began to cry. She went to a mirror and dried her eyes. Baxter followed. He put his arms around her. "Don't put your arms around me," she said, more in despair than in anger. "Nobody ever takes me seriously until they get their arms around me." She sat down again and Baxter sat near her. "But you're not stupid, Clarissa," he said. "You have a wonderful intelligence, a wonderful mind. I've often thought so. I've often felt that you must have a lot of very interesting opinions."

87   "Well, that's funny," she said, "because I do have a lot of opinions. Of course, I never dare say them to anyone, and Bob and Mother Ryan don't ever let me speak. They always interrupt me, as if they were ashamed of me. But I do have these opinions. I mean, I think we're like cogs in a wheel. I've concluded that we're like cogs in a wheel. Do you think we're like cogs in a wheel?"

88   "Oh, yes," he said. "Oh, yes, I do!"

89   "I think we're like cogs in a wheel," she said. "For instance, do you think that women should work? I've given that a lot of thought. My opinion is that I don't think married women should work. I mean, unless they have a lot of money, of course, but even then I think it's a full-time job to take care of a man. Or do you think that women should work?"

90   "What do you think?" he asked. "I'm terribly interested in knowing what you think."

91   "Well, my opinion is," she said timidly, "that you just have to hoe your row. I don't think that working or joining the church is going to change everything, or special diets, either. I don't put much stock in fancy diets. We have a friend who eats a quarter of a pound of meat at every meal. He has a scales right on the table and he weighs the meat. It makes the table look awful and I don't see what good it's going to do him. I buy what's

reasonable. If ham is reasonable, I buy ham. If lamb is reasonable, I buy lamb. Don't you think that's intelligent?''

"I think that's very intelligent."   92

"And progressive education," she said. "I don't have a good opinion of progressive   93
education. When we go to the Howards' for dinner, the children ride their tricycles
around the table all the time, and it's my opinion that they get this way from progressive
schools, and that children ought to be told what's nice and what isn't."

The sun that had lighted her hair was gone, but there was still enough light in the   94
room for Baxter to see that as she aired her opinions, her face suffused with color and
her pupils dilated. Baxter listened patiently, for he knew by then that she merely wanted
to be taken for something that she was not—that the poor girl was lost. "You're very
intelligent," he said, now and then. "You're so intelligent."

It was as simple as that.   95

Vocabulary

indolent (3)	noncommittal (22)
insular (3)	intimations (48)
monologue (4)	metamorphose (53)
unsavory (8)	ingenuous (58)
susceptible (18)	innuendoes (67)

Questions on Meaning and Technique

1. Why is Baxter attracted to Clarissa? What is your opinion of Baxter?

2. Although Clarissa is married, her husband never appears in the story. What effect does his absence have on the events in the story?

3. What does Clarissa desire above all else? Support your answer with quotations from the story. How does her desire create the story's conflict?

4. How do the citizens of Holly Cove regard Baxter? Do you agree with their assessment? Why or why not?

5. If there is an injured party in this story, who is it? Give reasons for your choice.

6. What is the horrible irony in this story? How does it affect the ending?

7. What details does the author provide to convince us of Clarissa's beauty? Point out specific passages.

8. What is Baxter's plan of attack in trying to seduce Clarissa? Will he succeed? Give reasons for your answer to the second question.

9. What makes the characters in the story seem realistic rather than fantastic?

Reading for Ideas

With characteristic poetic abruptness, this poem tells a moving story while drawing a sharp contrast between a dead father and his grieving son. Pay attention to the title as well as the basic dramatic elements in the poem: Ask yourself where the speaker is and why. How is the son like, and different from, his father? What is ironic about the comparison?

The Twins

Charles Bukowski

Charles Bukowski, American poet and writer, was born in 1920 in Andernach, Germany. He attended Los Angeles City College and worked at a variety of odd jobs for several years, including one long stint with the U.S. Postal Service. A prolific writer and best-selling author in West Germany, Bukowski is the author of numerous books including Flower Fist and Bestial Wail *(1959),* Long Shot Poems for Broke Players *(1961),* Mocking Bird, Wish Me Luck *(1972),* Hollywood *(1989), and the screenplay* Barfly *(1987).*

he hinted at times that I was a bastard and I told him to listen
to Brahms, and I told him to learn to paint and drink and not be
dominated by women and dollars
but he screamed at me, For Christ's sake remember your
         mother,

remember your country,
you'll kill us all! . . .

I move through my father's house (on which he owes
       $8,000 after 20
years on the same job) and look at his dead shoes
the way his feet curled the leather as if he were angry planting
           roses,
and he was, and I look at his dead cigarette, his last
         cigarette
and the last bed he slept in that night, and I feel I should
         remake it
but I can't, for a father is always your master even when he's
         gone;
I guess these things have happened time and again but I
        can't help
thinking
 to die on a kitchen floor at 7 o'clock in the morning
 while other people are frying eggs

is not so rough
unless it happens to you.

I go outside and pick an orange and peel back the bright
                                                  skin;
things are still living: the grass is growing quite well,
the sun sends down its rays circled by a Russian satellite;

a dog barks senselessly somewhere, the neighbors peek
                                          behind blinds:

I am a stranger here, and have been (I suppose) somewhat
                                                the rogue,

and I have no doubt he painted me quite well (the old
                                          boy and I

fought like mountain lions) and they say he left it all to
                                          some woman

in Duarte but I don't give a damn—she can have it: he was
                                          my old

man
     and he died.

inside, I try on a light blue suit
much better than anything I have ever worn
and I flap the arms like a scarecrow in the wind
but it's no good:
I can't keep him alive
no matter how much we hated each other.

we looked exactly alike, we could have been twins
the old man and I: that's what they
said. he had his bulbs on the screen
ready for planting
while I was laying with a whore from 3rd street.

very well. grant us this moment: standing before a mirror

     in my dead father's suit
     waiting also
     to die.

Questions on Meaning and Technique

1. How would you characterize the relationship between the speaker of the
   poem and his father?

2. What contrasts in life-style and temperament can you infer existed between this father and son?

3. How would you characterize the way the speaker feels about his dead father?

4. Although about two contrasting personalities, the poem is entitled "The Twins." In what way are the two personalities described in it twins?

5. In what way does this poem defy the traditional subject and treatment usually associated with poetry?

6. In what kind of verse is this poem written? Where is its rhyme?

7. The speaker says that he feels he should remake his father's bed but can't because "a father is always your master even when he's / gone." In what way is a "father always your master even when he's / gone"? Do you agree with this sentiment?

How to Write a Comparison/Contrast

In the context of the English classroom, an assignment to do a comparison usually means to write about both similarities and differences. Strictly speaking, however, there is a difference between a comparison and a contrast. A comparison reveals the similarities and differences between two items; a contrast focuses only on differences. Most of our private and public decisions are based on comparison and contrast: we buy a Buick rather than a Toyota because of differences we perceive between the two cars. An executive hires one secretary rather than another because of perceived differences in their skills. A student selects one history class over another because of the greater reputation of its professor. Although often carried out unsystematically with little forethought, comparison is still a necessary and familiar thinking process for most of us.

Nevertheless, you should be aware that in English departments *comparison* tends to be a blanket term used to cover both comparison and contrast. Many instructors have this more general meaning in mind when they assign a comparison. In other disciplines "comparison" tends to mean "compare only," whereas "contrast" tends to mean the opposite—contrast only. If you have any doubt about what a comparison assignment entails, ask the instructor. As for us, we use "comparison" in the sense of English departments, to mean a systematic discussion of both similarities and differences.

Writing Assignment

Compare and contrast two people who are totally different. Base your essay on the contrast between the attitudes they represent, taking into account such factors as attitude toward money, treatment of people, purpose in life, dependence on others, and any other important basis for comparison. Place the controlling idea at the end of the introductory paragraph, making sure that it expresses the general areas of contrast you will treat in your essay—for example, "Mark and John differ in their cultural values, their treatment of people, and their goals in life."

Specific Instructions

PREWRITING ON THE ASSIGNMENT.   The first step in prewriting about the topic is to make a list of likely subjects for your essay. Think of two acquaintances or friends or public figures you would like to compare/contrast. Because the ultimate aim is to gain fresh insight into your subjects through the process of matching them up against each other, you should select significant bases for the comparison/contrast. These bases or criteria should reveal telling, rather than trivial, similarities and differences. For example, a comparison between George Bush and Bill Clinton based on similarities in physical appearance would end up drawing trivial conclusions. On the other hand, if you used foreign policy accomplishments as your base, the search for similarities and differences would lead to more significant revelations.

Once you have selected your subjects, begin your list by heading two columns with their names. To the left, set down the bases for your comparison/contrast. Remember to use significant rather than trivial bases. The writer of the student essay decided to use the bases of appearances, manners, and recreational activities. Here is how his blank list looked:

Aben Tuasso   James Greenlaw

Appearances:

Manners:

Recreation:

Once you have prepared this blank list, you merely fill in the details systematically under each column, which you will later incorporate into your paragraphs.

Working from this kind of list promises a fair comparison that deals equally with both subjects. It is easy to see from this list, for example, whether you have amassed more details on one subject or the other, or whether you have entirely overlooked gathering material about, say, James's recreational activities. Such omissions are harder to spot in an essay itself.

LIMIT YOUR ESSAY TO MAJOR BASES FOR COMPARISON.   No doubt there are countless bases for comparing people—looks, talent, charm, intelligence, creativity, ability to make friends, athletic prowess, and so on. However, rambling over the infinity of

Controlling idea

differences and similarities you see between John and Mark will not necessarily give your essay structure, emphasis, or clarity. To write a structured, emphatic, and clear comparison of your two acquaintances, select the major points of difference and similarity between them and restrict your essay to a contrast based on these. Once chosen and enunciated in your controlling idea, these bases will give your essay unity and structure. You should not violate this unity and structure by slipping into areas not mentioned in the controlling idea. The following paragraph begins by announcing a comparison of two girls on the basis of looks, personality, and physical strength, and lives up to its promise:

Looks

Personality

Physical strength

Kora and Shery, though best friends, were as different as winter and summer in their looks, personality, and physical strength. Kora was tall and dark, with snappy black eyes and long silken braids that fell to her hips, whereas Shery looked almost frail, with soft blue eyes and a halo of golden curls framing her delicate face. Kora wasn't afraid of anyone or anything—not even Mr. Threllkeld, the burly principal. Without the slightest abashment she could confront even the town mayor and demand that he schedule the spring prom in the civic auditorium. Strangers didn't exist for Kora. She greeted them as she would an old acquaintance, without fear or reticence. On the other hand, Shery was painfully shy. To speak up in class was a nightmare for her, as could be seen from her high blush and whispered answers. She hated meeting new people and would always wait for Kora to take over the conversation. If someone she hardly knew attempted a conversation with her, she would begin to stammer, look confused, and eventually excuse herself and hurriedly leave. Then, too, Kora was physically stronger than Shery. The boys often asked her to practice basketball or baseball with them because she could hit a basket and swing a bat as well as any other tenth-grader. Unlike Kora, Shery feared any physical adventure. When Kora playfully threw her a basketball, Shery would cover her face with her hands and dodge it. When coaxed to go swimming, skating, or climbing, Shery would say, "I'm too chicken." Kora and Shery attracted each other as opposites, not as kindred spirits.

DECIDE ON THE ORGANIZATION OF YOUR COMPARISON.   Basically, there are two ways to organize a comparison assignment—vertically or horizontally. For example, you intend to compare John, who is rich, with Mark, who is poor, on the basis of their attitude toward money. Organized *vertically*, the elements of your outline would look like this:

    I. John has the rich boy's contempt for money.
      a. He expects it to be there when he needs it.
      b. He never hesitates over a purchase.
      c. He buys what he wants.
    II. Mark has the poor boy's reverence for money.
      a. He knows it is hard to come by.
      b. He hesitates and lingers over a purchase.
      c. He buys what he can afford.

Vertical organization requires that you first write about John on points a, b, and c, and then contrast Mark with John on these same points, as in this example:

Having always lived a life of luxury and comfort, John has a rich boy's contempt for money. He expects it to be there when he needs it; he sees it as having only a utility value, enabling him to do what he likes. He never lingers or hesitates over a purchase. For him, the object of shopping is not to agonize over the amount to be spent, but simply to find expeditiously the best, most suitable object that will satisfy all his wants. He has a high regard for quality, and a low regard for expense. He buys what suits him best, whether it is the most or least expensive item in the store.

Mark, on the other hand, has the poor boy's reverence and respect for money. It was not always there when he needed it; what little money he has acquired has cost him in labor, sweat, and drudgery. He spends an interminable amount of time on shopping trips, endlessly comparing prices, quality, and value and listening patiently to sales spiels and technical explanations. For him, the aim of shopping is to acquire the most for the least. He regards expense on a par with quality and usually ends up buying not his first choice or even his second, but sometimes his third, or fourth, or even fifth, the acquisition always being dictated by his budget and seldom by quality.

Here is an outline of this same contrast organized *horizontally*:

John has contempt for money; Mark has reverence for money.

John buys without hesitation; Mark hesitates and compares prices.

John buys what he wants; Mark buys what he can afford.

Here is the horizontally organized written contrast:

Having lived a life of luxury and comfort, John has the rich boy's contempt for money. Mark, on the other hand, has the poor boy's reverence for it. John expects money to be there when he needs it and sees it as having a utility value, enabling him to do as he pleases. Mark, however, knows that money is not always there when he needs it, and that what little money he has acquired has cost him in labor, sweat, and drudgery. A pronounced difference shows up in their behavior on shopping trips. John never lingers or hesitates over a purchase; he shops for what he wants, buying always the most suitable, the best object which will satisfy all his wants. It is just the opposite with Mark. For him, shopping means acquiring the most for the least. He must choose his purchases not by quality alone, but also by expense. Frequently he ends up buying not his first choice, or even his second or third, but his fourth or fifth choice, in every case the acquisition being dictated by budget rather than by quality. John buys the best if it suits him; Mark, to the contrary, buys what he can afford.

USE INDICATORS TO SHOW COMPARISON/CONTRAST.   A good comparison should be sprinkled with *indicators* that signal similarities and differences. For example:

Similarity	*Contrast*
likewise	but
the same as	yet
too/also	however
similarly	nevertheless
in like manner	on the contrary
	contrary to
	unlike
	the opposite of

The most common student error in comparison/contrast essays is to leave out the indicators and not complete the comparison. Consider the following:

> Benjamin Franklin was a more positive American than was Jonathan Edwards. For example, he had a much more developed sense of humor, as revealed in the numerous funny anecdotes in his autobiography. He could laugh at his own mistakes and at the stupidity of the world in general. Furthermore, he was much more successful in his work, becoming famous all over the world as an inventor, writer, and statesman. Then too, Franklin was more optimistic about America. His writings reflect confidence and security in America's future; they indicate an innate pride in America's potential as well as its accomplishments.

As you can see, the above comparison is hopelessly lopsided. Claiming to draw a contrast between Benjamin Franklin and Jonathan Edwards, the writer tells us only about Franklin, leaving us to guess about Edwards. Perhaps the student simply forgot that he was comparing two figures and that he was therefore obliged to give each equal treatment. However, one way to forestall this sort of lapse is to sprinkle the text mechanically and consciously with indicators that force a complete comparison with equal treatment to all parties:

> Benjamin Franklin was a more positive American than was Jonathan Edwards. First, Franklin had a developed sense of humor. He could laugh, as revealed in the numerous funny anecdotes of his autobiography. *In contrast,* the diaries of Jonathan Edwards are filled with passages in which he weeps and moans over his own sinful condition and the general wickedness of the world. Second, Benjamin Franklin was successful in everything he attempted, achieving worldwide fame as an inventor, writer, and statesman. *On the other hand,* Jonathan Edwards was doubted by most thinkers and despised by his own congregation; he ended his ministry as an outcast in the wilderness, helping the Indians. Third, Franklin was a much more optimistic man than was Jonathan Edwards. His writings show great confidence and security in America's future; they indicate an innate pride in America's potential as well as its accomplishments. *Unlike* Franklin, Edwards was burdened by a deep-seated pessimism. His sermons emphasize man's utter depravity and vileness. In his view, all men except the few elect were despicable worms and the world was damned to everlasting hell.

The second version provides a clearer contrast than the first because the contrast indicators remind the writer to treat both sides equally.

READING FOR IDEAS

This article by Highet describes a meeting between two sharply contrasting personalities in history—Alexander the Great (356–323 B.C.), king of Macedonia, and Greek Cynic philosopher Diogenes (c. 412–323 B.C.). As you read, notice how Highet organizes his contrasts and the implicit bases he uses. Notice also the tactful curtain line that Alexander uses to withdraw with face-saving dignity from the scene. What does Highet mean when he says that "only Alexander the conqueror and Diogenes the beggar were truly free"?

PROFESSIONAL MODEL

Diogenes and Alexander
GILBERT HIGHET

Gilbert Highet (1906–1978), Scottish-born writer and scholar, was educated at the University of Glasgow and Oxford University and became a naturalized American citizen in 1951. Highet was best known for his scholarly writings on the classics and on a wide range of literary topics. His works include The Classical Tradition *(1949) and* The Anatomy of Satire *(1962). Highet was married to novelist Helen MacInnes.*

Lying on the bare earth, shoeless, bearded, half-naked, he looked like a beggar or a lunatic. He was one, but not the other. He had opened his eyes with the sun at dawn, scratched, done his business like a dog at the roadside, washed at the public fountain, begged a piece of breakfast bread and a few olives, eaten them squatting on the ground, and washed them down with a few handfuls of water scooped from the spring. (Long ago he had owned a rough wooden cup, but he threw it away when he saw a boy drinking out of his hollowed hands.) Having no work to go to and no family to provide for, he was free. As the market place filled up with shoppers and merchants and gossipers and sharpers and slaves and foreigners, he had strolled through it for an hour or two. Everybody knew him, or knew of him. They would throw sharp questions at him and get sharper answers. Sometimes they threw jeers, and got jibes; sometimes bits of food, and got scant thanks; sometimes a mischievous pebble, and got a shower of stones and abuse. They were not quite sure whether he was mad or not. He knew they were mad, all mad, each in a different way; they amused him. Now he was back at his home.   1

It was not a house, not even a squatter's hut. He thought everybody lived far too elaborately, expensively, anxiously. What good is a house? No one needs privacy: natural acts are not shameful; we all do the same things, and need not hide them. No one needs   2 beds and chairs and such furniture; the animals live healthy lives and sleep on the ground. All we require, since nature did not dress us properly, is one garment to keep us warm, and some shelter from rain and wind. So he had one blanket—to dress him in the daytime and cover him at night—and he slept in a cask. His name was Diogenes. He was the founder of the creed called Cynicism (the word means "doggishness"); he spent much of his life in the rich, lazy, corrupt Greek city of Corinth, mocking and satirizing its people, and occasionally converting one of them.

3   His home was not a barrel made of wood: too expensive. It was a storage jar made of earthenware, something like a modern fuel tank—no doubt discarded because a break had made it useless. He was not the first to inhabit such a thing: the refugees driven into Athens by the Spartan invasion had been forced to sleep in casks. But he was the first who *ever* did so by choice, out of principle.

4   Diogenes was not a degenerate or a maniac. He was a philosopher who wrote plays and poems and essays expounding his doctrine; he talked to those who cared to listen; he had pupils who admired him. But he taught chiefly by example. All should live naturally, he said, for what is natural is normal and cannot possibly be evil or shameful. Live without conventions, which are artificial and false; escape complexities and superfluities and extravagances; only so can you live a free life. The rich man believes he possesses his big house with its many rooms and its elaborate furniture, his pictures and expensive clothes, his horses and his servants and his bank accounts. He does not. He depends on them, he worries about them, he spends most of his life's energy looking after them; the thought of losing them makes him sick with anxiety. They possess him. He is their slave. In order to procure a quantity of false, perishable goods he has sold the only true, lasting good, his own independence.

5   There have been many men who grew tired of human society with its complications, and went away to live simply—on a small farm, in a quiet village, in a hermit's cave, or in the darkness of anonymity. Not so Diogenes. He was not a recluse, or a stylite, or a beatnik. He was a missionary. His life's aim was clear to him; it was "to restamp the currency." (He and his father had once been convicted for counterfeiting, long before he turned to philosophy, and this phrase was Diogenes' bold, unembarrassed joke on the subject.) To restamp the currency; to take the clean metal of human life, to erase the old false conventional markings, and to imprint it with its true values.

6   The other great philosophers of the fourth century before Christ taught mainly their own private pupils. In the shady groves and cool sanctuaries of the Academy, Plato discoursed to a chosen few on the unreality of this contingent existence. Aristotle, among the books and instruments and specimens and archives and research-workers of his Lyceum, pursued investigations and gave lectures that were rightly named *esoteric,* "for those within the walls." But for Diogenes, laboratory and specimens and lecture halls and pupils were all to be found in a crowd of ordinary people. Therefore he chose to live in Athens or in the rich city of Corinth, where travelers from all over the Mediterranean world constantly came and went. And, by design, he publicly behaved in such ways as to show people what real life was. He would constantly take up their spiritual coin, ring it on a stone, and laugh at its false superscription.

7   He thought most people were only half-alive, most men only half-men. At bright noonday he walked through the market place carrying a lighted lamp and inspecting the

face of everyone he met. They asked him why. Diogenes answered, "I am trying to find a *man*."

To a gentleman whose servant was putting on his shoes for him, Diogenes said, "You won't be really happy until he wipes your nose for you: that will come after you lose the use of your hands." 8

Once there was a war scare so serious that it stirred even the lazy, profit-happy Corinthians. They began to drill, clean their weapons, and rebuild their neglected fortifications. Diogenes took his old cask and began to roll it up and down, back and forward. "When you are all so busy," he said, "I felt I ought to do *something*!" 9

And so he lived—like a dog, some said, because he cared nothing for privacy and other human conventions, and because he showed his teeth and barked at those whom he disliked. Now he was lying in the sunlight, as contented as a dog on the warm ground, happier (he himself used to boast) than the Shah of Persia. Although he knew he was going to have an important visitor, he would not move. 10

The little square began to fill with people. Page boys elegantly dressed, spearmen speaking a rough foreign dialect, discreet secretaries, hard-browed officers, suave diplomats, they all gradually formed a circle centered on Diogenes. He looked them over, as a sober man looks at a crowd of tottering drunks, and shook his head. He knew who they were. They were the attendants of the conqueror of Greece, the servants of Alexander, the Macedonian king, who was visiting his newly subdued realm. 11

Only twenty, Alexander was far older and wiser than his years. Like all Macedonians he loved drinking, but he could usually handle it; and toward women he was nobly restrained and chivalrous. Like all Macedonians he loved fighting; he was a magnificent commander, but he was not merely a military automaton. He could think. At thirteen he had become a pupil of the greatest mind in Greece, Aristotle. No exact record of his schooling survives. It is clear, though, that Aristotle took the passionate, half-barbarous boy and gave him the best of Greek culture. He taught Alexander poetry; the young prince slept with the *Iliad* under his pillow and longed to emulate Achilles, who brought the mighty power of Asia to ruin. He taught him philosophy, in particular the shapes and uses of political power: a few years later Alexander was to create a supranational empire that was not merely a power system but a vehicle for the exchange of Greek and Middle Eastern cultures. 12

Aristotle taught him the principles of scientific research: during his invasion of the Persian domains Alexander took with him a large corps of scientists, and shipped hundreds of zoological specimens back to Greece for study. Indeed, it was from Aristotle that Alexander learned to seek out everything strange which might be instructive. Jugglers and stunt artists and virtuosos of the absurd he dismissed with a shrug; but on reaching India he was to spend hours discussing the problems of life and death with naked Hindu mystics, and later to see one demonstrate Yoga self-command by burning himself impassively to death. 13

Now, Alexander was in Corinth to take command of the League of Greek States which, after conquering them, his father Philip had created as a disguise for the New Macedonian Order. He was welcomed and honored and flattered. He was the man of the hour, of the century: he was unanimously appointed commander-in-chief of a new expedition against old, rich, corrupt Asia. Nearly everyone crowded to Corinth in order 14 to congratulate him, to seek employment with him, even simply to see him: soldiers and statesmen, artists and merchants, poets and philosophers. He received their compliments graciously. Only Diogenes, although he lived in Corinth, did not visit the new monarch. With that generosity which Aristotle had taught him was a quality of the truly magnanimous man, Alexander determined to call upon Diogenes. Surely Dio-genes, the God-born, would acknowledge the conqueror's power by some gift of hoarded wisdom.

15   With his handsome face, his fiery glance, his strong supple body, his purple and gold cloak, and his air of destiny, he moved through the parting crowd, toward the Dog's kennel. When a king approaches, all rise in respect. Diogenes did not rise, he merely sat up on one elbow. When a monarch enters a precinct, all greet him with a bow or an acclamation. Diogenes said nothing.

16   There was silence. Some years later Alexander speared his best friend to the wall, for objecting to the exaggerated honors paid to His Majesty; but now he was still young and civil. He spoke first, with a kindly greeting. Looking at the poor broken cask, the single ragged garment, and the rough figure lying on the ground, he said, "Is there anything I can do for you, Diogenes?"

17   "Yes," said the Dog. "Stand to one side. You're blocking the sunlight."

18   There was silence, not the ominous silence preceding a burst of fury, but a hush of amazement. Slowly, Alexander turned away. A titter broke out from the elegant Greeks, who were already beginning to make jokes about the Cur that looked at the King. The Macedonian officers, after deciding that Diogenes was not worth the trouble of kicking, were starting to guffaw and nudge one another. Alexander was still silent. To those nearest him he said quietly, "If I were not Alexander, I should be Diogenes." They took it as a paradox, designed to close the awkward little scene with a polite curtain line. But Alexander meant it. He understood Cynicism as the others could not. Later he took one of Diogenes' pupils with him to India as a philosophical interpreter (it was he who spoke to the naked *saddhus*). He was what Diogenes called himself, a *cosmopolites*, "citizen of the world." Like Diogenes, he admired the heroic figure of Hercules, the mighty conqueror who labors to help mankind while others toil and sweat only for themselves. He knew that of all men then alive in the world only Alexander the conqueror and Diogenes the beggar were truly free.

Vocabulary

squatter (2)	superfluities (4)	fortifications (9)
Cynicism (2)	recluse (5)	barbarous (12)
satirizing (2)	stylite (5)	supranational (12)
degenerate (4)	Lyceum (6)	mystics (13)
maniac (4)	superscription (6)	ominous (18)

Questions on Meaning and Technique

1. What bases govern Highet's comparison of Diogenes and Alexander?
2. How does Highet present his comparison—vertically or horizontally?

3. In what paragraph does Highet first shift from one character to another? How is the shift accomplished?

4. What other contrast is drawn besides the contrast between Diogenes and Alexander? Point to specific passages.

5. What is the analogy used in paragraph 10?

6. What are some characteristics that Diogenes and Alexander share?

7. What are the most outstanding contrasts between the old philosopher and the young emperor?

STUDENT ESSAY

First Draft   Randy Varney

Aben and James

1   ~~People's social backgrounds affect their characters.~~ Aben Tuasso lives in a small Maori tribe on New Zealand's North Island. Aben's village is located on the shore of the Tasman Sea. He is single and twenty-six years old. His lifestyle is somewhat primitive and simple. (Insert A) Across the world/ ^from New Zealand^ in Boston, lives another young single man, James Greenlaw. His address is in a wealthy, snobbish community, where the average adult drives a luxury car and enjoys all of the modern conveniences people in his class are expected to own. (Insert B) The ~~social~~ backgrounds of these two men ~~has~~ ^have^ caused a marked difference in their appearance, ^their^ mannerisms, and ~~hobbies.~~ ^their recreational activities^

2   Aben and James's ~~looks~~ ^are^ set ~~them~~ completely apart/ ^by their looks^ Aben's tribal custom requires males over eighteen to wear black lava-lavas, a cloth ^the^ size of a large bath towel~~s~~ wrapped around the waist, and have colorful tattoos engraved with burning charcoal

This sentence works better at the end of the essay.

adds needed information about the Maori

smoother wording

(Insert A)

Sheltered from rain, wind, and occasional volcanic eruptions by a traditional Polynesian hut, Aben exists as if Captain James Cook had never brought English modernization to his part of the world. Protected by an eighteenth-century political treaty which guarantees the Maori that they can continue to live according to their tribal traditions, without interference from the British Crown, he today still leads a pristine life, herding sheep among beeches, palms, and bushy undergrowth—as did his forebears centuries ago.

(Insert B)

As a promising young city lawyer, he boards trains and planes in a hectic race for prestige and power.

*The purpose of this style is to retain the general look of a fiercely brave warring tribe.**

over most of their bodies. Unlike Aben, James dresses in expensive clothing designed

by his ~~own~~ tailor. In his society this dress code exemplifies success. James's social

status enables him to avoid hard manual labor, which accounts for his fair complexion

and his manicured fingernails. To keep sinewy and fit, James exercises one hour a day

in his personal exercise room, filled with gleaming equipment that he can pump, push,

or pull. ~~On the other hand,~~ Aben's darkly tanned, muscular body is the result of many

hours spent spear fishing in the bay, canoeing down rivers, and climbing jagged cliffs

along the seashore. His hands and feet bear thick calluses. *Move to * above*

Keep with description of Aben's looks.

Their ~~mannerisms~~ *of Aben and James* are distinctly different. Aben grunts and stares coldly when he is   3
also

makes transition to manners more precise

approached by another person. In his society an arrogant attitude connotes superior

manliness. He continually tries to impress the tribal women of his village by engaging

in physical combat with the other males of his tribe. James has an entirely different

approach toward people in his environment. Following the etiquette of his peers, he

greets new acquaintances with a smile, a warm handshake, and a deferential bow. He

impresses a woman by taking her to an elegant restaurant and then to the opera or

ballet. He dazzles his peers with his sophisticated style, his fluent command of three

languages, and his Harvard law degree. One similarity between these otherwise

different young men is that both are ambitious and reveal a fervent drive to excel. Aben

does it by bringing home trophies tracked down with his bow and arrow whereas

James does it by winning different court cases. Both Aben and James desire to be best.

recreational activities

Comparing Aben and James's ~~hobbies~~ also reveals some fascinating differences.   4

better term

Aben enjoys hunting with a bow and arrow and swimming in turbulent waters. He

loves diving for pearls deep beneath the surface of the sea. On special evenings, he

joins his fellow villagers in the "Haka," a ritual war dance, performed around a blazing

fire. This lusty dance is accompanied by loud singing and energetic foot stomping.

When the fire begins to die and only glowing coals are left, Aben swiftly volunteers to

walk across the hot coals in order to demonstrate his unqualified bravery. How different

lounge on a living room sofa,

are James's hobbies from those of Aben! James loves to read the works of Sir Walter
ing   *is*

Scott while listening to a Beethoven or Mozart symphony. On weekends he ~~can~~
recorded on an expensive compact disc

details added

inevitably ~~be~~ seen at the country club, where he will play a round of golf or a polo
with fellow sportsmen

match. James also loves to play the violin, which he started to master at the age of six.

birth and

5   A person's ~~social~~ background truly determines his or her character. [Insert C] If Aben and

James were to switch social backgrounds, would they adapt? Would James become a

fire dancer? Would Aben play the violin?

*This sentence
adds texture to
the conclusion.*

[Insert C]

*Aben and James are clear examples of this
incontrovertible truth. Both men are young, vigorous,
and ambitious, but their lifestyles have bred them
into two totally different people.*

STUDENT ESSAY

Final Draft   Randy Varney

Aben and James

Aben Tuasso lives in a small Maori tribe on New Zealand's North Island. Aben's village   1

is located on the shore of the Tasman Sea. He is single and twenty-six years old. His

lifestyle is somewhat primitive and simple. Sheltered from rain, wind, and occasional

volcanic eruptions by a traditional Polynesian hut, Aben exists as if Captain James

Cook had never brought English modernization to his part of the world. Protected by an

eighteenth-century political treaty which guarantees the Maori that they can continue

to live according to their tribal traditions, without interference from the British Crown,

he today still leads a pristine life, herding sheep among beeches, palms, and bushy

undergrowth—as did his forebears centuries ago. Across the world from New Zealand,

in Boston, lives another young single man, James Greenlaw. His address is in a

wealthy, snobbish community, where the average adult drives a luxury car and enjoys

all of the modern conveniences people in his class are expected to own. As a promising

young city lawyer, he boards trains and planes in a hectic race for prestige and power.

The backgrounds of these two men have caused a marked difference in their

appearance, their mannerisms, and their recreational activities.

Aben and James are set completely apart by their looks. Aben's tribal custom   2

requires males over eighteen to wear black lava-lavas, cloths the size of large bath

towels, wrapped around the waist, and have colorful tattoos engraved with burning

charcoal over most of their bodies. The purpose of this style is to retain the general look

of a fiercely brave warring tribe. Aben's darkly tanned, muscular body is the result of many hours spent spear fishing in the bay, canoeing down rivers, and climbing jagged cliffs along the seashore. His hands and feet bear thick calluses. Unlike Aben, James dresses in expensive clothing designed by his tailor. In his society this dress code exemplifies success. James's social status enables him to avoid hard manual labor, which accounts for his fair complexion and his manicured fingernails. To keep sinewy and fit, James exercises one hour a day in his personal exercise room, filled with gleaming equipment that he can pump, push, or pull.

3   The manners of Aben and James are also distinctively different. Aben grunts and stares coldly when he is approached by another person. In his society an arrogant attitude connotes superior manliness. He continually tries to impress the tribal women of his village by engaging in physical combat with the other males of his tribe. James has an entirely different approach toward people in his environment. Following the etiquette of his peers, he greets new acquaintances with a smile, a warm handshake, and a deferential bow. He impresses a woman by taking her to an elegant restaurant and then to the opera or ballet. He dazzles his peers with his sophisticated style, his fluent command of three languages, and his Harvard law degree. One similarity between these otherwise different young men is that both are ambitious and reveal a fervent drive to excel. Aben does it by bringing home trophies tracked down with his bow and arrow whereas James does it by winning difficult court cases. Both Aben and James desire to be best.

4   Comparing Aben and James's recreational activities also reveals some fascinating differences. Aben enjoys hunting with a bow and arrow and swimming in turbulent waters. He loves diving for pearls deep beneath the surface of the sea. On special evenings, he joins his fellow villagers in the "Haka," a ritual war dance, performed around a blazing fire. This lusty dance is accompanied by loud singing and energetic foot stomping. When the fire begins to die and only glowing coals are left, Aben swiftly volunteers to walk across the hot coals in order to demonstrate his unqualified bravery. How different are James's hobbies from those of Aben! James loves to lounge on a living room sofa, reading the works of Sir Walter Scott while listening to a Beethoven or Mozart symphony recorded on an expensive compact disc. On weekends he is

inevitably seen at the country club, where he will play a round of golf or a polo match with fellow sportsmen. James also loves to play the violin, which he started to master at the age of six.

A person's birth and background truly determine his or her character. Aben and 5
James are clear examples of this incontrovertible truth. Both men are young, vigorous, and ambitious; but their lifestyles have bred them into two totally different people. If Aben and James were to switch social backgrounds, would they adapt? Would James become a fire dancer? Would Aben play the violin?

READING FOR IDEAS

This touching tale contrasting the lives of two men—one rich, the other poor—comes from *All Creatures Great and Small* and demonstrates the reason for Herriot's enormous popularity. The contrast between the men is skillfully embedded in the context of a stirring narrative and tied together through the portraits of their two daughters. Ask yourself how such a rich and powerful man—admired by the world for his success—could come to merit the contempt of his wife and daughter. Also ask yourself what the poor farmer did to deserve the admiration and love of his daughter. Speculate on what you think the rich man has to do to win back his family's love and respect.

ALTERNATE READING

The Mansion and the Hut
James Herriot

James Herriot (b. 1916), veterinarian and writer, was born James Alfred Wight in Scotland and attended Glasgow Veterinary College. For over 40 years Herriot has practiced veterinary medicine in a Yorkshire village, acquiring a lifetime of experiences that he has chronicled in a series of beloved best-sellers, none of which was written until he was over 50. His enormously successful books, which have sold over 11 million copies, include All Creatures Great and Small *(1972),* All Things Bright and Beautiful *(1974),* All Things Wise and Wonderful *(1977),* The Lord God Made Them All *(1981), and* Dog Stories *(1986).*

Rheumatism is a terrible thing in a dog. It is painful enough in humans but an acute 1
attack can reduce an otherwise healthy dog to terrified, screaming immobility.

2   Very muscular animals suffered most and I went carefully as my fingers explored the bulging triceps and gluteals of the little Staffordshire bull terrier. Normally a tough little fellow, afraid of nothing, friendly, leaping high in an attempt to lick people's faces; but today, rigid, trembling, staring anxiously in front of him. Even to turn his head a little brought a shrill howl of agony.

3   Mercifully it was something you could put right and quickly too. I pulled the Novalgin into the syringe and injected it rapidly. The little dog, oblivious to everything but the knife-like stabbing of the rheumatism did not stir at the prick of the needle. I counted out some salicylate tablets into a box, wrote the directions on the lid and handed the box to the owner.

4   "Give him one of these as soon as the injection has eased him, Mr. Tavener. Then repeat in about four hours. I'm pretty sure he'll be greatly improved by then."

5   Mrs. Tavener snatched the box away as her husband began to read the directions. "Let me see it," she snapped. "No doubt I'll be the one who has the job to do."

6   It had been like that all the time, ever since I had entered the beautiful house with the terraced gardens leading down to the river. She had been at him ceaselessly while he was holding the dog for me. When the animal had yelped she had cried: "Really, Henry, don't grip the poor thing like that, you're hurting him!" She had kept him scuttling about for this and that and when he was out of the room she said: "You know, this is all my husband's fault. He will let the dog swim in the river. I knew this would happen."

7   Half-way through, daughter Julia had come in and it was clear from the start that she was firmly on Mama's side. She helped out with plenty of "How could you, Daddy!" and "For God's sake, Daddy!" and generally managed to fill in the gaps when her mother wasn't in full cry.

8   The Taveners were in their fifties. He was a big, floridly handsome man who had made millions in the Tyneside shipyards before pulling out of the smoke to this lovely place. I had taken an instant liking to him; I had expected a tough tycoon and had found a warm, friendly, curiously vulnerable man, obviously worried sick about his dog.

9   I had reservations about Mrs. Tavener despite her still considerable beauty. Her smile had a switched-on quality and there was a little too much steel in the blue of her eyes. She had seemed less concerned about the dog than with the necessity of taking it out on her husband.

10   Julia, a scaled-down model of her mother, drifted about the room with the aimless, bored look of the spoiled child; glancing blankly at the dog or me, staring without interest through the window at the smooth lawns, the tennis court, the dark band of river under the trees.

11   I gave the terrier a final reassuring pat on the head and got up from my knees. As I put away the syringe, Tavener took my arm. "Well, that's fine, Mr. Herriot. We're very grateful to you for relieving our minds. I must say I thought the old boy's time had come when he started yelling. And now you'll have a drink before you go."

12   The man's hand trembled on my arm as he spoke. It had been noticeable, too, when he had been holding the dog's head and I had wondered; maybe Parkinson's disease, or nerves, or just drink. Certainly he was pouring a generous measure of whisky into his glass, but as he tipped up the bottle his hand was seized by an even more violent tremor and he slopped the spirit on to the polished sideboard.

"Oh God! Oh God!" Mrs. Tavener burst out. There was a bitter note of oh no, not   13
again, in her cry and Julia struck her forehead with her hand and raised her eyes to
heaven. Tavener shot a single hunted look at the women then grinned as he handed me
my glass.

"Come and sit down, Mr. Herriot," he said. "I'm sure you have time to relax for a few   14
minutes."

We moved over to the fireside and Tavener talked pleasantly about dogs and the   15
countryside and the pictures which hung on the walls of the big room. Those pictures
were noted in the district; many of them were originals by famous painters and they had
become the main interest in Tavener's life. His other passion was clocks and as I looked
round the room at the rare and beautiful timepieces standing among elegant period
furniture it was easy to believe the rumours I had heard about the wealth within these
walls.

The women did not drink with us; they had disappeared when the whisky was brought   16
out, but as I drained my glass the door was pushed open and they stood there, looking
remarkably alike in expensive tweed coats and fur-trimmed hats. Mrs. Tavener pulling on
a pair of motoring gloves, looked with distaste at her husband. "We're going into
Brawton," she said. "Don't know when we'll be back."

Behind her, Julia stared coldly at her father; her lip curled slightly.   17

Tavener did not reply. He sat motionless as I listened to the roar of the car engine and   18
the spatter of whipped-up gravel beyond the window; then he looked out, blank-faced,
empty-eyed at the drifting cloud of exhaust smoke in the drive.

There was something in his expression which chilled me. I put down my glass and got   19
to my feet. "Afraid I must be moving on, Mr. Tavener. Thanks for the drink."

He seemed suddenly to be aware of my presence; the friendly smile returned. "Not at   20
all. Thank you for looking after the old boy. He seems better already."

In the driving mirror, the figure at the top of the steps looked small and alone till the   21
high shrubbery hid him from my view.

The next call was to a sick pig, high on Marstang Fell. The road took me at first along   22
the fertile valley floor, winding under the riverside trees past substantial farmhouses and
rich pastures; but as the car left the road and headed up a steep track the country began
to change. The transition was almost violent as the trees and bushes thinned out and gave
way to the bare, rocky hillside and the miles of limestone walls.

And though the valley had been rich with the fresh green of the new leaves, up here   23
the buds were unopened and the naked branches stretched against the sky still had the
look of winter.

Tim Alton's farm lay at the top of the track and as I pulled up at the gate I wondered   24
as I always did how the man could scrape a living from those few harsh acres with the
grass flattened and yellowed by the wind which always blew. At any rate, many
generations had accomplished the miracle and had lived and struggled and died in that
house with its outbuildings crouching in the lee of a group of stunted, wind-bent trees, its
massive stones crumbling under three centuries of fierce weathering.

Why should anybody want to build a farm in such a place? I turned as I opened the   25
gate and looked back at the track threading between the walls down and down to where
the white stones of the river glittered in the spring sunshine. Maybe the builder had stood

here and looked across the green vastness and breathed in the cold, sweet air and thought it was enough.

26   I saw Tim Alton coming across the yard. There had been no need to lay down concrete or cobbles here; they had just swept away the thin soil and there, between house and buildings was a sloping stretch of fissured rock. It was more than a durable surface—it was everlasting.

27   "It's your pig this time, then, Tim," I said and the farmer nodded seriously.

28   "Aye, right as owt yesterday and laid flat like a dead'un this morning. Never looked up when I filled his trough and by gaw when a pig won't tackle his grub there's summat fat wrong." Tim dug his hands inside the broad leather belt which encircled his oversized trousers and which always seemed to be about to nip his narrow frame in two and led the way gloomily into the sty. Despite the bitter poverty of his existence he was a man who took misfortune cheerfully. I had never seen him look like this and I thought I knew the reason; there is something personal about the family pig.

29   Smallholders like Tim Alton made their meagre living from a few cows; they sold their milk to the big dairies or made butter. And they killed a pig or two each year and cured it themselves for home consumption. On the poorer places it seemed to me that they ate little else; whatever meal I happened to stumble in on, the cooking smell was always the same—roasting fat bacon.

30   It appeared to be a matter of pride to make the pig as fat as possible; in fact, on these little wind-blown farms where the people and the cows and the dogs were lean and spare, the pig was about the only fat thing to be seen.

31   I had seen the Alton pig before. I had been stitching a cow's torn teat about a fortnight ago and Tim had patted me on the shoulder and whispered: "Now come along wi' me, Mr. Herriot and I'll show tha summat." We had looked into the sty at a twenty-five-stone monster effortlessly emptying a huge trough of wet meal. I could remember the pride in the farmer's eyes and the way he listened to the smacking and slobbering as if to great music.

32   It was different today. The pig looked, if possible, even more enormous as it lay on its side, eyes closed, filling the entire floor of the sty like a beached whale. Tim splashed a stick among the untouched meal in the trough and made encouraging noises but the animal never stirred. The farmer looked at me with haggard eyes.

33   "He's bad, Mr. Herriot. It's serious whatever it is."

34   I had been taking the temperature and when I read the thermometer I whistled. "A hundred and seven. That's some fever."

35   The colour drained from Tim's face. "Oh 'ell! A hundred and seven! It's hopeless, then. It's ower with him."

36   I had been feeling along the animal's side and smiled reassuringly. "No, don't worry, Tim. I think he's going to be all right. He's got erysipelas. Here, put your fingers along his back. You can feel a lot of flat swellings on his skin—those are the diamonds. He'll have a beautiful rash within a few hours but at the moment you can't see it, you can only feel it."

37   "And you can make him better?"

38   "I'm nearly sure I can. I'll give him a whacking dose of serum and I'd like to bet you he'll have his nose in that trough in a couple of days. Most of them get over it all right."

"Well that's a bit o' good news, any road," said Tim, a smile flooding over his face. 39
"You had me worried there with your hundred and seven, dang you!"

I laughed. "Sorry, Tim, didn't mean to frighten you. I'm often happier to see a high 40
temperature than a low one. But it's a funny time for erysipelas. We usually see it in late
summer."

"All right, I'll let ye off this time. Come in and wash your hands." 41

In the kitchen I ducked my head but couldn't avoid bumping the massive side of bacon 42
hanging from the beamed ceiling. The heavy mass rocked gently on its hooks; it was
about eight inches thick in parts—all pure white fat. Only by close inspection was it
possible to discern a thin strip of lean meat.

Mrs. Alton produced a cup of tea and as I sipped I looked across at Tim who had fallen 43
back into a chair and lay with his hands hanging down; for a moment he closed his eyes
and his face became a mask of weariness. I thought for the hundredth time about the
endless labour which made up the lives of these little farmers. Alton was only forty but his
body was already bent and ravaged by the constant demands he made on it; you could read
his story in the corded forearm, the rough, work-swollen fingers. He told me once that the
last time he missed a milking was twelve years ago and that was for his father's funeral.

I was taking my leave when I saw Jennie. She was the Altons' eldest child and was 44
pumping vigorously at the tyre of her bicycle which was leaning against the wall just
outside the kitchen door.

"Going somewhere?" I asked and the girl straightened up quickly, pushing back a few 45
strands of dark hair from her forehead. She was about eighteen with delicate features and
large, expressive eyes; in her wild, pinched prettiness there was something of the
wheeling curlews, the wind and sun, the wide emptiness of the moors.

"I'm going down to t'village." She stole a glance into the kitchen. "I'm going to get a 46
bottle of Guinness for dad."

"The village! It's a long way to go for a bottle of Guinness. It must be two miles and 47
then you've got to push back up this hill. Are you going all that way just for one bottle?"

"Aye, just one," she whispered, counting out a sixpence and some coppers into her 48
palm with calm absorption. "Dad's been up all night waiting for a heifer to calve—he's
tired out. I won't be long and he can have his Guinness with his dinner. That's what he
likes." She looked up at me conspiratorially, "It'll be a surprise for him."

As she spoke, her father, still sprawled in the chair, turned his head and looked at her; 49
he smiled and for a moment I saw a serenity in the steady eyes, a nobility in the seamed
face.

Jennie looked at him for a few seconds, a happy secret look from under her lowered 50
brows; then she turned quickly, mounted her bicycle and began to pedal down the track
at surprising speed.

I followed her more slowly, the car, in second gear, bumping and swaying over the 51
stones. I stared straight ahead, lost in thought. I couldn't stop my mind roaming between
the two houses I had visited; between the gracious mansion by the river and the
crumbling farmhouse I had just left; from Henry Tavener with his beautiful clothes, his
well-kept hands, his row of books and pictures and clocks to Tim Alton with his worn,
chest-high trousers nipped in by that great belt, his daily, monthly, yearly grind to stay
alive on that unrelenting hilltop.

52   But I kept coming back to the daughters; to the contempt in Julia Tavener's eyes when she looked at her father and the shining tenderness in Jennie Alton's.

53   It wasn't so easy to work out as it seemed; in fact it became increasingly difficult to decide who was getting the most out of their different lives. But as I guided the car over the last few yards of the track and pulled on to the smooth tarmac of the road it came to me with unexpected clarity. Taking it all in all, if I had the choice to make, I'd settle for the Guinness.

Vocabulary

rheumatism (1)	limestone (22)	ravaged (43)
immobility (1)	lee (24)	corded (43)
gluteals (2)	fissured (26)	curlews (45)
syringe (3)	durable (26)	moors (45)
oblivious (3)	smallholders (29)	absorption (48)
floridly (8)	consumption (29)	conspiratorially (48)
vulnerable (8)	spare (30)	seamed (49)
spatter (18)	haggard (32)	tarmac (53)
fertile (22)	serum (38)	

Questions on Meaning and Technique

1. What is being contrasted in this essay? What are the bases of the contrast?

2. What is the difference between Julia Tavener and Jennie Alton? What similarity is there?

3. Although Mr. Tavener and Mr. Alton lead totally different lives, what characteristics do they have in common?

4. In what way is the description of the little bull terrier's rheumatism related to the rest of the story? How effective is the description?

5. Why does the author state that he has "reservations" about Mrs. Tavener despite her beauty? After reading the story, do you share these reservations? Why or why not?

6. In paragraph 12, the author speculates on the possible reasons for the trembling of Mr. Tavener's hands. What comment seems to support one reason over the others?

7. In what way do the two houses reflect the women who live in them?

8. What is the difference between the two excursions taken by the women of both houses? What is the purpose of alluding to them?

9. The author claims that it was not easy to decide who was getting the most out of life, Tavener or Alton. Why was it difficult to decide? In the end what is the author's verdict? What does he mean when he says, "I'd settle for the Guinness"?

Writing Assignments

1. Using Herriot's story as a model, write a descriptive contrast between two people, one rich and one poor. To draw vivid portraits of the two, you may wish to use the block model of contrasting, in which you first describe one person and then the other, drawing the contrast between the two at the end.

2. Write an essay in which you compare or contrast the advantages of being poor with the advantages of being rich. Use specific examples to clarify the two sides.

READING FOR IDEAS

Despite the fact that this essay is well organized and conceptually clear, it requires concentration because it is written in a scholarly style, becoming to its author who is a university professor. Because the vocabulary may pose a few problems, be sure to look up all words with which you are not thoroughly familiar, focusing particularly on the vocabulary list on page 295. In this essay the author points out major differences between two cultures that meet in the southwestern part of the United States—the Anglo culture, stemming from English sources, and the Chicano culture, stemming from Hispanic sources. Notice that the author uses history, geography, and language to clarify how the differences between the two cultures make understanding of each other difficult.

ALTERNATE READING

Anglo vs. Chicano: Why?
Arthur L. Campa

Arthur L. Campa (1905–1978) was an American university professor and diplomat who was born to American missionaries in Mexico. His experience growing up in a foreign culture influenced him to study modern languages at the University of New Mexico in Albuquerque and also at Columbia University in New York. Eventually he was appointed professor and chairman of the Department of Modern Languages at the University of Denver. In a different vein, he also served as cultural attaché for several United States embassies. The selection reprinted below first appeared in the Western Review.

The cultural differences between Hispanic and Anglo-American people have been   1
dwelt upon by so many writers that we should all be well informed about the values of both. But audiences are usually of the same persuasion as the speakers, and those who consult published works are for the most part specialists looking for affirmation of what they believe. So, let us consider the same subject, exploring briefly some of the basic

cultural differences that cause conflict in the Southwest, where Hispanic and Anglo-American cultures meet.

2   Cultural differences are implicit in the conceptual content of the languages of these two civilizations, and their value systems stem from a long series of historical circumstances. Therefore, it may be well to consider some of the English and Spanish cultural configurations before these Europeans set foot on American soil. English culture was basically insular, geographically and ideologically; was more integrated on the whole, except for some strong theological differences; and was particularly zealous of its racial purity. Spanish culture was peninsular, a geographical circumstance that made it a catchall of Mediterranean, central European and north African peoples. The composite nature of the population produced a marked regionalism that prevented close integration, except for religion, and led to a strong sense of individualism. These differences were reflected in the colonizing enterprise of the two cultures. The English isolated themselves from the Indians physically and culturally; the Spanish, who had strong notions about *pureza de sangre* [purity of blood] among the nobility, were not collectively averse to adding one more strain to their racial cocktail. Cortés led the way by siring the first *mestizo*[1] in North America, and the rest of the conquistadores followed suit. The ultimate products of these two orientations meet today in the Southwest.

3   Anglo-American culture was absolutist at the onset; that is, all the dominant values were considered identical for all, regardless of time and place. Such values as justice, charity, honesty were considered the superior social order for all men and were later embodied in the American Constitution. The Spaniard brought with him a relativistic viewpoint and saw fewer moral implications in man's actions. Values were looked upon as the result of social and economic conditions.

4   The motives that brought Spaniards and Englishmen to America also differed. The former came on an enterprise of discovery, searching for a new route to India initially, and later for new lands to conquer, the fountain of youth, minerals, the Seven Cities of Cíbola and, in the case of the missionaries, new souls to win for the Kingdom of Heaven. The English came to escape religious persecution, and once having found a haven, they settled down to cultivate the soil and establish their homes. Since the Spaniards were not seeking a refuge or running away from anything, they continued their explorations and circled the globe 25 years after the discovery of the New World.

5   This peripatetic tendency of the Spaniard may be accounted for in part by the fact that he was the product of an equestrian culture. Men on foot do not venture far into the unknown. It was almost a century after the landing on Plymouth Rock that Governor Alexander Spotswood of Virginia crossed the Blue Ridge Mountains, and it was not until the nineteenth century that the Anglo-Americans began to move west of the Mississippi.

6   The Spaniard's equestrian role meant that he was not close to the soil, as was the Anglo-American pioneer, who tilled the land and built the greatest agricultural industry in history. The Spaniard cultivated the land only when he had Indians available to do it for him. The uses to which the horse was put also varied. The Spanish horse was essentially a mount, while the more robust English horse was used in cultivating the soil. It is therefore not surprising that the viewpoints of these two cultures should differ when we

---

[1]Mestizo—mixed blood.

consider that the pioneer is looking at the world at the level of his eyes while the *caballero* [horseman] is looking beyond and down at the rest of the world.

One of the most commonly quoted, and often misinterpreted, characteristics of   7
Hispanic peoples is the deeply ingrained individualism in all walks of life. Hispanic individualism is a revolt against the incursion of collectivity, strongly asserted when it is felt that the ego is being fenced in. This attitude leads to a deficiency in those social qualities based on collective standards, an attitude that Hispanos do not consider negative because it manifests a measure of resistance to standardization in order to achieve a measure of individual freedom. Naturally, such an attitude has no *reglas fijas* [fixed rules].

Anglo-Americans who achieve a measure of success and security through institutional   8
guidance not only do not mind a few fixed rules but demand them. The lack of a concerted plan of action, whether in business or in politics, appears unreasonable to Anglo-Americans. They have a sense of individualism, but they achieve it through action and self-determination. Spanish individualism is based on feeling, on something that is the result not of rules and collective standards but of a person's momentary, emotional reaction. And it is subject to change when the mood changes. In contrast to Spanish emotional individualism, the Anglo-American strives for objectivity when choosing a course of action or making a decision.

The Southwestern Hispanos voiced strong objections to the lack of courtesy of the   9
Anglo-Americans when they first met them in the early days of the Santa Fe trade. The same accusation is leveled at the *Americanos* today in many quarters of the Hispanic world. Some of this results from their different conceptions of polite behavior. Here too one can say that the Spanish have no *reglas fijas* because for them courtesy is simply an expression of the way one person feels toward another. To some they extend the hand, to some they bow and for the more *íntimos*[2] there is the well-known *abrazo*.[3] The concepts of "good or bad" or "right or wrong" in polite behavior are moral considerations of an absolutist culture.

Another cultural contrast appears in the way both cultures share part of their material   10
substance with others. The pragmatic Anglo-American contributes regularly to such institutions as the Red Cross, the United Fund and a myriad of associations. He also establishes foundations and quite often leaves millions to such institutions. The Hispano prefers to give his contribution directly to the recipient so he can see the person he is helping.

A century of association has inevitably acculturated both Hispanos and Anglo-   11
Americans to some extent, but there still persist a number of culture traits that neither group has relinquished altogether. Nothing is more disquieting to an Anglo-American who believes that time is money than the time perspective of Hispanos. They usually refer to this attitude as the "*mañana*[4] psychology." Actually, it is more of a "today psychology," because Hispanos cultivate the present to the exclusion of the future; because the latter has not arrived yet, it is not a reality. They are reluctant to relinquish the present, so they hold on to it until it becomes the past. To an Hispano, nine is nine

---

[2]Íntimos—intimates.
[3]Abrazo—embrace.
[4]Mañana—tomorrow.

until it is ten, so when he arrives at nine-thirty, he jubilantly exclaims: "*¡Justo!*" [right on time]. This may be why the clock is slowed down to a walk in Spanish while in English it runs. In the United States, our future-oriented civilization plans our lives so far in advance that the present loses its meaning. January magazine issues are out in December; 1973 cars have been out since October; cemetery plots and even funeral arrangements are bought on the installment plan. To a person engrossed in living today the very idea of planning his funeral sounds like the tolling of the bells.

12   It is a natural corollary that a person who is present oriented should be compensated by being good at improvising. An Anglo-American is told in advance to prepare for an "impromptu speech," but an Hispano usually can improvise a speech because "*Nosotros lo improvisamos todo*" [we improvise everything].

13   Another source of cultural conflict arises from the difference between *being* and *doing.* Even when trying to be individualistic, the Anglo-American achieves it by what he does. Today's young generation decided to be themselves, to get away from standardization, so they let their hair grow, wore ragged clothes and even went barefoot in order to be different from the Establishment. As a result they all ended up doing the same things and created another stereotype. The freedom enjoyed by the individuality of *being* makes it unnecessary for Hispanos to strive to be different.

14   In 1963 a team of psychologists from the University of Guadalajara in Mexico and the University of Michigan compared 74 upper-middle-class students from each university. Individualism and personalism were found to be central values for the Mexican students. This was explained by saying that a Mexican's value as a person lies in his *being* rather than, as is the case of the Anglo-Americans, in concrete accomplishments. Efficiency and accomplishments are derived characteristics that do not affect worthiness in the Mexican, whereas in the American it is equated with success, a value of highest priority in the American culture. Hispanic people disassociate themselves from material things or from actions that may impugn a person's sense of being, but the Anglo-American shows great concern for material things and assumes responsibility for his actions. This is expressed in the language of each culture. In Spanish one says, "*Se me cayó la taza*" [the cup fell away from me] instead of "I dropped the cup."

15   In English, one speaks of money, cash and all related transactions with frankness because material things of this high order do not trouble Anglo-Americans. In Spanish such materialistic concepts are circumvented by referring to cash as *efectivo* [effective] and when buying or selling as something *al contado* [counted out], and when without it by saying *No tengo fondos* [I have no funds]. This disassociation from material things is what produces *sobriedad* [sobriety] in the Spaniard according to Miguel de Unamuno, but in the Southwest the disassociation from materialism leads to *dejadez* [lassitude] and *desprendimiento* [disinterestedness]. A man may lose his life defending his honor but is unconcerned about the lack of material things. *Desprendimiento* causes a man to spend his last cent on a friend, which when added to lack of concern for the future may mean that tomorrow he will eat beans as a result of today's binge.

16   The implicit differences in words that appear to be identical in meaning are astonishing. Versatile is a compliment in English and an insult in Spanish. An Hispano student who is told to apologize cannot do it, because the word doesn't exist in Spanish. *Apología* means words in praise of a person. The Anglo-American either apologizes,

which is a form of retraction abhorrent in Spanish, or compromises, another concept foreign to Hispanic culture. *Compromiso* means a date, not a compromise. In colonial Mexico City, two hidalgos[5] once entered a narrow street from opposite sides, and when they could not go around, they sat in their coaches for three days until the viceroy ordered them to back out. All this because they could not work out a compromise.

It was that way then and to some extent now. Many of today's conflicts in the   17
Southwest have their roots in polarized cultural differences, which need not be irreconcilable when approached with mutual respect and understanding.

Vocabulary

affirmation (1)	conquistadores (2)	acculturated (11)
implicit (2)	absolutist (3)	corollary (12)
conceptual (2)	relativistic (3)	impugn (14)
configurations (2)	peripatetic (5)	circumvented (15)
insular (2)	equestrian (5)	versatile (16)
zealous (2)	incursion (7)	irreconcilable (17)
peninsular (2)	collectivity (7)	

Questions on Meaning and Technique

1. Where in the essay does Campa state his purpose? Where does he state his thesis? How well does the thesis relate to the purpose?

2. What sociological advantages, if any, accrue to a country on an island compared with a country that is part of the mainland? Which is more likely to produce people that could adapt to an entirely new society? Give reasons for your answers.

3. In paragraph 3, the author suggests that values such as justice, charity, and honesty were considered the "superior social order for all men" and were reflected in the constitution. What other values, if any, do you consider important as the basis for a successful society?

4. In your view, which is better for society—the insistence on individuality, as expressed by the Hispanic culture, or the need for fixed rules, as expressed by the Anglo culture? (Reread paragraphs 8 and 9.) Give reasons for your answer.

5. How does the author maintain coherence between paragraphs 4 and 5?

6. The author points out (see paragraph 9) that Hispanics to this day object to the Anglo lack of politeness. What is your definition of politeness in dealing with people? Provide examples of what you consider rude.

7. For the most part, how is the contrast organized—by using the alternating method of contrasting within a paragraph or by using the block method of

---

[5]Hidalgo—nobleman.

contrasting one paragraph with the next? Provide an example of the author's method.

8. What specific suggestions do you have for promoting respect and understanding among cultures in our society?

Writing Assignments

1. Write an essay in which you contrast two cultures with which you are familiar. Choose three or four clear bases for your contrast, considering such matters as social customs, food, religion, attitude toward education, and economics.

2. Compare and contrast two world figures, past or present, from totally different backgrounds. For instance, you might contrast Saddam Hussein with Bill Clinton, Queen Elizabeth I with Queen Elizabeth II, Pope John Paul II with Sheik Omar Abdul Rahman, Babe Ruth with Don Drysdale, or Michelangelo with Picasso. For your bases of contrast you might choose such areas as general popularity, social or political belief, influence on others, and personal taste.

READING FOR IDEAS

We are quite accustomed to hearing passionate complaints about how much of our money has to be spent on the underclass, those who beg on the streets, use drugs, live under bridges, or depend on welfare. But we rarely turn the spotlight to the overclass, another group in society that also spends our money to promote corporate raidings or other speculative schemes. In this essay the author points out not only the differences but also the similarities between the underclass and the overclass of our society. As you read, notice how the author smoothly shifts from one group to the other, thus highlighting the comparison/contrast.

ALTERNATE READING

A Class-ic Tale of America
ALICE STEINBACH

Alice Steinbach is an American reporter and columnist. She has written for the Baltimore Sun *and published an autobiographical essay titled "The Girl Who Loved the Win" in the November 1991 issue of the* Reader's Digest.

1   The man calling in to the radio talk show was angry. He was angry about almost everything, from the weather to the way the "liberal press" distorts the news.

But mostly the caller was angry about "the underclass" and the free ride he thinks   2
they're getting from the taxpayer.

"This is a segment of society that doesn't work, that lives on handouts from the   3
government and that won't assume any personal responsibility for their own lives," said
the caller. He laid the blame for many of the country's problems at the doorstep of the
underclass.

It's a popular theory, of course. The "lifestyle" of the so-called underclass—and its   4
consequences for the country—has been the subject of countless articles in magazines
and newspapers. Indeed, entire books have been devoted to analyzing how the
underclass got to be the underclass.

Given this kind of media coverage, you'd think some enterprising writer would have   5
realized by now that the underclass has been done. And that it's time to turn the spotlight
on a group that may be society's most overlooked minority: the overclass.

Which, because I abhor a vacuum, I am prepared to do.   6

The first thing to note about the overclass is that while there are many differences
between it and the underclass, there are also many similarities.

But let's do the differences first: 7

Unlike the underclass, which is basically a nameless group, members of the overclass   8
have names. Boesky, Milken, Trump, Keating and Helmsley spring to mind.

As a rule, the overclass is in need of constant legal counsel and therefore must   9
apportion a larger share of income toward legal fees than the underclass.

Because the underclass has no need for nannies, butlers and the like, they need less of   10
a budget for servants than the overclass.

But both classes, strangely enough, often wind up paying about the same—which is to   11
say, nothing—in Social Security employee taxes.

The overclass often lives in houses with names. Villa Favorita. Or Jasmine Hill. The   12
underclass, on the other hand, may live in places with names like Mission House or Circle
of Light Shelter.

Now for some similarities: 13

Just as there are the "undeserving poor" in the underclass, so too will you find the   14
"undeserving rich" in the overclass. Some good examples of the "undeserving rich"
might include: corporate raiders, Wall Street speculators, S&L criminals.

Both the underclass and the overclass enjoy betting the long shot. The underclass has   15
the lottery; the overclass has junk bonds.

Many members of both the underclass and the overclass develop their values in   16
response to "street culture." The underclass has violence and drugs on the streets where
they live; the overclass has Wall Street and insider trading.

Both the underclass and the overclass tend to live on credit. The underclass, if they can   17
get credit, may owe money to the neighborhood grocery store and the landlord. They are
expected to pay it off.

The overclass, however, may buy a large corporation without investing anything other   18
than "paper wealth." If the deal goes bad and they can't pay off, they can always exit
through the escape hatch of bankruptcy.

Generally speaking, it would seem that the overclass has taken to heart some of the   19
lessons society has tried to teach the underclass.

20   Self-help, for instance. As in: Why can't the undeserving poor help themselves more?

21   We have only to look to the S&L bandits who helped themselves to millions of dollars that didn't belong to them.

22   The concept of government entitlements is another area in which the overclass has excelled.

23   The overclass believe themselves to be entitled to million-dollar tax abatements. And they are willing to hold up cities and states for such tax advantages, threatening to move if such demands aren't met.

24   More and more, the overclass, like the underclass, produces less and less. The overclass now generates fewer jobs than ever before in our country's history.

25   What's generated is paper wealth, junk bonds and an increasing number of jobs for bankruptcy lawyers.

26   Maybe it's time to pin a note above society's desk, one that reads: It's the overclass, stupid!

Vocabulary

enterprising (5)
abhor (6)
apportion (9)
entitlements (22)
abatements (23)

Questions on Meaning and Technique

1. How does the author organize her essay? What is the sequence of her main segments? How does organization help the reader to follow her line of thought?

2. On what basis does the author draw her contrast between the underclass and the overclass? What method of contrast does she use—block or alternating? How well does the method work? Would you have preferred another method? If so, why?

3. On which part does the author spend more time—on the differences or on the similarities between the two classes? Why do you suppose she spent more time on one than the other? Do you agree with her comparison? Give reasons for your answer.

4. Twice during the essay the author uses allusion as a technique. What are these allusions? Explain them and indicate their function in the essay.

5. In paragraph 20, how does the author twist the usual meaning of the term *self-help*? What is her purpose?

6. In your view, who are the undeserving poor and the undeserving rich in the world? Which group do you consider worse? Would Steinbach agree with you? Give reasons for your answer.

7. How does the title of the essay function?

Photo Writing Assignment

Man lounging at Michelangelo Piazza. © 1960 F. B. Grunzweig/Photo Researchers, Inc., NYC.

Comparison points out similarities; *contrast* points out differences. As you scrutinize the photo of the man lying on the stone ledge of the Michelangelo monument in Florence, try first to see the similarities between him and the supine sculptures above him. Then analyze how the man differs from the statues. Write an essay in which you emphasize these similarities and differences between real life and art.

Writing Assignments

1. Write an essay in which you contrast the middle class with either the underclass or the overclass in your city, town, or neighborhood. Be sure to state clearly the basis of your contrast, providing appropriate examples to illustrate your contrast.

2. In a brief essay, answer the question, "How do the rich differ from the poor in our society?" Write your contrast so that you will favor one over the other.

Additional Writing Assignments

1. Develop an essay based on the following controlling idea: "Ignorance is different from stupidity."

2. Compare and contrast two love affairs you have had.

3. Write an essay contrasting envy with jealousy.

4. Compare and contrast respectability with self-respect.

5. Write an essay comparing and contrasting any two teachers you have ever had.

6. Based on your travels throughout the United States and abroad, choose two cities or towns that strike you as completely different from each other. Write an essay contrasting the two.

7. Compare and contrast erotica with pornography.

8. Write an essay specifying the differences between a romantic versus a realistic novel or movie.

9. From your general knowledge of U.S. history, contrast the eighteenth and twentieth centuries on three bases—hygiene, education, women's rights—supplying examples that stress their differences.

10. Compare and contrast the law-abiding person with the moral person.

Process

READING FOR IDEAS

As you read through the story "How Mr. Hogan Robbed a Bank," you might admire the meticulousness of Mr. Hogan's method even if you are repelled by his ethics. Ask yourself whether the means ever justifies an end. In other words, if the method is right, is the purpose also right? Also, think of some task you would like to accomplish and see if you can put together similar meticulous, easy-to-follow directions for this task.

How Mr. Hogan Robbed a Bank
JOHN STEINBECK

John Steinbeck (1902–1968), American novelist and writer, was known mainly for his sociological novels about the poor and downtrodden of American society. Born in Salinas, California, Steinbeck studied at Stanford. His novels include Tortilla Flat *(1935),* Of Mice and Men *(1937, also made into a play), and* The Grapes of Wrath *(1939; Pulitzer Prize). Steinbeck was awarded the Nobel Prize in literature in 1962.*

On Saturday before Labor Day, 1955, at 9:04½ A.M., Mr. Hogan robbed a bank. He   1
was forty-two years old, married, and the father of a boy and a girl, named John and Joan, twelve and thirteen respectively. Mrs. Hogan's name was Joan and Mr. Hogan's name was John, but since they called themselves Papa and Mama that left their names free for the children, who were considered very smart for their ages, each having jumped a grade in school. The Hogans lived at 215 East Maple Street, in a brown-shingle house

with white trim—there are two. 215 is the one across from the street light and it is the one with the big tree in the yard, either oak or elm—the biggest tree in the whole street, maybe in the whole town.

2   John and Joan were in bed at the time of the robbery, for it was Saturday. At 9:10 A.M., Mrs. Hogan was making the cup of tea she always had. Mr. Hogan went to work early. Mrs. Hogan drank her tea slowly, scalding hot, and read her fortune in the tea leaves. There was a cloud and a five-pointed star with two short points in the bottom of the cup, but that was at 9:12 and the robbery was all over by then.

3   The way Mr. Hogan went about robbing the bank was very interesting. He gave it a great deal of thought and had for a long time, but he did not discuss it with anyone. He just read his newspaper and kept his own counsel. But he worked it out to his own satisfaction that people went to too much trouble robbing banks and that got them in a mess. The simpler the better, he always thought. People went in for too much hullabaloo and hanky-panky. If you didn't do that, if you left hanky-panky out, robbing a bank would be a relatively sound venture—barring accidents, of course, of an improbable kind, but then they could happen to a man crossing the street or anything. Since Mr. Hogan's method worked fine, it proved that his thinking was sound. He often considered writing a little booklet on his technique when the how-to rage was running so high. He figured out the first sentence, which went: "To successfully rob a bank, forget all about hanky-panky."

4   Mr. Hogan was not just a clerk at Fettucci's grocery store. He was more like the manager. Mr. Hogan was in charge, even hired and fired the boy who delivered groceries after school. He even put in orders with the salesmen, sometimes when Mr. Fettucci was right in the store too, maybe talking to a customer. "You do it, John," he would say and he would nod at the customer, "John knows the ropes. Been with me—how long you been with me, John?"

5   "Sixteen years."

6   "Sixteen years. Knows the business as good as me. John, why he even banks the money."

7   And so he did. Whenever he had a moment, Mr. Hogan went into the storeroom on the alley, took off his apron, put on his necktie and coat, and went back through the store to the cash register. The checks and bills would be ready for him inside the bankbook with a rubber band around it. Then he went next door and stood at the teller's window and handed the checks and bankbook through to Mr. Cup and passed the time of day with him too. Then, when the bankbook was handed back, he checked the entry, put the rubber band around it, and walked next door to Fettucci's grocery and put the bankbook in the cash register, continued on to the storeroom, removed his coat and tie, put on his apron, and went back into the store ready for business. If there was no line at the teller's window, the whole thing didn't take more than five minutes, even passing the time of day.

8   Mr. Hogan was a man who noticed things, and when it came to robbing the bank, this trait stood him in good stead. He had noticed, for instance, where the big bills were kept right in the drawer under the counter and he had noticed also what days they were likely to be more than other days. Thursday was payday at the American Can Company's local plant, for instance, so there would be more then. Some Fridays people drew more

money to tide them over the weekend. But it was even Steven, maybe not a thousand dollars difference, between Thursdays and Fridays and Saturday mornings. Saturdays were not terribly good because people didn't come to get money that early in the morning, and the bank closed at noon. But he thought it over and came to the conclusion that the Saturday before a long weekend in the summer would be the best of all. People going on trips, vacations, people with relatives visiting, and the bank closed Monday. He thought it out and looked, and sure enough the Saturday morning before Labor Day the cash drawer had twice as much money in it—he saw it when Mr. Cup pulled out the drawer.

Mr. Hogan thought about it during all that year, not all the time, of course, but when he had some moments. It was a busy year too. That was the year John and Joan had the mumps and Mrs. Hogan got her teeth pulled and was fitted for a denture. That was the year when Mr. Hogan was Master of the Lodge, with all the time that takes. Larry Shield died that year—he was Mrs. Hogan's brother and was buried from the Hogan house at 215 East Maple. Larry was a bachelor and had a room in the Pine Tree House and he played pool nearly every night. He worked at the Silver Diner but that closed at nine and so Larry would go to Louie's and play pool for an hour. Therefore, it was a surprise when he left enough so that after funeral expenses there were twelve hundred dollars left. And even more surprising that he left a will in Mrs. Hogan's favor, but his double-barreled twelve-gauge shotgun he left to John Hogan, Jr. Mr. Hogan was pleased, although he never hunted. He put the shotgun away in the back of the closet in the bathroom, where he kept his things, to keep it for young John. He didn't want children handling guns and he never bought any shells. It was some of that twelve hundred that got Mrs. Hogan her dentures. Also, she bought a bicycle for John and a doll buggy and walking-talking doll for Joan—a doll with three changes of dresses and a little suitcase, complete with play make-up. Mr. Hogan thought it might spoil the children, but it didn't seem to. They made just as good marks in school and John even got a job delivering papers. It was a very busy year. Both John and Joan wanted to enter the W. R. Hearst National "I Love America" Contest and Mr. Hogan thought it was almost too much, but they promised to do the work during their summer vacation, so he finally agreed.

9

II

During that year, no one noticed any difference in Mr. Hogan. It was true, he was thinking about robbing the bank, but he only thought about it in the evening when there was neither a Lodge meeting nor a movie they wanted to go to, so it did not become an obsession and people noticed no change in him.

10

He had studied everything so carefully that the approach of Labor Day did not catch him unprepared or nervous. It was hot that summer and the hot spells were longer than usual. Saturday was the end of two weeks heat without a break and people were irritated with it and anxious to get out of town, although the country was just as hot. They didn't think of that. The children were excited because the "I Love America" Essay Contest was due to be concluded and the winners announced, and the first prize was an all-expense-paid two days trip to Washington, D.C., with every fixing—hotel room, three meals a day, and side trips in a limousine—not only for the winner, but for an accompanying

11

chaperone; visit to the White House—shake hands with the President—everything. Mr. Hogan thought they were getting their hopes too high and he said so.

12 "You've got to be prepared to lose," he told his children. "There're probably thousands and thousands entered. You get your hopes up and it might spoil the whole autumn. Now I don't want any long faces in this house after the contest is over."

13 "I was against it from the start," he told Mrs. Hogan. That was the morning she saw the Washington Monument in her teacup, but she didn't tell anybody about that except Ruth Tyler, Bob Tyler's wife. Ruthie brought over her cards and read them in the Hogan kitchen, but she didn't find a journey. She did tell Mrs. Hogan that the cards were often wrong. The cards had said Mrs. Winkle was going on a trip to Europe and the next week Mrs. Winkle got a fishbone in her throat and choked to death. Ruthie, just thinking out loud, wondered if there was any connection between the fishbone and the ocean voyage to Europe. "You've got to interpret them right." Ruthie did say she saw money coming to the Hogans.

14 "Oh, I got that already from poor Larry," Mrs. Hogan explained.

15 "I must have got the past and future cards mixed," said Ruthie. "You've got to interpret them right."

16 Saturday dawned a blaster. The early morning weather report on the radio said "Continued hot and humid, light scattered rain Sunday night and Monday." Mrs. Hogan said, "Wouldn't you know? Labor Day." And Mr. Hogan said, "I'm sure glad we didn't plan anything." He finished his egg and mopped the plate with his toast. Mrs. Hogan said, "Did I put coffee on the list?" He took the paper from his handkerchief pocket and consulted it. "Yes, coffee, it's here."

17 "I had a crazy idea I forgot to write it down," said Mrs. Hogan. "Ruth and I are going to Altar Guild this afternoon. It's at Mrs. Alfred Drake's. You know, they just came to town. I can't wait to see their furniture."

18 "They trade with us," said Mr. Hogan. "Opened an account last week. Are the milk bottles ready?"

19 "On the porch."

20 Mr. Hogan looked at his watch just before he picked up the bottles and it was five minutes to eight. He was about to go down the stairs, when he turned and looked back through the opened door at Mrs. Hogan. She said, "Want something, Papa?"

21 "No," he said. "No," and he walked down the steps.

22 He went down to the corner and turned right on Spooner, and Spooner runs into Main Street in two blocks, and right across from where it runs in, there is Fettucci's and the bank around the corner and the alley beside the bank. Mr. Hogan picked up a handbill in front of Fettucci's and unlocked the door. He went through to the storeroom, opened the door to the alley, and looked out. A cat tried to force its way in, but Mr. Hogan blocked it with his foot and leg and closed the door. He took off his coat and put on his long apron, tied the strings in a bowknot behind his back. Then he got the broom from behind the counter and swept out behind the counters and scooped the sweepings into a dustpan; and, going through the storeroom, he opened the door to the alley. The cat had gone away. He emptied the dustpan into the garbage can and tapped it smartly to dislodge a piece of lettuce leaf. Then he went back to the store and worked for a while on the order sheet. Mrs. Clooney came in for a half a pound of bacon. She said it was hot and Mr. Hogan agreed. "Summers are getting hotter," he said.

"I think so myself," said Mrs. Clooney. "How's Mrs. standing up?"   23

"Just fine," said Mr. Hogan. "She's going to Altar Guild."   24

"So am I. I just can't wait to see their furniture," said Mrs. Clooney, and she went out.   25

III

Mr. Hogan put a five-pound hunk of bacon on the slicer and stripped off the pieces   26
and laid them on wax paper and then he put the wax paper-covered squares in the cooler
cabinet. At ten minutes to nine, Mr. Hogan went to a shelf. He pushed a spaghetti box
aside and took down a cereal box, which he emptied in the little closet toilet. Then, with
a banana knife, he cut out the Mickey Mouse mask that was on the back. The rest of the
box he took to the toilet and tore up the cardboard and flushed it down. He went into the
store then and yanked a piece of string loose and tied the ends through the side holes of
the mask and then he looked at his watch—a large silver Hamilton with black hands. It
was two minutes to nine.

Perhaps the next four minutes were his only time of nervousness at all. At one minute   27
to nine, he took the broom and went out to sweep the sidewalk and he swept it very
rapidly—was sweeping it, in fact, when Mr. Warner unlocked the bank door. He said
good morning to Mr. Warner and a few seconds later the bank staff of four emerged from
the coffee shop. Mr. Hogan saw them across the street and he waved at them and they
waved back. He finished the sidewalk and went back in the store. He laid his watch on the
little step of the cash register. He sighed very deeply, more like a deep breath than a sigh.
He knew that Mr. Warner would have the safe open now and he would be carrying the
cash trays to the teller's window. Mr. Hogan looked at the watch on the cash register
step. Mr. Kenworthy paused in the store entrance, then shook his head vaguely and
walked on and Mr. Hogan let out his breath gradually. His left hand went behind his back
and pulled the bowknot on his apron, and then the black hand on his watch crept up on
the four-minute mark and covered it.

Mr. Hogan opened the charge account drawer and took out the store pistol, a   28
silver-colored Iver Johnson .38. He moved quickly to the storeroom, slipped off his
apron, put on his coat, and stuck the revolver in his side pocket. The Mickey Mouse mask
he shoved up under his coat where it didn't show. He opened the alley door and looked
up and down and stepped quickly out, leaving the door slightly ajar. It is sixty feet to
where the alley enters Main Street, and there he paused and looked up and down and
then he turned his head toward the center of the street as he passed the bank window. At
the bank's swinging door, he took out the mask from under his coat and put it on. Mr.
Warner was just entering his office and his back was to the door. The top of Will Cup's
head was visible through the teller's grill.

Mr. Hogan moved quickly and quietly around the end of the counter and into the   29
teller's cage. He had the revolver in his right hand now. When Will Cup turned his head
and saw the revolver, he froze. Mr. Hogan slipped his toe under the trigger of the floor
alarm and motioned Will Cup to the floor with the revolver and Will went down quick.
Then Mr. Hogan opened the cash drawer and with two quick movements he piled the
large bills from the tray together. He made a whipping motion to Will on the floor, to
indicate that he should turn over and face the wall, and Will did. Then Mr. Hogan stepped
back around the counter. At the door of the bank, he took off the mask, and as he passed

the window he turned his head toward the middle of the street. He moved into the alley, walked quickly to the storeroom and entered. The cat got in. It watched him from a pile of canned goods cartons. Mr. Hogan went to the toilet closet and tore up the mask and flushed it. He took off his coat and put on his apron. He looked out into the store and then moved to the cash register. The revolver went back into the charge account drawer. He punched No Sale and, lifting the top drawer, distributed the stolen money underneath the top tray and then pulled the tray forward and closed the register, and only then did he look at his watch and it was 9:07½.

30　　He was trying to get the cat out of the storeroom when the commotion boiled out of the bank. He took his broom and went out on the sidewalk. He heard all about it and offered his opinion when it was asked for. He said he didn't think the fellow could get away—where could he get to? Still, with the holiday coming up—

31　　It was an exciting day. Mr. Fettucci was as proud as though it were his bank. The sirens sounded around town for hours. Hundreds of holiday travelers had to stop at the roadblocks set up all around the edge of town and several sneaky-looking men had their cars searched.

32　　Mrs. Hogan heard about it over the phone and she dressed earlier than she would have ordinarily and came to the store on her way to Altar Guild. She hoped Mr. Hogan would have seen or heard something new, but he hadn't. "I don't see how the fellow can get away," he said.

33　　Mrs. Hogan was so excited, she forgot her own news. She only remembered when she got to Mrs. Drake's house, but she asked permission and phoned the store the first moment she could. "I forgot to tell you. John's won honorable mention."

34　　"What?"

"In the 'I Love America' Contest."

"What did he win?"

"Honorable mention."

"Fine. Fine—Anything come with it?"

35　　"Why, he'll get his picture and his name all over the country. Radio too. Maybe even television. They've already asked for a photograph of him."

36　　"Fine," said Mr. Hogan. "I hope it don't spoil him." He put up the receiver and said to Mr. Fettucci, "I guess we've got a celebrity in the family."

37　　Fettucci stayed open until nine on Saturdays. Mr. Hogan ate a few snacks from cold cuts, but not much, because Mrs. Hogan always kept his supper warming.

38　　It was 9:05 or :06, or :07, when he got back to the brown-shingle house at 215 East Maple. He went in through the front door and out to the kitchen where the family was waiting for him.

39　　"Got to wash up," he said, and went up to the bathroom. He turned the key in the bathroom door and then he flushed the toilet and turned on the water in the basin and tub while he counted the money. Eight thousand three hundred and twenty dollars. From the top shelf of the storage closet in the bathroom, he took down the big leather case that held his Knight Templar's uniform. The plumed hat lay there on its form. The white ostrich feather was a little yellow and needed changing. Mr. Hogan lifted out the hat and pried the form up from the bottom of the case. He put the money in the form and then he thought again and removed two bills and shoved them in his side pocket. Then he put the form back over the money and laid the hat on top and closed the case and shoved it back on the top shelf. Finally he washed his hands and turned off the water in the tub and the basin.

In the kitchen, Mrs. Hogan and the children faced him, beaming, "Guess what some   40
young man's going on?"

"What?" asked Mr. Hogan.   41

"Radio," said John. "Monday night. Eight o'clock."

"I guess we got a celebrity in the family," said Mr. Hogan.

Mrs. Hogan said, "I just hope some young lady hasn't got her nose out of joint."   42

Mr. Hogan pulled up to the table and stretched his legs. "Mama, I guess I got a fine   43
family," he said. He reached in his pocket and took out two five-dollar bills. He handed one to John. "That's for winning," he said. He poked the other bill at Joan. "And that's for being a good sport. One celebrity and one good sport. What a fine family!" He rubbed his hands together and lifted the lid of the covered dish. "Kidneys," he said. "Fine."

And that's how Mr. Hogan did it.   44

Questions on Meaning and Technique

1. What steps are taken by Mr. Hogan to rob the bank? State them in the order in which they occur.

2. What point does this story make?

3. What are some examples of the typical middle-class life of the Hogans?

4. What detail in paragraph 9 clearly indicates Mr. Hogan's double standard?

5. What is your response to the sentence in paragraph 3, ". . . if you left hanky-panky out, robbing a bank would be a relatively sound venture . . ."?

READING FOR IDEAS

"Tract" could well be considered a step-by-step process for how to perform a funeral that would be in harmony with nature. In the first stanza, notice whom the poet addresses, and be prepared to give reasons for his choice of audience. On a sheet of paper, list the instructions one by one and explain what they mean in a philosophical and psychological sense.

Tract

WILLIAM CARLOS WILLIAMS

William Carlos Williams (1883–1963), American poet and physician, was born in Rutherford, N.J., and educated at the University of Pennsylvania and the University of Leipzig. Among the most original American poets of this century, Williams wrote in a style close to the idioms and rhythms of natural speech, but with a poetic incisiveness. His works include Collected Poems *(1934),* Collected Later Poems *(1950), and* Pictures from Brueghel and Other Poems *(1963; Pulitzer Prize).*

1 I will teach you my townspeople
how to perform a funeral
for you have it over a troop
of artists—
unless one should scour the world—
you have the ground sense necessary.

2 See! the hearse leads.
I begin with a design for a hearse.
For Christ's sake not black—
nor white either—and not polished!
Let it be weathered—like a farm wagon—
with gilt wheels (this could be
applied fresh at small expense)
or no wheels at all:
a rough dray to drag over the ground.

3 Knock the glass out!
My God—glass, my townspeople!
For what purpose? Is it for the dead
to look out or for us to see
how well he is housed or to see
the flowers or the lack of them—
or what?
To keep the rain and snow from him?
He will have a heavier rain soon:
pebbles and dirt and what not.
Let there be no glass—
and no upholstery, phew!
and no little brass rollers
and small easy wheels on the bottom—
my townspeople what are you thinking of?

4 A rough plain hearse then
with gilt wheels and no top at all.
On this the coffin lies
by its own weight.

5   No wreaths please—
especially no hot house flowers.
Some common memento is better,
something he prized and is known by:
his old clothes—a few books perhaps—

God knows what! You realize
how we are about these things
my townspeople—
something will be found—anything
even flowers if he had come to that.
So much for the hearse.

For heaven's sake though see to the driver!   6
Take off the silk hat! In fact
that's no place at all for him—
up there unceremoniously
dragging our friend out to his own dignity!
Bring him down—bring him down!
Low and inconspicuous! I'd not have him ride
on the wagon at all—damn him—
the undertaker's understrapper!
Let him hold the reins
and walk at the side
and inconspicuously too!

Then briefly as to yourselves: 7
Walk behind—as they do in France,
seventh class, or if you ride
Hell take curtains! Go with some show
of inconvenience; sit openly—
to the weather as to grief.
Or do you think you can shut grief in?
What—from us? We who have perhaps
nothing to lose? Share with us
share with us—it will be money
in your pockets.
                              Go now
I think you are ready.

Vocabulary

> dray (2)
> memento (5)
> unceremoniously (6)
> understrapper (6)

Questions on Meaning and Technique

1. In giving advice on how to perform a funeral, what major steps does the speaker advocate? List them in the order in which they are mentioned.

2. What is the poet's general purpose in advocating this kind of funeral?

3. In stanza 2, why does the speaker suggest the gilt wheels, applied fresh?

4. Why doesn't the speaker want the coffin to ride along smoothly (stanza 3)?

5. Instead of wreaths of "hot house" flowers, what does the speaker suggest as a decoration for the coffin? Why?

6. What objections does the speaker have to the undertaker's driving the carriage in a silk top hat?

7. What is the most important thought contained in the final stanza?

HOW TO WRITE A PROCESS PAPER

A process is a sequence of operations or actions telling how something is done, is made, or happens. Describing a process, often called *process analysis,* is a common and indispensable assignment. Some process papers focus on "how-to-do-it" by giving step-by-step directions, such as for assembling a computer; others focus on "why-it-happened" by explaining how a certain situation came about, such as the 1990 savings and loan financial debacle. Most process papers that offer directions address the reader personally by using the pronoun *you:* "Before inserting the cartridge, *you* must clean off all excess grime." But other process papers, especially those explaining how a situation happened or will happen, are developed impersonally, in the third person: "The first step in the trend toward achieving a zero-growth society is the use of the pill, allowing women to feel secure from unwanted pregnancy."

Writing Assignment

Choose a process with which you are thoroughly familiar and give a specific, detailed set of instructions for doing it. Here are some sample process topics: "How to detect counterfeit money"; "How to train a dog in obedience"; "How to keep a journal"; "How to read a map"; "How to write a research paper"; "How to balance a budget"; "How to produce an antiflu serum." The assignment here involves a "how-to-do-it" process rather than a "how-it-happened" one.

Specific Instructions

PREWRITING ON THE ASSIGNMENT. Before starting to write, choose a process you are able to explain clearly. Mentally rehearse your day, and most likely a subject will come to mind. For instance, you have to do your morning exercises, make your bed, review for a biology exam, drive the busy freeway to work where you do manicures, or wait on tables, or help the elderly in a convalescent hospital, or deliver pizzas, or. . . . Each of these activities involves a process with which you are thoroughly acquainted. Choose an activity complicated enough to keep your reader's interest yet simple enough to be easily explained.

Once you have settled on a subject, you must figure out the major steps of the process involved. Most likely these major steps will contain substeps that also need explaining, but the major steps should be identified first. Let us consider a process with which all of us are familiar—making the bed. What are the major steps involved? First, airing the mattress; second, smoothing and fitting the bottom sheet; third, pulling up the bedding over the bed; fourth, fitting the corners so that the bed will have a finished look; fifth, adjusting the pillows and bedspread. Each of these major steps contains some steps of its own. An outline reveals them easily:

I. Air the mattress.
   A. Throw the pillows on the floor.
   B. Pull off the flat sheets, blankets, and bedspread.
   C. Shake the sheets and blankets.
II. Smooth and fit the bottom sheet.
   A. Get rid of all lumps or wrinkles.
   B. Make sure the corners are properly tucked under.
III. Pull the bedding over the bed.
   A. Pull the flat sheet up to the headboard, allowing a two-foot overlap.
   B. Bring the blankets to within a foot of the headboard.
   C. Allow the flat sheet to fold one foot over the blankets.
IV. Fit the corners.
   A. Smooth the blankets.
   B. Tuck in the sheets and blankets at the foot of the bed.
   C. Create symmetrical corners by pulling up the ends of the bedding and tucking them in, military style.
V. Adjust the bedspread and pillows.
   A. Align the pillows at the top of the bed.
   B. Pull up the bedspread, allowing the same length to hang down on each side and at the foot.
   C. Tuck about a foot of bedspread under the pillows to create a tailored effect.

Although the process of making a bed is admittedly a mundane subject, it is also one that cannot be well explained without organizing the individual steps into the sequence in which they must be performed. Writing a process is not so much a matter of finding exotic imagery or elegant words as choosing a methodical arrangement of events that your reader can follow.

The most common failing of process papers is the writer's assumption that a step is too self-evident to be included. For instance, if you are trying to explain how to set up camp and you leave out pitching the tent because you assume that everyone already knows that maneuver, then your process will be incomplete. This kind of omission becomes especially acute if left out of directions on how to assemble something. All of us are familiar with the frustration of creating a lopsided stool, or having a window shade not work because the instructions omitted a step.

We therefore recommend that in preparing for this assignment, you write a simple outline to make sure your process is clear and complete.

BEGIN WITH A CLEAR STATEMENT OF PURPOSE. A process paper should begin by announcing the process it intends to clarify. Here are some samples: "Assembling a dictionary involves four major steps." Or "The purpose of this paper is to show the easiest way to gather a good collection of rock music." Or "What follows is a summary of the basic steps involved in the scientific method of investigation." Or "A few simple steps in dealing with garbage will help us win the ecological battle to save the environment." This initial announcement alerts the reader to the purpose of a process paper, giving a context for the individual steps that follow. Such a clear statement of purpose takes the place of the thesis in a process paper.

ASSEMBLE ALL THE INFORMATION NECESSARY TO THE COMPLETE PROCESS. To give directions or explain the separate steps of a process is easier when you have accurate and complete information about it. If the process is unfamiliar and the information not at hand, you will need to do some research. Gather *all* the information you can. It is better to assemble more information than you will actually use than to overlook a detail that might help explain a step. Collect the facts and refer to them as you write the process.

DECIDE ON THE ORDER OF YOUR STEPS. Once the facts are collected, their order of presentation usually becomes apparent from the process. For example, if you are analyzing the steps in planting camellias, common sense tells you that the first step is preparing the soil. Similarly, if you are writing a paper on how a U.S. president is elected to office, you would begin not with the inauguration but with the election of local delegates in the primaries.

A reasonable way to begin a process paper is to outline all the steps in the order they will logically occur and to include those details necessary for a clear presentation of each step. An example of such an outline follows:

Controlling idea: My purpose is to list the basic steps in writing a book review.

   I. Read the book carefully.
    A. Look for major ideas.
    B. Mark essential pages.
  II. Think about the book.
    A. Figure out the purpose of the book.
    B. Judge the book according to how well it has fulfilled its purpose.
    C. Make mental notes of both strengths and weaknesses.
 III. Write a fair review.
    A. State the purpose of the book.
    B. Give a brief summary of the book.
    C. Explain major passages, using quotations to give a flavor of the author's style.
    D. Pass judgment on the book.

Although the sequence of a process may be extremely simple, consisting of only one or two steps, each step may be complicated by many details. For example, the process of writing good advertising copy contains two steps complicated by details:

Controlling idea: The purpose of this paper is to show how to write good advertising copy.

I. Begin with a strong headline.
  A. Flag down all possible customers.
  B. Include key words associated with the product.
  C. Appeal to the reader's self-interest.
  D. Make the produce sound new.
II. Write the body as if you were answering someone's questions.
  A. Go straight to the point.
  B. Be factual and specific.
  C. Include testimonials.
  D. Give the reader some helpful advice.
  E. Write in colloquial language.

The outline makes the process easier to write by highlighting each step along with its cluster of details. Without the aid of the outline, the writer could easily become confused.

EACH INDIVIDUAL STEP MUST BE CLEAR AND COMPLETE.   Each step in the process must be clearly enumerated and explained; one poorly explained step can confuse an entire process. For example, suppose the third step in producing an antivenom for snake bites is to collect the serum by bleeding a horse that has been injected with the venom. A clear explanation of this step, with all the necessary details beautifully aligned, is of little use if step 1 —collecting the venom by milking a snake—is never explained. A clear step-by-step presentation of material is crucial in a process paper.

READING FOR IDEAS

Mayleas's essay provides a visual structure to help you read purposefully. Take advantage, for instance, of the numbering system and italic headings used. The best way to approach the content of this essay is to ponder the advice presented and to apply it to job markets of interest to you. For example, one piece of advice is to compose "a better résumé." To make sure you understand the author's suggestions, translate them into a résumé you might use to apply for a summer job while in college. Let us say that you wish to work in the car pickup section of Sears Roebuck. Do as the author states and mentally list the personal traits you possess that would be helpful in such a position: You are courteous, patient, diligent, and honest. You have held other jobs that required muscular strength, and you enjoy working with people. Think of action words to describe past jobs and accomplishments. Here are examples, with the action words italicized: "For several summers, I *helped unload* lumber for Brock Brothers, a large development firm in Los Angeles." "During last Christmas vacation, I *staffed* the information desk of J. C. Penney, dealing with inquisitive, lost, or angry customers." "While attending high school, I spent much of my spare time *filing* requisition forms for my father, who owns a locksmith store."

PROFESSIONAL MODEL

How to Land the Job You Want
Davidyne Mayleas

Davidyne Mayleas is a freelance journalist and social critic whose work has appeared in Reader's Digest, Esquire, *and numerous other popular magazines. She attended the University of Chicago and then New York University, majoring in banking and finance. She is married to William Mayleas, a well-known entrepreneur, investment consultant, economist, and writer. Among the books she has written are* The Hidden Job Market for the 80's *(1981) and* By Appointment Only *(1989).*

1   Louis Albert, 39, lost his job as an electrical engineer when his firm made extensive cutbacks. He spent two months answering classified ads and visiting employment agencies—with zero results. Albert might still be hunting if a friend, a specialist in the employment field, had not shown him how to be his own job counselor. Albert learned how to research unlisted openings, write a forceful résumé, perform smoothly in an interview, even transform a turndown into a job.

2   Although there seemed to be a shortage of engineering jobs, Albert realized that he still persuaded potential employers to see him. This taught him something—that his naturally outgoing personality might be as great an asset as his engineering degree. When the production head of a small electronics company told him that they did not have an immediate opening, Albert told his interviewer, "You people make a fine product. I think you could use additional sales representation—someone like me who understands and talks electrical engineer's language, and who enjoys selling." The interviewer decided to send Albert to a senior vice president. Albert got a job in sales.

3   You too can be your own counselor if you put the same vigorous effort into *getting* a job as you would into *keeping* one. Follow these three basic rules, developed by placement experts:

4   1. FIND THE HIDDEN JOB MARKET. Classified ads and agency listings reveal only a small percentage of available jobs. Some of the openings that occur through promotions, retirements and reorganization never reach the personnel department. There are three ways to get in touch with this hidden market:

5   *Write a strong résumé with a well-directed cover letter and mail it to the appropriate department manager in the company where you'd like to work.* Don't

worry whether there's a current opening. Many managers fill vacancies by reviewing the résumés already in their files. Dennis Mollura, press-relations manager in the public-relations department of American Telephone and Telegraph, says, "In my own case, the company called me months after I sent in my résumé."

Get in touch with people who work in or know the companies that interest you.   6
Jobs are so often filled through personal referral that Charles R. Lops, executive employment manager of the J. C. Penney Co., says, "Probably our best source for outside people comes from recommendations made by Penney associates themselves."

"Drop in" on the company. Lillian Reveille, employment manager of Equitable Life   7
Assurance Society of the United States, reports: "A large percentage of the applicants we see are 'walk-ins'—and we do employ many of these people."

2. LOCATE HIDDEN OPENINGS. This step requires energy and determination to make   8
telephone calls, see people, do research, and to keep moving despite turndowns.

Contact anyone who may know of openings, including relatives, friends, teachers,   9
bank officers, insurance agents—anyone you know in your own or an adjacent field. When the teachers' union and employment agencies produced no teaching openings, Eric Olson, an unemployed high-school math instructor, reviewed his talent and decided that where an analytical math mind was useful, there he'd find a job. He called his insurance agent, who set up an interview with the actuarial department of one of the companies he represented. They hired Olson.

It's a good idea to contact not only professional or trade associations in your field, but   10
also your local chamber of commerce and people involved in community activities. After Laura Bailey lost her job as retirement counselor in a bank's personnel department, she found a position in customer relations in another bank. Her contact: a member of the senior-citizens club that Mrs. Bailey ran on a volunteer basis.

Use local or business-school libraries. Almost every field has its own directory of   11
companies, which provides names, addresses, products and/or services, and lists officers and other executives. Write to the company president or to the executive to whom you'd report. The vice president of personnel at Warner-Lambert Co. says, "When a résumé of someone we could use—now or in the near future—shows up 'cold' in my in-basket, that's luck for both of us."

Consult telephone directories. Sometimes the telephone company will send you free   12
the telephone directories of various cities. Also, good-sized public libraries often have many city directories. Fred Lewis, a cabinet maker, checked the telephone directories of nine different cities where he knew furniture was manufactured. At the end of five weeks he had a sizable telephone bill, some travel expenses—and ten interviews which resulted in three job offers.

3. AFTER YOU FIND THE OPENING, GET THE JOB. The applicants who actually get hired are   13
those who polish these six job-getting skills to perfection:

Compose a better résumé. A résumé is a self-advertisement, designed to get you an   14
interview. Start by putting yourself in an employer's place. Take stock of your job history and personal achievements. Make an inventory of your skills and accomplishments that might be useful from the employer's standpoint. Choose the most important and

describe them in words that stress accomplishments. Avoid such phrases as "my duties included . . ." Use action words like planned, sold, trained, managed.

15   Ask a knowledgeable business friend to review your résumé. Does it stress accomplishment rather than duties? Does it tell an employer what you can do for him? Can it be shortened? (One or two pages should suffice.) Generally, it's not wise to mention salary requirements.

16   *Write a convincing cover letter.* While the résumé may be a copy, the cover letter must be personal. Sy Mann, director of research for Aceto Chemical Co., says: "When I see a mimeographed letter that states, 'Dear Sir, I'm sincerely interested in working for your company,' I wonder, 'How many other companies got this valentine?' " Use the name and title of the person who can give you the interview, and be absolutely certain of accuracy here. Using a wrong title or misspelling a prospective employer's name may route your correspondence directly to an automatic turndown.

17   *Prepare specifically for each interview.* Research the company thoroughly; know its history and competition. Try to grasp the problems of the job you're applying for. For example, a line in an industry journal that a food company was "developing a new geriatric food" convinced one man that he should emphasize his marketing experience with vitamins rather than with frozen foods.

18   You'll increase your edge by anticipating questions the interviewer might raise. Why do you want to work for us? What can you offer us that someone else cannot? Why did you leave your last position? What are your salary requirements?

19   An employer holds an interview to get a clearer picture of your work history and accomplishments, and to look for characteristics he considers valuable. These vary with jobs. Does the position require emphasis on attention to detail or on creativity? Perseverance or aggressiveness? Prior to the interview decide what traits are most in demand. And always send a thank-you note immediately after the interview.

20   *Follow-up.* They said you would hear in a week; now it's two. Call them. Don't wait and hope. Hope and act.

21   *Supply additional information.* That's the way Karen Halloway got her job as fashion director with a department store. "After my interview I sensed that the merchandise manager felt I was short on retail experience. So I wrote to him describing the 25 fashion shows I'd staged yearly for the pattern company I'd worked for."

22   *Don't take no for an answer.* Hank Newell called to find out why he had been turned down. The credit manager felt he had insufficient collection experience. Hank thanked him for his time and frankness. The next day, Hank called back saying, "My collection experience is limited, but I don't think I fully emphasized my training in credit checking." They explored this area and found Hank still not qualified. But the credit manager was so impressed with how well Hank took criticism that when Hank asked him if he could suggest other employers, he did, even going so far as to call one. Probing for leads when an interview or follow-up turns negative is a prime technique for getting personal referrals.

23   The challenge of finding a job, approached in an active, organized, realistic way, can be a valuable personal adventure. You can meet new people, develop new ideas about yourself and your career goals, and improve your skills in dealing with individuals. These in turn can contribute to your long-term job security.

Vocabulary

actuarial (9)

Questions on Meaning and Technique

1. What is the purpose of the anecdote given in paragraph 1?

2. The author suggests three ways to find hidden job markets. Of the three, which do you consider the most important? Which the most difficult to perform?

3. In addition to those suggested by the author, what other ways of finding hidden markets can you suggest?

4. What does the author state about the length of a résumé? Do you agree with her? Why or why not?

5. What is the difference between a cover letter and a résumé? If one had to be deleted, which would it be?

6. What good, if any, do you attach to interviews that did not land you a job?

7. What makes this essay a process essay? How effective is it?

8. Examine paragraph 17. What technique does the author use to clarify her suggestion? Point to other passages where the same technique is used.

STUDENT ESSAY

First Draft   Monica Esparza

Driving to Preserve Your Car

~~Driving~~   *more precise title*

Amazingly

1   ~~It is amazing how~~ few people realize that their driving styles affect ~~how long their~~   *cuts deadwood;*
the durability and   *their automobiles*   *more concise*
~~automobile will last and what the~~ cost of ~~operating it will be~~. It behooves drivers to use
and safely
their cars as efficiently as possible to preserve them from deterioration and accidents.

Accidents are the number one reason for junking cars.

2   Here are some simple instructions that, if followed, will make your car run better and   *punctuation*

last longer.

First and most important, concentrate on your driving so that you make good

judgments, especially in critical circumstances. If you have driven five or ten miles and

3   suddenly you can't remember where you are or where you are going, you have probably

been daydreaming. Wake up and concentrate on the road.

numbering each instruction adds clarity to the process

cuts deadwood

Second,

ᴧAvoid sudden accelerations; they cause excessive wear and tear on your car by   4

unnecessarily forcing the engine. Emergencies are exceptions, but you can minimize the

likelihood of their occurrence if you ~~allow yourself thinking time by~~ concentrating on

your driving environment.

creates subordination for better emphasis

adds necessary information

more specific

Third,   using them

ᴧStay off the brakes., ~~Use the brakes~~ as seldomly and ~~as~~ lightly as possible. This is the   5

single most important technique you can learn. Brakes waste the momentum on your car.

(Insert A)   the flow of

In all driving, try hard to match your speed to traffic ~~speed~~ so that you need not step on

                                    in fits and starts

either your brakes or on the gas ~~constantly~~. Many times this is impossible, but at least

try. By avoiding sudden stops and starts, you save more gas (money!) than through most

of the expensive mechanical modifications installed on cars to save fuel.

more direct

Fourth,

ᴧLooking ahead and ~~being~~ cautious ~~is important~~. Drive as smoothly as possible by   6

punctuation

anticipating traffic as much as a quarter of a mile away on city streets,and as far as you

can see on country roads or on freeways.

adds useful example to drive home the point

more direct and concise

Fifth,

ᴧKeep your emotions under control while driving. Competitive and angry driving   7

                                                                        (Insert B)

not only increases the wear and tear on your car, but also the chance of an accident.

Sixth, drive strategically.

ᴧ~~There is one other large area that directly affects the life of the car, and that is road~~   8

                        are doubtless familiar with   and

~~strategy~~. You ~~know pretty well~~ all of the shortcuts ~~as well as~~ obstacles involved in

getting from where you live to where you work because you found out by trial and error.

Your trip to work is probably well executed. Now, get into the habit of planning all trips

to unfamiliar places as well, no matter how near. Take into account ~~the fact~~ that the

type of road on which you travel can either cost or save gas. Choose the best route. A

(Insert A)

Moreover, they increase the risk of someone's ramming
into you from the rear.

(Insert B)

For instance, when you respond with feelings of aggressive
revenge to a driver who has just cut you off, given you an
obscene sign, or in some other way irritated you, your
mental acuity is sidetracked to plot a get-even act, leaving
you and your car less protected. The smarter reaction is to
dismiss this numbskull from your mind so that you can stay
cool and rational at the steering wheel.

8   potholed or patched road may cost up to fifteen percent fuel penalty, and stretches of

loose gravel can cost up to thirty-five percent. When you have a choice, always drive on

a smooth road, maintained by a concerned local highway department.

9   Finally, ~~look at~~ ^{view} yourself as the ultimate control mechanism in the machinery that

transports you. Take extra precautions to become a better driver, thus ~~give long lasting~~   *increasing the useful lifespan of your car.*

~~life to your car.~~

more precise restatement of thesis

STUDENT ESSAY

Final Draft   Monica Esparza

Driving to Preserve Your Car

1   Amazingly few people realize that their driving styles affect the durability and cost of their automobiles. It behooves drivers to use their cars as efficiently and safely as possible to preserve them from deterioration and accidents. Accidents are the number one reason for junking cars.

2   Here are some simple instructions that, if followed, will make your car run better and last longer.

3   First and most important, concentrate on your driving so that you make good judgments, especially in critical circumstances. If you have driven five or ten miles and suddenly you can't remember where you are or where you are going, you have probably been daydreaming. Wake up and concentrate on the road.

4   Second, avoid sudden accelerations; they cause excessive wear and tear on your car by unnecessarily forcing the engine. Emergencies are exceptions, but you can minimize the likelihood of their occurrence if you concentrate on your driving environment.

5   Third, stay off the brakes, using them as seldom and lightly as possible. This is the single most important technique you can learn. Brakes waste the momentum on your car. Moreover, they increase the risk of someone's ramming into you from the rear. In all driving, try hard to match your speed to the flow of traffic so that you need not step on either your brakes or on the gas in fits and starts. Many times this is impossible, but at least try. By avoiding sudden stops and starts, you save more gas (money!) than through most of the expensive mechanical modifications installed on cars to save fuel.

6   Fourth, look ahead and be cautious. Drive as smoothly as possible by anticipating traffic as much as a quarter of a mile away on city streets, and as far as you can see on country roads or on freeways.

7   Fifth, keep your emotions under control while driving. Competitive and angry driving increases not only the wear and tear on your car, but also the chance of an accident. For instance, when you respond with feelings of aggressive revenge to a driver who has just cut you off, given you an obscene sign, or in some other way irritated you, your mental acuity is sidetracked to plot a get-even act, leaving you and your car less protected. The smarter reaction is to dismiss this numbskull from your mind so that you can stay cool and rational at the steering wheel.

8   Sixth, drive strategically. You are doubtless familiar with all of the shortcuts and obstacles involved in getting from where you live to where you work because you found out by trial and error. Your trip to work is probably well executed. Now, get into the habit of planning all trips to unfamiliar places as well, no matter how near. Take into account that the type of road on which you travel can either cost or save gas. Choose the best route. A potholed or patched road may cost up to fifteen percent fuel penalty, and stretches of loose gravel can cost up to thirty-five percent. When you have a choice, always drive on a smooth road, maintained by a concerned local highway department.

9   Finally, view yourself as the ultimate control mechanism in the machinery that transports you. Take extra precautions to become a better driver, thus increasing the useful lifespan of your car.

READING FOR IDEAS

This essay was originally published in *Harper's Magazine*, whose reading audience consists mostly of cultured and educated people but not necessarily experts about medical surgery. The essay outlines in layperson's language the intricate and delicate process of taking out a brain tumor that had damaged the patient's eyesight and might have caused complete blindness. As you follow each step involved in this complex surgery, try to imagine the process from both the patient's and the physician's point of view. After reading the essay, think about all the personal qualities required by a surgeon about to start a surgical operation with so many possible life-threatening consequences.

ALTERNATE READING

A Delicate Operation
Roy C. Selby, Jr.

Roy C. Selby, Jr. (b. 1930) is a practicing neurologist and neurosurgeon in the Chicago area. Since his graduation from the University of Arkansas Medical School, he has specialized in diseases connected with the brain and has written numerous essays about this field of specialty.

In the autumn of 1973 a woman in her early fifties noticed, upon closing one eye   1
while reading, that she was unable to see clearly. Her eyesight grew slowly worse. Changing her eye-glasses did not help. She saw an ophthalmologist, who found that her vision was seriously impaired in both eyes. She then saw a neurologist, who confirmed the finding and obtained X-rays of the skull and an EMI scan—a photograph of the patient's head. The latter revealed a tumor growing between the optic nerves at the base of the brain. The woman was admitted to the hospital by a neurosurgeon.

Further diagnosis, based on angiography, a detailed X-ray study of the circulatory   2
system, showed the tumor to be about two inches in diameter and supplied by many small blood vessels. It rested beneath the brain, just above the pituitary gland, stretching the optic nerves to either side and intimately close to the major blood vessels supplying the brain. Removing it would pose many technical problems. Probably benign and slow-growing, it may have been present for several years. If let alone it would continue to grow and produce blindness and might become impossible to remove completely. Removing it, however, might not improve the patient's vision and could make it worse. A major blood vessel could be damaged, causing a stroke. Damage to the undersurface of the brain could cause impairment of memory and changes in mood and personality. The hypothalamus, a most important structure of the brain, could be injured, causing coma, high fever, bleeding from the stomach, and death.

The neurosurgeon met with the patient and her husband and discussed the various   3
possibilities. The common decision was to operate.

The patient's hair was shampooed for two nights before surgery. She was given a   4
cortisonelike drug to reduce the risk of damage to the brain during surgery. Five units of blood were cross-matched, as a contingency against hemorrhage. At 1:00 P.M. the operation began. After the patient was anesthetized her hair was completely clipped and shaved from the scalp. Her head was prepped with an organic iodine solution for ten minutes. Drapes were placed over her, leaving exposed only the forehead and crown of the skull. All the routine instruments were brought up—the electrocautery used to coagulate areas of bleeding, bipolar coagulation forceps to arrest bleeding from individual blood vessels without damaging adjacent tissues, and small suction tubes to remove blood and cerebrospinal fluid from the head, thus giving the surgeon a better view of the tumor and surrounding areas.

A curved incision was made behind the hairline so it would be concealed when the hair   5
grew back. It extended almost from ear to ear. Plastic clips were applied to the cut edges

of the scalp to arrest bleeding. The scalp was folded back to the level of the eyebrows. Incisions were made in the muscle of the right temple, and three sets of holes were drilled near the temple and the top of the head because the tumor had to be approached from directly in front. The drill, powered by nitrogen, was replaced with a fluted steel blade, and the holes were connected. The incised piece of skull was pried loose and held out of the way by a large sponge.

6   Beneath the bone is a yellowish leatherlike membrane, the dura, that surrounds the brain. Down the middle of the head the dura carries a large vein, but in the area near the nose the vein is small. At that point the vein and dura were cut, and clips made of tantalum, a hard metal, were applied to arrest and prevent bleeding. Sutures were put into the dura and tied to the scalp to keep the dura open and retracted. A malleable silver retractor, resembling the blade of a butter knife, was inserted between the brain and skull. The anesthesiologist began to administer a drug to relax the brain by removing some of its water, making it easier for the surgeon to manipulate the retractor, hold the brain back, and see the tumor. The nerve tracts for smell were cut on both sides to provide additional room. The tumor was seen approximately two-and-one-half inches behind the base of the nose. It was pink in color. On touching it, it proved to be very fibrous and tough. A special retractor was attached to the skull, enabling the other retractor blades to be held automatically and freeing the surgeon's hands. With further displacement of the frontal lobes of the brain, the tumor could be seen better, but no normal structures—the carotid arteries, their branches, and the optic nerves—were visible. The tumor obscured them.

7   A surgical microscope was placed above the wound. The surgeon had selected the lenses and focal length prior to the operation. Looking through the microscope, he could see some of the small vessels supplying the tumor and he coagulated them. He incised the tumor to attempt to remove its core and thus collapse it, but the substance of the tumor was too firm to be removed in this fashion. He then began to slowly dissect the tumor from the adjacent brain tissue and from where he believed the normal structures to be.

8   Using small squares of cotton, he began to separate the tumor from very loose fibrous bands connecting it to the brain and to the right side of the part of the skull where the pituitary gland lies. The right optic nerve and carotid artery came into view, both displaced considerably to the right. The optic nerve had a normal appearance. He protected these structures with cotton compresses placed between them and the tumor. He began to raise the tumor from the skull and slowly to reach the point of its origin and attachment—just in front of the pituitary gland and medial to the left optic nerve, which still could not be seen. The small blood vessels entering the tumor were cauterized. The upper portion of the tumor was gradually separated from the brain, and the branches of the carotid arteries and the branches to the tumor were coagulated. The tumor was slowly and gently lifted from its bed, and for the first time the left carotid artery and optic nerve could be seen. Part of the tumor adhered to this nerve. The bulk of the tumor was amputated, leaving a small bit attached to the nerve. Very slowly and carefully the tumor fragment was resected.

9   The tumor now removed, a most impressive sight came into view—the pituitary gland and its stalk of attachment to the hypothalamus, the hypothalamus itself, and the

brainstem, which conveys nerve impulses between the body and the brain. As far as could be determined, no damage had been done to these structures or other vital centers, but the left optic nerve, from chronic pressure of the tumor, appeared gray and thin. Probably it would not completely recover its function.

After making certain there was no bleeding, the surgeon closed the wounds and placed wire mesh over the holes in the skull to prevent dimpling of the scalp over the points that had been drilled. A gauze dressing was applied to the patient's head. She was awakened and sent to the recovery room.   10

Even with the microscope, damage might still have occurred to the cerebral cortex and hypothalamus. It would require at least a day to be reasonably certain there was none, and about seventy-two hours to monitor for the major postoperative dangers—swelling of the brain and blood clots forming over the surface of the brain. The surgeon explained this to the patient's husband, and both of them waited anxiously. The operation had required seven hours. A glass of orange juice had given the surgeon some additional energy during the closure of the wound. Though exhausted, he could not fall asleep until after two in the morning, momentarily expecting a call from the nurse in the intensive care unit announcing deterioration of the patient's condition.   11

At 8:00 A.M. the surgeon saw the patient in the intensive care unit. She was alert, oriented, and showed no sign of additional damage to the optic nerves or the brain. She appeared to be in better shape than the surgeon or her husband.   12

Vocabulary

ophthalmologist (1)	organic (4)	coagulated (7)
neurologist (1)	malleable (6)	incised (7)
neurosurgeon (1)	anesthesiologist (6)	dissect (7)
circulatory (2)	manipulate (6)	adjacent (7)
pituitary (2)	retractor (6)	compresses (8)
optic (2)	fibrous (6)	resected (8)
benign (2)	lobes (6)	postoperative (11)
impairment (2)	obscured (6)	oriented (12)
contingency (4)		

Questions on Meaning and Technique

1. How does the author, who as a physician is familiar with medical terminology, assure that his readers will understand the scientific terms in his process analysis?

2. How important do you consider the conversation among the physician, patient, and patient's husband, mentioned in paragraph 3? Give reasons for your answer.

3. Given the possibility of death as one of the results of operating, would you have made the same decision as the patient in Selby's essay had you been in her place? Why or why not?

4. How many major steps are there in this surgical procedure? List them one at a time and then include some substeps.

5. *Incise, dissect,* and *resect* are all verbs meaning some kind of cutting. Why do you suppose the author uses three different words?

6. What image of the surgeon do you have after reading this essay? Do you find him cold and objective or does he have a sensitive, human side? Support your answer with examples from the text.

7. What importance do details have in this essay? Cite a paragraph where details are particularly obvious.

8. Much of the essay is written in the passive voice (see paragraphs 5 and 6, for example). How do you account for this uninvolved style? Who do you think performed the surgery?

Writing Assignments

1. Using the step-by-step method, describe the process of having your teeth cleaned by a dentist or a hygienist.

2. In a precisely organized essay describe how to accomplish some task that requires a step-by-step approach. Consider such tasks as learning how to use a computer for word processing, how to dissect a frog, how to balance a bank account, how to organize a protest against chopping down trees or demolishing a historical building, or how to classify your personal library.

READING FOR IDEAS

This is the heart-rending, disturbing yet comforting story of one man's personal journey toward poetic birth. In a rare opportunity we are allowed to see deep into a man's scarred and demon-filled soul to witness how he faces the horrors of prison life, including solitary confinement and the mental ward. We are privileged to feel the depths of torment he feels—the hellish despair—but finally we also hear about the birth of faith and hope as he finds his purpose as a poet. Read every line with compassion and you will emerge enlightened not only about how a person learns to write, but how a human being overcame crime and violence through the beauty of language.

ALTERNATE READING

Coming Into Language
JIMMY SANTIAGO BACA

Jimmy Santiago Baca (b. 1952) is one of the greatly admired Barrio writers, so-called because they emerged from the terrors of barrio life to portray their environments with vigor and artistic power. An ex-convict, he taught himself to read and write while in prison, eventually winning the American Book Award of 1988. Part Chicano and part Indian, Baca was abandoned by his parents when he was two and lived with his grandparents. By the time he was five, his mother had been murdered by her second husband, his father was dead of alcoholism, and Baca lived in an orphanage, which he escaped to survive on the streets. In time he landed in prison on a drug charge (which he claims was false) and was sent to maximum security and later placed in isolation because of his combative nature. Through an outside mentor his writings gradually received international attention, and he was released from prison. Despite his tragic life, his poetry dwells on rebirth rather than on bitterness. Among his works are the following books of poetry: Immigrants in Our Own Land *(1979),* Swords of Darkness *(1981),* What's Happening? *(1982),* Martin and Meditations on the South Valley *(1987),* Black Mesa Poems *(1989), and* Working in the Dark: Reflections of a Poet of the Barrio *(1990), from which the essay below is taken.*

On weekend graveyard shifts at St. Joseph's Hospital I worked the emergency room, 1 mopping up pools of blood and carting plastic bags stuffed with arms, legs, and hands to the outdoor incinerator. I enjoyed the quiet, away from the screams of shotgunned, knifed, and mangled kids writhing on gurneys outside the operating rooms. Ambulance sirens shrieked and squad car lights reddened the cool nights, flashing against the hospital walls: gray—red, gray—red. On slow nights, I would lock the door of the administration office, search the reference library for a book on female anatomy and, with my feet propped on the desk, leaf through the illustrations, smoking my cigarette. I was seventeen.

One night my eye was caught by a familiar-looking word on the spine of a book. The 2 title was *450 Years of Chicano History in Pictures.* On the cover were black-and-white photos: Padre Hidalgo exhorting Mexican peasants to revolt against the Spanish dictators; Anglo vigilantes hanging two Mexicans from a tree; a young Mexican woman with rifle and ammunition belts crisscrossing her breast; César Chávez and field workers marching for fair wages; Chicano railroad workers laying creosote ties; Chicanas laboring at machines in textile factories; Chicanas picketing and hoisting boycott signs.

From the time I was seven, teachers had been punishing me for not knowing my 3 lessons by making me stick my nose in a circle chalked on the blackboard. Ashamed of not understanding and fearful of asking questions, I dropped out of school in the ninth grade. At seventeen I still didn't know how to read, but those pictures confirmed my identity. I stole the book that night, stashing it for safety under the slopsink until I got off work. Back at my boardinghouse, I showed the book to friends. All of us were amazed; this book told us we were alive. We, too, had defended ourselves with our fists against hostile Anglos, gasping for breath in fights with the policemen who outnumbered us. The book reflected back to us our struggle in a way that made us proud.

Most of my life I felt like a target in the cross hairs of a hunter's rifle. When strangers 4 and outsiders questioned me I felt the hang-rope tighten around my neck and the trapdoor creak beneath my feet. There was nothing so humiliating as being unable to express myself, and my inarticulateness increased my sense of jeopardy, of being endangered. I felt intimidated and vulnerable, ridiculed and scorned. Behind a mask of humility, I seethed with mute rebellion.

5   Before I was eighteen, I was arrested on suspicion of murder after refusing to explain a deep cut on my forearm. With shocking speed I found myself handcuffed to a chain gang of inmates and bused to a holding facility to await trial. There I met men, prisoners, who read aloud to each other the works of Neruda, Paz, Sabines, Nemerov, and Hemingway. Never had I felt such freedom as in that dormitory. Listening to the words of these writers, I felt that invisible threat from without lessen—my sense of teetering on a rotting plank over swamp water where famished alligators clapped their horny snouts for my blood. While I listened to the words of the poets, the alligators slumbered powerless in their lairs. Their language was the magic that could liberate me from myself, transform me into another person, transport me to other places far away.

6   And when they closed the books, these Chicanos, and went into their own Chicano language, they made barrio life come alive for me in the fullness of its vitality. I began to learn my own language, the bilingual words and phrases explaining to me my place in the universe. Every day I felt like the paper boy taking delivery of the latest news of the day.

7   Months later I was released, as I had suspected I would be. I had been guilty of nothing but shattering the windshield of my girlfriend's car in a fit of rage.

8   Two years passed. I was twenty now, and behind bars again. The federal marshals had failed to provide convincing evidence to extradite me to Arizona on a drug charge, but still I was being held. They had ninety days to prove I was guilty. The only evidence against me was that my girlfriend had been at the scene of the crime with my driver's license in her purse. They had to come up with something else. But there was nothing else. Eventually they negotiated a deal with the actual drug dealer, who took the stand against me. When the judge hit me with a million-dollar bail, I emptied my pockets on his booking desk: twenty-six cents.

9   One night in my third month in the county jail, I was mopping the floor in front of the booking desk. Some detectives had kneed an old drunk and handcuffed him to the booking bars. His shrill screams raked my nerves like a hacksaw on bone, the desperate protest of his dignity against their inhumanity. But the detectives just laughed as he tried to rise and kicked him to his knees. When they went to the bathroom to pee and the desk attendant walked to the file cabinet to pull the arrest record, I shot my arm through the bars, grabbed one of the attendant's university textbooks, and tucked it in my overalls. It was the only way I had of protesting.

10   It was late when I returned to my cell. Under my blanket I switched on a pen flashlight and opened the thick book at random, scanning the pages. I could hear the jailer making his rounds on the other tiers. The jangle of his keys and the sharp click of his boot heels intensified my solitude. Slowly I enunciated the words . . . p-o-n-d, ri-pple. It scared me that I had been reduced to this to find comfort. I always had thought reading a waste of time, that nothing could be gained by it. Only by action, by moving out into the world and confronting and challenging the obstacles, could one learn anything worth knowing.

11   Even as I tried to convince myself that I was merely curious, I became so absorbed in how the sounds created music in me and happiness, I forgot where I was. Memories began to quiver in me, glowing with a strange but familiar intimacy in which I found refuge. For a while, a deep sadness overcame me, as if I had chanced on a long-lost friend and mourned the years of separation. But soon the heartache of having missed so much of life, that had numbed me since I was a child, gave way, as if a grave illness lifted

itself from me and I was cured, innocently believing in the beauty of life again. I stumblingly repeated the author's name as I fell asleep, saying it over and over in the dark: Words-worth, Words-worth.

Before long my sister came to visit me, and I joked about taking her to a place called 12 Kubla Khan and getting her a blind date with this *vato* named Coleridge who lived on the seacoast and was *malias* on morphine. When I asked her to make a trip into enemy territory to buy me a grammar book, she said she couldn't. Bookstores intimidated her, because she, too, could neither read nor write.

Days later, with a stub pencil I whittled sharp with my teeth, I propped a Red Chief 13 notebook on my knees and wrote my first words. From that moment, a hunger for poetry possessed me.

Until then, I had felt as if I had been born into a raging ocean where I swam 14 relentlessly, flailing my arms in hope of rescue, of reaching a shoreline I never sighted. Never solid ground beneath me, never a resting place. I had lived with only the desperate hope to stay afloat; that and nothing more.

But when at last I wrote my first words on the page, I felt an island rising beneath my 15 feet like the back of a whale. As more and more words emerged, I could finally rest: I had a place to stand for the first time in my life. The island grew, with each page, into a continent inhabited by people I knew and mapped with the life I lived.

I wrote about it all—about people I had loved or hated, about the brutalities and 16 ecstasies of my life. And, for the first time, the child in me who had witnessed and endured unspeakable terrors cried out not just in impotent despair, but with the power of language. Suddenly, through language, through writing, my grief and my joy could be shared with anyone who would listen. And I could do this all alone; I could do it anywhere. I was no longer a captive of demons eating away at me, no longer a victim of other people's mockery and loathing, that had made me clench my fist white with rage and grit my teeth to silence. Words now pleaded back with the bleak lucidity of hurt. They were wrong, those others, and now I could say it.

Through language I was free. I could respond, escape, indulge; embrace or reject earth 17 or the cosmos. I was launched on an endless journey without boundaries or rules, in which I could salvage the floating fragments of my past, or be born anew in the spontaneous ignition of understanding some heretofore concealed aspect of myself. Each word steamed with the hot lava juices of my primordial making, and I crawled out of stanzas dripping with birth-blood, reborn and freed from the chaos of my life. The child in the dark room of my heart, that had never been able to find or reach the light switch, flicked it on now; and I found in the room a stranger, myself, who had waited so many years to speak again. My words struck in me lightning crackles of elation and thunderhead storms of grief.

When I had been in the county jail longer than anyone else, I was made a trustee. One 18 morning, after a fist fight, I went to the unlocked and unoccupied office used for lawyer-client meetings, to think. The bare white room with its fluorescent tube lighting seemed to expose and illuminate my dark and worthless life. And yet, for the first time, I had something to lose—my chance to read, to write; a way to live with dignity and meaning, that had opened for me when I stole that scuffed, second-hand book about the Romantic poets. In prison, the abscess had been lanced.

19   "I will never do any work in this prison system as long as I am not allowed to get my G.E.D." That's what I told the reclassification panel. The captain flicked off the tape recorder. He looked at me hard and said, "You'll never walk outta here alive. Oh, you'll work, put a copper penny on that, you'll work."

20   After that interview I was confined to deadlock maximum security in a subterranean dungeon, with ground-level chicken-wired windows painted gray. Twenty-three hours a day I was in that cell. I kept sane by borrowing books from the other cons on the tier. Then, just before Christmas, I received a letter from Harry, a charity house samaritan who doled out hot soup to the homeless in Phoenix. He had picked my name from a list of cons who had no one to write to them. I wrote back asking for a grammar book, and a week later received one of Mary Baker Eddy's treatises on salvation and redemption, with Spanish and English on opposing pages. Pacing my cell all day and most of each night, I grappled with grammar until I was able to write a long true-romance confession for a con to send to his pen pal. He paid me with a pack of smokes. Soon I had a thriving barter business, exchanging my poems and letters for novels, commissary pencils, and writing tablets.

21   One day I tore two flaps from the cardboard box that held all my belongings and punctured holes along the edge of each flap and along the border of a ream of state-issue paper. After I had aligned them to form a spine, I threaded the holes with a shoestring, and sketched on the cover a hummingbird fluttering above a rose. This was my first journal.

22   Whole afternoons I wrote, unconscious of passing time or whether it was day or night. Sunbursts exploded from the lead tip of my pencil, words that grafted me into awareness of who I was; peeled back to a burning core of bleak terror, an embryo floating in the image of water, I cracked out of the shell wide-eyed and insane. Trees grew out of the palms of my hands, the threatening otherness of life dissolved, and I became one with the air and sky, the dirt and the iron and concrete. There was no longer any distinction between the other and I. Language made bridges of fire between me and everything I saw. I entered into the blade of grass, the basketball, the con's eye and child's soul.

23   At night I flew. I conversed with floating heads in my cell, and visited strange houses where lonely women brewed tea and rocked in wicker rocking chairs listening to sad Joni Mitchell songs.

24   Before long I was frayed like a rope carrying too much weight, that suddenly snaps. I quit talking. Bars, walls, steel bunk and floor bristled with millions of poem-making sparks. My face was no longer familiar to me. The only reality was the swirling cornucopia of images in my mind, the voices in the air. Mid-air a cactus blossom would appear, a snake-flame in blinding dance around it, stunning me like a guard's fist striking my neck from behind.

25   The prison administrators tried several tactics to get me to work. For six months, after the next monthly prison board review, they sent cons to my cell to hassle me. When the guard would open my cell door to let one of them in, I'd leap out and fight him—and get sent to thirty-day isolation. I did a lot of isolation time. But I honed my image-making talents in that sensory-deprived solitude. Finally they moved me to death row, and after that to "nut-run," the tier that housed the mentally disturbed.

As the months passed, I became more and more sluggish. My eyelids were heavy, I   26
could no longer write or read. I slept all the time.

One day a guard took me out to the exercise field. For the first time in years I felt grass   27
and earth under my feet. It was spring. The sun warmed my face as I sat on the bleachers
watching the cons box and run, hit the handball, lift weights. Some of them stopped to
ask how I was, but I found it impossible to utter a syllable. My tongue would not move,
saliva drooled from the corners of my mouth. I had been so heavily medicated I could not
summon the slightest gesture. Yet inside me a small voice cried out, I am fine! I am hurt
now but I will come back! I am fine!

Back in my cell, for weeks I refused to eat. Styrofoam cups of urine and hot water   28
were hurled at me. Other things happened. There were beatings, shock therapy,
intimidation.

Later, I regained some clarity of mind. But there was a place in my heart where I had   29
died. My life had compressed itself into an unbearable dread of being. The strain had
been too much. I had stepped over that line where a human being had lost more than he
can bear, where the pain is too intense, and he knows he is changed forever. I was now
capable of killing, coldly and without feeling. I was empty, as I have never, before or
since, known emptiness. I had no connection to this life.

But then, the encroaching darkness that began to envelop me forced me to re-form   30
and give birth to myself again in the chaos. I withdrew even deeper into the world of
language, cleaving the diamonds of verbs and nouns, plunging into the brilliant light of
poetry's regenerative mystery. Words gave off rings of white energy, radar signals from
powers beyond me that infused me with truth. I believed what I wrote, because I wrote
what was true. My words did not come from books or textual formulas, but from a deep
faith in the voice of my heart.

I had been steeped in self-loathing and rejected by everyone and everything—society,   31
family, cons, God and demons. But now I had become as the burning ember floating in
darkness that descends on a dry leaf and sets flame to forests. The word was the ember
and the forest was my life.

I was born a poet one noon, gazing at weeds and creosoted grass at the base of a   32
telephone pole outside my grilled cell window. The words I wrote then sailed me out of
myself, and I was transported and metamorphosed into the images they made. From the
dirty brown blades of grass came bolts of electrical light that jolted loose my old self;
through the top of my head that self was released and reshaped in the clump of scrawny
grass. Through language I became the grass, speaking its language and feeling its green
feelings and black root sensations. Earth was my mother and I bathed in sunshine.
Minuscule speckles of sunlight passed through my green skin and metabolized in my blood.

Writing bridged my divided life of prisoner and free man. I wrote of the emotional   33
butchery of prisons, and of my acute gratitude for poetry. Where my blind doubt and
spontaneous trust in life met, I discovered empathy and compassion. The power to
express myself was a welcome storm rasping at tendril roots, flooding my soul's cracked
dirt. Writing was water that cleansed the wound and fed the parched root of my heart.

I wrote to sublimate my rage, from a place where all hope is gone, from a madness of   34
having been damaged too much, from a silence of killing rage. I wrote to avenge the

betrayals of a lifetime, to purge the bitterness of injustice. I wrote with a deep groan of doom in my blood, bewildered and dumbstruck; from an indestructible love of life, to affirm breath and laughter and the abiding innocence of things. I wrote the way I wept, and danced, and made love.

Vocabulary

incinerator (1)   primordial (17)   regenerative (30)
inarticulateness (4)   subterranean (20)   creosoted (32)
lairs (5)   samaritan (20)   metamorphosed (32)
extradite (8)   treatises (20)   tendril (33)
enunciated (10)

Questions on Meaning and Technique

1. Who is the voice in this essay? What kind of person do you judge him to be? How do you feel about him? Why does he seem to be writing the essay?

2. The author's experience can be divided into separate, discernible steps. What are these steps? List and summarize each step, one by one as it occurred in the total process.

3. Which part of the author's artistic journey do you consider the climax of his experience, that is, the point at which he sees the possibility of language? Give reasons for your choice.

4. Where in this essay does the author reveal his poetic talent? Use specific examples of poetic utterances.

5. How can you explain the author's seeming grasp of English mechanics and grammar despite the fact that he is a school dropout?

6. How does the author indicate the passage of time?

7. If paragraph 34 were taken as the summary of the writer's life so far, then what do you consider the essence of his past? How did writing figure in this life?

8. What do you think was the reason for the author's sluggishness as described in paragraph 26? Is the reason plausible? Be specific in your answer.

9. What is your opinion of the punishment meted out by the grade school teachers described in paragraph 3? Is this punishment related to the reasons why Baca dropped out in ninth grade? If so, what did the punishment contribute?

10. How do you explain the title of the essay? What other title might you suggest?

Writing Assignments

1. Write an essay delineating step by step the process of how you learned something at which you now excel.

2. Suggest a step-by-step process for getting prison inmates—especially hardened criminals—interested in literature.

READING FOR IDEAS

Advice to students about how to write fills college bookstores, but no advice has been more practical or humorous than Roberts's essay. With great flair and wit this English professor leads you through a tangle of typical false starts and missteps, then cleverly shows you, by rule and example, how the typical college writing assignment can be mastered. Pay serious attention to the rules listed in the form of headings and try to understand clearly how the examples provided fit into these rules.

ALTERNATE READING

How to Say Nothing in 500 Words
PAUL ROBERTS

Paul McHenry Roberts (1917–1967) was an English teacher and writer of textbooks whose work enjoyed immense popularity. He taught at San Jose State University and Cornell University and was the author of many books on English and linguistics, among them Understanding Grammar *(1954),* Patterns of English *(1956), and* Understanding English *(1958).*

It's Friday afternoon, and you have almost survived another week of classes. You are just looking forward dreamily to the weekend when the English instructor says: "For Monday you will turn in a five-hundred-word composition on college football." 1

Well, that puts a good hole in the weekend. You don't have any strong views on college football one way or the other. You get rather excited during the season and go to all the home games and find it rather more fun than not. On the other hand, the class has been reading Robert Hutchins in the anthology and perhaps Shaw's "Eighty-Yard Run," and from the class discussion you have got the idea that the instructor thinks college football is for the birds. You are no fool. You can figure out what side to take. 2

After dinner you get out the portable typewriter that you got for high school graduation. You might as well get it over with and enjoy Saturday and Sunday. Five hundred words is about two double-spaced pages with normal margins. You put in a sheet of paper, think up a title and you're off: 3

WHY COLLEGE FOOTBALL SHOULD BE ABOLISHED

College football should be abolished because it's bad for the school and also for the players. The players are so busy practicing that they don't have any time for their studies.

This, you feel, is a mighty good start. The only trouble is that it's only thirty-two words. You still have four hundred and sixty-eight to go, and you've pretty well exhausted the 4 subject. It comes to you that you do your best thinking in the morning, so you put away the typewriter and go to the movies. But the next morning you have to do your washing and some math problems, and in the afternoon you go to the game. The English instructor turns up too, and you wonder if you've taken the right side after all. Saturday night you have a date, and Sunday morning you have to go to church. (You can't let English assignments interfere with your religion.) What with one thing and another, it's ten o'clock Sunday night before you get out the typewriter again. You make a pot of coffee and start to fill out your views on college football. Put a little meat on the bones.

WHY COLLEGE FOOTBALL SHOULD BE ABOLISHED

In my opinion, it seems to me that college football should be abolished. The reason why I think this to be true is because I feel that football is bad for the college in nearly every respect. As Robert Hutchins says in his article in our anthology in which he discusses college football, it would be better if the colleges had race horses and had races with one another, because then the horses would not have to attend classes. I firmly agree with Mr. Hutchins on this point, and I am sure that many other students would agree too.

One reason why it seems to me that college football is bad is that it has become too commercial. In the olden times when people played football just for the fun of it, maybe college football was all right, but they do not play football just for the fun of it now as they used to in the old days. Nowadays college football is what you might call a big business. Maybe this is not true at all schools, and I don't think it is especially true here at State, but certainly this is the case at most colleges and universities in America nowadays, as Mr. Hutchins points out in his very interesting article. Actually the coaches and alumni go around to the high schools and offer the high school stars large salaries to come to their colleges and play football for them. There was one case where a high school star was offered a convertible if he would play football for a certain college.

Another reason for abolishing college football is that it is bad for the players. They do not have time to get a college education, because they are so busy playing football. A football player has to practice every afternoon from three to six and then he is so tired that he can't concentrate on his studies. He just feels like dropping off to sleep after dinner, and then the next day he goes to his classes without having studied and maybe he fails the test.

(Good ripe stuff, so far, but you're still a hundred and fifty-one words from home. One more push.)

Also I think college football is bad for the colleges and the universities because not very many students get to participate in it. Out of a college of ten thousand students only seventy-five or a hundred play football, if that many. Football is what you might call a spectator sport. That means that most people go to watch it but do not play it themselves.

(Four hundred and fifteen. Well, you still have the conclusion, and when you retype it, you can make the margins a little wider.)

These are the reasons why I agree with Mr. Hutchins that college football should be abolished in American colleges and universities.

On Monday you turn it in, moderately hopeful, and on Friday it comes back marked "weak in content" and sporting a big "D."   5

This essay is exaggerated a little, not much. The English instructor will recognize it as   6 reasonably typical of what an assignment on college football will bring in. He knows that nearly half of the class will contrive in five hundred words to say that college football is too commercial and bad for the players. Most of the other half will inform him that college football builds character and prepares one for life and brings prestige to the school. As he reads paper after paper all saying the same thing in almost the same words, he wonders how he allowed himself to get trapped into teaching English when he might have had a happy and interesting life as an electrician or a confidence man.

Well, you may ask, what can you do about it? The subject is one on which you have   7 few convictions and little information. Can you be expected to make a dull subject interesting? As a matter of fact, this is precisely what you are expected to do. This is the writer's essential task. All subjects, except sex, are dull until somebody makes them interesting. The writer's job is to find the argument, the approach, the angle, the wording that will take the reader with him. This is seldom easy, and it is particularly hard in subjects that have been much discussed: College Football, Fraternities, Popular Music, Is Chivalry Dead?, and the like. You will feel that there is nothing you can do with such subjects except repeat the old bromides. But there are some things you can do which will make your papers, if not throbbingly alive, at least less insufferably tedious than they might otherwise be.

AVOID THE OBVIOUS CONTENT

Say the assignment is college football. Say that you've decided to be against it. Begin   8 by putting down the arguments that come to your mind: it is too commercial, it takes the students' minds off their studies, it is hard on the players, it makes the university a kind of circus instead of an intellectual center, for most schools it is financially ruinous. Can you think of any more arguments, just off hand? All right. Now when you write your paper, *make sure that you don't use any of the material on this list*. If these are the points that leap to your mind, they will leap to everyone else's too, and whether you get a "C" or a "D" may depend on whether the instructor reads your paper early when he is fresh and tolerant or late, when the sentence "In my opinion, college football has become too commercial," inexorably repeated, has brought him to the brink of lunacy.

Be against college football for some reason or reasons of your own. If they are keen   9 and perceptive ones, that's splendid. But even if they are trivial or foolish or indefensible, you are still ahead so long as they are not everybody else's reasons too. Be against it because the colleges don't spend enough money on it to make it worthwhile, because it is bad for the characters of the spectators, because the players are forced to attend classes, because the football stars hog all the beautiful women, because it competes with baseball and is therefore un-American and possibly Communist-inspired. There are lots of more or less unused reasons for being against college football.

10 Sometimes it is a good idea to sum up and dispose of the trite and conventional points before going on to your own. This has the advantage of indicating to the reader that you are going to be neither trite nor conventional. Something like this:

> We are often told that college football should be abolished because it has become too commercial or because it is bad for the players. These arguments are no doubt very cogent, but they don't really go to the heart of the matter.

Then you go to the heart of the matter.

TAKE THE LESS USUAL SIDE

11 One rather simple way of getting into your paper is to take the side of the argument that most of the citizens will want to avoid. If the assignment is an essay on dogs, you can, if you choose, explain that dogs are faithful and lovable companions, intelligent, useful as guardians of the house and protectors of children, indispensable in police work—in short, when all is said and done, man's best friends. Or you can suggest that those big brown eyes conceal, more often than not, a vacuity of mind and an inconstancy of purpose; that the dogs you have known most intimately have been mangy, ill-tempered brutes, incapable of instruction; and that only your nobility of mind and fear of arrest prevent you from kicking the flea-ridden animals when you pass them on the street.

12 Naturally personal convictions will sometimes dictate your approach. If the assigned subject is "Is Methodism Rewarding to the Individual?" and you are a pious Methodist, you have really no choice. But few assigned subjects, if any, will fall in this category. Most of them will lie in broad areas of discussion with much to be said on both sides. They are intellectual exercises, and it is legitimate to argue now one way and now another, as debaters do in similar circumstances. Always take the side that looks to you hardest, least defensible. It will almost always turn out to be easier to write interestingly on that side.

13 This general advice applies where you have a choice of subjects. If you are to choose among "The Value of Fraternities" and "My Favorite High School Teacher" and "What I Think about Beetles," by all means plump for the beetles. By the time the instructor gets to your paper, he will be up to his ears in tedious tales about a French teacher at Bloombury High and assertions about how fraternities build character and prepare one for life. Your view on beetles, whatever they are, are bound to be a refreshing change.

14 Don't worry too much about figuring out what the instructor thinks about the subject so that you can cuddle up with him. Chances are his views are no stronger than yours. If he does have convictions and you oppose him, his problem is to keep from grading you higher than you deserve in order to show he is not biased. This doesn't mean that you should always cantankerously dissent from what the instructor says; that gets tiresome too. And if the subject assigned is "My Pet Peeve," do not begin, "My pet peeve is the

English instructor who assigns papers on 'my pet peeve.' " This was still funny during the War of 1812, but it has sort of lost its edge since then. It is in general good manners to avoid personalities.

SLIP OUT OF ABSTRACTION

If you will study the essay on college football [near the beginning of this essay], you will perceive that one reason for its appalling dullness is that it never gets down to particulars. It is just a series of not very glittering generalities: "football is bad for the colleges," "it has become too commercial," "football is big business," "it is bad for the players," and so on. Such round phrases thudding against the reader's brain are unlikely to convince him, though they may well render him unconscious.   15

If you want the reader to believe that college football is bad for the players, you have to do more than say so. You have to display the evil. Take your roommate, Alfred Simkins, the second-string center. Picture poor old Alfy coming home from football practice every evening, bruised and aching, agonizingly tired, scarcely able to shovel the mashed potatoes into his mouth. Let us see him staggering up to the room, getting out his econ textbook, peering desperately at it with his good eye, falling asleep and failing the test in the morning. Let us share his unbearable tension as Saturday draws near. Will he fail, be demoted, lose his monthly allowance, be forced to return to the coal mines? And if he succeeds, what will be his reward? Perhaps a slight ripple of applause when the third-string center replaces him, a moment of elation in the locker room if the team wins, or despair if it loses. What will he look back on when he graduates from college? Toil and torn ligaments. And what will be his future? He is not good enough for pro football, and he is too obscure and weak in econ to succeed in stocks and bonds. College football is tearing the heart from Alfy Simkins and, when it finishes with him, will callously toss aside the shattered hulk.   16

This is no doubt a weak enough argument for the abolition of college football, but it is a sight better than saying, in three or four variations, that college football (in your opinion) is bad for the players.   17

Look at the work of any professional writer and notice how constantly he is moving from the generality, the abstract statement, to the concrete example, the facts and figures, the illustrations. If he is writing on juvenile delinquency, he does not just tell you that juveniles are (it seems to him) delinquent and that (in his opinion) something should be done about it. He shows you juveniles being delinquent, tearing up movie theatres in Buffalo, stabbing high school principals in Dallas, smoking marijuana in Palo Alto. And more than likely he is moving toward some specific remedy, not just a general wringing of the hands.   18

It is no doubt possible to be too concrete, too illustrative or anecdotal, but few inexperienced writers err this way. For most the soundest advice is to be seeking always for the picture, to be always turning general remarks into seeable examples. Don't say, "Sororities teach girls the social graces." Say, "Sorority life teaches a girl how to carry on a conversation while pouring tea, without sloshing the tea into the saucer." Don't say, "I like certain kinds of popular music very much." Say, "Whenever I hear Gerber Sprinklittle play 'Mississippi Man' on the trombone, my socks creep up my ankles."   19

GET RID OF OBVIOUS PADDING

20   The student toiling away at his weekly English theme is too often tormented by a figure: five hundred words. How, he asks himself, is he to achieve this staggering total? Obviously by never using one word when he can somehow work in ten.

21   He is therefore seldom content with a plain statement like "Fast driving is dangerous." This has only four words in it. He takes thought, and the sentence becomes:

In my opinion, fast driving is dangerous.

Better, but he can do better still:

In my opinion, fast driving would seem to be rather dangerous.

If he is really adept, it may come out:

In my humble opinion, though I do not claim to be an expert on this complicated subject, fast driving, in most circumstances, would seem to be rather dangerous in many respects, or at least so it would seem to me.

Thus four words have been turned into forty, and not an iota of content has been added.

22   Now this is a way to go about reaching five hundred words, and if you are content with a "D" grade, it is as good a way as any. But if you aim higher, you must work differently. Instead of stuffing your sentences with straw, you must try steadily to get rid of the padding, to make your sentences lean and tough. If you are really working at it, your first draft will greatly exceed the required total, and then you will work it down, thus:

It is thought in some quarters that fraternities do not contribute as much as might be expected to campus life.
    Some people think that fraternities contribute little to campus life.
    The average doctor who practices in small towns or in the country must toil night and day to heal the sick.
    Most country doctors work long hours.
    When I was a little girl, I suffered from shyness and embarrassment in the presence of others.
    I was a shy little girl.
    It is absolutely necessary for the person employed as a marine fireman to give the matter of steam pressure his undivided attention at all times.
    The fireman has to keep his eye on the steam gauge.

23   You may ask how you can arrive at five hundred words at this rate. Simple. You dig up more real content. Instead of taking a couple of obvious points off the surface of the topic and then circling warily around them for six paragraphs, you work in and explore, figure out the details. You illustrate. You say that fast driving is dangerous, and then you prove it. How long does it take to stop a car at forty and at eighty? How far can you see at

night? What happens when a tire blows? What happens in a head-on collision at fifty miles an hour? Pretty soon your paper will be full of broken glass and blood and headless torsos, and reaching five hundred words will not really be a problem.

CALL A FOOL A FOOL

Some of the padding in freshman themes is to be blamed not on anxiety about the word minimum but on excessive timidity. The student writes "In my opinion, the principal of my high school acted in ways that I believe every unbiased person would have to call foolish." This isn't exactly what he means. What he means is, "My high school principal was a fool." If he was a fool, call him a fool. Hedging the thing about with "in-my-opinion's" and "it-seems-to-me's" and "as-I-see-it's" and "at-least-from-my-point-of-view's" gains you nothing. Delete these phrases whenever they creep into your paper.   24

The student's tendency to hedge stems from a modesty that in other circumstances would be commendable. He is, he realizes, young and inexperienced, and he half suspects that he is dopey and fuzzy-minded beyond the average. Probably only too true. But it doesn't help to announce your incompetence six times in every paragraph. Decide what you want to say and say it as vigorously as possible, without apology and in plain words.   25

Linguistic diffidence can take various forms. One is what we call *euphemism*. This is the tendency to call a spade "a certain garden implement" or women's underwear "unmentionables." It is stronger in some areas than others and in some people than others but it always operates more or less in subjects that are touchy or taboo: death, sex, madness, and so on. Thus we shrink from saying "He died last night" but say instead "passed away," "left us," "joined his Maker," "went to his reward." Or we try to take off the tension with a lighter cliché: "kicked the bucket," "cashed in his chips," "handed in his dinner pail." We have found all sorts of ways to avoid saying *mad:* "mentally ill," "touched," "not quite right upstairs," "feebleminded," "innocent," "simple," "off his trolley," "not in his right mind." Even such a now plain word as *insane* began as a euphemism with the meaning "not healthy."   26

Modern science, particularly psychology, contributes many polysyllables in which we can wrap our thoughts and blunt their force. To many writers there is no such thing as a bad schoolboy. Schoolboys are maladjusted or unoriented or misunderstood or in the need of guidance or lacking in continued success toward satisfactory integration of the personality as a social unit, but they are never bad. Psychology no doubt makes us better men and women, more sympathetic and tolerant, but it doesn't make writing any easier. Had Shakespeare been confronted with psychology, "To be or not to be" might have come out, "To continue as a social unit or not to do so. That is the personality problem. Whether 'tis a better sign of integration at the conscious level to display a psychic tolerance toward the maladjustments and repressions induced by one's lack of orientation in one's environment or—" But Hamlet would never have finished the soliloquy.   27

Writing in the modern world, you cannot altogether avoid modern jargon. Nor, in an effort to get away from euphemism, should you salt your paper with four-letter words. But you can do much if you will mount guard against those roundabout phrases, those echoing polysyllables that tend to slip into your writing to rob it of its crispness and force.   28

BEWARE OF PAT EXPRESSIONS

29   Other things being equal, avoid phrases like "other things being equal." Those sentences that come to you whole, or in two or three doughy lumps, are sure to be bad sentences. They are no creation of yours but pieces of common thought floating in the community soup.

30   Pat expressions are hard, often impossible to avoid, because they come too easily to be noticed and seem too necessary to be dispensed with. No writer avoids them altogether, but good writers avoid them more often than poor writers.

31   By "pat expressions" we mean such tags as "to all practical intents and purposes," "the pure and simple truth," "from where I sit," "the time of his life," "to the ends of the earth," "in the twinkling of an eye," "as sure as you're born," "over my dead body," "under cover of darkness," "took the easy way out," "when all is said and done," "stand up and be counted," "gave him the best years of her life," "worked her fingers to the bone." Like other clichés, these expressions were once forceful. Now we should use them only when we can't possibly think of anything else.

32   Some pat expressions stand like a wall between the writer and thought. Such a one is "the American way of life." Many student writers feel that when they have said that something accords with the American way of life or does not they have exhausted the subject. Actually, they have stopped at the highest level of abstraction. The American way of life is the complicated set of bonds between a hundred and eighty million ways. All of us know this when we think about it, but the tag phrase too often keeps us from thinking about it.

33   So with many another phrase dear to the politician: "this great land of ours," "the man in the street," "our national heritage." These may prove our patriotism or give a clue to our political beliefs, but otherwise they add nothing to the paper except words.

COLORFUL WORDS

34   The writer builds with words, and no builder uses a raw material more slippery and elusive and treacherous. A writer's work is a constant struggle to get the right word in the right place, to find that particular word that will convey his meaning exactly, that will persuade the reader or soothe him or startle or amuse him. He never succeeds altogether—sometimes he feels that he scarcely succeeds at all—but such successes as he has are what make the thing worth doing.

35   There is no book of rules for this game. One progresses through everlasting experiment on the basis of ever-widening experience. There are few useful generalizations that one can make about words as words, but there are perhaps a few.

36   Some words are what we call "colorful." By this we mean that they are calculated to produce a picture or induce an emotion. They are dressy instead of plain, specific instead of general, loud instead of soft. Thus, in place of "Her heart beat," we may write, "Her heart *pounded, throbbed, fluttered, danced.*" Instead of "He sat in his chair," we may say, "He *lounged, sprawled, coiled.*" Instead of "It was hot," we may say, "It was *blistering, sultry, muggy, suffocating, steamy, wilting.*"

37   However, it should not be supposed that the fancy word is always better. Often it is as well to write "Her heart beat" or "It was hot" if that is all it did or all it was. Ages differ

in how they like their prose. The nineteenth century liked it rich and smoky. The twentieth has usually preferred it lean and cool. The twentieth century writer, like all writers, is forever seeking the exact word, but he is wary of sounding feverish. He tends to pitch it low, to understate it, to throw it away. He knows that if he gets too colorful, the audience is likely to giggle.

See how this strikes you: "As the rich, golden glow of the sunset died away along the   38
eternal western hills, Angela's limpid blue eyes looked softly and trustingly into Montague's flashing brown ones, and her heart pounded like a drum in time with the joyous songs surging in her soul." Some people like that sort of thing, but most modern readers would say, "Good grief," and turn on the television.

COLORED WORDS

Some words we would call not so much colorful as colored—that is, loaded with   39
associations, good or bad. All words—except perhaps structure words—have associations of some sort. We have said that the meaning of a word is the sum of the contexts in which it occurs. When we hear a word, we hear with it an echo of all the situations in which we have heard it before.

In some words, these echoes are obvious and discussable. The word *mother*, for   40
example, has, for most people, agreeable associations. When you hear *mother* you probably think of home, safety, love, food, and various other pleasant things. If one writes, "She was like a mother to me," he gets an effect which he would not get in "She was like an aunt to me." The advertiser makes use of the associations of *mother* by working it in when he talks about his product. The politician works it in when he talks about himself.

So also with such words as *home, liberty, fireside, contentment, patriot, tender-*   41
ness, sacrifice, childlike, manly, bluff, limpid. All of these words are loaded with associations that would be rather hard to indicate in a straightforward definition. There is more than a literal difference between "They sat around the fireside" and "They sat around the stove." They might have been equally warm and happy around the stove, but *fireside* suggests leisure, grace, quiet tradition, congenial company, and *stove* does not.

Conversely, some words have bad associations. *Mother* suggests pleasant things, but   42
mother-in-law does not. Many mothers-in-law are heroically lovable and some mothers drink gin all day and beat their children insensible, but these facts of life are beside the point. The point is that *mother* sounds good and *mother-in-law* does not.

Or consider the word *intellectual.* This would seem to be a complimentary term, but   43
in point of fact it is not, for it has picked up associations of impracticality and ineffectuality and general dopiness. So also such words as *liberal, reactionary, Commu-*
nist, socialist, capitalist, radical, schoolteacher, truck driver, undertaker, operator,
salesman, huckster, speculator. These convey meaning on the literal level, but beyond that—sometimes, in some places—they convey contempt on the part of the speaker.

The question of whether to use loaded words or not depends on what is being written.   44
The scientist, the scholar, try to avoid them; for the poet, the advertising writer, the public speaker, they are standard equipment. But *every* writer should take care that they do not substitute for thought. If you write, "Anyone who thinks that is nothing but a Socialist (or Communist or capitalist)" you have said nothing except that you don't like people who

think that, and such remarks are effective only with the most naive readers. It is always a bad mistake to think your readers more naive than they really are.

COLORLESS WORDS

45   But probably most student writers come to grief not with words that are colorful or those that are colored but with those that have no color at all. A pet example is *nice,* a word we would find it hard to dispense with in casual conversation but which is no longer capable of adding much to a description. Colorless words are those of such general meaning that in a particular sentence they mean nothing. Slang adjectives like *cool* ("That's real cool") tend to explode all over the language. They are applied to everything, lose their original force, and quickly die.

46   Beware also of nouns of very general meaning, like *circumstances, cases, instances, aspects, factors, relationships, attitudes, eventualities,* etc. In most circumstances you will find that those cases of writing which contain too many instances of words like these will in this and other aspects have factors leading to unsatisfactory relationships with the reader resulting in unfavorable attitudes on his part and perhaps other eventualities, like a grade of "D." Notice also what *etc.* means. It means "I'd like to make this longer, but I can't think of any more examples."

Vocabulary

contrive (6)   cogent (10)   diffidence (26)
bromides (7)   vacuity (11)   repressions (27)
inexorably (8)   cantankerously (14) limpid (41)

Questions on Meaning and Technique

1. How does the author's opening draw us in? Comment on the effectiveness of his technique.

2. How did the student proceed with writing the essay on college football? Do you regard the author's description of this hypothetical attempt as exaggerated, or does it strike you as true to life? How does it compare with your own attempts at writing essays?

3. Do you think the "D" allegedly earned by the essay on college football is overly harsh or deserved? Justify your answer.

4. A characteristic of this famous essay is the hold it manages to exert over most readers. How does the author achieve this effect?

5. The author advises that you list the arguments that come immediately to mind on a topic and then never use any of them. How do you think the author would reply to the objection that a student might deeply believe in one of the clichéd arguments on the list?

6. The author urges the student writer always to take the less than usual side of a topic. Do you think this advice ethical? Why or why not?

7. What purpose do the questions at the beginning of paragraph 7 serve?

8. In paragraph 19 the author suggests that "Whenever I hear Gerber Sprink-little play 'Mississippi Man' on the trombone, my socks creep up my ankles" is better than, "I like popular music very much." What objection might an English instructor raise to the Sprinklittle sentence?

9. In paragraph 25, the author writes: "He is, he realizes, young and inexperienced, and he half suspects that he is dopey and fuzzy-minded beyond the average. Probably only too true." What is grammatically wrong with the second assertion? What justification can the author have for using it?

10. "The student toiling away at his weekly English theme is too often tormented by a figure: five hundred words. How, he asks himself, is he to achieve this staggering total? Obviously by never using one word when he can somehow work in ten." What obvious—and to some, offensive—assumption does the wording of this passage make? How might a modern textbook writer word this same idea?

Writing Assignments

1. Inverting Roberts's approach, write an essay titled "How to Say Something in 500 Words." Like Roberts, use examples to support your thesis.

2. Write an essay in which you outline the proper steps involved in writing a journal entry and using it later in a fully developed essay.

Additional Writing Assignments

1. You would like to have a balanced budget at the end of each month. Write a process paper on how to set up your ledger sheets. Use an approach that suits your spending needs and style.

2. Write a "how-to" process paper of the way your state senators are elected.

3. Write a process paper on how to prepare for a trip to a foreign country.

4. Renting a room or an apartment often proves disastrous for students. Write a process paper indicating how to rent an appropriate room or apartment.

5. Choose your favorite hobby or sport and write a process paper on how to excel at this activity.

6. Pretend that you are planning your wedding. Develop a process essay in which you analyze chronologically the major steps involved.

7. If you were a first-grade teacher, what events would you plan for the first hour of school? Explain them in a process essay that could serve as a lesson plan.

8. Through library research, accumulate the proper information to write an essay in which you describe the major events that led to one of the following:

the Battle of Waterloo, the bombing of Pearl Harbor, the war in Vietnam, or the 1990 Iraqi invasion of Kuwait.

9. Write a process essay suggesting the steps one must take to overcome one of the following bad habits: eating too many desserts, smoking, talking without listening, being stingy.

Photo Writing Assignment

Coretta Scott King mourning her husband, Martin Luther King, Jr. UPI/Bettmann Newsphotos.

Process involves a sequence of steps telling how something is done or how something happened. This photo shows Coretta Scott King attending the funeral service for her husband, Martin Luther King, Jr. Think about what steps in the grieving process this woman will need to take in order to recover from her agony. Write an essay suggesting the successive steps.

343

Classification/Division

READING FOR IDEAS

In the science fiction story that follows, the author asks you to imagine that all human differences have been outlawed by a government intent on achieving complete equality. All citizens who show extraordinary talents or brain power are immediately handicapped to reduce them to the desired uniformity. As you read, ask yourself if any of the characters in the story resemble people you know. What does the story teach you about possible future trends, especially related to individuality? Try to classify the handicaps described and think about the chances of that kind of equality ever succeeding.

Harrison Bergeron
KURT VONNEGUT, JR.

Kurt Vonnegut, Jr. (b. 1922) is a writer whose science fiction, fantasy, and political satire have been especially popular on college campuses. During World War II, he was a prisoner of war in Germany, an experience reflected in many of his novels and essays. Recently Mr. Vonnegut has combined writing with university teaching. Among his best works are The Sirens of Titan *(1961),* Cat's Cradle *(1963),* Slaughterhouse Five *(1969),* Breakfast of Champions *(1972),* Slapstick *(1976),* Jailbird *(1979), and* Bluebeard *(1990).*

1   The year was 2081, and everybody was finally equal. They weren't only equal before God and the law. They were equal in every which way. Nobody was smarter than

anybody else. Nobody was better looking than anybody else. Nobody was stronger or quicker than anybody else. All this equality was due to the 211th, 212th, and 213th Amendments to the Constitution, and to the unceasing vigilance of agents of the United States Handicapper General.

Some things about living still weren't quite right, though. April, for instance, still drove   2
people crazy by not being springtime. And it was in that clammy month that the H-G men took George and Hazel Bergeron's fourteen-year-old son, Harrison, away.

It was tragic, all right, but George and Hazel couldn't think about it very hard. Hazel   3
had a perfectly average intelligence, which meant she couldn't think about anything except in short bursts. And George, while his intelligence was way above normal, had a little mental handicap radio in his ear. He was required by law to wear it at all times. It was tuned to a government transmitter. Every twenty seconds or so, the transmitter would send out some sharp noise to keep people like George from taking unfair advantage of their brains.

George and Hazel were watching television. There were tears on Hazel's cheeks, but   4
she'd forgotten for the moment what they were about.

On the television screen were ballerinas.   5

A buzzer sounded in George's head. His thoughts fled in panic, like bandits from a   6
burglar alarm.

"That was a real pretty dance, that dance they just did," said Hazel.   7

"Huh?" said George.   8

"That dance—it was nice," said Hazel.   9

"Yup," said George. He tried to think a little about the ballerinas. They weren't really   10
very good—no better than anybody else would have been anyway. They were burdened with sash-weights and bags of birdshot, and their faces were masked, so that no one, seeing a free and graceful gesture or a pretty face, would feel like something the cat drug in. George was toying with the vague notion that maybe dancers shouldn't be handi-capped. But he didn't get very far with it before another noise in his ear radio scattered his thoughts.

George winced. So did two out of the eight ballerinas.   11

Hazel saw him wince. Having no mental handicap herself, she had to ask George   12
what the latest sound had been.

"Sounded like somebody hitting a milk bottle with a ball peen hammer," said George.   13

"I'd think it would be real interesting, hearing all the different sounds," said Hazel, a   14
little envious. "All the things they think up."

"Um," said George.   15

"Only, if I was Handicapper General, you know what I would do?" said Hazel. Hazel,   16
as a matter of fact, bore a strong resemblance to the Handicapper General, a woman named Diana Moon Glampers. "If I was Diana Moon Glampers," said Hazel, "I'd have chimes on Sunday—just chimes. Kind of in honor of religion."

"I could think, if it was just chimes," said George.   17

"Well—maybe make 'em real loud," said Hazel. "I think I'd make a good Handicap-   18
per General."

"Good as anybody else," said George.   19

20   "Who knows better'n I do what normal is?" said Hazel.

21   "Right," said George. He began to think glimmeringly about his abnormal son who was now in jail, about Harrison, but a twenty-one-gun salute in his head stopped that.

22   "Boy!" said Hazel, "that was a doozy, wasn't it?"

23   It was such a doozy that George was white and trembling, and tears stood on the rims of his red eyes. Two of the eight ballerinas had collapsed to the studio floor, were holding their temples.

24   "All of a sudden you look so tired," said Hazel. "Why don't you stretch out on the sofa, so's you can rest your handicap bag on the pillows, honeybunch." She was referring to the forty-seven pounds of birdshot in a canvas bag, which was padlocked around George's neck. "Go on and rest the bag for a little while," she said. "I don't care if you're not equal to me for a while."

25   George weighed the bag with his hands. "I don't mind it," he said. "I don't notice it any more. It's just a part of me."

26   "You've been so tired lately—kind of wore out," said Hazel. "If there was just some way we could make a little hole in the bottom of the bag, and just take out a few of them lead balls, just a few."

27   "Two years in prison and two thousand dollars fine for every ball I took out," said George. "I don't call that a bargain."

28   "If you could just take a few out when you came home from work," said Hazel. "I mean—you don't compete with anybody around here. You just set around."

29   "If I tried to get away with it," said George, "then other people'd get away with it—and pretty soon we'd be right back to the dark ages again, with everybody competing against everybody else. You wouldn't like that, would you?"

30   "I'd hate it," said Hazel.

31   "There you are," said George. "The minute people start cheating on laws, what do you think happens to society?"

32   If Hazel hadn't been able to come up with an answer to this question, George couldn't have supplied one. A siren was going off in his head.

33   "Reckon it'd fall all apart," said Hazel.

34   "What would?" said George blankly.

35   "Society," said Hazel uncertainly. "Wasn't that what you just said?"

36   "Who knows?" said George.

37   The television program was suddenly interrupted for a news bulletin. It wasn't clear at first as to what the bulletin was about, since the announcer, like all announcers, had a serious speech impediment. For about half a minute, and in a state of high excitement, the announcer tried to say, "Ladies and gentlemen—"

38   He finally gave up, handed the bulletin to a ballerina to read.

39   "That's all right—" Hazel said to the announcer, "he tried. That's the big thing. He tried to do the best he could with what God gave him. He should get a nice raise for trying so hard."

40   "Ladies and gentlemen—" said the ballerina, reading the bulletin. She must have been extraordinarily beautiful because the mask she wore was hideous. And it was easy to see that she was the strongest and most graceful of all the dancers, for her handicap bags were as big as those worn by two-hundred-pound men.

And she had to apologize at once for her voice, which was a very unfair voice for a   41
woman to use. Her voice was warm, luminous, timeless, melody. "Excuse me—" she
said, and she began again, making her voice absolutely uncompetitive.

"Harrison Bergeron, age fourteen," she said in a grackle squawk, "has just escaped   42
from jail, where he was held on suspicion of plotting to overthrow the government. He
is a genius and an athlete, is underhandicapped, and should be regarded as extremely
dangerous."

A police photograph of Harrison Bergeron was flashed on the screen upside down,   43
then sideways, upside down again, then right side up. The picture showed the full length
of Harrison against a background calibrated in feet and inches. He was exactly seven feet
tall.

The rest of Harrison's appearance was Halloween and hardware. Nobody had ever   44
borne heavier handicaps. He had outgrown hindrances faster than the H-G men could
think them up. Instead of a little ear radio for a mental handicap, he wore a tremendous
pair of earphones, and spectacles with thick wavy lenses. The spectacles were intended
to make him not only half blind, but to give him whanging headaches besides.

Scrap metal was hung all over him. Ordinarily, there was a certain symmetry, a   45
military neatness to the handicaps issued to strong people, but Harrison looked like a
walking junkyard. In the race of life, Harrison carried three hundred pounds.

And to offset his good looks, the H-G men required that he wear at all times a red   46
rubber ball for a nose, keep his eyebrows shaved off, and cover his even white teeth with
black caps at snaggletooth random.

"If you see this boy," said the ballerina, "do not—I repeat, do not—try to reason with   47
him."

There was the shriek of a door being torn from its hinges.   48

Screams and barking cries of consternation came from the television set. The   49
photograph of Harrison Bergeron on the screen jumped again and again, as though
dancing to the tune of an earthquake.

George Bergeron correctly identified the earthquake, and well he might have—for   50
many was the time his own home had danced to the same crashing tune. "My God—"
said George, "that must be Harrison!"

The realization was blasted from his mind instantly by the sound of an automobile   51
collision in his head.

When George could open his eyes again, the photograph of Harrison was gone. A   52
living, breathing Harrison filled the screen.

Clanking, clownish, and huge, Harrison stood in the center of the studio. The knob of   53
the uprooted studio door was still in his hand. Ballerinas, technicians, musicians, and
announcers cowered on their knees before him, expecting to die.

"I am the Emperor!" cried Harrison. "Do you hear? I am the Emperor! Everybody   54
must do what I say at once!" He stamped his foot and the studio shook.

"Even as I stand here—" he bellowed, "crippled, hobbled, sickened—I am a greater   55
ruler than any man who ever lived! Now watch me become what I *can* become!"

Harrison tore the straps of his handicap harness like wet tissue paper, tore straps   56
guaranteed to support five thousand pounds.

Harrison's scrap-iron handicaps crashed to the floor.   57

58   Harrison thrust his thumbs under the bar of the padlock that secured his head harness. The bar snapped like celery. Harrison smashed his headphones and spectacles against the wall.

59   He flung away his rubber-ball nose, revealed a man that would have awed Thor, the god of thunder.

60   "I shall now select my Empress!" he said, looking down on the cowering people. "Let the first woman who dares rise to her feet claim her mate and her throne!"

61   A moment passed, and then a ballerina arose, swaying like a willow.

62   Harrison plucked the mental handicap from her ear, snapped off her physical handicaps with marvelous delicacy. Last of all, he removed her mask.

63   She was blindingly beautiful.

64   "Now—" said Harrison, taking her hand, "shall we show the people the meaning of the word dance? Music!" he commanded.

65   The musicians scrambled back into their chairs, and Harrison stripped them of their handicaps, too. "Play your best," he told them, "and I'll make you barons and dukes and earls."

66   The music began. It was normal at first—cheap, silly, false. But Harrison snatched two musicians from their chairs, waved them like batons as he sang the music as he wanted it played. He slammed them back into their chairs.

67   The music began again and was much improved.

68   Harrison and his Empress merely listened to the music for a while—listened gravely, as though synchronizing their heartbeats with it.

69   They shifted their weights to their toes.

70   Harrison placed his big hand on the girl's tiny waist, letting her sense the weightlessness that would soon be hers.

71   And then, in an explosion of joy and grace, into the air they sprang!

72   Not only were the laws of the land abandoned, but the law of gravity and the laws of motion as well.

73   They reeled, whirled, swiveled, flounced, capered, gamboled, and spun.

74   They leaped like deer on the moon.

75   The studio ceiling was thirty feet high, but each leap brought the dancers nearer to it.

76   It became their obvious intention to kiss the ceiling.

77   They kissed it.

78   And then, neutralizing gravity with love and pure will, they remained suspended in air inches below the ceiling, and they kissed each other for a long, long time.

79   It was then that Diana Moon Glampers, the Handicapper General, came into the studio with a double-barreled 10-gauge shotgun. She fired twice, and the Emperor and the Empress were dead before they hit the floor.

80   Diana Moon Glampers loaded the gun again. She aimed it at the musicians and told them they had ten seconds to get their handicaps back on.

81   It was then that the Bergeron's television tube burned out.

82   Hazel turned to comment about the blackout to George. But George had gone out into the kitchen for a can of beer.

83   George came back in with the beer, paused while a handicap signal shook him up. And then he sat down again. "You been crying?" he said to Hazel.

84   "Yup," she said.

"What about?" he said.   85

"I forget," she said. "Something real sad on television."   86

"What was it?" he said.   87

"It's all kind of mixed up in my mind," said Hazel.   88

"Forget sad things," said George.   89

"I always do," said Hazel.   90

"That's my girl," said George. He winced. There was the sound of a riveting gun in   91
his head.

"Gee—I could tell that one was a doozy," said Hazel.   92

"You can say that again," said George.   93

"Gee—" said Hazel, "I could tell that one was a doozy."   94

Vocabulary

unceasing (1)	winced (11)	luminous (41)	consternation (49)
vigilance (1)	glimmeringly (21)	grackle (42)	cowered (53)
transmitter (3)	doozy (22)	calibrated (43)	capered (73)
sash-weights (10)	impediment (37)	symmetry (45)	gamboled (73)

Questions on Meaning and Technique

1. To classify the handicaps presented in this story, what general categories would you list?

2. Which handicap, if any, do you consider the most harmful to society? Give reasons for your answer.

3. How do George and Hazel differ? What importance is attached to their differences?

4. What is *equality* as defined in Vonnegut's story? What is the narrator's point of view about the kind of equality described? Rely on specific passages to support your answer.

5. In your opinion, can a society succeed whose mission is to achieve the kind of equality described in this story? Why or why not?

6. What purposes does the opening paragraph serve? What is the narrator's tone?

7. What difference would it make if the story were narrated from Harrison's point of view?

8. How does the author achieve a sense of movement in the studio scene (paragraphs 69–75)?

READING FOR IDEAS

Taken from one of Shakespeare's most popular comedies, *As You Like It,* the poem is a monologue spoken by Jacques, a melancholy gentleman who has escaped court politics to live in the forest. He views life as a meaningless process of decay governed by inexorable time. In the words that follow, Jacques divides life into stages, with each stage being dominated by a type of man.

All the World's a Stage
William Shakespeare

From As You Like It *(Act 2, Scene 7)*

William Shakespeare (1564–1616) is generally considered the greatest literary genius of the English language. Despite his world renown, little is known about Shakespeare's personal life. Born in Stratford-on-Avon, England, the son of a successful businessman who also held the office of alderman and bailiff, Shakespeare probably attended the local grammar school, where he learned some Latin and Greek. At the age of 18, he married Anne Hathaway, eight years his senior, who bore him three children. The vast legacy of his writing includes 36 plays, 154 sonnets, and 5 epic poems.

All the world's a stage,

And all the men and women merely players.
They have their exits and their entrances,
And one man in his time plays many parts,
5   His acts being seven ages. At first, the infant,
Mewling and puking in the nurse's arms.
Then the whining schoolboy, with his satchel
And shining morning face, creeping like snail
Unwillingly to school. And then the lover,
10   Sighing like furnace, with a woful ballad
Made to his mistress' eyebrow. Then a soldier,
Full of strange oaths and bearded like the pard,[1]
Jealous in honour, sudden and quick in quarrel,
Seeking the bubble reputation
15   Even in the cannon's mouth. And then the justice,
In fair round belly with good capon lin'd,
With eyes severe and beard of formal cut,
Full of wise saws and modern instances;
And so he plays his part. The sixth age shifts
20   Into the lean and slipper'd pantaloon,
With spectacles on nose and pouch on side;
His youthful hose, well sav'd, a world too wide
For his shrunk shank, and his big manly voice,
Turning again toward childish treble, pipes

---

[1] Leopard.

And whistles in his sound. Last scene of all,   25
That ends this strange eventful history,
Is second childishness and mere oblivion,
Sans² teeth, sans eyes, sans taste, sans everything.

Vocabulary

mewling (line 6)	pantaloon (line 20)	shank (line 23)
puking (line 6)	pound (line 21)	treble (line 24)
capon (line 16)		

Questions on Meaning and Technique

1. In the first line, what metaphor is used to describe life? What other metaphor might be appropriate?

2. What name can you give to each of the seven stages of life as depicted by Jacques? Classify each character into the proper stage.

3. What does the simile "Sighing like furnace" reveal?

4. What characteristics typify the soldier? Are these characteristics typical of soldiers today?

5. In the final lines, how does Jacques portray life? Do you agree with his portrayal? Give reasons for your answer.

HOW TO WRITE A CLASSIFICATION/DIVISION

Classification or division means sorting people, objects, data, or ideas into various types and groups. It is a method of thinking that helps to impose order on the enormous jumble in the world. Classification and division are so closely related that writers often use them together because they are opposite sides of the same coin.

Classification means placing an individual part into a category with other similar parts, whereas division means separating a large subject into divisible parts. Thus, biologists, for example, classify a wolf as a canine (dog family), whereas a tiger is classified as a feline (cat family). The field of anthropology is divided into the subfields of archaeology, ethnography, and linguistics, whereas botany classifies every plant into the family to which it belongs. In each case an attempt is made to impose order by division or classification—that is, reducing the many to the few.

Division means starting from the opposite point of view. Thus, we might divide a subject like the Nobel Prize into its types: (1) the Nobel Peace Prize, (2) the Nobel Prize in chemistry, (3) the Nobel Prize in physics, (4) the Nobel Prize in medicine, (5) the Nobel Prize in literature, and (6) the Nobel Prize in economics. Dividing a subject into smaller, related parts makes it easier to comprehend and handle.

---

²French for "without."

As civilized humans, we are entirely addicted to thinking by classification/division. We carry classes, types, and categories on the tips of our tongues. A car is not merely a car; it is a coupe, a sedan, or a convertible—classified by body type. Its engine is a four, a six, or an eight—classified by number of cylinders. Its make is either domestic or foreign—classified by country of manufacture—giving rise to further subtyping as either a Ford, Chevrolet, Mercedes, Toyota, or one of the other kinds of cars. With little reflection, almost all of us can discern similar groupings and categories lurking about the simplest object. "What type of person is he?" we commonly ask, presuming that people can be sorted into recognizable types, such as introvert, extrovert, egoist, miser, and so forth.

Writing Assignment

After reading Kurt Vonnegut's "Harrison Bergeron," classify all the handicaps in our society by placing them in appropriate categories and illustrating each type with examples. Somewhere in your opening paragraph, provide a clear statement of your classifications. For instance, you might write, "All handicaps in our society can be classified into one of three types—catastrophic, severe, or mild." Then develop this controlling idea by discussing each type of handicap individually, trying to portray it vividly. Your final paragraph might include your views about whether such handicaps help or hinder society. In preparation for this conclusion, ask yourself what society would be like if no handicapped people existed.

Specific Instructions

PREWRITING ON THE ASSIGNMENT.   Before putting any of your ideas on paper, clarify for yourself what the term *handicap* means. The dictionary tells us that it means "a deficiency that prevents or restricts normal achievement." With this definition in mind, you might make a list of deficiencies you have encountered. Think, for example, of people whose ambitions for job advancement were ruined and ask yourself what devastated their progress. Keep your thoughts rolling by writing them down uncensored on paper. Your list might start out like this:

students with dyslexia

people in wheelchairs because of paralysis or maiming

excessive laziness

lack of self-confidence

self-centered behavior

mental retardation

phobias

being physically unattractive

lacking social skills

having a grating personality

anorexia nervosa

excessive obesity

trying to beat the system through dishonest means

blindness

lack of self-discipline

Make your list as long as you wish. Then analyze it for ways to group the handicaps. Even the brief list above reveals quickly that some handicaps are physical: dyslexia, paralysis, mental retardation, ugliness, and blindness; whereas other handicaps are emotional: laziness, phobias, lack of self-confidence, and certain eating disorders such as anorexia or obesity. Then again, some handicaps seem to result from moral lapses: self-indulgence, dishonesty, arrogance, chronic rudeness. Almost any list you compile will allow you to cluster the entries into compartments of related items. Your classification will be well on its way as soon as you have drawn your compartments and filled them with approximately the same number of handicaps to keep the categories balanced rather than lopsided.

Once your groups have been chosen, you have a ready-made thesis: "Handicaps that make it difficult for individuals to fulfill their life's ambitions fall mostly into three areas—physical, emotional, and moral."

Because the assignment also asks you to draw some conclusion from having classified handicaps, you need to mull over your views on the subject. Do handicaps have to be defeating, or can they actually spur a sufferer on to perform heroic or outstanding feats? Can talents be developed regardless of handicaps? In fact, would our society be better off if no one had a handicap? All these questions will help you clarify your own attitudes so that you can end your paper with a strong concluding statement.

BASE YOUR CLASSIFICATION ON A SINGLE PRINCIPLE.   In the division/classification essay, as in most nonfiction writing, clarity and intensity are children of a pure purpose. If you set out to do one thing and one thing only in an essay, you have a good chance of successfully doing it. But if you try to do two or three different things at once—unless you are a highly skilled writer—you are most likely to muddle the assignment.

To be clear and consistent, a division/classification should therefore be made according to a single principle. This simply means that once you have selected a criterion for making your division, you should concentrate exclusively on developing the categories that are thereby yielded. You should not, halfway through, switch to another principle that is likely to spawn further categories. For example, if you were writing an essay classifying cars according to their body types and suddenly switched to a classification based on number of cylinders, overlapping categories would result. Some coupes have eight cylinders; so do some sedans and some convertibles. The effect would be a tiresome double count.

The choice of a division/classification principle is sometimes dictated by the wording of an assignment but often is left entirely to the discretion of the writer. An essay that divides and classifies is as much a thinking as a writing assignment. Say, for example, that you are asked to write an essay dividing/classifying people. Numerous criteria could be used for sorting them into categories. You could, for instance, choose degree of intimacy as your selection principle, in which case you might have an opening sentence like this:

> Three major kinds of relationships tie people to each other: acquaintance, friendship, and love.

So far so good. If you stick to degree of intimacy as your dividing principle, you will have an essay that is at least structurally sound. But another criterion, yielding entirely different categories, could have been used. You could, for instance, have chosen to divide/classify the people you know on the basis of their politics, in which case your thesis might have read:

> Most people fall into four different political groups: radical, liberal, conservative, and indifferent.

Or you might have classified them on the basis of social class:

> People are classifiable into three distinct classes, each with its own peculiar way of behaving: lower class, middle class, and upper class.

Or humorously, on the basis of physique:

> My friends, relatives, and acquaintances fall neatly into three groups: the were-fats, the are-fats, and the will-be-fats.

In sum, you may make an entirely different essay out of the same assignment, depending on the principle you use to divide/classify.

But which principle should you have used? That is an unanswerable question. It depends entirely on what you can do and on what purpose you wish to achieve in your essay. If you are the solemn sort who writes stately and serious essays, you would probably do well classifying people by their politics. If you are the jolly sort and can write in a humorous vein, you might tackle the essay that lumps people into fat categories. If you are the affectionate sort who values friendship, you might use degree of intimacy as your dividing principle. What matters is that, in a serious essay, you use an important principle for dividing/classifying and that you practice it consistently throughout. In other words, if you were doing a classification of books on the best-seller list, you should not base your essay on a principle as trivial as, say, whether or not the books had pictures in them. Such an essay, if meant to be serious, would be unintentionally humorous.

Finally, the use of a single principle for division/classification should be observed in the essay as a whole as well as in individual paragraphs. Here, for instance, are three paragraphs, each based on a single principle of division:

There are five venereal diseases, all of which can cause death. Three of these have been eliminated by modern medicine, while the other two, syphilis and gonorrhea, are on the rise once more all over the world. Both of these diseases are mainly contracted through sexual relations. These germs spread to all parts of the body and, therefore, anything the infected person uses is possibly an immediate carrier. These germs can spread to another human by an open cut if it comes in contact with the germs of an infected person.

The symptoms of these diseases are usually disregarded by their victims. In infectious syphilis there are three definite stages, with a few weeks lapsing between the first two. The first stage consists of a hard chancre (SHANKer) sore in the genital area. The second stage is a rash accompanied by headaches, fever, sore throat, or loss of hair. The third stage, after a seemingly dormant period of 10 to 25 years, makes its presence known by rendering its victim blind, crippled, insane, sterile, or dead.

Unlike its counterpart, gonorrhea's latent stages are more easily noticed by its victims. The first symptom is usually a burning pain during urination. The remaining factors of this disease are similar to those of syphilis, and the results are equally as devastating.

> Mary Kathrine Wayman, "The Unmentionable Diseases"
> *Contemporary American Speeches,* 1969

The first paragraph is a division/classification of kinds of venereal diseases; the second, of symptoms of syphilis; the third, of symptoms of gonorrhea. Because it is based on a single principle of division/classification, each paragraph is unswervingly purposeful and clear.

DIVIDE THE WHOLE PIE.   Once you have been given a subject to divide/classify, be sure you discuss the entire subject. Don't leave out a single piece. For example, if you were to classify literature into short story, drama, and poetry, a significant category would be missing: the novel. The entire subject must be included if a division/classification is to be complete.

But sometimes, especially when the division/classification is of an abstract subject whose parts are not readily apparent, it is left to the ingenuity of the writer to give an illusion of completeness. For example, consider this paragraph:

> There are three kinds of book owners. The first has all the standard sets and best-sellers—unread, untouched. (This deluded individual owns wood-pulp and ink, not books.) The second has a great many books—a few of them read through, most of them dipped into, but all of them as clean and shiny as the day they were bought. (This person would probably like to make books his own, but is restrained by a false respect for their physical appearance.) The third has a few books or many—every one of them dog-eared and dilapidated, shaken and loosened by continual use, marked and scribbled in from front to back. (This man owns books.)

> Mortimer J. Adler, "How to Mark a Book"
> *Saturday Review,* 6 July 1940

The division, the categories yielded, and the entire subject are obviously idiosyncratic. One cannot pounce on this piece of writing as if one knew with absolute certainty exactly what kinds of book owners there are in the world. Yet the paragraph contains recognizable types and gives the illusion of completeness. What we mean to illustrate is simply that division/classification, especially of an abstract subject, is a highly imaginative exercise. It is less a question of *being* right in such a division and more a matter of *seeming* right. The preceding paragraph contains a sensible division supported by appropriate detail and delivered in a sparklingly clear style, all of which combine to give it a sense of authenticity.

MAKE EACH CATEGORY IN A CLASSIFICATION SEPARATE FROM THE OTHERS.   A classification whose segments overlap acquires a fuzziness that is the mark of an inferior essay. Notice the overlapping teaching methods here:

   a. Lecture
   b. Discussion
   c. Question-answer

Question-answer and discussion overlap: there is no clear distinction between them. A discussion lesson may involve questions and answers, and a question-answer lesson may involve discussion. The classification should either be limited to lecture and discussion or include a third, clearly separate segment:

   a. Lecture
   b. Discussion
   c. Quizzes

GIVE EQUAL IMPORTANCE TO EACH SEGMENT OF THE CLASSIFICATION.   Balance plays an important role in a division essay. You must curb the tendency to pamper one segment with elaborate details while paring down another to a few barren lines. Treat each segment with equal emphasis or your essay will become obviously lopsided.

READING FOR IDEAS

In a humorous tone, the author appeals to a common human frustration—dealing with inanimate objects that seem to defy our desires for using them. He begins by dividing these objects into three easily recognized categories. Then he continues by supplying examples of each category, and these too are instantly recognized. Notice how soon (in the opening paragraph) the author announces his purpose and how scrupulously he follows the rules for division/classification. The result is clarity and simplicity within the context of laughter.

PROFESSIONAL MODEL

The Plot Against People
RUSSELL BAKER

Russell Baker (b. 1925) is a Pulitzer Prize-winning journalist who began his career as a reporter for the Baltimore Sun *and later moved to the prestigious* New York Times, *where he still writes a regular column titled "The Observer." In 1982 he captured a large reading audience with his autobiography,* Growing Up, *which appealed to the middle-class generation of the 1940s and 1950s because it captured that era so accurately and with nostalgia. This work was followed with another autobiography,* The Good Times *(1989). But Baker is best known for his informal essays—like the one below—about life in the United States.*

Inanimate objects are classified scientifically into three major categories—those that break down, those that get lost, and those that don't work. 1

The goal of all inanimate objects is to resist man and ultimately to defeat him, and the three major classifications are based on the method each object uses to achieve its purpose. As a general rule, any object capable of breaking down at the moment when it is most needed will do so. The automobile is typical of the category. 2

With the cunning peculiar to its breed, the automobile never breaks down while entering a filling station which has a large staff of idle mechanics. It waits until it reaches a downtown intersection in the middle of the rush hour, or until it is fully loaded with family and luggage on the Ohio Turnpike. Thus it creates maximum inconvenience, frustration, and irritability, thereby reducing its owner's lifespan. 3

Washing machines, garbage disposals, lawn mowers, furnaces, TV sets, tape recorders, slide projectors—all are in league with the automobile to take their turn at breaking down whenever life threatens to flow smoothly for their enemies. 4

Many inanimate objects, of course, find it extremely difficult to break down. Pliers, for example, and gloves and keys are almost totally incapable of breaking down. Therefore, they have had to evolve a different technique for resisting man. 5

They get lost. Science has still not solved the mystery of how they do it, and no man has ever caught one of them in the act. The most plausible theory is that they have developed a secret method of locomotion which they are able to conceal from human eyes. 6

It is not uncommon for a pair of pliers to climb all the way from the cellar to the attic in its single-minded determination to raise its owner's blood pressure. Keys have been known to burrow three feet under mattresses. Women's purses, despite their great weight, frequently travel through six or seven rooms to find hiding space under a couch. 7

Scientists have been struck by the fact that things that break down virtually never get lost, while things that get lost hardly ever break down. A furnace, for example, will invariably break down at the depth of the first winter cold wave, but it will never get lost. A woman's purse hardly ever breaks down; it almost invariably chooses to get lost. 8

9   Some persons believe this constitutes evidence that inanimate objects are not entirely hostile to man. After all, they point out, a furnace could infuriate a man even more thoroughly by getting lost than by breaking down, just as a glove could upset him far more by breaking down than by getting lost.

10   Not everyone agrees, however, that this indicates a conciliatory attitude. Many say it merely proves that furnaces, gloves and pliers are incredibly stupid.

11   The third class of objects—those that don't work—is the most curious of all. These include such objects as barometers, car clocks, cigarette lighters, flashlights and toy-train locomotives. It is inaccurate, of course, to say that they *never* work. They work once, usually for the first few hours after being brought home, and then quit. Thereafter, they never work again.

12   In fact, it is widely assumed that they are built for the purpose of not working. Some people have reached advanced ages without ever seeing some of these objects— barometers, for example—in working order.

13   Science is utterly baffled by the entire category. There are many theories about it. The most interesting holds that the things that don't work have attained the highest state possible for an inanimate object, the state to which things that break down and things that get lost can still only aspire.

14   They have truly defeated man by conditioning him never to expect anything of them. When his cigarette lighter won't light or his flashlight fails to illuminate, it does not raise his blood pressure. Objects that don't work have given man the only peace he receives from inanimate society.

Vocabulary

inanimate (1)	conciliatory (10)
plausible (6)	illuminate (14)
burrow (7)	

Questions on Meaning and Technique

1. On what implausible idea is the tongue-in-cheek attitude of this essay based? What conclusion does the author reach?

2. What basis does Baker use for his classification? What other basis can you suggest?

3. What is the purpose of the disagreement described in paragraph 10? How important is it to know which side is right?

4. How does Baker indicate that he is moving from the first to the second category of objects? Where does the shift take place?

5. What words or phrases does the author use to make inanimate objects appear to be human?

6. Why do you think inanimate objects often infuriate humans? Is there a solution to this problem? If so, what is it? If there is no solution, how should humans adjust to the inevitable?

7. Considering that so many objects tend to break down, do you believe that society would be better off with fewer inanimate objects to contend with? Why or why not?

8. What is the purpose of Baker's brief opening paragraph?

STUDENT ESSAY

First Draft   David Beckham

Handicaps

Insert A

1   Every human being could be said to have a handicap of some sort. These handicaps could be divided into three categories: intellectual handicaps, emotional handicaps, and physical handicaps. No one is likely to be immune from one or more of these handicaps.

Rewrite to create a more gripping opening. Also, add one more category—"aesthetic handicaps"—to complete the classification.

2   Intellectual handicaps ~~come~~ exist in a wide variety of types. The type ~~most~~ immediately thought of by most people is stupidity, --not to be confused with ignorance ~~and it is certainly a handicap.~~ Stupidity is often ~~characterized by being~~ made the butt of jokes by the slightly less stupid ~~persons in one's environment~~. Although ~~Indeed,~~ stupidity is a difficult handicap, ~~but~~ it is far from the only intellectual handicap a person can ~~labor under~~ have. Brilliance, ~~for example~~ ironically, is another intellectual handicap. The brilliant person may be able to ~~see~~ grasp immediately the cause, effect, and cure of a particular problem ~~at school or at work~~, but be unable to ~~get anyone else to understand what is so obvious to this keen intellect~~ communicate this insight to anyone else. This trait alone can cause unpopularity with one's associates and foster frustration within one's self. Such Brilliance is ~~apt to subject one to hostility of~~ likely to cause serious resentment from those who are part of the problem. ~~a far less humorous kind than stupidity does.~~ Another broad subdivision of intellectual handicap might be called the "skewed intellect." For this sufferer, the problem is one of

This paragraph needs tightening throughout.

Moving this passage up makes for better logic.

Use quotation marks to indicate usage.

Insert A

Kurt Vonnegut, Jr., began his disturbing futuristic fantasy, "Harrison Bergeron," with some descriptive remarks: "The year was 2081, and everybody was finally equal. They weren't only equal before God and the law. They were equal in every which way." This amazing state of affairs was due to the tireless efforts, Vonnegut tells us, of the "United States Handicapper General." Well, it is only the last decade of the twentieth century, and everybody is already handicapped. No one is likely to be immune to all of these handicaps, and these handicaps can be divided into four categories: intellectual handicaps, emotional handicaps, physical handicaps, and aesthetic handicaps.

seeing what other people see in a quite different light. Mark Twain's humor provides numerous examples of this type of mind. From these few examples it is obvious that the possible intellectual handicaps are many and varied. ← Insert B

3

Emotional handicaps abound ~~within the human population of the earth~~ in society today. The two most obvious are excessive emotionalism and inadequate emotional response. ~~In the first case,~~ Excessively emotional people burst into tears at the slightest provocation-- a delightful sunset, a disheveled beggar, or a delicate hummingbird. ~~the sufferer, and anyone in the immediate area, is apt to be damp with the copious tears~~ ~~shed over all the sadness and misery that meets the eye at every turn. This sad case~~ ~~suffers for everyone more or less equally, and quickly becomes a bore to anyone who~~ ~~must remain associated with him or her.~~ The emotionally ~~unresponsive,~~ inadequate conversely, ~~are~~ ~~shunned because they~~ display little or no human feeling, ~~for anyone,~~ no matter ~~in~~ what straits confront them. dire ~~straights they may be found. This unfeeling defective seems to believe that he or~~ The earthquake victim, the lonely orphan, the jobless person-- all receive the same cold shoulder. ~~she is not, or should not be affected by the suffering of anyone else in any circumstance.~~

Rewrite for more correct language and for conciseness.

Correct subject-verb disagreement. Rewrite for smoothness, concreteness, and less awkwardness in avoiding sexist language.

Beyond these broad categories lie almost infinite varieties of more narrow emotional handicaps. The person who is obsessive about a pet snake, for instance, or the person who is focused on saving the walrus to the exclusion of all other earthly problems can be said to manifest an unfortunate emotional handicap.

Delete so as not to belabor the point.

4

Physical handicaps draw ~~a lot of~~ attention because they are ~~often~~ usually obvious. Paraplegics and quadriplegics, for example, have clearly recognizable handicaps, for which, in the United States at least, much public accommodation has been made. But consider the seven footers ~~that~~ who cannot ~~can't~~ walk upright through a normal door, and the four footers ~~that can't~~ who cannot reach the top two shelves anywhere; these people, too, have physical handicaps. The ninety-seven pound weakling who ~~can't~~ is unable to open the doors at public buildings, and the muscle-bound weight lifter who splits the seams in his or her jacket when offering assistance are alike physically handicapped. ~~The aforementioned~~ These examples are obvious because they involve

Correct comma splice.

Avoid sexist language.

Insert B

Mark Twain said that being a director of an accident insurance company in Hartford gave him a whole new outlook on accidents. When he added the statement that "There is nothing quite so seraphic as the expression on the face of a newly maimed accident victim when he reaches into his vest pocket and finds his accident ticket still intact," Twain was clearly displaying the "skewed intellect."

observable

the ∧ mechanical operations of life. A ~~closely related~~ handicap ~~is the~~ aesthetic handicap ~~which must be differentiated from the physical.~~

closely related to the physical, yet differentiated from it, is the

> New paragraph is needed for new idea.

5   Excessive ugliness or beauty, which ∧ effects the way others react to one, is a handicap as ~~significant~~ as intellectual or emotional handicaps. In fact, aesthetic handicaps often lead to concatenations of problems with the intellect and emotions. And by the way, ~~the~~ features are not the only possible aesthetic handicap. Fat can certainly be an aesthetic handicap, as can body odor, halitosis, shrillness of voice, or even misplaced regional accents.

a (above "effects")
damaging (above "significant")
facial (above "the")

> No paragraph.
>
> Improve diction.

6   In ~~sum~~, we all labor under some kind of handicap. That ~~fact~~ provide⟨s⟩ a sort of balance among the members of the human species. Rather than concerning ourselves with trying to make everyone equal, ~~it would behoove us to learn to appreciate the handicaps with which others live. Doing so might make our own particular difficulties more tolerable.~~

truth (above "sum")
does not make everyone equal, but it does (above "That fact provides")
we should relish the diversity that exists. Moreover, the recognition that each of us is handicapped can lead us to admiration and respect for the accomplishments of others.

> Rewrite to expand on topic sentence.
>
> Delete final sentence because it introduces a new idea that is never developed.

STUDENT ESSAY

Final Draft   David Beckham

Handicaps

Kurt Vonnegut, Jr., began his disturbing futuristic fantasy, "Harrison Bergeron," with some descriptive remarks: "The year was 2081, and everybody was finally equal. They weren't only equal before God and the law. They were equal in every which way." This amazing state of affairs was due to the tireless efforts, Vonnegut tells us, of the "United States Handicapper General." Well, it is only the last decade of the twentieth century, and everybody is already handicapped. No one is likely to be immune from all of these handicaps, and these handicaps can be divided into four categories: intellectual handicaps, emotional handicaps, physical handicaps, and aesthetic handicaps.   1

Intellectual handicaps exist in a wide variety. The type immediately thought of by most people is stupidity--not to be confused with ignorance. Stupidity is often made the butt of jokes by the slightly less stupid. Although stupidity is a difficult handicap, it is far from the only intellectual handicap a person can have. Brilliance, ironically, is   2 another intellectual handicap. The brilliant person may be able to grasp immediately the cause, effect, and cure of a particular problem, but be unable to communicate this insight to anyone else. Such brilliance is likely to cause serious resentment from those who are part of the problem. This trait alone can cause unpopularity with one's associates and foster frustration within one's self. Another broad subdivision of intellectual handicap might be called the "skewed intellect." For this sufferer, the problem is one of seeing what other people see in a quite different light. Mark Twain said that being a director of an accident insurance company in Hartford gave him a whole new outlook on accidents. When he added the statement that "There is nothing quite so seraphic as the expression on the face of a newly maimed accident victim when he reaches into his vest pocket and finds his accident ticket still intact," Twain was clearly displaying the "skewed intellect."

3   Emotional handicaps abound in society today. The two most obvious are excessive emotionalism and inadequate emotional response. Excessively emotional people burst into tears at the slightest provocation--a delightful sunset, a disheveled beggar, or a delicate hummingbird. The emotionally inadequate, conversely, display little or no human feeling, no matter what dire straits confront them. The earthquake victim, the lonely orphan, the jobless person--all receive the same cold shoulder.

4   Physical handicaps draw attention because they are usually obvious. Paraplegics and quadriplegics, for example, have clearly recognizable handicaps, for which, in the United States at least, much public accommodation has been made. But consider the seven footers who cannot walk upright through a normal door, and the four footers who cannot reach the top two shelves anywhere; these people, too, have physical handicaps. The ninety-seven pound weakling who is unable to open the doors of public buildings, and the muscle-bound weight lifter who splits the seams in his or her jacket when offering assistance are alike physically handicapped. These examples are obvious because they involve the observable mechanical operations of life.

5   A handicap closely related to the physical, yet differentiated from it, is the aesthetic handicap. Excessive ugliness or beauty, which affects the way others react to one, is a handicap as damaging as intellectual or emotional handicaps. In fact, aesthetic handicaps often lead to concatenations of problems with the intellect and emotions.

And by the way, facial features are not the only possible aesthetic handicap. Fat can certainly be an aesthetic handicap, as can body odor, halitosis, shrillness of voice, or even misplaced regional accents.

In truth, we all labor under some kind of handicap. That does not make everyone   6 equal, but it does provide a sort of balance among the members of the human species. Rather than concerning ourselves with trying to make everyone equal, we should relish the diversity that exists. Moreover, the recognition that each one of us is handicapped can lead us to admiration and respect for the accomplishments of others.

READING FOR IDEAS

In 1956 Dr. King gained a major victory in his battle for civil rights when the bus system of Montgomery, Alabama, was desegregated. Dr. King's philosophy of nonviolent resistance, as outlined in the following selection, led to his arrest on numerous occasions and eventually to his assassination on April 4, 1968. In June 1990, another great civil rights leader, Nelson Mandela of South Africa, visited the United States and praised King while insisting that nonviolence may have to be discarded as a philosophy if it does not bring results. As you study King's principles, ask yourself what stand you are willing to take on this matter.

ALTERNATE READING

Three Types of Resistance to Oppression
MARTIN LUTHER KING, JR.

Martin Luther King, Jr. (1929–1968), was an American clergyman and black civil rights leader of the 1960s. He was born in Atlanta and educated at Morehouse College, Crozer Theological Seminary, and Boston University. Dr. King advocated a philosophy of passive resistance to the evils of segregation and racial inequality in American society. He was responsible for the boycott by blacks of the Montgomery, Alabama, segregated bus system (1955–1956) and for a massive march on Washington, D.C., in 1963. In 1964 Dr. King won the Nobel Peace Prize.

Oppressed people deal with their oppression in three characteristic ways. One way is   1 acquiescence: the oppressed resign themselves to their doom. They tacitly adjust themselves to oppression, and thereby become conditioned to it. In every movement toward freedom some of the oppressed prefer to remain oppressed. Almost 2800 years ago Moses set out to lead the children of Israel from the slavery of Egypt to the freedom of the promised land. He soon discovered that slaves do not always welcome their deliverers. They become accustomed to being slaves. They would rather bear those ills they have, as Shakespeare pointed out, than flee to others that they know not of. They prefer the "fleshpots of Egypt" to the ordeals of emancipation.

2   There is such a thing as the freedom of exhaustion. Some people are so worn down by the yoke of oppression that they give up. A few years ago in the slum areas of Atlanta, a Negro guitarist used to sing almost daily: "Been down so long that down don't bother me." This is the type of negative freedom and resignation that often engulfs the life of the oppressed.

3   But this is not the way out. To accept passively an unjust system is to coöperate with that system; thereby the oppressed become as evil as the oppressor. Noncoöperation with evil is as much a moral obligation as is coöperation with good. The oppressed must never allow the conscience of the oppressor to slumber. Religion reminds every man that he is his brother's keeper. To accept injustice or segregation passively is to say to the oppressor that his actions are morally right. It is a way of allowing his conscience to fall asleep. At this moment the oppressed fails to be his brother's keeper. So acquiescence—while often the easier way—is not the moral way. It is the way of the coward. The Negro cannot win the respect of his oppressor by acquiescing; he merely increases the oppressor's arrogance and contempt. Acquiescence is interpreted as proof of the Negro's inferiority. The Negro cannot win the respect of the white people of the South or the peoples of the world if he is willing to sell the future of his children for this personal and immediate comfort and safety.

4   A second way that oppressed people sometimes deal with oppression is to resort to physical violence and corroding hatred. Violence often brings about momentary results. Nations have frequently won their independence in battle. But in spite of temporary victories, violence never brings permanent peace. It solves no social problem; it merely creates new and more complicated ones.

5   Violence as a way of achieving racial justice is both impractical and immoral. It is impractical because it is a descending spiral ending in destruction for all. The old law of an eye for an eye leaves everybody blind. It is immoral because it seeks to humiliate the opponent rather than win his understanding; it seeks to annihilate rather than to convert. Violence is immoral because it thrives on hatred rather than love. It destroys community and makes brotherhood impossible. It leaves society in monologue rather than dialogue. Violence ends by defeating itself. It creates bitterness in the survivors and brutality in the destroyers. A voice echoes through time saying to every potential Peter, "Put up your sword." History is cluttered with the wreckage of nations that failed to follow this command.

6   If the American Negro and other victims of oppression succumb to the temptation of using violence in the struggle for freedom, future generations will be the recipients of a desolate night of bitterness, and our chief legacy to them will be an endless reign of meaningless chaos. Violence is not the way.

7   The third way open to oppressed people in their quest for freedom is the way of nonviolent resistance. Like the synthesis in Hegelian philosophy, the principle of nonviolent resistance seeks to reconcile the truths of two opposites—acquiescence and violence—while avoiding the extremes and immoralities of both. The nonviolent resister agrees with the person who acquiesces that one should not be physically aggressive toward his opponent; but he balances the equation by agreeing with the person of

violence that evil must be resisted. He avoids the nonresistance of the former and the violent resistance of the latter. With nonviolent resistance, no individual or group need submit to any wrong, nor need anyone resort to violence in order to right a wrong.

It seems to me that this is the method that must guide the actions of the Negro in the 8
present crisis in race relations. Through nonviolent resistance the Negro will be able to rise to the noble height of opposing the unjust system while loving the prepetrators of the system. The Negro must work passionately and unrelentingly for full stature as a citizen, but he must not use inferior methods to gain it. He must never come to terms with falsehood, malice, hate, or destruction.

Nonviolent resistance makes it possible for the Negro to remain in the South and 9
struggle for his rights. The Negro's problem will not be solved by running away. He cannot listen to the glib suggestion of those who would urge him to migrate en masse to other sections of the country. By grasping his great opportunity in the South he can make a lasting contribution to the moral strength of the nation and set a sublime example of courage for generations yet unborn.

By nonviolent resistance, the Negro can also enlist all men of good will in his struggle 10
for equality. The problem is not a purely racial one, with Negroes set against whites. In the end, it is not a struggle between people at all, but a tension between justice and injustice. Nonviolent resistance is not aimed against oppressors but against oppression. Under its banner consciences, not racial groups, are enlisted.

If the Negro is to achieve the goal of integration, he must organize himself into a 11
militant and nonviolent mass movement. All three elements are indispensable. The movement for equality and justice can only be a success if it has both a mass and militant character; the barriers to be overcome require both. Nonviolence is an imperative in order to bring about ultimate community.

A mass movement of militant quality that is not at the same time committed to 12
nonviolence tends to generate conflict, which in turn breeds anarchy. The support of the participants and the sympathy of the uncommitted are both inhibited by the threat that bloodshed will engulf the community. This reaction in turn encourages the opposition to threaten and resort to force. When, however, the mass movement repudiates violence while moving resolutely toward its goal, its opponents are revealed as the instigators and practitioners of violence if it occurs. Then public support is magnetically attracted to the advocates of nonviolence, while those who employ violence are literally disarmed by overwhelming sentiment against their stand.

Vocabulary

acquiescence (1)	legacy (6)	anarchy (12)	tacitly (1)
Hegelian (7)	inhibited (12)	corroding (4)	perpetrators (8)
repudiates (12)	annihilate (5)	unrelentingly (8)	

Questions on Meaning and Technique

1. What is the basis of division in this selection?
2. What are the three characteristic ways in which oppressed people deal with their oppression?

3. What did Moses discover about the nature of slaves?

4. What is the author's criticism of acquiescence? What moral objection does he raise against it?

5. Why does the author object to violence? Why does he regard it as immoral?

6. How does nonviolent resistance reconcile the truths of two opposites? What are these opposites?

7. To what noble height does the author claim nonviolent resistance will raise the Negro?

8. What three elements are indispensable for successful nonviolent resistance?

9. According to King, what will Negroes gain by repudiating violence while resolutely moving toward their goal?

Writing Assignments

1. Write an essay in which you divide types of oppressors. Use your own imagination and reasoning to choose the principle by which you do your division.

2. Write an essay in which you classify people who are oppressed, placing them in the proper category to which they belong. For instance, one type might be the poor; another type might be the handicapped; yet another type might be the revolutionary. Be sure to include all types that belong in the general subject being classified.

READING FOR IDEAS

While reading this delightful classification of uncles, you will want to pause now and then to remember certain memorable characters in your own family, for each of us has a relative who qualifies as the family clown, the family rebel, or the family beauty. In this case the author divides his mother's brothers—his uncles—into distinct types, painting a lifelike verbal portrait of each. If you pay close attention, you will be able to understand the essence of each of these uncle's unique personality, and you will be able to visualize him in action.

ALTERNATE READING

The Uncles
LAURIE LEE

Laurie Lee (b. 1914) is a British poet and prose writer. After working as a clerk and a builder's laborer in London, he became a documentary filmmaker for the Post Office Film Unit in Cyprus and Assam. At the age of nineteen, Lee left his home in

Stroud, Gloucester, and walked to London, taking with him only a few belongings and his violin, determined never again to have an employer. He planned to write and, if writing failed him, to play the violin. Both his writing and his violin have been part of his life ever since. Among Lee's best-known works are the following poetry collections: The Sun My Monument *(1944),* The Bloom of Candles *(1947), and* My Many-Coated Man *(1955). His prose writings include a collection of essays written over a period of 30 years, titled,* I Can't Stay Long *(1975), and a memoir of his boyhood,* Cider with Rosie *(1959), from which the selection below is taken. He also wrote numerous magazine articles.*

Our family was large, even by the full-bred standards of those days, and we were especially well endowed with uncles. Not so much by their numbers as by their qualities of behaviour, which transformed them for us boys into figures of legend, and filled the girls with distress and excitement. Uncle George—our father's brother—was a thin, whiskered rogue, who sold newspapers in the streets, lived for the most part in rags, and was said to have a fortune in gold. But on my Mother's side there were these five more uncles: squat, hard-hitting, heavy-drinking heroes whom we loved and who were the kings of our youth. For the affection we bore them and the pride we took in them, I hope they'll not be displeased by what follows. 1

Grandfather Light—who had the handsomest legs of any coachman in Gloucestershire—raised his five sons in a world of horses; and they inherited much of his skill. Two of them fought against the Boers;[1] and all five were cavalrymen in the First World War, where they survived the massacres of Mons and Ypres, quick-witted their way through some others, and returned at last to peace and salvation with shrapnel in each of their bodies. I remember them first as khaki ghosts coming home on leave from the fighting, square and huge with their legs in puttees, smelling sweetly of leather and oats. They appeared as warriors stained with battle; they slept like the dead all day, then blackened their boots and brassed their buttons and returned again to the war. They were men of great strength, of bloody deeds, a fist of uncles aimed at the foe, riders of hell and apocalypse, each one half man, half horse. 2

Not until after the war did that brotherhood of avengers detach itself in my mind, so that I was able to see each one separate and human and to know at last who they were. The sons of John Light, the five Light brothers, illuminated many a local myth, were admired for their wildness, their force of arms, and for their leisurely, boasting wit. "We come from the oldest family in the world. We're down in the Book of Genesis. The Almighty said: 'Let there be Light'—and *that* was long afore Adam. . . ." 3

The uncles were all of them bred as coachmen and intended to follow their father; but the army released them to a different world, and by the time I was old enough to register what they were up to only one worked with horses; the others followed separate careers: one with trees, one with motors, another with ships, and the last building Canadian railways. 4

---

[1]Dutch colonists in South Africa.

5 Uncle Charlie, the eldest, was most like my grandfather. He had the same long face and shapely gaitered legs, the same tobacco-kippered[2] smell about him, the same slow storytelling voice heavy with Gloucester bass notes. He told us long tales of war and endurance, of taming horses in Flanders mud, of tricks of survival in the battlefield which scorned conventional heroism. He recounted these histories with stone-faced humour, with a cool self-knowing dryness, so that the surmounting of each of his life-and-death dilemmas sounded no more than a slick win at cards.

6 Now that he had returned at last from his mysterious wars he had taken up work as a forester, living in the depths of various local woods with a wife and four beautiful children. As he moved around, each cottage he settled in took on the same woody stamp of his calling, putting me in mind of charcoal burners and the lost forest huts of Grimm. We boys loved to visit the Uncle Charles family, to track them down in the forest. The house would be wrapped in aromatic smoke, with winter logs piled in the yard, while from eaves and door posts hung stoats'[3] tails, fox skins, crow bones, gin traps and mice. In the kitchen there were axes and guns on the walls, a stone jar of ginger in the corner, and on the mountainous fire a bubbling stew pot of pigeon or perhaps a new-skinned hare.

7 There was some curious riddle about Uncle Charlie's early life which not even our Mother could explain. When the Boer War ended he had worked for a time in a Rand diamond town as a barman. Those were wide-open days when a barman's duties included an ability to knock drunks cold. Uncle Charlie was obviously suited to this, for he was a lion of a man in his youth. The miners would descend from their sweating camps, pockets heavy with diamond dust, buy up barrels of whisky, drink themselves crazy, then start to burn down the saloon. . . . This was where Uncle Charles came in, the kingfish of those swilling bars, whose muscled bottle-swinging arm would lay them out in rows. But even he was no superman and suffered his share of damage. The men used him one night as a battering ram to break open a liquor store. He lay for two days with a broken skull, and still had a fine bump to prove it.

8 Then for two or three years he disappeared completely and went underground in the Johannesburg stews.[4] No letters or news were received during that time, and what happened was never explained. Then suddenly, without warning, he turned up in Stroud, pale and thin and penniless. He wouldn't say where he'd been, or discuss what he'd done, but he'd finished his wanderings, he said. So a girl from our district, handsome Fanny Causon, took him and married him.

9 He settled then in the local forests and became one of the best woodsmen in the Cotswolds.[5] His employer flattered, cherished, and under-paid him; but he was content among his trees. He raised his family on labourer's pay, fed them on game from the woods, gave his daughters no discipline other than his humour, and taught his sons the skill of his heart.

10 It was a revelation of mystery to see him at work, somewhere in a cleared spread of the woods, handling seedlings like new-hatched birds, shaking out delicately their fibrous

---

[2]Smoked like Kippers.
[3]Ermine.
[4]Brothels.
[5]Area in Southwestern England.

claws, and setting them firmly along the banks and hollows in the nests that his fingers had made. His gestures were caressive yet instinctive with power, and the plants settled ravenously to his touch, seemed to spread their small leaves with immediate life and to become rooted for ever where he left them.

The new woods rising in Horsley now, in Sheepscombe, in Rendcombe and Colne,   11
are the forests my Uncle Charlie planted on thirty-five shillings a week. His are those mansions of summer shade, lifting skylines of leaves and birds, those blocks of new green now climbing our hills to restore their remembered perspectives. He died last year, and so did his wife—they died within a week of each other. But Uncle Charlie has left a mark on our landscape as permanent as he could wish.

The next of the Lights was Uncle Tom, a dark, quiet talker, full of hidden strength,   12
who possessed a way with women. As I first remember him he was coachman-gardener at an old house in Woodchester. He was married by then to my Auntie Minnie—a tiny, pretty, parted-down-the-middle woman who resembled a Cruikshank[6] drawing. Life in their small, neat stable yard—surrounded by potted ferns, high-stepping ponies, and bright-painted traps and carriages—always seemed to me more toylike than human, and to visit them was to change one's scale and to leave the ponderous world behind.

Uncle Tom was well-mannered, something of a dandy, and he did peculiar things with   13
his eyebrows. He could slide them independently up and down his forehead, and the habit was strangely suggestive. In moments of silence he did it constantly, as though to assure us he wished us well; and to this trick was ascribed much of his success with women—to this and to his dignified presence. As a bachelor he had suffered almost continuous pursuit; but though slow in manner he was fleet of foot and had given the girls a long run. Our Mother was proud of his successes. "He was a cut above the usual," she'd say. "A proper gentleman. Just like King Edward. He thought nothing of spending a pound."

When he was young the girls died for him daily and bribed our Mother to plead their   14
cause. They were always inviting her out to tea and things, and sending him messages, and ardent letters, wrapped up in bright scarves for herself. "I was the most popular girl in the district," she said. "Our Tom was so refined. . . ."

For years Uncle Tom played a wily game and avoided entanglements. Then he met his   15
match in Effie Mansell, a girl as ruthless as she was plain. According to Mother, Effie M. was a monster, six foot high and as strong as a farm horse. No sooner had she decided that she wanted Uncle Tom than she knocked him off his bicycle and told him. The very next morning he ran away to Worcester and took a job as a tram conductor. He would have done far better to have gone down the mines, for the girl followed hot on his heels. She began to ride up and down all day long on his tram, where she had him at her mercy; and what made it worse, he had to pay her fares; he had never been so humiliated. In the end his nerve broke, he muddled the change, got the sack, and went to hide in a brick quarry. But the danger passed, Effie married an inspector, and Uncle Tom returned to his horses.

---

[6]George Cruikshank (1792–1878) was a popular English artist and caricaturist who won fame by illustrating Dickens' books.

16   By now he was chastened, and the stables reassured him—you could escape on a horse, not a tram. But what he wished for more than anything was a good woman's protection; he had found the pace too hot. So very soon after, he married the Minnie of his choice, abandoned his bachelor successes, and settled for good with a sigh of relief and a few astonishing runs on his eyebrows.

17   From then on Uncle Tom lived quietly and gratefully, like a prince in deliberate exile, merely dressing his face, from time to time, in those mantles of majesty and charm, those solemn winks and knowing convulsions of the brow which were all that remained of past grandeurs. . . .

18   My first encounter with Uncle Ray—prospector, dynamiter, buffalo fighter, and builder of transcontinental railways—was an occasion of memorable suddenness. One moment he was a legend at the other end of the world, the next he was in my bed. Accustomed only to the satiny bodies of my younger brother and sisters, I awoke one morning to find snoring beside me a huge and scaly man. I touched the thick legs and knotted arms and pondered the barbs on his chin, felt the crocodile flesh of this magnificent creature and wondered what it could be.

19   "It's your Uncle Ray come home," whispered Mother. "Get up now and let him sleep."

20   I saw a rust-brown face, a gaunt Indian nose, and smelt a reek of cigars and train oil. Here was the hero of our school-boasting days, and to look on him was no disappointment. He was shiny as iron, worn as a rock, and lay like a chieftain sleeping. He'd come home on a visit from building his railway, loaded with money and thirst, and the days he spent at our house that time were full of wonder and conflagration.

21   For one thing he was unlike any other man we'd ever seen—or heard of, if it came to that. With his leather-beaten face, wide teeth-crammed mouth, and far-seeing ice-blue eyes, he looked like some wigwam warrior stained with suns and heroic slaughter. He spoke the Canadian dialect of the railway camps in a drawl through his resonant nose. His body was tattooed in every quarter—ships in full sail, flags of all nations, reptiles and round-eyed maidens. By cunning flexings of his muscled flesh he could sail these ships, wave the flags in the wind, and coil snakes round the quivering girls.

22   Uncle Ray was a gift of the devil to us, a monstrous toy, a good-natured freak, more exotic than a circus ape. He would sit quite still while we examined him and absorb all our punishment. If we hit him he howled, if we pinched him he sobbed; he bore our aches and cramps like a Caliban. Or at a word he'd swing us round by our feet, or stand us upon his stomach, or lift us in pairs, one on either hand, and bump our heads on the ceiling.

23   But sooner or later he always said:

24   "Waal, boys, I gotta be going."

25   He'd stand up and shake us off like fleas and start slowly to lick his lips.

26   "Where you got to go to, Uncle?"

27   "See a man 'bout a mule."

28   "You ain't! Where you going? What for?"

29   "Get my fingers pressed. Tongue starched. Back oiled."

30   "It ain't true! You're fibbing! Uncle! . . ."

31   "Just *got* to, boys. See you all in the oven. Scrub yer elbows. Be good. So long."

Off he'd go at a run, though the Lord knew where: *we* couldn't think of any place to   32
go to. Then he'd come back much later, perhaps the following night, wet through, with
a dog-like grin. He'd be unable to see properly, couldn't hang up his coat, couldn't find
the latch on the door. He'd sit by the fire and steam and sing and flirt with the squawking
girls. "You'd best get to bed," Mother would say severely; at which he'd burst into theatrical
sobs. "Annie, I can't! I can't move an inch. Got a bone in me leg. . . . Mebbe two."

One night, after he'd been missing for a couple of days, he came home on a bicycle,   33
and rode it straight down the bank in the stormy darkness and crashed into the lavatory
door. The girls ran out and fetched him indoors, howling and streaming with blood. They
lay him full-length on the kitchen table, then took off his boots and washed him. "What
a state he's in," they giggled, shocked. "It's whisky or something, Mother." He began to
sing. "O, Dolly dear . . ." then started to eat the soap. He sang and blew bubbles, and we
crowded round him, never having had any man in our house like this.

Word soon got round that Ray Light was home, laden with Canadian gold. He was set   34
on by toughs, hunted by girls, and warned several times by the police. He took most of
this in his powerful stride, but the girls had him worried at times. A well-bred young
seamstress whom he was cuddling in the picture palace stole his dollar-crammed purse in
the dark. Then one morning Beatie Burroughs arrived on our doorstep and announced
that he'd promised to marry her. Under the Stroud Brewery arches, she said—just to
clinch it. He had to hide for three days in our attic. . . .

But drunk or sober, Uncle Ray was the same; a great shaggy animal wagging off to his   35
pleasures; a helpless giant, amiable, naïve, sentimental and straightforwardly lustful. He
startled my sisters, but even so they adored him; as for us boys, what more could we want?
He even taught us how to tie him up, boasting that no knots could hold him. So we tied
him one night to a kitchen chair, watched him struggle, and then went to bed. Mother
found him next morning on his hands and knees, still tied up and fast asleep.

That visit of Uncle Ray's with its games and exhibitions, was like a prolonged   36
Christmas Day in the house. Routine, discipline and normal behaviour were suspended
during that time. We stayed up late, took liberties, and shared his intoxications; while he
bounded about, disappeared on his errands, returned in a tousled daze, fumbled the girls,
sang songs, fell down, got up and handed dollars all around. Mother was by turns prim
and indulgent with him, either clicking her tongue or giggling. And the girls were as
excited and assailed as we, though in a different, whispering way; saying, Would you
believe it? I never! How awful! or, Did you hear what he said to me then?

When he got through his money he went back to Canada, back to the railway camps,   37
leaving behind him several broken heads, some fat innkeepers and well-set-up girls. Soon
after, while working in the snow-capped Rockies, he blew himself up with dynamite. He
fell ninety feet down the Kicking Horse Pass and into a frozen lake. A Tamworth
schoolteacher—now my Auntie Elsie—travelled four thousand miles to repair him. Having
plucked him from the ice and thawed him out, she married him and brought him home.
And that was the end of the pioneer days of that bounding prairie dog, without whom the
Canadian Pacific Railroad would never have reached the Pacific—at least, so we believe.

Moody, majestic Uncle Sid was the fourth, but not least, of the brothers. This small   38
powerful man, at first a champion cricketer, had a history blighted by rheumatism. He

was a bus driver, too, after he left the army, put in charge of our first double-deckers. Those solid-tyred, open-topped, passenger chariots were the leviathans of the roads at that time, staggering siege-towers which often ran wild and got their top decks caught under bridges. Our Uncle Sid, one of the élite of the drivers, became a famous sight in the district. It was a thing of pride and some alarm to watch him go thundering by, perched up high in his reeking cabin, his face sweating beer and effort, while he wrenched and wrestled at the steering wheel to hold the great bus on its course. Each trip through the town destroyed roof tiles and gutters and shook the gas mantles out of the lamps, but he always took pains to avoid women and children and scarcely ever mounted the pavements. Runaway roarer, freighted with human souls, stampeder of policemen and horses—it was Uncle Sid with his mighty hands who mastered its mad career. Uncle Sid's story, like Uncle Charlie's, began in the South African War. As a private soldier he had earned a reputation for silence, cunning and strength. His talent for cricket, learned on the molehills of Sheepscombe, also endowed him with special privileges. Quite soon he was chosen to play for the army and was being fed on the choicest rations. The hell-bent technique of his village game worked havoc among the officers. On a flat pitch at last, with a scorched dry wicket, after the hillocks and cow dung of home, he was projected straightaway into regions of greatness and broke records and nerves galore. His murderous bowling reduced heroes to panic; they just waved him good-bye and ran; and when he came in to bat, men covered their heads and retired piecemeal to the boundaries. In an old Transvaal newspaper, hoarded by my Mother, I once found a scorecard which went something like this:

ARMY V. TRANSVAAL. PRETORIA. 1899.

Army

Col. "Tigger" Ffoukes-Wyte		1
Brig. Fletcher		0
Maj. T. W. G. Staggerton-Hake		12
Capt. V. O. Spillingham		0
Major Lyle	(not)	31
Pte. S. Light	(not)	126
Extras		7
	Total	177 for 4 dec.

Transvaal 21 all out (Pte. S. Light 7 for 5)

39   I can picture that squat little whizzing man knocking the cricket ball out of the ground, his face congested with brick-red fury, his shoulders bursting out of his braces. I can see him crouch for the next delivery, then spin on his short bowed legs, and clout it again half-way to Johannesburg while he heard far-off Sheepscombe cheer. This was probably the peak of Uncle Sid's glory, the time he would most wish to remember. From then on his tale shows a certain fall—though it still flared up on occasions.

40   There was, for instance, the day of the Outing, when our village took three charabancs[7] to Clevedon, with Uncle Sid driving the leading one, a crate of beer at his

---

[7]Large buses.

feet. "Put her in top, Uncle Sid!" we cried, as we roared through the summer country. Guzzling with one hand, steering with the other, he drove through the flying winds, while we bounced and soared above the tops of the hedges, made airborne by this man at the wheel. . . .

Then on our way home, at the end of the day, we were stopped by a woman's 41 screams. She stood by the roadside with a child in her arms, cringing from a threatening man. The tableau froze for us all to see: the wild-haired woman, the wailing child, the man with his arm upraised. Our charabancs came to a shuddering halt and we all started shouting at once. We leaned over the sides of our open wagons and berated the man for a scoundrel. Our men from their seats insulted him roundly; they suggested he leave the poor woman alone. But our Uncle Sid just folded his coat, climbed down from his cab without speaking, walked up to the bully, swung back his arm, and knocked the man straight through the hedge. Life to him was black and white and he had reacted to it simply. Scowling with pride he returned to the wheel and drove us home, a hero.

Uncle Sid differed in no way from his other brothers in chivalry, temper and drink. He 42 could knock down a man or a glass of beer as readily and as neatly as they. But his job as a bus driver (and his rheumatism) both increased—and obstructed—his thirst. The result exposed him to official censure, and it was here that the fates laid him low.

When he married my Aunt Alice, and became the father of two children, his job 43 promised to anchor his wildness. But the law was against him and he soon got into scrapes. He was the best double-decker driver in Stroud, without doubt; even safer, more inspired, when he drank. Everybody knew this—except the bus company. He began to get lectures, admonitions, stern warnings, and finally suspensions without pay.

When this last thing happened, out of respect for Aunt Alice, he always committed 44 suicide. Indeed he committed suicide more than any man I know, but always in the most reasonable manner. If he drowned himself, then the canal was dry; if he jumped down a well, so was that; and when he drank disinfectant there was always an antidote ready, clearly marked, to save everyone trouble. He reasoned, quite rightly, that Aunt Alice's anger, on hearing of another suspension, would be swallowed up by her larger anxiety on finding him again near to death. And Auntie Alice never failed him in this, and forgave him each time he recovered.

The bus company were almost equally forgiving; they took him back again and again. 45 Then one night, having brought his bus safely home, they found him fast asleep at the wheel, reeking of malt and stone-jar cider; and they gave him the sack for good.

We were sitting in the kitchen rather late that night, when a loud knock came at the 46 door. A hollow voice called "Annie! Annie!" and we knew that something had happened. Then the kitchen door crept slowly open and revealed three dark-clad figures. It was Auntie Alice and her two small daughters, each dressed in their Sunday best. They stood at the foot of the kitchen steps, silent as apparitions, and Auntie Alice's face, with its huge drawn eyes, wore a mantle of tragic doom.

"He's done it this time," she intoned at last. "That's what. I know he has." 47

Her voice had a churchlike incantation which dropped crystals of ice down my back. 48 She held the small pretty girls in a majestic embrace while they squirmed and sniffed and giggled.

49   "He never came home. They must have give him the sack. Now he's gone off to end it all."

50   "No, no," cried out Mother. "Come and sit down, my dear." And she drew her towards the fire.

51   Auntie Alice sat stiffly, like a Gothic image, still clutching her wriggling children.

52   "Where else could I go, Annie? He's gone down to Deadcombe. . . . He always told me he would. . . ."

53   She suddenly turned and seized Mother's hands, her dark eyes rolling madly.

54   "Annie! Annie! He'll do himself in. Your boys—they just *got* to find him! . . ."

55   So Jack and I put on caps and coats and went out into the half-moon night. From so much emotion I felt light-headed; I wanted to laugh or hide. But Jack was his cool, intrepid self, tight-lipped as a gunboat commander. We were men in a crisis, on a secret mission; life and death seemed to hang on our hands. So we stuck close together and trudged up the valley, heading for Deadcombe Wood.

56   The wood was a waste of rotting silence, transformed by its mask of midnight; a fine rain was falling, wet ferns soaked our legs, leaves shuddered with owls and water. What were we supposed to do? we wondered. Why had we come, anyway? We beat up and down through the dripping trees, calling "Uncle!" in chill, flat voices. . . . What should we find? Perhaps nothing at all. Or worse, what we had come to seek. . . . But we remembered the women, waiting fearfully at home. Our duty, though dismal, was clear.

57   So we stumbled and splashed through invisible brooks, followed paths, skirted ominous shadows. We poked bits of stick into piles of old leaves, prodded fox-holes, searched the length of the wood. There was nothing there but the fungoid darkness, nothing at all but our fear.

58   We were about to go home, and gladly enough, when suddenly we saw him. He was standing—tiptoe under a great dead oak with his braces around his neck. The elastic noose, looped to the branch above him, made him bob up and down like a puppet. We approached the contorted figure with dread; saw his baleful eye fixed on us.

59   Our Uncle Sid was in a terrible temper.

60   "You've been a bloody long time!" he said.

61   Uncle Sid never drove any buses again but took a job as a gardener in Sheepscombe. All the uncles now, from their wilder beginnings, had resettled their roots near home—all, that is, save Insurance Fred, whom we lost through prosperity and distance. These men reflected many of Mother's qualities, were foolish, fantastical, moody; but in spite of their follies they remained for me the true heroes of my early life. I think of them still in the image they gave me; they were bards and oracles each, like a ring of squat megaliths on some local hill, bruised by weather and scarred with old glories. They were the horsemen and brawlers of another age, and their lives spoke its long farewell. Spoke, too, of campaigns on desert marches, of Kruger's cannon and Flanders mud; of a world that still moved at the same pace as Caesar's, and of that empire greater than his—through which they had fought, sharp-eyed and anonymous, and seen the first outposts crumble. . . .

Vocabulary

rogue (1)	assailed (36)	molehills (38)	intrepid (55)
apocalypse (2)	leviathans (38)	apparitions (46)	fungoid (57)
avengers (3)	siege (38)	intoned (47)	baleful ((58)
gaitered (5)	elite (38)	incantation (48)	megaliths (61)
aromatic (6)			

Questions on Meaning and Technique

1. Because division/classification is always conceived as dividing a whole into its specific parts, what is the whole being divided in this essay?

2. What brief phrase would you use to describe each category in the division? The phrase should capture the essence of the category.

3. Of the five uncles, which one appeals most to your imagination? Which do you consider the most acceptable in a society that values propriety and manners?

4. Why do you suppose the author begins with a description of Uncle George, his father's brother?

5. What wit is involved in the Light brothers' boast at the end of paragraph 3?

6. How did the underground experience in Johannesburg change Uncle Charlie? What do you suppose happened in Johannesburg?

7. After Tom married, what were the only remaining signs of his former charm? What purpose is served in mentioning these?

8. How does the author move from one category to the next? Is this necessary?

9. What does the author mean when he says, in the final paragraph, that the uncles lived in a world "that still moved at the same pace as Caesar's"? What is the mood at the end of the essay?

Writing Assignments

1. Write an essay in which you divide all of your relatives into types based on certain traits, such as their personalities, their philosophies toward life, their life-styles, or their looks.

2. Using Lee's essay as a model, write an essay in which you capture the essence of your three or four best friends. What you would be doing is dividing your best friends into types or categories.

READING FOR IDEAS

The topic of this article is a common complaint of many people today—fatigue, the chronic feeling of always being tired and worn-out. Brody's division and classification is based on the principle of underlying causation, which she uses to devise a crisp, no-frills journalistic analysis. Remedies for fatigue constitute her secondary topic, also organized as a division/classification. As you read, notice how the classification strategy imposes order and predictability on Brody's discussion, making the material easily accessible to busy newspaper readers.

ALTERNATE READING

Fatigue

JANE BRODY

Jane Brody (b. 1941) writes a popular health and fitness column for The New York Times. *She was educated at Cornell University (B.S., 1962) and the University of Wisconsin, Madison (M.A., 1963). She is the author of, among other works,* Secrets of Good Health *(1970, with her husband, Richard Engquist),* You Can Fight Cancer and Win *(1978, with Arthur Holleb), and* Jane Brody's Nutrition Book *(1981).*

"It doesn't seem to matter how long I sleep—I'm more tired when I wake up than when I went to bed."

"Some of my friends come home from work and jog for several miles or swim laps. I don't know how they do it. I'm completely exhausted at the end of a day at the office."

"I thought I was weary because of the holidays, but now that they're over, I'm even worse. I can barely get through the week, and on the weekend I don't even have the strength to get dressed. I wonder if I'm anemic or something."

"I don't know what's wrong with me lately, but I've been so collapsed that I haven't made a proper meal for the family for a week. We've been living on TV dinners and packaged mixes. I was finally forced to do a laundry because the kids ran out of underwear."

1 Fatigue is one of the most common complaints brought to doctors, as well as to friends and relatives, from whom the above examples were gleaned. You'd think in this era of labor-saving devices and convenient transportation that few people would have reason to be so tired. But, if anything, more people complain of fatigue today than when hay was baled by hand and laundry scrubbed on a washboard.

2 The causes of modern-day fatigue are diverse, and only rarely related to excessive physical exertion. The relatively few people who do heavy labor all day long almost never complain about being tired—perhaps because they expect to be! Today, physicians report, tiredness is more likely a consequence of underexertion than of wearing yourself down with overactivity. In fact, increased physical activity is often prescribed as a cure for sagging energy.

3 There are three main categories of fatigue:

4 **Physical.** This is the well-known result of overworking your muscles to the point where metabolic waste products—carbon dioxide and lactic acid—accumulate in your blood and sap your strength. Your muscles can't continue to work efficiently in a bath of these chemicals.

Physical fatigue is usually a pleasant tiredness, such as you might experience after 5 playing a hard set of tennis, chopping wood or climbing a mountain. The cure is simple and fast—you rest, giving your body a chance to get rid of accumulated wastes and restore muscle fuel.

Pathological. Here fatigue is a warning sign or consequence of some underlying 6 physical disorder, perhaps the common cold or flu or something more serious like diabetes or cancer. Usually, other symptoms besides fatigue are present that suggest the true cause.

Even after an illness has passed, you're likely to feel "dragged out" for a week or 7 more. Take it as a signal to go slow while your body has a chance to recover fully, even if all you had was a cold. Pushing yourself to resume full activity too soon could precipitate a relapse and almost certainly will prolong your period of fatigue.

Even though illness is not a frequent cause of prolonged fatigue, it's very important 8 that it not be overlooked. Therefore, anyone who feels drained of energy for weeks on end should have a thorough physical checkup. But if nothing shows up as a result of the various medical tests, that doesn't mean there's nothing wrong with you.

Unfortunately, too often a medical workup ends with a battery of negative test results, 9 and the true cause of serious fatigue goes undetected. As Dr. John Bulette, a psychiatrist at the Medical College of Pennsylvania Hospital in Philadelphia, tells it, this is what happened to a Pennsylvania woman who had lost nearly 50 pounds and was "almost dead—so tired she could hardly lift her head up."

The doctors who first examined the woman were sure she had cancer. But no matter 10 how hard they looked, they could find no sign of malignancy, nor of any other disease that could account for her wasting away.

Finally, she was brought to the college hospital, where doctors noted that she was 11 severely depressed. They questioned her about her life and discovered that her troubles had begun two years earlier after her husband had died. Once treated for depression, the woman quickly perked up, gained 10 pounds in just a few weeks, then returned home to continue her recovery through psychotherapy.

Psychological. Emotional problems and conflicts, especially depression and anxiety, 12 are by far the most common causes of prolonged fatigue. Fatigue may represent a defense mechanism that prevents you from having to face the true cause of your depression, such as the fact that you hate your job. It is also your body's safety valve for expressing repressed emotional conflicts, such as feeling trapped in an ungratifying role or an unhappy marriage.

When such feelings are not expressed openly, they often come out as physical 13 symptoms, with fatigue as one of the most common manifestations. "Many people who are extremely fatigued don't even know they're depressed," Dr. Bulette says. "They're so busy distracting themselves or just worrying about being tired that they don't recognize their depression."

One of these situations is so common it's been given a name—tired housewife 14 syndrome. The victims are commonly young mothers who day in and day out face the predictable tedium of caring for a home and small children, fixing meals, dealing with repairmen, and generally having no one interesting to talk to and nothing enjoyable to look forward to at the end of their boring and unrewarding day. The tired housewife may be inwardly resentful, envious of her husband's job, and guilty about her feelings. But rather than face them head on, she becomes extremely fatigued.

15   Today, with nearly half the mothers of young children working outside the home, the tired housewife syndrome has taken on a new twist—that of conflicting roles and responsibilities and guilt over leaving the children, often with an overlay of genuine physical exhaustion from trying to be all things to all people.

16   Compounding emotionally induced fatigue may be the problem of sleep disturbance that results from the underlying psychological conflict. A person may develop insomnia, or may sleep the requisite number of hours but fitfully, tossing and turning all night, having disturbing dreams and awakening, as one woman put it, feeling as if she had "been run over by a truck."

17   Understanding the underlying emotional problem is the crucial first step toward curing psychological fatigue, and by itself often results in considerable lessening of the tiredness. Professional psychological help or career or marriage counseling may be needed. But there is also a great deal you can do on your own to deal with both severe prolonged fatigue and periodic "washed-out" feelings.

18   Vitamins and tranquilizers are almost never the right answer, sleeping pills and alcohol are counterproductive, and caffeine is at best a temporary solution that can backfire with abuse and cause life-disrupting symptoms of anxiety. Instead you might try:

19   **Diet.** If you eat a skimpy breakfast or none at all, you're likely to experience midmorning fatigue, the result of a drop in blood sugar, which your body and brain depend on for energy. For peak energy in the morning, be sure to eat a proper breakfast, low in sugar and high in protein, which will provide a steady supply of blood sugar through the morning. Coffee and a doughnut are almost worse than nothing.

20   The same goes for the rest of the day: frequent snacking on sweets is a false pick-me-up that soon lets you down lower than you were to begin with. Stick to regular, satisfying, well-balanced meals.

21   Extra weight is tiring both physically and psychologically. Getting your weight down to normal can go a long way toward revitalizing you.

22   **Exercise.** Contrary to what you may think, exercise enhances, rather than saps, energy. Regular conditioning exercise, such as jogging, cycling or swimming, helps you resist fatigue by increasing your ability to handle more of a workload. At a given level of work, you get tired less quickly because your capability is greater.

23   Exercise also has a well-recognized tranquilizing effect, which helps you work in a more relaxed fashion and be less dragged down by the tensions of your day. At the end of a day, exercise can relieve accumulated tensions, give you more energy in the evening and help you sleep more restfully.

24   **Sleep.** If you know you're tired because you haven't been getting enough sleep, the solution is simple: get to bed earlier. There's no right amount of sleep for everyone and, generally, sleep requirements decline with age. Find the amount that suits you best and aim for it. Insomnia and other sleep disorders should not be treated with sleeping pills, alcohol or tranquilizers, which can actually make the problem worse.

25   **Know yourself.** Try to schedule your most taxing jobs for the time of day when you're at your peak. Some are "morning people" who tire by midafternoon; others do their best

work in the evening. Don't overextend yourself, trying to climb the ladder of success at a record pace or to meet everyone's demands or expectations.

Decide what you want to do and can handle comfortably and learn to say no to   26
additional requests. Recognize your energy cycles and plan accordingly. Many women have a low point premenstrually, during which extra sleep may be needed and demanding activities are particularly exhausting.

Take breaks. No matter how interesting or demanding your work, you'll be able to do   27
it with more vigor if now and again you stop, stretch and change the scenery. Instead of coffee and a sweet roll on your break, try meditation, yoga, calisthenics or a brisk walk. Even running up and down the staircase can provide refreshment for a sedentary job. If your job is physically demanding, relax in a quiet place for a while. The do-something-different rule also applies to vacations.

Vocabulary

gleaned (1)   repressed (12)   syndrome (14)   enhances (22)
precipitate (7)   manifestations (13)   compounding (16)   sedentary (27)

Questions on Meaning and Technique

1. What is the value in a newspaper column such as Brody writes of opening an article with quotations on the topic from friends and relatives?

2. Where does Brody establish the principle on which her classification is based? Why is she not more explicit about this principle?

3. In writing about pathological fatigue, what other strategy does Brody use to organize and enliven her discussion?

4. What other topic does Brody divide and classify, and what underlying principle does she use for this secondary discussion?

5. Brody aims her article mainly at a discussion of psychological fatigue, with considerably less ink devoted to fatigue of the physical and pathological kind. What is the rationale behind this ordering of topics?

6. What kind of evidence does Brody primarily cite in support of her discussion?

7. Brody's lead-ins to her discussions of the types of fatigue are skimpy and abrupt. How can she justify using this kind of skimpy lead-in?

8. What other strategy do you think Brody might have used to organize this discussion of fatigue?

Writing Assignments

1. Write an essay in which you classify the different types of exercises to combat fatigue.

2. Divide unmotivated students into three or four different types, describing each vividly and, if possible, humorously.

Additional Writing Assignments

1. Review the architecture of your neighborhood. Then write a paper classifying the various types of buildings using such aspects as size, age, and style as a basis for creating the various categories.

2. Classify one species of domesticated animal according to three or four general types, supplying vivid examples of each type. For instance, if you are a cat lover, you might use these categories: affectionate cats, sly cats, aloof cats, vicious cats.

3. How many major kinds of entertainment are there? Who indulges in each? Write a classification essay answering these questions.

4. Think about your friends in terms of their attitudes toward church attendance. Then classify these attitudes in a way that will shed light on why people attend or do not attend church.

5. Divide current television shows into three to five major types, supplying examples of each type.

6. Looking back over the list of teachers you have had, classify them into different types according to their personalities and ways of relating to students.

7. Humans communicate with each other by various means, some including language, some not. Classify the ways humans communicate and supply examples of each way.

8. A stereotype is a classification applied unthinkingly and without taking into account individual differences. Compose a popular stereotype of one of the following: Harvard students, rock stars, male ballet dancers, car salespersons, suburban housewives, female police officers.

9. All working societies pay homage to some kind of authority. Classify the major kinds of authorities and describe the characteristics of each.

10. Clouds are a fascinating and mysterious phenomenon of nature. Divide all clouds into three or four major types and describe each type in vivid, even poetic, language.

Photo Writing Assignment

Babe Ruth's last appearance at Yankee Stadium, June 1948. Harry Harris, AP/Wide World Photos.

The photo pictures Babe Ruth, the famous baseball player, in his last appearance at New York's Yankee Stadium in June of 1948. Two weeks later, Ruth was dead from cancer. Write an essay classifying the kinds of emotions that must have been experienced by the players, officials, reporters, and onlookers in this photograph.

Causal Analysis

READING FOR IDEAS

Read "The Girls in Their Summer Dresses." See whether you can describe and explain the kind of relationship that exists between Michael and Frances. Pay attention to bits of conversation and details. Try to probe the causes of behavior in Michael and Frances.

The Girls in Their Summer Dresses
IRWIN SHAW

Irwin Shaw (1913–1984), novelist, playwright, and short story writer, was born in New York City and educated at Brooklyn College. A former drama critic for the New Republic, *Shaw was known for his clear characterization and crisp plotting in the short story. He was also widely known as an author of popular novels. Many of these—such as* The Young Lions *(1948)—were made into movies or—like* Rich Man, Poor Man *(1969)—into highly rated television shows. His other works include* Bury the Dead *(play, 1936),* Sailor off Bremen *(short story collection, 1939),* The Troubled Air *(1951), and* Two Weeks in Another Town *(1960).*

1   Fifth Avenue was shining in the sun when they left the Brevoort. The sun was warm, even though it was February, and everything looked like Sunday morning—the buses and the well-dressed people walking slowly in couples and the quiet buildings with the windows closed.

Michael held Frances' arm tightly as they walked toward Washington Square in the sunlight.   2
They walked lightly, almost smiling, because they had slept late and had a good breakfast and
it was Sunday. Michael unbuttoned his coat and let it flap around him in the mild wind.

"Look out," Frances said as they crossed Eighth Street. "You'll break your neck."   3

Michael laughed and Frances laughed with him.   4

"She's not so pretty," Frances said. "Anyway, not pretty enough to take a chance of
breaking your neck."

Michael laughed again. "How did you know I was looking at her?"

Frances cocked her head to one side and smiled at her husband under the brim of her   5
hat. "Mike, darling," she said.

"O.K.," he said. "Excuse me."

Frances patted his arm lightly and pulled him along a little faster toward Washington   6
Square. "Let's not see anybody all day," she said. "Let's just hang around with each
other. You and me. We're always up to our neck in people, drinking their Scotch or
drinking our Scotch; we only see each other in bed. I want to go out with my husband all
day long. I want him to talk only to me and listen only to me."

"What's to stop us?" Michael asked.   7

"The Stevensons. They want us to drop by around one o'clock and they'll drive us into
the country."

"The cunning Stevensons," Mike said. "Transparent. They can whistle. They can go
driving in the country by themselves."

"Is it a date?"

"It's a date."

Frances leaned over and kissed him on the tip of the ear.   8

"Darling," Michael said, "this is Fifth Avenue."

"Let me arrange a program," Frances said. "A planned Sunday in New York for a
young couple with money to throw away."

"Go easy."

"First let's go to the Metropolitan Museum of Art," Frances suggested, because
Michael had said during the week he wanted to go. "I haven't been there in three years
and there're at least ten pictures I want to see again. Then we can take the bus down to
Radio City and watch them skate. And later we'll go down to Cavanagh's and get a steak
as big as a blacksmith's apron, with a bottle of wine, and after that there's a French
picture at the Filmarte that everybody says—say, are you listening to me?"

"Sure," he said. He took his eyes off the hatless girl with the dark hair, cut dancerstyle   9
like a helmet, who was walking past him.

"That's the program for the day," Frances said flatly. "Or maybe you'd just rather   10
walk up and down Fifth Avenue."

"No," Michael said. "Not at all."

"You always look at other women," Frances said. "Everywhere. Every damned place
we go."

"Now, darling," Michael said, "I look at everything. God gave me eyes and I look at
women and men and subway excavations and moving pictures and the little flowers of the
field. I casually inspect the universe."

"You ought to see the look in your eye," Frances said, "as you casually inspect the universe on Fifth Avenue."

"I'm a happily married man." Michael pressed her elbow tenderly. "Example for the whole twentieth century—Mr. and Mrs. Mike Loomis. Hey, let's have a drink," he said, stopping.

"We just had breakfast."

"Now listen, darling," Mike said, choosing his words with care, "it's a nice day and we both felt good and there's no reason why we have to break it up. Let's have a nice Sunday."

"All right. I don't know why I started this. Let's drop it. Let's have a good time."

11   They joined hands consciously and walked without talking among the baby carriages and the old Italian men in their Sunday clothes and the young women with Scotties in Washington Square Park.

12   "At least once a year everyone should go to the Metropolitan Museum of Art," Frances said after a while, her tone a good imitation of the tone she had used at breakfast and at the beginning of their walk. "And it's nice on Sunday. There's a lot of people looking at the pictures and you get the feeling maybe Art isn't on the decline in New York City, after all—"

13   "I want to tell you something," Michael said very seriously. "I have not touched another woman. Not once. In all the five years."

"All right," Frances said.

"You believe that, don't you."

"All right."

14   They walked between the crowded benches, under the scrubby city-park trees.

"I try not to notice it," Frances said, "but I feel rotten inside, in my stomach, when we pass a woman and you look at her and I see that look in your eye and that's the way you looked at me the first time. In Alice Maxwell's house. Standing there in the living room, next to the radio, with a green hat on and all those people."

"I remember the hat," Michael said.

"The same look," Frances said. "And it makes me feel bad. It makes me feel terrible."

"Sh-h-h, please, darling, sh-h-h."

"I think I would like a drink now," Frances said.

15   They walked over to a bar on Eighth Street, not saying anything, Michael automatically helping her over curbstones and guiding her past automobiles. They sat near a window in the bar and the sun streamed in and there was a small, cheerful fire in the fireplace. A little Japanese waiter came over and put down some pretzels and smiled happily at them.

"What do you order after breakfast?" Michael asked.

"Brandy, I suppose," Frances said.

"Courvoisier," Michael told the waiter. "Two Courvoisiers."

16   The waiter came with the glasses and they sat drinking the brandy in the sunlight. Michael finished half his and drank a little water.

"I look at women," he said. "Correct. I don't say it's wrong or right. I look at them. If I pass them on the street and I don't look at them, I'm fooling you, I'm fooling myself."

"You look at them as though you want them," Frances said, playing with her brandy glass. "Every one of them."

"In a way," Michael said, speaking softly and not to his wife, "in a way that's true. I don't do anything about it, but it's true."

"I know it. That's why I feel bad."

"Another brandy," Michael called. "Waiter, two more brandies."

He sighed and closed his eyes and rubbed them gently with his fingertips. "I love the 17 way women look. One of the things I like best about New York is the battalions of women. When I first came to New York from Ohio that was the first thing I noticed, the million wonderful women, all over the city. I walked around with my heart in my throat."

"A kid," Frances said, "that's a kid's feeling."

"Guess again," Michael said, "guess again. I'm older now, I'm a man getting near middle age, putting on a little fat and I still love to walk along Fifth Avenue at three o'clock on the east side of the street between Fiftieth and Fifty-seventh Streets. They're all out then, shopping, in their furs and their crazy hats, everything all concentrated from all over the world into seven blocks—the best furs, the best clothes, the handsomest women, out to spend money and feeling good about it."

The Japanese waiter put the two drinks down, smiling with great happiness. 18

"Everything is all right?" he asked.

"Everything is wonderful," Michael said.

"If it's just a couple of fur coats," Frances said, "and forty-five-dollar hats—"

"It's not the fur coats. Or the hats. That's just the scenery for that particular kind of woman. Understand," he said, "you don't have to listen to this."

"I want to listen."

"I like the girls in the offices. Neat, with their eyeglasses, smart, chipper, knowing what everything is about. I like the girls on Forty-fourth Street at lunchtime, the actresses, all dressed up on nothing a week. I like the salesgirls in the stores, paying attention to you first because you're a man, leaving lady customers waiting. I got all this stuff accumulated in me because I've been thinking about it for ten years and now you've asked for it and here it is."

"Go ahead," Frances said.

"When I think of New York City, I think of all the girls on parade in the city. I don't know whether it's something special with me or whether every man in the city walks around with the same feeling inside him, but I feel as though I'm at a picnic in this city. I like to sit near the women in the theatres, the famous beauties who've taken six hours to get ready and look it. And the young girls at the football games, with the red cheeks, and when the warm weather comes, the girls in their summer dresses." He finished his drink. "That's the story."

Frances finished her drink and swallowed two or three times extra. "You say you love 19 me?"

"I love you."

"I'm pretty, too," Frances said. "As pretty as any of them."

"You're beautiful," Michael said.

"I'm good for you," Frances said, pleading. "I've made a good wife, a good housekeeper, a good friend. I'd do any damn thing for you."

"I know," Michael said. He put his hand out and grasped hers.

"You'd like to be free to—" Frances said.

"Sh-h-h."

"Tell the truth." She took her hand away from under his.

Michael flicked the edge of his glass with his finger. "O.K.," he said gently. "Sometimes I feel I would like to be free."

"Well," Frances said, "any time you say."

"Don't be foolish." Michael swung his chair around to her side of the table and patted her thigh.

20   She began to cry silently into her handkerchief, bent over just enough so that nobody else in the bar would notice. "Someday," she said, crying, "you're going to make a move."

21   Michael didn't say anything. He sat watching the bartender slowly peel a lemon.

"Aren't you?" Frances asked harshly. "Come on, tell me. Talk. Aren't you?"

"Maybe," Michael said. He moved his chair back again. "How the hell do I know?"

"You know," Frances persisted. "Don't you know?"

"Yes," Michael said after a while, "I know."

22   Frances stopped crying then. Two or three snuffles into the handkerchief and she put it away and her face didn't tell anything to anybody. "At least do me one favor," she said.

"Sure."

"Stop talking about how pretty this woman is or that one. Nice eyes, nice breasts, a pretty figure, good voice." She mimicked his voice. "Keep it to yourself. I'm not interested."

23   Michael waved to the waiter. "I'll keep it to myself," he said.

Frances flicked the corners of her eyes. "Another brandy," she told the waiter.

"Two," Michael said.

"Yes, ma'am, yes, sir," said the waiter, backing away.

24   Frances regarded Michael coolly across the table. "Do you want me to call the Stevensons?" she asked. "It'll be nice in the country."

"Sure," Michael said, "call them."

25   She got up from the table and walked across the room toward the telephone. Michael watched her walk, thinking what a pretty girl, what nice legs.

Questions on Meaning and Technique

1. How does Frances feel about Michael? Why does she feel this way? State both the *way she feels* and the *reasons* for it in a single sentence that could serve as the controlling idea for an essay about the story.

2. What role do the "girls in their summer dresses" play in the story?

3. How does Michael feel toward Frances? Support your conclusion with evidence from the story.

4. How does Michael make Frances feel when he looks at other women? Why?

5. What would your advice be to a wife whose husband looks at other women the way Michael does? Should she ignore him? Be happy that he enjoys beauty and life? Scold him? Flirt with men in order to get even? Why? Give your reasons.

6. What is your prediction about Michael and Frances's future together? Will they eventually divorce? Will the marriage survive? Why or why not?

7. Do you believe that Michael is unusual, or do his feelings toward women represent the feelings of most men?

8. What advice might you give the young couple?

READING FOR IDEAS

Crucial to the understanding of the poem is the analogy being drawn. Figure out to what the poet is comparing money, and the rest of the poem's meaning will follow.

Money

VICTOR CONTOSKI

Victor Contoski (b. 1936) is a poet born in St. Paul, Minnesota, of Polish origin. He studied at the University of Minnesota and Ohio State for his B.A. and M.A., but received his Ph.D. from the University of Wisconsin in 1969. He has taught American literature at the University of Lodz in Poland, was a Fulbright Professor from 1963 to 1964, and is currently Professor of English at the University of Kansas in Lawrence. Among his writings are a bilingual edition of literary criticism, titled Four Contemporary Polish Poets *(1967), a volume of poetry,* Broken Treaties *(1973), editorship of* Blood of Their Blood: An Anthology of Polish-American Poetry *(1980), and essays contributed to numerous magazines. He is presently working on an anthology of his collected poems.*

At first it will seem tame,   1
willing to be domesticated.

It will nest   2
in your pocket
or curl up in a corner
reciting softly to itself
the names of the presidents.

It will delight your friends,   3
shake hands with men
like a dog and lick
the legs of women.

But like an amoeba   4
it makes love
in secret
only to itself.

5   Its food is normal
American food.
Fold it frequently;
it needs exercise.

6   Water it every three days
and it will repay you
with displays of affection.

7   Then one day when you think
you are its master
it will turn its head
as if for a kiss
and bite you gently
on the hand.

8   There will be no pain
but in thirty seconds
the poison will reach your heart.

Vocabulary

domesticated (1)
amoeba (4)

Questions on Meaning and Technique

1. What is the theme (lesson about life) of the poem, and where is it stated?
2. What is the predominant figure of speech used in the poem? How effective do you consider it? Give reasons to support your answer.
3. What allusion is used in stanza 3? Why?
4. Do you agree with the poet's opinion concerning the malevolence of money? Is it possible for money to bring true benefit to its owner? How or why not?
5. What is the meaning of the opening stanza? What clue helps you recognize immediately that the reference to "It" is money?
6. Why is the destruction so sudden and so painless?

HOW TO WRITE AN ANALYSIS OF CAUSE

Causal analysis is the expression used for finding connections between events. Unconsciously, you make causal analyses every day of your life. For example, you are doing causal analysis when you try to figure out why you did poorly on an exam. You also are doing causal analysis when you decide to wear warm clothing on a mountain trip so that you won't catch a cold. In the first case, you are looking at the past to find causes; in the second case, you are looking at the future to predict results.

During your college career, you often will be required to write essays that analyze cause. Your history teacher may ask you to give the causes for the Crimean War; your health teacher may ask you to name three results of a rattlesnake bite; your meteorology teacher may ask you to cite the major causes for hurricanes. Such assignments are rigorous, but you can fulfill them by drawing data and facts from textbooks or lecture notes. On occasion, you will also be asked to draw causal connections of your own and these will require particularly careful thought.

Causal analysis is tricky. Few situations can be traced directly to a single, clear cause, and for this reason even experts disagree about cause. It is commonplace to read about a murder trial in which eminent psychiatrists and psychologists disagree vehemently about a defendant's motive and state of mind. Economists argue vainly about the causes of inflation and recession; medical people constantly debate the causes of cancer. Most effects have not one but several causes, and often it is difficult, if not impossible, to determine the main cause of any event.

An effect may often be preceded by a whole chain of causes so that when you try to find the real cause, you are simply pushed farther and farther back from one cause to another. For instance, what is the cause of air pollution? Industrial waste. But industrial waste is caused by industry. Industry is caused by the growing needs of our exploding population. The exploding population is caused by lack of birth control, which results in part from religious beliefs. Religious beliefs come from writings in the Bible. The Bible is the word of God. Therefore, God is the cause of air pollution.

This conclusion is obviously silly. It illustrates, however, how an attempt at tracing causation can quickly lead to absurdity and serves to warn you against making haphazard, hit-or-miss, or hasty causal connections. Investigate your subject thoroughly, either from firsthand experience or by doing research. The causes for your parents' happy or miserable marriage can be identified through personal experience, but the causes of complex problems such as urban poverty or juvenile crime will require some research.

Writing Assignment

Write an essay analyzing the causes of a condition, event, or situation in society. First, describe the condition, event, or situation. Then probe the causes, listing them one by one and making sure that each cause is directly connected to the subject being described.

Specific Instructions

PREWRITING ON THE ASSIGNMENT.   Before you can begin to write, you have to choose a condition, event, or situation that has occurred as a result of identifiable causes. Situations do exist to which no absolute cause can be assigned, and these will be difficult to write about in any essay. For instance, scientists are still arguing over what caused the dinosaurs to disappear or the Egyptian mummies to be so well preserved. Better to choose a subject whose causes are definite and traceable. Follow your natural inclinations. If you are of a scientific bent, write about a scientific subject. One student, for example, wrote an excellent paper on what causes fireflies to light up, explaining that the light is produced by organs located on the fly's abdomen. The student then went into details about the nerve evolvement and role of reflector cells. Another student, majoring in political science, wrote a paper identifying the control of oil production, different interpretations of Islam, and a historical distrust of one another as the major causes of quarreling among Arab states. In either case, the basic idea is to choose a subject whose causes are traceable and discussable. Here are some topics to consider: the growing number of "bag women" in large cities; the increase in polluted lakes; the resistance to ordination of women as ministers or priests; the popularity of gangs and resultant killings; or the importance of the coffee break.

Once you have chosen your topic, jot down on a piece of paper its major causes or begin the research necessary to trace them. For instance, let us assume that you want to write about the growing number of "bag women" in large cities. Finding out why their numbers have increased will require some research, which, combined with experience and common sense, may lead you to the following summary: (1) Many people suffering from mental illness are no longer sheltered in medical institutions, (2) the population of large cities has become callous to the plight of homeless people, (3) some "bag women" want the independence of roaming the streets. Summing up these three causes could lead to this thesis for your essay: "Three major causes contribute to the growing number of 'bag women' roaming the streets of our large cities: the government's unwillingness to shelter all mentally ill persons, callousness to the plight of the homeless, and a sense of stubborn independence on the part of these indigents." You are now ready to begin writing the actual essay.

USE THE PROPER WORD INDICATORS TO SHOW CAUSATION

Wrong
: Admissions quotas based on sex, ethnic background, or age are bad. They discriminate against the capable student.

Right
: Admissions quotas based on sex, ethnic background, or age are bad *because* they discriminate against the capable student.

Whether you are listing the effects or causes of a situation, warn your reader that you intend to do a causal analysis by using such expressions as *because, therefore, since, the reason is, due to, as a result, consequently,* and *thus.* Here are some examples of causal sentences:

Chaucer is difficult to read *because* he uses antiquated English.

Because living human cells are constantly breaking down, they are in a constant state of reconstructing themselves through nutrients.

Walter is talented, practices the violin five hours a day and, *as a result,* won the Luba Lefcowitz prize for violin.

The present chaos in the world may have the following *results:* the extinction of human life, a reversion to barbarism after an atomic explosion, or the peaceful establishment of a world government.

If you are listing several causes for a certain situation, it is well to number them as in these examples:

The first cause is. . . .
The second cause is. . . .
The third cause is. . . .

As a matter of course, professional writers often use various expressions that signal what they are about to do before they do it. If they are about to define a term, they say so. If they intend to describe a vista, they tell the reader. If they are analyzing effect, they announce this in advance. It is really a commonsense strategy, and one that is highly effective. Readers are more likely to comprehend a passage whose purpose is clear to them. Here, for instance, is a paragraph that analyzes why, after the Norman Conquest, French did not replace English in England:

> One might wonder why, after the Norman Conquest, French did not become the national language, replacing English entirely. The reason is that the Conquest was not a national migration, as the earlier Anglo-Saxon invasion had been. Great numbers of Normans came to England, but they came as rulers and landlords. French became the language of the court, the language of the nobility, the language of polite society, the language of literature. But it did not replace English as the language of the people. There must always have been hundreds of towns and villages in which French was never heard except when visitors of high station passed through.
>
> Paul Roberts, *Understanding English*

If you are similarly analyzing the cause of a thing, or its effect, you should advise your reader that that is what you are going to do. Then you do it.

AMPLIFY ON THE ANALYSIS OF CAUSE.   Of all assignments you will be asked to write, the analysis of cause requires the most diversity of skills because it often mixes strategies. You will almost certainly—in the course of doing an essay on cause— have to write paragraphs that define, describe, and exemplify. For in any analysis of cause, it is necessary to supply background material. You may have to describe the problem, define key terms, and possibly divide and classify, even though the thrust of your essay is to explain cause or to predict effect.

It is not surprising that this is so. Essays are written with a dominant purpose or intent conceived in the mind of the writer. But a translation of this dominant intent onto the page generally requires many different kinds of paragraphs. It is a little like baking a chocolate cake. One uses not only chocolate, but also flour, butter, baking powder, milk, eggs, and sugar. Yet, when the cake comes out of the oven, it is indisputably a chocolate cake though made of different kinds of ingredients. Essays likewise have distinct and recognizable purposes. Some are intended primarily to describe; others set out to narrate; still others are written to analyze cause. Yet most are constructed of different kinds of paragraphs.

For instance, a writer is attempting to explain why humans sleep. He is, to begin with, obliged to talk about the principal human states of mind: waking, sleeping, and dreaming. The paragraph that does this is developed by *classification/division*. But, he asks, what is sleep good for? He surveys the animal kingdom and finds that although some animals—sloths, armadillos, opossums, and bats—sleep between nineteen and twenty hours a day, there are others, such as the shrew and the porpoise, that sleep very little. He also mentions the case of some humans who require only an hour or two of sleep. The paragraph that serves up all this intriguing information has been developed by *example*. He then turns his attention to the kinds of sleep—dreaming and dreamless—and discusses the results of research into each. Again, the paragraph is developed by *classification/division*. He is now ready to suggest a reason for sleep. The paragraph is developed by causal analysis:

Analysis of cause

> Perhaps one useful hint about the original function of sleep is to be found in the fact that dolphins and whales and aquatic mammals in general seem to sleep very little. There is, by and large, no place to hide in the ocean. Could it be that, rather than increasing an animal's vulnerability, the function of sleep is to *decrease* it? Wilse Webb of the University of Florida and Ray Meddis of London University have suggested this to be the case. The sleeping style of each organism is exquisitely adapted to the ecology of the animal. It is conceivable that animals who are too stupid to be quiet on their own initiative are, during periods of high risk, immobilized by the implacable arm of sleep. The point seems particularly clear for the young of predatory animals; not only are baby tigers covered with a superbly effective protective coloration, they also sleep a great deal. This is an interesting notion and probably at least partly true. It does not explain everything. Why do lions, who have few natural enemies, sleep? The question is not a very damaging objection because lions may have evolved from animals that were not the king of beasts. Likewise, adolescent gorillas, who have little to fear, nevertheless construct nests each night—perhaps because they evolved from more vulnerable predecessors. Or perhaps, once, the ancestors of lions and gorillas feared still more formidable predators.

> Carl Sagan, *The Dragons of Eden*

The remainder of the discussion goes on to expand on this notion and to find applications of its truthfulness in the animal kingdom.

Such a paragraph mix is quite typical of an analysis of cause. The writer, however, must strive to keep on the straight-and-narrow path in pursuing the dominant purpose of the essay. It is all very well and good to sidestep to define a term or to give an example of concept, but you must not allow these excursions to seduce you from your dominant purpose—which is to explain cause.

BE CAUTIOUS.   Don't be dogmatic or simplistic in drawing causal connections. Because very few events are sufficient in themselves to bring about a result, it is prudent to qualify your assertions with "a major cause," "it appears that," or "evidence indicates that." These qualifiers show you realize that the connection between events may be probable rather than certain, and they will enhance your credibility to the reader. On the other hand, if your causal analysis is a result of a personal opinion arrived at after much research and thought, have the courage of your convictions. For example, do not say, "It appears that the 1989 murder of 16-year-old Yusuf Hawkins in Brooklyn may have been racially motivated." Instead, say, "The Brooklyn murder of 16-year-old Yusuf Hawkins adds yet another page to our history of racial hatred."

WHENEVER POSSIBLE, FOCUS ON IMMEDIATE RATHER THAN REMOTE CAUSE.   Causation, we pointed out earlier, has a way of multiplying back in time, with one cause leading to another and then to another, until God becomes the cause of smog. To avoid entanglement in infinity, always focus on immediate rather than remote causation. For instance, one cause of overcrowded freeways is the population explosion, but a more immediate cause is the lack of rapid transit facilities. Focusing on the immediate cause has a better chance of resulting in an effective, convincing essay. Of course, some immediate causes are too deeply rooted in remote causes for the connection to be ignored. An example is the continuing conflict between Jews and Arabs in the Middle East. Whatever immediate causes—desire for oil, a Palestinian homeland, or national sovereignty—have led to this conflict, the remote causes implicit in the centuries-old rift between Arab and Jew since the days of Abraham should also be discussed.

AVOID CIRCULAR REASONING ABOUT CAUSE.   The following causal statements are circular:

> The freeways are overcrowded because there are too many cars.
>
> Lung cancer is caused by the rapid and uncontrolled growth of abnormal cells in the lungs.
>
> Beauty pageants are dehumanizing because ugly women never win them.

Each statement simply restates in the second half what is already implied in the first. Overcrowded freeways obviously have too many cars on them; lung cancer is, by definition, uncontrolled cell growth in the lungs; beauty pageants are called beauty pageants because they judge women for beauty. These revisions are better:

> The freeways are overcrowded because they are inadequately engineered for need, and because rapid transit facilities are poor.
>
> Cigarette smoking is the major cause of lung cancer.
>
> Beauty pageants are dehumanizing because they evaluate a woman as a sex object rather than as a whole, functioning person.

BEWARE OF IDEOLOGY IN ASSIGNING CAUSE. Here is an example of two causal statements based on ideology:

> The high divorce rate in Southern California is caused by the fact that the devil has chosen this section of the country for his own and has been especially busy working among couples here.
>
> The high divorce rate in California is caused by an astrological opposition between Neptune and the Moon, and by a weak but dangerous sextile relationship between Mars and the Sun.

In a complex universe, neither statement is refutable nor demonstrable, unless one is in ideological agreement with the writer. General essays on causation, however, ought not to exert any special ideological requirement on a reader.

STRUCTURING A CAUSAL ANALYSIS ESSAY. Now that you fully understand all the factors involved in assigning effect or probing cause, you are ready to organize your paper. Do not neglect this step in the process because without organization a causal analysis paper can easily disintegrate into a mass of disorderly information that cannot be sorted out by the average reader. Here is an important question you need to answer: Do I wish to emphasize cause, effect, or both? Assuming, for instance, that you have chosen to write a paper on women who have been molested as children by a male, you can decide to focus on the causes of this problem, on its effects, or on both the causes and the effects. Let us further assume you have decided that the effects on the victim are more important than the causes and that you will dwell on this aspect. Begin, then, by listing the effects you wish to consider:

1. Inability of the victim to relate lovingly to her husband
2. The victim's excessive fear or hostility toward all men
3. The victim's lack of self-esteem because of unconscious feelings that somehow she could have prevented the molestation

You have three clear effects that can be developed in the order listed. Moreover, your thesis statement can be formulated based on the three effects:

> Women who were molested during their childhood often cannot erase the harm done at that early stage in their lives and, in fact, may have to have years of psychotherapy to counteract the effects of not being able to relate lovingly to their husbands, of harboring excessive fear or hostility in relating to men in general, and of lacking a sense of self-esteem for having allowed the molestation to take place.

Once your thesis is in place, you can develop the essay by carefully describing the three effects, including facts, statistics, examples, case histories, and other supportive details. The structure you built will help give your essay movement and coherence.

Another way to structure the essay is to begin with molestation as an effect and then trace the causes of this effect. Here are four possible causes, listed in order of their relative importance:

1. The molester himself was abused as a child.
2. The molester molests as a substitute for trying to find love.
3. The molester victimizes a child, who is too weak to resist, thus achieving a sense of control over the world.
4. The molester has never assimilated the normal sexual taboos of his society.

The thesis statement for this essay might read as follows:

> Research psychologists tell us that the major causes of little girls being molested by an adult male can all be traced to the male's own development: having been abused as a child, trying to find love, wanting to gain control over a world that victimized him, and never having assimilated the normal sexual taboos of his society.

The causal analysis essay is rooted in our elemental need to make connections between events and to understand how the events came about. A well-structured causal analysis essay may well uncover some surprising truths that help make sense out of a tangled situation.

Reading for Ideas

Why do some works, even those that require a struggle from a modern reader, persist in popularity over the centuries? This is the question Bennett sets out to analyze and answer. His answer is surprisingly simple. See if you can summarize that answer in one short sentence and then think of ideas that either agree or disagree with Bennett's answer.

PROFESSIONAL MODEL

Why a Classic Is a Classic
Arnold Bennett

Arnold Bennett (1867–1931) was an English novelist and playwright best known for his "Five Towns" novels about an imaginary manufacturing district in northern England. As a young man Bennett served as an editor and literary reviewer before embarking on his career as a novelist. Among his best-known novels are Anna of the Five Towns *(1902) and* The Old Wives' Tale *(1908). His most successful play was* Milestones *(1912), with Edward Knoblock.*

1   The large majority of our fellow citizens care as much about literature as they care about archaeology or the program of the Legislature. They do not ignore it; they are not quite indifferent to it. But their interest in it is faint and perfunctory; or, if their interest happens to be violent, it is spasmodic. Ask the two hundred thousand persons whose enthusiasm made the vogue of a popular novel ten years ago what they think of that novel now, and you will gather that they have utterly forgotten it, and that they would no more dream of reading it again than of reading Bishop Stubb's *Select Charters*.[1] Probably if they did read it again they would not enjoy it—not because the said novel is a whit worse now than it was ten years ago; not because their taste has improved—but because they have not had sufficient practice to be able to rely on their taste as a means of permanent pleasure. They simply don't know from one day to the next what will please them.

2   In the face of this one may ask: Why does the great and universal fame of classical authors continue? The answer is that the fame of classical authors is entirely independent of the majority. Do you suppose that if the fame of Shakespeare depended on the man in the street it would survive a fortnight? The fame of classical authors is originally made, and it is maintained, by a passionate few. Even when a first-class author has enjoyed immense success during his lifetime, the majority have never appreciated him so sincerely as they have appreciated second-rate men. He has always been reinforced by the ardor of the passionate few. And in the case of an author who has emerged into glory after his death the happy sequel has been due solely to the obstinate perseverance of the few. They could not leave him alone; they would not. They kept on savoring him, and talking about him, and buying him, and they generally behaved with such eager zeal, and they were so authoritative and sure of themselves, that at last the majority grew accustomed to the sound of his name and placidly agreed to the proposition that he was a genius; the majority really did not care very much either way.

3   And it is by the passionate few that the renown of genius is kept alive from one generation to another. These few are always at work. They are always rediscovering genius. Their curiosity and enthusiasm are exhaustless, so that there is little chance of genius being ignored. And, moreover, they are always working either for or against the verdicts of the majority. The majority can make a reputation, but it is too careless to maintain it. If, by accident, the passionate few agree with the majority in a particular instance, they will frequently remind the majority that such and such a reputation has been made, and the majority will idly concur: "Ah, yes. By the way, we must not forget that such and such a reputation exists." Without that persistent memory-jogging the reputation would quickly fall into oblivion which is death. The passionate few only have their way by reason of the fact that they are genuinely interested in literature, that literature matters to them. They conquer by their obstinacy alone, by their eternal repetition of the same statements. Do you suppose they could prove to the man in the street that Shakespeare was a great artist? The said man would not even understand the terms they employed. But when he is told ten thousand times, and generation after generation, that Shakespeare was a great artist, the said man believes—not by reason, but by faith. And he too repeats that Shakespeare was a great artist, and he buys the

---

[1]A medieval history text published in 1870.

complete works of Shakespeare and puts them on his shelves, and he goes to see the marvellous stage effects which accompany *King Lear* or *Hamlet,* and comes back religiously convinced that Shakespeare was a great artist. All because the passionate few could not keep their admiration of Shakespeare to themselves. This is not cynicism; but truth. And it is important that those who wish to form their literary taste should grasp it.

What causes the passionate few to make such a fuss about literature? There can be   4 only one reply. They find a keen and lasting pleasure in literature. They enjoy literature as some men enjoy beer. The recurrence of this pleasure naturally keeps their interest in literature very much alive. They are forever making new researches, forever practising on themselves. They learn to understand themselves. They learn to know what they want. Their taste becomes surer and surer as their experience lengthens. They do not enjoy today what will seem tedious to them tomorrow. When they find a book tedious, no amount of popular clatter will persuade them that it is pleasurable; and when they find it pleasurable no chill silence of the street crowds will affect their conviction that the book is good and permanent. They have faith in themselves. What are the qualities in a book which give keen and lasting pleasure to the passionate few? This is a question so difficult that it has never yet been completely answered. You may talk lightly about truth, insight, knowledge, wisdom, humor, and beauty, but these comfortable words do not really carry you very far, for each of them has to be defined, especially the first and last. It is all very well for Keats in his airy manner to assert that beauty is truth, truth beauty, and that that is all he knows or needs to know. I, for one, need to know a lot more. And I shall never know. Nobody, not even Hazlitt[2] nor Sainte-Beuve,[3] has ever finally explained why he thought a book beautiful. I take the first fine lines that come to hand—

> The woods of Arcady are dead,
> And over is their antique joy—

and I say that those lines are beautiful, because they give me pleasure. But why? No answer! I only know that the passionate few will, broadly, agree with me in deriving this mysterious pleasure from those lines. I am only convinced that the liveliness of our pleasure in those and many other lines by the same author will ultimately cause the majority to believe, by faith, that W. B. Yeats[4] is a genius. The one reassuring aspect of the literary affair is that the passionate few are passionate about the same things. A continuance of interest does, in actual practice, lead ultimately to the same judgments. There is only the difference in width of interest. Some of the passionate few lack catholicity, or, rather, the whole of their interest is confined to one narrow channel; they have none left over. These men help specially to vitalize the reputations of the narrower geniuses: such as Crashaw.[5] But their active predilections never contradict the general verdict of the passionate few; rather they reinforce it.

A classic is a work which gives pleasure to the minority which is intensely and   5 permanently interested in literature. It lives on because the minority, eager to renew the

---

[2]William Hazlitt (1778–1830), English essayist.
[3]Charles Sainte-Beuve (1804–1869), French literary critic and writer.
[4]William Butler Yeats (1865–1939), Irish poet, playwright, and essayist.
[5]Richard Crashaw (1613?–1649), English religious poet.

sensation of pleasure, is eternally curious and is therefore engaged in an eternal process of rediscovery. A classic does not survive for any ethical reason. It does not survive because it conforms to certain canons, or because neglect would not kill it. It survives because it is a source of pleasure, and because the passionate few can no more neglect it than a bee can neglect a flower. The passionate few do not read "the right things" because they are right. That is to put the cart before the horse. "The right things" are the right things solely because the passionate few *like* reading them. Hence—and I now arrive at my point—the one primary essential to literary taste is a hot interest in literature. If you have that, all the rest will come. It matters nothing that at present you fail to find pleasure in certain classics. The driving impulse of your interest will force you to acquire experience, and experience will teach you the use of the means of pleasure. You do not know the secret ways of yourself: that is all. A continuance of interest must inevitably bring you to the keenest joys. But, of course, experience may be acquired judiciously or injudiciously, just as Putney may be reached via Walham Green or via Moscow.[6]

Vocabulary

perfunctory (1)	concur (3)	predilections (4)
spasmodic (1)	catholicity (4)	canons (5)

Questions on Meaning and Technique

1. What is the attitude of the large majority of people toward literature?
2. Why can't the large majority of people rely on their literary taste as a means of permanent pleasure?
3. What is the basis for the great fame that classical authors enjoy? Where is this stated in the essay?
4. Throughout the essay, the author frequently poses questions to himself, which he then answers. What does this self-questioning technique contribute to the essay?
5. Why do the passionate few have their way in literary matters?
6. Why does the man on the street believe the proposition that Shakespeare is a great artist?
7. Why do the passionate few take such an interest in literature?
8. One man has a greater interest in literature than another. Does it follow that the literary taste of the first man is superior to that of the second? Justify your reasoning.
9. Why does a classic survive? What causes the passionate few to agree that a work is a classic?

---

[6]Putney and Walham Green are adjoining districts in London. Putney may be reached via Walham Green or via Moscow in the same way that a person in Los Angeles can fly to New York via Chicago or Buenos Aires—in other words, directly or indirectly.

10. What is essential to the formation of literary taste?
11. How does the author develop his causal analysis?

STUDENT ESSAY

First Draft   Letitia Sanchez

Crooks, Fools, and Congressmen

1   *Possibly the greatest American scandal of the last decade of the twentieth century is the* ~~The Savings and Loan scandal of the last decade of the Twentieth Century was a~~ *collapse of the Savings and Loan system.* ~~terrible thing.~~ The costs of paying off the depositors and cleaning up the mess may run as high as $500,000,000,000.00 ~~(five hundred billion dollars)~~. Our children and grandchildren will *suffer* ~~feel~~ the effects of paying off such a huge loss ~~in severely diminished maintenance on the infrastructure of the country~~. They will not enjoy the quality of roads, bridges, water systems, and schools they should have been able to afford. The causes of this debacle are ~~cupidity, stupidity, perfidy, and impecunity~~ *greed and her sisters profligacy, stupidity, and dishonesty*.

    First, consider the profligacy involved.
2   If it were not for the ~~impecunity~~ *extravagance* of the United States federal government, the situation ~~which~~ *that* precipitated the S & Ls' problems would never have ~~existed~~ *unfolded*. For many years these institutions took in deposits from private individuals and other sources, and made loans, mostly mortgages, to individual families for home building or purchase. They paid interest on the deposits, and charged a little higher rate of interest on the loans. Banking laws allowed them to leverage their loans by ~~loaning~~ *lending* out the same money several times. Most loans were paid back in good order, *and* ~~There~~ was no need for keeping large reserves to offset bad loans. But the picture changed *when* ~~The~~ Federal *g*overnment ~~spent~~ *through spending* far more than its income, ~~It~~ became the biggest borrower in the history of the world. As the government gobbled up more and more of the available money, interest rates ~~went up~~ *soared*, and the depositors began to withdraw their money from S & Ls and put it in more attractive "money-market funds" ~~which~~ *that* bought Treasury bills ~~that paid~~ *yielding* as much as twenty percent interest, *limited to paying less than half that rate of interest on deposits, were* ~~The S & Ls couldn't pay half that much~~. *quickly in deep trouble.*

(Insert A)

By July 1990, over four hundred and fifty of these formerly respectable institutions had been seized by the federal government for insolvency (about one-fourth of the estimated total thought to be bankrupt).

Margin notes:

- Revise for an opening that grabs better.
- More background needed.
- Delete bureaucratic tone.
- Focus on key points of thesis.
- Number the key ideas to clarify them for the reader.
- Too choppy. Combine ideas through subordination.

More detailed
explanation
needed.
Correct
vagueness.
Make subject
agree with verb.
Specify who
"they" is.
Specify
reference.

of the equation

The stupidity part also belongs to the federal government. In 1981–82, while trying   3

by federal borrowing

to solve the problem it created. Congress passed legislation to allow S & Ls to raise the

rate of interest paid on deposits. But the S & Ls could not earn enough to pay the new

because   many

rates, since so much of their assets were tied up in long-term fixed-rate mortgages. So

Congress and the Federal Home Loan Bank Board

~~they~~ decided to encourage rapid growth by changing the rules that S & Ls operated

rapid growth

under. This would allow the thrift institutions to make enough to pay the exorbitant

lend

interest rates the government had caused in the first place. S & Ls were allowed to ~~loan~~

money on much more speculative projects, and even to invest directly in speculative

opportunities

"Things" is too
general.

~~things~~. In order to make this new game work, accepted accounting procedures were

changed, and S & L institutions became able to hide losses deep in the "investment

The new accounting procedures

portfolios" while declaring profits on those speculations that worked out well. ~~This~~

created a ~~very~~ false picture of the health of the whole industry. ~~Such changes were~~

Either delete or
explain further.

~~instituted at the same time the sizes of Federal Regulatory Agencies dealing with S & Ls~~

~~were cut down.~~

Parallelism too
artificial.

dishonesty involved

The ~~stupidity part of the equation~~ belongs to Wall Street investment banks, large   4

accounting firms, large law firms, academics in the fields of economics and business, and

the owners of the S & Ls who profited from the strange new laws. An alliance of these

This information
is not necessary.

players kept the government's mistake from being corrected for most of a decade, until

the cost of correcting the situation had reached enormous levels. The brokerage houses

made money on each purchase or sale of paper assets by speculating S & Ls. The

accounting firms earned huge fees finding and cynically exploiting the loopholes in the

changing regulations. The big law firms gleefully resisted Congress's efforts to rectify

its mistakes, while charging fat fees for their efforts. A lot of people were getting rich off

the system, and they did not want it changed.

The perfidy seems equally distributed over the playing field. Cynical accountants   5

building a fence

okayed as "improvements" such minor efforts as ~~fencing raw land~~ or bulldozing a dirt

road ~~down the middle of it~~, in order to allow the S & L to "capitalize" the interest it had

paid out on the money used to buy the land. Such "assets" became more and more

spurious

~~phony~~ as the accounting practices adjusted the institution's basis in them. As assets

diminished in actual worth, more deposits, at ever higher rates of interest, were sought.

With each escalation of the process, more and more   made.
~~More~~ speculative investments were ~~indulged in with each escalation of the process. As~~
Because of the high failure rate on
~~the failure rate is higher with~~ more speculative investments, more losses had to be
         For instance,
hidden with ever more creative accounting procedures, ~~U~~ncollected loan fees were
      A classic case in point is
allowed to be declared as income, making the S & Ls look good on paper. Vernon Savings
    which in 1985
and Loan, in Texas, was proclaimed the most profitable large S & L in the country ~~in 1985~~.
     were appalled to
When it folded in 1987, examiners, discovered that ninety-six percent of its loans were
  Worse yet,
worthless, ~~W~~hen regulators tried to prevent such abuses, the S & Ls hired major national
      bribed   to help cover up the disaster
law firms to block them. They also ~~hired~~ Congressmen and bureaucrats ~~where they were~~

~~available.~~

6   shabby spectacle   obsolete as an
    Perhaps the ~~matter~~ of the S & L industry will show that greed is ~~no longer a viable~~
     Although   was
operating basis for business in the United States. ~~While~~ greed ~~is a force that may have~~
          has
~~been very~~ influential in contributing to the initial growth of the country, it ~~may have~~
      profligacy, stupidity and dishonesty,
outlived its usefulness. Certainly, when accompanied by ~~companions like stupidity,~~
it is a flawed instrument for shaping national policy. When the results produced by an instrument
~~perfidy, and governmental impecunity it is an untrustworthy instrument for shaping~~
are so defective, shouldn't the instrument be discarded?
~~national policy.~~

Margin notes:

Rewrite for smoother flow of thought.

Transition needed.

Transition needed.

Be more specific.

Use same order of key words as in thesis.

Rewrite for stronger conclusion.

STUDENT ESSAY

Final Draft   Letitia Sanchez

Crooks, Fools, and Congressmen

Possibly the greatest American scandal of the last decade of the twentieth century is   1

the collapse of the Savings and Loan system. By July 1990, over four hundred and fifty

of these formerly respectable institutions had been seized by the federal government

for insolvency (about one-fourth of the estimated total thought to be bankrupt). The

costs of paying off the depositors and cleaning up the mess may run as high as five

hundred billion dollars. Our children and grandchildren will suffer the effects of paying

off such a huge loss. They will not enjoy the quality of roads, bridges, water systems,

and schools they should have been able to afford. The causes of this debacle are greed

and her sisters profligacy, stupidity, and dishonesty.

    First, consider the profligacy involved. If it were not for the extravagance of the   2

United States federal government, the situation that precipitated the S & Ls' problems would never have unfolded. For many years these institutions took in deposits from private individuals and other sources, and made loans, mostly mortgages, to individual families for home building or purchase. They paid interest on the deposits and charged a little higher rate of interest on the loans. Banking laws allowed them to leverage their loans by lending out the same money several times. Most loans were paid back in good order, and there was no need for keeping large reserves to offset bad loans. But the picture changed when the federal government, through spending far more than its income, became the biggest borrower in the history of the world. As the government gobbled up more and more of the available money, interest rates soared, and the depositors began to withdraw their money from S & Ls and put it in more attractive "money-market funds" that bought Treasury bills yielding as much as twenty percent interest. The S & Ls, limited to paying less than half that rate of interest on deposits, were quickly in deep trouble.

3   The stupidity part of the equation also belongs to the federal government. In 1981–82, while trying to solve the problem created by federal borrowing, Congress passed legislation to allow S & Ls to raise the rate of interest paid on deposits. But the S & Ls could not earn enough to pay the new rates because so many of their assets were tied up in long-term fixed-rate mortgages. So Congress and the Federal Home Loan Bank Board decided to encourage rapid growth by changing the rules the S & Ls operated under. This rapid growth would allow the thrift institutions to make enough to pay the exorbitant interest rates the government had caused in the first place. S & Ls were allowed to lend money on much more speculative projects, and even to invest directly in speculative opportunities. In order to make this new game work, accepted accounting procedures were changed, and S & L institutions became able to hide losses deep in their "investment portfolios" while declaring profits on those speculations that worked out well. The new accounting procedures created a false picture of the health of the whole industry.

4   The dishonesty involved belongs to Wall Street investment banks, large accounting firms, large law firms, academics in the fields of economics and business, and the

owners of the S & Ls who profited from the strange new laws. Cynical accountants okayed as "improvements" such minor efforts as building a fence or bulldozing a dirt road in order to allow the S & L to "capitalize" the interest it had paid out on the money used to buy the land. Such "assets" became more and more spurious as the accounting practices adjusted the institution's basis in them. As assets diminished in actual worth, more deposits, at ever higher rates of interest, were sought. With each escalation of the process, more and more speculative investments were made. Because of the high failure rate on more speculative investments, more losses had to be hidden with ever more creative accounting procedures. For instance, uncollected loan fees were allowed to be declared as income, making the S & Ls look good on paper. A classic case in point is Vernon Savings and Loan, in Texas, which in 1985 was proclaimed the most profitable large S & L in the country. When it folded in 1987, examiners were appalled to discover that ninety-six percent of its loans were worthless. Worse yet, when regulators tried to prevent such abuses, the S & Ls hired major national law firms to block them. They also bribed Congressmen and bureaucrats to help cover up the disaster.

Perhaps the shabby spectacle of the S & L industry will show that greed is obsolete   5
as an operating basis for business in the United States. Although greed was influential in contributing to the initial growth of the country, it has outlived its usefulness. Certainly, when accompanied by profligacy, stupidity, and dishonesty, it is a flawed instrument for shaping national policy. When the results produced by an instrument are so defective, shouldn't the instrument be discarded?

READING FOR IDEAS

Have you been dreaming about a life like Crocodile Dundee's or Robinson Crusoe's—a life free from the usual hassles and restrictions imposed by civilized life? Well, in the essay that follows, Marilyn Geewax describes graphically the down side of this kind of freedom. Pay close attention to her essay and then ask yourself just how much fun total freedom would be. In fact, ask yourself if total freedom is possible.

Freedom's Another Word for Nothing Left to Lose
Marilyn Geewax

Marilyn Geewax (b. 1955) is a regular editorial writer for the Atlanta Constitution.

1   About a decade ago, I traveled to Ireland by myself. I was happy to have no schedule, no reservations, no one expecting me to do anything. I'd just pick up my backpack and wander.

2   At first, I was thrilled by my sense of weightlessness. I was not tethered to the Earth by the usual forms of social gravity—a work schedule, a lunch date, a promise to walk a friend's dog.

3   The novelty wore off quickly. After a few days, I missed having my family worry about me. I wanted my boss to call and my friends to expect me at dinner. I never traveled alone again.

4   Drifting is unnatural. We homo sapiens survived in the primeval savannahs because we learned to take care of one another and look out for our group.

5   The lonely drifter may be a romantic figure in Westerns, but in real life, a person who stops connecting with society is bound to become a loser.

6   Recently, I was reminded of how sad life is for people who are "free" from responsibilities.

7   I spent the night in a Downtown shelter for the homeless. My task was to help watch over 26 men sprawled on cots in a church basement.

8   At 5:30 a.m., I was to turn on the lights, hand the men bagged lunches and see that everyone cleared out.

9   When the fluorescent lights flickered on, the men rose slowly and drifted silently toward the door. It was a damp, cold Saturday. Though some men work during the week, few have anywhere to go on weekends.

10   That day, their idle hours would slip away with the raindrops. That night, they'd return to the long rows of cots.

11   During the quiet predawn hours there, I tried to imagine what it would be like to have no phone number, no bills to pay, no friend's birthday to remember. These men were not enjoying a weeklong adventure in weightlessness; they were facing a lifetime of disconnected days.

12   For some, this hard life was unavoidable. A factory closed, a house burned down, a medical bill wiped out the rent money. For others, the first step on the way to the church basement was a deliberate one—a decision to drop out of school and leave home, a choice to start drinking.

13   No matter how their social ties got severed, the job of reconnecting them is nearly impossible. Just think of the obstacles one of these men would face climbing back into society. He would have to wake up and put on the same dirty clothes he'd worn the day before. He couldn't give the job interviewer a phone number. He couldn't list an address.

He wouldn't have a calendar to remind him of his new work schedule. He'd have no reliable transportation.

The path up from a basement cot to a decent home is so strewn with roadblocks that even a sober, sane person likely would stumble and fall back. After a few years of drifting, few people could stay sober or sane. 14

What a strange culture we have. In songs and stories, we glorify the loner—the guy who demands his "freedom" and who isn't afraid to tell his boss to "take this job and shove it." 15

Look closely at what happens to those who, through their own failings or through unfortunate circumstances, ended up free—free of bills and neckties and timeclocks and nagging wives. 16

Those burdens the rest of us bear every day—paying our taxes, packing lunches, getting to work on time—save our souls from the hell of such freedom. 17

Vocabulary

homo sapiens (4)
primeval (4)
savannahs (4)

Questions on Meaning and Technique

1. What is the author's thesis? Where is it stated? Is this a good placement? Does it always work? Support your answer with reasons.

2. How did the author come to her conclusion about freedom? Do you think you would reach the same conclusion? Support your answer with examples and details from your own experience.

3. What is your opinion of the freedom associated with the life of the homeless? Is any aspect of it enviable? Are these people really free?

4. What strategy does the author use to develop her thesis? How effective is she?

5. What irony is expressed in paragraphs 15 through 17?

Writing Assignments

1. In a reversal of Geewax's point, write an essay in which you illustrate the effect of having no personal freedom whatsoever.

2. Write an essay in which you probe the major causes of homelessness in our cities. Support your thesis with examples or details from urban life.

READING FOR IDEAS

You may disagree with the author, but if you read her carefully, you will find many of her ideas worth considering—if only to reject them. The author's point is that we have been much too hard on our bodies, expecting miracles and heroic feats from them when in reality they cannot live up to our fantastic expectations. As you read, notice what causes Ehrenreich blames for our mistreatment of the human flesh.

ALTERNATE READING

Why Don't We Like the Human Body?
Barbara Ehrenreich

Barbara Ehrenreich (b. 1941) is an outspoken feminist whose writing crusades for social justice, especially toward women. From 1969 to 1977 she was a staff member working for the Health Policy Advisory Center in New York. Following that position, she became a professor of health sciences at the State University of New York College at Old Westbury. Presently she is co-chair of the Democrat Socialists of America. Her writings include the following books: Long March, Short Spring: The Student Uprising at Home and Abroad *(1969), written with her husband, John Ehrenreich;* The Hearts of American Men: American Dreams and the Flight from Commitment *(1983);* Fear of Falling: The Inner Life of the Middle Class *(1989); and* The Worst Years of Our Lives: Irreverent Notes from a Decade of Greed *(1990). Ehrenreich has also contributed essays to numerous magazines, including* Time, *from which the essay below is taken.*

1   There's something wrong when a $7 movie in the mall can leave you with post-traumatic stress syndrome. In the old days killers merely stalked and slashed and strangled. Today they flay their victims and stash the rotting, skinless corpses. Or they eat them filleted, with a glass of wine, or live and with the skin still on when there's no time to cook. It's not even the body count that matters anymore. What counts is the number of ways to trash the body: decapitation, dismemberment, impalings and (ranging into the realm of the printed word) eye gougings, power drillings and the application of hungry rodents to some poor victim's innards.

2   All right, terrible things do happen. Real life is filled with serial killers, mass murderers and sickos of all degrees. Much of the 20th century, it could be argued, has been devoted to ingenious production and disposal of human corpses. But the scary thing is not that eye gougings and vivisections and meals of human flesh may, occasionally, happen. The scary thing, the thing that ought to make the heart pound and the skin go cold and tingly, is that somehow we find this fun to watch.

3   There are some theories, of course. In what might be called the testosterone theory, a congenital error in the wiring of the male brain leads to a confusion between violence and sex. Men get off on hideous mayhem, and women, supposedly, cover their eyes. Then there's the raging puritan theory, which is based on the statistical fact that those who get slashed or eaten on the screen are usually guilty of a little fooling around themselves. It's only a tingle of rectitude we feel, according to this, when the bad girl finally gets hers. There's even an invidious comparison theory: we enjoy seeing other people get sautéed or chain-sawed because at least it's not happening to us.

The truth could be so much simpler that it's staring us in the face. There's always been   4
a market for scary stories and vicarious acts of violence. But true horror can be bloodless,
as in Henry James' matchless tale, *The Turn of the Screw*. Even reckless violence, as in
the old-time western, need not debauch the human form. No, if offerings like *American
Psycho* and *The Silence of the Lambs* have anything to tell us about ourselves, it must
be that at this particular historical moment, we have come to hate the body.

Think about it. Only a couple of decades ago, we could conceive of better uses for the   5
body than as a source of meat or leather. Sex, for example. Sex was considered a valid
source of thrills even if both parties were alive and remained so throughout the act.
Therapists urged us to "get in touch with our bodies"; feminists celebrated "our bodies,
ourselves." Minimally, the body was a cuddly personal habitat that could be shared with
special loved ones. Maximally, it was a powerhouse offering multiple orgasms and
glowing mind-body epiphanies. Skin was something to massage or gently stroke.

Then, for good reasons or bad, we lost sex. It turned out to spread deadly viruses. It   6
offended the born-again puritans. It led to messy entanglements that interfered with
networking and power lunching. Since there was no way to undress for success, we
switched in the mid-'80s to food. When we weren't eating, we were watching food-porn
starring Julia Child or working off calories on the Stairmaster. The body wasn't perfect,
but it could, with effort and willpower, be turned into a lean, mean eating machine.

And then we lost food. First they took the red meat, the white bread and the   7
Chocolate Decadence desserts. Then they came for the pink meat, the cheese, the
butter, the tropical oils and, of course, the whipped cream. Finally, they wanted all
protein abolished, all fat and uncomplex carbohydrates, leaving us with broccoli and
Metamucil. Everything else, as we know, is transformed by our treacherous bodies into
insidious, slow-acting toxins.

So no wonder we enjoy seeing the human body being shredded, quartered, flayed,   8
filleted and dissolved in vats of acid. It let us down. No wonder we love heroes and
megavillains like RoboCop and the Terminator, in whom all soft, unreliable tissue has
been replaced by metal alloys. Or that we like reading (even in articles deeply critical of
the violence they manage to summarize) about diabolical new uses for human flesh. It's
been, let's face it, a big disappointment. May as well feed it to the rats or to any
cannibalistically inclined killer still reckless enough to indulge in red meat.

No, it's time for a truce with the soft and wayward flesh. Maybe violent imagery feeds the   9
obsessions of real-life sickos. Or maybe, as some argue, it drains their sickness off into
harmless fantasy. But surely it cheapens our sense of ourselves to think that others, even
fictional others, could see us as little more than meat. And it's hard to believe all this carnage
doesn't dull our response to the global wastage of human flesh in famine, flood and war.

We could start by admitting that our '70s-era expectations were absurdly high. The   10
body is not a reliable source of ecstasy or transcendental insight. For most of our lives, it's
a shambling, jury-rigged affair, filled with innate tensions, contradictions, broken springs.
Hollywood could help by promoting better uses for the body, like real sex, by which I
mean sex between people who are often wrinkled and overweight and sometimes even
fond of each other. The health meanies could relax and acknowledge that one of the
most marvelous functions of the body is, in fact, to absorb small doses of whipped cream
and other illicit substances.

11   Then maybe we can start making friends with our bodies again. They need nurture and care, but they should also be good for a romp now and then, by which I mean something involving dancing or petting as opposed to dicing and flaying. But even ''friends'' is another weirdly alienated image. The truth, which we have almost forgotten, is that Bodies ''R'' Us.

Vocabulary

flay (1)	invidious (3)
filleted (1)	epiphanies (5)
decapitation (1)	insidious (7)
dismemberment (1)	vats (8)
testosterone (3)	carnage (9)

Questions on Meaning and Technique

1. What details does the author provide to convince us that lately movies have gone too far in their display of scenes that debase rather than elevate the human body?

2. What is the author's thesis? Where is it stated?

3. In paragraph 3 the author lists some theories that suggest causes for the fun so many people get out of the heart-pounding gore in present-day movies. Which theory do you consider the most plausible? Do you have your own theory? If so, explain it.

4. What does the author suggest as her own views on the causes for the mistreatment of the human body? What is your reaction to her views?

5. At what point in the essay does the author move from some theories about violence to what she thinks is the truth? How dogmatic is she?

6. Like the author, do you too find it "hard to believe all this carnage doesn't dull our response to the global wastage of human flesh in famine, flood and war"? What evidence can you produce for your opinion?

7. How does the author achieve coherence between paragraphs 5, 6, and 7?

8. Why do you suppose the author worded the title of her essay in the form of a question? State the advantages, if any, of this format.

Writing Assignments

1. Write an essay in which you explore the causes of people's obsession with having a perfect body.

2. In a 500-word essay do a causal analysis of why violent movies do so well at the box office. Be sure to provide specific examples from movies you have seen or from reviews you have read.

READING FOR IDEAS

In his book *Anatomy of an Illness,* Cousins proposes that a positive attitude can contribute significantly to recovery from illness. He himself claims to have overcome a serious disease through laughter and optimism. Keep these ideas in mind while reading the essay that follows. Notice how the author prefers to focus on the human body's ability to heal itself rather than give so much credit to physicians or hospitals. Does your own experience support Cousins's views? In the event of a serious illness, would you rather just follow your doctor's instructions or try to heal yourself with a positive attitude? Focus your memory on times when you felt pain and on how you reacted psychologically.

ALTERNATE READING

Nation of Hypochondriacs
NORMAN COUSINS

Norman Cousins (1912–1990) was an influential author, editor, and essayist associated with the New York Post, Current History, *and the* Saturday Review. *Among his many books are* Modern Man is Obsolete *(1945),* Dr. Schweitzer of Lambarene *(1960), and* Anatomy of an Illness *(1970). Because of his writings on medical ethics and how the human mind and body can cure themselves, Cousins was appointed a member of the medical faculty at the University of California in Los Angeles, where he served until his death.*

The main impression growing out of twelve years on the faculty of a medical school is   1
that the No. 1 health problem in the U.S. today, even more than AIDS or cancer, is that we don't know how to think about health and illness. Our reactions are formed on the terror level. We fear the worst, expect the worst, thus invite the worst. The result is that we are becoming a nation of weaklings and hypochondriacs, a self-medicating society incapable of distinguishing between casual, everyday symptoms and those that require professional attention.

Somewhere in our early education we become addicted to the notion that pain means   2
sickness. We fail to learn that pain is the body's way of informing the mind that we are doing something wrong, not necessarily that something is wrong. We don't understand that pain may be telling us that we are eating too much or the wrong things; or that we are smoking too much or drinking too much; or that there is too much emotional congestion in our lives; or that we are being worn down by having to cope daily with overcrowded streets and highways, the pounding noise of garbage grinders, or the cosmic distance between the entrance to the airport and the departure gate. We get the message of pain all wrong. Instead of addressing ourselves to the cause, we become pushovers for pills, driving the pain underground and inviting it to return with increased authority.

3   Early in life, too, we become seized with the bizarre idea that we are constantly assaulted by invisible monsters called germs, and that we have to be on constant alert to protect ourselves against their fury. Equal emphasis, however, is not given to the presiding fact that our bodies are superbly equipped to deal with the little demons, and that the best way of forestalling an attack is to maintain a sensible life-style.

4   The most significant single statement about health to appear in the medical journals during the past decade is by Dr. Franz Ingelfinger, the late and former editor of the *New England Journal of Medicine.* Ingelfinger noted that almost all illnesses are self-limiting. That is, the human body is capable of handling them without outside intervention. The thrust of the article was that we need not feel we are helpless if disease tries to tear away at our bodies, and that we can have greater confidence in the reality of a healing system that is beautifully designed to meet most of its problems. And even when outside help is required, our own resources have something of value to offer in a combined strategy of treatment.

5   No one gets out of this world alive, and few people come through life without at least one serious illness. If we are given a serious diagnosis, it is useful to try to remain free of panic and depression. Panic can constrict the blood vessels and impose an additional burden on the heart. Depression, as medical researchers all the way back to Galen[1] have observed, can set the stage for other illnesses or intensify existing ones. It is no surprise that so many patients who learn that they have cancer or heart disease—or any other catastrophic disease—become worse at the time of diagnosis. The moment they have a label to attach to their symptoms, the illness deepens. All the terrible things they have heard about disease produce the kind of despair that in turn complicates the underlying condition. It is not unnatural to be severely apprehensive about a serious diagnosis, but a reasonable confidence is justified. Cancer today, for example, is largely a treatable disease. A heavily damaged heart can be reconditioned. Even a positive HIV diagnosis does not necessarily mean that the illness will move into the active stage.

6   One of the interesting things researchers at the UCLA medical center have discovered is that the environment of medical treatment can actually be enhanced if seriously ill patients can be kept free of depression. In a project involving 75 malignant-melanoma patients, it was learned that a direct connection exists between the mental state of the patient and the ability of the immune system to do its job. In a condition of emotional devastation, immune function is impaired. Conversely, liberation from depression and panic is frequently accompanied by an increase in the body's interleukins, vital substances in the immune system that help activate cancer-killing immune cells. The wise physician, therefore, is conscious of both the physical and emotional needs of the patient.

7   People who have heart attacks are especially prone to despair. After they come through the emergency phase of the episode, they begin to reflect on all the things they think they will be unable to do. They wonder whether they will be able to continue at their jobs, whether they will be able to perform satisfactorily at sex, whether they can play tennis or golf again. In short, they contemplate an existence drained of usefulness and joy. The spark goes out of their souls. It may help for these people to know that in addition to the miracles that modern medicine can perform, the heart can make its own

[1]Greek physician (c. A.D. 130–200), founder of experimental physiology.

bypass around the occluded arteries and that collateral circulation can provide a rich supply of oxygen. A heart attack need not be regarded as consignment to a mincing life-style. Under circumstances of good nutrition, a reasonable amount of exercise and a decrease in the wear and tear of stressful events, life expectancy need not be curtailed.

Plainly, the American people need to be re-educated about their health. They need to know that they are the possessors of a remarkably robust mechanism. They need to be de-intimidated about disease. They need to understand the concept of a patient-physician partnership in which the best that medical science has to offer is combined with the magnificent resources of mind and body.   8

We need not wait, of course, for a catastrophic illness before we develop confidence in our ability to rise to a serious challenge. Confidence is useful on the everyday level. We are stronger than we think. Much stronger.   9

Vocabulary

hypochondriacs (1)	immune (6)	collateral (7)
catastrophic (5)	devastation (6)	mincing (7)
apprehensive (5)	occluded (7)	curtailed (7)

Questions on Meaning and Technique

1. In the opening paragraph, why does the author mention that he has served on a medical faculty for twelve years?

2. What is the author's thesis, summarized in one sentence?

3. How important is the information given in paragraphs 2 and 3 to the thesis of Cousins's essay? Would the essay be seriously affected if these paragraphs were deleted? Why or why not?

4. What purpose does the Ingelfinger reference serve in paragraph 4?

5. If the author's statement that panic or depression may cause deterioration in a patient is correct, how can these feelings be prevented?

6. The author mentions that heart attack victims are especially prone to despair. How is a heart attack different from any other serious disease?

7. If you agree with the author that Americans need to be reeducated about their health, how would you propose to go about this reeducation process?

8. What audience is targeted in this essay? How can you tell?

9. How does the author avoid medical terminology that might not be understood by readers?

10. What cause-effect relationship is made clear by the end of the essay?

Writing Assignments

1. Write an essay probing the major causes for general good health. Provide examples of each cause.

2. Write an essay listing all of the positive effects that come from having good health. Areas to consider are the workplace, family life, psychological welfare, and recreation.

Additional Writing Assignments

1. Why do students seek a higher education? Write a causal analysis in which you offer the most important reasons why students continue their education, often beyond college into graduate school.

2. Write an essay in which you analyze the influence (effects) of your closest friend on your life. Be sure to supply vivid examples to enhance your essay.

3. What do you consider the major causes of the recent increase in juvenile gang crimes? Develop an essay in which you deal with this question.

4. Think of the public figure whom you most dislike or distrust. Describe the trait that makes you dislike him or her and find reasons for this trait. State both the trait and reasons for it in your thesis.

5. Political actions always have an effect on society—good or bad. Analyze the effect of the following political actions, were they to take place: free housing for all poor people, automatic capital punishment for all first-degree murderers, compulsory military service for women, legalization of drugs, automobile taxes based on fuel consumption.

6. Explore the major causes for the high dropout rate in college. Summarize these causes in your thesis and develop them into an essay.

7. Explore the major causes of the high divorce rate in the United States.

8. Most major cities in our country are becoming increasingly culturally diverse owing to large-scale immigration. Write an essay in which you explore the effects of this cultural diversity.

9. Write an essay indicating how the human personality is influenced by the early socialization one receives as a female or male.

10. Write an essay analyzing the good or bad effects of any recent medical discovery, such as the Salk vaccine, chemotherapy, or dental bonding.

11. With the help of some library research, write a causal analysis on one of the following historical events:
    a. the Salem witch trials
    b. the Aaron Burr–Alexander Hamilton duel
    c. Fauvism as a movement in painting
    d. the creation of labor unions
    e. the 1930 depression
    f. the civil rights movement of the 1950s

12. Write an essay delineating the causes for the modern movement toward nonsexist language in printed matter.

13. Write an essay stating the reasons so many people refuse to learn word processing. (Or state the major effects of using word processing.)

Photo Writing Assignment

Blind father and his assistant, his son. © 1986 by Carlos Ugalde, personal collection.

Causal analysis attempts to find physical or psychological connections between events to establish the reasons that something happened. In the photo, taken in Nicaragua, try to see a connection between the plight of the blind father with his son and the society in which they live. Write an essay exploring the causes of the extreme poverty and suffering depicted.

413

Argumentation

READING FOR IDEAS

The short story "War," by Luigi Pirandello, is a subtle and moving argument against war that resurrects the universal questions people have always asked: Is war glorious? Is war worth the sacrifice of a loved one? Is there honor in dying at war? As the story progresses, you will see that it is an eloquent and persuasive argument. Use the story as a springboard to an argument of your own. Ask yourself what traditions, institutions, customs, or stereotypes bother you. Why do you dislike them? If you could do away with them, would you? Why?

War

LUIGI PIRANDELLO

Luigi Pirandello (1867–1936), Italian author and playwright, is regarded as one of the great playwrights of the twentieth-century European theater. Born in Sicily, Pirandello became professor of Italian literature at the Normal College for Women in Rome. He wrote seven novels and nearly three hundred stories, but he is best known for his grotesquely humorous plays such as Right You Are If You Think You Are *(1922),* The Pleasure of Honesty *(1923), and* Six Characters in Search of an Author *(1922). Pirandello won the Nobel Prize in literature in 1934.*

1   The passengers who had left Rome by the night express had had to stop until dawn at the small station of Fabriano in order to continue their journey by the small old-fashioned local joining the main line with Sulmona.

At dawn, in a stuffy and smoky second-class carriage in which five people had already   2
spent the night, a bulky woman in deep mourning was hoisted in—almost like a
shapeless bundle. Behind her—puffing and moaning, followed her husband—a tiny man,
thin and weakly, his face death-white, his eyes small and bright and looking shy and
uneasy.

Having at last taken a seat he politely thanked the passengers who had helped his wife   3
and who had made room for her; then he turned round to the woman trying to pull down
the collar of her coat, and politely inquired:

"Are you all right, dear?"   4

The wife, instead of answering, pulled up her collar again to her eyes, so as to hide her   5
face.

"Nasty world," muttered the husband with a sad smile.   6

And he felt it his duty to explain to his traveling companions that the poor woman was   7
to be pitied for the war was taking away from her her only son, a boy of twenty to whom
both had devoted their entire life, even breaking up their home at Sulmona to follow him
to Rome, where he had to go as a student, then allowing him to volunteer for war with
an assurance, however, that at least for six months he would not be sent to the front and
now, all of a sudden, receiving a wire that he was due to leave in three days' time and
asking them to go and see him off.

The woman under the big coat was twisting and wriggling, at times growling like a wild   8
animal, feeling certain that all those explanations would not have aroused even a shadow
of sympathy from those people who—most likely—were in the same plight as herself.
One of them, who had been listening with particular attention, said:

"You should thank God that your son is only leaving now for the front. Mine has been   9
sent there the first day of the war. He has already come back twice wounded and been
sent back again to the front."

"What about me? I have two sons and three nephews at the front," said another   10
passenger.

"Maybe, but in our case it is our only son," ventured the husband.   11

"What difference can it make? You may spoil your only son with excessive attentions,   12
but you cannot love him more than you would all your other children if you had any.
Paternal love is not like bread that can be broken into pieces and split amongst the
children in equal shares. A father gives *all* his love to each one of his children without
discrimination, whether it be one or ten, and if I am suffering now for my two sons, I am
not suffering half for each of them but double . . . "

"True . . . true . . . " sighed the embarrassed husband, "but suppose (of course we all   13
hope it will never be your case) a father has two sons at the front and he loses one of
them, there is still one left to console him . . . while . . . "

"Yes," answered the other, getting cross, "a son left to console him but also a son left   14
for whom he must survive, while in the case of the father of an only son if the son dies
the father can die too and put an end to his distress. Which of the two positions is the
worse? Don't you see how my case would be worse than yours?"

"Nonsense," interrupted another traveler, a fat, red-faced man with bloodshot eyes of   15
the palest gray.

16 He was panting. From his bulging eyes seemed to spurt inner violence of an uncontrolled vitality which his weakened body could hardly contain.

17 "Nonsense," he repeated, trying to cover his mouth with his hand so as to hide the two missing front teeth. "Nonsense. Do we give life to our children for our own benefit?"

18 The other travelers stared at him in distress. The one who had had his son at the front since the first day of the war sighed: "You are right. Our children do not belong to us, they belong to the Country. . . . "

19 "Bosh," retorted the fat traveler. "Do we think of the Country when we give life to our children? Our sons are born because . . . well, because they must be born and when they come to life they take our own life with them. This is the truth. We belong to them but they never belong to us. And when they reach twenty they are exactly what we were at their age. We too had a father and mother, but there were so many other things as well . . . girls, cigarettes, illusions, new ties . . . and the Country, of course, whose call we would have answered—when we were twenty—even if father and mother had said no. Now, at our age, the love of our Country is still great, of course, but stronger than it is the love for our children. Is there any one of us here who wouldn't gladly take his son's place at the front if he could?"

20 There was a silence all round, everybody nodding as to approve.

21 "Why then," continued the fat man, "shouldn't we consider the feelings of our children when they are twenty? Isn't it natural that at their age they should consider the love for their Country (I am speaking of decent boys, of course) even greater than the love for us? Isn't it natural that it should be so, as after all they must look upon old boys who cannot move any more and must stay at home? If Country exists, if Country is a natural necessity, like bread, of which each of us must eat in order not to die of hunger, somebody must go to defend it. And our sons go, when they are twenty, and they don't want tears, because if they die, they die inflamed and happy (I am speaking, of course, of decent boys). Now, if one dies young and happy, without having the ugly sides of life, the boredom of it, the pettiness, the bitterness of disillusion . . . what more can we ask for him? Everyone should stop crying; everyone should laugh, as I do . . . or at least thank God—as I do—because my son, before dying, sent me a message saying that he was dying satisfied at having ended his life in the best way he could have wished. That is why, as you see, I do not even wear mourning. . . . "

22 He shook his light fawn coat as to show it; his livid lip over his missing teeth was trembling, his eyes were watery and motionless, and soon after he ended with a shrill laugh which might well have been a sob.

23 "Quite so . . . quite so . . . " agreed the others.

24 The woman who, bundled in a corner under her coat, had been sitting and listening had—for the last three months—tried to find in the words of her husband and her friends something to console her in her deep sorrow, something that might show her how a mother should resign herself to send her son not even to death but to a probable danger of life. Yet not a word had she found amongst the many which had been said . . . and her grief had been greater in seeing that nobody—as she thought—could share her feelings.

25 But now the words of the traveler amazed and almost stunned her. She suddenly realized that it wasn't the others who were wrong and could not understand her but herself who could not rise up to the same height of those fathers and mothers willing to

resign themselves, without crying, not only to the departure of their sons but even to their death.

She lifted her head, she bent over from her corner trying to listen with great attention   26
to the details which the fat man was giving to his companions about the way his son had fallen as a hero, for his King and his Country, happy and without regrets. It seemed to her that she had stumbled into a world she had never dreamed of, a world so far unknown to her and she was so pleased to hear everyone joining in congratulating that brave father who could so stoically speak of his child's death.

Then suddenly, just as if she had heard nothing of what had been said and almost as   27
if waking up from a dream, she turned to the old man, asking him:

"Then . . . is your son really dead?"   28

Everybody stared at her. The old man, too, turned to look at her, fixing his great,   29
bulging, horribly watery light gray eyes, deep in her face. For some little time he tried to answer, but words failed him. He looked and looked at her, almost as if only then—at that silly incongruous question—he had suddenly realized at last that his son was really dead—gone forever—forever. His face contracted, became horribly distorted; then he snatched in haste a handkerchief from his pocket and, to the amazement of everyone, broke into harrowing, heartrending, uncontrollable sobs.

Vocabulary

livid (22)	incongruous (29)
stoically (26)	harrowing (29)

Questions on Meaning and Technique

1. What is the controlling idea of the story? State it in one concise sentence.
2. What is the fat man's *pretended* attitude toward the loss of a son at war? How does this contrast with his *real* attitude?
3. The story contains little action. What is the conflict of the story?
4. What exactly triggers the sudden change in the fat man's attitude?
5. Is there any hint earlier in the story that the fat man was not as sure of his argument as he claimed to be?
6. How would you counter the fat man's argument?

READING FOR IDEAS

In the poem, Dooley, a convicted murderer, advances an ironic argument against going to war. Compare his argument with your own. Try to formulate a clear view of how you feel about soldiers being compelled to fight wars. Think about the following questions: Are there some causes worth killing for? Is it cowardly to hate war and perhaps even refuse to carry arms? Can there be glory in war?

Dooley Is a Traitor

JAMES MICHIE

James Michie (b. 1927), a British poet and translator, was for many years director of
The Bodley Head Ltd., a British publisher, and was a lecturer at London University.
Michie's work includes Possible Laughter *(1959),* The Odes of Horace *(translation;*
1964), and The Epigrams of Martial *(translation; 1973).*

1 "So then you won't fight?"
   "Yes, your Honour," I said, "that's right."
   "Now is it that you simply aren't willing,
   Or have you a fundamental moral objection to killing?"
   Says the judge, blowing his nose
   And making his words stand to attention in long rows.
   I stand to attention too, but with half a grin
   (In my time I've done a good many in).
   "No objection at all, sir," I said.
   "There's a deal of the world I'd rather see dead—
   Such as Johnny Stubbs or Fred Settle or my last landlord, Mr. Syme.
   Give me a gun and your blessing, your Honour, and I'll be killing
      them all the time.

2 But my conscience says a clear no
   To killing a crowd of gentlemen I don't know.
   Why, I'd as soon think of killing a worshipful judge,
   High-court, like yourself (against whom, God knows, I've got no grudge—
   So far), as murder a heap of foreign folk.
   If you've got no grudge, you've got no joke
   To laugh at after." Now the words never come flowing

3 Proper for me till I get the old pipe going.
   And just as I was poking
   Down baccy, the judge looks up sharp with "No smoking,
   Mr. Dooley. We're not fighting this war for fun.
   And we want a clearer reason why you refuse to carry a gun.
   This war is not a personal feud, it's a fight
   Against wrong ideas on behalf of the Right.
   Mr. Dooley, won't you help to destroy evil ideas?"

4 "Ah, your Honour, here's
   The tragedy," I said. "I'm not a man of the mind.
   I couldn't find it in my heart to be unkind
   To an idea. I wouldn't know one if I saw one. I haven't one of my own.

5 So I'd best be leaving other people's alone."
   "Indeed," he sneers at me, "this defence is

Curious for someone with convictions in two senses.
A criminal invokes conscience to his aid
To support an individual withdrawal from a communal crusade.
Sanctioned by God, led by the Church, against a godless, churchless nation!''

I asked his Honour for a translation.   6
''You talk of conscience,'' he said. ''What do you know of the Christian creed?''
''Nothing, sir, except what I can read,
That's the most you can hope for from us jail-birds.
I just open the Book here and there and look at the words.
And I find when the Lord himself misliked an evil notion
He turned it into a pig and drove it squealing over a cliff into the ocean,

And the loony ran away   7
And lived to think another day.
There was a clean job done and no blood shed!
Everybody happy and forty wicked thoughts drowned dead.
A neat and Christian murder. None of your mad slaughter
Throwing away the brains with the blood and the baby with the bathwater.

Now I look at the war as a sportsman. It's a matter of choosing   8
The decentest way of losing.
Heads or tails, losers or winners,
We all lose, we're all damned sinners.
And I'd rather be with the poor cold people at the wall that's shot
Than the bloody guilty devils in the firing-line, in Hell and keeping hot.''
''But what right, Dooley, what right,'' he cried,
''Have you to say the Lord is on your side?''
''That's a dirty crooked question,'' back I roared.
''I said not the Lord was on my side, but I was on the side of the Lord.''
Then he was up at me and shouting.

But by and by he calms: ''Now we're not doubting   9
Your sincerity, Dooley, only your arguments,
Which don't make sense.''
('Hullo,' I thought, 'that's the wrong way round.
I may be skylarking a bit, but my brainpan's sound.')
Then biting his nail and sugaring his words sweet:
''Keep your head, Mr. Dooley. Religion is clearly not up your street.
But let me ask you as a plain patriotic fellow
Whether you'd stand there so smug and yellow
If the foe were attacking your own dear sister.''
''I'd knock their brains out, mister,
On the floor,'' I said. ''There,'' he says kindly, ''I knew you were no pacifist.

It's your straight duty as a man to enlist.   10
The enemy is at the door.'' You could have downed

Me with a feather. "Where?" I gasp, looking round.
"Not this door," he says angered. "Don't play the clown.
But they're two thousand miles away planning to do us down."

Questions on Meaning and Technique

1. Dooley is labeled a traitor because he refuses to join the army and fight in the war. What is the controlling idea of his objection?
2. What is the judge's counterargument to Dooley's position?
3. When the judge tries to trick Dooley by bringing up the Christian creed (paragraph 6), what does Dooley answer? Why?
4. When the judge tries to trick Dooley again by asking what he would do if an enemy were suddenly to attack Dooley's sister, what is Dooley's answer?
5. How would you characterize Dooley's logic? How does his logic differ from the judge's?
6. According to Dooley, who wins in a war?
7. What supportive evidence can you present to advance either Dooley's or the judge's argument?
8. Dooley is a confessed murderer and criminal. What effect does this have on his view about war?

How to Write an Argument

An argument is a discussion in which disagreement is expressed about a subject. Argumentation always assumes the possibility of a debate, with one side arguing from one position and the other side arguing from another.

To write an effective argument, you must reason logically, support your case by evidence, and anticipate the opposition. In a spoken debate, all these things may take place in the give-and-take of arguing. But in a written debate, the writer is the sole expositor of the case who must not only air personal views, but must also raise and rebut any foreseeable counterclaims by critics.

Some arguments convince because of the merits of their evidence; others, because they are persuasively presented. Unfortunately, the merit of an argument is not necessarily related to its rightness. Many crooks have been glib and convincing in advancing their fraudulent schemes and views, whereas many saints have had their ideas rejected for lack of persuasiveness. In short, to write or state a convincing argument, you need to be more than just "right"; you also need to know how to argue persuasively.

Writing Assignment

Select a tradition, custom, institution, or stereotype that you distrust or dislike and write an argument against it. Begin with a controlling idea that clearly expresses the hub of your opposition—for example, "Now that the Cold War is over, NATO should invite the members of the former Soviet Union to join its league as an ally, rather than continuing the animosity of the past." Or, "The white wedding gown is outmoded and hypocritical." Or, "Handicapped students can usually adjust well to mainstream college education when given a chance." Once expressed, the controlling idea should be supported by logic, evidence, and expert testimony; moreover, the argument should take into account and parry the expected replies of the opposition.

Specific Instructions

PREWRITING ON THE ASSIGNMENT.   A good way to get started on this assignment is to sit with a friend and discuss the issues in the present world that really bother you. Ask yourself what changes you would like to see in your home state, your city, your school, or your society. About what reform do you feel strongly enough to invest time in helping it to succeed? You will have a better chance of writing a successful essay if you choose an issue to which you have some emotional commitment. The last time we asked our classes to suggest some "hot" issues, the following seemed to evoke the strongest responses: toxic waste, population control, better transit systems, improved relations with immigrants, peace in the Middle East, stronger family ties, better elementary education, Americans' craving for drugs, obscenity in film or popular music, and attracting a higher quality of candidates to run for public office. These, of course, are big issues. You might be more interested in some narrower or more focused issue, such as the despoiling developers in your neighborhood, ugly billboards along the freeways, female ministers in your church, the increase in the price of clothing as a result of shoplifting, or the lack of a streamlined registration process for college classes.

Avoid arguments for which logical proof does not exist. You may feel strongly that the unborn fetus has a soul, but to prove that view in scientific or logical terms is impossible.

BASE YOUR ARGUMENT ON SOUND PREMISES.   A premise is a basic assertion that serves as the starting point of an argument. Consider, for example, the premise of a speech given by Benjamin Franklin at the Constitutional Convention held in 1787. The Convention was mulling over whether or not executive officers of the newly minted federal government should be paid for their services. Franklin made an impassioned speech against the idea of payment, beginning with the following premise:

> Sir, there are two passions which have a powerful influence in the affairs of men. These are *ambition* and *avarice:* the love of power and the love of money. Separately, each of these has great force in prompting men to action: but when united in view of the same object, they have in many minds the most violent effect.

The premise of Franklin's argument consists of his assertions about the wicked influences of ambition and avarice. He then proceeds to give examples of what he foresaw as the harmful consequences of salaried federal offices on these weaknesses in human nature. Greedy, grasping candidates would aspire to office, not for love of country, but for love of money. The best would not be called upon to serve, only the greediest. Once Franklin's premise is aired, the remainder of the argument consists mainly of demonstrating the havoc that payment to federal officers would wreak on the national character.

With some justification, the premise of an argument has often been compared to the foundation of a house. The structure of a house rests on its foundation; the integrity of an argument rests on its premise. Indeed, the premise is what the argument begins by asserting and often ends by proving. It is also the point of contention to which an opponent will most often direct a counterattack. For instance, a possible rebuttal of the Franklin argument would deny that people are as corruptible and venal as the premise implies. One might argue, instead, that good men and women are as much motivated by patriotism, morality, and/or duty as they are by avarice and ambition. And, no doubt, a strong argument could be waged on both sides, for it is the nature of premises that consist of grand assertions about human nature to be "slippery" and hard to prove or disprove.

Premises are as varied and complex as the individuals who assert them. We hold premises about the effects of the planets upon our lives, about the causes of the common cold, or about global warming. Some premises, like Franklin's, are plainly stated in the body of an argument, whereas others are merely implied.

Here, for example, are the theses of various arguments whose premises are implied:

Thesis	A prime reason for the increase in crime has been the reduced severity of jail sentences.
Implied premise	Severe jail sentences deter crimes.
Thesis	Abortion is a great wickedness that is in blatant opposition to the laws of God.
Implied premise	God exists, and His Laws must be obeyed.
Thesis	We oppose busing because we support quality education in our schools.
Implied premise	Busing decreases the quality of education.

Obviously, the argument built on a shaky premise will not stand. To refute such an argument, an opponent needs merely to show that its premise is untrue or inaccurate. Few premises, however, are black-and-white, and therefore few arguments end with a clear victory on one side or the other.

A premise, we said, is a summary assertion about reality. Capital punishment deters crime, energy policies affect global warming, sunspots affect the world's economy—these and other generalizing statements become premises when they are used as the launching point of an argument. How do we come to believe in such generalizations? We do so by two reasoning processes—*induction* and *deduction*. Inductive and deductive reasoning are two natural thought patterns everyone uses to draw conclusions about the world and to make decisions. A closer look at each of these patterns may be helpful.

INDUCTION.   Induction is a way of coming to a general principle from particular facts or experiences. Take the case of Mr. Cochran, a gourmet cook. One day he made a mistake and stewed beef in tea, which he mistook for broth. He discovered, to his surprise, that the meat turned out especially tender. A week later, he deliberately repeated his "error," with the same tender and savory result. Further trials again confirmed a conclusion that Mr. Cochran had begun to suspect: Meat is tenderized when it is stewed in tea.

Though homespun and trivial, the example of Mr. Cochran is not far removed in method from the way induction is practiced by scientists. Whether conducted in the kitchen by a gourmet cook or in the laboratory by a scientist, induction involves the investigation of specific cases and the drawing of general conclusions from them. Here, for instance, is a newspaper report of a medical finding derived from the inductive method:

Thousands of children are needlessly denying themselves milk and other common foods because of allergies they don't have, a research team at the National Jewish Hospital and Research Center has concluded.

    Conclusion

Dr. Charles D. May and Dr. S. Allan Bock, co-directors of a major clinical and research program in food allergies at the Denver hospital, said that of 71 children they have studied who were thought to have food allergies, only 25 actually had such allergies.

"That isn't to say that there aren't children who are allergic to such things as strawberries, tomatoes and chocolate," Bock said, "but it apparently is very much less common than people think."

In the NJH research, which is continuing, children between the ages of 3 and 16 are "challenged" with food to which they are believed to be allergic, and their reactions are observed.

    Inductive method used to reach conclusion

Possible bias is eliminated through the use of a double-blind technique in which neither the children nor the observers know what the patients are getting. The food is given to the patients in the form of opaque capsules. Only the person supervising the test knows what is in each capsule. It could be milk, shrimp, tomato, or one of two placebos—known whimsically as "spider teeth" and "bat wings."

The capsules are administered initially in small doses, but the dosage is increased gradually, and the patients' reactions are monitored and their reactions recorded hour by hour.

"These techniques . . . sometimes indicate that the patient can safely eat small amounts of food which, in larger quantities, might trigger reactions."

But the most significant result of the study so far is the revelation that possibly only one-third of children thought to have food allergies actually have such allergies.

    Discussion of the conclusions

This result caused May and Bock to become concerned that some people may be living with "unwarranted restrictions on optimal nutrition" because of an incorrect diagnosis of food sensitivity.

The research, if its findings are confirmed by further testing, could mean that many "allergy sufferers" can enjoy more palatable and nourishing diets.

"Doctors Find Two-Thirds of 'Allergic' Kids Aren't,"
Atlanta Constitution, 19 March 1979, p. 13A

Notice that Mr. Cochran induced his findings about the tenderizing qualities of tea after a number of experiments. Similarly, from the study of only 71 children, the doctors induced that *thousands* of children thought to have allergies do not. In both cases, random samples—of meat tenderized after stewing in tea and of children who were thought to have allergies but didn't—are taken to represent characteristics of the whole. Mr. Cochran assumes that if tea tenderizes stewed meat in fifteen trials it will do so in umpteen other instances; the doctors assume that if only 25 percent of a random sample of children thought to have allergies actually do, then this percentage should also apply to the larger population.

When structuring your own arguments, you may need to use inductive reasoning; when you do, you should be aware of how to evaluate the soundness of your inductive conclusion. Study the chart below to understand induction.

CHARACTERISTICS OF INDUCTIVE REASONING

1. Inductive reasoning moves from the specific to the general, beginning with the observation of specific facts or experiences to draw a general conclusion.
2. Induction leads to new truths by using old observations to make new ones.
3. An inductive conclusion is reliable only if the facts and observations leading to it are also reliable.

DEDUCTION.   Deduction is the opposite of induction, moving from general observations to specific ones. Once one has discovered a general principle, it is useful only if it can be applied to different, specific cases. In other words, one can often discover valuable new principles derived from an already established and accepted principle. Consider, for instance, the possible reaction of a doctor familiar with the Denver hospital research to whom a mother has brought a child she suspects of having a food allergy. The doctor's first response is likely to be of doubt and disbelief. His thinking will doubtless run along these lines: Only 25 percent of the children thought to have allergies in the Denver experiment actually did; therefore, it is unlikely that this particular child has a food allergy. Using this line of reasoning, the doctor will probably try to isolate some other cause for the mother's worry, rather than subject the child to expensive and time-consuming allergy tests.

Many scenarios may be imagined in which Mr. Cochran also makes deductions from his inductively acquired premise about the tenderizing properties of tea. There had been a dinner party, hosted by one of Mr. Cochran's friends, to whom he had imparted his findings about the tea. Mr. Cochran arrived early only to be greeted at the door by the fretful host. The stew meat was of dreadful quality, the host told Mr. Cochran. No doubt it will be extremely chewy and tough. The party will be ruined. Mr. Cochran asked the host whether or not he'd taken his advice and stewed the meat in tea. The host replied affirmatively, adding that the meat, however, was gristly and bad. Nevertheless, Mr. Cochran was able to reassure the host that the meat, if it had been stewed in tea, will be tender. His reasoning ran something like this: "All meat stewed in tea is tenderized; this meat was stewed in tea; therefore this meat has been tenderized."

This rather simple example demonstrates the everyday use of a *syllogism,* which is a common form of reasoning used to make deductions. Many syllogisms deduce characteristics about unknowns by classifying them in categories whose properties are known. The syllogism proposed by the Greek philosopher Socrates is a classic example:

All men are mortal.   Major premise

Socrates is a man.   Minor premise

Therefore Socrates is mortal.   Conclusion

Once identified as belonging to the category of "man," Socrates immediately assumes the known properties of that category, which include mortality.

On paper, this is a rather clear-cut example of a syllogism hardly likely to puzzle even the amateur logician. But not all deductive reasoning is as clean and simple. Here, for instance, is a piece of pure deductive reasoning that consists of a complicated series of syllogistic steps made in rapid succession:

Freud once told the story of how an East European Jew . . . observed in the train which was taking him home to his village a young man who seemed to be going there too. As the two sat alone in the compartment, the Jew, puzzled about the stranger, began to work things out: "Only peasants and Jews live there. He is not dressed like either, but still, he is reading a book, so he must be Jewish. But why to our village? Only fifty families live there, and most are poor. Oh, but wait, Mr. Shmuel, the merchant, has two daughters: one of them is married, but for the other he has been seeking a husband. Mr. Shmuel is rich, and lately has acquired airs, so he would not want anyone from the village for his daughter. He must have asked the marriage broker to find a son-in-law from the outside. But Mr. Shmuel is old and cannot travel to meet a new family, so he would probably want a son-in-law from a family he knows. This means it would have to be one that had lived in the village but moved away. Who? The Cohen family had a son. Twenty years ago they moved to Budapest. What can a Jewish boy do there? Become a doctor. Mr. Shmuel would like a doctor in the family. A doctor needs a large dowry. The boy opposite is neat, but not well dressed. Dr. Cohen. But in Budapest, Cohen wouldn't do. Probably changed his name. In Budapest? To Kovacs—a name which comes as naturally to Hungarians as Cohen to Jews."

As the train drew into the village station, the old Jew said to the young man: "Excuse me, Dr. Kovacs, if Mr. Shmuel is not waiting for you at the station, I'll take you to his home and introduce you to your betrothed." Replied the astonished young man: "How do you know who I am and where I'm going? Not a word has passed between us."

"How do I know?" said the old man with a smile. "It stands to reason."

David Abrahamsen, *Nixon Versus Nixon*

This is the sort of reasoning with which Sherlock Holmes made a name for himself. Using a series of premises that he had formulated from his life in the village, the old man was able to deduce the unknown from the known.

In practice, our daily processes of reasoning consist of innumerable leaps of induction and deduction. When you observe, year after year, that anyone who goes out into the rain gets wet, you are reasoning *inductively;* but when you decide to wear a raincoat to keep you from getting wet in the rain, you are reasoning *deductively.* Both forms of reasoning are essential to logical thinking. Overreliance on deductive reasoning alone leads eventually to bigoted, stereotyped thinking, because it is only a matter of time before the premises we have accumulated in our heads become stale and inaccurate. The other side of the coin is induction practiced to an obsessive degree, in which the reasoner accepts no premises not directly yielded by his own experiments and observations. Such an insistence would create a chronic doubting Thomas, hardly able to function in a complicated world where men and women constantly presume the basic truth and accuracy of one another's reports.

Again, here is a chart that summarizes the way deduction works.

CHARACTERISTICS OF DEDUCTIVE REASONING

1. Deductive reasoning moves from the general to the specific.
2. A deductive argument consists of three parts: major premise, minor premise, and conclusion.
3. A deductive argument is valid if the conclusion logically follows from the premises.
4. A deductive conclusion may be judged true or false depending on whether the premises are true or false. If both premises are true, the conclusion must be true.

AVOID COMMON FALLACIES OF THINKING.   Arguments may be corrupted in a nearly inexhaustible number of ways. But some of these ways have become well enough recognized as to be assembled into categories. The most common fallacies are listed below under their English and Latin names.

Arguing in circles (*petitio principii*). An argument is illogical if its conclusion merely repeats its major premise. Such an argument is said to "beg the question," or to be "circular." Here is an example:

The Bible is the word of God. How do I know it is the word of God? Because in verse after verse the Old as well as the New Testament tells us that it is God speaking. When God says it's His word, that's good enough for me.

In effect, the speaker says that the Bible is the word of God because the Bible says so. A variation on this same error is shown below:

"The citizens of New York are more sophisticated than the citizens of Los Angeles."

"How do you know?"

"Because New Yorkers are far less crude and boorish."

Or, in other words, New Yorkers are more sophisticated than Angelenos because New Yorkers are more sophisticated.

Being irrelevant (*ignoratio elenchi*). Varieties of this error exist, many of which are to be commonly found in political speeches. The aim of the arguer who uses such tactics is to divert the reader's or listener's attention from the issue and focus it instead on unrelated matters. Different ruses may be brought to bear. The *red herring* is a favorite tactic of demagogues and unscrupulous debaters. The term comes from a practice in hunting, where the strong scent of a herring was sometimes used to distract hounds on the trail of game. Here is an example of the red-herring tactic:

Now certain government leaders tell us that we must not display Nativity scenes in our store windows at Christmas time. The question is, do we want to be governed by godless men?

That is not the question at all, nor does it follow that people opposed to Nativity scenes are godless; they may simply be sensitive to religions other than Christianity.

Another typical error of irrelevancy is the *ad hominem* argument, which attacks a person instead of an issue. Here is an example:

Don't give Mr. Finchley a penny when he tries to collect money for a mobile unit to be used by the school to teach students fire prevention. Mr. Finchley is an avowed atheist who lives openly with a mistress.

Entirely overlooked are the pros and cons of the usefulness of the mobile unit.

The *ad populum* technique uses a similar diverting device. But here the diversion is created by an appeal to popular, though irrelevant, sentiment:

Virgil Pettis is bound to be a wonderful president. He overcame polio when he was a teenager and he has always stuck up for the rights of little people and victims of tyranny. He is a man cut from the cloth of Lincoln and Jefferson.

This argument hopes to persuade voters to cast their lots for a candidate by dazzling them with appeals to pity and patriotic nostalgia rather than by citing the candidates' abilities, experience in government, or intelligence.

BE HARD-HEADED IN YOUR USE OF EVIDENCE.   Nothing takes the place of facts, experience, statistics, or exhibits that supply a finite, definite, and incontestable edge to your assertions. Naturally, no one is an expert on all things, and hard evidence is often difficult to come by. However, the campus library is still a storehouse of innumerable facts, uncountable numbers, and irrefutable data. Look up the information you need. Here are some assertions of mush and assertions of granite:

Mush   Hot dogs are horrible things to eat and have been proven to be very bad for you because they are very high in fat and chemicals.

Granite   According to the U.S. Department of Agriculture, since 1937 the frankfurter has gone from 19% fat and 19.6% protein to 28% fat and only 11.7% protein. (The rest is water, salt, spices and preservatives.) This deterioration is yet another of technology's ambiguous gifts.

"The Decline and Fill of the American Hotdog," *Time*

Mush   People can reduce and lose weight. Many celebrities, including well-known actors, athletes, and politicians, have successfully lost weight. If they can, so can everyone.

Granite   People can reduce and lose weight. Alfred Hitchcock went from 365 lbs. to a weight of 200 lbs. by eating only steak and cutting down on liquor; Jackie Gleason scaled down from 280 lbs. to 221 lbs. Maria Callas likewise went from a tumorous 215 lbs. to a trim 135 lbs. Even Lyndon Johnson, when he was Vice President, lost 31 lbs. in less than 10 weeks after being elected to the post in 1961.

Jean Meyer, *Overweight: Causes, Cost, and Control*

Your evidence must be specific. All factual prose writing depends on specifics. Pack a series of pinpoint specifics in a paragraph, and it will acquire a zesty sting that will do honor to your wit and style. When the paragraph is part of an argument whose intent is to convince and persuade a reader, the specifics are even more indispensable. This applies not only to the use of facts, but to the use of general details.

Some arguments fare badly with facts, but do better with overall detail. For instance, if you were writing an essay opposing beauty contests, facts about them would probably not dissuade your reader. Love or hate for beauty contests is not usually founded on fact alone, but on a person's underlying values. You may hate beauty contests because you think they *degrade* a woman into a sex object, whereas another person may think that they *elevate* a woman into an art object. A remorseless barrage of facts about the number of beauty contests held in America will probably not change your reader's mind about them. What you must do is draw a graphic picture showing the grotesque side of beauty contests. To do this, you desperately need specific, graphic detail. Here are two examples of arguments against beauty contests. The first is mush in its use of details:

I am against beauty pageants because they degrade women. They show the superficial side of the contestants. They never really evaluate the inside person. The whole deal is about bosoms and legs. Then all the women watching the contestants feel inferior because they don't feel as beautiful and desirable as the girls up on the stage. To me that is degrading womanhood. When the time comes for the winner to receive the flowers and the crown, I feel depressed that our country wastes its time and money on beauty pageants.

The argument starts out with a strong controlling idea but has not amounted to two sentences before we realize that the writer has little to say. His details are weak or nonexistent. One has the urge to yell: "Prove to me that you are right! Show me!" The following has a better beginning and is sharper and more specific in the use of details:

> I am against beauty pageants because they degrade women. By "degrade" I mean they force women to be less than what they really are. What the audience sees is a beautifully proportioned smiling mannequin, parading gracefully up and down a light-flooded ramp, to the tune of some lilting band music. Her smile is fixed, her beauty is lacquered. The master of ceremonies asks her some inane question, such as: "How does it feel to be a runner-up in the Miss Rootbeer of Indiana Contest?" The mannequin twirps a delighted giggle and spreads her lips into a wide smile that exhibits gleamingly white teeth. If the girl has an I.Q., the judges could never discern it because she is treated as if she were made of plastic, not flesh and blood. Each year, 150 such pageants are held in California alone, sponsored as advertising by big companies that sell every sort of commodity from oranges to toothpaste. And in each pageant between ten and fifty girls must go through this degrading demotion to mannequin status. The last pageant I attended was the Miss International Trade competition. And when the girls walked out on stage, I almost expected them to jump through circus hoops held by the M.C., some honey-voiced executive who stood to gain from the advertising of the pageant.

The grotesqueness of beauty contests is hammered home by effective use of details. The author appears to have actually attended beauty pageants and to know some facts about them—the number in California each year, what questions the women are asked, the names of certain pageants, and who profits from them. If you thought that beauty contests elevate women, here is an argument showing how they degrade. Chances are that this passage—replete with vivid details and graphic adjectives—is more likely to persuade you than the first.

Evidence is gathered through work. Checking library sources, consulting encyclopedias, and plodding through stacks of articles, books, or pamphlets is work, no question about that. But if you want to formulate a strong argument, that is what you will have to do.

QUOTE AUTHORITIES. An argument is strengthened by the support of an *authority*—a person who is generally accepted by his or her peers as an expert. Usually, he or she is an authority on a particular subject and is known to be fair and objective. For example, Jack Landau, a respected journalist known for his support of a free press, might be quoted in an argument against the gag rule that is sometimes invoked in certain trials. Or Steffi Graf might be quoted in an argument that advocates equivalent tournament purses for both male and female tennis players.

How do you find authorities and experts? By reading and by checking library sources such as the *Reader's Guide to Periodical Literature*, encyclopedias, *Who's Who*, and other reference books. Relevant personal experiences may also be used as testimonial evidence. For instance, in an argument against the legalization of marijuana, you may wish to quote a former user of the drug who has had bad experiences with it. Or in an argument against the welfare system, you may wish to cite the case of a mother of four who has been debased and ill-treated by the system. Your own experience may also be worth quoting, providing you do not base your entire argument on it. Few arguments are flimsier than the one that waxes contentiously on the basis of a single, unrepresentative experience. Here are some examples of how testimonial evidence may be incorporated into an argument:

No authority	Thomas Jefferson was not the moral saint students study in grade school.
With authority	Thomas Jefferson, far from being the moral saint studied by grade school students, was a man attracted to forbidden women, as indicated by Fawn Brodie's intimate history entitled *Thomas Jefferson*.
No authority	The quality of medical care in America varies with how much you can afford to pay, and how quickly you can demonstrate your ability to pay. Accident victims are sometimes turned away by hospitals because they have no insurance or proof of financial ability to pay.
With authority	The quality of medical care in America varies with how much you can afford to pay and how quickly you can demonstrate your ability to pay. Last summer, for instance, while climbing El Capitan in Yosemite, I fell and broke my leg. I was rescued by a group of passing hikers and driven to the nearest hospital, which refused to admit me because I had no proof of insurance. I was dressed in mountain climbing gear and sported a five-day growth of stubble on my face; my clothes had been shredded by the fall. To all appearances, I was a penniless tramp. Before the admitting nurse could dispatch me to a county hospital, one of the hikers, a well-known businessman in the area, vouched for my ability to pay. Only then was I admitted.

In sum, testimonial evidence allows you to incorporate into your argument a consensus of opinions supportive of your own views. Moreover, it permits you to add a human dimension to what might otherwise be a cut-and-dried recital of facts, figures, and statistics.

ANTICIPATE THE OPPOSITION.   A well-shaped argument does not ignore the opposition but anticipates refutations or objections by identifying them clearly and then showing their unreasonableness. This alerts the reader to the writer's knowledge of opposing arguments. If you neglect this step in arguing, you lay yourself wide open to the accusation of ignorance. In the following argument against the wasteful extravagance of using paper grocery bags, notice how the writer anticipates two major arguments of the opposition:

Can you believe that in the most well-educated, cultured nation in the world we consume and destroy a vital part of our natural resources without a second thought? Consider the average brown paper grocery bag, which is made from the pulp of trees. One of our most vital resources is transformed into a convenience that is used no place else in the world with such careless extravagance as here in the United States. And for what? To move groceries from store to car to home—to be used briefly as a trash bag and then to be pulverized by chemical action into a city sewage plant. How foolish and spoiled we are. A billion tons of lovely trees are destroyed annually, just to satisfy our compulsive need for convenience. How shallow we are to make this tradeoff from lush green beauty to tacky brown bags. One day in the future, people will have to look at pictures to be reminded that the Ozark Mountains were breathlessly beautiful in the fall as the deep green leaves turned to shimmering gold. Personal memories they will not have.

Of course, the big industries try to make us think that high living standards are more important than beauty. For example, George I. Kneeland, Chairman of the Board and Executive Officer of the St. Regis Paper Company, insists that "providing the highest possible standard of living for America is an urgent national priority." But I ask, what kind of value system is it that places higher priority on a trivial convenience than on the survival of Mother Earth?

Another argument is that paper is biodegradable and consequently not as polluting as plastic. But plastic bags do not have to be the substitute. People all over the world adapt to grocery carts, fishnet bags, or cloth containers. We could get into the habit of doing this too and we would be stopping our insane path of ecological mass murder.

Reading for Ideas

The idea of stopping the population explosion is not new and, in fact, has been proposed by numerous organizations concerned with the inability of our planet to continue feeding and housing the increasing masses of humans. Asimov's statistics are frightening and convincing. As you read, ask ourself what you are willing to do to avoid the catastrophe so persuasively foretold. What plan would you be willing to follow? Would your friends go along with your plan? If not, how could you sway them to your side?

PROFESSIONAL MODEL

The Case Against Man
Isaac Asimov

Isaac Asimov (b. 1920) is a Russian-born American biochemist, educator, and prolific writer. He is best known for his science fiction works, among them I, Robot *(1950),* The Caves of Steel *(1954),* The Gods Themselves *(1973),* Out of Everywhere *(1990), and* Atom: A Journey Across the Subatomic Cosmos *(1991). A popularizer of science, Asimov is the author of over a hundred books and a staggering variety of articles on nearly every imaginable topic.*

1   The first mistake is to think of mankind as a thing in itself. It isn't. It is part of an intricate web of life. And we can't think even of life as a thing in itself. It isn't. It is part of the intricate structure of a planet bathed by energy from the Sun.

2   The Earth, in the nearly 5 billion years since it assumed approximately its present form, has undergone a vast evolution. When it first came into being, it very likely lacked what we would today call an ocean and an atmosphere. These were formed by the gradual outward movement of material as the solid interior settled together.

3   Nor were ocean, atmosphere, and solid crust independent of each other after formation. There is interaction always: evaporation, condensation, solution, weathering. Far within the solid crust there are slow, continuing changes, too, of which hot springs, volcanoes, and earthquakes are the more noticeable manifestations here on the surface.

4   Between 2 billion and 3 billion years ago, portions of the surface water, bathed by the energetic radiation from the Sun, developed complicated compounds in organization sufficiently versatile to qualify as what we call "life." Life forms have become more complex and more various ever since.

5   But the life forms are as much part of the structure of the Earth as any inanimate portion is. It is all an inseparable part of a whole. If any animal is isolated totally from other forms of life, then death by starvation will surely follow. If isolated from water, death by dehydration will follow even faster. If isolated from air, whether free or dissolved in water, death by asphyxiation will follow still faster. If isolated from the Sun, animals will survive for a time, but plants would die, and if all plants died, all animals would starve.

6   It works in reverse, too, for the inanimate portion of Earth is shaped and molded by life. The nature of the atmosphere has been changed by plant activity (which adds to the air the free oxygen it could not otherwise retain). The soil is turned by earthworms, while enormous ocean reefs are formed by coral.

7   The entire planet, plus solar energy, is one enormous intricately interrelated system. The entire planet is a life form made up of nonliving portions and a large variety of living portions (as our own body is made up of nonliving crystals in bones and nonliving water in blood, as well as of a large variety of living portions).

8   In fact, we can pursue the analogy. A man is composed of 50 trillion cells of a variety of types, all interrelated and interdependent. Loss of some of those cells, such as those making up an entire leg, will seriously handicap all the rest of the organism: serious damage to a relatively few cells in an organ, such as the heart or kidneys, may end by killing all 50 trillion.

9   In the same way, on a planetary scale, the chopping down of an entire forest may not threaten Earth's life in general, but it will produce serious changes in the life forms of the region and even in the nature of the water runoff and, therefore, in the details of geological structure. A serious decline in the bee population will affect the numbers of those plants that depend on bees for fertilization, then the numbers of those animals that depend on those particular bee-fertilized plants, and so on.

10   Or consider cell growth. Cells in those organs that suffer constant wear and tear—as in the skin or in the intestinal lining—grow and multiply all life long. Other cells, not so exposed, as in nerve and muscle, do not multiply at all in the adult, under any circumstances. Still other organs, ordinarily quiescent, as liver and bone, stand ready to grow if that is necessary to replace damage. When the proper repairs are made, growth stops.

In a much looser and more flexible way, the same is true of the "planet organism"   11
(which we study in the science called ecology). If cougars grow too numerous, the deer
they live on are decimated, and some of the cougars die of starvation, so that their
"proper number" is restored. If too many cougars die, then the deer multiply with
particular rapidity, and cougars multiply quickly in turn, till the additional predators bring
down the number of deer again. Barring interference from outside, the eaters and the
eaten retain their proper numbers, and both are the better for it. (If the cougars are all
killed off, deer would multiply to the point where they destroy the plants they live off, and
more would then die of starvation than would have died of cougars.)

The neat economy of growth within an organism such as a human being is   12
sometimes—for what reason, we know not—disrupted, and a group of cells begins
growing without limit. This is the dread disease of cancer, and unless that growing group
of cells is somehow stopped, the wild growth will throw all the body structure out of true
and end by killing the organism itself.

In ecology, the same would happen if, for some reason, one particular type of   13
organism began to multiply without limit, killing its competitors and increasing its own
food supply at the expense of that of others. That, too, could end in the destruction of the
larger system—most or all of life and even of certain aspects of the inanimate
environment.

And this is exactly what is happening at this moment. For thousands of years, the   14
single species Homo sapiens, to which you and I have the dubious honor of belonging,
has been increasing in numbers. In the past couple of centuries, the rate of increase has
itself increased explosively.

At the time of Julius Caesar, when Earth's human population is estimated to have   15
been 150 million, that population was increasing at a rate such that it would double in
1,000 years if that rate remained steady. Today, with Earth's population estimated at
about 4,000 million (26 times what it was in Caesar's time), it is increasing at a rate
which, if steady, will cause it to double in 35 years.

The present rate of increase of Earth's swarming human population qualifies Homo   16
sapiens as an ecological cancer, which will destroy the ecology just as surely as any
ordinary cancer would destroy an organism.

The cure? Just what it is for any cancer. The cancerous growth must somehow be   17
stopped.

Of course, it will be. If we do nothing at all, the growth will stop, as a cancerous   18
growth in a man will stop if nothing is done. The man dies and the cancer dies with him.
And, analogously, the ecology will die and man will die with it.

How can the human population explosion be stopped? By raising the deathrate, or by   19
lowering the birthrate. There are no other alternatives. The deathrate will rise spontaneously and finally catastrophically, if we do nothing—and that within a few decades. To
make the birthrate fall, somehow (almost *any* how, in fact), is surely preferable, and that
is therefore the first order of mankind's business today.

Failing this, mankind would stand at the bar of abstract justice (for there may be no   20
posterity to judge) as the mass murderer of life generally, his own included, and mass
disrupter of the intricate planetary development that made life in its present glory
possible in the first place.

21   Am I too pessimistic? Can we allow the present rate of population increase to continue indefinitely, or at least for a good long time? Can we count on science to develop methods for cleaning up as we pollute, for replacing wasted resources with substitutes, for finding new food, new materials, more and better life for our waxing numbers?

22   Impossible! If the numbers continue to wax at the present rate.

23   Let us begin with a few estimates (admittedly not precise, but in the rough neighborhood of the truth).

24   The total mass of living objects on Earth is perhaps 20 trillion tons. There is usually a balance between eaters and eaten that is about 1 to 10 in favor of the eaten. There would therefore be about 10 times as much plant life (the eaten) as animal life (the eaters) on Earth. There is, in other words, just a little under 2 trillion tons of animal life on Earth.

25   But this is all the animal life that can exist, given the present quantity of plant life. If more animal life is somehow produced, it will strip down the plant life, reduce the food supply, and then enough animals will starve to restore the balance. If one species of animal life increases in mass, it can only be because other species correspondingly decrease. For every additional pound of human flesh on Earth, a pound of some other form of flesh must disappear.

26   The total mass of humanity now on Earth may be estimated at about 200 million tons, or one ten-thousandth the mass of all animal life. If mankind increases in numbers ten thousandfold, then Homo sapiens will be, perforce, the *only* animal species alive on Earth. It will be a world without elephants or lions, without cats or dogs, without fish or lobsters, without worms or bugs. What's more, to support the mass of human life, all the plant world must be put to service. Only plants edible to man must remain, and only those plants most concentratedly edible and with minimum waste.

27   At the present moment, the average density of population of the Earth's land surface is about 73 people per square mile. Increase that ten thousandfold and the average density will become 730,000 people per square mile, or more than seven times the density of the workday population of Manhattan. Even if we assume that mankind will somehow spread itself into vast cities floating on the ocean surface (or resting on the ocean floor), the average density of human life at the time when the last nonhuman animal must be killed would be 310,000 people per square mile over all the world, land and sea alike, or a little better than three times the density of modern Manhattan at noon.

28   We have the vision, then, of high-rise apartments, higher and more thickly spaced than in Manhattan at present, spreading all over the world, across all the mountains, across the Sahara Desert, across Antarctica, across all the oceans; all with their load of humanity and with no other form of animal life beside. And on the roof of all those buildings are the algae farms, with little plant cells exposed to the Sun so that they might grow rapidly and, without waste, form protein for all the mighty population of 35 trillion human beings.

29   Is that tolerable? Even if science produced all the energy and materials mankind could want, kept them all fed with algae, all educated, all amused—is the planetary high-rise tolerable?

30   And if it were, can we double the population further in 35 more years? And then double it again in another 35 years? Where will the food come from? What will persuade

the algae to multiply faster than the light energy they absorb makes possible? What will speed up the Sun to add the energy to make it possible? And if vast supplies of fusion energy are added to supplement the Sun, how will we get rid of the equally vast supplies of heat that will be produced? And after the icecaps are melted and the oceans boiled into steam, what?

Can we bleed off the mass of humanity to other worlds? Right now, the number of human beings on Earth is increasing by 80 million per year, and each year that number goes up by 1 and a fraction percent. Can we really suppose that we can send 80 million people per year to the Moon, Mars, and elsewhere, and engineer those worlds to support those people? And even so, merely remain in the same place ourselves? 31

No! Not the most optimistic visionary in the world could honestly convince himself that space travel is the solution to our population problem, if the present rate of increase is sustained. 32

But when will this planetary high-rise culture come about? How long will it take to increase Earth's population to that impossible point at the present doubling rate of once every 35 years? If it will take 1 million years or even 100,000, then, for goodness sake, let's not worry just yet. 33

Well, we don't have that kind of time. We will reach that dead end in no more than 460 years. 34

At the rate we are going, without birth control, then even if science serves us in an absolutely ideal way, we will reach the planetary high-rise with no animals but man, with no plants but algae, with no room for even one more person, by A.D. 2430. 35

And if science serves us in less than an ideal way (as it certainly will), the end will come sooner, much sooner, and mankind will start fading long, long before he is forced to construct that building that will cover all the Earth's surface. 36

So if birth control *must* come by A.D. 2430 at the very latest, even in an ideal world of advancing science, let it come *now,* in heaven's name, while there are still oak trees in the world and daisies and tigers and butterflies, and while there is still open land and space, and before the cancer called man proves fatal to life and the planet. 37

Vocabulary

quiescent (10)	decimated (11)	waxing (21)
ecology (11)	catastrophically (19)	fusion (30)

Questions on Meaning and Technique

1. What is the author's main argument? Where is it explicitly stated? What advantage does such placement have?

2. According to the author, what conditions will prevail on earth by A.D. 2430 if matters keep going the way they are?

3. How does the author use cancer as a way to clarify the problem of ecological imbalance?

4. What similarities does the author draw between the life processes of a person and those of the planet?

5. What do the statistics and mathematical calculations add to the argument?

6. According to the author, why is moving to other planets not a plausible answer?

7. Do you agree with Asimov's sense of urgency? What other world problem, if any, do you consider more important? Why?

STUDENT ESSAY

First Draft   Francis Shriver

Against Fraternities

As portrayed in the 1977 hit movie <u>Animal House,</u> college fraternities are a hotbed of   1

in real life,

excessive drinking, casual sex, vandalism, and generally licentious behavior. But, unlike

the movie, the results of such conduct are hardly laughable. Even though nationwide

in various fraternities

membership is at an all-time high of 350,000, fraternities are meeting with harsh criticism

from university leaders and civic authorities alike. In the face of several recent incidents,

fraternity behavior can no longer be viewed as harmless schoolboy high jinks , (Insert A)

Adds focus and force to the proposition.

At the center of the controversy is the problem of hazing, an initiation ritual that has   2

for   the

been around as long as fraternities themselves. Hazing occurs when brothers physically

that is,

or mentally abuse pledges, or candidates for membership. When I was a pledge, I was

elegant

commanded to drink excessively, appear in boxer shorts at an alumni function, and run

absurd

to the grocery store on late-night errands for brothers. I became so disillusioned with the

whole fraternity system that I withdrew my pledgeship. Luckily, I was not physically

pledges

Transition adds coherence.

harmed by the hazing process, but others have not been so fortunate. At Long Island

for example,

University, a pledge was hospitalized with broken ribs after being beaten by brothers

who acted in the name of an initiation tradition. A pledge at Oklahoma State University

by forcing him to

claimed that brothers tried to build "unity through terror" ~~after he~~ endured hours of

(Insert B)

Adds details to stress the humiliation involved.

humiliating criticism. The Phi Gamma Deltas, or Fijis, at Arizona State University

(Insert A)

but must be seen for what it truly is--a dangerous
threat to the lives of innocent students.

(Insert B)

including sarcastic attacks on his intelligence, looks,
and personality.

frequently forced pledges to vomit and regularly interrupted their sleep ~~by shaking them during the night~~. At North
Carolina ~~A. and T.,~~ *Agricultural and Technical State University,* ~~a predominantly black college,~~ an Omega Psi Phi member was
convicted on seven counts of assault with a deadly weapon after participating in his
fraternity's "Turn Back Night." During this infamous Omega tradition, pledges were
treated to a meal of dog food and cheap wine, several paddlings, and a midnight trip to
a densely wooded area, far from the campus, where they were abandoned and told to
find their way home. At Chopin State University in Baltimore, a pledge took a fraternity
to court after his flesh was branded with a Greek insignia.

3   As despicable as these incidents seem, others with more serious consequences have
occurred. In *For instance,* February of 1988 a Rutgers University freshman died after an induction
ceremony at the Lambda Chi House. At the behest of his soon-to-be brothers, James
Callahan, *aged* 18, ~~was drinking excessively until~~ *drank so much liquor that* he collapsed. According to Eileen Stevens,
President of CHUCK (Committee to Halt Useless College Killings), 43 deaths of this
nature have occurred since 1978, including that of her own brother. This is a terrifyingly
high price to pay for the maintenance of ~~needless~~ *useless* macho traditions.

4   ~~While~~ *Although* not as immediately dangerous as hazing, racism among fraternities is a ~~growing~~ problem
~~that is growing.~~ At the University of Southern California, in 1986, members of a rival
fraternity spray painted anti-Semitic slogans on the sidewalk in front of a Jewish
fraternity house. *In another disgraceful episode,* Sigma Alpha Epsilon brothers (at Oklahoma State *University,*) were reprimanded
after holding a "plantation party," during which several members masqueraded as black
slaves. Kappa Alpha chapters, traditionally strong in the Southeast, hold "Old South"
parties annually. At these parties, females dress as southern belles while the K.A.s don
Confederate Army uniforms *in a satirical reenactment of the days when slavery prevailed*. A Fiji Island party at the University of Wisconsin was halted
after college officials deemed the tropical garb and black makeup worn by the brothers
as *racially* offensive. Similarly, the Delta Kappa Epsilons at *Louisiana's* Tulane University blackened their
faces during the 30th annual "Debutramp" Parade. Then, at a party following this event,
brothers carrying torches allegedly attacked several black women and tore apart their
clothing while yelling racist epithets.

5   Two years ago, at the University of Alabama, I witnessed a campus-wide furor over a
racist incident that involved the fraternities. When a black sorority was allowed to
occupy a house on the previously all-white sorority row, some students reacted by

Transition adds coherence.

Substitute clause is more direct and therefore forceful.

Better transition to next example.

Explanation added.

burning crosses on the lawn of that house. The identity of the culprits [~~remains anonymous~~] *has never been disclosed*, but their behavior is indicative of the racist attitudes of the majority of brothers in Tuscaloosa. This point is underscored by the disparity in the size of the houses of white and black fraternities. Whereas white fraternity brothers dwell in centrally located, columned houses with manicured lawns, blacks are relegated to tiny decrepit buildings out in the woods.

Although subtle [~~While~~] racist attitudes *within* [~~among~~] fraternities may be hard to control, blatantly criminal 7 activities should be eradicated. (Insert C) Fortunately, the Alpha Tau Omegas at the University of Georgia were expelled from the campus last year, after a young woman was sexually abused in their fraternity house. This young woman woke up in the basement of the fraternity house, (naked,) after an all-night party with fraternity-supplied booze. Her family sued *the university for damages and won*. At the University of Illinois, home of the nation's most active fraternity system--with 52 houses and 3,500 members--two brothers were accused of sexually assaulting a 15-year-old girl who happened to be at a pre-football game party at the Lambda Chi Alpha house. Furthermore, the university health center has reported that over half of the 25 rape victims they counsel each semester are raped by fraternity members. The fact that these cases are being taken to court is a good sign, indicating that some people are so outraged that they are no longer willing to cover up for the arrogant criminality of certain fraternities. *Concerned citizens* [~~They~~] do not want fraternities to become the breeding ground for individual, racist, or sexual violence.

Lest the Greek letters on fraternity T-shirts be replaced by prison numbers, fraternities simply must clean up their act. To their credit, some are currently doing [~~this~~] *so* *replacing fraternity pranks with* by [~~holding~~] charity benefits, *such as* [~~like~~] dance contests and marathon sporting events. Others are visiting nursing homes and renovating dilapidated houses for the poor. Tim Mourigan, President of the University of Southern California's Sigma Chi Chapter, recently commented, "We're really trying to break the party animal mold." The national leadership

The additional comments strengthen the proposition.

Misplaced modifier corrected.

Reference needed.

Wording makes point clearer.

(Insert C)

All civilized Americans must rally to close any fraternity exhibiting the slightest tendency toward cruelty, racism, or any other barbaric behavior. We must insist on a strict code of decency in fraternity activities.

of the eight black fraternities, which had particularly serious problems with hazing and resultant lawsuits, recently went a step further by banning the entire pledge system. How fraternities will select new members is not known, but Georgia State's Omega Psi Phi chapter offers a possible model. This chapter chooses prospective brothers based on *the* criteria of *high* academic *achievement* and *altruistic* community service.

8　Pressure for fraternity reform is coming from ~~other sources~~ *state legislatures* as well. Twenty-eight states, including Georgia, have enacted anti-hazing legislation. In order to keep control of the fraternities, authorities now must strictly enforce ~~this legislation~~ *these laws*.

Specifics.

9　The greatest responsibility lies with the universities themselves. Some are responding to it, others are fleeing from it. Nevertheless, statistics form a hopeful picture. Whereas in 1985, according to the Center for the Study of the College Fraternity, only 15 percent of the colleges or universities claimed responsibility for their fraternities, in 1986 that figure climbed to 32 percent. ~~In 1983 less than two per cent of the surveyed colleges had a completely independent fraternity system.~~ In 1986, almost 35 percent of the schools had a laisez-faire policy toward their "Greeks." *Today,* More and more universities are imposing strict standards on their fraternities. A case in point is Rutgers, where all of the fraternities' activities have been indefinitely suspended because of the death of James Callahan. At Oklahoma State *University* officials have brought in a representative from the U.S. Justice Department to help ease racial tensions among the fraternities. At the University of Southern California, fraternities have been forced by the administration to check the age of all party goers and display signs ~~stating the~~ *announcing legal* drinking age. The fraternities are supplying buses and limousines for brothers and their dates. ~~This~~ preclude*s to* the possibility of drunk driving lawsuits. ~~and~~ *This new attitude* shows responsible thinking--a much needed change on the part of fraternities.

Deletes irrelevant information.

10　I am not arguing for the ~~demise~~ *dismantling* of fraternities because these organizations can provide an important function--that of bringing together college freshmen and ~~providing~~ *giving* them ~~with~~ a support group and some lifelong friendships. ~~Being a social organization that sponsors violent and lurid acts is one thing, but being a positive and productive organization is~~ *The fraternity as one thing, but* quite another. At this time more *strictly enforced* regulation by all involved parties is needed to ensure that no more innocent people are hurt by the careless "Greek" life-style.

Transposition makes for better logic.

STUDENT ESSAY

Final Draft   Francis Shriver

Against Fraternities

1   As portrayed in the 1977 hit movie *Animal House,* college fraternities are a hotbed of excessive drinking, casual sex, vandalism, and generally licentious behavior. But, in real life, unlike the movie, the results of such conduct are hardly laughable. Even though nationwide membership in various fraternities is at an all-time high of 350,000, fraternities are meeting with harsh criticism from university leaders and civic authorities alike. In the face of several recent incidents, fraternity behavior can no longer be viewed as harmless schoolboy high jinks, but must be seen for what it truly is—a dangerous threat to the lives of innocent students.

2   At the center of the controversy is the problem of hazing, an initiation ritual that has been around for as long as the fraternities themselves. Hazing occurs when brothers physically or mentally abuse pledges, that is, candidates for membership. When I was a pledge, I was commanded to drink excessively, appear in boxer shorts at an elegant alumni function, and run to the grocery store on absurd late-night errands for brothers. I became so disillusioned with the whole fraternity system that I withdrew my pledgeship. Luckily, I was not physically harmed by the hazing process, but other pledges have not been so fortunate. At Long Island University, for example, a pledge was hospitalized with broken ribs after being beaten by brothers who acted in the name of an initiation tradition. A pledge at Oklahoma State University claimed that brothers tried to build "unity through terror" by forcing him to endure hours of humiliating criticism, including sarcastic attacks on his intelligence, looks, and personality. The Phi Gamma Deltas, or Fijis, at Arizona State University frequently forced pledges to vomit and regularly interrupted their sleep by shaking them during the night. At North Carolina Agricultural and Technical State University, an Omega Psi Phi member was convicted on seven counts of assault with a deadly weapon after participating in his fraternity's "Turn Back Night." During this infamous Omega tradition, pledges were treated to a meal of dog food and cheap wine, several paddlings, and a midnight trip to a densely wooded area, far from the campus, where

they were abandoned and told to find their way home. At Chopin State University in Baltimore, a pledge took a fraternity to court after his flesh was branded with a Greek insignia.

As despicable as these incidents seem, others with more serious consequences have occurred. For instance, in February of 1988 a Rutgers University freshman died after an induction ceremony at the Lambda Chi house. At the behest of his soon-to-be brothers, James Callahan, aged 18, drank so much liquor that he collapsed. According to Eileen Stevens, President of CHUCK (Committee to Halt Useless College Killings), 43 deaths of this nature have occurred since 1978, including that of her own brother. This is a terrifyingly high price to pay for the maintenance of useless macho traditions.

Although not as immediately dangerous as hazing, racism among fraternities is a growing problem. At the University of Southern California, in 1986, members of a rival fraternity spray painted anti-Semitic slogans on the sidewalk in front of a Jewish fraternity house. In another disgraceful episode, at Oklahoma State University, Sigma Alpha Epsilon brothers were reprimanded after holding a "plantation party," during which several members masqueraded as black slaves. Kappa Alpha chapters, traditionally strong in the Southeast, hold "Old South" parties annually. At these parties, females dress as southern belles while the K.A.s don Confederate Army uniforms in a satirical reenactment of the days when slavery prevailed. A Fiji Island party at the University of Wisconsin was halted after college officials deemed the tropical garb and black makeup worn by the brothers as racially offensive. Similarly, the Delta Kappa Epsilons at Louisiana's Tulane University blackened their faces during the 30th annual "Debutramp" Parade. Then, at a party following this event, brothers carrying torches allegedly attacked several black women and tore apart their clothing while yelling racist epithets.

Two years ago, at the University of Alabama, I witnessed a campus-wide furor over a racist incident that involved the fraternities. When a black sorority was allowed to occupy a house on the previously all-white sorority row, some students reacted by burning crosses on the lawn of that house. The identity of the culprits has never been disclosed, but their behavior is indicative of the racist attitudes of the majority of brothers in Tuscaloosa. This point is underscored by the disparity in the size of the houses of white and black fraternities. Whereas white fraternity brothers dwell in centrally located columned houses with manicured lawns, blacks are relegated to tiny, decrepit buildings out in the woods.

6   Although subtle racist attitudes within fraternities may be hard to control, blatantly criminal activities should be eradicated. All civilized Americans must rally to close any fraternity exhibiting the slightest tendency toward cruelty, racism, or any other barbaric behavior. We must insist on a strict code of decency in fraternity activities. Fortunately, the Alpha Tau Omegas at the University of Georgia were expelled from the campus last year, after a young woman was sexually abused in their fraternity house. This young woman woke up, naked, in the basement of the fraternity house after an all-night party with fraternity-supplied booze. Her family sued the university for damages and won. At the University of Illinois, home of the nation's most active fraternity system—with 52 houses and 3,500 members—two brothers were accused of sexually assaulting a 15-year-old girl who happened to be at a pre-football game party at the Lambda Chi Alpha house. Furthermore, the university health center has reported that over half of the 25 rape victims they counsel each semester are raped by fraternity members. The fact that these cases are being taken to court is a good sign, indicating that some people are so outraged that they are no longer willing to cover up for the arrogant criminality of certain fraternities. Concerned citizens do not want fraternities to become the breeding ground for individual, racist, or sexual violence.

7   Lest the Greek letters on fraternity T-shirts be replaced by prison numbers, fraternities simply must clean up their act. To their credit, some are currently doing so by replacing fraternity pranks with charity benefits, such as dance contests and marathon sporting events. Others are visiting nursing homes and renovating dilapidated houses for the poor. Tim Mourigan, President of the University of Southern California's Sigma Chi Chapter, recently commented, "We're really trying to break the party animal mold." The national leadership of the eight black fraternities, which had particularly serious problems with hazing and resultant lawsuits, recently went a step further by banning the entire pledge system. How fraternities will select new members is not known, but Georgia State's Omega Psi Phi chapter offers a possible model. This chapter chooses prospective brothers based on the criteria of high academic achievement and altruistic community service.

Pressure for fraternity reform is coming from state legislatures as well. Twenty-eight   8
states, including Georgia, have enacted anti-hazing legislation. In order to keep control
of the fraternities, authorities now must strictly enforce these laws.

The greatest responsibility lies with the universities themselves. Some are responding   9
to it, others are fleeing from it. Nevertheless, statistics form a hopeful picture. Whereas in
1985, according to the Center for the Study of the College Fraternity, only 15 percent of
the colleges or universities claimed responsibility for their fraternities, in 1986 that figure
climbed to 32 percent. In 1986, almost 35 percent of the schools had a laissez-faire policy
toward their "Greeks." Today, more and more universities are imposing strict standards
on their fraternities. A case in point is Rutgers, where all of the fraternities' activities
have been indefinitely suspended because of the death of James Callahan. At Oklahoma
State University, officials have brought in a representative from the U.S. Justice Department to help ease racial tensions among the fraternities. At the University of Southern
California, fraternities have been forced by the administration to check the age of all
party goers and display signs announcing the legal drinking age. The fraternities are supplying buses and limousines for brothers and their dates to preclude the possibility of
drunk driving lawsuits. This new attitude shows responsible thinking—a much needed
change on the part of fraternities.

I am not arguing for the dismantling of fraternities, because these organizations can   10
provide an important function—that of bringing together college freshmen and giving
them a support group and some lifelong friendships. The fraternity as a positive and
productive organization is one thing, but being a social organization that sponsors
violent and lurid acts is quite another. At this time more strictly enforced regulations by
all involved parties is needed to ensure that no more innocent people are hurt by the
careless "Greek" life-style.

READING FOR IDEAS

This essay argues against bilingualism, a touchy subject with many immigrant
groups, especially Hispanics, the largest bloc of immigrants in the United States
whose native language is not English. The author argues that bilingualism eventually leads to separatism and separatist sentiments. Canada, for example, struggled

for years with the problem of whether French should be acknowledged as a primary language. Because the problem was never solved, Quebec voted in 1990 to secede from Canada and declare French as its native language. For our own country the problem has grown in complexity during the last decade as more and more immigrants, speaking various languages, have sought refuge here. We are told that some colleges educate students representing as many as 100 different languages. You need to think seriously about the melting-pot effect of so much ethnic diversity in our country. How can we turn ethnic diversity into a social advantage? What can be done to ensure that students from foreign countries acquire excellent English language skills while maintaining their cultural heritage?

ALTERNATE READING

Against a Confusion of Tongues
William A. Henry III

William Alfred Henry III (b. 1950) was born in South Orange, New Jersey, and educated at Yale (B.A. 1971). Henry has been an art critic and editorial writer for the Boston Globe. *Since 1981 he has been an associate editor with* Time. *He is the author of several books, including* The Insider's Guide to the Colleges *(1970) and* The Blue Football Book *(1971). In 1980 he won the Pulitzer Prize for criticism.*

"We have room for but one language here, and that is the English language, for we intend to see that the crucible turns our people out as Americans and not as dwellers in a polyglot boarding house."—Theodore Roosevelt

1   In the store windows of Los Angeles, gathering place of the world's aspiring peoples, the signs today ought to read, "English spoken here." Supermarket price tags are often written in Korean, restaurant menus in Chinese, employment-office signs in Spanish. In the new city of dreams, where gold can be earned if not found on the sidewalk, there are laborers and businessmen who have lived five, ten, 20 years in America without learning to speak English. English is not the common denominator for many of these new Americans. Disturbingly, some of them insist it need not be.

2   America's image of itself as a melting pot, enriched by every culture yet subsuming all of them, dates back far beyond the huddled yearning masses at the Baja California border and Ellis Island, beyond the passage in steerage of victims of the potato famine and the high-minded Teutonic settlements in the nascent Midwest. Just months after the Revolution was won, in 1782, French-American writer Michel-Guillaume-Jean de Crèvecoeur said of his adopted land: "Individuals of all nations are melted into a new race of men." Americans embittered by the wars of Europe knew that fusing diversity into unity was more than a poetic ideal, it was a practical necessity. In 1820 future Congressman Edward Everett warned, "From the days of the Tower of Babel, confusion of tongues has ever been one of the most active causes of political misunderstanding."

The successive waves of immigrants did not readily embrace the new culture, even   3
when intimidated by the xenophobia of the know-nothing era or two World Wars. Says
historian James Banks: "Each nationality group tried desperately to remake North
America in the image of its native land." When the question arose of making the U.S.
multilingual or multicultural in public affairs, however, Congress stood firm. In the 1790s,
1840s, and 1860s, the lawmakers voted down pleas to print Government documents in
German. Predominantly French-speaking Louisiana sought statehood in 1812; the state
constitution that it submitted for approval specified that its official language would be
English. A century later, New Mexico was welcomed into the union, but only after an
influx of settlers from the North and East had made English, not Spanish, the majority
tongue.

Occasional concentrations of immigrants were able to win local recognition of their   4
language and thereby enforce an early form of affirmative action: by 1899 nearly 18,000
pupils in Cincinnati divided their school time between courses in German and in English,
thus providing employment for 186 German-speaking teachers. In 1917 San Francisco
taught German in eight primary schools, Italian in six, French in four and Spanish in two.
Yet when most cities consented to teach immigrant children in their native Chinese or
Polish or Yiddish or Gujarati, the clearly stated goal was to transform the students as
quickly as possible into speakers of English and full participants in society.

Now, however, a new bilingualism and biculturalism is being promulgated that would   5
deliberately fragment the nation into separate, unassimilated groups. The movement
seems to take much of its ideology from the black separatism of the 1960s but derives its
political force from the unprecedented raw numbers—15 million or more—of a group
linked to a single tongue, Spanish. The new metaphor is not the melting pot but the salad
bowl, with each element distinct. The biculturalists seek to use public services, particularly
schools, not to Americanize the young but to heighten their consciousness of belonging
to another heritage. Contends Thomás A. Arciniega, vice president for academic affairs
at California State University at Fresno: "The promotion of cultural differences has to be
recognized as a valid and legitimate educational goal." Miguel Gonzalez-Pando, director
of the Center for Latino Education at Florida International University in Miami, says: "I
speak Spanish at home, my social relations are mostly in Spanish, and I am raising my
daughter as a Cuban American. It is a question of freedom of choice." In Gonzalez-
Pando's city, where Hispanics outnumber whites, the anti-assimilationist theory has
become accepted practice: Miami's youth can take twelve years of bilingual public
schooling with no pretense made that the program is transitional toward anything. The
potential for separatism is greater in Los Angeles. Philip Hawley, president of the Carter
Hawley Hale retail store chain, cautions: "This is the only area in the U.S. that over the
next 50 years could have a polarization into two distinct cultures, of the kind that brought
about the Quebec situation in Canada." Professor Rodolfo Acuña of California State
University at Northridge concurs. Says Acuña: "Talk of secession may come when there
are shrinking economic resources and rising expectations among have-not Hispanics."

Already the separatists who resist accepting English have won laws and court cases   6
mandating provision of social services, some government instructions, even election
ballots in Spanish. The legitimizing effect of these decisions can be seen in the
proliferation of billboards, roadside signs and other public communications posted in

Spanish. Acknowledges Professor Ramon Ruiz of the University of California at San Diego: "The separatism question is with us already." The most portentous evidence is in the classrooms. Like its political cousins, equal opportunity and social justice, bilingual education is a catchall term that means what the speaker wishes it to mean.

7   There are at least four ways for schools to teach students who speak another language at home:

8   1) Total immersion in English, which relies on the proven ability of children to master new languages. Advocates of bilingual education argue that this approach disorients children and sometimes impedes their progress in other subjects, because those who have already mastered several grades' worth of material in their first language may be compelled to take English-language classes with much younger or slower students.

9   2) Short-term bilingual education, which may offer a full curriculum but is directed toward moving students into English-language classes as rapidly as possible. In a report last month by a Twentieth Century Fund task force, members who were disillusioned with the performance of elaborate bilingual programs urged diversion of federal funds to the teaching of English. The panel held: "Schoolchildren will never swim in the American mainstream unless they are fluent in English."

10   3) Dual curriculum, which permits students to spend several years making the transition. This is the method urged by many moderate Hispanic, Chinese and other ethnic minority leaders. Says historian Ruiz: "The direct approach destroys children's feelings of security. Bilingual education eases them from something they know to something they do not."

11   4) Language and cultural maintenance, which seeks to enhance students' mastery of their first language while also teaching them English. In Hispanic communities, the language training is often accompanied by courses in ethnic heritage. Argues Miami attorney Manuel Diaz, a vice chairman of the Spanish American League Against Discrimination: "Cultural diversity makes this country strong. It is not a disease."

12   The rhetoric of supporters of bilingualism suggests that theirs may be a political solution to an educational problem. Indeed, some of them acknowledge that they view bilingual programs as a source of jobs for Hispanic administrators, teachers and aides. In cities with large minority enrollments, says a Chicago school principal who requested anonymity, "those of us who consider bilingual education ineffective are afraid that if we say so we will lose our jobs." Lawrence Uzzell, president of Learn Inc., a Washington-based research foundation, contends that Hispanic educational activists are cynically protecting their own careers. Says Uzzell: "The more the Hispanic child grows up isolated, the easier it is for politicians to manipulate him as part of an ethnic voting bloc."

13   The signal political success for bilingualism has been won at the U.S. Department of Education. After the Supreme Court ruled in 1974 that Chinese-speaking students were entitled to some instruction in a language they could understand, the DOE issued "informal" rules that now bind more than 400 school districts. Immersion in English, even rapid transition to English, does not satisfy the DOE; the rules compel school systems to offer a full curriculum to any group of 20 or more students who share a foreign language. The DOE rules have survived three presidencies, although Jesse Soriano, director of the Reagan Administration's $138 million bilingual program, concedes, "This is money that could be spent more effectively." About half of students

from Spanish-speaking homes drop out before the end of high school; of the ones who remain, 30% eventually score two or more years below their age group on standardized tests. But it is hard to demonstrate the value of any bilingual approach in aiding those students. In 1982 Iris Rotberg reported in the *Harvard Education Review:* "Research findings have shown that bilingual programs are neither better nor worse than other instructional methods." Indeed, the DOE's review found that of all methods for teaching bilingual students English and mathematics, only total immersion in English clearly worked.

One major problem in assessing the worth of bilingual programs is that they often   14
employ teachers who are less than competent in either English or Spanish, or in the specific subjects they teach. In a 1976 test of 136 teachers and aides in bilingual programs in New Mexico, only 13 could read and write Spanish at third-grade level. Says former Boston school superintendent Robert Wood: "Many bilingual teachers do not have a command of English, and after three years of instruction under them, children also emerge without a command of English." Another complicating factor is the inability of researchers to determine whether the problems of Hispanic students stem more from language difficulty or from their economic class. Many Hispanic children who are unable to speak English have parents with little education who hold unskilled jobs; in school performance, these students are much like poor blacks and whites. Notes Harvard's Nathan Glazer: "If these students do poorly in English, they may be doing poorly in a foreign language."

Even if the educational value of bilingual programs were beyond dispute, there would   15
remain questions about their psychic value to children. Among the sharpest critics of bilingualism is author Richard Rodriguez, who holds a Berkeley Ph.D. in literature and grew up in a Spanish-speaking, working-class household; in his autobiography *Hunger of Memory,* Rodriguez argues that the separation from his family that a Hispanic child feels on becoming fluent in English is necessary to develop a sense of belonging to American society. Writes Rodriguez: "Bilingualists do not seem to realize that there are two ways a person is individualized. While one suffers a diminished sense of private individuality by becoming assimilated into public society, such assimilation makes possible the achievement of public individuality." By Rodriguez's reasoning, the discomfort of giving up the language of home is far less significant than the isolation of being unable to speak the language of the larger world.

The dubious value of bilingualism to students is only part of America's valid concern   16
about how to absorb the Hispanic minority. The U.S. despite its exceptional diversity, has been spared most of the ethnic tensions that beset even such industrialized nations as Belgium and Spain. The rise of a large group, detached from the main population by language and custom, could affect the social stability of the country. Hispanic leaders, moreover, acknowledge that their constituents have been less inclined to become assimilated than previous foreign-language communities, in part because many of them anticipated that after earning and saving, they would return to Puerto Rico, Mexico, South America or Cuba. Says historian Doyce Nunis of the University of Southern California: "For the first time in American experience, a large immigrant group may be electing to bypass the processes of acculturation." Miami Mayor Maurice Ferré, a Puerto Rican, claims that in his city a resident can go from birth through school and working life

to death without ever having to speak English. But most Hispanic intellectuals claim that their communities, like other immigrant groups before them, cling together only to combat discrimination.

17   The disruptive potential of bilingualism and biculturalism is still worrisome: millions of voters cut off from the main sources of information, millions of potential draftees inculcated with dual ethnic loyalties, millions of would-be employees ill at ease in the language of their workmates. Former Senator S.I. Hayakawa of California was laughed at for proposing a constitutional amendment to make English the official language of the U.S. It was a gesture of little practical consequence but great symbolic significance: many Americans mistakenly feel there is something racist, or oppressive, in expecting newcomers to share the nation's language and folkways.

18   Beyond practical politics and economics, separatism belittles the all-embracing culture that America has embodied for the world. Says writer Irving Howe, a scholar of literature and the Jewish immigrant experience: "The province, the ethnic nest, remains the point from which everything begins, but it must be transcended." That transcendence does not mean disappearance. It is possible to eat a Mexican meal, dance a Polish polka, sing in a Rumanian choir, preserve one's ethnicity however one wishes, and still share fully in the English-speaking common society. Just as American language, food and popular culture reflect the past groups who landed in the U.S., so future American culture will reflect the Hispanics, Asians and many other groups who are replanting their roots. As author Rodriguez observes after his journey into the mainstream, "Culture survives whether you want it to or not."

Vocabulary

aspiring (1)	xenophobia (3)	mandating (6)	impedes (8)
denominator (1)	promulgated (5)	proliferation (6)	acculturation (16)
subsuming (2)	unassimilated (5)	portentous (6)	inculcated (17)
nascent (2)	secession (5)	disorients (8)	transcended (18)

Questions on Meaning and Technique

1. How old is America's image of itself as a melting pot? What bearing on the author's argument does the age of this image have?

2. *Time* magazine is known for using the techniques of fiction to report the news. Where in the early stages of this essay can you find an example of the use of fictional techniques?

3. What is "xenophobia"? What is the origin of this curious word?

4. Up until now, what was the implicit goal in the teaching of a foreign language in American classrooms? What difference does the author detect in the teaching of foreign languages today?

5. What is the purpose of the first four paragraphs of this essay?

6. From what ideology does the movement for bilingualism and biculturalism draw its main force?

7. What is the connection between bilingualism and biculturalism? Do you agree that the one necessarily goes hand-in-hand with the other? Why, or why not?

8. Generally, what kind of evidence does the author cite in asserting his argument against bilingualism?

9. The author quotes liberally from a Hispanic writer, Richard Rodriguez, who opposes bilingualism. What value does a Hispanic background add to Rodriguez's opinion?

Writing Assignments

1. In 500 words or less, argue for having all children taught a second language in elementary school, beginning with first grade. Support your argument with logic, facts, experience, and expert testimony.

2. Write an argument for a constitutional amendment that would make English the official language of the United States. Support your argument with logic, facts, experience, and expert testimony.

READING FOR IDEAS

You should be intensely interested in the basic argument of this essay because it involves you as a student at the university. If you are enrolled in a community college, you are not experiencing the teaching assistant syndrome described in the essay below because at these institutions all the teaching is done by experienced teachers, who are continuously evaluated by their administrators, their peers, and their students. However, once you transfer to the university, especially in your freshman or sophomore year, you are likely to face another student who will be teaching your class. As you read, imagine yourself in the classroom or lecture hall of one of these teaching assistants, who may be just a few semesters ahead of you in biology, psychology, history, or whatever class you are taking. Knowing the teaching assistant's experience, will you feel confident that you are getting the quality education for which you have paid or received a scholarship? It is a good question to ponder seriously.

ALTERNATE READING

Academia's Dirty Secret

MARTIN ANDERSON

Martin Anderson (b. 1936) has taught at Columbia University's Graduate School of Business and is now a senior fellow at Stanford University's Hoover Institution, where advanced studies are conducted on the social and political developments resulting from war. He is the author of Impostors in the Temple *(1992), a book exposing policies and behavior unworthy of the university. The essay below was reprinted from this work.*

1   The critical problem with universities today is not so much that many professors don't teach very well, but that so few of them teach at all. A significant part of the crucial teaching responsibilities of our universities has been handed over to people who are unqualified.

2   It is the shame of the academic intellectuals, a shabby secret they are loath to discuss publicly.

3   If senior professors were lecturing only six hours a week to a hundred or so students, but were preparing those lectures thoughtfully and thoroughly, grading the students individually with care, and counseling them wisely, then we would have no complaints.

4   But more and more professors are not teaching or grading or counseling. As a former Stanford professor, John Kaplan, an excellent teacher himself, once observed, "Professors feel that students are the crabgrass on the lawn of academia."[1]

5   Professors don't lecture or lead classroom discussion? Don't grade? Don't counsel? Then who does?

6   Students.

TEACHING ASSISTANTS A SOLUTION?

7   The clever solution that professors have come up with for the teaching albatross that grew around their necks in the 1960s and 1970s is the teaching assistant. These young men and women, usually graduate students, but sometimes undergraduates, do a large part of the teaching work of many of our universities. You won't find them listed in any college or university catalog by name, but they lecture, they lead classroom discussions, they make up examinations and grade them, and they counsel their fellow students.

8   We have recently had a growing problem in this country with children having children, a practice that threatens the stability of family life. We now have what may be an even worse problem, students "teaching" students, children teaching children.

9   The extent of the scandal is difficult to know precisely because the records of student teaching are not publicized. Pick up any university catalog and you will find only the vaguest of references to these student teachers. Look at the detailed schedule of courses and you will not find their names among the listed instructors. They are nameless and unknown, unhonored and unsung in their own universities.

10   Why don't students complain? Why are they so docile about being taught and graded by other students?

STUDENTS TRAPPED

11   Basically, they don't have much choice. Who are they going to complain to—the professors and administrators who set the system up and who ultimately determine whether or not the student gets a degree?

---

[1] Society of scholars.

One explanation was offered by Ernest Boyer, president of the Carnegie Foundation 12 for the Advancement of Teaching. These kids arrive "all wide eyes and hopeful," he said. "Then they begin to see that they are not being well-served and a certain resignation sets in. They figure, 'If these are the ground rules, and if I'll get a blue-chip degree and will have a good time in the process, let's go for it.' Instead these students should march into the dean's office and demand what the catalog promised them."

This is what they should do, but how many undergraduates are that strong? 13

The university world will argue that many student teachers are qualified, that they do 14 possess the knowledge, the teaching skills, and the maturity to teach undergraduates.

In some cases that may be true, but then we should insist that the university do the 15 right thing: promote them to the faculty, pay them a decent wage, and give them the title for the work they do. Or stop pretending.

PROHIBIT STUDENT TEACHING

The seamy practice of allowing, and sometimes coercing, students to teach students is 16 one of the most significant forms of academic corruption, and one of the easiest to correct.

Prohibit all student teaching. Simply adopt a policy that says all classes will be taught 17 by professors, all discussion sections will be led by professors, all examinations will be made up by professors, all examinations will be graded by professors, and all counseling of students will be done by professors.

There is nothing radical about this. A few major schools—Amherst College and 18 Dartmouth College, for example—have always done it this way. In fact, most people in America think that professors already do this.

Such a simple change would have an immediate, far-reaching impact. Students and 19 parents would no longer feel cheated, duped by the rhetoric in the college catalogs. Students might even take more interest in their courses if they were taught by real professors, not one of their beer-drinking buddies.

Because students, graduate students especially, would be prohibited from teaching, 20 they could devote more time to their own studies, complete their degrees earlier, and add to the pool of professors available for teaching. Professors, required to spend more time on what they were originally hired to do, would have less time to spend on spurious research and writing, thus tending to increase the quality of intellectual output.

PROFESSORS WON'T LIKE IT

Any attempt to banish the widespread use of student teachers can be expected to 21 meet adamant hostility from professors. Much of this opposition stems from the fact that so many of today's professors do not have the temperament of teachers.

Teaching is an old and honorable profession, but many professors consider teaching 22 no longer a fitting vocation once they get to be 35 or 40 years old. These are the academic intellectuals who are excited by the play of ideas among equals or near-equals. Publishing an article in a prestigious academic journal, participating in an advanced seminar, debating colleagues in a panel discussion—these are what stimulate their intellectual juices.

23   Students are not qualified to teach. They do not possess enough knowledge. They do not have enough judgment and maturity. They rarely know how to teach. They have powerful conflicts of interest, for in many cases they must teach and grade some of their friends, or even the young men and women they date.

24   To pretend that students are qualified to lecture other students a scant few years behind them, to grade and judge them, and to counsel them is to mock the essence of higher education.

25   Children teaching children is unconscionable.

Vocabulary

academia (title, 4)
albatross (7)
docile (10)
spurious (20)
adamant (21)
unconscionable (25)

Questions on Meaning and Technique

1. What is the proposition of this argument? Where is it stated? How clear is it?

2. What expertise, if any, does the author bring to his argument? Do you consider him qualified to take the stand he does?

3. How does the author go about proving that he is right in objecting to students teaching at the university?

4. What negative connotations does the author attach to what is going on at the university? What words does he use to strengthen this connotation? Provide specific examples.

5. Do you agree with the author that the reason students do not complain is that they feel trapped and they are resigned to being docile and not making waves lest they be prevented from getting their degrees? If you could, would you protest the present system? If so, how would you go about your protest?

6. What advantages can you give for having teaching assistants? What can they add to a classroom lecture or discussion that a senior tenured member may not? What financial impact on the university do they have? How can they help the regular professors?

7. What tone does the author use? Is it appropriate to his purpose?

8. Does the author simply castigate the present system or does he also offer an answer to the problem? What answer, if any, does he offer?

Writing Assignments

1. Write an essay in which you argue for the use of teaching assistants. Be sure to bolster your argument with logic, facts, experience, and expert testimony.

2. Drawing heavily from objective views on the subject, argue against a university system that forces its tenured faculty to "publish or perish."

or

Argue in favor of all the research done at the universities. You may need to do some research of your own to write a forceful paper on this subject.

READING FOR IDEAS

Many educational theorists have criticized the present education system, accusing it of deficiency and suggesting various practical remedies for improvement. Krishnamurti, on the other hand, paints a philosophical and idealized picture of what education should do for the individual, but gives no concrete steps for implementing what he proposes. Ask yourself as you read whether it is possible for any public education system to incorporate these ideas and survive. If not, why not?

The Function of Education

JIDDU KRISHNAMURTI

Jiddu Krishnamurti (1895–1986), Indian philosopher and teacher, was a prolific author of books, primarily of his lectures and dialogues. He was highly influential in his day and commanded respect from many of the world's best thinkers, including Bertrand Russell and Aldous Huxley. Reportedly, Greta Garbo renounced her career in the movies after listening to one of his lectures. Krishnamurti taught that "truth is a pathless land" and cannot be approached by "any religion, any sect. . . . " His writings include The Songs of Life *(1931),* Commentaries on Living *(1956–1960),* The Urgency of Change *(1970), and* The Awakening of Intelligence *(1974).*

I wonder if we have ever asked ourselves what education means. Why do we go to school, why do we learn various subjects, why do we pass examinations and compete with each other for better grades? What does this so-called education mean, and what is it all about? This is really a very important question, not only for the students, but also for the parents, for the teachers, and for everyone who loves this earth. Why do we go through the struggle to be educated? Is it merely in order to pass some examinations and get a job? Or is it the function of education to prepare us while we are young to understand the whole process of life? Having a job and earning one's livelihood is necessary—but is that all? Are we being educated only for that? Surely, life is not merely a job, an occupation; life is something extraordinarily wide and profound, it is a great mystery, a vast realm in which we function as human beings. If we merely prepare ourselves to earn a livelihood, we shall miss the whole point of life; and to understand life is much more important than merely to prepare for examinations and become very proficient in mathematics, physics, or what you will. 1

So, whether we are teachers or students, is it not important to ask ourselves why we are educating or being educated? And what does life mean? Is not life an extraordinary 2 thing? The birds, the flowers, the flourishing trees, the heavens, the stars, the rivers and the fish therein—all this is life. Life is the poor and the rich; life is the constant battle between groups, races and nations; life is meditation; life is what we call religion, and it is also the subtle, hidden things of the mind—the envies, the ambitions, the passions, the fears, fulfillments and anxieties. All this and much more is life. But we generally prepare ourselves to understand only one small corner of it. We pass certain examinations, find a job, get married, have children, and then become more and more like machines. We remain fearful, anxious, frightened of life. So, is it the function of education to help us understand the whole process of life, or is it merely to prepare us for a vocation, for the best job we can get?

3   What is going to happen to all of us when we grow to be men and women? Have you ever asked yourselves what you are going to do when you grow up? In all likelihood you will get married, and before you know where you are you will be mothers and fathers; and you will then be tied to a job, or to the kitchen, in which you will gradually wither away. Is that all that *your* life is going to be? Have you ever asked yourselves this question? Should you not ask it? If your family is wealthy you may have a fairly good position already assured, your father may give you a comfortable job, or you may get richly married; but there also you will decay, deteriorate. Do you see?

4   Surely, education has no meaning unless it helps you to understand the vast expanse of life with all its subtleties, with its extraordinary beauty, its sorrows and joys. You may earn degrees, you may have a series of letters after your name and land a very good job; but then what? What is the point of it all if in the process your mind becomes dull, weary, stupid? So, while you are young, must you not seek to find out what life is all about? And is it not the true function of education to cultivate in you the intelligence which will try to find the answer to all these problems? Do you know what intelligence is? It is the capacity, surely, to think freely, without fear, without a formula, so that you begin to discover for yourself what is real, what is true; but if you are frightened you will never be intelligent. Any form of ambition, spiritual or mundane, breeds anxiety, fear; therefore ambition does not help to bring about a mind that is clear, simple, direct, and hence intelligent.

5   You know, it is really very important while you are young to live in an environment in which there is no fear. Most of us, as we grow older, become frightened; we are afraid of living, afraid of losing a job, afraid of tradition, afraid of what the neighbours, or what the wife or husband would say, afraid of death. Most of us have fear in one form or another; and where there is fear there is no intelligence. And is it not possible for all of us, while we are young, to be in an environment where there is no fear but rather an atmosphere of freedom—freedom, not just to do what we like, but to understand the whole process of living? Life is really very beautiful, it is not this ugly thing that we have made of it; and you can appreciate its richness, its depth, its extraordinary loveliness only when you revolt against everything—against organized religion, against tradition, against the present rotten society—so that you as a human being find out for yourself what is true. Not to imitate but to discover—*that* is education, is it not? It is very easy to conform to what your society or your parents and teachers tell you. That is a safe and easy way of existing; but that is not living, because in it there is fear, decay, death. To live is to find out for yourself what is true, and you can do this only when there is freedom, when there is continuous revolution inwardly, within yourself.

But you are not encouraged to do this; no one tells you to question, to find out for   6
yourself . . . , because if you were to rebel you would become a danger to all that is false.
Your parents and society want you to live safely, and you also want to live safely. Living
safely generally means living in imitation and therefore in fear. Surely, the function of
education is to help each one of us to live freely and without fear, is it not? And to create
an atmosphere in which there is no fear requires a great deal of thinking on your part as
well as on the part of the teacher, the educator.

Do you know what this means—what an extraordinary thing it would be to create an   7
atmosphere in which there is no fear? And we *must* create it, because we see that the
world is caught up in endless wars; it is guided by politicians who are always seeking
power; it is a world of lawyers, policemen and soldiers, of ambitious men and women all
wanting position and all fighting each other to get it. Then there are the so-called saints,
the religious *gurus* with their followers; they also want power, position, here or in the
next life. It is a mad world, completely confused, in which the communist is fighting the
capitalist, the socialist is resisting both, and everybody is against somebody, struggling to
arrive at a safe place, a position of power or comfort. The world is torn by conflicting
beliefs, by caste and class distinctions, by separative nationalities, by every form of
stupidity and cruelty—and this is the world you are being educated to fit into. You are
encouraged to fit into the framework of this disastrous society; your parents want you to
do that, and you also want to fit in.

Now, is it the function of education merely to help you to conform to the pattern of   8
this rotten social order, or is it to give you freedom—complete freedom to grow and
create a different society, a new world? We want to have this freedom, not in the future,
but now, otherwise we may all be destroyed. We must create immediately an atmosphere
of freedom so that you can live and find out for yourselves what is true, so that you
become intelligent, so that you are able to face the world and understand it, not just
conform to it, so that inwardly, deeply, psychologically you are in constant revolt;
because it is only those who are in constant revolt that discover what is true, not the man
who conforms, who follows some tradition. . . .

. . . The question is: if all individuals were in revolt, would not the world be in chaos?   9
But is the present society in such perfect order that chaos would result if everyone revolted
against it? Is there not chaos *now?* Is everything beautiful, uncorrupted? Is everyone living
happily, fully, richly? Is man not against man? Is there not ambition, ruthless competition?
So the world is already in chaos, that is the first thing to realize. Don't take it for granted
that this is an orderly society; don't mesmerize yourself with words. Whether, here in
Europe, in America or Russia, the world is in a process of decay. If you see the decay, you
have a challenge: you are challenged to find a way of solving this urgent problem. And how
you respond to the challenge is important, is it not? If you respond as a Hindu or a
Buddhist, a Christian or a communist, then your response is very limited—which is no
response at all. You can respond fully, adequately only if there is no fear in you, only if you
don't think as a Hindu, a communist or a capitalist, but as a total human being who is trying
to solve this problem; and you cannot solve it unless you yourself are in revolt against the
whole thing, against the ambitious acquisitiveness on which society is based. When you
yourself are not ambitious, not acquisitive, not clinging to your own security—only then
can you respond to the challenge and create a new world. . . .

10   Do you know what it means to learn? When you are really learning you are learning throughout your life and there is no one special teacher to learn from. Then everything teaches you—a dead leaf, a bird in flight, a smell, a tear, the rich and the poor, those who are crying, the smile of a woman, the haughtiness of a man. You learn from everything, therefore there is no guide, no philosopher, no guru. Life itself is your teacher, and you are in a state of constant learning. . . .

11   Do you know what attention is? Let us find out. In a class room, when you stare out of the window or pull somebody's hair, the teacher tells you to pay attention. Which means what? That you are not interested in what you are studying and so the teacher compels you to pay attention—which is not attention at all. Attention comes when you are deeply interested in something, for then you love to find out all about it; then your whole mind, your whole being is there. . . . When you are doing something with your whole being, not because you want to get somewhere, or have more profit, or greater results, but simply because you love to do it—in that there is no ambition, is there? In that there is no competition; you are not struggling with anyone for first place. And should not education help you to find out what you really love to do so that from the beginning to the end of your life you are working at something which you feel is worth while and which for you has deep significance? Otherwise, for the rest of your days, you will be miserable. Not knowing what you really want to do, your mind falls into a routine in which there is only boredom, decay and death. That is why it is very important to find out while you are young what it is you really *love* to do; and this is the only way to create a new society. . . .

Vocabulary

proficient (1)
mundane (4)
mesmerize (9)

Questions on Meaning and Technique

1. What is the author's definition of education? In what way does this definition differ from our usual understanding of the word? Do you agree with his definition?

2. What rhetorical technique does the author repeatedly use to make his main points? With what other major Western philosopher is this particular technique identified?

3. What do you think would be the likely practical consequences to any student presently in high school or college who insisted that he or she be given the kind of education advocated by Krishnamurti?

4. What objection do you think a religious fundamentalist of any persuasion would have to Krishnamurti's teaching on education?

5. In paragraph 2, the author writes: "So, is it the function of education to help us understand the whole process of life, or is it merely to prepare us for a vocation, for the best job we can get?" What apparent logical fallacy is evident in this question?

6. The author says that "if you are frightened you will never be intelligent." What is your opinion of this statement? Why does this necessarily follow?

7. What objection does the author raise to ambition? What is your attitude toward these objections?

8. What one practical suggestion can you make that would help your present school incorporate Krishnamurti's ideas in your education?

Writing Assignments

1. Write an essay suggesting at least two practical steps that a school could take to implement Krishnamurti's vision of education.

2. Write an essay supporting or attacking the ideas presented in this article.

Additional Writing Assignments

1. Write an argument either for or against dorm life for college students.

2. Write a paper in which you argue the urgent necessity for recycling trash by individual families.

3. It is often stated that newspapers give a distorted view of life because they report only the sensational. Argue for or against this proposition.

4. Should art galleries be censored for "pornographic" exhibits? Answer this question in the form of an argument either for or against censorship of art.

5. "Instructors of political science should never express their own political opinions in class." Argue for or against this proposition.

6. Some experts of educational theory indicate that bright and slow students should be separated to learn at a maximum level; others state that slow learners can learn from bright ones without harm to the bright. Take a position on this issue and argue it.

7. Write an argument supporting the view that the American consumer is a victim of planned obsolescence.

8. Read through the opinion section in several issues of your local newspaper until you find an article containing a proposition with which you disagree. Counter with your own argument.

9. Argue either for or against living wills—that is, the idea that while individuals are still of sound mind they should sign a legal document forbidding extraordinary medical methods in case they suffer from an illness that renders them into vegetablelike beings.

10. Write an essay arguing in favor of buying American-made cars to bolster the American economy.

11. Write an argument persuading your readers to carry an earthquake safety kit in the trunks of their cars.

12. As persuasively as you can, argue for or against a research paper requirement for freshman English.

13. There is no constitutionally mandated national language of the United States. Argue for or against amending the Constitution to make English the official language.

14. Once the U.S. government has identified another country as an enemy, should we send humanitarian aid to it in the event of a natural disaster such as an earthquake, flood, or famine? Answer in the form of a persuasive argument.

Prochoice versus antiabortion demonstrators, New York City. © 1992 Barbara Rios/Photo Researchers, Inc., NYC.

Argument always implies two sides of an issue. After studying the photo about
abortion, try to see clearly both sides depicted. Then choose the side that best
represents your own view and write a 500-word essay supporting that side. Be
sure to clarify the opposition and to support your side with convincing evidence.

The Essay Examination

Preparing for the Essay Examination

HOW TO DO WELL ON ESSAY EXAMINATIONS

Anyone who attends college will sooner or later face the ordeal of the essay exam, usually with the outcome decisively influencing the final grade. To excel at the essay exam requires that you (1) know your subject, (2) be able to demonstrate your knowledge in your essay, (3) and organize your answer so it is easy for an overworked grader to follow. This last observation is not meant to be cynical but is a realistic requirement the student writer must take into account in writing essay exams. Teachers who grade them are looking for particular points organized in specific sequence. And the student who delivers these points in the expected order with a minimum of wordiness is likely to evoke a response of immense gratitude from any weary instructor who must plod through a stack of essays.

To perform well on essay exams, you should observe these commonsense cautions.

Read the Question Carefully, At Least Twice

Simplistic as this advice may sound, it remains a fact that the commonest error students make on essay exams is to misread the question. If more than one essay answer is required, read each one so that you get an overview of the questions and are able to budget the correct time for each. Consider this question from a History of Western Europe class:

Define the Franco-Prussian War, placing it in its proper age, describing who the participants were, and explaining the causes that led up to it.

Implied in this question are three rhetorical objectives that the writer must meet and that the reader expects:

1. A *definition* of the war
2. A *description* of its major participants
3. An *explanation* of the causes leading up to the war

A good answer will not only present the appropriate facts, but do so *exactly in the order asked* by the question. If you scramble the order of the question, you make your answer harder to read and will likely suffer a penalty. As an exam taker your aim should be not only to deliver the answers asked for by the question, but also to do so in a way that is most helpful to your reader. And once you have established that the question calls for a definition followed by a description and a causal analysis, the rest is a straightforward presentation of the facts in comprehensible and readable prose.

Give the Question Some Thought Before Starting to Write

In a hundred-yard sprint the first runner out of the block is generally the one who wins, but not so in an essay exam. Finishing before the deadline earns you no extra credits, and it is pointless to try to beat the clock by superficially glancing at the question and plunging as quickly as possible into the actual writing. Instead, sit back and think about the question and how you plan to answer it, including the points you must cover and the facts you intend to cite. If you have a choice of questions, answer the one you know best. And once you have made your selection, be absolutely sure that your answer sticks to the question, no matter how much you might know and yearn to say about a side issue. For instance, if the question asks you to explain the causes of the Civil War, do not write at length about its devastating effects. Always do exactly what the question asks.

Organize Your Thoughts Through Prewriting

Some students can organize their thoughts systematically and logically as they write, but most cannot and perform better on an essay exam when they prewrite. The prewriting may be as simple as jotting down a few key words on a separate piece of notepaper to ensure the inclusion of all important points. A rough outline may also be helpful, such as this one explaining the causes of the Franco-Prussian War:

A. Bismarck's desire to unify Germany
B. Napoleon III's fear of an alliance against him
C. France's fear of a Prussian prince on the Spanish throne

Exam taking is nerve wracking, and jotting down major ideas on a slip of paper can keep you from drifting or forgetting to make an important point.

Time Yourself Carefully

Because most examinations allot a time limit to every question, you cannot afford to ramble or throw in information not asked for by the question. Nor do you get any more points for doing so. Pay attention, therefore, to such phrases as "in a brief paragraph" "in 200 words or less" or "in approximately two pages." Pay particularly close attention to the number of points an answer is worth. Nothing is gained by wasting one hour on a 10-point question in a two-hour 100-point examination. Nor is anything achieved by demonstrating your knowledge on a topic not included in the question. For example, if a history question asks you to define Pickett's Charge at the Civil War Battle of Gettysburg, you earn no bonus by throwing in details about the conduct of Union General Meade.

USING RHETORICAL STRATEGIES IN ESSAY EXAMINATIONS

The rhetorical strategies can help a student under pressure quickly organize answers to an essay exam. If you know in the abstract how to write, say, a definition, you will find it easy to write one in the particular. However, although some questions will clearly specify the most appropriate rhetorical strategy to be used in an answer, others will not. What you must do is look for key words in the essay question that will tell you which strategy you should use in your answer. Here are some examples of essay examination questions, followed by a discussion of the best strategy for answering them.

FROM LITERATURE

Question

Typical of many of Shakespeare's plays, *Othello* is filled with dramatic irony. Point out at least three *instances* of this technique in the play and *discuss* how they intensify the conflict or suspense.

Although the key words in this question are *instances* and *discuss*, common sense tells us that the logical opening for an essay answering this question is to define dramatic irony, which occurs in a play when the audience knows something that the stage character does not. Having defined dramatic irony, you can then cite three specific examples of it in *Othello*. The question further asks for a *discussion* of how dramatic irony intensifies conflict or suspense. *Discuss* is a catch-all term that often masks the use of various possible strategies—example, effect, argument, and so on. In this case, the question is asking that you demonstrate the *effect* of specific instances of irony on the dramatic tension in the play. In other words, you need to show how Othello's blindness to his wife's virtue intensifies emotion in the audience watching the tragic unraveling of events in the play.

Question
    Use one paragraph to answer the following questions: What is the Federal Reserve System? How did it originate and what is its purpose?

A question that begins with "What is . . .?" almost always requires the strategy of *definition*. Your answer might begin as follows: "The Federal Reserve System is the central banking authority for the United States," which gives a nuts-and-bolts definition of the system. The second part of the question, on the *origin* and *purpose* of the Federal Reserve System, calls for an unclassifiable response based partly on narration. You might write: "It originated in 1913 as part of the Federal Reserve Act, and its purpose is to stimulate economic activity by buying securities and allowing banks to expand and thus to increase their money lending. The system may also slow down economic activity by selling securities and thus contracting bank reserves and reducing lending. Moreover, the system controls the interest rates at which member banks may borrow from it."
    Because the question asks for an answer in only a single paragraph, you must stick to the required length and bridle any urge to gush for pages.

Question
    Using *Park in Tangier, The Purple Robe,* and *Seated Blue Nude* as examples, *show* how Henri Matisse's experimentation with color eventually led to the Fauve movement.

Show as used in this question is a synonym for *describe*. A good way to begin the answer is to describe in specific detail how color is used in the Matisse paintings named. You should also describe how Matisse's paintings foreshadowed the Fauves, a group of painters such as Derain, Braque, and Rouault, who were devoted to the use of violent, uncontrolled, brilliant color.

Question
    What major powers competed for influence in the Caribbean region and what territories did they acquire? What were these colonial powers seeking?

Buried in this question is an implicit division and classification of the powers that colonized the Caribbean and the territories they captured. You must divide the Caribbean into the various Spanish, British, Dutch, and French colonies. The second part of the question—what the colonial powers were seeking—can be answered by a strategy of *causal analysis* specifying the reasons behind these Caribbean acquisitions. Notice that the wording of this question does not make it particularly clear which rhetorical strategy you should use. But with a little thought, the most appropriate strategy can easily be inferred.

FROM SOCIOLOGY

Question
   From your own experience or from reading the newspaper, *narrate* an incident that illustrates the unresponsive bystander syndrome in densely populated urban areas.

This question calls for a narration from your own experience. But if it is to be answered with purpose, the incident chosen must be paced to show how and why people in large cities might witness a crime or an accident and refuse to help or get involved. You must avoid redundancy or irrelevant rambling by focusing sharply on the question.

FROM PHILOSOPHY

Question
   What is virtue as revealed in Spinoza's *Foundations of the Moral Life* and in the Hindu *Bhagavadgita*? How do the concepts of virtue differ in each philosophy? Cite incidents from your own experience to bolster the respective concepts and to indicate that you understand them.

Although it does not explicitly say so, this question is calling for three different strategies: the first, a *definition* of virtue in Spinoza and in the *Bhagavadgita*; the second, a *comparison/contrast* of the differing meanings of virtue in each philosophy; the third, the use of personal *examples* to illustrate your understanding of both concepts. For instance, you might begin by writing, "Spinoza defines virtue as self-preservation, whereas the *Bhagavadgita* defines virtue as self-denial. Clearly, the two definitions stand in stark contrast to each other."

FROM CHEMISTRY

Question
   (1) Differentiate, first, between starch and glycogen and, second, between cellulose and starch. (2) High-compression automobile engines that operate at high temperatures are designed to oxidize hydrocarbons completely to carbon dioxide and water. In the process of attempting to completely oxidize the hydrocarbons, a non-carbon-containing pollutant is produced. What types of compounds are produced and why do high-compression engines favor the formation of these compounds?

At first you may think that the first question gives you no clues as to what strategy to use. However, on closer look you will see that the question is asking for a comparison/contrast. You must answer by explaining how starch is different from glycogen, and cellulose from starch. Here is an excerpt from a student answer to this question:

> Both starch and glycogen are disaccharides, but starch has a d-glycosidic bond that doesn't allow a great extent of H-bonding. Therefore starch is easier to break down than glycogen. Starch is found mainly in plants, whereas glycogen exists mainly in animals. Glycogen is the monomer unit of most fatty acids.

Although this is a technical answer, it is still easy to see that the student is systematically comparing and contrasting. She uses contrasting terms such as *but* and *whereas*. She says how starch and glycogen are similar and how they are different.

Consider the second chemistry question on high-compression automobile engines. Your answer should consist of paragraphs that divide and classify—specifying the types of compounds produced—as well as paragraphs that analyze cause—saying why high-compression engines produce them.

FROM POLITICAL SCIENCE

Question

In an essay of approximately 300 words, argue for or against this proposition: "If parents choose to send their children to private school rather than public school, then the government should provide them with a voucher equivalent to the cost of a public school education."

This question is clearly asking for an argumentative essay. All you have to do is take a side and knuckle down to the work of supporting your argument with the right facts, expert testimony, and logic.

To sum up, although it is not always clear what rhetorical strategy you might best use in writing an essay exam, most of the time you can make a reasonable inference from the wording of the question. Your answer, for that matter, may not always neatly fall into any specific rhetorical strategy. Indeed, most of the time your answer is likely to call for a mixed strategy. In any case, instructors do not judge essay exams on the relative purity of their rhetorical strategies, but on such sensible criteria as whether the question is fully answered and cites a wealth of factual details.

Sample Essay Exams

To give you an idea of the difference between an "A" and a "C" essay written for an exam, we are including below two actual student essay answers written for a history class. Notice the instructor's annotations.

Dr. M. Renner   Fall, 1992

Glendale Community College

FINAL EXAMINATION QUESTION

History 111—Women in American History

<u>100-point question</u>

Women have not always agreed on their role and function in society. Some women have   1

emphasized the domestic role, basing their support of this role on religious principles.

Others have cast a wider net and justified their arguments on political, economic,

religious, or other social grounds. Your task is to select four of the women listed below

whose attitudes and practices best reveal those differences historically. Discuss the

female role(s) they promoted, the values and attitudes that underlay their ideas, and

the grounds they used to justify their arguments. End your essay with a discussion of

one specific woman who, you believe, has had the most dramatic impact on modern

women.

   a. Anne Hutchinson

   b. Sarah Grimke

   c. Judith Sargent Murray

   d. Elizabeth Murray Smith

   e. Alice Paul

   f. Charlotte P. Gilman

   g. M. Carey Thomas

   h. Elizabeth Cady Stanton

<u>C ANSWER</u>   74 pts

by Elizabeth Caraballo

1   The role of women in society for the Puritans was being a wife, mother, and home

maintainer. Women were supposed to grow up and learn how to cook, clean, keep

house, and tend to their husbands' needs. Religion played an enormous part in the

Puritans' lives. Women were good and righteous. They went to church and prayed all

Your opening paragraph is weak. You state the obvious without focusing on the role of women as a challenge.

day on Sunday. Men also went to church and prayed all day on Sunday. Wives had to make their own bread and butter, milk their own cows, and clothe the entire family. These Puritan women also bore many children, one child approximately every two years.

Anne Hutchinson was a Puritan woman who changed or at least sparked an interest 2 in change in the lives of the Puritans. She would gather with other women and speak and teach them things. Hutchinson was a midwife; therefore, she was always with young women and influenced them a great deal. She was a vocal woman who spoke out on what she believed. She was friends with a pastor who was disliked by the Puritan Church. The Puritan Church passed a law forbidding anyone to keep a person in their home. Hutchinson was keeping this pastor in her home and was caught. Later she was exiled from the Puritan community, and some followers left with her. ~~Anne Hutchinson was a very outspoken women who spoke out on what she believed.~~ The Puritan Church did not believe that women should be heard so they got rid of her. She is a clear example of a woman who believed that she should do something more than stay home and cook or clean.

not specific enough

What did she believe? What was her challenge?

What was the issue?

You have already said this

Explain

As the years passed, many women began to speak out about how they felt and what 3 they believed. For instance, the Grimke sisters were the daughters of an attorney and they learned a lot from situations their father encountered. Sarah Grimke would later speak about slavery and how wrong it was. She would speak in public. Since this was not acceptable, the Church wrote her a letter, called the "Pastoral letter." This letter told Sarah that it was unacceptable behavior for a woman to be doing what she was doing. This letter told her that her place was in the home and that it would be in her best interest to do that. She wrote back to the Church and published the letters so everyone could read them. Grimke came a step closer to becoming someone different from what she was supposed to be.

Vague
Do you mean his court trials?

What was the main content of her letters? Again, you hint rather than offer specific information. What did she actually gain?

The Abolition Movement sparked women's interest more than almost any other issue. 4 Many women believed that slavery was not right. Elizabeth Cady Stanton was a woman who was educated in private schools. She married Henry Stanton but remained a very independent woman. She fought for married women's right to own their own property.

She went to court to try to get *ref* it passed. Finally *ref* it was passed that married women could own property, but five years later *ref* it was reversed. The point was that she was heard and later on in history women would be able to own property. Elizabeth Cady Stanton's name appears throughout many years of women's history. <u>She attended the Women's Convention</u>, which would convene every year with more and more participants. She would fight for women's education. She and her husband would spend their lives trying to <u>change things.</u>

You might have mentioned the decades. What was its purpose? Consider Stanton's fight for suffrage. What specifically did they want to change?

5   During this same period, Elizabeth Murray Smith had a prenuptial agreement written so that her husband-to-be could not acquire all of her wealth after they were married.

needs further development

6   The ideas that Elizabeth Cady Stanton and Elizabeth Murray Smith portrayed were ideas suggesting that women could do other things besides just staying home. The man was not necessarily the boss. <u>These women believed that women were important as individuals.</u>

Careful! They could have been individuals at home.

7   Religion was the basis of life according to most historical accounts throughout the eighteenth and nineteenth centuries. In the twentieth century religion was still important, but it did not seem as important as in earlier days. Women could gain the right to vote through the strides of many women in many societies. <u>Now</u> women had a say in what would happen to them. Many women were opposed to women's voting and so were many men. Some groups tried to make women believe that good and righteous women should not vote. They also established voting places in bars, where respectable women did not dare go. However, matters changed slowly, and by the mid-1900s many women were voting.

When?

8   Alice Paul wrote the Equal Rights Amendment. She tried to get women's pay and education equal to those of men. She also tried to get rid of protective legislation that harmed women and their goal of equality in general. This amendment was rewritten many times—the last time in the 1970s—but it has never been passed. The ERA, though, put a spark in the government. They did agree that women were treated differently. This kind of brings us up to date.

Who?

9   Women in the 1990s are more independent than ever. They still do not have everything they deserve, <u>but all things happen in due time.</u>

Do they? "Things happen" because people struggle hard for change.

*Nevertheless, the
exam requires that
you select one
woman and explain
her dramatic
impact.*

I believe that any woman who fights for a cause she believes in is incredible. <u>It is very</u>   10
<u>hard for me to isolate just one woman</u> who made the most dramatic impact on modern

society, but Elizabeth Cady Stanton was the woman who impressed me the most. It may

be just because her name popped up more than any other woman's name, but she was

an incredible woman.

*good extra
comment*

NOTE: We did not discuss Sandra Day O'Connor, the only woman ever to be a justice   11

on the U.S. Supreme Court, but I admire her and believe her to be the woman who has

made quite an impact on modern women.

A   ANSWER

by Melissa Barcelona

95 pts

Through the course of time, women, like men, have held disparate views on what   1

role a woman should play in society and on what constitutes appropriate conduct for

her. Some women have made their point in subtle ways whereas others have been

*You have re-
sponded to the
question in an ex-
emplary way, fo-
cusing on the roles
of four women and
what each one
specifically contrib-
uted to the Wom-
en's Movement in
the U.S. Your es-
say is well orga-
nized, and your
thesis is well sup-
ported.*

flamboyant and outspoken. These varying attitudes probably depended on the times in

which they were presented and the principles they defended.

In the beginning of the Colonial Period here in America, women stood staunchly   2

behind religious principles in defining their roles as women. The world of these women

was based on the Bible, which they knew well and taught faithfully to their children.

One of these women was Anne Hutchinson, a strong Puritan woman, who based her

views of a woman's role on the Bible, but who also became a mighty spokeswoman for

the theological belief that people were saved by Grace. Although she believed in the

Biblical injunctions concerning a woman and her role, Anne Hutchinson did not accept

every dogma of the Puritan Church—predestination, for example. But most obvious, she

was not a quietly obsequious Puritan woman who remained in the background of public

life the way women of her day were supposed to. By speaking in public on women's

issues, she broke the rules of what was expected of a woman. So, although Anne

Hutchinson's opinion of a woman's role was based on her understanding of Scripture,

her view on how women should function in society contrasted sharply with the Biblical

interpretation of her society. Claiming the Bible as her guide, Anne Hutchinson promoted the role of domesticity for women, but one could argue that as a spokeswoman at a time when women were to remain in the background of debate, she clearly broke her own rules.

Sarah Grimke was another woman who clearly stood behind religious principles in her view of women's role; however, this belief was tinged with political overtones. For instance, when she read the Bible and came cross the words, "Man and woman are created equal," she took this passage at face value. Sarah Grimke began to write letters on the equality of women. Despite an unfavorable response from her church in the form of a scolding pastoral letter, Sarah Grimke did not back down, just as Anne Hutchinson had not. Grimke not only argued for the equality of women with men, but she also focused on the fair treatment of Blacks. It was her strong moral convictions that provoked her to pursue the issue of equality among men, women, and Blacks. It is difficult to know whether or not Grimke really supported the role of domesticity for women, but it is easy to see that she believed in a woman's right to choose her role and to have equal rights with men. 3

Alice Paul is another woman who espoused equality for women; however, she did not base her stand on religious principles, but on political and economic motivation. She felt that women should have a choice in the role they chose and that they should be treated with equality. Standing squarely behind the Equal Rights Amendment, Alice Paul promoted the idea that women should not have limitations forced on them by the laws of the day. Her argument was that while some of these laws did indeed make life easier for women, so far as job duties and time on the job were concerned, they also limited women by restricting job availability. Paul also took a stand on women's right to vote and thus have a voice in government. She was responsible for reorganizing the National Woman's Party into the League of Women Voters. 4

Like Alice Paul, Elizabeth Cady Stanton was also politically and economically oriented in her views of woman's role and position in society. She stood with the National Woman's Party by writing documents based on the Party's platform. She also took a stand on equality in the roles of women and men. Her values were based on the Bible, but she also wrote her own Bible to demonstrate her strong belief in equality, 5 going so far as to change the wording of certain Biblical passages to support her beliefs.

6   Needless to say, women like Elizabeth Cady Stanton and Alice Paul did not support the traditional woman's role of being in the home as other women of their day did. Instead, they felt women should have a choice and, regardless of their choice, they should be treated fairly and equal with men.

7   Out of these four women, Alice Paul has had the most dramatic and lasting impact on modern women. She was the originator of equal rights. She fought wholeheartedly for the Equal Rights Amendment, long before the battle became a popular cause. Her contribution will not be forgotten by history. I think Alice Paul would fit with ease into today's political arena.

The Research Paper

The Research Paper

WHAT IS A RESEARCH PAPER?

Students often anticipate the research paper with fear and trembling, but for no good reason. From the French verb *rechercher,* meaning "to investigate," research requires a student to comb the library in an exhilarating and suspenseful search for information. The end product of this search is a research paper, a typewritten or word-processed manuscript in which you present your views and findings on a chosen topic. Most of the information contained in your paper will reflect the ideas of other people to whom you must give credit for all borrowed material. Your task is to read on a restricted topic, to evaluate the material you find, and to meld the uncovered information into a well-focused, clearly organized, and coherently developed paper. You benefit from this exercise by learning to think, to organize, to discriminate among library sources, to summarize or paraphrase, and to conceive of a research project from start to finish.

HOW IS A RESEARCH PAPER DIFFERENT FROM OTHER ESSAYS?

The research paper differs in format from other assignments you may be asked to write. Research papers must be written in a conventional format based on specific guidelines, such as those laid down by the Modern Language Association (MLA) for papers in language and literature or other areas of the humanities, and by the American Psychological Association (APA) for papers in the social sciences. These guidelines cover every aspect of the paper's format, including placement of title, width of margins, punctuation, and listing of references. Guidelines such as the

477

MLA and APA styles are agreed upon and used by scholars to encourage consistency in papers published in journals.

Over the past 25 years the MLA has made several changes in a determined effort to simplify the format of the research paper. Latin labels were dropped from papers in language and literature and replaced by English equivalents; footnotes were replaced by the simpler endnotes. Then, in 1984, came the most sweeping change of all—parenthetical documentation, which we propose using for all freshman papers.

Parenthetical documentation is essentially a simplification of all earlier systems. It requires that a citation to a quoted work be given in parentheses in the text, rather than in either a footnote or an endnote. Under the old style, for example, the following citation format was used:

Old Style

Cleanth Brooks believes that all literature is "ultimately metaphorical and symbolic."[3]

The elevated "3" refers the reader to a footnote or to an endnote where the following citation would be found:

Footnote

[3]Cleanth Brooks, "The Formalist Critics," *The Kenyon Review* 13 (Winter 1951): 52.

Endnote

[3]Cleanth Brooks, "The Formalist Critics," *The Kenyon Review* 13 (Winter 1951): 52.

Footnotes differ from endnotes only in placement and spacing. Footnotes appear single spaced at the bottom of the page on which the citation actually occurs; endnotes are collected and typed double spaced on a separate page at the end of the paper. In either case, the citations are also listed in alphabetical order and on a separate bibliography page, which is usually titled "Works Cited." Here, for example, is how the Cleanth Brooks citation would appear on the "Works Cited" page:

Brooks, Cleanth. "The Formalist Critics." *The Kenyon Review* 13 (Winter 1951): 52.

The obvious disadvantage of this traditional style is its duplicate effort. Every work must be cited twice—once in either an endnote or footnote, and then again in the "Works Cited" listing. But it is a disadvantage entirely eliminated by the parenthetical system. Here is an example of how the parenthetical style treats citations:

For Gilbert Murray, Greek literature has a direct bearing on modern politics, morals, and culture. For instance, in *An Unfinished Biography* he comments on Euripides: "His contemporary public denounced him as dull, because he tortured them with personal problems; as malignant, because he made them see truths they wished not to see; as blasphemous and foul-minded, because he made demands on their spiritual and religious nature which they could neither satisfy nor overlook" (155).

The text briefly introduces the author and work, with a page number supplied in parentheses. The entire citation appears only once in "Works Cited" at the end of the paper:

Murray, Gilbert. *An Unfinished Biography.* New York: Oxford, 1960.

Simplicity is the clear advantage of this parenthetical style. Only one citation is given for each work. No footnotes have to be laboriously typed at the bottom of each page. Endnotes and duplicate citations are also done away with. This simpler parenthetical style is the one we will introduce and explain throughout this chapter. We will take you through all the steps involved in doing a research paper, from digging for essential sources to framing the outline and writing the first draft.

CHOOSING A TOPIC

You may be assigned a specific research topic, such as a comparison of the social problems in *Oliver Twist* and *Great Expectations*, two novels by Charles Dickens. More often, however, the freshman term paper leaves the task of finding a workable topic to the student. Let us assume that your teacher has given a typical assignment—to write a 10-page research paper on a topic of your choice within the humanities or general sciences. The first problem is to find a specific topic that is challenging enough to support a 10-page research paper.

The rule of thumb is to choose a topic that cries out for research, one that demands citations from several sources. Begin by browsing through the library. Mammoth topics such as "Famine in Africa," "Prisons of the World," or "Greek Mythology" may occur to you first, but eventually a chance opinion encountered in your browsing will suggest a narrower topic. Let us assume, for example, that your library browsing has led you to books about the Comanche Indians. After skimming some sources, you begin to wonder, "What special contributions did the Comanche make to the culture of the other Plains Indians?" To answer that question, you will have to begin a more minute search of the available sources. One student who asked herself that question eventually ended up with this narrowed topic: "The Peyote Ritual: A Contribution of the Comanche to Other Plains Indians."

Sheridan Baker, a well-known rhetorician and writer, suggests that every good topic has an "argumentative edge," some point that needs proving or disproving. For example, the general topic "Contagious Diseases of the Past," which is admittedly both overly broad and bland, could be honed to an argumentative edge and become a paper with this cutting title: "The Black Death: Reducer of Overpopulation in Europe." Or, the overdone topic of child abuse could be given an argumentative twist by arguing that in some cases child abuse turns into parent abuse. The point is to turn your research assignment into a hunt for treasure, not into grave digging.

Topics to Avoid

TOPICS THAT ARE OVERLY BROAD.   A 10-page term paper, about the length of a short magazine article, cannot accommodate such massive topics as "The History of Painting," "Novels During the Victorian Age," or "The Life of Joseph Stalin." To be properly covered, such topics would require an entire book.

TOPICS BASED ON PERSONAL OPINIONS.   Personal opinions are frequently not supportable by fact and are therefore seldom appropriate research paper topics. "The German Expressionists Were Bad Artists" or "Why the Counselors at Swanee College Are Stodgy Dressers" are not documentable enough to be usable topics.

TOPICS THAT ARE TRIVIAL.   A trivial topic is a waste of time—yours and your reader's. Avoid such pointless topics as "The Advantages of a Supermarket over a Small Local Grocery" or "Why America Needs Good Mothers." The first is intellectually empty, the second is self-evident. Try, instead, for a topic that leads somewhere, that suggests ideas, theories, and perhaps even ignites a spark of controversy.

TOPICS THAT ARE HACKNEYED.   Certain research topics are so commonplace as to be utterly uninspiring and humdrum. The following, especially, crop up year after year in research papers all over the United States: "The Case against Capital Punishment," "Legalizing Marijuana," "Abortion: Good or Bad?" "Euthanasia." For the past 20 or so years, these shopworn topics have stupefied instructors who grade research papers. Anything you write on such well-used topics had better be altogether superior, for your instructor is most likely already so utterly sated with them as to regard your paper with venom and dread. Better, then, to choose a topic that is fresh to your reader and critic, one that he or she has not seen before, or only rarely. "The Counterfeit Coin Business" is, for that reason, a better choice for a paper than is any variation on the topic of capital punishment. For the same reason, the topic "Nicolas Poussin's Intellectual Approach to Painting" is a better choice than one on abortion.

TOPICS THAT ARE TOO TECHNICAL.   Avoid topics replete with technical terms and data that neither you nor your reader really understands. Papers on such topics as "Laser Geodynamic Satellites and Their Functions" or "Seismological Computations of Dilatancy in the Palmdale Bulge" generally end up as garbled horrors, hard to write and painful to read.

TOPICS THAT CAN BE DEVELOPED FROM A SINGLE SOURCE.   "How to Make Your Own Soap" is one such topic. So is "Steps in Learning How to Use a Word Processor." Such topics can be documented from a single accurate source and therefore inspire no research. Biographical topics, depending on how they are worded, are likewise easily documented from a single source. Most merely chronological narratives of a famous life fall into this category. If you are doing a biographical paper, then, be sure to choose an angle that requires some digging and thought. For example, instead of merely writing the life story of Florence Nightingale, which can be paraphrased from any good biography about her, choose some subtheme like "How Florence Nightingale Influenced Nursing for the Laboring Classes."

GETTING ACQUAINTED WITH THE LIBRARY

Nothing teaches the efficient use of the library better than the practical experience of actual research. The following is a review of the basic research tools available in the library.

The Computer

The computer is fast becoming an invaluable research tool in the library. Information is stored in databases and accessed through a terminal. Library computers are designed to manage vast amounts of cataloged materials and can perform numerous helpful functions for any researcher willing to learn how to use them. The computer terminal, consisting of a video screen and typewriter keyboard, is the focal point for researchers working in a computerized library. Most library terminals are "user-friendly" and give simple directions onscreen about how to call up such items as a subject heading list, bibliographic information, or, in sophisticated libraries with online databases, the actual works themselves. With the help of databases, computerized libraries can also retrieve vast quantities of stored information. However, many libraries control access to these databases or charge researchers fees for using them. The most common databases are: DIALOG and BRS (Bibliographic Retrieval Services) for general information in the fields of government, health, education, social and physical sciences, humanities, and business; Mead Data Control for legal information; ERIC (Educational Research Information Center) for education; NYTIS (New York Times Information Center) for abstracts of many general interest publications; and OCLC (Online Computer Library Center) for collections in member libraries, including the Library of Congress. Many libraries have interlibrary loan arrangements that allow students access to works in other libraries.

Be sure to acquaint yourself with the computer facilities in your library (if it has them).

DOING A COMPUTER SEARCH.   A computer search on a topic of enough importance to be online and in a database can yield gems of information almost instantaneously.

Most librarians ask you to follow these steps in doing a computer search:

1. Determine the best subject heading to be used (e.g., "Graffiti," "Child Abuse," "Third-World Hunger," "Chemical Waste," "Angelou, Maya," "Gettysburg").
2. Fill out a search request form.
3. Contact the librarian in charge of computer searches.
4. With the librarian's assistance, do a database search, and see if you want the information in a printout.

Many libraries charge students for computer searches, so be sure to cost out the search before agreeing to have it done. For extensive, in-depth research you may wish to do an online search through DIALOG. However, such a search may be expensive because you pay for every minute you log online. The advantage of DIALOG is that it has access to thousands of articles in 700 databases. A more common and less expensive system to use is Academic Abstracts or InfoTrac, both CD-ROM systems. We suggest InfoTrac if your library has the software, because it not only contains the familiar *Guide to Periodical Literature* on disk, but also provides abstracts of all articles. InfoTrac has access to two files: the *National Newspaper Index* and the *Magazine Index*. These can be profiled to show that the library has holdings of the periodical in question.

Here is a sample printout from a computer search based on DIALOG. The information came from *Social Scisearch*, database number 7.

SAMPLE PRINTOUT FROM DIALOG

```
File   7:SOCIAL SCISEARCH(R)   1972-1993/Nov W1
       (c) 1993 ISI Inc.
    Set   Items   Description
? s graffiti
    S1      93  GRAFFITI
? t s1/5/1
 1/5/1
02542519   Genuine Article#: MB426   Number of References: 5
Title: GENDER DIFFERENCES IN THE JUDGED ACCEPTABILITY OF
GRAFFITI
Author(s): MCMENEMY P; CORNISH IM
Corporate Source: UNIV WAIKATO,DEPT EDUC STUDIES,PRIVATE BAG
    3105/HAMILTON//NEW ZEALAND/; UNIV WAIKATO,DEPT EDUC
    STUDIES,PRIVATE BAG
    3105/HAMILTON//NEW ZEALAND/; UNIV ULSTER/COLERAINE//
    NORTH IRELAND/
Journal: PERCEPTUAL AND MOTOR SKILLS, 1993, V77, N2 (OCT),
P622
ISSN: 0031-5125
Language: ENGLISH   Document Type: ARTICLE
Subfile: SocSearch; CC SOCS--Current Contents, Social &
Behavioral Sciences
Journal Subject Category: PSYCHOLOGY, EXPERIMENTAL
Abstract: Mean ratings of the social acceptability of
collected graffiti
    showed no gender differences for 22 men and 22 women
undergraduates
    in Northern Ireland. The bases for gender differences in
content must lie
    elsewhere.
Cited References:
    ARLUKE A, 1987, V16, P1, SEX ROLES
```

```
    LANDY EE, 1967, V25, P711, PERCEPT MOTOR SKILL
    OLOWU AA, 1983, V52, P986, PSYCHOL REP
    SCHWARTZ MJ, 1984, V59, P395, PERCEPT MOTOR SKILL
    SOLOMON H, 1975, V97, P149, J SOC PSYCHOL
logoff
        29nov93 12:05:19 User118452 Session D33.2
            $1.92    0.016 Hrs File7
              $0.90  1 Type(s) in Format  5
              $0.90  1 Types
     $2.82  Estimated cost File7
     $0.14  TYMNET
     $2.96  Estimated cost this search
     $3.13  Estimated total session cost   0.024 Hrs.
Logoff: level 31.10.01 D  12:05:20
```

Here is a sample printout from a computer search based on InfoTrac. The student selected the subdivision "Social aspects" to obtain these samples.

SAMPLE PRINTOUT FROM INFOTRAC

```
InfoTrac * National Newspaper Index ~ 1990 - Oct 1993
  Heading:   GRAFFITI
              -Social aspects
    1.    Clothing ads hit as glorifying taggers. (Orange
      County, California, Transit Authority officials want
      removal of Tag Rag clothes advertisements from bus
      shelters, claiming the ads encourage graffiti vandals)
      by Jeffrey A. Perlman il 9 col in. v112 Los Angeles
      Times June 29 '93 pA3 col 6
        HEADINGS, LIBRARY HOLDS
    2.    Leaving their mark. (youths risk arrest to tag
      Southern California surfaces with graffiti; includes
      list of tagger terms) by John M. Glionna il 44 col in.
      v112 Los Angeles Times March 10 '93 pB1 col 2
        HEADINGS, LIBRARY HOLDS
    3.    Pals in the posse; teen culture has seized the
      word as a hip name for groups; not all are harmless.
      by John M. Glionna il 34 col in. v112 Los Angeles
      Times Feb 26 '93 pB1 col 2
        HEADINGS, LIBRARY HOLDS
InfoTrac * Magazine Index Plus    (Backfile) ~ 1986 - Oct 1993
  Heading:   GRAFFITI
              -Social aspects
    1.    Can you read the handwriting on the wall? (gang
      graffiti; preventing gang activities) by Paul Conklin
      il v57 U.S. Catholic Dec '92 p28(7)
```

```
        67D3975
        ABSTRACT / HEADINGS
    2.     Harassment in the halls. (sexual harassment in
        schools) by Adrian Nicole LeBlanc v51 Seventeen Sept
        '92 p162(5)
        ABSTRACT / HEADINGS
    5.     Welcome to my nightmare; the graffiti of homeless
        youth. by G. Cajetan Luna il v24 Society Sept-Oct '87
        p73(6)
           41A2450
        HEADINGS, LIBRARY HOLDS
```

The Card Catalog

The card catalog is an alphabetical index of all books in the library, the starting point for any research. Ask a librarian to point out the location of the card catalog, which lists all library books on three separate cards, by author, title, and subject. The cards usually are stored in small, labeled drawers. In many libraries this information is stored on some microform device such as a microfilm reader or scanner. Basically, however, the same information found on the traditional card will also occur on microform.

Following are three sample cards. Technical information, useful only to the librarian, is listed on the bottom half of the card. The top half of the card contains the book title, author's name, publication data, and the call number, which indicates the location of the book in the library.

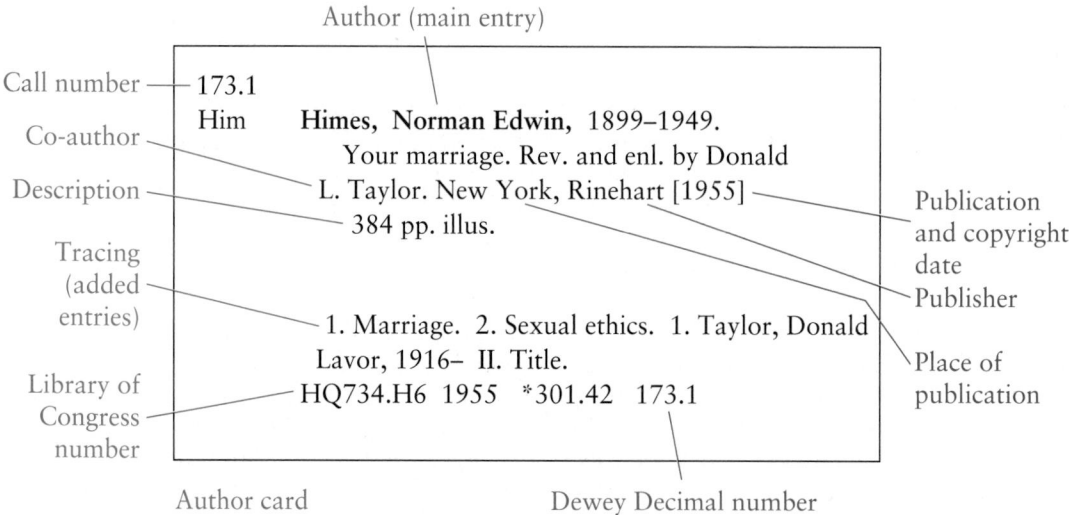

173.1   Your marriage.
Him   **Himes, Norman Edwin.** 1899–1949
         Your marriage. Rev. and enl. by Donald
     L. Taylor. New York, Rinehart [1955]
      384 pp. illus.

         1. Marriage. 2. Sexual ethics. I. Taylor,
    Donald Lavor, 1916– II. Title.
    HQ734.H6 1955 *301.42 173.1

Title card

173.1   MARRIAGE
Him   **Himes, Norman Edwin,** 1899–1949.
         Your marriage. Rev. and enl. by Donald
     L. Taylor. New York, Rinehart [1955]
      384 pp. illus.

         1. Marriage. 2. Sexual ethics. I. Taylor,
    Donald Lavor, 1916– II. Title.
    HQ734.H6 1955 *301.42 173.1

Subject card

The Stacks

The stacks are the actual library shelves on which books, magazines, and other materials are stored. Some large universities do not permit undergraduate readers into the stacks, preferring instead to dispense requested books through a librarian. In some libraries, commonly used works are available in the main library area, with the remainder of the collection stored in stacks and available through the librarian. If your school library allows access into the stacks, be aware that important books missing from the shelves may be on loan, in a special collection, or on reserve.

Whether admitted into the stacks or not, every college student should know the systems by which library books are organized. Through these systems, a single title can be located among vast numbers of books. American libraries use two systems for organizing books: (a) the Library of Congress System and (b) the Dewey Decimal System. Both systems assign each book a specific "call number," marked on its spine and listed on all catalog cards for that book.

Most large libraries today use the Library of Congress System, which contains 21 major categories, broken down as follows:

A . General works, Polygraphy

B . Philosophy, Religion

C . History, Auxiliary sciences

D . History, Topography (except America)

E . America (general), United States (general)

F . United States (local), America (except the United States)

G . Geography, Anthropology

H . Social Sciences (general), Statistics, Economics, Sociology

J . Political Science

K . Law

L . Education

M . Music

N . Fine Arts

P . Language and Literature

Q . Science

R . Medicine

S . Agriculture

T . Technology

U . Military Science

V . Naval Science

Z . Bibliography, Library Science

Further subdivisions are created by the addition of a letter. For example, Agriculture (S) is subdivided as follows:

SB   General plant culture, soils, fertilizer, implements
SD   Forestry
SF   Animal culture, veterinary medicine
SH   Fish culture, fisheries
SK   Hunting, game protection

Under the Dewey Decimal System, all knowledge is divided into ten general categories and indicated by decimal notation:

000–099	General works	500–599	Pure Science
100–199	Philosophy	600–699	Applied Arts and Sciences
200–299	Religion	700–799	Fine Arts, Recreation
300–399	Social Sciences	800–899	Literature
400–499	Philology	900–999	History, Geography, Travel

Every general area of knowledge is subdivided into tens. For example, Pure Science (500–599) is subdivided as follows:

510–519	Mathematics	560–569	Paleontology
520–529	Astronomy	570–579	Biology
530–539	Physics	580–589	Botany
540–549	Chemistry	590–599	Zoology
550–559	Geology		

Additional subcategories are designated as in this example:

511   Arithmetic
511.1   Systems

Invented in the 1870s, the Dewey Decimal System does not contain enough categories to adequately classify the knowledge that has accumulated since that time, especially in the sciences. Consequently, classifications are often long and awkward.

The Reference Room

Reference material consists of a variety of books and indexes that synopsize and classify information and its location. Usually stored on open shelves, reference material cannot be checked out and taken home.

The *Reader's Guide to Periodical Literature,* issued monthly, is the most important and useful index in the reference room. It lists magazine and journal articles in specific subject areas according to author, title, and subject. The monthly indexes are bound into a hardcover volume at the end of each year and stored alongside other volumes, which go back to the nineteenth century. The facsimile of a page from *Reader's Guide* (p. 488) will help you interpret its listings. Following is a list of other useful indexes:

Indexes

Applied Science and Technology Index
Art Index
Bibliographic Index
Biography Index
Book Review Digest
Dramatic Index
Education Index
Index to the London Times
Monthly Catalog of United States Government Publications
Music Index
New York Times Index
Social Sciences and Humanities Index

CHILDREN, Adoption of. See Adoption
CHILDREN, Exceptional
    See also
  Children, Handicapped
CHILDREN, Gifted
                Education
  Gifted programs for the culturally different. E. M. Bernal, Jr. Educ
    Digest 41:28-31 My '76
CHILDREN, Handicapped
  Thelma Boston. miracle worker. M. G. Crawford. il pors Good H 182:40+ Je '76
    See also
  Cerebral palsied children
                Education
  Education for all handicapped children. H. A. Williams, Jr. por
    Parents Mag 51:20 Je '76
  Education of the handicapped today. il Am Educ 12:6-8 Je '76
CHILDREN, Psychotic. See Mentally ill children
CHILDREN and alcohol. See Alcohol and youth
CHILDREN and television. See Television and children
CHILDREN as stockholders
  Teaching children about stocks. C. Kirk. Parents Mag 51:14 Je '76
CHILDRENS art
  Student art. See issues of School arts
    See also
  Paperwork
                Exhibitions
  Art gallery in the lobby. K. Thompson. il Sch Arts 75:35 Je '76
CHILDRENS exhibitions
    See also
  Childrens art-Exhibitions
CHILDRENS homes. See Homes, Institutional
CHILDRENS librarians
  Old strengths and new weaknesses. E. L. Heins. Horn Bk 52-250-1 Je '76
  Skimming of memory; ed by M. Hodges. F. C. Sayers. il Horn Bk 52:270-5 Je '76
CHILDRENS literature
    See also
  Fairy tales
                Authorship
  Books that say yes. M. L'Engle. Writer 89:9-12 Je '76
  Sprezzatura: a kind of excellence; excerpts from address. April 12, 1975. E. L.
    Konigsburg. Horn Bk 52:253-61 Je '76
              Awards, prizes, etc.
  Memories of childhood; awarded to J. Reiss. A. Wolff. Sat R 3:8 Je 12 '76
                Bibliography
  Books for the reluctant reader. A. R. Zinck and K. J. Hawkins. il
    Wilson Lib Bull 50:722-4 My '76
  Children's books: the best of the season. W. Cole. il Sat R 3:36-9 My 15 '76
CHILDRENS sayings. See Children-Sayings
CHILDRENS stories
      See name of author for full entry
  Peachy pig. J. O'Reilly
CHILE
                Commerce
  Ray of hope from an export pickup. Bus W p48-9 My 24 '76
            Economic conditions
  Ray of hope from an export pickup. Bus W p48-9 My 24 '76
          Politics and government
  Protest in Chile. A. Bono. Commonweal 103:390-1 Je 18 '76
CHILEANS in the United States
    See also
  California-Foreign population
CHIMERAS (biology) See Mosaics (biology)
CHIMES, Electric
  Door chime. W. D. Leckey. il Pop Mech 145:107 My '76
CHINA (People's Republic)
    See also
  Agriculture-China (People's Republic)
  Education-China (People's Republic)

Subject

Title of article

Volume, pages, issue

Magazine

Cross-references

Cross-references subdividing a topic

The following reference list was prepared by John de la Fontaine, Acquisitions Assistant at Occidental College in Los Angeles, California.

Consult the following works for information about books currently in print:

Booksellers' lists

Books in Print. New York: R. R. Bowker, 1948–. Separate volumes for listings by author and title. Accompanied by: *Subject Guide to Books in Print* (1957–).

Books in Print Plus with Book Reviews Plus [CD-ROM]. New York: R. R. Bowker, 1986–.

Cumulative Book Index. Minneapolis: H. W. Wilson, 1908–.

Paperbound Books in Print. New York: R. R. Bowker, 1971–.

Encyclopedias give a general overview of a subject. The best-known encyclopedias are:

General encyclopedias

Academic American Encyclopedia, 21 v. Danbury, CT: Grolier, 1993.

Collier's Encyclopedia, 24 v. New York: P. F. Collier, 1993.

The Columbia Encyclopedia. 5th ed. New York: Columbia University Press, 1993.

Compton's Multimedia Encyclopedia [CD-ROM], version 2.00. Carlsbad, CA: Compton's NewMedia, 1993.

Encyclopedia Americana, 30 v. Danbury, CT: Grolier, 1993.

New Encyclopaedia Britannica. 15th ed., 32 v. Chicago: Encyclopaedia Britannica, 1993.

For facts and figures, consult the following:

Almanacs and fact books

Facts on File. New York: Facts on File, 1940–, updated weekly.

Information Please Almanac, Atlas and Yearbook. New York: McGraw-Hill, 1960–, annual.

New York Public Library Desk Reference. New York: Webster's New World, 1989.

World Almanac and Book of Facts. New York: Press Pub., 1923–, annual.

Atlases and gazetteers give information about places. An atlas is a collection of maps; a gazetteer is a dictionary of places. Be sure the atlas or gazetteer you use is up to date.

Atlases and gazetteers

Cambridge World Gazetteer: A Geographical Dictionary. New York: Cambridge University Press, 1990.

Hammond Atlas of the World. Maplewood, NJ: Hammond, 1993.

National Geographic Atlas of the World. Rev. 6th ed. Washington, DC: National Geographic Society, 1992.

Omni Gazetteer of the United States of America [CD-ROM]. Detroit, MI: Omnigraphics, 1992.

Rand McNally Commercial Atlas and Marketing Guide. 123rd ed. Chicago: Rand McNally, 1992, annual.

Shepherd, William R. *Shepherd's Historical Atlas.* 9th ed. rev. Totowa, NJ: Barnes & Noble, 1980.

Times Atlas of the World. 9th comp. ed. New York: Times Books, 1992.

Today's World: A New World Atlas from the Cartographers of Rand McNally. Rev. ed. Chicago: Rand McNally, 1993.

Webster's New Geographical Dictionary. Springfield, MA: Merriam-Webster, 1988.

Biography

General information about well-known persons is listed in the following sources:

Bio-Base [microform]. Detroit: Gale Research, 1978–. A master index listing where a person's biography can be found among all the retrospective and current sources.

Biography and Genealogy Master Index [CD-ROM]. Detroit: Gale Research, 1993.

Biography Index. New York: H. W. Wilson, 1946– [also on CD-ROM]. Quarterly. Cumulated annually and every three years. An index to books and magazines.

Cambridge Biographical Dictionary. New York: Cambridge University Press, 1990.

Current Biography. Bronx, NY: H. W. Wilson, 1940–. Monthly except August. Cumulated annually. Articles about living persons. Especially useful for current celebrities. See the index in each volume, which covers preceding years.

Dictionary of American Biography, 22 v. + supplements. New York: C. Scribner's, 1928–58. Authoritative articles on Americans no longer living who have made significant contributions to American life.

Dictionary of National Biography, 66 v. + supplements. London: Smith, Elder, 1885–1901. The basic source of bibliographical information about Englishmen no longer living.

Encyclopedia of World Biography: An International Reference Work, 12 v. + 20th-century supplement in progress, New York: McGraw-Hill, 1973.

International Who's Who. London: Europa Publications, 1935–.

National Cyclopaedia of American Biography, 63 v. + current series in progress. New York: T. White, 1893–19–. The most comprehensive source of information about Americans no longer living.

Obituary Index. Westport, CT: Meckler, 1988–. Companion title: *New York Times Obituary Index.*

Webster's New Biographical Dictionary. Springfield, MA: Merriam-Webster, 1988.

Who's Who in America. Chicago: Marquis Who's Who, 1899–.

Who's Who of American Women. Chicago: Marquis Who's Who, 1970–.

Who Was Who in America. Chicago: Marquis Who's Who, 1899–. Reprints discontinued entries from *Who's Who in America.*

Information about words, their meanings, and their histories is found in one or more of the following dictionaries:

Dictionaries

American Heritage Dictionary of the English Language. 3rd ed. Boston: Houghton Mifflin, 1992.

Craigie, William A. *Dictionary of American English on Historical Principles,* 4 v. Chicago: University of Chicago Press, 1938–44. A historical dictionary of American words and meanings, modeled after *The Oxford English Dictionary.*

Merriam-Webster Dictionary of Synonyms and Antonyms. Springfield, MA: Merriam-Webster, 1992.

Oxford English Dictionary. 2nd ed. 20 v. New York: Oxford University Press, 1989. The great English dictionary based on historical principles. Also on CD-ROM.

Random House Dictionary of the English Language. 2nd ed. New York: Random House, 1987.

Webster's Third New International Dictionary of the English Language. Springfield, MA: Merriam-Webster, 1993.

To verify the source of a quotation, check one of the following dictionaries of quotations:

Quotations

Bartlett, John. *Familiar Quotations: A Collection of Passages, Phrases, and Proverbs Traced to Their Sources in Ancient and Modern Literature.* 16th ed. Boston: Little, Brown, 1992.

H. L. Mencken's Dictionary of Quotations: On Historical Principles from Ancient and Modern Sources. London: Collins, 1982,

Oxford Dictionary of Quotations. 4th ed. New York: Oxford University Press, 1992.

Webster's New World Dictionary of Quotable Definitions. 2nd ed. Englewood Cliffs, NJ: Prentice Hall, 1988.

For articles on current events and general interest articles, consult the following:

Periodical and newspaper indexes

Humanities Index. New York: H. W. Wilson, 1974–. Also on CD-ROM.

National Newspaper Index. Magazine index. Foster City, CA: Information Access, 1988–. These two titles form the InfoTrac service, which is on CD-ROM.

Readers' Guide to Periodical Literature. Minneapolis: H. W. Wilson, 1905–. Also on CD-ROM.

Social Sciences Index. New York: H. W. Wilson, 1974–. Also on CD-ROM.

Reference works for special fields

A list of all the works that survey special fields would consume an entire volume. The following is a list, by subject area, of frequently used reference works:

ART

Artbibliographies Modern. Santa Barbara, CA: Clio Press, 1989–.

Art Index. New York, H. W. Wilson, 1929–. Also on CD-ROM. Issued quarterly with annual and biennial cumulations. An author-subject index to periodicals.

Cowan, Henry J. *Dictionary of Architectural and Building Technology.* New York: Elsevier Applied Science Publishers, 1986.

Ehresmann, Donald L. *The Fine Arts: A Bibliographic Guide to Basic Reference Works, Histories, and Handbooks.* 3rd ed. Englewood, CO: Libraries Unlimited, 1990.

Encyclopedia of Architecture: Design, Engineering & Construction. New York: Wiley, 1988–.

Encyclopedia of World Art, 17 v. New York: McGraw-Hill, 1959–1987.

Gardner, Helen. *Gardner's Art Through the Ages.* 9th ed. San Diego: Harcourt Brace Jovanovich, 1991.

International Dictionary of Art and Artists, 2 v. Chicago: St. James Press, 1990.

Lucie-Smith, Edward. *Thames and Hudson Dictionary of Art Terms.* New York: Thames and Hudson, 1984.

Oxford Dictionary of Art. New York: Oxford University Press, 1988.

Thames and Hudson Dictionary of Art and Artists. Rev. ed. New York: Thames and Hudson, 1985.

BIOLOGY

Biological Abstracts. Philadelphia: BioSciences Information Service of Biological Abstracts, 1926–. Semimonthly with annual cumulations.

Biological & Agricultural Index. New York: H. W. Wilson, 1964–. Also on CD-ROM. Monthly except August, cumulated annually.

Cambridge Dictionary of Biology. New York: Cambridge University Press, 1989.

Current Contents: Life Sciences. Philadelphia: Institute for Scientific Information, 1967–. Weekly, lists tables of contents for journals.

Encyclopedia of Animal Biology. New York: Facts on File, 1987.

Encyclopedia of Human Biology, 8 v. San Diego: Academic Press, 1991.

Facts on File Dictionary of Botany. New York: Facts on File, 1984.

Gray, Peter. *Encyclopedia of the Biological Sciences.* Huntington, NY: R. E. Krieger, 1981.

Grzimek's Encyclopedia of Mammals. New York: Van Nostrand Reinhold, 1988. Also on CD-ROM.

Henderson, I. F. *Henderson's Dictionary of Biological Terms*. 10th ed. New York: Wiley, 1989.

Information Sources in the Life Sciences. 3rd ed. Boston: Butterworths, 1987.

Little, R. John. *Dictionary of Botany*. New York: Van Nostrand Reinhold, 1980.

Nowak, Ronald M. *Walker's Mammals of the World*. 5th ed., 2 v. Baltimore: Johns Hopkins University Press, 1991.

BUSINESS

ABI/Inform [CD-ROM]. Ann Arbor, MI: U.M.I., 1989–. Contains abstracts and indexing to more than 800 business and management periodicals.

Accountants' Index. New York: American Institute of Accountants, 1921. Biennially.

Berle, Gustav. *Business Information Sourcebook*. New York: Wiley, 1991.

Business Periodicals Index. New York: H. W. Wilson Co., 1958–. Also on CD-ROM. Monthly except August with annual cumulations.

Directory of Corporate Affiliations. Skokie, IL: National Register, 1973–. "Who owns whom, the family tree of every major corporation in America."

Encyclopedia of Banking & Finance. 9th ed., rev. and expanded, 3 v. Pasadena, CA: Salem Press, 1993.

Encyclopedia of Business Information Sources. 9th ed. Detroit, MI: Gale Research, 1992.

Financial Handbook. 5th ed. New York: Wiley, 1981.

Rosenberg, Jerry Martin. *Dictionary of Business and Management*. New York: Wiley, 1993.

Shim, Jae K. *Encyclopedic Dictionary of Accounting and Finance*. Englewood Cliffs, NJ: Prentice Hall, 1989.

Standard & Poor's Register of Corporations, Directors and Executives. New York: Standard & Poor's, 1928–. Annual.

CHEMISTRY

Chemical Abstracts. Columbus, OH: American Chemical Society, 1907–. Semimonthly, indexed annually and every ten years.

Concise Chemical and Technical Dictionary. 4th enlarged ed. New York: Chemical Publishing, 1986.

Dean, John Aurie. *Lange's Handbook of Chemistry*. 14th ed. New York: McGraw-Hill, 1992.

Hackh, Ingo W. D. *Grant & Hackh's Chemical Dictionary*. 5th ed. New York: McGraw-Hill, 1987.

Index Chemicus. Philadelphia, PA: Institute for Scientific Information, 1987–.

Maizell, Robert E. *How to Find Chemical Information: A Guide for Practicing Chemists, Educators, and Students.* 2nd ed. New York: Wiley, 1987.

Van Nostrand Reinhold Encyclopedia of Chemistry. 4th ed. New York: Van Nostrand Reinhold, 1984.

Wiggins, Gary. *Chemical Information Sources.* New York: McGraw-Hill, 1991.

COMPUTER SCIENCE

Computer Literature Index. Phoenix, AZ: Applied Computer Research, 1970–.

Cortada, James W. *A Bibliographic Guide to the History of Computing, Computers, and the Information Processing Industry.* New York: Greenwood Press, 1990.

Encyclopedia of Computer Science. 3rd ed. New York: Van Nostrand Reinhold, 1993.

Freedman, Alan. *The Computer Glossary: The Complete Illustrated Desk Reference.* 6th ed. New York: AMACOM, 1993.

Hildebrandt, Darlene Myers. *Computing Information Directory: A Comprehensive Guide to the Computing Literature.* 10th ed. Collville, WA: Computer Information Directory, 1993.

Rosenberg, Jerry Martin. *McGraw-Hill Dictionary of Information Technology and Computer Acronyms, Initials, and Abbreviations.* New York: McGraw-Hill, 1992.

The Software Encyclopedia. New York: Bowker, 1985–.

ECONOMICS

Block, Walter. *Lexicon of Economic Thought.* Vancouver, B.C., Canada: Fraser Institute, 1989.

Freeman, Michael J. *Atlas of the World Economy.* New York: Simon & Schuster, 1991.

Frumkin, Norman. *Guide to Economic Indicators.* Armonk, NY: M. E. Sharpe, 1990.

The HarperCollins Dictionary of Economics. New York: HarperPerennial, 1991.

International Economic Indicators. Washington, DC: Dept. of Commerce, International Trade Administration, 1978–.

Knopf, Kenyon A. *A Lexicon of Economics.* San Diego: Academic Press, 1991.

Rutherford, Donald. *Dictionary of Economics.* New York: Routledge, 1992.

Survey of Current Business. Washington, DC: Depart. of Commerce, 1921–.

EDUCATION

Barrow, Robin. *A Critical Dictionary of Educational Concepts: An Appraisal of Selected Ideas and Issues in Educational Theory and Practice.* 2nd ed. New York: Teachers College Press, 1990.

Buttlar, Lois. *Education: A Guide to Reference and Information Sources.* Englewood, CO: Libraries Unlimited, 1989.

Current Contents: Social and Behavioral Sciences. Weekly. Philadelphia: Institute for Scientific Information, 1974–.

Current Index to Journals in Education. Phoenix, AZ: Oryx Press, 1969–. Monthly with semiannual and annual indexes.

Education Index. New York: H. W. Wilson, 1929–. Also on CD-ROM. Monthly except July and August, annual cumulations.

The Encyclopedia of Comparative Education and National Systems of Education. New York: Pergamon Press, 1988.

Encyclopedia of Educational Research. 6th ed., 4 v. New York: Macmillan, 1992.

ERIC [CD-ROM]. Boston: SilverPlatter, 1988–. Corresponds to two printed publications: *Resources in Education* and *Current Index to Journals in Education.*

Freed, Melvyn N. *The Educator's Desk Reference (EDR): A Sourcebook of Educational Information and Research.* New York: American Council on Education, 1989.

The International Encyclopedia of Education [CD-ROM]. London: Pergamon, 1988. New edition due Spring 1994.

The International Encyclopedia of Educational Technology. New York: Pergamon Press, 1989.

Palmer, James C. *Dictionary of Educational Acronyms, Abbreviations, and Initialisms.* 2nd ed. Phoenix, AZ: Oryx Press, 1985.

Resources in Education. Washington, DC: Dept. of Health, Education, and Welfare, National Institute of Education, 1975–. Monthly, abstracts prepared by the Educational Research Information Center.

Shafritz, Jay M. *The Facts on File Dictionary of Education.* New York: Facts on File, 1988.

World Education Encyclopedia, 3 v. New York: Facts on File, 1988.

ENGINEERING

ASM Materials Engineering Dictionary. Metals Park, OH: ASM International, 1992.

Compendex Plus [CD-ROM] Palo Alto, CA: Dialog Information Services, 1989–.

The Engineering Index. New York: Engineering Index, 1962–. Monthly with annual cumulations, includes abstracts.

Eshbach, Ovid W. *Eshbach's Handbook of Engineering Fundamentals.* 4th ed. New York: Wiley, 1990.

Information Sources in Engineering. 2nd ed. Boston: Butterworths, 1985.

Melaragno, Michele G. *Quantification in Science: The VNR Dictionary of Engineering Units and Measures.* New York: Van Nostrand Reinhold, 1991.

New York Public Library. Research Libraries. *Bibliographic Guide to Technology.* Boston: G. K. Hall, 1975–.

GEOLOGY

Bates, Robert Latimer. *Glossary of Geology.* 3rd ed. Alexandria, VA: American Geological Institute, 1987.

Challinor, John. *Challinor's Dictionary of Geology.* 6th ed. New York: Oxford University Press, 1986.

The Concise Oxford Dictionary of Earth Sciences. New York: Oxford University Press, 1990.

Encyclopedia of Earth Sciences Series. Stroudsburg, PA: Dowden, Hutchinson & Ross, 1986–.

GeoRef [CD-ROM]. Boston: SilverPlatter Information System, 1990–.

Information Sources in the Earth Sciences. 2nd ed. New York: Bowker-Saur, 1989.

Magill's Survey of Science. Earth Science Series. Pasadena, CA: Salem Press, 1990–.

McGraw-Hill Encyclopedia of the Geological Sciences. 2nd ed. New York: McGraw-Hill, 1988.

HISTORY

Adams, James Truslow. *Dictionary of American History.* 2d ed. rev. New York: C. Scribner's, 1968.

America, History and Life. Santa Barbara, CA: Clio Press, 1964–. Also on CD-ROM, monthly.

Atlas of World History. Chicago: Rand McNally, 1993.

Barzun, Jacques. *The Modern Researcher.* 5th ed. Boston: Houghton Mifflin, 1992.

Beeching, Cyril Leslie. *A Dictionary of Dates.* New York: Oxford University Press, 1993.

Cook, Chris. *Dictionary of Historical Terms.* 2nd ed. New York: Peter Bedrick Books, 1990.

Documents of American History. 10th ed. Englewood Cliffs, NJ: Prentice Hall, 1988.

Encyclopedia of American History. 6th ed. New York: Harper & Row, 1982.

Fritze, Ronald H. *Reference Sources in History: An Introductory Guide.* Santa Barbara, CA: ABC-Clio, 1990.

The Harper Atlas of World History. Rev. ed. New York: HarperCollins, 1992.

Historical Abstracts. Part A, Modern History Abstracts, 1775–1914. Part B, Twentieth Century Abstracts, 1914–. Santa Barbara, CA: ABC-Clio, 1971–.

Prucha, Francis Paul. *Handbook for Research in American History: A Guide to Bibliographies and Other Reference Works.* Lincoln: University of Nebraska Press, 1987.

Ritter, Harry. *Dictionary of Concepts in History.* Westport, CT: Greenwood Press, 1986.

The Times Atlas of World History. 4th ed. Maplewood, NJ: Hammond, 1993.

Wetterau, Bruce. *The New York Public Library Book of Chronologies.* New York: Prentice Hall, 1990.

LITERATURE

Abrams, M. H. *A Glossary of Literary Terms*. 5th ed. New York: Holt, Rinehart, and Winston, 1988.

Abstracts of English Studies. Boulder, CO: National Council of Teachers of English, 1958–. Ten issues a year.

Benet's Reader's Encyclopedia. 3rd ed. New York: Harper & Row, 1987.

Benet's Reader's Encyclopedia of American Literature. New York: HarperCollins Publishers, 1991.

Brewer's Dictionary of 20th-Century Phrase and Fable. Boston: Houghton Mifflin, 1992.

The Cambridge History of American Literature, 4 v. New York: G. P. Putnam's Sons, 1917–21.

The Cambridge History of English Literature, 15 v. New York: Macmillan, 1932.

Cohen, Ralph. *New Literary History: International Bibliography of Literary Theory and Criticism*. Baltimore: Johns Hopkins University Press, 1988.

Columbia Dictionary of Modern European Literature. 2nd ed. New York: Columbia University Press, 1980.

Dictionary of Literary Biography. Detroit: Gale Research, 1978–.

Drabble, Margaret. *The Oxford Companion to English Literature*. 5th ed. New York: Oxford University Press, 1985.

Essay and General Literature Index. New York: H. W. Wilson, 1933–.

Grote, David. *Common Knowledge: A Reader's Guide to Literary Allusions*. New York: Greenwood Press, 1987.

Hart, James David. *The Oxford Companion to American Literature*. 5th ed. New York: Oxford University Press, 1983.

Holman, C. Hugh. *A Handbook to Literature*. 6th ed. New York: Macmillan, 1992. Thorough revision of a standard reference work with the same title by Thrall and Hibbard.

Howatson, M. C. *The Oxford Companion to Classical Literature*. 2nd ed. New York: Oxford University Press, 1989.

Leary, Lewis Gaston. *Articles on American Literature, 1900–1950*. Durham, NC: Duke University Press, 1954.

Leary, Lewis Gaston. *Articles on American Literature, 1950–1967*. Durham, NC: Duke University Press, 1970.

Leary, Lewis Gaston. *Articles on American Literature, 1968–1975*. Durham, NC: Duke University Press, 1979.

Magill, Frank Northen. *Cyclopedia of Literary Characters II*, 4 v. Pasadena, CA: Salem Press, 1990.

Magill, Frank Northen. *Magill's Bibliography of Literary Criticism: Selected Sources for the Study of More than 2,500 Outstanding Works of Western Literature,* 4 v. Englewood Cliffs, NJ: Salem Press, 1979.

MLA International Bibliography of Books and Articles on the Modern Languages and Literatures. New York: Modern Language Association, 1970–. Also on CD-ROM.

The New Cambridge Bibliography of English Literature. 5 v. Cambridge: Cambridge University Press, 1969–77.

Patterson, Margaret C. *Literary Research Guide.* 2nd ed. New York: Modern Language Association, 1983.

Thompson, George. *Key Sources in Comparative and World Literature: An Annotated Guide to Reference Materials.* New York: F. Ungar, 1982.

The Year's Work in English Studies. London: Published for the English Association by John Murray, 1919/20–. Annual critical surveys.

MUSIC

Baker, Theodore. *Baker's Biographical Dictionary of Musicians.* 8th ed. New York: Schirmer Books, 1992.

Brockman, William S. *Music: A Guide to the Reference Literature.* Littleton, CO: Libraries Unlimited, 1987.

Cary, Tristram. *Dictionary of Musical Technology.* New York: Greenwood Press, 1992.

Duckles, Vincent H. *Music Reference and Research Materials: An Annotated Bibliography.* 4th ed. New York: Schirmer Books, 1992.

Ewen, David. *The New Encyclopedia of the Opera.* New York: Hill and Wang, 1971.

Grove, George. *Grove's Dictionary of Music and Musicians.* 5th ed., 10 v. New York: St. Martin's, 1975. The standard encyclopedia of music since 1879.

Morehead, Philip D. *The New American Dictionary of Music.* New York: Dutton, 1991.

The Music Index. Detroit: Information Coordinators, 1949–. Monthly with annual cumulations.

The Music Index on CD-ROM. Alexandria, VA: Chadwyck-Healey, 1981–.

The New Harvard Dictionary of Music. Cambridge, MA: Belknap Press of Harvard University Press, 1986.

The Norton/Grove Concise Encyclopedia of Music. New York: W. W. Norton, 1991.

Scholes, Percy Alfred. *The Oxford Companion to Music.* 10th ed. New York: Oxford University Press, 1990.

MYTHOLOGY AND FOLKLORE

Ashliman, D. L. *A Guide to Folktales in the English Language: Based on the Aarne-Thompson Classification System.* New York: Greenwood Press, 1987.

Bulfinch, Thomas. *Bulfinch's Mythology.* New York: Modern Library, 1993. A reprint of three works: *The Age of Fable; The Age of Chivalry; Legends of Charlemagne.* Originally written and published separately, the classic reference in the field.

Diehl, Katharine Smith. *Religions, Mythologies, Folklores: An Annotated Bibliography.* 2d ed. New York: Scarecrow Press, 1962.

Frazer, James George. *The Golden Bough: A Study in Magic and Religion.* 3rd ed., 9 v. in 13. New York: St. Martin's, 1990. Reprint. Originally published: London: Macmillan, 1911–1915.

Funk & Wagnalls Standard Dictionary of Folklore, Mythology and Legend. London: New English Library, 1975.

Man, Myth & Magic: The Illustrated Encyclopedia of Mythology, Religion, and the Unknown. New ed., 12 v. New York: Marshall Cavendish, 1983.

Mythical and Fabulous Creatures: A Source Book and Research Guide. New York: Greenwood Press, 1987.

The Mythology of All Races, 13 v. Boston: Marshall Jones Company, 1916–32.

Radford, Edwin. *Encyclopaedia of Superstitions.* Chester Springs, PA: Dufour Editions 1969.

Thompson, Stith. *Motif-Index of Folk-Literature: A Classification of Narrative Elements in Folktales, Ballads, Myths, Fables, Mediaeval Romances, Exempla, Fabliaux, Jestbooks, and Local Legends.* Rev ed., 6 v. Bloomington, IN: Indiana University Press, 1989.

PHILOSOPHY

Bynagle, Hans E. *Philosophy: A Guide to the Reference Literature.* Littleton, CO: Libraries Unlimited, 1986.

The Concise Encyclopedia of Western Philosophy and Philosophers. New ed. Boston: Unwin Hyman, 1989.

De George, Richard T. *The Philosopher's Guide to Sources, Research Tools, Professional Life, and Related Fields.* Lawrence: Regents Press of Kansas, 1980.

Dictionary of Philosophy. New York: International Publishers, 1984.

Dictionary of the History of Ideas; Studies of Selected Pivotal Ideas, 5 v. New York: Scribner, 1973–74.

The Encyclopedia of Eastern Philosophy and Religion: Buddhism, Hinduism, Taoism, Zen. Boston: Shambhala, 1989.

The Encyclopedia of Philosophy, 8 v. in 4. New York: Macmillan, 1972.

The Handbook of Western Philosophy. New York: Macmillan, 1988.

Handbook of World Philosophy: Contemporary Developments Since 1945. Westport, CT: Greenwood Press, 1980.

The Oxford Companion to the Mind. New York: Oxford University Press, 1987.

The Philosopher's Index. Bowling Green, OH: Philosophy Documentation Center, 1967–. Quarterly.

Tice, Terrence N. Research Guide to Philosophy. Chicago: American Library Association, 1983.

PHYSICS

Ballentyne, D. W. G. A Dictionary of Named Effects and Laws in Chemistry, Physics, and Mathematics. 4th ed. London: Chapman and Hall, 1980.

CRC Handbook of Chemistry and Physics. Cleveland, OH: CRC Press, 1977–. Annual.

Current Contents: Physical, Chemical & Earth Sciences. Philadelphia, PA: Institute for Scientific Information, 1979–.

Current Physics Index. New York: American Institute of Physics, 1975–.

Encyclopedia of Physics. 2nd ed. New York: VCH, 1991.

The Facts on File Dictionary of Physics. 2nd ed. New York: Facts on File, 1981.

INSPEC Ondisc [CD-ROM]. Ann Arbor, MI: U.M.I., 1989–.

Lord, M. P. Macmillan Dictionary of Physics. London: Macmillan Reference, 1986.

A Physicist's Desk Reference. New York: American Institute of Physics, 1989.

Physics Abstracts. London: Institution of Electrical Engineers, 1903–.

Physics Briefs. Weinheim: Physik Verlag, 1979–.

POLITICAL SCIENCE

The Blackwell Encyclopaedia of Political Institutions. New York: Blackwell Reference, 1987.

The Blackwell Encyclopaedia of Political Thought. New York: B. Blackwell, 1991.

The Book of the States. Lexington, KY: Council of State Governments, 1935–.

Congressional Record: Proceedings and Debates of the . . . Congress. Washington: Govt. Print. Off., 1874–. Daily, cumulated for each session, annual index.

Dictionary of Modern Political Ideologies. New York: St. Martin's Press, 1987.

Encyclopedia of the Third World. 4th ed., 3 v. New York: Facts on File, 1992.

Evans, Graham. The Dictionary of World Politics: A Reference Guide to Concepts, Ideas, and Institutions. New York: Simon & Schuster, 1990.

Holler, Frederick L. *Information Sources of Political Science*. 4th ed. Santa Barbara, CA: ABC-Clio, 1986.

Kalvelage, Carl. *Bridges to Knowledge in Political Science: A Handbook for Research*. Pacific Palisades, CA: Palisades Publishers, 1984.

PAIS on CD-ROM. New York: Public Affairs Information Service, 1986–. Print version since 1915.

Plano, Jack C. *The American Political Dictionary*. 9th ed. Fort Worth: Harcourt Brace, 1993.

Plano, Jack C. *The International Relations Dictionary*. 4th ed. Santa Barbara, CA: ABC-Clio, 1988.

Political Handbook of the World. New York: McGraw-Hill, 1975–.

Robertson, David. *A Dictionary of Modern Politics*. 2nd ed. London: Europa Publications, 1993.

Worldmark Encyclopedia of the Nations. 7th ed., 5 v. New York: Worldmark Press, 1988.

York, Henry E. *Political Science: A Guide to Reference and Information Sources*. Englewood, CO: Libraries Unlimited, 1990.

PSYCHOLOGY

Campbell, Robert Jean. *Psychiatric Dictionary*. 6th ed. New York: Oxford University Press, 1989.

Chaplin, James Patrick. *Dictionary of Psychology*. 2nd rev. ed. New York: Laurel, 1985.

Dictionary of Behavioral Science. 2nd ed. San Diego: Academic Press, 1989.

The Encyclopedic Dictionary of Psychology. Cambridge, MA: MIT Press, 1983.

Encyclopedia of Psychology. 2nd ed. New York: Wiley, 1994.

Kahn, Ada P. *The Encyclopedia of Mental Health*. New York: Facts on File, 1993.

The Oxford Companion to the Mind. New York: Oxford University Press, 1987.

Popplestone, John A. *Dictionary of Concepts in General Psychology*. New York: Greenwood Press, 1988.

PsychLit [CD-ROM]. Peabody, MA: EBSCO Pub., 1991–. Psychological Abstracts on CD-ROM.

Psychological Abstracts. Washington: American Psychological Association, 1927–.

Sutherland, N. S. *The International Dictionary of Psychology*. New York: Continuum, 1989.

RELIGION

The Dictionary of Bible and Religion. Nashville: Abingdon, 1986.

Encyclopaedia Judaica, 16 v. New York: Macmillan, 1971–72.

The Encyclopedia of Islam. New ed. Leyden: E. J. Brill; London: Luzac & Co., 1954–.

The Encyclopedia of Religion, 16 v. New York: Macmillan, 1987.

Encyclopaedia of Religion and Ethics, 13 v. New York: Scribner, 1910–34. Often referred to by its editor's name—Hastings.

Geddes, C. L. *Guide to Reference Books for Islamic Studies.* Denver, CO: American Institute of Islamic Studies, 1985.

Illustrated Dictionary & Concordance of the Bible. New York: Macmillan, 1986.

The Interpreter's Dictionary of the Bible, 5 v. New York: Abingdon Press, 1962.

Kennedy, James R. *Library Research Guide to Religion and Theology: Illustrated Search Strategy and Sources.* 2nd ed., rev. Ann Arbor, MI: Pierian Press, 1984.

Kennedy, Richard. *The International Dictionary of Religion: A Profusely Illustrated Guide to the Beliefs of the World.* New York: Crossroad, 1984.

Mead, Frank Spencer. *Handbook of Denominations in the United States,* 7th ed. Nashville: Abingdon, 1980.

Melton, J. Gordon. *Encyclopedia of American Religions,* 4th ed. Detroit: Gale Research, 1993.

Melton, J. Gordon. *Magic, Witchcraft, and Paganism in America: A bibliography.* New York: Garland, 1982.

New Catholic Encyclopedia, 17 v. New York: McGraw-Hill, 1967–79.

The Oxford Dictionary of the Christian Church. 2d ed. New York: Oxford University Press, 1974.

Religion Indexes [CD-ROM]. Bronx, NY: H. W. Wilson, 1989–. CD-ROM version of *Religion Index One.*

Religion Index One: Periodicals. Chicago: American Theological Library Association, 1977–. Continues: *Index to Religious Periodical Literature.*

Religious and Theological Abstracts. Myerstown, PA: Religious and Theologial Abstracts, 1958–. Also available on CD-ROM.

Stutley, Margaret. *The Illustrated Dictionary of Hindu Iconography.* Boston: Routledge & Kegan Paul, 1985.

Tucker, Dennis C. *Finding Religion (in the library): A Student Manual of Information Retrieval and Utilization Skills.* Bristol, IN: Wyndham Hall Press, 1989.

SOCIOLOGY

Aby, Stephen H. *Sociology: A Guide to Reference and Information Sources.* Littleton, CO: Libraries Unlimited, 1987.

Boudon, Raymond. *A Critical Dictionary of Sociology.* Chicago: University of Chicago Press, 1989.

Brown, Samuel R. *Finding the Source in Sociology and Anthropology: A Thesaurus-Index to the Reference Collection.* New York: Greenwood Press, 1987.

Encyclopedia of Social Work. 18th ed. Silver Spring, MD: National Association of
     Social Workers, 1987.

Encyclopedia of Sociology, 4 v. New York: Macmillan, 1992.

Handbook of Sociology. Newbury Park, CA: Sage Publications, 1988.

The International Encyclopedia of Sociology. New York: Continuum, 1984.

Sociofile [CD-ROM]. Wellesley Hills, MA: Silver Platter Information Services,
     1986–. CD-ROM version of *Sociological Abstracts.*

Sociological Abstracts. San Diego: Sociological Abstracts, 1952/53–.

COLLECTING PERTINENT INFORMATION

COMPILE A BIBLIOGRAPHY.   You now have a research topic, and you know how and
where to collect information on it. The next step is to compile a *bibliography,* a list
of useful sources of information on the topic. Purposeful reading is now one of the
most important skills you can develop. You must learn to separate useless from
useful information without a wasteful and slow page-by-page analysis of the
source.

Skim book chapters and magazine articles to see if they contain material relevant
to the topic. Read tables of contents, index pages, and subtitles of books; read the
topic sentences of paragraphs. Mark pertinent passages in pencil if the source
belongs to you, or if it is a library source, place a paperclip on the page. When you
are reasonably sure that the source will be useful, list it on a 3 × 5 bibliography
card. A typical bibliography card looks like this:

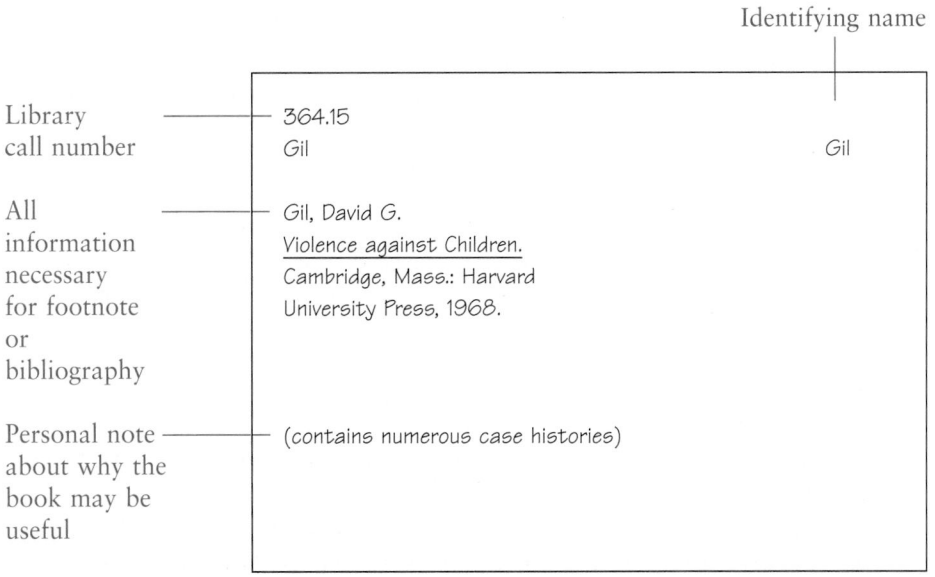

Identifying name

Library
call number

All
information
necessary
for footnote
or
bibliography

Personal note
about why the
book may be
useful

364.15
Gil

Gil, David G.
Violence against Children.
Cambridge, Mass.: Harvard
University Press, 1968.

(contains numerous case histories)

Gil

It will save you valuable time later if you note the call number of a book and the date and title of a magazine article on the bibliography card. Use a separate card for each source to simplify changes in your preliminary bibliography. To add a source, make a new card; to delete a source, remove the card on which it is entered.

EVALUATE THE EVIDENCE. Assessing the authenticity and accuracy of uncovered sources is part of your job as a researcher. You cannot simply take for granted the fairness and accuracy of a source. Lies appear as often in print as they do in speech. The information in some sources (possibly even in most sources) will be found to be truthful, current, and accurate for their time. But there's the rub. Earlier generations were often mistaken (our own generation will no doubt appear likewise to our descendants). And a writer may have published some notion as hard and fast fact that was truthful for the time but is nowadays regarded as myth or nonsense. Novice researcher or not, you are the only possible judge of a source's worthiness for inclusion in your paper. Here are some practical rules that will help you evaluate sources:

1. Check one opinion against another. If, for example, one source insists that the painter Raphael Santi was influenced by Michelangelo, confirm this opinion in another source. As you read on your chosen topic, you'll quickly discover a consensus among the experts that will enable you to separate fact from speculation.

2. Notice the publication date of the source. The fact of one generation is very often the myth of another. If the source is very old, its views and ideas may be outdated and wrong. If you have two equivalent sources on the same topic, use the later one.

3. Check your own opinions and evaluations against the views of professionals. For instance, you may think that the poetry of Edgar Guest is far superior to any you have read, only to find that experienced critics rate his work as mediocre. The *Book Review Digest* is a good source for critical opinions on books. The credentials of an author can be checked in the various biographical dictionaries or *Who's Who* volumes.

4. Beware of statistics. They can be out of date and they can also be inaccurate. You should immediately question a source that uses exaggerated numbers, such as "Millions of children are allowed to view pornography on the streets of New York." Such exaggerated numbers are often used as figurative language to make a point. Make sure that any study using statistics is from a source known to be systematic and careful.

5. Check to see who published the source. If you have never heard of the publishing house, check its name in *Literary Market Place (LMP)*. This reference work will tell you what kinds of material a house usually publishes, who its audience is, and what its standards are for accepting new work. Another reference work to help you evaluate books is *Book Review Digest*, which cites selected reviews of works of literature and nonfiction books in all

fields. Alphabetized by the author of the reviewed book, its citations include a brief description of the book, quotations from selected reviews, and references to other reviews.

TAKE NOTES.   By now, considerable skimming and reading should have given you an overall view of the topic. Quite likely, you have already formulated a controlling idea and are ready to begin taking notes from the sources you will use. The importance of careful note-taking cannot be overstated: Accuracy and thoroughness at this stage will save literally hours of work in assembling the first draft of your paper.

Make notes on 4 × 6 cards. Any information, data, or quotation to be incorporated into the paper should be listed on the 4 × 6 note cards; call numbers and publication information on books or magazine articles should be listed on the bibliography cards. Therefore, there will be both a note card and a bibliography card for each source consulted.

The four primary forms of note-taking are: summarizing, paraphrasing, quoting, and a mixture of these.

To *summarize* means to condense. A condensation uses fewer words than the original. A book may be condensed into one paragraph; a paragraph may be condensed into one sentence. For example, a book citing numerous examples of child battering in the schools of Sumer, five thousand years ago, might be summarized like this on a note card:

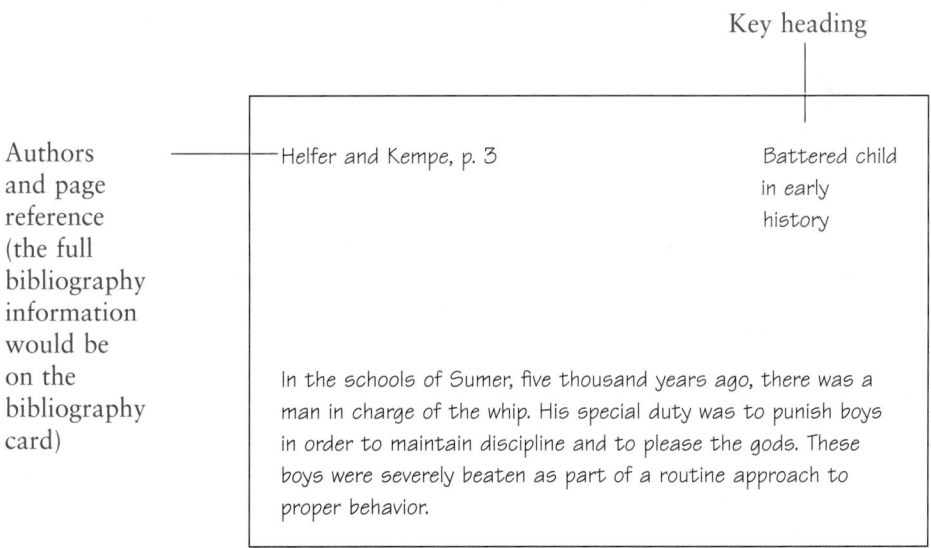

Key heading

Authors and page reference (the full bibliography information would be on the bibliography card)

Helfer and Kempe, p. 3

Battered child in early history

In the schools of Sumer, five thousand years ago, there was a man in charge of the whip. His special duty was to punish boys in order to maintain discipline and to please the gods. These boys were severely beaten as part of a routine approach to proper behavior.

To *paraphrase* means to restate an original source in your own words using nearly the same amount of space as the original. Here is an example of a paraphrase:

The general public is not fully aware of the seriousness and prevalence of cruelty to children. The knowledge that babies suffer severe injury or death at the hands of their parents is repugnant and extremely hard to accept. Abuse of children, the

Original

greatest cause of death among children under the age of three, causes more deaths than auto accidents, leukemia, and muscular dystrophy.

Earl, *Today's Health*, p. 27

Society's feelings toward child abuse

Paraphrase ——————— Because society feels repelled by the idea of child battering, it remains unaware of the extent and seriousness of the problem. Decent people tend to ignore the ugly truth that children are often seriously injured and even killed by their own parents. Few people realize that in fact child abuse is the greatest cause of death among children under the age of three, causing more deaths than car accidents or serious diseases like leukemia.

To *quote* means to use exactly the same words as the original. Many passages may be quoted in the notes, but as few quotations as possible should appear in the actual paper. A good research paper should reveal that the writer has assimilated the information and data and therefore need not rely on the words of others. Frequent quotations also give writing a choppy effect. Use quotations only when:

1. You want authoritative support for a statement.
2. Something is said with exceptional literary taste.
3. The quotation is needed for accuracy.

Quotations must meticulously include every comma and every word in the original. Check quotations for accuracy. Oddities of spelling or phrasing in the original should be copied exactly and followed by a bracketed [*sic*], which indicates, "This is the way the text reads in the original." Any omitted portion of the original quotation is indicated by ellipses (. . .) as in this example:

> It is thought that because of crowding in small quarters and because of having larger families, "the working-class parent uses . . . punishment more than the middle-class parent."

Ellipses are not used if the quotation is integrated into a sentence and the omission is made at the beginning or end of the original. Here is an example:

Quotation to be used

> Many sociologists have noted that the working-class parent uses physical punishment more than the middle-class parent.

Quotation as it appears in the paper

> It is thought that because of crowding in smaller quarters and because of having larger families, "the working-class parent uses physical punishment more than the middle-class parent."

Quotations in the final paper must fit coherently into the flow of writing. Transitional sentences, based on a thorough understanding of both the quotation and its context, should be used to introduce the quotation and move the reader on to succeeding material. A well-prepared note card, with author and subject identified, will help you effectively use a quotation:

Neill, p. 102   An authority's
                                                 view on
                                                 punishment

A. S. Neill suggests that "Perhaps we punish because we are a
Christian civilization. If you sin, punishment awaits you in the here
and now, and Hell awaits you in the future."

Here are some additional suggestions for writing useful note cards:

1. Write in ink, not pencil, or the note cards will smudge when you shuffle them. Do not type note cards. Many libraries do not allow the use of typewriters on their premises; moreover, transcribing notes on a typewriter later wastes time and causes copying errors.

2. Use one card per idea. With one idea on each card, an outline can be created by shuffling the cards and arranging them in a logical sequence. To save money, cut your own note cards from regular paper.

3. In copying or paraphrasing material from more than one page in an original source, indicate all pages on the note card. This information is needed for footnotes or endnotes.

4. Write notes legibly or you may have to go back to an original source to decipher what you meant. (See also "Avoid Plagiarism," pp. 511–12).

Formulating the Thesis, Outlining the Paper, and Writing the Abstract

THE THESIS.   Sometime during your note-taking, you will begin to lean toward an assumption, an opinion, a point of view about your topic. This leaning will eventually result in your thesis, a one-sentence summary of the main idea in your paper. The thesis is, in effect, the conclusion to which you have been brought by your research; it is the imprint of your mind on the subject.

Generally, but not always, the thesis will have an argumentative edge; it will reflect the stand you have chosen to take on the material, the viewpoint you will argue or advocate. But not all research papers are argumentative. Some papers are framed as reports rather than as arguments. The following examples will clarify the difference between the intent of a *report paper* and an *argumentative paper*.

Report thesis

Most Egyptologists today conclude that the Great Pyramid was built by Egyptian citizens using the simplest of tools and technology.

This paper will simply report on the techniques used by ancient Egyptians to build the pyramids.

Argumentative thesis

Although supporters of animal experiments claim that any reduction would jeopardize scientific progress, scientists should stop abusing animals in an attempt to improve human lives.

This paper will not report; it will argue in defense of its main idea that cruel scientific experiments on animals should be stopped. The writer of this thesis has clearly taken a stand whose rightness the paper must prove and defend.

The thesis is possibly the single most important sentence of your paper; it is literally the scaffolding on which all the ideas in the paper must hang. You should therefore do your utmost to make the thesis sentence as clear and incisive as possible. A muddled thesis starts the paper off on the wrong foot, from which lame beginning it may never recover.

THE OUTLINE. If you are writing a paper for the humanities, the next step is to outline the paper. (See "Abstract," p. 556 if you are writing a social science paper.) A simple procedure for creating an outline is to assemble the note cards according to the logical sequence of their major ideas. All information relating to one major idea is placed in the same stack. For example, in the paper on child abuse, perhaps the note cards could be logically grouped into three stacks based on the following major ideas:

I. Violence against children by adults has been practiced throughout history.

II. A wide variety of child-abuse cases exist today and for numerous reasons.

III. Some effective action has been taken against child abuse, but more social cooperation and legal sanctions are needed to overcome the problem.

These three points could then be condensed into a controlling idea such as the following:

Adult violence against children, commonly practiced throughout history, occurs today for a variety of reasons in countless cases of child abuse and can be corrected only through social cooperation and legal sanctions.

A controlling idea containing three major divisions is now established. Arrange the note cards within each division into a logical sequence of information, examples, and other data. If necessary, add or delete cards. Translate the logical arrangement of the cards into an outline as in this example:

Child Abuse

Adult violence against children, commonly practiced throughout history, occurs today for a variety of reasons in countless cases of child abuse and can be corrected only through social cooperation and legal sanctions.   Thesis

I. Adult violence against children is common throughout history.
   A. The Sumerians beat children with whips to discipline them.
   B. The Romans flogged boys before the altars of Diana as a religious practice.
   C. Early Christians whipped their children on Innocents Day in memory of King Herod's massacre.
   D. During the Middle Ages, children's eyes were gouged and their bodies mutilated to make them effective beggars.
   E. The factory system allowed foremen to beat children mercilessly if they didn't work hard enough.

II. Countless cases of child abuse exist today for a variety of reasons.
   A. Numerous child-abuse cases have been recorded.
      1. On record are thousands of cases of planned falls, strangulations, and sexual assaults.
      2. Parents have assaulted children with instruments ranging from plastic bags to baseball bats.
      3. Disciplinary measures may include cigarette burns, plunges into boiling water, or starvation.
   B. Child-abuse cases exist for a variety of reasons.
      1. In a study of sixty families with beaten children, all the persecuting parents were beaten as children, indicating a revenge pattern.
      2. Some parents become abusive because they expect more love and affection from their child than the child is able to deliver.
      3. A frustrated parent will use the child's bad behavior to justify abuses.
      4. Unsatisfactory marital relationships are another frequent cause of child abuse.

III. Social cooperation and legal sanctions are needed to overcome the problem of child abuse.
   A. Although little was heard of the battered child syndrome before 1960, today all the states have adopted legislation governing reporting of battered children.
   B. But only two states, Maryland and New Jersey, have laws specifically prohibiting the use of physical force on children.

C. Doctors and other people fear slander suits if they notify police of child abuse and an investigation does not support the charge.

D. The other parent often protects the one inflicting the harm so that proof of battering is difficult to obtain.

E. Society and its legal system must make further advances toward curbing child abuse.

Avoid an overly detailed outline. The rule of thumb is two pages of outline for every ten pages of writing.

THE ABSTRACT.   An abstract is a summary of your paper which, for the benefit of the reader, lists the main points of your research. Unlike the introduction, your abstract is no place to entice, shock, or hint. Use it only to state in the clearest, most concise language what your paper is about.

If you are required to write an abstract, center the heading "Abstract" one inch down from the top of the paper. First, clarify the purpose of your paper and then state its major points in narrative, not outline, form (see example in social science student paper). Next, place the abstract page immediately after the title page but before the paper itself.

Writing and Documenting the Paper

With the outline or abstract completed, you are now ready to write the paper. First, arrange the note cards in the topic sequence of the outline. Once the cards are assembled in the right order, you can expand on the notes, insert appropriate transitions, and write the first draft. Remember, however, that the information in the research paper, although compiled from borrowed sources, must be thoroughly reorganized and expressed in your own style. Your job is to meld your own words with the materials uncovered in your research—the quotations, facts, and opinions of others—into an original paper.

Documenting the paper requires that you cite any source from which you have derived information or ideas. You do not have to document your own insights and opinions, obviously. But just as obviously you should give credit for the ideas of others uncovered in your research and expressed as summaries, paraphrases, or quotations in your paper. A paper containing material improperly documented is regarded as plagiarized (stolen) and, in many English departments, automatically earns an irrevocable "F" (see example of plagiarism on page 512).

Two main styles of documentation are now in use: (1) the author/work system approved by the Modern Language Association (MLA) and used in most subjects of the humanities. (Art, history, literature, music, and philosophy require MLA style.) (2) the author/date system approved by the American Psychological Association (APA) and used in the social sciences. (Anthropology, economics, political science, psychology, sociology, and biology require APA style.) Both systems are widely used by freshman composition students, who must often write papers for both social science and the humanities. We consequently discuss both the MLA and the APA systems of documentation in the following pages. We do not, however, cover either footnotes or endnotes because both have been largely replaced by the simpler parenthetical systems.

In writing and documenting the paper, there are some pitfalls to avoid.

AVOID THE "STRING OF PEARLS" EFFECT.   The "string of pearls" effect occurs when a writer strings together one quotation after another with no original writing, interpretation, or clear purpose. Here is an example:

> "The greatest influence of Latin upon Old English was occasioned by the
> introduction of Christianity by St. Augustine into Britain in 597" (Baugh 98).
>
> "At the time England shared the religion of other Teutonic tribes and this
> religion was often in sharp contrast with Christianity" (Baugh 98).
>
> "One of the main problems was that the Teutonic religions exalted loyalty to
> one's tribe to the point of leaving no wrong unavenged, and men were admired
> when they went to war to avenge their tribe" (Baugh 99).
>
> "Christianity, on the other hand, preached a philosophy of kindness and mercy
> towards one's enemy" (Baugh 101).
>
> "The many new conceptions that came along with this new religion naturally
> had to be translated into the Anglo-Saxon language in order to be expressed"
> (Baugh 102).

Consisting of one unassimilated note after another, this excerpt seems choppy and undeveloped. The writer should have assimilated the notes into a single unified paragraph with one citation:

> The introduction of Christianity into Britain in A.D. 597 by Augustine caused Latin
> to become an important part of the English language. The infiltration was gradual
> but dramatic because Christianity changed the philosophy of the Anglo-Saxons by
> substituting the Christian notions of kindness and mercy for the Teutonic notions
> of tribal revenge through physical combat. New words had to be found to give
> expression to this new philosophy of love and these words were in Latin (Baugh
> 97–102).

AVOID PLAGIARISM.   Plagiarism is the act of fraudulently passing off another's words, ideas, and interpretations as your own. Sometimes students plagiarize unintentionally because they are unaware of the scholarly rules governing the use of another's work. Here is an example of plagiarism. The original is on the left, the plagiarized version on the right:

Original version	Plagiarized version
The relation between master and slave thus frankly conceived by the Greeks, did not necessarily imply, though it was quite compatible with brutality of treatment. The slave might be badly treated, no doubt, and very frequently was, for his master had almost absolute control over him, life and limb; but, as we should expect, it was clearly recognized by the best Greeks that the treatment should be genial and humane (Dickinson 77).	In Greece the relationship between master and slave did not necessarily imply brutality of treatment. The slave might be badly treated, and frequently was because the master had complete control over the life and limb of the slave; however, it was clearly recognized by the kindest Greeks that slaves should be treated in a genial and humane way (Dickinson 77).

Even though a citation is given, the version on the right is plagiarized because it is nearly identical to the original passage. The words used come, in the main, from the source and not from the writer. Here is an acceptable rendering of the original paragraph:

Although slaves were considered a natural part of the Greek economy, much like agricultural tools, and although every slave belonged body and soul to his master, the best and most ethical Greeks believed firmly that slaves should be treated humanely and should neither be insulted nor outraged (Dickinson 77).

DOCUMENTING THE HUMANITIES PAPER (MLA)

Using Parenthetical Documentation (MLA)

The parenthetical style of documentation requires that you provide full documentation only once for each source cited. This will be done in "Works Cited" at the end of the paper. Within the paper itself you will give only brief references, in parentheses, to any sources cited.

Begin the parenthetical documentation one space after the material cited. Except for closing quotation marks, no punctuation of any kind should come between the material cited and the parentheses. Periods, commas, and semicolons go after the parentheses:

> According to William Zinsser, most writers work from a spacious design, trying to
>
> get a lot of material down on paper, but they are not "hung up on starting at the
>
> beginning" (106).

One exception is quotations set off from the text. In such a case, skip two spaces after the concluding punctuation mark of the quotation and insert the parenthetical reference with no punctuation mark following. Here is an example:

> Writing is never an act conducted in a vacuum. In fact it is a highly personal
>
> transaction that takes place on paper:
>
>> It is one person talking to another person. Readers identify first with the
>>
>> person who is writing, not with what the person is writing about. Often,
>>
>> in fact, we will read about a subject that really doesn't interest us
>>
>> because we like the writer. We like the warmth or humor or humanity
>>
>> that he brings to his subject. (Zinsser 112)

See also example on page 515.
Some guidelines about how to use parenthetical citations follow.

WHEN YOU GIVE THE AUTHOR'S NAME IN THE TEXT.   If you give the author's name when referring to a source, then provide only the pagination within parentheses:

> In his best-seller <u>Restoring the American Dream</u>, Robert J. Ringer states
>
> emphatically that a fundamental law of economics, one that politicians refuse to
>
> accept, is, "There is no such thing as something for nothing" (53).

WHEN YOU DON'T GIVE THE AUTHOR'S NAME IN THE TEXT.   If in your text you have introduced a source without giving the author's name, give the author's last name and the pagination within parentheses:

> As one great pedagogue put it, "No one can bear young people all the time."
>
> Occasionally every teacher loves to escape into a cool library or garden—away
>
> from the noise of pupils (Highet 27).

WHEN YOU ARE CITING MORE THAN ONE WORK BY THE SAME AUTHOR.   If you are citing more than one work by the same author, but you do not mention the author's name in your text, give the author's name, an abbreviated title, and the pagination within parentheses:

> One point of view is that all writing is "a deeply personal process, full of mystery
>
> and surprise" (Zinsser, <u>Word Processor</u> 96).

If, however, you *do* mention the author's name in your text, then supply within parentheses only a short title followed by the pagination:

> William Zinsser insists that the word processor can help writers to achieve three
>
> cardinal goals of good writing—"clarity, simplicity and humanity" (<u>Word Processor</u>
>
> 112).

WHEN YOU ARE USING A WORK BY MORE THAN ONE AUTHOR. When citing a work with up to three authors whose names you have not mentioned in the text, give all last names within parentheses, followed by the pagination:

> It should be pointed out that the God of the Hebrews is distinct from matter
>
> whereas the God of the Babylonians co-existed with matter (McNeil and
>
> Sedlar 4).

Use "et al." or "and others" when citing a work by more than three authors:

> The Norman Conquest united the practical and enterprising qualities of the
>
> Norman and their French instinct for symmetry with the Anglo-Saxon character to
>
> form a new race (Baugh et al. 111). <u>Or:</u> (Baugh and others 111).

WHEN YOU ARE USING A WORK WITH A CORPORATE AUTHOR. If a work is authored by a committee, an institution, a corporation, or a government agency, the full or shortened name of the author should appear within parentheses if you did not mention it in your text:

> "Students are encouraged to attend all worship services and to dress according to
>
> code" (Pacific Union College 6).

In the case of long and cumbersome corporate names, abbreviations are acceptable in subsequent citations as long as the name is recognized and understood:

First citation (National Institutes of Mental Health 22).

Subsequent citation (NIMH 23).

WHEN YOU ARE USING A WORK WITH MORE THAN ONE VOLUME.   For works with more than one volume, use a colon (followed by a space) to separate the volume number from the pagination:

> Browning's poems often portray "lovers who let the good minute pass without
>
> acting upon it" (Harrison 2: 473).

If, however, you are referring to an entire volume of a multivolume work, and there is no need to give pagination, place a comma after the author's name and include the abbreviation "vol.":

> (Durant and Durant, vol. 2).

WHEN YOU ARE USING QUOTED MATERIAL SET OFF FROM THE TEXT.   Quotations longer than four lines must be indented ten spaces and set off from the text. In such cases, place the parenthetical citation after the final period:

> Brodie finds an ironic contradiction in Jefferson's so-called agrarian period:
>
> > But if one looks at the private life of Thomas Jefferson in precisely
> >
> > those years in which he committed himself totally to the rustic life, some
> >
> > curious contradictions emerge. What exactly did Jefferson mean by virtue,
> >
> > by corruption, and by morality? For if Jefferson truly believed, as he wrote
> >
> > in 1781, that laboring in the earth kept a man's morals free from corruption,
> >
> > how do we square this with the fact that the finality of Jefferson's settling
> >
> > into rural living in 1767–68 coincided with his attempt or attempts at the
> >
> > seduction of the wife of his good friend and near neighbor John Walker?
> >
> > This is an episode that is still somewhat obscure, and somewhat comic. (73)

WHEN YOU ARE USING A PLAY CITED BY ACT, SCENE, AND LINE.   When citing a play by act, scene, and line numbers, use arabic numerals divided by periods. For instance, a quotation from Act 1, Scene 3, lines 43–46 of Shakespeare's *The Merchant of Venice* would be treated as follows:

> In an aside to the audience, Shylock reveals his mean character early in the play:
>
> > I hate him for he is a Christian.
> >
> > But more for that in low simplicity
> >
> > He lends out money gratis and brings down
> >
> > The rate of usance here with us in Venice.
> >
> > (Merchant 1.3.43–46)

Notice that the final period comes before the parentheses and that you may use an abbreviated title as long as it is not ambiguous. Some teachers prefer the old-style use of roman numerals. If so, use a capital roman numeral for the act, a lower case roman numeral for the scene, and arabic numerals for the lines:

(<u>Merchant</u> I.iii.43–46)

WHEN YOU ARE USING A LONG CLASSICAL POEM DIVIDED INTO BOOKS OR CANTOS. A poem divided into books or cantos should be treated as follows:

Pyrochles finds his brother Cymochles in the Bower of Acrasia, indulging in a

passionless kind of titillation:

And now he has pourd out his ydle mynd

In daintie delices, and lavish joyes

Having his warlike weapons cast behynd,

And flowes in pleasures and vaine pleasing toyes

Mingled emongst loose Ladies and lascivious boyes.

(<u>Fairie Queene</u> 2.5.5–9)

If your teachers insist on roman numerals, then the parenthetical reference would be as follows:

(<u>Fairie Queene</u> II.v.5–9)

WHEN YOU ARE USING A POEM. When quoting lines of poetry in stanzaic form, use the words "line" or "lines," not "1." or "11.":

The superiority of feeling over intellect is asserted by e. e. cummings:

wholly to be a fool

while Spring is in the world

my blood approves

and kisses are a better fate

than wisdom. (lines 5–9)

When quoting poetry, be sure to copy the stanzas, lines, and words exactly as found in the original. For example, cummings's unorthodox capitalization and punctuation must be faithfully reproduced.

WHEN YOU ARE USING THE BIBLE. A reference to the Bible is placed within parentheses immediately following the quotation and is cited by book, chapter, and verse; no other documentation is needed:

> Job has reached the nadir of his despair when he cries out, "I am repulsive to my
>
> wife, loathsome to the sons of my own mother. Even young children despise me"
>
> (Job 19.17–18).

WHEN YOU ARE CITING AN INDIRECT SOURCE. Scholars try whenever possible to deal with the original source of an idea or a quotation; however, sometimes the only source available is an indirect one, as in the case of one author quoting another. In such a case, place the abbreviation "qtd. in" ("quoted in") before the indirect source in your parenthetical reference:

> Homosexual males experience a high degree of social alienation, caused by the
>
> fact that they are a minority group at odds with the majority of society. In an
>
> interview, after having declared his homosexuality publicly, Congressman Gerry E.
>
> Studds said, "To grow up and enter adulthood as a gay person in this country is
>
> to be in a situation where all the messages one receives with respect to the
>
> deepest feelings inside oneself tell one that those feelings are not legitimate at
>
> best, and that they are sinful and evil at worst" (qtd. in Meredith 59–60).

The parenthetical reference does not give the source of the Studds quotation.

Using Content Notes (MLA)

Material related to your research but not important enough to be part of the main body of the paper can be placed in a content note, either at the bottom of the page to which the information belongs, or gathered at the end of the paper before the "Works Cited" page. The following rules apply to preparing content notes:

1. Indent the first line of each note five spaces.
2. Double space content notes gathered at the end of the paper, but single space those shown at the foot of a page. In the latter case be sure to allow for enough space for the entire note. Begin the note four lines below the text. Do *not* type a solid line between the text and the note because this would indicate a note continued from the previous page when space ran out. Single space the note but double space between notes if there is more than one note.

3. In your text, roll up a half space at the relevant place and strike your note number, followed by one space, as in the following example:

> In the last decade 15 million unborn children have had their lives abbreviated by someone's decision to have an abortion.[6] All of the combined . . .

The note at the foot of the page adds the following comment without interrupting the flow of the text:

> [6] In 1973 the Supreme Court decision of <u>Roe v. Wade</u> made abortions legal.

Content notes can be used to explain a term or a procedure, to expand on an idea, to acknowledge assistance, or to refer the reader to another source. If a content note refers to another source, full documentation of that source must appear in "Works Cited":

> [12] In 1984 President Ronald Reagan directed the Departments of Justice and Health and Human Services to apply civil rights regulations to protect handicapped newborns (15).

"Works Cited" would then have the following entry:

> Reagan, Ronald. <u>Abortion and the Conscience of the Nation.</u> New York: Thomas Nelson, Publishers, 1984.

Preparing the List of "Works Cited" (MLA)

At the end of your paper, you must compile a complete list of the sources used in your paper. Title this list "Works Cited" and include on it all sources cited either in the text or in content notes. The entries must be arranged in alphabetical order by the authors' last names. Where several works by the same author appear, list these alphabetically by title. Don't repeat the author's name, but simply use three hyphens, followed by a period. Here is an example:

> Trayers, Scott. "Altered Coins." <u>Coinage</u> June 1984: 88–94.
>
> ---. "Counterfeits." <u>Coinage</u> August 1984: 64–68.

If the work has no author, as in the case of some magazine articles, alphabetize by the first word of the title, excluding articles such as "The" or "A." The format of the "Works Cited" page follows:

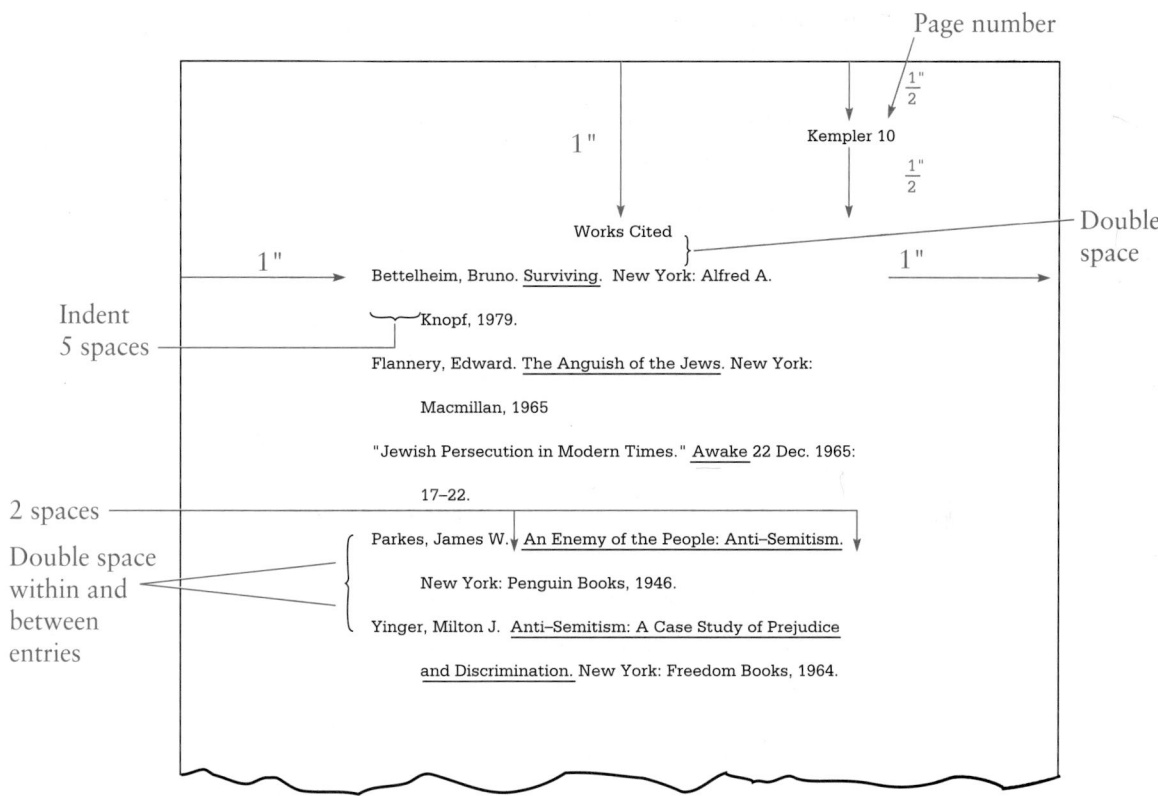

STANDARD SOURCES.   Listed below are examples of most standard sources you will encounter in your research. Adhere to the format rigorously. Should you encounter a source for which you find no model, use the format of a similar source or consult your teacher. All sources below follow the MLA style.

Brodie, Fawn M. Thomas Jefferson: An Intimate History. New York: Norton, 1974.

Book by a single author

1. For easy alphabetizing, the author's name is inverted and followed by a period.

2. Then comes the title, given in full, followed by a period.

3. A subtitle is separated from the main title by a colon. The full title must be underlined (see first example).

4. Next is the place of publication, followed by a colon and the name of the publisher, a comma, the date of publication, and then a period. If more than one place is given, use only the first. Copy the publisher's name as it is listed on the title page of the book. Well-known publishers' names should be

abbreviated. For instance, "W. W. Norton & Company, 1973" is shortened to "Norton, 1973."

However, always supply the full name of a university press, abbreviating the words "University Press" as "UP" (Oxford UP, 1980). Always use the original publication date unless the book is a new edition, in which case you must give the date of the edition being used. If no date is given, use the latest copyright date or state "n.d."

Book by two or three authors	Hallberg, Edmond C., and William G. Thomas. <u>When I Was Your Age.</u> New York: Free, 1974.

The names of the second (and third) authors are not inverted. Give the names of the authors in the order in which they appear on the title page.

Book by more than three authors	Masotti, Louis H., et al. <u>A Time to Burn? An Evaluation of the Present Crisis in Race Relations.</u> Chicago: Rand, 1969.

Et al. may be replaced by the English "and others" if you prefer. This form for multiple authors should be used only for books by more than three authors.

Book by a corporate author	American Institute of Physics. <u>Handbook.</u> 3rd ed. New York: McGraw, 1972.

If the publisher is the same as the author, repeat the information:

Defense Language Institute. <u>Academic Policy Standards.</u> Monterey: Defense Language Institute, 1982.

Book with an editor	Arnold, Matthew. <u>Culture and Anarchy.</u> Ed. J. Dover Wilson. Cambridge: Cambridge UP, 1961.

If the editor's contribution is being cited in your paper, his name goes first:

Wilson, J. Dover, ed. <u>Culture and Anarchy.</u> By Matthew Arnold. Cambridge: Cambridge UP, 1961.

Title in an edited collection	Thoreau, Henry David. "Observation." <u>The Norton Reader.</u> 3rd ed. Ed. Arthur M. Eastman, et al. New York: Norton, 1973.
Title in a collection by same author	Thomas Lewis. "The Wonderful Mistake." <u>The Medusa and the Snail: More Notes of a Biology Watcher.</u> New York: Viking, 1974.
Translation	Alighieri, Dante. <u>The Inferno.</u> Trans. John Ciardi. New York: New American Library, 1954.

As in the case of an editor, if you wish to stress the translator's work, place the name of the translator first:

Ciardi, John, trans. <u>The Inferno.</u> By Dante Alighieri. New York: New American Library,

   1954.

McCrimmon, James M. <u>Writing with a Purpose.</u> 5th ed. Boston: Houghton Mifflin,

   1974.

> A second or later edition

Other editions could be as follows: "Rev. ed." (revised edition), "2nd ed." (second edition), "Rev. and enl. ed." (revised and enlarged edition).

Knowles, John. <u>A Separate Peace.</u> 1959. New York: Bantam, 1966.

> Republished book

The original edition appeared in 1959; the writer of the paper used the 1966 Bantam edition.

Harrison, G. B., et al., eds. <u>Major British Writers.</u> 2 vols. New York: Harcourt, 1959.

> A work of more than one volume

This form is appropriate if you are using all of the volumes in the series; however, if you are using a specific volume only, give the number of the volume used at the end of the entry:

Harrison, G. B., et al., eds. <u>Major British Writers.</u> 2 vols. New York: Harcourt, 1959,

   Vol. 2.

Paolucci, Anne. "Comedy and Paradox in Pirandello's Plays." <u>Modern Drama</u> 20 (1977):

   321–39.

> Article in a periodical with continuous pagination throughout the year

The following sequence must be observed for periodicals numbered continuously through the year: Author, title of article, name of journal, volume number (in arabic numerals), year of issue (within parentheses) followed by a colon, and finally the pages of the entire article.

Cappe, Walter H. "Humanities at Large." <u>The Center Magazine</u> 11.2 (1978): 2–6.

> Article in a periodical with separate pagination of each issue.

When each issue of a periodical is paged separately, include the issue number (or month or season). Page numbers alone will not locate the article because every issue begins with page 1.

Berger, Brigitte. "The Coming Age of People Work." <u>Change</u> May 1976: 24–30.

Davis, Flora, and Julia Orange. "The Strange Case of the Children Who Invented Their

   Own Language." <u>Redbook</u> Mar. 1978: 113, 165–67.

> Article in a monthly magazine

Article in a weekly magazine	Barthelme, Donald. "The Captured Woman." <u>The New Yorker</u> 28 June 1976: 22–25.

For periodicals that have no volume numbers, supply the exact date.

Unsigned article	"Philadelphia's Way of Stopping the Shoplifter." <u>Business Week</u> 6 Mar. 1972: 57–59.

When the article is unsigned, begin with the title of the article.

Newspaper article	Gergen, David. "White House Weakens Its Vital Center." <u>Los Angeles Times</u> 13 January 1985, pt. 4: 1.

Give the name of the newspaper as it appears on the masthead, omitting any introductory article (*New York Times*, not *The New York Times*). Specify the part or section if one is given. Because different editions contain different materials, give the edition when one is given on the masthead:

Southerland, Daniel. "Carter Plans Firm Stand With Begin." <u>Christian Science Monitor</u> 9 Mar. 1978, western ed.: 1, 9.

An editorial	Futrell, William. "The Inner City Frontier." Editorial. <u>Sierra</u> 63.2 (1978): 5.
Letter to the éditor	Miller, Donald, E. P. Letter. <u>Time</u> 14 Jan. 1985: 8.

If the author is replying to a letter, write "Reply to letter of Nora Newhaus." Do not underline this information or place it in quotation marks.

Article from an encyclopedia	Nicholas, Herbert George. "Churchill, Sir Winston Leonard Spencer." <u>Encyclopaedia Britannica</u> 1968 ed.

or more commonly

"Churchill, Sir Winston Leonard Spencer." <u>Encyclopaedia Britannica</u> 1969 ed.

1. The authors of encyclopedia articles are usually listed by initials at the end of the articles; these initials are clarified in the index.
2. Not all facts of publication are necessary; year and volume number suffice.
3. Watch the various spellings of *encyclopedia*.

Public document or pamphlet	<u>Cong. Rec.</u> 10 June 1975: 2520–21.
	<u>Social Security Programs in the United States.</u> U.S. Department of Health, Education, and Welfare. Washington: GPO, 1968.

Note that most federal publications emanate from the Government Printing Office (GPO).

Kruger, Jane. <u>Teaching as an Art</u>. A Conference Syllabus published by Maryland

    University, 1970.

<u>1976 Foreign Currency Converter</u>, published by Deak and Co. of Los Angeles, 1976.

Because pamphlets are distributed by many organizations in a variety of nonstandard forms, the best you can do is treat them as much like books as possible, supplying place of publication, publisher, and date.

Marcus, Greil. "Limits." Rev. of <u>Meridian</u>, by Alice Walker. <u>The New Yorker</u> 7 June 1976:   Critical review

    133–36.

If the review is untitled, proceed directly with "Rev. of . . ."

<u>The Hearst and Davies Affair</u>. Dir. David Rich. Prod. Paul Pompia. With Robert Mitchum   Radio or

    and Virginia Madsen. ABC. KABC, Los Angeles: 14 Jan. 1985.   television
    program

The information for a radio or television program should be listed in the following order:

1. Title of program, underlined
2. Director, producer, narrator, composer, host, etc.
3. Star performers, preceded by "With"
4. Network (e.g., CBS)
5. Local station (followed by a comma) and its city (e.g., KETC, St. Louis)
6. Date of broadcast

If you want to list an episode, it should precede the title of the program and should appear within quotation marks:

"The Exchange Student." <u>Schoolbreak Special</u>. With Neeta Puri. CBS. KCBS, Los

    Angeles. 22 Jan. 1985.

<u>The River</u>. Dir. Mark Rydell. Prod. Edward Lewis. Writ. Robert Dillon and Julian Barry.   Film

    With Sissy Spacek and Mel Gibson. Universal Pictures, 1985.

A film citation requires information in the following order:

1. Title of film, underlined
2. Director, producer, writer—each followed by a period
3. Names of stars, preceded by "With"
4. Name of studio distributing the film, followed by a comma and the year the movie came out

If the director, writer, or producer's work is being stressed, it should appear first:

Rydell, Mark, dir. The River. Prod. Edward Lewis. Writ. Robert Dillon and Julian Barry.

With Sissy Spacek and Mel Gibson. Universal Pictures, 1985.

Recording or tape

Osborn, Alex, narr. Applied Imagination. Cassette. Prod. Success Motivation Institute,

Inc., San Francisco, 1972.

Roosevelt, Eleanor, narr. My Life with F.D.R. Cassette. Glendale, Calif.: Glendale

Community College Library, 1981.

Hampton, Lionel, cond. Lionel Hampton and His Big Band. New York: Glad-Hamp

Record, Inc., GHS 1023, 1983.

The order of information listed when citing a recording depends on the desired emphasis. Usually, however, the composer, narrator, or conductor will appear first. Other information to include is the title of the record (underlined), the artist(s) or orchestra, the manufacturer, the catalog number, and the year of issue. If you are using a tape recording, indicate the medium (e.g., "cassette" or "audiotape"). If you wish to include the titles of individual musical works on the record, then omit the general title and place the work cited in quotation marks; however, do not underline or place in quotation marks the title of musical compositions identified only by form, number, and key:

Miller, Glenn, cond. "Moonlight Serenade." Glenn Miller Orchestra. New York: RCA,

LSP–1192(e), 1960.

Bach, Johann Sebastian. Toccata and Fugue in D minor; Toccata, Adagio, and Fugue in

C major; Passacaglia and Fugue in C minor. Cond. Eugene Ormandy. Philadelphia

Orchestra. New York: Columbia, MS 6003, n.d.

Private letter

Woolley, Morton. Letter to the author. 12 Feb. 1976.

Interview

Hirshberg, Jennifer A. Personal interview on College Grading Standards. Glendale,

California, 19 Feb. 1976.

Manuscript

Zimmerman, Fred M. "Speculation: Los Angeles–1985." A working paper for the Los

Angeles Goals Program. Los Angeles City Hall: Planning Department Library, 1967.

No specific rules exist for the documentation of manuscripts. When using this kind of material, stick as closely as you can to the form for books or magazines. The titles of unpublished works, no matter how long, are enclosed in quotation marks.

Kelly, James E., Jr. <u>Readability Analyzer.</u> Computer software. Acorn Software Products,

1984. IBM-PC-DOS 2.10.

Computer
software

Entries for computer software should contain the following information:

1. Writer of the program, if known
2. Title of the program, underlined
3. Descriptive label "Computer software," neither underlined nor in quotation marks
4. Distributor and year of publication
5. Other pertinent information, if available

Separate all items with periods, except the distributor and year, which are separated by a comma. At the end of the entry add any other pertinent information, such as the computer for which the program was designed (e.g., Apple), the number of kilobytes or units of memory (e.g., 12 KB), the operating system (e.g., IBM-PC-DOS 2.10, CP/17 2.2), and the form of program (disk). Separate these items with commas and end the entry with a period.

Bassan, Fernande. "The Translation of Hamlet by Alexandre Dumas and Paul Meurice,

and its Development, 1846–96." <u>Australian Journal of French Studies</u> (Australia)

1982 19 (1): 11–31. DIALOG file 39, item 1078171 35A–01672.

Material from a
computer
database

Material from a computer database, such as BRS, DIALOG, or OCLC, should be treated like other printed material, except that you must add a reference to the service at the end of the entry. Give the publication information as provided by the service, the name of the vendor, and any identifying number within the service.

DOCUMENTING THE SOCIAL SCIENCE PAPER (APA)

With the current emphasis on across-the-curriculum writing, freshmen composition students are encouraged to write research papers in areas other than the humanities. Many of these papers will focus on the social sciences, a field primarily concerned with how human beings, and sometimes other animals, relate to each other. Universities have not come to an absolute agreement on what constitutes a social science, but most often it includes the following studies: anthropology, economics, political science, and psychology. History and philosophy are included in the social sciences when they take a scientific approach, but when they deal with the joys, sufferings, and aspirations of humanity—especially in nonscientific terms—they are likely to be considered as part of the humanities. Appropriate topics on which college students can do research abound in the social sciences. For instance, you might do a paper on typical fears experienced by elementary school children (psychology), or on the attitude of the Kalahari Desert !Kung people toward marriage (anthropology), or on how the 1987 stock market crash came about (economics). Most projects suitable for the time limitations of an academic term and for the resources available to beginning writers involve studying and synthesizing secondary materials. Beginning students in the social sciences traditionally work with the written papers, reports, articles, and books of experts in the area they are studying. They will not be expected to write a paper based on original behavioral studies, answers to questionnaires, statistical evidence, or administered surveys. In short, your paper in the social sciences will probably not require you to do primary research.

Everything we have said so far in this chapter about research techniques applies to your social science paper. You will need to choose a narrowed topic, get acquainted with the library, collect pertinent information, evaluate your sources, and formulate a thesis, which you then support. The main difference is one of form rather than approach. For instance, instead of an outline, you will submit an abstract, and instead of using the Modern Language Association (MLA) rules as your style sheet, you will use the rules of the American Psychological Association (APA). Widely used in the social sciences, APA documentation is an author and date system that is parenthetical and similar to the MLA system. If you understand the MLA system, you will find it easy to make the shift to the APA system. The essential difference between them is the APA system's requirement that an author's name be followed by the date of publication—an ever-important fact in scientific (especially clinical) research. Full information about the sources cited within the paper will then be contained under a heading called "References" at the end of the paper. Here are some useful hints you will want to follow.

Using Parenthetical Documentation (APA)

BE CLEAR AND UNCLUTTERED.   Whenever possible, give the necessary documentation within your main text. If this seems awkward, then give it in parentheses:

> In 1971, Arthur Miller came out with *The Assault on Privacy,* a book pointing out the problems in a society where private information is so accessible.

> LeMond and Fry (1975) exposed the widespread use of computer records in various federal agencies.

> All kinds of attorneys, government agencies, and business people have access to the personal files of individuals because these files are open to people who know how to get at them (Neier, 1975, p. 190).

If you mention the name(s) of the author(s) in your text, all you need in parentheses is the date and page. But in your reference list you must include the names of all authors.

If you are referring to an entire work, you do not need to include a page reference; however, if you are referring to information on a specific page, include the page. It is better to include the page reference whenever helpful for retrieval of information.

WHEN YOU ARE USING A SOURCE WITH A SINGLE AUTHOR.   As a general rule, place the date of publication as close to the name of the author as possible, followed by the page number to facilitate retrieval of the citation.

> Bachman (1983, p. 86) explains the result of a survey of how American high
>
> school students view the military.
>
> American high school students generally wish they could avoid the military
>
> (Bachman, 1983).

WHEN YOU ARE USING A SOURCE IN WHICH THE AUTHORS HAVE THE SAME LAST NAME. When a source refers to two different authors who have the same last name (James Jones and Carl Jones), use the first initial to distinguish the two.

> Other authors disagree (J. Jones & C. Jones, 1988).

If the two authors are known to be related, no initial is needed: (Durant & Durant, 1975).

Use an ampersand (&) to connect the two names when placed within parentheses. No ampersand is needed for in-text references not within parentheses (see example under the next heading).

WHEN YOU ARE USING A SOURCE WITH MORE THAN TWO AUTHORS.   When citing a work by three or more authors, give all names the first time you refer to the work. In subsequent references to this work, use the last name of the first author, followed by "et al."

> Turco, Toon, Ackerman, Pollack, and Sagan (1983) list the global consequences of
>
> a nuclear explosion.
>
> The global consequences of a nuclear explosion are so immense as to be
>
> indescribable (Turco et al., 1983).

If your reference list has more than one work by Turco and any other co-authors, do not shorten any citations to Turco, lest you confuse the reader.

WHEN YOU ARE USING A SOURCE WITH A CORPORATE AUTHOR.   A corporate author is any organization, such as the Carnegie Foundation, National Academy of Sciences, or some governmental agency. Write out the full name of the corporate author for the first citation. You can, however, abbreviate the citation in subsequent references.

> Many breeding programs for birds in captivity are proving successful (National
>
> Geographic Society, 1988).

Subsequent references to this source are abbreviated:

> (NGS, 1988).

WHEN YOU ARE USING A SOURCE REFERRED TO IN A SECONDARY SOURCE. In your research, you will often depend on comments or quotations found in your books or journals. For instance, the author of a psychology book you are using as one of your sources may quote Sigmund Freud. The quotation itself comes from a primary source, but the book in which it is quoted is a secondary source. When you cite this material in the text of your paper, give the author of the original work first, followed by a parenthetical reference to the work in which you found the citation. Begin the parenthetical reference with "cited in . . ."

> Greenway (cited in Alvin, 1966, p. 24) indicated that . . .

Your reference list will then contain the following entry:

> Alvin, J. (1966). *Music therapy.* New York: Humanities Press.

If you are quoting a statement made by an author in 1862 but contained in a work published in 1949, it is common sense to indicate in your text the time of the original statement. Here is how you can handle it:

> In 1862 Otto von Bismarck became chancellor of Prussia. He worshipped force,
>
> saying, "Germany does not look to Prussia's liberalism, but to her power" (cited in
>
> Wallbank and Taylor, 1949, vol. 2, p. 214).

WHEN YOU ARE USING A MULTIVOLUME SOURCE. When referring to a work that is part of a multivolume set, include the volume number and page number, separating the volume number from the page number with a colon.

> Approval of the project had been unanimous (Harrison, 1988, vol. 3: p. 180).

When referring to a specific table or section of a work, include this information in your citation, as follows:

> (Clark, 1988, fig. 5).

> (Winstein, 1986, sec. 8).

WHEN YOU ARE CITING TWO OR MORE SOURCES WITHIN THE SAME PARENTHESES. If your paper requires you to cite within parentheses two or more works supporting the same point, list the citations in the same order in which they appear in the reference list.

Research during the past two years (Roth, 1987 & Quincy, 1988) has given rise to

some serious doubt.

Using Content Notes (APA)

Content notes consist of information that does not belong in the main flow of your text. They should be used sparingly, but when they are necessary, they should conform to the following rules:

1. Immediately following the material to which the note refers, place a numeral elevated one-half space above the line, with no space between the numeral and the last word or punctuation mark. Here is an example:

   In the second experiment, the researchers used voice feedback by recording

   all of the vocal protests resulting from the shock that had been introduced.[2]

   As in the first situation, . . .

   A complete reference will then appear on your content notes page.

2. Begin all content notes on a separate page following the last page of your text. Label this page "Footnotes," centered at the top of the page. See sample student paper for the social sciences, page 564.

3. Here are some typical examples of content notes:

   References to other sources:

   [3] On this point see also P. Marler and S. Peters (1981), who raised 16 male

   swamp sparrows by hand in acoustic isolation. They were taken from the

   field as 2- and 10-day old nestlings.

Your "References" must include any works referred to in your content notes. Comments related to the subject being discussed:

[6] In this paper the term artificial intelligence will be used to mean a language

developed from a set of rules determined before the language is put into use.

Major source requiring frequent in-text citation:

[12] All quotations of Hubert Dreyfus are from his book <u>What Computers Can't Do</u> (1979).

Your "References" must include any version referred to in your content notes.

Preparing the List of "References" (APA)

At the end of your paper, you will have a list of all sources actually cited as documentation; this list will be entitled "References." Each entry will contain four units, in the following order: (1) author, (2) year of publication, (3) title, and (4) publication facts. End all units with periods and separate them from each other by a single typewriter space.

Several APA conventions differ from those of MLA. In general, the differences have to do with punctuation and capitalization. Here are some of the APA conventions you must follow:

1. Center the word "References" at the top of a new page. Start the first line of each entry at the left margin, but indent the second and succeeding lines three spaces from that margin. Type the list double spaced throughout, in alphabetical order by author (or title, if no author is shown). Alphabetize corporate authorship by the first significant word in the name.

2. Give the surname and initials of all authors, no matter how many there are. Separate the names with commas and use an ampersand (&) between the last two names. List the names in the order listed on the source you are citing.

3. If a book is the work of one or more editors, enclose the abbreviation "Ed." or "Eds." in parentheses after the name of the last editor:

   Baker, J. (Ed.).

   Daniels, M. & Miller, D. (Eds.).

4. Enclose the date of publication in parentheses. For magazines and newspapers, place a comma after the year, then the month—written out in full—and the date:

Book   Fishman, J. (1988).

Magazine   Gonzales, P. (1987, January 15).

5. Capitalize only the first word of a book or article title (and the first word of a subtitle if there is one). Type the remaining words in lowercase letters. However, capitalize each word in the title of a periodical:

Book   <u>AIDS: The ultimate challenge.</u>

Periodical   <u>Journal of Applied Psychology.</u>

6. Underline the titles of books and periodicals. Do not use quotation marks around the titles of articles within these longer works.

> Linden, E. (1988, March 28). Putting knowledge to work. <u>Time</u>, pp. 60–63.

7. The actual page numbers on which a newspaper article appears are shown following the name of the paper and a comma. Use the abbreviation "p." or "pp." Separate page numbers by commas and end the item with a period:

> pp. 50, 51, 63–67.

8. When you are using an essay or chapter within a book, list the author, date, and title of the primary source on the "References" page. Then, place "In" followed by the author or editor's name, the book title, then parentheses enclosing the abbreviation "pp." and the exact page numbers of the article or chapter you have referred to. Finally, give the publisher's location and name, followed by a period. See sample in number 10.

9. Show the state in which a publisher is located, unless the city is well known, such as New York, Chicago, Boston, Paris, or London. Use the standard two-letter postal abbreviation for states. Place a colon after the location:

> Belmont, CA: Wadsworth.

Be as brief as possible in giving the name of the publisher, omitting such words as "Company" or "Incorporated." Do spell out the names of associations or university presses:

> Macmillan
>
> Oxford University Press
>
> National Audubon Society

10. If your reference list contains more than one work by the same author, use three hyphens, followed by a period, in place of the author's name for all works after the first one listed:

> Beardsley, W., & Mack, J. E. (1982). The impact on children and adolescents
>
>   of nuclear development. In <u>Psychological Aspects of Nuclear</u>
>
>   <u>Developments</u>. Washington, DC: American Psychiatric Association.
>
> ---. (1983). Adolescents and the threat of nuclear war: The evolution of a
>
>   perspective. <u>Yale Journal of Biology and Medicine</u>, 56, 79–91.

Both of the works are authored by W. Beardsley and J. E. Mack.

STANDARD SOURCES. Listed below are examples of most standard sources you will encounter in your research. Adhere to the format rigorously. Should you encounter a source for which you find no model, use the format of a similar source or consult your teacher. All sources below follow the APA style.

Book by a single author

Jackson, S. W. (1988). <u>Melancholia and depression: From Hippocratic times to modern times</u>. New Haven: Yale University Press.

Book by two or more authors

Cole, D. M., & Scarfo, R. G. (1965). <u>Beyond tomorrow</u>. Amherst, WI: Amherst Press.

Book by a corporate author

U.S. Congress. Office of Technology Assessment (1982). <u>World population and fertility planning technologies: The next twenty years</u>. Washington, DC: U.S. Government Printing Office.

When the publisher is the same as the author, write "author" where the publisher belongs:

South-Western Publishing Co. (1976). <u>Fair and balanced treatment of minorities and women</u>. Cincinnati, OH: Author.

Book edited by an individual or group

Friedman, R. J., & Katz, M. M. (Eds.). (1974). <u>The psychology of depression: Contemporary theory and research</u>. New York: Wiley.

Chapter in an edited book

Salter, R. M. (1979). Transplanetary subway systems. In F. P. Davidson, L. J. Giacoletto, & R. Salkeld (Eds.), <u>Macroengineering and the infrastructure of tomorrow</u>. Boulder, CO: Westview Press.

The names of the editors following "In" are not inverted.

Edition, other than first, of a book

Lester, J. D. (1971). <u>Writing research papers: A complete guide</u> (4th ed.). Glenview, IL: Scott, Foresman.

Book in translation

La Boetie, E. (1975). <u>The politics of obedience: The discourse of voluntary servitude</u> (H. Kurz, Trans.). Montreal, Canada: Black Rose Books. (Original work published 1971)

Reference to the entire set of a multivolume set

Lindzey, G., & Aronson, E. (Eds.). (1969). <u>The handbook of social psychology</u> (2nd ed., Vols. 1–5). Reading, MA: Addison-Wesley.

Reference to an article in one volume of a multivolume set

Moore, W. E. (1969). Social structure and behavior. In G. Lindzey & E. Aronson (Eds.), <u>The handbook of social psychology: Vol. 4. Group psychology and phenomena of interaction</u> (pp. 283–322). (2nd ed.). Reading, MA: Addison-Wesley.

Encyclopaedia Britannica. (1963), s.v. "Torture," by J. Williams, & G. W. Keeton.

The New Columbia Encyclopedia (1975), s.v. "Granger movement."

Signed article in an encyclopedia or dictionary
Unsigned article in an encyclopedia or dictionary

The abbreviation "s.v." stands for *sub verbo* (Latin meaning "under the word"). Most encyclopedias and dictionaries are arranged in alphabetical order according to key words.

Penfield, W. (1952). Memory mechanisms. A.M.A. Archives of Neurology and Psychiatry, 67, 178–198.

Article from a journal paginated continuously throughout a volume

The volume number is underlined, followed by the page numbers of the entire article.

Nicholson, T. D. (1988). Down in the dumps. Natural History, 97(4), 8–12.

Article from a journal with separate pagination of each issue

The volume number is underlined and the issue number is placed within parentheses.

Baum, A. (1968, April). Disasters, natural and otherwise. Psychology Today, pp. 57–60.

Magazine article in monthly periodical

APA uses "p." and "pp." to indicate pages for magazines, newspapers, and books, but not for journals.

Schnur, S. (1988, March 28). In New Jersey: Day care with a lot of caring. Time, pp. 8–10.

Magazine article in weekly periodical

Miller, A. (1968, June 16). The trouble with our country. San Francisco Chronicle, p. 2.

Not proved. (1988, April 10). Los Angeles Times, part 5, p. 4.

Newspaper article with author
Newspaper article without author

Give part or section of the paper when it is helpful.

The space limits of this book will not allow us to cover every single possibility for materials you might use in your research, especially if these materials are from nonprint sources, such as feature films, video recordings, or computer programs. APA does not require that lectures or interviews be listed in the list of references, but, of course, they must be acknowledged in your text. The general rule for any nonprint material is to take down all information available on the source. State the kind of source within brackets following the title. Here are samples for three common types of sources.

Redford, R. (Director), Ward, D., & Nichols, J. (Writers). (1988). The Milagro beanfield war [Film]. Los Angeles: Universal.

Film

Jennings, P. (Anchorman). (1988). Drugs: A plague upon the land [Video recording]. New York: ABC.

Computer
program

Brose, E. D. (1987). <u>Treaty of Versailles</u> [Computer program]. Palo Alto, CA: Stanford

University. (Macintosh, 128k, with finder, version 4.1).

Best Bits and Bytes. (1986). <u>Tenants' rights</u> [Computer program]. Van Nuys, CA: Author.

(For IBM compatibles).

Begin with the author, date, and title of the program. Place the label "computer program" in brackets, followed by the place and publisher of the material. Next, list the computer for which the software is designed. If available, list also the kilobytes and other information useful for retrieving the program.

Source retrieved
from a data bank

Salk, J. E. (1983). <u>American men and women of science</u>. 15th ed. New York: Bowker.

DIALOG 236, item 0090936.

When citing material from a computer service, such as DIALOG, ERIC, or BRS, use the same format as for books or periodicals, but add a reference to the service and the numbers identifying the database and the particular item being referenced.

DEVELOPING THE PROPER WRITING STYLE

The informalities, eccentricities, or inaccuracies tolerated in more spontaneous writing assignments are usually disallowed in research papers, whose writing is expected to be more formal and orderly. Your challenge will be to hold the reader's interest while producing writing based on a mixture of sources written by others. You should aim for language suitable to an educated audience while avoiding jargon, overblown diction, and tortured sentences. Writing with accuracy and clarity, which should be your aim, means mastering all the concepts you have digested and are attempting to discuss. Here are some stylistic flaws to avoid:

1. Excessive use of the passive voice
   The passive voice, when used unnecessarily, makes writing abstract and boring. It also tends to make you seem unsure of your own opinions, observations, and conclusions.
   Passive: The decline of the whooping crane population was found by the Wildlife Research Center in Maryland to have been accelerated by destruction of habitat and by hunting.
   Active: The Wildlife Research Center in Maryland found that destruction of habitat and hunting accelerated the decline of the whooping crane population.
2. Abstractions
   Whenever possible, use concrete nouns and verbs to keep your language from sounding ponderous and pedantic.
   Abstract: The junior populations in third-world countries suffer great necessity for nutritional supplements of high protein content.

Concrete: Children and adolescents in third-world countries are starving for proteins such as beans, chicken, and fish.

3. Vague language

Vague expressions are also imprecise and tend to make you seem careless.

Vague: China used to have a terrible time with famines, but today this heavily populated country feeds its people quite adequately.

Precise: Although the China of 500 million people used to suffer famine occurring nearly every year, today's China—whose population exceeds 800 million—provides its people with an average of 2,300 calories per day per capita—more than the U.S. Recommended Daily Allowance.

4. Sexist language

Avoid a masculine or feminine bias in pronouns or other words that indicate gender. Most often, the simplest way to avoid this bias is to write in the plural.

Sexist: A doctor must make sure that his diagnosis is correct.

Nonsexist: Doctors must make sure that their diagnoses are correct.

Sexist: Congressman Shirley Pettis agreed.

Nonsexist: Congressperson Shirley Pettis agreed. *Or,* Representative Shirley Pettis agreed.

5. Confusing shifts in verb tense

Hopping from the past tense to the present tense when the shift is inappropriate places a mental burden on your reader. Generally, the past tense should be used when you are reporting research already completed:

> Recently Del Monte opened a new plantation in Kenya so that the British could enjoy "jet-fresh" pineapples.

However, the present tense is appropriate if you are addressing your reader with your own speculation or observation:

> This is not surprising when we consider that on a Kenya plantation a pineapple brings only a few cents, but on the English market, it brings $1.50.

Furthermore, identify source material in the past tense, but treat its substance in the present tense:

> Browning *wrote* "My Last Duchess." The poem *reveals* a marked contrast between the speaker and his wife.
>
> Wolfgang Amadeus Mozart *was* born in Austria. A remarkable prodigy, he *was taught* to play the harpsichord, violin, and organ by his father, and *began* composing before he was five. His work, combining luminous beauty of sound with classical grace, *represents* one of the great peaks in the history of music.

What Mozart accomplished as a young boy is discussed in the past tense; the Mozart qualities that prevail in his work to this day are treated in the present tense.

Preparing the Final Copy (MLA)

The final copy of your paper should be clean and free of errors. Don't skimp on revising or proofreading time. If you do not type reasonably well, pay a good typist to type your paper, for many a good paper has been ruined by messy erasures or typographical errors. Students who know how to use the computer for word processing will have an advantage as they edit. Carefully observe the following rules.

1. Type
   a. Type on one side of the paper only.
   b. Avoid typewriters with fancy script; instead use a plain type, such as pica, which is easy to read.
   c. Use a fresh, black ribbon and clean type.

2. Paper
   a. Use white twenty-pound 8½-inch × 11-inch bond. Avoid erasable paper because it smudges.

3. Margins
   a. Except for page numbers, leave one-inch margins at the top, bottom, and both sides of the paper.
   b. Indent the first word in each new paragraph five spaces.
   c. Quotations of four or more typewritten lines must be set off from the text by double spacing, indented ten spaces, and double spaced. A colon ends the sentence preceding them. Skip two spaces after the concluding punctuation mark of the quotation and insert the parenthetical reference:

      At one point in her life Sylvia Plath was deeply moved by a French motion

      picture about the temptation of Joan of Arc. She gives this account of her

      reaction:

         After it was all over, I couldn't look at anyone. I was crying

         because it was like a purge, the buildup of unbelievable tension,

         then the release, as of the soul of Joan at the stake. (96)

4. Spacing
   a. Double space the research paper throughout, including the outline, the heading, the title (if it is longer than one line), quotations, and the bibliography. Quadruple space between the title and the first line of the body of the paper. See sample student paper.

5. First page
   a. A research paper does not need a separate title page. Beginning one inch from the top of the first page and flush with the left margin, type

your name, your instructor's name, the course number, and the date. The first page of the outline should also contain this information.

b. Center the title. Do not underline your title or put it in quotation marks or type it in all capital letters. Follow the format given here:

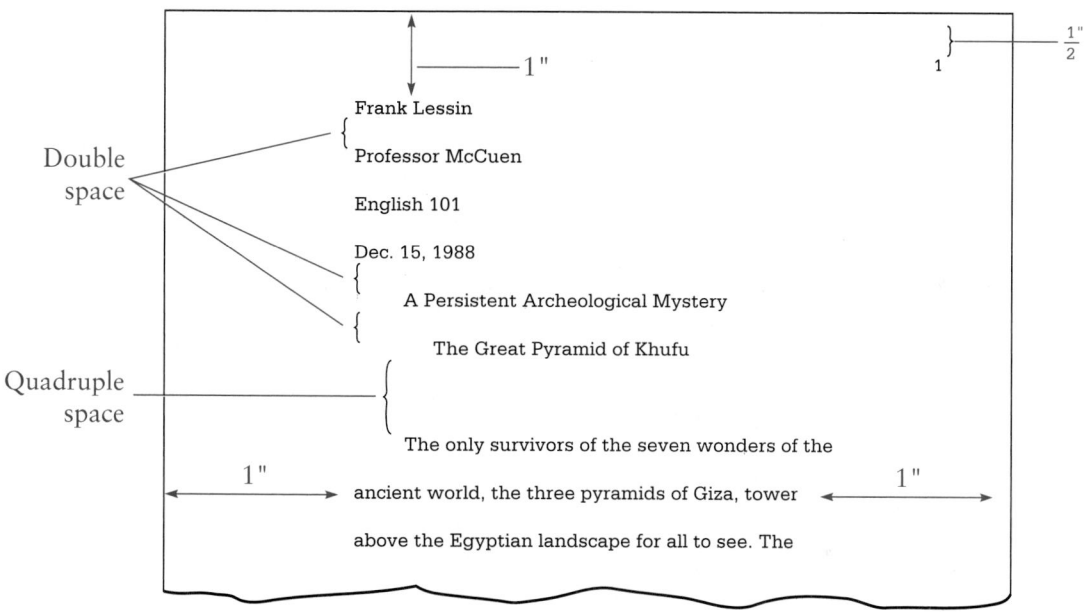

6. Pagination

a. Number all pages consecutively throughout the manuscript.

b. Place each page numeral in the upper right-hand corner, one-half inch from the top.

c. Beginning with page 2, place your name in front of the page number to prevent confusion in case part of your paper gets lost. See below:

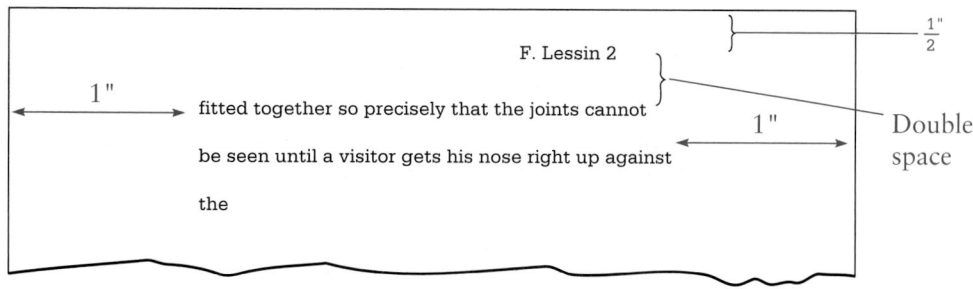

    d. Number the pages of the outline separately and with small roman numerals. See sample student paper. Do not add a hyphen, a parenthesis, or any other punctuation mark or symbol to the page number.

7. Binding

Many students try to make their research papers look attractive by placing them in a folder or cover of some kind; however, such bindings tend to be a nuisance to the teacher trying to analyze the paper and comment on it. Better to submit the paper held together with a good paper clip, which the teacher can remove and replace at will.

Preparing the Final Copy (APA)

The same rules apply to typing a research paper for the social sciences as a research paper for the humanities. That is, use good paper, type on one side only, double space throughout the paper, observe the proper margins, and so forth. However, a research paper following the APA style has three special differences: (1) it has a title page, (2) it has an abstract, and (3) each page has a running head (shortened form of the title) rather than the name of the author in the top right-hand side of the paper. Follow the form used in the student sample paper, pages 555–65.

List of the Most Common Abbreviations

Use abbreviations often and consistently in your notes and bibliography, but avoid them in your text.

A.D.	(*Anno Domini*). Refers to years after Christ's birth, as in "A.D. 200."
anon.	Anonymous.
art., arts.	Article(s).
B.C.	Before Christ. Refers to years before Christ's birth, as in "50 B.C."
bk., bks.	Book(s).
ca.	(*Circa*). About, used to indicate an approximate date, as in "ca. 1730."
cf	Confer. Compare one source with another.
ch., chs.	Chapter(s).
col., cols.	Column(s).
comp.	Compiled by, compiler.
diss.	Dissertation.

ed., eds.	Editor(s), edition, or edited by.
e.g.	(*Exempli gratia*). For example—preceded and followed by a comma.
enl.	enlarged, as in "enl. ed."
et al.	(*Et alii*). And others, as in "John Smith et al."
f., ff.	Page(s) following, as in "pp. 8 f." meaning page 8 and the following page.
i.e.	(*id est*). That is—preceded and followed by a comma.
l., ll.	Line(s).
ms, mss	Manuscript(s).
n.d.	No date.
no., nos.	Number(s)
n.p.	No place.
p., pp.	Page(s).
passim	Here and there throughout the work, as in "pp. 67, 72, et passim."
pseud.	Pseudonym.
pt., pts.	Part(s).
rev.	Revised, revision, reviewed, review.
rpt.	Reprint, reprinted.
sec., secs.	Section(s).
sic	Thus—placed in brackets to indicate that an error exists in the passage being quoted, as in "sevral [sic]."
st., sts.	Stanza(s).
trans.	Translator, translated, translation.
vol., vols.	Volume(s).

Acceptable shortened forms of publishers' names include the following:

Abrams	Harry N. Abrams, Inc.
Acad. for Educ. Dev.	Academy for Educational Development, Inc.
Allen	George Allen and Unwin Publishers, Inc.
Allyn	Allyn and Bacon, Inc.
Appleton	Appleton-Century-Crofts
Ballantine	Ballantine Books, Inc.
Bantam	Bantam Books, Inc.
Barnes	Barnes and Noble Books
Basic	Basic Books
Beacon	Beacon Press, Inc.
Benn	Ernest Benn, Ltd.
Bobbs	The Bobbs-Merrill Co., Inc.
Bowker	R. R. Bowker Co.
CAL	Center for Applied Linguistics

Cambridge UP	Cambridge University Press
Clarendon	Clarendon Press
Columbia UP	Columbia University Press
Cornell UP	Cornell University Press
Dell	Dell Publishing Co., Inc.
Dodd	Dodd, Mead, and Co.
Doubleday	Doubleday and Co., Inc.
Dover	Dover Publications, Inc.
Dutton	E. P. Dutton, Inc.
Farrar	Farrar, Straus, and Giroux, Inc.
Feminist	The Feminist Press
Free	The Free Press
Funk	Funk and Wagnalls, Inc.
Gale	Gale Research Co.
GPO	Government Printing Office
Harcourt	Harcourt Brace Jovanovich, Inc.
Harper	Harper and Row Publishers, Inc.
Harvard Law Rev. Assn.	Harvard Law Review Association
Harvard UP	Harvard University Press
Heath	D. C. Heath and Co.
HMSO	Her (His) Majesty's Stationery Office
Holt	Holt, Rinehart, and Winston, Inc.
Houghton	Houghton Mifflin Co.
Humanities	Humanities Press, Inc.
Indiana UP	Indiana University Press
Johns Hopkins UP	The Johns Hopkins University Press
Knopf	Alfred A. Knopf, Inc.
Larousse	Librairie Larousse
Lippincott	J. B. Lippincott Co.
Little	Little, Brown and Co.
Macmillan	Macmillan Publishing Co., Inc.
McGraw	McGraw-Hill, Inc.
MIT P	The MIT Press
MLA	The Modern Language Association of America
NAL	The New American Library, Inc.
NCTE	The National Council of Teachers of English
NEA	The National Education Association
New York Graphic Soc.	New York Graphic Society
Norton	W. W. Norton and Co., Inc.
Oxford UP	Oxford University Press, Inc.
Penguin	Penguin Books, Inc.
Pocket	Pocket Books
Popular	The Popular Press
Prentice	Prentice-Hall, Inc.
Princeton UP	Princeton University Press

Putnam's	G. P. Putnam's Sons
Rand	Rand McNally and Co.
Random	Random House
Rizzoli	Rizzoli Editore
St. Martin's	St. Martin's Press, Inc.
Scott	Scott, Foresman and Co.
Scribner's	Charles Scribner's Sons
Simon	Simon and Schuster, Inc.
State U of New York P	State University of New York Press
UMI	University Microfilms International
U of Chicago P	University of Chicago Press
U of Toronto P	University of Toronto Press
UP of Florida	The University Presses of Florida
Viking	The Viking Press, Inc.
Yale UP	Yale University Press

Postal Abbreviations

Alabama	AL	Florida	FL
Alaska	AK	Georgia	GA
Arizona	AZ	Guam	GU
Arkansas	AR	Hawaii	HI
California	CA	Idaho	ID
Colorado	CO	Illinois	IL
Connecticut	CT	Indiana	IN
Delaware	DE	Iowa	IA
District of Columbia	DC	Kansas	KS
Kentucky	KY	Ohio	OH
Louisiana	LA	Oklahoma	OK
Maine	ME	Oregon	OR
Maryland	MD	Pennsylvania	PA
Massachusetts	MA	Puerto Rico	PR
Michigan	MI	Rhode Island	RI
Minnesota	MN	South Carolina	SC
Mississippi	MS	South Dakota	SD
Missouri	MO	Tennessee	TN
Montana	MT	Texas	TX
Nebraska	NB	Utah	UT
Nevada	NV	Vermont	VT
New Hampshire	NH	Virgin Islands	VI
New Jersey	NJ	Virginia	VA
New Mexico	NM	Washington	WA
New York	NY	West Virginia	WV
North Carolina	NC	Wisconsin	WI
North Dakota	ND	Wyoming	WY

Exercises

A. Unscramble the following bibliographical facts and arrange them in the proper bibliographical form for "Works Cited."

1. A book by E. L. Doctorow, published by Random House of New York in 1975. The title of the book is *Ragtime*.

2. An article entitled "What Is the Federal Cup?" published in volume 23 of *World Tennis,* the August 1976 issue, covering pages 32–34.

3. "Good Country People," a story by Flannery O'Connor, taken from an anthology entitled *The Modern Tradition* (second edition), edited by Daniel F. Howard and published in 1972 by Little, Brown and Company of Boston.

4. Feodor Dostoevsky's famous novel *Crime and Punishment,* published by Oxford University Press, Inc. of New York (1953), in a translation by Jessie Coulson.

5. "The Dutiful Child's Promises," a selection from an anthology entitled *Readings from American Literature,* edited by Mary Edwards Calhoun and Emma Lenore MacAlarney, published by Ginn and Company of Boston, 1915.

6. A two-volume work entitled *Civilization—Past and Present,* coauthored by T. Walter Wallbank and Alastair M. Taylor, published in 1949 by Scott, Foresman and Company of Chicago.

7. An unsigned encyclopedia article under the heading "Tiryns," found in volume 22 of the 1963 edition of the *Encyclopaedia Britannica,* pp. 247–248.

8. The sixth edition of Karl C. Garrison's book entitled *Psychology of Adolescence,* published in 1965 by Prentice-Hall, of Englewood Cliffs, New Jersey.

9. An article without author from the August 9, 1976, issue of *Time.* The article appears on pages 16 and 19 and is entitled "To Plains with the Boys in the Bus."

10. A feature article by Jim Murray, entitled "The Real Olympian," which appeared in Part III of the *Los Angeles Times,* pp. 1 and 7 (Wednesday, August 4, 1976).

B. Unscramble the following bibliographical facts and arrange them in the proper form for "References."

1. A work put out by the Canadian Tax Foundation. It is entitled *Provincial and Municipal Finances* and was published in Toronto, Canada in 1979.

2. An article entitled "Boom & Doom on Wall Street," authored by Berkeley Rice. It was published in the April of 1988 issue of *Psychology Today,* on pages 52–54.

3. A journal article by the following authors: B. Kerr, J. Davison, J. Nelson, and S. Haley. The article appeared in the year 1982, in

volume 34, number 3 of *Journal of Experimental Child Psychology.* The entire article took up pages 526–541. The journal numbers its pages continuously throughout a volume.
4. "Beyond Freedom and Dignity," an essay by the psychologist B. F. Skinner, who was born in 1904. The essay is reprinted in an anthology entitled *The Tradition of Philosophy,* edited by Harrison Hall and Norma B. Bowie and published in Belmont, California, by the Wadsworth Publishing Company. The full article takes up p. 321 to p. 325.
5. An unsigned article in the *New Columbia Encyclopedia,* published in 1975, entitled "Athlete's heart." The encyclopedia is edited by William H. Harris and Judith S. Levey. It is published in New York by the Columbia University Press. The article appears on page 176.

C. Using the bibliographical information provided in exercise A, convert the items below into a proper sequence of parenthetical notes for either MLA or APA style.
1. Page 25 of the book by Karl C. Garrison.
2. Page 50 of that same book.
3. Page 30 of volume one of the book by T. Walter Wallbank and Alastair M. Taylor.
4. Page 31 of that same book.
5. Page 90 of the book edited by Mary Edwards Calhoun and Emma Lenore MacAlarney.
6. Page 1 of the *Los Angeles Times* article.
7. Page 248 of the encyclopedia article.
8. Page 48 of Feodor Dostoevsky's novel.
9. Page 507 of Flannery O'Connor's story.
10. Page 46 of *Ragtime.*

D. From the works mentioned in this unit, compile a list of sources that you would consult if you were to write on one of the following topics:
1. The last year of Thomas Jefferson's life
2. Research regarding the education of blind children
3. The novels of William Makepeace Thackeray
4. The myth of Europa
5. The rise of Mao Tse-tung
6. Safety in nuclear plants
7. The art of Jacques Louis David
8. Famous quotations about the value of education
9. The murder of Stanford White by Harry K. Thaw
10. The philosophy of Bertrand Russell

E. Summarize the following paragraph in one sentence:
Those who are awed by their surrounding do not think of change, no matter how miserable their condition. When our mode of life is so

precarious as to make it patent that we cannot control the circumstances of our existence, we tend to stick to the proven and the familiar. We counteract a deep feeling of insecurity by making of our existence a fixed routine. We hereby acquire the illusion that we have tamed the unpredictable. Fisherfolk, nomads and farmers who have to contend with the willful elements, the creative worker who depends on inspiration, the savage awed by his surroundings—they all fear change. They face the world as they would an all-powerful jury. The abjectly poor, too, stand in awe of the world around them and are not hospitable to change. It is a dangerous life we live when hunger and cold are at our heels. There is thus a conservatism of the destitute as profound as the conservatism of the privileged, and the former is as much a factor in the perpetuation of a social order as the latter.

Eric Hoffer, The True Believer

F. Paraphrase the following paragraph so that it sounds like you.

The urge for a touch of class, for something better than others have, has put new pressure on that classic Russian institution—the queue. Customers the world-over wait in lines, but Soviet queues have a dimension all their own, like the Egyptian pyramids. They reveal a lot about the Russian predicament and the Russian psyche. And their operation is far more intricate than first meets the eye. To the passerby they look like nearly motionless files of mortals doomed to some commercial purgatory for their humble purchases. But what the outsider misses is the hidden magnetism of lines for Russians, their inner dynamics, their special etiquette.

Hedrick Smith, The Russians

Sample Student Papers

The two student research papers included on the following pages will give you an idea of what good student papers look like. The first paper scrutinizes a period in American history when our government acted cruelly and unfairly toward American citizens of Japanese descent. It follows the format of humanities papers as proposed by the Modern Language Association (MLA). The second paper is about how the body and mind interact. It is more scientific than the first and therefore follows the rules proposed by the American Psychological Association (APA). Your instructor will tell you which format your paper should follow. We have not supplied samples of footnotes or endnotes because these have been abandoned by the majority of instructors. Both papers were written by college freshmen and demonstrate what any conscientious student can achieve with effort and diligence.

i

Diane L. Thomas

Professor McCuen

English 101

May 1, 1992

The Internment of Japanese Americans during World War II

Thesis: The internment of Japanese Americans during World War II was an abomi-

nable violation of American ideals.

I. The United States government abused the rights of an entire group.

A. Guaranteed constitutional rights were suspended.

B. The Japanese Americans were judged by their ancestry rather than by

individual acts.

1. German and Italian aliens suspected of disloyalty were treated more fairly

than were the Japanese Americans.

2. Efforts on the part of Japanese Americans to demonstrate loyalty and pa-

triotism were futile.

II. In a land where "all men are created equal," the underlying force behind the in-

ternment was extreme racial prejudice.

A. There was a history of anti-Japanese feeling and actions in the United States

prior to World War II.

1. The stereotyped Japanese were viewed as a threat to Americans.

2. Anti-Japanese legislation was already in existence.

B. With racism to back it up, the hysteria that followed the attack on Pearl Harbor

was aggravated by politicians, anti-Japanese groups, and the press.

ii

III. The unjust suffering that Japanese Americans faced seems a paradox in a country where "justice for all" is proclaimed.

   A. Japanese Americans suffered severe economic losses as a result of the relocation.

   B. The facilities in the camps were inadequate.

   C. While Japanese Americans were living in internment camps, Japanese-American soldiers were serving the United States in the war effort.

   D. The psychological and emotional suffering was perhaps the most tragic.

1

Diane L. Thomas

Professor McCuen

English 101

May 1, 1992

The Internment of Japanese Americans during World War II

On February 19, 1942, President Franklin D. Roosevelt signed an executive order that allowed the United States government to begin the evacuation and incarceration of 110,000 Japanese Americans. The order for relocation applied to "all persons of Japanese ancestry" and, of the total number of evacuees, 70,000 were American-born citizens. Forced to leave behind their homes, lands, and businesses, they were herded off to ten desolate camps scattered throughout the United States, surrounded by barbed wire and under military guard, where they made their homes for nearly three years. The possibility of sabotage or espionage from among these people was the primary rationale behind this mass removal of the entire Japanese-American population in California, western Washington, Oregon, and Arizona (Myer xiii). It is difficult to imagine how this unhappy event could have happened in these United States, but it did happen. Our history books often seem to imply that we are heroes without guilt and the protectors of freedom carried on by the democratic principles for which we stand. The mass incarceration of Japanese Americans during World War II, however, is a part of our history that Americans cannot be proud of. Without a doubt, at that point in our history democracy was operating at its worst. Racial prejudice, wartime hysteria, fear, and outrage made the evacuation decision a popular one that caused us to commit what Roger Daniels called "our worst wartime mistake" (xi–xii). The internment of Japanese Americans during World War II was an abominable violation of American ideals.

D. Thomas 2

By allowing the evacuation, the United States government abused the rights of an entire group. Writing for the *National Review,* correspondent William Petersen claimed there was no question that the evacuation of men, women, and children from their homes without being charged with any crime, without trials or hearings, was a drastic invasion of the constitutional rights of citizens (49). Another journalist, Janet Stevenson, pointed out that guarantees covered under the Fourteenth Amendment were ignored, depriving Japanese Americans of liberty and property without due process and the "equal protection of the laws" afforded other citizens (24). All of this was done out of "military necessity" because the Japanese Americans were thought to be potentially disloyal. Even if there were saboteurs among them, such a fact does not justify suspending the rights of an entire group because of the possible guilt of a few (McWilliams 109–10). There was not, however, one actual case of any act of sabotage or disloyalty by Japanese Americans during the entire war.

The government further abused the rights of Japanese Americans by judging them by their ancestry rather than by individual acts. Aliens and citizens alike were lumped together as a racial group whereas German and Italian aliens suspected of sabotage or espionage were handled on an individual basis. It is worth noting that, with few exceptions, the Japanese alien residents that were interned had lived in the United States from twenty to thirty years, having arrived prior to the Japanese Exclusion Act of 1924. Amazingly, the discriminating laws that were in effect made Japanese immigrants ineligible for citizenship, whereas a large percentage of German and Italian immigrants had become naturalized American citizens and, therefore, exempt from the "enemy alien" classification (Thomas 5). Army General John L. DeWitt had said, "a Jap's a Jap," (qtd. in Haak 23) and it appears that this was the attitude that shaped prevailing policy.

D. Thomas 3

Despite numerous efforts, Japanese Americans found that attempts to prove their loyalty and patriotism were futile. For example, immediately following Pearl Harbor, the Japanese American Citizens League wired President Roosevelt pledging their cooperation: ". . . We, in our hearts are Americans—loyal to America. We must prove that to all of you" (qtd. in Conrat 57). Other Japanese Americans bought defense bonds, donated to the Red Cross, and volunteered for civil defense and intelligence work in an effort to prove their loyalty (Girdner and Loftis 11). These patriotic actions were apparently meaningless because these same people would soon find themselves identified as the enemy and placed in barbed-wire enclosures.

In a land where "all men are created equal," the underlying force behind the internment was extreme racial prejudice. Even prior to the evacuation in 1942 the Japanese had been the victims of racism in America, particularly on the West Coast where their population was most concentrated. When immigrants from Japan began to arrive in the United States after 1890, they were stereotyped, along with other Orientals, and viewed as a threat to Americans. There was a general feeling that the Japanese would eventually overpopulate the country and conquer the Caucasians (Daniels 2). Economically, they were resented because of competition in agriculture, business, and labor. The development of Japan as a world power also contributed to this irrational fear and hatred of the Japanese, who were described as the "yellow peril" (Myer 11–12).

The anti-Japanese movement in America goes back to the turn of the century when the United States Industrial Commission made the following claim:

> The Japanese are more servile than the Chinese, but less obedient and far less desirable. They have most of the vices of the Chinese with none

D. Thomas 4

> of the virtues. They underbid the Chinese in everything and are as a
> class tricky, unreliable and dishonest. (Qtd. in Conrat 18)

At about the same time, the slogan of politician and labor leader Dennis Kearney was "The Japs must go!" The mayor of San Francisco insisted that it was impossible for the Japanese to assimilate into our culture and that they were "not the stuff of which American citizens can be made" (qtd. in Daniels 9–10). Appropriately, the Japanese and Korean Exclusion League was formed in 1905, and a number of other anti-Japanese societies followed. There were scattered cases of individual and mob violence directed against the Japanese, the press made verbal racist attacks, and the "yellow peril" concept continued to gain credibility (Myer 11–14).

With the agitation against the Japanese came continual proposals of anti-Japanese legislation. Indeed every session of the California legislature between 1905 and 1945 attempted to pass at least one piece of anti-Japanese legislation (Daniels 11). They were successful in 1913 when the Alien Land Law was passed, preventing Japanese from purchasing or leasing land for more than three years. In most of the western states, residence choice was restricted by covenants, intermarriage with Caucasians was forbidden, and free access to certain public places was forbidden (Thomas 2). Finally, in 1924 the agitation subsided temporarily when an exclusion act was passed specifically preventing further Japanese immigration.

With years of racism to back it up, the hysteria that persisted after Pearl Harbor was aggravated by politicians, anti-Japanese groups, and the press. Newspapers led the already frightened public to believe that Japanese saboteurs were lurking everywhere, publishing headlines like "JAP BOAT FLASHES MESSAGE

ASHORE," "JAPANESE HERE SENT VITAL DATA TO TOKYO," and "JAPS PLAN COAST ATTACK IN APRIL WARNS CHIEF OF KOREAN SPY BAND" (Daniels 33). The stories, of course, were totally unfounded. Analyzing the situation in 1970 for *Transaction* magazine, Ronald Haak referred to the role of Supreme Court Justice Earl Warren, who added to the panic when he was still attorney general by testifying that American-born Japanese were even more dangerous to the security of the United States than alien Japanese (23). Emotional demands for action by leaders like Representative John Rankin helped make up the minds of the public: "I'm for catching every Japanese in America, Alaska, and Hawaii now and putting them in concentration camps. Damn them! Let's get rid of them now!" (Qtd. in Conrat 21). The pressure increased, more unfounded rumors were spread, and the fear of invasion and suspicion of sabotage eventually led to the imprisonment of 110,000 Japanese Americans.

Considering the unjust suffering that Japanese Americans faced, it seemed a paradox that it took place in a country where there is "justice for all." The economic losses suffered by Japanese Americans as a result of the internment have been nearly impossible to calculate. Given only a matter of days or a few weeks between notification and evacuation, they were forced to sell their property at prices far below its real value. Far away at relocation centers and unable to protect their interests back home, their property that had been stored or left to trustees was often stolen, vandalized, or sold (Conrat 21). It is impossible to calculate the lost wages, income, and interest; but the property losses have been estimated to be worth $400,000,000. The United States government has repaid Japanese Americans a portion of this amount, and in 1967 the Supreme Court ruled that an additional

D. Thomas 6

$10,000,000 was owed to Japanese Americans whose dollar savings had been con-
fiscated during the internment (*Time* 31).

To add to the miserable plight of the internees, the camps themselves were inadequate. Small, semi-private barracks were hastily built with wood and tar paper and
often located in desolate, out-of-the-way deserts and wastelands. There were no
cooking or plumbing facilities in the barracks, but each block had a mess hall and a
building with latrines, showers, and laundry facilities (Myer 30–32). Sanitation and
protection from the elements were simply not adequate. In spite of these obstacles,
cooperating communities were established in the camps and, through a lot of hard
work and determination, they led a reasonably comfortable existence (Conrat 22).

It is ironic that while the internees were overcoming these conditions within their
barbed wire enclosures, Japanese-American soldiers were serving the United States
in the war effort. The 442nd Combat Team, an all-Japanese volunteer unit, distinguished themselves on the battle front in Italy with more casualties and decorations
than any other unit of similar size and length of service in the history of the army
(Conrat 23). It seems incredible that while Japanese soldiers were being injured and
killed overseas, their brothers, sisters, mothers, and fathers were back in the states
imprisoned by the very country they were fighting for. Knowing this, many members
of the 442nd Combat Team must have found it frustrating when, at an honorary citation ceremony, President Truman said to them: "You are to be congratulated for
what you have done for this great country. I think it was my predecessor who said
that Americanism is not a matter of race or creed, it is a matter of the heart . . ."
(qtd. in Myer 148).

Perhaps the most tragic of the injustices inflicted upon Japanese Americans was
the psychological and emotional suffering they experienced. The internment was

morale-killing, humiliating, and frustrating. The internees had to live with the knowledge that they were being regarded as traitors to their country and that they would
always be judged by their ancestry rather than their actions. For those Americans, it
is fair to conclude that the imprisonment represents a very bad memory that is permanently engraved in their minds.

    Today the internment of 100,000 Japanese Americans in the United States is diffi-
cult to imagine, but forty-three years ago it was a cold reality. Every aspect of it was
diametrically opposed to the treasured ideals of America. That such a tragedy could
have taken place in this country illustrates that prejudice, hate, and fear can cause
us to ignore completely the rights and freedoms of which we are so proud. It should
also serve as a ghastly reminder that such a tragedy should never be allowed to
happen again.

Works Cited

Conrat, Maisie. Executive Order 9066. Los Angeles: California Historical Society,

    1972.

Daniels, Roger. Concentration Camps U.S.A. New York: Holt, 1972.

Girdner, Audrie, and Anne Loftis. The Great Betrayal. London: Macmillan, 1969.

Haak, Ronald O. "Co-opting the Oppressors: The Case of the Japanese Americans."

    Transaction Oct. 1970: 23–31.

McWilliams, Carey. Prejudice. Boston: Little, 1944.

Myer, Dillion S. Uprooted Americans. Tucson: U of Arizona P, 1971.

Petersen, William. "Incarceration of Japanese Americans." National Review 9 Dec.

    1972: 49–50.

Stevenson, Janet. "Before the Colors Fade: The Return of the Exiles." American Heri-

    tage June 1969: 22–25.

Thomas, Dorothy Swaine. The Spoilage. Los Angeles: U of California P, 1946.

"Tule Lake Thirty Years Later." Time 10 June 1974: 31.

1

The Mind and the Body:

Do They Interact?

Pauline Huzau

Philosophy 101

Professor Parker

June 6, 1992

Abstract

The modern field of psychosomatics has challenged and contradicted the traditional philosophy of dualism, which in varying degrees insisted that the mind and body are separate entities with little influence of one on the other. The purpose of this paper is to show how recent discoveries in medicine strongly support the idea that the mind does influence and control the body as well as vice versa. Specifically, Norman Cousins's personal experience refutes Descartes; biofeedback refutes Thomas Huxley; and recent studies on the immune system refute C. D. Broad.

The Mind and the Body:

Do They Interact?

Since the beginning of civilization, and perhaps even earlier, no subject has captured the human imagination more than knowledge about self. One fascinating
question seriously probed throughout the centuries is this: How does the mind affect the body and vice versa? Attempting to answer these questions, the philosophers Thomas Huxley, Rene Descartes, and C. D. Broad developed a system of concepts that eventually became known as dualism. Dualism holds that humans are
composed of two distinct substances, mind and body. Different versions of this
theory claim different levels of separateness between mind and body, but ultimately,
dualism refuses to see the mind and body as interacting freely with each other. Dualism was the accepted scientific view for many decades; however, the advent of
modern science, with its emphasis on the scientific method and heavy clinical research, has proposed another view: the belief in the integrity and wholeness of mind
and body. In short, today we must take a new look at the human mind and its connection with the body to see if new evidence incontrovertibly proves that the mind
and body are not separate entities, but a unified whole.[1]

Recently, one particular field of study, psychosomatics, has most strongly contradicted the theories of dualism. Dorland's *Illustrated Medical Dictionary* (1965) defines
psychosomatics as "having bodily symptoms of psychic, emotional, or mental origin."
The etymology of the term can be traced to the Greek *psyche,* meaning "soul," and
soma, meaning "body." In other words, psychosomatics is the study of the influence
of the mind on the body as revealed in physical illness. Lewis and Lewis (1972) con-

sider psychosomatics a total approach to health that views the person as a mind-body unity, taking into consideration one's whole way of life when health is scrutinized. According to these two scientists, the idea of a mind-body interrelationship is not really new, but can be traced back at least 4,500 years, to the Yellow Emperor of China, Huang Ti, who authored a famous manuscript dealing with internal medicine. In it he claimed that "frustration can make people physically ill" (cited in Lewis & Lewis, 1972, p. 5). Later on, in the fourth century B.C., Socrates returned from military service to tell his Greek countrymen that the barbaric Thracians were culturally advanced because they believed that "the body could not be cured without the mind" (cited in Lewis & Lewis, 1970, p. 5). Despite these early historical views pointing toward an influence of mind on body and body on mind, the dualistic theories prevailed—with individual modifications—until just recently, when a wave of modern research has challenged them seriously. This paper will present a brief summary of the three major dualistic positions and will show how each has been superseded by a modern, clinically proved theory that renders them outmoded.

One of the purest dualistic theories was proposed in 1649 by René Descartes, whose treatise "The Passions of the Soul" argued that the physical world is mechanistic and entirely divorced from the mind, the only connection between the two being by intervention of God. He proposed that since all emotions were physical, if one would control the physical expression of emotions, such as trembling, one would control the emotion itself. While Descartes agreed that bodily injury could cause mental pain and that mental pain could cause the body to respond, he insisted that the two entities operated separately. For example, if the foot was injured, the mind would immediately become excited "to do its utmost to remove the cause of evil as dangerous and hurtful to the foot" (cited in Hall & Bowie, 1986, p. 149). In other words, Descartes limits his belief to an instinctive level of interaction between mind and body, insisting that the mind reacts instinctively when the body is in danger: "I have a body which is adversely affected when I feel pain" (cited in Hall & Bowie, 1986, p. 147). Descartes did not attempt to hide the fact that at one point he was not even sure if he *had* a body. Thus, one can only imagine what difficulties he had in trying to philosophize about a relationship between something that he knew existed and something he was not sure existed at all.

Descartes' view that mind and body react to each other as mere reflexes is seriously challenged by occurrences of healing having taken place because of the will to heal oneself despite the actual physical incapability of the body to do so. One well-publicized example is the miraculous recovery from a fatal disease of Norman Cousins, the influential essayist and editor associated with the *New York Post* and *Saturday Review.* His experience was published in the December 1966 issue of the *New England Journal of Medicine.* Cousins caused a national sensation when he claimed he had used his mind to heal his body. In 1964, after a trip to the Soviet Union, where he was apparently poisoned by jet exhaust, he was hospitalized and lay dying from a collagen disease. He found the hospital stay highly uncomfortable and felt that it was contributing to his body's wasting away. When told that he had only one in five hundred chances of living, he decided that "it was time to get into the act" (Cousins, 1966, p. 1459). He diagnosed the cause of his illness and researched its possible cures. "Assuming my hypothesis true, I had to get my adrenal glands functioning properly again" (Cousins, 1966, p. 1460). He found that adrenal exhaustion could be caused by tension, frustration, or suppressed rage. He then reasoned

Mind and Body 6

that if he could get rid of these emotions, he could put his physical body back in or-

der. Thus, he went on to wean himself from pain medication and other massive

doses of drugs by using an emotion—laughter—and by checking himself out of the

hospital environment, which he found deeply depressing. Norman Cousins claimed

to have cured himself of his terrible affliction by using his mind to help his body

(Cousins, 1966, pp. 1460–1463). Such a life-threatening or life-saving interaction be-

tween the mind and the body is impossible to assimilate into Descartes' reflex-

action theory.[2]

Another theory of dualism is the theory of epiphenomenalism, upheld by Thomas

Huxley. This theory suggests that a causal connection exists between mind and

body, but that it only goes in one direction—from body to mind, not from mind to

body. After reporting in detail clinical experiments involving severed spinal cords in

animals and observing the results, Huxley concluded that some physical events do

indeed cause mental states, but that mental states themselves have no power what-

soever to cause either mental or physical states. In "Evolution and Ethics" (1931),

Huxley declared that things going on in the body, especially in the nervous system,

do give rise to conscious mental states, but that mental states exert no influence on

the body.

Today, Huxley's view is being strongly challenged by supporters of biofeedback, a

quickly growing clinical method that is being used to reduce the effects of stress on

the body, especially in patients with severe migraine headaches. Biofeedback is

based on three major principles: 1) any biological function that can be monitored by

electronic instrumentation can be regulated by the individual, 2) every change in the

emotional state is accompanied by a change in the physiological state, and 3) the

Mind and Body 7

reduction of stress can be achieved through relaxation and visualization. Research on biofeedback has now proven that many involuntary functions of the nervous system, such as brain waves, body temperature, or heart rate, can be brought under control by the individual. An example of the use of biofeedback in medical treatment is revealed in the following case history, documented by Pelletier (1977, p. 280): A 19-year-old male patient, almost completely paralyzed on the left side of his body because of a severe neck fracture, was found to have the entire left side of his body 15 degrees lower in temperature than his right side, causing a severe reduction in the use of his muscles. Using biofeedback methods, the young man was eventually able to use his will to raise the temperature on the left side of his body to within 2 degrees of the right side—an increase of 13 degrees. He then experienced amazing success in the muscular coordination of his previously useless muscles. Now, according to Huxley's theory of dualism this change would be impossible; yet, it is a medically documented fact. Biofeedback is one area of study that clearly demonstrates that Huxley's claims are being questioned.

Somewhere between the thinking of Descartes and that of Huxley lies the philosophy of C. D. Broad, who propounded a modified version of dualism. He argued that indeed certain states in the mind and body *seem* to coincide. For instance, when one steps on a pin, one feels pain. But for him, such incidences were simply a sophisticated, pre-established harmony between the separate mind and body, preset by God. He believed that perhaps this was God's way of keeping human beings informed of what is physically going on in their bodies. Broad appeals to common sense in his argument, insisting that if minds or mental events and bodies or bodily events are "just what enlightened common-sense thinks them to be and nothing more, the two are extremely unlike." Going one step further, he concludes:

Mind and Body 8

". . . however closely correlated certain pairs of events in mind and body respectively may be, they cannot be causally connected" (cited in Hall & Bowie, 1986, p. 151). Again, numerous modern, well-documented case histories exist to prove an action on the part of the mind *before* an action on the part of the body, not coinciding with it. For example, in Australia during 1970 a Dr. R. W. Bartrop and his associates studied the effects of bereavement on the body's ability to fight off illness and disease. They found that the immune systems of spouses grieving over the deaths of their marriage partners had weakened considerably during this mourning period. Almost two decades later, in 1987, Ornstein and Sobel confirmed specifically that widows or widowers had clinically proven lower activity levels of what are known as "T-cells"— blood cells that resist intruders in the body (p. 48). The Ornstein and Sobel study was one of the first scientifically controlled experiments that showed a measurable weakening of the body's defense system *following* severe stress in a real-life situation. Here one clearly sees that, instead of a physical act being accompanied by a coincidental emotional feeling, the emotions occurred first and the action on the physical system followed. Grief is only one of many other clinical examples that directly contradict Broad's view that the mind is totally separate from the body and is simply God's way of keeping the human being informed of what occurs in the body. Many clinical experiments have concluded that the mind is often the primary action.

Philosophers such as Descartes, Huxley, and Broad are fascinating to study, but their theories of dualism, once deemed profound and sophisticated, now seem almost simplistic. They have signaled scientists to go on and explore further the true relationship between these two remarkable entities we know as mind and body. We

Mind and Body 8

live in exciting times, when scientific exploration and medical research are at their

most advanced stages ever, and it is up to us to use the abundance of information

never before available in philosophic research to expound upon the mind/body theo-

ries of the past. The heroes of tomorrow are those philosophers or scientists who

will discover new sources of power and healing in the interrelationship between the

mind and the body—making the world a better place in which to live.

Footnotes

[1] Owing to space constraints and the complex nature of the subject, this paper will not deal with the recent field of functionalism, which takes into account the latest research in artificial intelligence and cognitive science. For further information on this new era of knowledge about the mind-body connection, see the works of Jerry A. Fodor and Hubert Dreyfus.

[2] Similar experiences have been narrated by a number of patients who claim to have cured cancer by using positive thinking. Oncologist Carl Simonton established a clinic in Houston, Texas, and in Santa Monica, California, based on the concept of imaging—imagining oneself being cured. For instance, a cancer patient might imagine a medieval knight on a white horse, representing the immune system inside his body physically doing battle with the destructive cancer cells. The Simonton clinic has drawn patients from all over the world. While not accepted by all members of the medical community, the idea of imaging has gained some enthusiastic proponents. For more on this subject, see Dr. Simonton's book, *Getting Well Again.*

Mind and Body 10

References

Broad, C. D. (1986). The traditional problem of body and mind. In H. Hall & N. E.
Bowie (Eds.), The tradition of philosophy (pp. 150–158). Belmont, CA: Wadsworth.

Cousins, N. (1966, December). Anatomy of an illness. The New England Journal of
Medicine, 295(26), 1458–1468.

Descartes, R. (1986). The distinction between the mind and body of man. In H. Hall
& N. E. Bowie (Eds.), The tradition of philosophy (pp. 146–149). Belmont, CA:
Wadsworth.

Descartes, R. (1958). The passions of the soul. In N. K. Smith (Ed. & Trans.), Descartes' philosophical writings (pp. 34–45). New York: Modern Library.

Dorland's illustrated medical dictionary. 1965 ed., s.v. "Psychosomatic."

Huxley, T. E. (1986). Animals as conscious automata. In H. Hall & N. E. Bowie (Eds.),
The tradition of philosophy (pp. 159–166). Belmont, CA: Wadsworth.

Huxley, T. E. (1931). Evolution and ethics. In C. W. Thomas (Ed.), Essays in contemporary civilization (pp. 363–396). New York: Macmillan.

Lewis, H. R., & Lewis, M. E. (1972). Psychosomatics. New York: Viking.

Ornstein, R., & Sobel, D. (1987, March). The healing brain. Psychology Today, pp. 48–
52.

Pelletier, K. R. (1977). Mind as healer, mind as slayer. New York: Delacorte.

Simonton, C. (1978). Getting well again: A step-by-step self-help guide to overcoming cancer for patients and their families. New York: Tarcher.

English Usage

Grammar Fundamentals

THE SENTENCE

A sentence is *a group of words that expresses a complete thought*. "Because I'm happy" and "singing in the rain" do not express complete thoughts and are therefore not sentences. The following express complete thoughts and are therefore classified as sentences:

1. Because I am happy, I like to see other people happy.
2. John is singing in the rain.

The Subject and Predicate

Every sentence is divisible into two parts—a *subject* and a *predicate*. The subject is the word or word group about which something is said; the predicate is the word or word group that asserts something about the subject:

SUBJECT	PREDICATE
The bird	fell out of the sky.
It	angered him deeply.
All the boys	left without saying a word.

The *simple subject* of a sentence is the single word—usually a noun or pronoun—about which the sentence says something:

1. The *beggar* suddenly blinked his eyes.
2. The ugly *frog* turned into a handsome young prince.

The *simple predicate* is the verb or verb phrase that makes a statement about the subject:

1. Fred *decided* to play in the tournament.
2. Before dinner we *had welcomed* all the guests.

Complete Subjects and Predicates

The *complete subject* is the simple subject and all the words associated with it. The *complete predicate* is the simple predicate and all the words associated with it. A vertical line divides the complete subject from the complete predicate in these sentences:

1. Diseases of the mind | are often caused by the pressures of city living.
2. The regular bus driver | knows his passengers by name.

Learning to distinguish between the simple subject and simple predicate and between the complete subject and complete predicate will help you learn to construct and punctuate sentences.

Compound Subjects and Predicates

A *compound subject* is made up of two or more nouns or pronouns tied together; a *compound predicate* is made up of two or more verbs tied together:

1. *Terror and hate* were in their eyes.   COMPOUND SUBJECT
2. The soldier *stopped and saluted.*   COMPOUND PREDICATE
3. *Ghosts and witches* were the main characters in the story.   COMPOUND SUBJECT
4. In the recesses of his mind, the villain *remembered and felt guilty.*   COMPOUND PREDICATE
5. *John and Mary laughed and sang.*   COMPOUND SUBJECT/COMPOUND PREDICATE

Exercises

Underline the simple subject once and the simple predicate twice in the following sentences. Identify the verb first. To find the subject, ask "Who or what performs the action of the verb?"

1. The teacher arrived ten minutes after the class was to begin.
2. Mary believes in the intelligence and honesty of dogs.
3. After seeing the movie twice, Alice was sure she was in love with Robert Redford.
4. At the end of the first act, the big star made his appearance.

5. People all over the world expect America to feed them.

6. Ted was elected to run as vice-president.

7. We danced in the hallway, in the cellar, and on the patio.

8. Grace, her voice controlled and her head held high, debated the issues with her rival.

9. My father, a business consultant, is going to New York on Friday.

10. At the end of the examination, Bill breathed a sigh of relief.

In the following sentences, draw a vertical line between the complete subject and the complete predicate.

1. Jane arranged her schedule to allow for study.

2. As an usher as well as a waiter, Bruce worked to save $300.

3. Alaska, with all of its natural beauty, appealed to the Smiths.

4. Playing a guitar demands skill and sensitivity.

5. Angry and tired, the dean arrived and was hit with a water balloon.

6. Separate wills are recommended for couples who have been married twice.

7. The top of Mt. Whitney offers a breathtaking view of the Sierras.

8. The undefeatable Johnson was dropped from the squad.

9. Horses, covered with flies, stood scratching their backs on the fence.

10. Honor is more important than love.

Self-Grading Exercise 1

Underline the simple subject once and the simple predicate twice in the following sentences. To find the subject, ask "Who or what performs the action of the verb?" After completing the exercise, turn to the appendix for the correct answers.

1. Libraries contain the wisdom of civilization.

2. In the district of Wymar, burglars were ransacking the stores.

3. In Hemingway's novels matadors are highly respected.

4. A clear conscience is the best sleeping pill.

5. The silver-gray vest suited his taciturn personality.

6. Most middle-class homes in the Southwest are built with air conditioning.

7. The outdoor markets in Europe attract numerous tourists.

8. Noise pollution in towns and cities blots out the sounds and silences of the outdoor world.

9. A cup of good tea or coffee must be brought to me early each morning.

10. I wish to describe two kinds of tours available.

Self-Grading Exercise 2

In the following sentences, draw a vertical line between the complete subject and the complete predicate. After completing the exercise, turn to the appendix for the correct answers.

1. Television has contributed to the decline of reading skills.
2. Incensed by their rudeness, the senator left.
3. Michelangelo's work continues to attract admirers all over the world.
4. Wars go on endlessly.
5. Divorce affects children most of all.
6. Professional tennis has become big business in the United States.
7. Most people insist on paying their bills on time.
8. Within five weeks one hundred polio victims had been claimed.
9. Spain is no longer a strong world power.
10. Many areas of Saudi Arabia have experienced droughts.

CLAUSES AND PHRASES

The Clause

A clause is *a group of related words that forms part of a sentence*. Every clause has a subject and a predicate. There are two types of clauses: *independent* and *dependent*. An independent clause expresses a complete thought by making a complete statement, asking a question, giving a command, or making an exclamation. An independent clause, therefore, could stand alone as a complete sentence, but it is combined with other independent or dependent clauses to form a full sentence, as in the following examples:

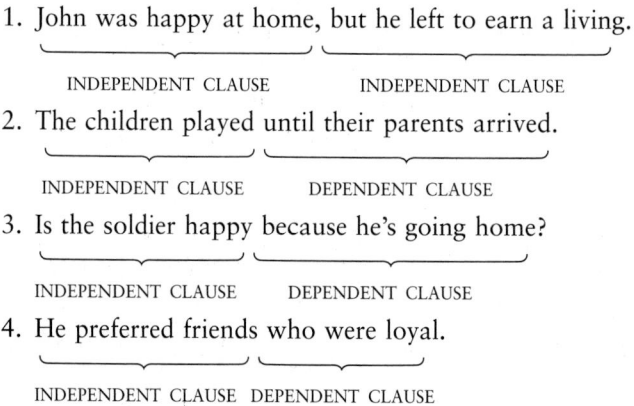

1. John was happy at home, but he left to earn a living.
   INDEPENDENT CLAUSE   INDEPENDENT CLAUSE

2. The children played until their parents arrived.
   INDEPENDENT CLAUSE   DEPENDENT CLAUSE

3. Is the soldier happy because he's going home?
   INDEPENDENT CLAUSE   DEPENDENT CLAUSE

4. He preferred friends who were loyal.
   INDEPENDENT CLAUSE   DEPENDENT CLAUSE

5. The accused claimed that she was innocent.

INDEPENDENT CLAUSE   DEPENDENT CLAUSE

There is a crucial difference between an independent and a dependent clause: Standing alone, an independent clause makes sense, but a dependent clause does not. A dependent clause depends for its meaning on an independent clause that either precedes or follows it. Dependent clauses are therefore said to be *subordinate* to independent clauses.

The Phrase

A phrase is *a group of two or more associated words having neither subject nor predicate*. A phrase does not make a complete statement, is never a clause, and is certainly not a sentence. A phrase is only part of a clause or a sentence. The following groups of words are phrases:

1. for his fiftieth birthday
2. practicing the flute
3. under the table
4. after a long time

Exercises

Label the following passages as *I* (independent clause), *D* (dependent clause), or *P* (phrase).

1. Spring has begun   _____
2. Since their parents died   _____
3. Although Sam is an atheist   _____
4. Follow the main road for a mile   _____
5. Between the two houses   _____
6. Everyone told him to stay home   _____
7. For your country   _____
8. If Mary enrolled in the class   _____
9. You may wish to return the picture today   _____
10. People who attend religious services   _____
11. Begging her to love him   _____
12. Flowers blossom   _____
13. Have you seen the five napkins   _____
14. He seldom speaks his mind   _____
15. Because she grew up in Poland   _____

Self-Grading Exercise 3

Label the following passages as *I* (independent clause), *D* (dependent clause), or *P* (phrase). After completing the exercise, turn to the appendix for the correct answers.

1. Such is my ideal   _____
2. The return from the walk should coincide with the serving of tea   _____
3. Not all books being suitable for mealtime reading   _____
4. What one does not want is a gossipy, superficial book   _____
5. Because self-concern and self-pity filled all their thoughts   _____
6. The letters from his brother, now longer, arrived daily   _____
7. One of the happiest men and most pleasing companions   _____
8. Either condition will destroy the psyche in the end   _____
9. Whenever they have set about rectifying the error   _____
10. As if in all ages they had been surrounded by barbarism   _____
11. He has little doubt that they should have succeeded equally well   _____
12. The country was given absolute freedom   _____
13. Plunged into an inferno of torturous extremes   _____
14. Here their methods were the same   _____
15. When I called Cleopatra a "Circe" and her love affairs "business deals"   _____
16. But Homer came first   _____
17. Who romanticize the worst poverty   _____
18. My deep appreciation for my parents   _____
19. Some discotheques don't allow clients older than twenty   _____
20. With the lining of her full-length lynx coat   _____

SENTENCE TYPES

Sentences are punctuated according to their function and their form. The examples in this section will assist you in recognizing the function a sentence serves and the forms it can take.

Classification According to Function

A *declarative sentence* states a fact or a possibility and ends with a period:

1. The pilot died in the crash. (fact)
2. The stock market may go up tomorrow. (possibility)

An *interrogative sentence* asks a question and ends with a question mark:

1. Is it true what they say about Dixie?
2. Have you decided which courses you will take?

An *imperative sentence* makes a request or gives an order:

1. Don't park your car here.
2. Turn over the cash to the cashier.

An imperative sentence ends with a period unless the command is filled with strong emotion, in which case it ends with an exclamation mark:

1. Shut your mouth, you fool!
2. It's an earthquake! Fall to the floor!

An *exclamatory sentence* expresses strong or sudden feeling and ends with an exclamation mark:

1. Oh, the pain is terrible!
2. How cruel you are!

Classification According to Form

A *simple sentence* consists of one independent clause that contains one subject and one predicate and expresses one complete thought:

1. The tree fell.
2. The heavens declare the glory of God.
3. There is no peace in being greedy.

Although a simple sentence has only one subject and one predicate, either the subject or the predicate or both may be compound. Not all simple sentences are short, for both the subject and the predicate may have many modifying words:

Staggering from his wound, inflicted during the heat of battle, and exhausted from the endless trudging through jungles, the young marine found a place near a brook shaded by trees and sat down to rest.

A *compound sentence* consists of two or more independent clauses connected by one of the following coordinating conjunctions: *and, or, nor, but, yet, for, as.* For example:

1. The flowers were blossoming, but patches of snow still covered the earth.
2. He studied hard for the examination, yet he failed.
3. Jim smiled and Fred frowned.

Occasionally, a semicolon separates the independent clauses:

He's superstitious; he never opens an umbrella inside the house.

A *complex sentence* consists of one independent clause to which one or more dependent clauses have been connected:

1. The foreman ordered the men to work because five days had elapsed. ONE DEPENDENT CLAUSE

2. Because life is not perfect, we must expect to find that difficulties will confront us as we attempt to achieve our goals. THREE DEPENDENT CLAUSES

A *compound-complex sentence* consists of two or more independent clauses and at least one dependent clause.

1. The company figured the values of all the pieces of property that lay within the city limits, and the manager then wrote each property owner a letter that explained the cost of curbing.

2. The world's petroleum supply is expected to last about 30 years; although some countries are exploring alternate energy sources, others are not.

Exercises

Place the appropriate punctuation mark at the end of each of the following sentences.

1. Oh, crime and violence, how long will you continue to rob us of peace
2. This is the time for all good men to come to the aid of their country
3. Come here this minute
4. Have you, by chance, already met this gentleman
5. Help I am caught in a mousetrap
6. Go to the store and buy me a quart of milk
7. If I need you, will you be available
8. What an exciting evening
9. Should we never meet again, I wish you the best of luck
10. I asked him if he had been paid for his time

Classify each of the following sentences as (A) simple, (B) compound, (C) complex, (D) compound-complex. Justify your classification by identifying the various clauses.

1. At the end of the day, Alice made an appearance; however, she did not smile once. _____

2. Because the winter was nearly over, Maxine arranged to be home with her mother, her grandmother, and her sisters. _____

3. After he had reached the end of the road, Mr. Leffingwell began to cross the bridge.   _____

4. Big Tom was dropped from the club after one month of membership; he now is trying out for the swimming team.   _____

5. At the end of the race, Jane let out a yell, for she had finished in third place.   _____

6. Maybelle operated an elevator for three years to save enough money to go to night school, to buy a new car, and to pay her mother's doctor bills.   _____

7. In the top drawer you will find two pairs of old gloves, three torn sweaters, and a yellowed picture album.   _____

8. We all believe that the U.S. Constitution must be preserved, because our liberties, which our ancestors paid for with their lives, must be nurtured with care.   _____

9. After freezing all night, Nancy decided she should have worn a sweater.   _____

10. When my family left for New Orleans, I thought they would return within two weeks; instead, they stayed there a full year.   _____

11. My uncle, a famous poet, gave me a handwritten manuscript and asked me to take care of it for him.   _____

12. Your letter was delightful; I am sure that it offended no one.   _____

13. Because Tom gave the most forceful pep talk, he was asked to represent the senior class at the fine arts festival.   _____

14. The mayor, his voice trembling with rage, denounced his opponent, Jack Wilson.   _____

15. He flew to New York, and she drove to Chicago because she was afraid to fly with him.   _____

Self-Grading Exercise 4

Place the appropriate punctuation mark at the end of each of the following sentences. After completing the exercise, turn to the appendix for the correct answers.

1. We asked him if he would be willing to do it alone
2. Are you usually alert to the problems of older people
3. Sound the alarm Then run for your life
4. I am as angry as a cornered cat
5. Do you mean to tell me that all of the money simply disappeared
6. They inquired as to whether or not we would accompany the performers
7. Heavens What a way to get attention

8. Go straight down the aisle and interrupt his conversation
9. Would you be so kind as to direct me to the British Museum
10. Whew What a terrible odor

Self-Grading Exercise 5

Classify each of the following sentences as (A) simple, (B) compound, (C) complex, (D) compound-complex. After completing the exercise, turn to the appendix for the correct answers.

1. In Paris we lived near the Louvre. _____
2. The whole school was a great temple for the worship of these mortal gods, and no boy ever went there unprepared to worship. _____
3. If you have not visited a German *Gymnasium* (high school), you may be confused about the German school system. _____
4. Their position was emphasized by special rituals; nevertheless, we refused to remain in their mansion because the atmosphere was stern and oppressive. _____
5. Strength and popularity were not enough to keep them in the club if they were not recommended by at least two members. _____
6. It is vital that they attempt a revolution when the time is ripe. _____
7. They tried to accelerate their social progress by flattering the existing leaders. _____
8. The doors opened into the study, but no one passed through them because the room was too dark to be used. _____
9. As we sat around our table, we felt the silence; however, no one ever spoke up because silence was an absolute rule. _____
10. Each study imitated the cluttered appearance of an Edwardian drawing room. _____
11. They were not like slaves, for their favors were nearly always solicited rather than compelled. _____
12. After games, gallantry was the principal topic of polite conversation. _____
13. I thought about it then, and I am still thinking about it. _____
14. He really insists that the candidate insulted him; yet, he remained seated on the podium as if he had received a compliment. _____
15. Dean Metzger has three lovely daughters, a beautiful home, and a free airline pass to travel all over the world. _____
16. I became a marked man, but that never stopped me from speaking my mind. _____
17. What takes so much time is waiting in line for the tickets or lining up to get in. _____

18. One must not conclude that the housekeeper's signature was forged, even though two experts testified against her.   _____

19. There are two reasons for such an unusual conclusion.   _____

20. The modern world is the child of doubt and inquiry, as the ancient world was the child of fear and faith.   _____

PARTS OF SPEECH

The Verb

A verb is a word that suggests *action*, a *state of being*, or a *condition*:

1. The cat *leaped* off the roof.   ACTION
2. The antique cup *sat* on the lace cloth.   STATE OF BEING
3. Her eyes *were* big and luminous.   CONDITION

A verb functions as the predicate or as part of the predicate in a sentence:

1. The blind man *hears*.
2. The blind man *has heard*.
3. The blind man *is* still *hearing*.

Note that verbals (participles, gerunds, or infinitives) cannot function as predicates of a sentence:

1. Participle: "*Heard* melodies are sweet . . ."   *HEARD* FUNCTIONS AS AN ADJECTIVE.
2. Gerund: His *hearing* is bad.   *HEARING* FUNCTIONS AS A NOUN.
3. Infinitive: *To hear* is important.   *TO HEAR* FUNCTIONS AS A NOUN.

The Noun

Nouns are *names* of persons, animals, things, places, characteristics, or ideas. The following are nouns:

engineer	Westwood Village
dog	jealousy
box	communism

You should know the following terms that describe nouns:

1. *concrete* nouns: tangible things, such as *men, cat, towns, teachers, coat*
2. *abstract* nouns: qualities or concepts, such as *love, justice, hate, credibility, intimacy*

3. *proper* nouns: specific persons, places, things, organizations, and events, which are capitalized, such as *Mt. Everest, Mary, French, Mr. Jones, the Eiffel Tower*

4. *common* nouns: general nouns that are not capitalized, such as *chair, kite, happiness, team*

5. *collective* nouns: words that are singular, but involve a group or imply a plural meaning, such as *jury, group, family, council, committee*

Understanding these terms will help you to avoid common errors in capitalization, agreement of subject and predicate, and agreement of pronouns with their *antecedents*—the words the pronouns stand for.

The Pronoun

Pronouns are words used *in place of nouns*. For example, you may use the pronoun *she* instead of the noun *mother*. You may speak of "the *children's* toys" or *"those"* or *"theirs."* There are nine kinds of pronouns, listed below. Although it is not important that you be able to name each kind, you should be able to recognize each as a pronoun:

1. personal   *You* and *they* will help *us*.
2. interrogative   *Who* is it? *What* do you want? *Which* is best?
3. relative   The man *who* killed her is the one *that* I saw.
4. demonstrative   *This* is older than *that*.
5. indefinite   *Each* of us must accomplish *something*.
6. reciprocal   Let us help *each other* and trust *one another*.
7. reflexive   John did it *himself*. I blame *myself*.
8. intensive   I *myself* heard him. *We* need money *ourselves*.
9. possessive   Is that book *yours* or *mine?*

The Adjective

Adjectives are words that *modify* (describe or qualify) nouns and pronouns:

1. The *shiny, black* cat   THE NOUN *CAT* IS MODIFIED.
2. *Morose* and *depressed*, he sat in the corner.   THE PRONOUN *HE* IS MODIFIED.
3. The beggar wanted *five* nickels.   THE WORD *NICKELS* IS MODIFIED.

Adjectives usually precede, but sometimes follow, the nouns they modify (a *tall, handsome* man). *Appositive adjectives* immediately follow a noun and are set off by commas from the nouns they follow:

1. The attorney, *pale* with anger, jumped forward.
2. The little boy, *dusty* and *tired,* fell asleep.

Sometimes the adjective follows the predicate, in which case it is called a *predicate adjective:*

1. The sunset looks *splendid.*
2. The newlyweds seem *happy.*
3. Women are *strong.*

Occasionally, the adjective modifies the object of the sentence, in which case it is called an *objective complement:*

1. The cream sauce made her *sick.*
2. The sun turned him *crimson red.*

Possessive and demonstrative adjectives precede the nouns they point out or specify:

1. We visited *their* mansion.
2. She bought *that* coat.

The Article

The article is a kind of adjective that *limits* a noun; *the* is a definite article and *a* and *an* are indefinite articles.

1. *the* people
2. *a* balloon, *an* orange

The Adverb

Adverbs modify verbs, adjectives, and other adverbs. They are next to verbs and nouns in importance. Effective writers tend to use more adverbs than adjectives. Note the use of adverbs in the following sentences:

1. Cecil will work *slowly* and *deliberately.*   ADVERB MODIFYING A VERB
2. My mother inherited a *surprisingly* old clock.   ADVERB MODIFYING AN ADJECTIVE
3. She succeeded *quite* well.   ADVERB MODIFYING AN ADVERB

Most adverbs indicate time (we must leave *now*), place (they stayed *over there*), manner (she walks *awkwardly*), or degree (all the relatives were *extraordinarily* kind). Some nouns function as adverbs and are called *adverbial nouns* (he left home *Monday*).

A special group of adverbs are the *conjunctive adverbs.* The primary conjunctive adverbs are the following:

accordingly	furthermore	instead	still
also	hence	likewise	then
anyhow	henceforth	meanwhile	therefore
besides	however	nevertheless	thus
consequently	indeed	otherwise	

When used to connect independent clauses, the conjunctive adverb is preceded by a semicolon:

1. We doubted their word; *nevertheless,* we went along with the plan.
2. Something about the garden pleased us; *however,* we did not wish to purchase the house.
3. The manager was harsh; *moreover,* he owed us our salaries.

When a conjunctive adverb is used parenthetically, it is set off by commas:

1. You can see, *moreover,* why this is important.
2. She, *however,* denied the truth.
3. This time, *furthermore,* he was forbidden to speak.

When the adverb *there* is used to introduce a sentence, it is called an *expletive: There* is a city in Algeria where bazaars appear everywhere.

Most adverbs end in *-ly.* The few that do not are called *flat* adverbs:

1. He walked *far.*
2. He walks too *fast.*
3. They work *hard.*

The Preposition

A preposition is used to show the relationship of a noun or pronoun to some other word in the sentence. For example, in "The airplane flew *above* the clouds," the preposition *above* shows the relationship between the clouds and the airplane. Stating anything else that an airplane can do when approaching clouds is likely to involve a preposition:

1. The airplane flew *into* the clouds.
2. The airplane flew *through* the clouds.
3. The airplane flew *across* the clouds.
4. The airplane flew *behind* the clouds.
5. The airplane flew *between* the clouds.

6. The airplane flew *after* the clouds.
7. The airplane flew *by* the clouds.
8. The airplane flew *over/under* the clouds.
9. The airplane flew *with* the clouds.
10. The airplane flew *out* of the clouds.
11. The airplane flew *near* the clouds.

Some prepositions, such as *for, at,* and *of,* will not work in this example.

Some words, such as *off, on, out, in, over,* and *up* may be used as prepositions, adverbs, or verbs:

1. He climbed *up* the ladder.   PREPOSITION
2. All of us looked *up*.   ADVERB
3. When I arrived in New York, I *looked* him *up*.   VERB
4. He ran *out* the door.   PREPOSITION
5. Reach *out* with your hand.   ADVERB
6. We must *watch out* for fires.   VERB

The preposition and its object form a *prepositional phrase*:

1. The dog remained *inside his kennel.*
2. Every morning he looked *underneath the table.*
3. The thief lurked *near the car.*

The Conjunction

Conjunctions are connectors and can be classified into two types: *coordinating* conjunctions and *subordinating* conjunctions. Coordinating conjunctions *(and, or, nor, but, yet, for)* are used to connect words, phrases, and clauses that are of equal importance:

1. apples *and* oranges   WORDS
2. with them, *but* not with us   PHRASES
3. I love my son, *yet* he must obey me.   CLAUSES

Subordinating conjunctions *(after, although, as, because, before, if, since, until, when, while, then)* are used to connect main clauses with subordinate clauses:

1. That man never looked us straight in the eye *when* he talked with us.
2. *If* you don't believe him, tell him so.
3. The bridge collapsed *because* it was so old.
4. She is stronger *than* any of the men are.

Relative pronouns can function as subordinators:

1. I firmly believe *that* you are wrong.
2. John returned the gift to the person *who* had given it to him.
3. He demands to know *whose* door is squeaking.

Often subordinating conjunctions consist of more than one word:

1. The sky was pitch black *even though* it was noon.
2. The doctor came *as soon as* he was called.
3. Nothing works out, *no matter how* hard I try.

A special kind of conjunction is the *correlative* conjunction, which is used in pairs:

1. They were *not only* kind *but also* generous.
2. They *neither* complained *nor* cared.

The Interjection

Interjections are words or phrases used to express strong or sudden feelings that attract attention:

1. *Hurray!* They've won.
2. *Ouch!* The horse stepped on my foot.
3. *Whew!* That's hard work.

Context and the Parts of Speech

The role of the word in a sentence always determines the part of speech it is. Context may change the role of a word:

1. He must *round* the corner at top speed.   VERB
2. The audience gave the orchestra a *round* of applause.   NOUN
3. The baby had a perfectly *round* face.   ADJECTIVE
4. Her fiance lives *round* the corner.   PREPOSITION

Exercises

Identify the part of speech of each italicized word in the following paragraphs:

I[1] went back to the *Devon School*[2] not long ago, *and*[3] *found*[4] it looking *oddly*[5] newer than *when*[6] I was a student *there*[7] fifteen years before. It seemed *more*[8] sedate *than*[9] I remembered it, more *perpendicular*[10] and straitlaced, *with*[11] *narrower*[12] windows and shinier woodwork, *as though*[13] a coat *of*[14] varnish *had been put*[15] *over*[16] everything for better preservation. *But,*[17] of course, fifteen years *before*[18] there had been a war going on. Perhaps the school wasn't as *well*[19] kept up in those days; *perhaps*[20] varnish, *along with*[21] every-*thing*[22] else, had gone to war.

I didn't *entirely*[23] like this glossy new *surface,*[24] *because*[25] it made the school look *like*[26] a museum, and that's exactly *what*[27] it was to me, and what I did not want it to be. In the deep, tacit way in which *feeling*[28] becomes stronger than thought, I had always *felt*[29] *that*[30] the Devon School came *into*[31] existence the *day*[32] I entered it, was vibrantly *real*[33] *while*[34] I was a student there, and then blinked out like a candle *the*[35] day I left.

John Knowles, *A Separate Peace*

1._____	19._____
2._____	20._____
3._____	21._____
4._____	22._____
5._____	23._____
6._____	24._____
7._____	25._____
8._____	26._____
9._____	27._____
10._____	28._____
11._____	29._____
12._____	30._____
13._____	31._____
14._____	32._____
15._____	33._____
16._____	34._____
17._____	35._____
18._____	

Self-Grading Exercise 6

Identify the part of speech of each italicized word in the following paragraphs. After completing the exercise, turn to the appendix for the correct answers.

A few years ago, an *Englishman*[1] named John David Potter *was rushed*[2] to the Newcastle General Hospital after suffering *extensive*[3] brain damage *in*[4] a brawl. Fourteen hours *later,*[5] he stopped breathing. Ordinarily, the man *would have been declared*[6] dead, *but*[7] at that moment a kidney was needed *for*[8] transplant, and Potter was an *obvious*[9] donor.

A respirator *was applied,*[10] and *it*[11] *artificially*[12] revived Potter's *breathing.*[13] *This*[14] in turn restored his failing *heartbeat*[15] *and*[16] circulation, *thus*[17] preserving *the*[18] kidneys. These vital organs, *now*[19] strictly *dependent*[20] *upon*[21] the respirator, *were kept*[22] going 24 hours, *even though*[23] the doctors *knew*[24] *that*[25] Potter *had*[26] no chance *of*[27] *recovery.*[28] *Meanwhile,*[29] Mrs. Potter *had granted*[30] permission to remove *a*[31] kidney *for*[32] *transplant.*[33] *When*[34] *this*[35] *was done,*[36] the attending *physician*[37] ordered the respirator *turned*[38] off. For the second time, Potter *ceased*[39] breathing, and his heart stopped *forever.*[40]

Leonard A. Stevens, "When Is Death?" *Reader's Digest*, May 1969

1._____	21._____
2._____	22._____
3._____	23._____
4._____	24._____
5._____	25._____
6._____	26._____
7._____	27._____
8._____	28._____
9._____	29._____
10._____	30._____
11._____	31._____
12._____	32._____
13._____	33._____
14._____	34._____
15._____	35._____
16._____	36._____
17._____	37._____
18._____	38._____
19._____	39._____
20._____	40._____

Correcting Common Errors

This unit presents the most common errors found in student essays. Most teachers use handwritten symbols to indicate student errors. For an explanation of your own errors and how to correct them, match the symbols in the margin of your paper with those provided in this unit.

A sentence *fragment* results when a phrase or a dependent clause is treated as if it were a complete sentence. Correct a fragment either by attaching it to the previous sentence or by adding enough words to the fragment to make it a complete sentence:

frag

We thought about the weather. Decided to cancel the picnic.	Error
We thought about the weather and decided to cancel the picnic.	Correction
Lonely house on the block.	Error
There was a lonely house on the block.	Correction
A man doesn't call a wall warped. Unless he knows what a straight wall is.	Error
A man doesn't call a wall warped unless he knows what a straight wall is.	Correction
Birds chirping, bees buzzing, the smell of honey in the air. I knew that spring was here.	Error
Birds were chirping, bees were buzzing, and the smell of honey hung in the air. I knew that spring was here.	Correction

A *comma splice* occurs when two independent clauses are separated by a comma instead of a period or a semicolon. There are four ways of correcting a comma splice:

cs

1. Separate the independent clauses with a period.

I was deeply shaken, my favorite cousin lay ill with cancer.	Error
I was deeply shaken. My favorite cousin lay ill with cancer.	Correction

587

2. Separate the independent clauses with a semicolon.

Error The backyard was full of plums, our family ate them all.

Correction The backyard was full of plums; our family ate them all.

3. Join the independent clauses by a comma and a coordinating conjunction.

Error Anyone can stick flowers in a vase, few can achieve an artistic arrangement.

Correction Anyone can stick flowers in a vase, but few can achieve an artistic arrangement.

4. Subordinate one independent clause to the other.

Error You failed to come to dinner, I ate alone.

Correction Because you failed to come to dinner, I ate alone.

Don't let a conjunctive adverb trick you into a comma splice:

Error I hate cold weather, however, the Rocky Mountains are good for my asthma.

Correction I hate cold weather; however, the Rocky Mountains are good for my asthma.

rt A *run-together sentence* occurs when one sentence is piled on another without any kind of punctuation, often resulting in an incoherent passage. Correct a run-together sentence by placing a period or a conjunction between the two sentences.

Error This map also predicts California's future the San Andreas fault, which underlies Los Angeles, is heading out to sea.

Correction This map also predicts California's future. The San Andreas fault, which underlies Los Angeles, is heading out to sea.

Error I like her attitude she is a solid person.

Correction I like her attitude. She is a solid person.

Error The first year of marriage is never easy I made it harder than need be.

Correction The first year of marriage is never easy, but I made it harder than need be.

Exercises

In the blanks at the right, enter *C* if the sentence is correct, *Frag* if it is a fragment, *CS* if it is a comma splice, or *RT* if it is a run-together sentence. Correct any sentence that is incorrect.

1. People must eat. _____C_____
2. The countless women who need jobs. _____FRAG_____
3. Chicago being a city riddled with crime. _____FRAG_____
4. The rivers overflowed their banks the trees were swept away. _____RT_____
5. Houses were destroyed, and homes were burned. _____C_____

6. Pet lovers in our country as well as abroad.   _FRAG_

7. In particular the mayor, who had supported a transit system when he spoke to the legislature.   _FRAG_

8. Irresistible also were the lovely orchards surrounding the swimming pool.   _C_

9. However, some crowds were vengeful.   _C_

10. "I cannot marry you," said the princess, "I am too ugly."   _CS_

11. Every one of us felt the loss.   _C_

12. The Vietnam War was senseless it gained us nothing.   _RT_

13. Run as fast as you can you need the practice.   _RT_

14. Recalling his visit to Paris, my uncle smiled.   _C_

15. All of us visited the statue, few of us admired it.   _CS_

16. Originally made in Taiwan but then transported to the United States.   _FRAG_

17. Soon giving up trying.   _FRAG_

18. She was as delicate as a butterfly.   _C_

19. I want to excel not only as a musician, but also as a human being.   _C_

20. The car weighed a ton; they could not lift it.   _C_

Self-Grading Exercise 7

In the blanks at the right, enter *C* if the sentence is correct, *Frag* if it is a fragment, *CS* if it is a comma splice, or *RT* if it is a run-together sentence. After completing the exercise, turn to the appendix for the correct answers.

1. Hardly as big as a powderpuff and no bigger.   _____

2. Quietly this cat dozes by the fire or on her lap.   _____

3. He will not sell himself for any amount of money, he will not enter into an allegiance.   _____

4. Because psychologists have learned a great deal about abnormal human behavior.   _____

5. There is nothing difficult here if you found this article in a children's book, you would not be surprised.   _____

6. Nevertheless, the writer has prepared you for a number of questions.   _____

7. Although necessity is the mother of invention.   _____

8. We believe.   _____

9. Once you have noted the topic sentence, the paragraph is easy to follow.   _____

10. Putting your own ideas into words.   _____

11. All creatures living in the wild are subject to attack by predators, their survival depends on their ability to fend off such attacks.   _____

12. "I'm telling you one last time," said the policeman, "Show me your driver's license."   _____

13. The battle lines are firmly drawn between the chiropractors and their foes; accordingly, the public must decide on which side to be.   _____

14. Everybody knows about Chicago, the "windy city."   _____

15. Consciously ignoring the poor, alienating the old, and forgetting the handicapped.   _____

16. Express your thesis concisely, however, do not leave out any key words.   _____

17. Of course, there is much more to reading any piece of prose, even a popular magazine article, than understanding the opening paragraph.   _____

18. The manager taught them time-saving techniques and helped them improve their skills.   _____

19. The winter has arrived you should get out your snow boots.   _____

20. Many tourists stand admiringly in front of the *Mona Lisa,* few leave quickly.   _____

agr   An *error in agreement* occurs when the subject does not agree with the verb or when a pronoun does not agree with its antecedent. Avoid errors in subject–verb agreement by learning to recognize the subject of a sentence. To avoid errors in pronoun agreement, learn which pronouns are plural and which are singular.

Errors with Verbs

Error   My family, together with numerous other families, were checked for excess baggage.

Correction   My family, together with numerous other families, was checked for excess baggage.   THE SUBJECT IS *FAMILY*.

Error   The main issue are high taxes.

Correction   The main issue *is* high taxes.   THE SUBJECT IS *ISSUE*.

My list of errors were so long that the teacher shook her head in despair.   Error

My list of errors *was* so long that the teacher shook her head in despair.   THE   Correction
SUBJECT IS *LIST*.

Either John alone or all of the boys together has to show up at the entrance.   Error

Either John alone or all of the boys together *have* to show up at the entrance.   THE   Correction
SUBJECT IS *ALL*. WHEN TWO SUBJECTS, ONE SINGULAR AND ONE PLURAL, ARE CONNECTED BY
OR, *NOR*, OR *EITHER*, THE VERB MUST AGREE WITH THE NEARER SUBJECT.

Mary is among the girls who has collected funds to build a memorial hall.   Error

Mary is among the girls who *have* collected funds to build a memorial hall.   *WHO*,   Correction
SUBJECT OF THE DEPENDENT CLAUSE, REFERS TO *GIRLS*, NOT *MARY*.

Unemployment as well as inflation affect the voters.   Error

Unemployment as well as inflation *affects* the voters.   THE ADDITION OF EXPRESSIONS   Correction
SUCH AS *TOGETHER WITH*, *ALONG WITH*, *AS WELL AS*, *INCLUDING*, AND *LIKE* DOES NOT
ALTER THE NUMBER OF THE SUBJECT.

A pair of scissors and some thread is standard equipment for seamstresses.   Error

A pair of scissors and some thread *are* standard equipment for seamstresses.   Correction
SUBJECTS JOINED BY *AND* REQUIRE A PLURAL VERB. EXCEPTIONS ARE COMPOUND SUBJECTS
REFERRING TO A SINGLE PERSON: "MY LOVER AND BEST FRIEND *HAS* LEFT ME." *LOVER* AND
FRIEND ARE THE SAME PERSON.

Exercises

In the following sentences, change each verb that does not agree with its subject.
Write the correct form in the blank, or if the sentence is correct, write *C.*

1. Neither storms nor illness delay our newspapers.   _____
2. His five children and their education was his main worry.   _____
3. There's much to be said for simplicity.   _____
4. The importance of words are being stressed in all newspapers.   _____
5. My chief concern this summer are my expenses.   _____
6. Taste in books differs from student to student.   _____
7. *The Three Stooges* are a wonderful movie.   _____
8. Mathematics is one of my worst subjects.   _____
9. Either you or I am mistaken.   _____
10. My brothers as well as my sister is coming to visit me.   _____

Self-Grading Exercise 8

In the following sentences, change each verb that does not agree with its subject.
Write the correct form in the blank, or if the sentence is correct, write *C.* After
completing the exercise, turn to the appendix for the correct answers.

1. Just one error in those endless columns of figures make the project unacceptable. _____

2. These kinds of books is pleasant to read. _____

3. Everything in this nation, world, and universe have a reason for existence. _____

4. Neither the winner nor the loser was injured. _____

5. The rate of inflation, along with the scarcity of oil, cause people to go into debt. _____

6. Not only they but also I am unhappy. _____

7. Either they or he are to drive. _____

8. There is several active ingredients in the mixture. _____

9. All three of the courses Mike is taking requires a final essay examination. _____

10. Make sure that either your sister or your brothers go. _____

11. What is her arguments supposed to prove? _____

12. The diseases we are investigating cause severe anxiety. _____

13. Does a man and a woman have to agree? _____

14. The committee has submitted a fine report. _____

15. Physics are so difficult when one uses obscure problem-solving methods. _____

16. The main problem are all of the prostitutes in town. _____

17. No matter how dreadful the weather, a cluster of onlookers watch the surfers. _____

18. The tragedy—and main argument—of the novel is that love can fail miserably. _____

19. There on the park bench sits Fritz and Jane. _____

20. Surprisingly enough, law, not medicine or architecture, appeal to Jim. _____

Errors with Pronouns

The following pronouns, when used as subjects, always require a singular verb: *each, either, neither, another, anyone, anybody, anything, someone, somebody, something, one, everyone, everybody, everything, nobody, nothing.*

Error   Each of the prizes were spectacular.

Correction   Each of the prizes *was* spectacular.   DON'T LET PREPOSITIONAL PHRASES TRICK YOU INTO AN AGREEMENT ERROR. IN THE ABOVE CASE, *EACH* IS THE SUBJECT.

Behind all the managers stand their president.	Error
Behind all the managers *stands* their president.	Correction
Everyone in that room care sincerely.	Error
Everyone in that room *cares* sincerely.	Correction
Neither of the twins plan to go to private school.	Error
Neither of the twins *plans* to go to private school.	Correction

A pronoun must agree in number with its antecedent:

Everyone who accepted the money knew that they would have to return it.	Error
Everyone who accepted the money knew that *he* would have to return it.	Correction
Anyone who visits the principal will find that they are welcome.	Error
Anyone who visits the principal will find that *he* is welcome.	Correction
Every woman who wrote demanding a ticket knew that they would get one.	Error
Every woman who wrote demanding a ticket knew that *she* would get one.	Correction

The rule that regards such indefinite pronouns as *everyone, someone, somebody, everybody* as singular and therefore replaceable by *he* has been challenged by feminist writers and linguists, who contend that gender-neutral pronouns such as *they* and *their* are far better replacements. Feminists argue that while the sentence *Anyone who visits the principal will find that he is welcome* may be traditionally correct, it is also sexually biased against the possibility of the "anyone" being a woman. Many writers are sympathetic to the feminist argument, which carries considerable logic, and formal usage of *they* and *their* as substitutes for *everyone, someone, somebody, everybody* is becoming increasingly popular.

Collective nouns are replaced by singular pronouns if they denote a single unit, but by plural pronouns if they denote a group acting separately and individually.

1. The jury rendered *its* verdict.   ACTING AS A SINGLE UNIT
2. The jury could not reach an agreement; *they* argued all day.   ACTING INDIVIDUALLY
3. The whole family gave *its* view.   ACTING AS A SINGLE UNIT
4. The family have gone their separate ways.   ACTING INDIVIDUALLY

Case errors most commonly occur when a student fails to distinguish between the subjective and objective cases. The subject is always a noun or pronoun that the predicate says something about. The subject answers who? or what? about the predicate. The object, on the other hand, receives the action of the verb and is not the same as the subject. Study the following diagrams:

case

SUBJECT	VERB	OBJECT
The patient	*watches*	*the sunset*

The patient initiates the action of the verb *watched,* whereas the sunset being watched receives it. Two further examples will reinforce the difference between subject and object:

SUBJECT	VERB	OBJECT	SUBJECT	VERB	OBJECT
My brother	*hit*	*the dog*	*Americans*	*love*	*their country*

Problems in case arise when nouns are replaced by pronouns of the wrong case. The pronouns below are listed in the subjective case at left and in the objective case at right:

SUBJECTIVE	OBJECTIVE
I	me
you	you
he, she, it	him, her, it
we	us
they	them
who, whoever	whom, whomever

In the sentences,

1. John bit the dog.
2. The dog bit John.

a pronoun substituted for *John* must reflect in its case whether John is the subject or object of the verb *bit*—whether he initiates the action or receives it:

1. He bit the dog.
2. The dog bit him.

The subjective pronoun *he* is used in place of *John* when *John* functions in the sentence as a subject. The objective pronoun *him* is used in place of *John* when *John* functions in the sentence as an object.

Error
: The coach called *he* and *I.*

Correction
: The coach called *him* and *me.*   HIM AND ME ARE OBJECTS BECAUSE THEY TAKE THE ACTION FROM THE VERB CALLED.

Error
: Ellen and *me* decided to wear platform heels.

Correction
: *Ellen and I* decided to wear platform heels.   ELLEN AND I IS A COMPOUND SUBJECT.

Prepositions always require the objective case.

Error
: The teacher got a better understanding of him and *I.*

Correction
: The teacher got a better understanding of him and *me.*

Between you and *I*, the whole matter was a joke.   Error
Between you and *me*, the whole matter was a joke.   Correction

Special care must be taken to use the right case with pronouns in apposition. An appositive must be in the same case as the noun or pronoun it qualifies.

They told both of us—my mother and *I*—that the sale was over.   Error
They told both of us—my mother and *me*—that the sale was over.   ME IS IN THE   Correction
OBJECTIVE CASE BECAUSE IT IS IN APPOSITION WITH US.

Let's you and *I* make sure that the bill is paid.   Error
Let's you and *me* make sure that the bill is paid.   LET US—YOU AND ME.   Correction
MUST BE IN THE OBJECTIVE CASE BECAUSE THEY ARE IN APPOSITION WITH US.

The case of pronouns used in clauses must be determined by treating each clause as a separate part.

I shall vote for whoever I like.   Error
I shall vote for *whomever* I like.   WHOMEVER I LIKE MUST BE TREATED AS A SEPARATE
PART. WHOMEVER IS THE OBJECT OF THE VERB LIKE.   Correction
Give the job to whomever is willing to work.
Give the job to *whoever* is willing to work.   WHOEVER IS WILLING TO WORK MUST BE   Error
TREATED AS A SEPARATE PART. WHOEVER IS THE SUBJECT OF THE VERB IS.   Correction

Don't allow a parenthetical expression to trick you into a wrong pronoun case.

The Smiths are people whom I think will make good neighbors.
The Smiths are people *who*, I think, will make good neighbors.   WHO IS THE   Error
SUBJECT OF WILL MAKE.   Correction
The Pennsylvania Dutch are people who, they say, we can trust.
The Pennsylvania Dutch are people *whom*, they say, we can trust.   WHOM IS THE   Error
OBJECT OF VERB CAN TRUST.   Correction

A pronoun following *than* or *as* is the subjective or the objective case depending on the implied verb:

1. He admires him more than (he admires) *her*.
2. He admires him more than *she* (admires him).
3. We are happier than *they* (are).

Use the subjective case when the pronoun follows the verb *to be*:

1. Answer the phone; it may be *she*.   NOT HER
2. It was *they* who rang the bell.   NOT THEM

A possessive adjective, not an object pronoun, is used immediately in front of a gerund (noun used as a verb, such as *singing, talking, thinking*). The following are possessive adjectives:

my	our
your	their
his, her, its	whose

Error   *Him* lying is what tipped off the police.

Correction *His* lying is what tipped off the police.

Error   *Us* checking the score helped.

Correction *Our* checking the score helped.

Exercises

Underline the correct form of the pronoun in each of the following sentences:

1. I am more to be pitied than (he, him).
2. The saleslady (who, whom) they think stole the stockings lives next to us.
3. You must praise (whoever, whomever) does the best job.
4. During the Vietnam War some of (we, us) football players felt guilty.
5. Florence insists that I was later than (he, him).
6. Was it (she, her) who called you the other day?
7. The candidate made an excellent impression on us—my Dad and (I, me).
8. (Who, whom) do you think will set a better example?
9. We were relieved by (his, him) paying the bill.
10. Between you and (me, I), is she innocent or guilty?
11. The coach said that I swim better than (him, he).
12. (Him, his) daydreaming affected his work negatively.
13. Bud doesn't care (who, whom) he gives his cold to.
14. The pinecones were divided among the three of us—John, Bill, and (me, I).
15. (Our, us) leaving the inner city was a blessing in disguise.
16. Do you remember (me, my) telling you?
17. Can you tell me the rank of the general (who, whom), it is said, struck one of his soldiers?
18. (Whom, who) the Cubs will play next is unknown.
19. Marilyn Monroe, (who, whom) most women envied, was unhappy.
20. Give the papers to (he and I, him and me).

Self-Grading Exercise 9

Underline the correct form of the pronoun in each of the following sentences. After completing the exercise, turn to the appendix for the correct answers.

1. No one cares except (he, him).
2. I need to call (whomever, whoever) should be at the celebration.
3. His memory was so bad that he no longer knew (whom, who) she was.
4. Was it (he or she/him or her) who asked the question?
5. Between you and (I, me), the entire plan is vicious.
6. Despite the political problems in the Middle East, (him and I, he and I) traveled to Jerusalem.
7. Do you remember (my, me) getting the measles?
8. The television set was donated to the fraternity for (its, their) members.
9. (Them, Their) escaping the accident was a miracle.
10. By (who, whom) was this fabulous cake baked?
11. They may well ask (you or I, you or me) about the burglary.
12. He has no political views of his own; he will vote for (whomever, whoever) others support.
13. Robert Frost was a poet (whom, who) I admired greatly.
14. After his divorce, he consulted a psychiatrist (who, whom) he had met socially.
15. We admire you every bit as much as we do (she, her).
16. They did not wish to frighten James or (she, her).
17. (Us, We) football players require a great deal of protein.
18. It seems to me that (whomever, whoever) has the biggest car should drive.
19. Both of us—Fred and (I, me)—received an A.
20. (Who, Whom) do you trust completely?

Errors in *point of view* occur when the writer needlessly shifts person, tense, mood, voice, discourse, or key words.   *pv*

Person

We have come to the place where one should either fish or cut bait. SHIFT FROM *WE* TO *ONE*		Error
We have come to the place where *we* should either fish or cut bait.		Correction
If you turn right on LaFollet Street, one will see the sign on one's right. SHIFT FROM *YOU* TO *ONE*		Error
If you turn right on LaFollet Street, *you* will see the sign on your right.		Correction

Tense

Error	The weather suddenly turned windy, and clouds arise. SHIFT FROM PAST TO PRESENT
Correction	The weather suddenly turned windy, and clouds *arose*.
Error	William Tell takes the apple, places it on his son's head, and shot an arrow right through the middle. SHIFT FROM PRESENT TO PAST
Correction	William Tell takes the apple, places it on his son's head, and *shoots* an arrow right through the middle.
Error	His face turned purple with rage, and he would strike his friend. SHIFT FROM PAST TO CONDITIONAL
Correction	His face turned purple with rage, and he *struck* his friend.

Mood

Error	People of America, why do you wait? Protect your environment and you should vote against nuclear plants. SHIFT FROM IMPERATIVE TO INDICATIVE
Correction	People of America, why do you wait? Protect your environment. *Vote* against nuclear plants.

Voice

Error	John carried Mary's pack, and her tent was also pitched by him. SHIFT FROM ACTIVE TO PASSIVE VOICE
Correction	John carried Mary's pack, and he also *pitched* her tent.

Discourse

Error	The minister asked Bill if he loved his fiancée and will he treat her with devotion. SHIFT FROM INDIRECT TO DIRECT DISCOURSE
Correction	The minister asked Bill if he loved his fiancée and if he *would treat* her with devotion.

or

The minister asked Bill, "Do you love your fiancée and will you treat her with devotion?"

Key Words

Error	Because everyone has a primary goal in life, I too have an outstanding goal. SHIFT FROM *PRIMARY* TO *OUTSTANDING*
Correction	Like everyone else, I have a primary goal in life.
Error	I want to be a perfect human being. God made me, so why not be worthwhile? SHIFT FROM *PERFECT* TO *WORTHWHILE*
Correction	I want to be a perfect human being. God made me, so why not be perfect?

Exercises

In the following sentences correct all shifts in (A) person, (B) tense, (C) mood, (D) discourse, (E) voice, or (F) key word. Identify the shift by placing the appropriate letter in the blank at the right.

1. Everyone must live according to your conscience. _____

2. She insisted loudly that "I am opposed to abortions." _____

3. A good meal is enjoyed by all of us and we like fresh air, too. _____

4. She revealed that an unknown intruder is in the room. _____

5. So far we have not mentioned poverty. So let me discuss it now. _____

6. Truth is a principle everyone should cherish because you can be a better person when we adhere to it. _____

7. Lock the door and you should turn out the lights. _____

8. The robber stole her jewelry and she was mugged by him, too. _____

9. Slowly he crept toward me and grabs for my wallet. _____

10. A straightforward question to ask the salesman is, "Why people should buy his razors?" _____

11. He helped me out by pointing out where one could find an inexpensive hotel. _____

12. The doorman opened the door; then my baggage was picked up by a porter. _____

13. In his memory he heard the melody of that old song and knew that time is passing quickly. _____

14. She was a spoiled brat, it always seems to me. _____

15. The senator's question was an intelligent one; the chairman's answer was also a wise one. _____

Self-Grading Exercise 10

In the following sentences correct all shifts in (A) person, (B) tense, (C) mood, (D) discourse, (E) voice, or (F) key word. Identify the shift by placing the appropriate letter in the blank at the right. After completing the exercise, turn to the appendix for the answers (there is more than one possible way to correct each item).

1. As they listened to the music, Sir Peregrine remarked about the success of the races while his wife dreams about love. _____

2. A person must accept the fact that you can't always win. _____

3. Every secretary who worked in the office was asked to give their opinion and to say how they felt. _____

4. The airline attendants wondered why so many passengers were standing in the aisle and who gave them permission to leave their seats? _____

5. If I were wealthy and if I was living in Zaire, I'd tell Mobutu a thing or two. _____

6. He pored over all of his notes, and many library books were checked out by him. _____

7. Mrs. Olson walks into strangers' kitchens and they are told by her how to make coffee. _____

8. The professor informed us that the test would be given and asked if we are ready. _____

9. First the insane man quoted lines from Richard Lovelace; then he recites a passage from the "Song of Solomon." _____

10. "Raise the property tax—and you must impose rent control!" he yelled with fervor. _____

11. When we buy a foreign car, you have to expect poor service. _____

12. The matter suddenly came to a crisis, but just as suddenly the situation was resolved. _____

13. It is essential that he bring the document with him and that he is here by noon. _____

14. We fear the unknown whereas the known is often welcomed by us. _____

15. Our Constitution protects our right to pursue happiness; however, it does not guarantee that we shall find this satisfaction, no matter how diligently we pursue it. _____

16. The tenant claims that he paid the rent and would I convey this fact to the landlord? _____

17. The skylark gracefully lifts itself into the sky, lets out a joyful warble, and disappeared into a cloud. _____

18. The sea breeze is blowing harder and felt colder. _____

19. As you walked into the slaughterhouse, one could see hundreds of carcasses hanging on hooks. _____

20. Because most of the children loved to go swimming, the group goes to the beach. _____

ref   *Reference* errors occur with the use of pronouns that do not stand for anything specific. Every pronoun must have an unmistaken *antecedent*.

Error   No one is perfect, but that doesn't mean that I shouldn't try to be *one*.   THE PRONOUN *ONE* HAS NO ANTECEDENT, NO SPECIFIC NOUN FOR WHICH IT STANDS.

Correction   No one is perfect, but that doesn't mean that I shouldn't try to be.

She keeps her files well organized; she gets along well with her employers; and she has ethical integrity; however, this is not enough to convince us to hire her. THE ANTECEDENT OF *THIS* IS TOO BROAD AND IT NEEDS TO BE PINPOINTED.	Error
She keeps her files well organized; she gets along well with her employers; and she has ethical integrity; however, these qualities are not enough to convince us to hire her.	Correction
Our neighbor, Mrs. Irwin, told my mother that *she* had not chosen the proper dress. WHO HAD NOT CHOSEN THE PROPER DRESS—MRS. IRWIN OR THE MOTHER? THE REFERENCE IS UNCLEAR.	Error
Our neighbor, Mrs. Irwin, told my mother, "I have not chosen the proper dress." TURNING THE CLAUSE INTO DIRECT ADDRESS IS THE SIMPLEST WAY TO CORRECT THIS KIND OF REFERENCE ERROR.	Correction
His clothes were scattered all across the room which needed folding. CONFUSION ARISES BECAUSE THE MISPLACED *WHICH* IMPLIES THAT THE ROOM NEEDED FOLDING.	Error
His clothes, which needed folding, were scattered all across the room.	Correction
In Europe they often claim that Americans eat too much ice cream. AVOID USING *THEY* OR *YOU* AS A REFERENCE TO PEOPLE IN GENERAL.	Error
Europeans often claim that Americans eat too much ice cream.	Correction
When the Godfather dies, it is due to a heart attack. *IT* HAS ONLY AN IMPLIED REFERENCE.	Error
The Godfather's death is due to a heart attack.	Correction
Arthur Ashe swung his racket hard, but it went into the net. *IT* STANDS FOR BALL, BUT THE WORD *BALL* NEVER SHOWS UP.	Error
Arthur Ashe swung his racket hard, but the ball went into the net.	Correction
When Elmer Cole's restaurant was opened, he invited all the townspeople for a free meal. A PRONOUN IN THE SUBJECTIVE CASE MUST NOT REFER TO AN ANTECEDENT IN THE POSSESSIVE CASE.	Error
When Elmer Cole opened his restaurant, he invited all the townspeople for a free meal.	Correction

Exercises

Rewrite the following sentences to avoid confusing, implied, nonexistent, or vague pronoun references:

1. Many people are emotional but have difficulty showing them.

   _____

   _____

2. At the factory where I work at night, they say not to ask for salary advances.

   _____

   _____

3. My dad warned my brother that he would not get a promotion.

   _____

   _____

4. She sat by the window knitting, which was too small to let in any light.

   _____

   _____

5. The nuclear bomb was developed in the twentieth century; this completely changed man's approach to war.

   _____

   _____

6. The leading baritone didn't show up for the opening night, which caused all kinds of gossip.

   _____

   _____

7. In the South, you aren't understood if you have a New York accent.

   _____

   _____

8. Life is a cycle of happiness followed by misery, but I want to have them in equal portions.

   _____

   _____

9. Although it is muddy down by the river, it looks inviting.

   _____

   _____

10. The first chapter awakens the reader's interest in mining, which continues until the Camerons move to America.

   _____

   _____

11. The American colonists refused to pay taxes without being represented. This was the major cause of the 1776 revolution.

   _____

   _____

12. Tomorrow it may rain and damage our roof, and it should be protected.

_____

_____

13. The guests were perspiring and fanning themselves with the printed program; it really bothered them.

_____

_____

14. The rose garden in Hoover Park is spectacular. Some of them are deep purple, almost black.

_____

_____

15. I went over my check stubs three times, but it never balanced properly.

_____

_____

Self-Grading Exercise 11

Rewrite the following sentences to avoid confusing, implied, nonexistent, or vague pronoun references. After completing the exercise, turn to the appendix for the answers (there is more than one possible answer for each item).

1. We are now expected to drive less and use public transportation; we are asked to conserve heating fuel. This is realistic.

_____

_____

2. They say that a tablespoon of vinegar in some sugar and oil will reduce the appetite.

_____

_____

3. In the newspaper it said that a rebirth of great art is taking place in China.

_____

_____

4. Byron carried on a lively correspondence with Shelley when he was on the Continent.

_____

_____

5. When Golda Meir died, the world was expecting it.

_____

_____

6. My brother is enormously talented, but he does not make full use of it.

_____

_____

7. During lunch John always sat alone while the other students sat together chatting away. This didn't last long, however.

_____

_____

8. In Mahatma Gandhi's room, he wanted only the sparsest of furniture.

_____

_____

9. In an interview with a group of millionaires, the master of ceremonies told the audience that they were very articulate.

_____

_____

10. Melissa invited Ruth to travel to Spain with her because she thought she was interested in Spanish history.

_____

_____

11. A psychologist has no right discussing his patients' personal problems with his friends because they could be embarrassed if their identities were discovered.

_____

_____

12. The passerby noticed a young boy dashing out of the store and running down the street, which made him wonder about it.

_____

_____

13. On our flight across the Atlantic it was beautiful.

_____

_____

14. Inside the Blue Grotto of Capri, the water was rough and dark, but it was splendid anyway.

_____

_____

15. My friend John loves to watch basketball for hours on end, but his wife doesn't approve of it.

_____

_____

Dangling modifiers occur when words or phrases are used that have no logical relationship to any other element in the sentence. These words simply "dangle" in front of the reader, causing mystification and mirth. The most frequent dangling errors are caused by (1) misused verbal phrases, and (2) misused subordinate clauses. To correct dangling elements, assign the logical subject to all verbal phrases or subordinate clauses.

dang

Falling in love with Carole Lombard made me envy Clarke Gable. FOR THIS SENTENCE TO MAKE SENSE, CLARK GABLE MUST BE THE SUBJECT OF THE PHRASE "FALLING IN LOVE WITH CAROLE LOMBARD."   Dangling

I envied Clark Gable's falling in love with Carole Lombard.   Correct

Upon reaching the age of six, my grandfather took me to school. THE SENTENCE IMPLIES THAT THE GRANDFATHER WAS SIX YEARS OLD WHEN HE TOOK HIS GRANDCHILD TO SCHOOL.   Dangling

When I reached the age of six, my grandfather took me to school.   Correct

To understand why fat people eat, a study of self-hatred is necessary. IN THIS SENTENCE, *A STUDY* BECOMES THE SUBJECT OF THE INFINITIVE *TO UNDERSTAND*, WHICH IS OBVIOUSLY SILLY BECAUSE A STUDY CAN'T "UNDERSTAND."   Dangling

To understand why fat people eat, we must study self-hatred.   Correct

Although loved by Americans, historians deny the truth of many anecdotes involving Abraham Lincoln. THIS SENTENCE IMPLIES THAT HISTORIANS ARE LOVED BY AMERICANS.   Dangling

Although loved by Americans, many anecdotes involving Abraham Lincoln have been labeled as historically untrue.   Correct

Misplaced modifiers occur when modifying words, phrases, or clauses are not placed as close as possible to the words they modify. Confusing, illogical, or awkward sentences are caused by misplaced modifiers.

misp

Confusing	We looked inside the car with our friends for the package. WERE THE FRIENDS INSIDE OR OUTSIDE THE CAR?
Correct	With our friends we looked inside the car for the package.
Illogical	Visitors to France can see the Eiffel Tower floating down the Seine River on a barge. IN THIS SENTENCE, THE EIFFEL TOWER IS FLOATING ON A BARGE.
Correct	Floating down the Seine River on a barge, visitors to Paris can see the Eiffel Tower.
Awkward	My husband and I expect you to instantly pay for the damage to our car. IT IS BEST NOT TO SEPARATE TO FROM ITS VERB.
Correct	My husband and I expect you to pay for the damage to our car instantly.

The error noted above is grounded in the split infinitive rule, which says that a word should never be interposed between *to* and its verb. This rule evolved from the work of earliest grammarians, who had in mind the Latin model where the infinitive is always a single word. As arbitrary as it may now sound, these grammarians reasoned that if a Latin verb such as *amare* could not be split that it was also wrong to split its English equivalent, *to love*. With this logic they deduced that *to passionately love* must be ungrammatical because *passionately* comes between *to* and the verb. We think this rule silly as observing it often leads to incongruous sounding phrases such as *really to understand* instead of *to really understand*. In classroom usage, however, some instructors remain adamant about never splitting infinitives.

Exercises

Rewrite the following sentences to eliminate the dangling or misplaced modifiers.

1. Looking down in horror the snake crawled away.

   _____

   _____

2. To guarantee their rights, collective bargaining was organized by the teachers.

   _____

   _____

3. She did not realize that he had had major surgery until Friday.

   _____

   _____

4. John had looked forward to getting married for two weeks to Mary Ellen.

   _____

   _____

5. Responding to consumer demands for better gasoline milage, the Honda was promoted.

_____

_____

6. We bought ice cream cones at a small stand that cost forty cents.

_____

_____

7. She decided to immediately telephone her friend.

_____

_____

8. Arriving at the pack station, our dried food had been stolen.

_____

_____

9. I held my breath as the car slid into the curb that had raced ahead suddenly.

_____

_____

10. While dreaming about the future, lightning flashed and the rain began to pour.

_____

_____

11. My mother consented to let me use her car reluctantly.

_____

_____

12. Continue to whip the cream until tired.

_____

_____

13. To understand T. S. Eliot, the classics must be read.

_____

_____

14. Drilling my teeth, I could tell he was an excellent dentist.

_____

_____

15. He was not willing to completely give up drinking.

_____

_____

16. Looking at the mountain range from the valley, a lovely rainbow could be seen.

_____

_____

17. My uncle had warned me never to leave a gun in my car that had not been unloaded.

_____

_____

18. Now is the time to, if you want a Democrat in the White House, vote for our governor.

_____

_____

19. At the party hors d'oeuvres were served to all of the guests on silver trays.

_____

_____

Self-Grading Exercise 12

Rewrite the following sentences to eliminate the dangling or misplaced modifiers. After completing the exercise, turn to the appendix for the answers (there is more than one possible answer to each item).

1. Bowing to the audience, his violin fell to the floor.

_____

_____

2. The tiny kitten sat shivering in the corner filled with terror.

_____

_____

3. Watching from behind a bush, a camera in hand, the bears seemed like harmless pets.

_____

_____

4. What the teacher needs is a list of students neatly typed.

_____

_____

5. Students will not need to pass the three conversation examinations that speak French fluently.

_____

_____

6. During World War II the Nazis only gave Jewish prisoners cabbage to eat, nothing else.

_____

_____

7. Instead of asking forgiveness, a piece of chocolate cake was her sign of repentance.

_____

_____

8. Even when confronted with the full truth, the facts were ignored.

_____

_____

9. Hearing the bell ring, the boxer's glove was flung to the ground triumphantly.

_____

_____

10. Out of breath, the lover ran up the stairs revealing a look of anxiety.

_____

_____

11. The day drew to a close with anguish, praying that God would spare the infant.

_____

_____

12. We not only enjoy music, but also painting and sculpture.

_____

_____

13. After adjourning Congress, the law was enacted immediately.

_____

_____

14. Scorched by the sizzling heat, jumping into the river made a great deal of sense.

_____

_____

15. We tried on some Givenchy pants at a Neiman-Marcus store that cost $150.

_____

_____

// *Lack of parallelism* occurs when similar grammatical constructions are not used to express parallel ideas. The result is a disruptive break in the rhythm of writing.

Not parallel	I love swimming, hiking, and to ski. THE SENTENCE STARTS WITH TWO GERUNDS (-ING WORDS) BUT SUDDENLY SWITCHES TO AN INFINITIVE (TO + A VERB).
Parallel	I love swimming, hiking, and skiing.
Not parallel	Community colleges are necessary because they give late bloomers a second chance; they provide free tuition for the poor; and they always encouraged the vocational trades. THE SENTENCE STARTS WITH TWO VERBS IN THE PRESENT TENSE, BUT SUDDENLY SWITCHES TO THE PAST TENSE.
Parallel	Community colleges are necessary because they give late bloomers a second chance; they provide free tuition for the poor; and they encourage the vocational trades.
Not parallel	For days the president of the club wondered whether he should pay the bills or to resign. "HE SHOULD" IS FOLLOWED BY "TO RESIGN."
Parallel	For days the president of the club wondered whether to pay the bills or to resign.
Not parallel	Whether tired or when he is rested, he reads the paper.
Parallel	Whether tired or rested, he reads the paper.

Exercises

Rewrite the following sentences to improve parallel structure. Join participles with participles, infinitives with infinitives, noun phrases with noun phrases, and so on.

1. Bright sun gleams on the water, dark shadows across the cliffs, and the delicate flowers that blossomed in the desert created a memorable picture.

_____

_____

2. I prefer to attend small dinners than going to big banquets.

_____

_____

3. What we claim to believe rarely coincides with the things we actually do.

   _____ _____

   _____

4. The anthropologist traveled into heated jungles, along insect-infested rivers, and he ventured up steep mountain trails.

   _____

   _____

5. I tried to explain that time was short, that the firm wanted an answer, and the importance of efficiency.

   _____

   _____

6. Most women's fashions come from Paris, Rome, and also from New York.

   _____

   _____

7. As we watched through the bars of the cage we could see the monkeys eating bananas, scratching their fur, and they swung on rails.

   _____

   _____

8. Most teachers try not only to engage the students' attention but they also want to say something important.

   _____

   _____

9. Victor Hugo was a statesman and who also wrote novels, including *Les Misérables*.

   _____

   _____

10. Bigger Social Security checks would allow senior citizens to pay for decent living quarters, to get proper medical help, and they could afford sound nutrition.

    _____

    _____

11. Basketball, football, and the game of baseball are favorite American spectator sports.

    _____

    _____

12. I admire the songs of Diana Ross, formerly a member of the Supremes, but who is now on her own.

_____

_____

13. Their divorce was due to his stressful job, his hot temper, and because he disliked her friends.

_____

_____

14. You have two choices: You must take either the exam or to write a research paper.

_____

_____

Self-Grading Exercise 13

Rewrite the following sentences to improve parallel structure. Join participles with participles, infinitives with infinitives, noun phrases with noun phrases, and so on. After completing the exercise, turn to the appendix for the answers (there is more than one possible answer for each item).

1. He wanted to marry her because she was bright, pleasant, and never placed herself first.

_____

_____

2. Her boss fired her because her letters were sloppy, ungrammatical, and she didn't type well.

_____

_____

3. The handbook revealed two ways in which the unity of a paragraph could be broken: (1) one could stray from the topic sentence, (2) excessive details obscuring the central thought.

_____

_____

4. By exercising daily, by eating proper food, and if he avoids stress, he can regain his health.

_____

_____

5. This simple man did not doubt that after death there was a paradise for good people and a hell for people who had been bad.

_____

_____

6. Most of them were either athletic or had great strength.

_____

_____

7. Handing out oil coupons seemed both intelligent and a necessity.

_____

_____

8. She insisted that he must leave and never to return.

_____

_____

9. The man is either an idealist or foolish.

_____

_____

10. Today pocket calculators are inexpensive, durable, and it is easy to obtain them.

_____

_____

11. The Byronic hero was a man who felt alienated from mainstream society, who withdrew into haughty superiority, loved passionately, and felt an element of self-pity.

_____

_____

12. This is the case not only with policemen but also of firemen.

_____

_____

13. Here is what you will need to know: how to open a bank account, how to judge a contract, and selling equipment.

_____

_____

14. He climbed Mount Whitney not because he wanted to test his endurance, but out of a sense of arrogance.

_____

_____

15. To err is human; forgiving is divine.

_____

_____

d *Poor diction* (also called poor word usage) refers to the use of a word to mean something other than its dictionary definition or the use of a word in a way unacceptable according to the standards of users of *ideal English. Ideal English* can be defined as language spoken or written according to standards of educated people. It is the language of good books, magazines, and newspapers. People who follow precise standard usage rules are using ideal English, although they probably express themselves less formally in day-to-day communication—on the bus, in the laundromat, or at the supermarket.

Ideal English is the language of concentrated formality. Dun J. Li, introducing a textbook on Chinese civilization, uses *ideal English* when he states: "Of all ideologies that influenced the thinking and life of traditional China none was more important than Confucianism." On the other hand, the irate factory worker complaining about his wages uses colloquial English when he writes, "If you wasn't so darn pigheaded, you'd raise our pay." Both messages are clear, but the difference is in their levels of formality.

Use the Correct Word

Because it is highly precise, *ideal English* is generally required in student writing. Colloquial, substandard, or slang words are unacceptable in ideal English. If you are unsure about a word's meaning, we suggest that you look it up. The following glossary will help you avoid expressions that are unacceptable in ideal English.

Glossary of Word Choice

ACCEPT, EXCEPT. To *accept* is to *receive;* to *except* is to *exclude.* (We *accepted* her into the group; we didn't let him in because C students were *excepted.*) *Except* is a preposition meaning *other than, with the exception of.* (Everyone arrived on time *except* Jim.)

ACCIDENTLY. No such word exists. The correct word is *accidentally.*

ADVICE, ADVISE. *Advice* is a noun; *advise* is a verb. (A person receives *advice,* but he will *advise* another.)

AFFECT, EFFECT. *Affect* means to *influence*. (It will *affect* my health.) *Effect* is both a verb and a noun. To *effect* is to *produce, cause,* or *bring about*. (He *effected* a change.) An *effect* is a *result*. (The *effect* of the paint was ugly.)

AGGRAVATE. *Aggravate* means *make worse*. It should not be used for *provoke* or *irritate*.

AGREE TO, AGREE WITH. One agrees *to* a proposal but *with* a person. (I agreed *to* his plan. I agreed *with* Nancy.)

AIN'T. Considered substandard.

ALL READY, ALREADY. *All ready* means that all are ready. (The guests were *all ready*.) *Already* means *previously* or *before now*. (He had *already* moved away from town.)

ALL TOGETHER, ALTOGETHER. *All together* means *all of a number* considered as a group. (She scolded them *all together*.) *Altogether* means *entirely, completely*. (The officer was *altogether* correct.)

ALLUSION, ILLUSION. *Allusion* means *hint* or *indirect reference*. (The comment was an *allusion* to World War II.) *Illusion* means *false impression* or *belief*. (She is under the *illusion* that she is beautiful.)

AMONG, BETWEEN. *Among* is used for more than two people or objects. (We searched *among* the many guests.) *Between* is used for two people or objects. (Divide the money *between* the two workers.)

AMOUNT, NUMBER. *Amount* refers to uncountable things (a large *amount* of cement). *Number* refers to countable things (a large *number* of houses).

ANY PLACE, NO PLACE. Corruptions of *anywhere, nowhere*.

ANYWHERES, NOWHERES, SOMEWHERES. Corruptions of *anywhere, nowhere, somewhere*.

APPRAISE, APPRISE. *Appraise* means *estimate* (the *appraised* value of the car). *Apprise* means *inform*. (*Apprise* me of your decision.)

APT, LIABLE, LIKELY. *Apt* means *suitable, qualified, capable* (an *apt* phrase, a man *apt* in his work). *Liable* means *susceptible, prone, responsible* (*liable* to be injured, *liable* for damages). *Likely* means *credible, probable, probably*. (He had a *likely* excuse. It is *likely* to rain.)

AWFUL. Colloquial when used for *disagreeable* or *very*.

BAD, BADLY. *Bad* is an adjective, *badly* an adverb. (He has a *bad* cold; he sings *badly*.)

BEING AS. Corruption of *since* or *inasmuch as*.

BESIDE, BESIDES. *Beside* is a preposition meaning *by the side of, in addition to,* or *aside from*. (He sat down *beside* her.) *Besides* is a preposition meaning *except* (he had little *besides* his good looks) and an adverb meaning *in addition, moreover*. (He received a trip and fifty dollars *besides*.)

BLAME ON. Correct idiom calls for the use of *to blame* with *for*, not *on*. (They *blamed* the driver *for* the accident, not They *blamed* the accident *on* the driver.) *Blame on* is colloquial.

BURST, BURSTED, BUST. The principal parts of the verb *burst* are *burst, burst, burst*. The use of *bursted* or *busted* for the past tense is incorrect. *Bust* is either a piece of sculpture, a part of the human body, or a slang expression for *failure*. It is sometimes incorrectly used instead of *burst* or *break*.

BUT WHAT. Use *that* instead of *but what*. (They had no doubt *that* he won the New York primary.)

CANNOT HELP BUT. This is a mixed construction. *Cannot help* and *cannot but* are separate expressions, either of which is correct. (*He cannot but attempt it,* or *He cannot help attempting it.*) Do not write, "He *cannot help but* lose."

CAPITAL, CAPITOL. *Capital* is a city; *capitol* is a building. *Capital* is also an adjective, usually meaning *chief* or *excellent*. As a noun, *capital* means accumulated assets or wealth.

CENSOR, CENSURE. To *censor* means to *subject to censorship*. (The Vietnamese military *censored* his mail.) To *censure* means to *criticize severely*. (He was *censured* by the church.)

CHOOSE, CHOSE. *Choose* is the present tense. (Today I *choose* to stay.) *Chose* is the past tense. (Yesterday I *chose* to stay.)

CITE, SITE. To *cite* means to *quote*. (He *cited* Abraham Lincoln.) *Site* means *place* or *location*. (It was a grassy, green *site*.)

COMPLEMENT, COMPLIMENT. In its usual sense, *complement* means *something that completes*. (His suggestion was a *complement* to the general plan.) A *compliment* is an expression of courtesy or praise. (My *compliments* to the chef.)

CONSIDERABLE. The word is an adjective meaning *worthy of consideration, important*. (The idea is at least *considerable*.) When used to denote a great deal or a great many, *considerable* is colloquial or informal.

CONTINUAL, CONTINUOUS. *Continual* means *repeated often*. (The interruptions were *continual*.) *Continuous* means *going on without interruption*. (For two days the pain was *continuous*.)

CONVINCE, PERSUADE. Do not use *convince* or *persuade*, as in "I *convinced* him to do it." *Convince* means to *overcome a doubt*. (I *convinced* him of the soundness of my plan.) *Persuade* means to *induce*. (I *persuaded* him to do it.)

COUNCIL, COUNSEL. *Council* means an *assembly*. (The *council* discussed taxes.) *Counsel* means *advice*. (The teacher gave him good *counsel*.)

CREDIBLE, CREDITABLE. *Credible* means *believable*. (His evidence was not *credible*.) *Creditable* means *deserving esteem* or *admiration*. (The male lead gave a *creditable* performance.)

DIFFERENT THAN. Most authorities on usage prefer *different from* to *different than*.

DISINTERESTED. Often confused with *uninterested, disinterested* means *unbiased, impartial*. (The judge was *disinterested*.) *Uninterested* means *bored with*. (She was *uninterested* in politics.)

DON'T. A contraction of *do not*. Do not write *he, she,* or *it don't*.

EITHER. Used only with two items, not three or more. (*Either* the teacher or the book was wrong. *Not: Either* the teacher, the book, or I was wrong.)

EMIGRANT, IMMIGRANT. A person who moves from one country to another is both an *emigrant* and an *immigrant*. He *emigrates from* one place and *immigrates to* the other.

ENTHUSED. The word is colloquial and almost always unacceptable.

EQUALLY AS. Do not use these words together; omit either *equally* or *as*. Do not write "Water is equally as necessary as air," but rather "Water is as necessary as air" or "Water and air are equally necessary."

ETC. An abbreviation of Latin *et* (and) and *cetera* (other things). It should not be preceded by *and*, nor should it be used to avoid a clear and exact ending of an idea or a sentence.

EVERYONE. This singular pronoun takes a singular verb. (Everyone *is* going.)

EXAM. Colloquial for examination. Compare *gym, lab, dorm, soph, prof*.

EXPECT. The word means *look forward to* or *foresee*. Do not use it for *suspect* or *suppose*.

FEWER, LESS. Use *fewer* to refer to items that can be numbered and *less* to refer to amount. (Where there are *fewer* machines, there is *less* noise.)

FORMALLY, FORMERLY. *Formally* means *in a formal manner*. (He was *formally* initiated last night.) *Formerly* means *at a former time*. (They *formerly* lived in Ohio.)

FUNNY. When used to mean *strange* or *queer*, *funny* is colloquial.

FURTHER, FARTHER. *Further* is used for ideas. (We studied the question *further*.) *Farther* is used for geographical location (*farther* down the street).

GOT. This is a correct past tense and past participle of the verb *to get*. (He *got* three traffic tickets in two days.) *Gotten* is the alternative past participle of *get*. (He had *gotten* three tickets the week before.)

GUESS. Colloquial when used for *suppose* or *believe*.

GUY. Slang when used for *boy* or *man*.

HAD OUGHT, HADN'T OUGHT. Do not use for *ought* and *ought not*.

HARDLY, SCARCELY. Do not use with a negative. "I *can't hardly* see it" borders on the illiterate. Write "I *can hardly* see it" or (if you cannot see it at all) "I *can't* see it."

HEALTHFUL, HEALTHY. Places are *healthful* (conducive to health) if persons living in them are *healthy* (having good health).

IMPLY, INFER. *Imply* means *suggest*. (His grin *implied* that he was teasing.) *Infer* means *conclude*. (I *inferred* from her look that she was teasing.)

INCIDENTLY. There is no such word. The correct form is *incidentally*, which is derived from the adjective *incidental*.

INSIDE OF. In expressions of time, *inside of* is colloquial for *within*. (He will return *within* a week).

IRREGARDLESS. No such word exists. Use *regardless*.

ITS, IT'S. The form *its* is possessive. (*Its* cover is gray.) *It's* is a contraction of *it is*. (*It's* your fault.)

IT'S ME. Formal English requires *It is I. It's me* is informal or colloquial.

KIND OF, SORT OF. Do not use these to mean *rather* as in "He was *kind of* (or *sort of*) stupid."

KIND, SORT. These are singular forms of nouns and should be modified accordingly (*this kind, that sort*). Do not write "*these* kind."

LAST, LATEST. *Last* implies that there will be no more; *latest* means *most recent*. (After reading his *latest* book, I hope that it is his *last*.)

LEAVE, LET. The use of *leave* for *let* in expressions like *leave him go* is incorrect.

LIKE, AS. Confusion in the use of these words results from using *like* as a conjunction—"He talks *like* a gentlemen should. She spends money *like* she had a fortune." Use *as* or *as if* instead. (He talks *as* a gentlemen should. She spends money *as if* she had a fortune.)

LOOSE, LOSE. *Loose* means *not tight, not attached*. (The button is *loose*.) *Lose* means to *be unable to keep or find*. (Did she *lose* her diamond ring?)

LOT, LOTS. Colloquial or informal when used to mean *many* or *much*.

MAD. The meaning of *mad* is *insane*. Used to mean *angry*, it is informal.

MAY BE, MAYBE. *May be* is a verb phrase. (They *may be* late.) *Maybe* used as an adverb means *perhaps*. (*Maybe* they will buy a boat.)

MEAN. Used informally for *disagreeable*. (He has a *mean* face.) It is slang when used to mean *skillful, expert*. (He plays a *mean* tennis game.)

MEDIA. *Media* is the plural of *medium*—a means, agency, or instrument. It is often used *incorrectly* as though it were singular, as in "The *media* is playing a big role in political races this year."

MOST. Do not use for *almost*. "*Almost* all my friends appeared" is the correct form.

MYSELF. Incorrect when used as a substitute for *I* or *me*, as in "He and *myself* did it." It is correctly used as an intensifier (*I myself* shall do it) and in the reflexive (I blame only *myself*).

NONE, NO ONE. Singular pronouns taking irregular verb forms. (None of his reasons *is* valid. No one *is* going.)

OF. Unnecessary after such prepositions as *off, inside,* or *outside*. (He fell *off* the chair. They waited *inside* the house.)

ON ACCOUNT OF. Do not use as a conjunction. The phrase should be followed by an object of the preposition *of* (*on account of* his illness). "He was absent *on account of* he was sick" is poor English.

ORAL, VERBAL. *Oral* means *spoken* rather than written; *verbal* means *associated with words*. When referring to an agreement or commitment that is not in writing, *oral* should be used.

OVER WITH. The *with* is unnecessary in such expressions as "The concert was *over with* by five o'clock."

PAST, PASSED. *Past* is a noun, adjective, or preposition (to remember the *past;* in the *past* two weeks; one block *past* the pharmacy). *Passed* is a verb. (She *passed* by his house.)

PERSONAL, PERSONNEL. Personal means *private.* (She expressed her *personal* view.) *Personnel* is a *body of employed people.* (The *personnel* demanded higher wages.)

PLAN ON. Omit *on.* Standard practice calls for an infinitive or a direct object after *plan.* (They *planned to go.* They *planned a reception.*)

PRINCIPAL, PRINCIPLE. Principal is both adjective and noun (*principal* parts, *principal* of the school, interest and *principal*). *Principle* is a noun only, meaning *code of conduct, fundamental truth or assumption* (*principles* of morality, a person of *principle*).

QUITE. The word means *altogether, entirely.* (He was *quite* exhausted from his exertion.) It is colloquial when used for *moderately* or *very* and in expressions like *quite a few, quite a number.*

RAISE, RISE. *Raise* requires an object. (She *raised* the cover.) *Rise* is not used with an object. (Let us *rise* and sing.)

REASON IS BECAUSE, REASON WHY. These are not correct forms in English. Examples of correct usage are "The *reason* I stayed home is *that* I was sick," "The *reason* (not *why*) they invited us is that . . ."

RESPECTFULLY, RESPECTIVELY. Respectfully means *with respect.* (The young used to act *respectfully* toward their elders.) *Respectively* is used to clarify antecedents in a sentence. (The *men and women* took their seats on the right and left, *respectively.*)

RIGHT. In the sense of *very* or *extremely, right* is colloquial. Do not write, "I'm *right* glad to know you."

SAME. The word is an adjective, not a pronoun. Do not use it as in "We received your order and shall give *same* our immediate attention." Substitute *it* for *same.*

SET, SIT. *Set* requires an object. (She *set* the cup on the table.) *Sit* is not used with an object. (You must *sit* in the chair.)

SHOULD OF, WOULD OF. Do not use these forms for *should have, would have.*

SOME. Do not use for *somewhat,* as in "She is *some* better after her illness."

STATIONARY, STATIONERY. *Stationary* means *fixed, not moving. Stationery* means paper and other materials for writing letters.

STATUE, STATURE, STATUTE. A *statue* is a piece of sculpture. *Stature* is bodily height, often used figuratively to mean *level of achievement, status,* or *importance.* A *statute* is a law or regulation.

SURE, SURELY. *Sure* is an adjective, and *surely* is an adverb. (I am *sure* that he will arrive, but he *surely* annoys me.)

SUSPICION. This word is a noun and should not be used for the verb *to suspect.* (His *suspicion* was right; they *suspected* the butler.)

TRY AND. Use *try to,* not *try and,* in such expressions as "*Try to* be kind."

TYPE. Colloquial in expressions like "this *type* book." Write "this *type of* book."

UNIQUE. If referring to something as the *only* one of its kind, you may correctly use *unique.* (The Grand Canyon is *unique.*) The word does not mean *rare, strange,* or *remarkable,* and there are no degrees of uniqueness: Nothing can be *extremely* (almost, nearly, virtually) *unique.*

USE (USED) TO COULD. Do not use for *once could* or *used to be able.*

VERY. Do not use as a modifier of a past participle, as in *very burned.* English idiom calls for *badly burned* or *very badly burned.*

WAIT FOR, WAIT ON. To *wait for* means *to look forward to, to expect.* (For days, I *have waited for* you.) To *wait on* means *to serve.* (The hostess *waited on* the guests.)

WANT IN, WANT OFF, WANT OUT. These forms are dialectal. Do not use them for *want to come in, want to get off, want to get out.*

WAY. Colloquial when used for *away,* as in "*way* out West."

WAYS. Colloquial when used for *way,* as in "a long *ways* to go."

WHOSE, WHO'S. The possessive form is *whose.* (*Whose* money is this?) *Who's* is a contraction of *who is.* (*Who's* there?)

WISE. Unacceptable when appended to a noun to convert it to an adverb as in *businesswise.*

YOUR, YOU'RE. The possessive form is *your.* (Give me *your* address.) *You're* is a contraction of *you are.*

Exercises

Underline the correct term in each of the following sentences:

1. When they arrived at West Point, they received some practical (advise, advice) regarding the honor system.
2. During his lecture, the professor made an (allusion, illusion) to Abraham Lincoln.
3. The prime minister's illness was so (aggravated, irritated) by his drinking that he needed surgery.
4. My aunt does a (credible, creditable) job of sewing evening gowns.
5. In the past, interviewers were (disinterested, uninterested) when they interviewed candidates; now they are biased.
6. I was (enthusiastic, enthused) when they told me about the new director.
7. When we heard about the theft, we immediately (suspicioned, suspected) collusion within the company.
8. They received the news that he would return (within, inside of) a week.

9. Chris Evert's (latest, last) match gave the world of tennis something to rave about.

10. Be careful not to (loose, lose) the keys.

11. We drank the spring water (as if, like) we would never drink water again in our lives.

12. That information seriously (affects, effects) the decision.

13. The agreement was (oral, verbal), so it will not hold up in court.

14. The reason grades are necessary (is that, is because) they are a point of reference for students.

15. If I had known you were coming, I (would of, would have) baked a cake.

16. Most people improve (somewhat, some) the moment they take one spoonful of Kay's cough syrup.

17. For Christmas, I sent mother some blue (stationary, stationery) so she could write to her friends.

18. Never use a large (number, amount) of words when (less, fewer) will do.

19. We still had a long (way, ways) to trudge uphill, but none of the students complained.

20. Will the person (who's, whose) wallet this is please claim it at the front ticket booth?

21. Before the tall buildings were built, we (used to could, used to be able) to see the ocean.

22. That scandal in her (passed, past) may keep her from getting the promotion.

23. Many Americans want to return to old-fashioned, religious (principals, principles).

24. (Regardless, irregardless) of the consequences, the ambassador stood by his post.

25. The glint in her eye (implied, inferred) more clearly than words how she really felt.

Self-Grading Exercise 14

Underline the correct term in each of the following sentences. After completing the exercise, turn to the appendix for the correct answers.

1. After noticing that the watch and the bedspread were gone, they immediately (suspicioned, suspected) his stepdaughter.

2. Dorothy insisted keeping her (personnel, personal) opinions hidden from her students.

3. The hiring committee preferred communicating by telephone because they believed in (oral, verbal) interviews.

4. I was always told that (this type, this type of) novel was cheap and aimed at the sensation seekers.

5. (Sit, set) the flower pot in front of the brick wall, where it will look lovely.

6. The (amount, number) of registered students varies from semester to semester.

7. In the upper left-hand corner of his (stationery, stationary) one could clearly discern three modest initials.

8. Earl Warren was considered a Supreme Court justice of immense (stature, statue, statute).

9. The team that climbed Mt. Whitney included (quite a number, a rather large number) of women.

10. Twenty years and six children later, the marriage was finally (over, over with).

11. Day after day his fiancee waited (for, on) him to return from the war.

12. Thank you for the (complement, compliment)—how kind!

13. (Your, you're) either for us or against us.

14. He never returned the suitcase (like, as) he was asked to do.

15. We (can hardly, can't hardly) distinguish one twin from the other.

16. The (farther, further) he delved into St. Paul's theology, the more fascinated he became.

17. When the real estate agent had received a firm bid, he (appraised, apprised) his clients of the fact.

18. He could never be (persuaded, convinced) to travel overseas on an airplane.

19. The (site, cite) for the international hotel was near the center of town.

20. While he was in Vietnam, all of his mail was (censured, censored).

Use Concrete Words

A word is *concrete* when it refers to a *specific* object, quality, or action. "He *limped* across the road" is more concrete than "He *went* across the road." "*One hundred women* attended the dinner" is more concrete than "*Quite a few people* attended the dinner." (See also Unit 1, the section on using details.)

Vague	I like her because she is such a *nice* girl.
Concrete	I like her because she is *witty* and *vivacious*.
Vague	The lyrics of Paul Simon are *relevant*.
Concrete	The lyrics of Paul Simon *expose many fears felt by the people in our society*.
Vague	I dislike my teacher's *negative attitude* toward old people.
Concrete	I dislike my teacher's *contempt* for old people.

Exercises

Improve the following sentences by replacing the italicized vague words with more concrete words or phrases.

1. John *got* on his horse and quickly *went* away.

   _____

   _____

2. Eloise always wears such sloppy *apparel.*

   _____

   _____

3. The streets of Amsterdam are crowded with *vehicles.*

   _____

   _____

4. The lecturer was most *uninteresting.*

   _____

   _____

5. She *ate* her food *quickly.*

   _____

   _____

6. It was fascinating to watch the children *being active* on the school playground.

   _____

   _____

7. I was upset by this whole *business.*

   _____

   _____

8. What a *great* idea!

   _____

   _____

9. We expect to have a *wonderful* time in Palm Springs.

   _____

   _____

10. Eskimos are *unusual* in many *ways*.

_____

_____

11. I couldn't follow the complicated *setup* in his church.

_____

_____

12. My psychology class was one of the most *worthwhile* experiences of my college days.

_____

_____

13. Spanking is an important *element* of child rearing.

_____

_____

14. The *negative aspects* of driving huge cars outweigh the *positive aspects*.

_____

_____

15. *All the President's Men* is a *tremendous* movie.

_____

_____

16. Here are the *things* that bother me about assigning grades.

_____

_____

Self-Grading Exercise 15

Improve the following sentences by replacing the italicized vague words with more concrete words or phrases. After completing the exercise, turn to the appendix for the answers (there is more than one possible answer for each item).

1. To add to our depression, a period of *unfavorable weather* set in.

_____

_____

2. Vicky *showed great satisfaction* as she walked off the stage with her gold medal.

_____

_____

3. I liked *the advantages of living* in the city.

_____

_____

4. His extreme selfishness *had some negative consequences on his life.*

_____

_____

5. He chewed his food noisily, he talked with his mouth full, and he wiped his lips with his hand; in short, his manners were *deficient.*

_____

_____

6. For six days and nights, he *participated in a combat* with fever and death.

_____

_____

7. A delicate sea shell is a *nice thing.*

_____

_____

8. All of the fun at Joe's birthday party was ruined because the children *behaved badly.*

_____

_____

9. The Mohave Desert of California and the Sinai Desert of Egypt *have certain characteristics in common.*

_____

_____

10. Every large city *has its problems.*

_____

_____

11. She was a hopeless, desiccated old lady *going across* the street with her cane, her *entire posture* serving as a symbol of her despair.

   _____

   _____

12. In 1925, a terrible dust storm *went* across the Midwest, *causing considerable destruction*.

   _____

   _____

13. Many of the old Tin Pan Alley songs reveal poignantly *some regrettable aspects of* American life.

   _____

   _____

14. We tried various cleaning solutions, but the kitchen floor remained *unsightly*.

   _____

   _____

15. People who throw *all kinds of stuff* out of their car windows while they drive along our highways reveal a disgusting kind of vulgarity.

   _____

   _____

W   *Wordiness* results when writing is burdened with redundant or wasted expressions. Prune your rough draft of such redundancies.

Wordy	He spent *all of his entire* life in freezing temperatures. ALL AND ENTIRE ARE REDUNDANT.
Correct	He spent his entire life in freezing temperatures.
Wordy	After *the end of* the flood, Noah released the dove. THE END OF IS WASTED.
Correct	After the flood, Noah released the dove.
Wordy	My dress was pink and yellow *in color*. THE TERM *IN COLOR* IS WASTED; PINK AND YELLOW ARE OBVIOUSLY COLORS.

Other redundancies of this kind are

short *in length*	*necessary* requirements
circle *around*	*and* etc.
still persist	combined *together*
many *in number*	now *at this time*

The Oldsmobile that was parked behind the supermarket was smeared with mud.   Wordy

The Oldsmobile parked behind the supermarket was smeared with mud.   Correct

Often, relative clauses can be trimmed. Note the following:

the judge *who was seated* on the bench
the judge on the bench

the man *who was* accused
the accused man

Exercises

Revise the following sentences for economy by eliminating redundancies or wasted words.

1. The secretary who sat behind the big mahogany desk of wood seemed to be efficient.

    _____

    _____

2. Most people find it difficult to express the emotion of tenderness toward other people.

    _____

    _____

3. The winner was timid and reticent about accepting the trophy.

    _____

    _____

4. Her coat, which is of the fur type, cost $2,000.

    _____

    _____

5. Worshiping ancestors is a venerable, sacred, old religious tradition among the Chinese.

    _____

    _____

6. My study of history leads me to believe that the Danes were a militant people who loved war.

    _____

    _____

7. Probably paying decent wages is usually the right thing to do in the majority of cases.

_____

_____

8. Workers who are employed shouldn't be allowed to collect food stamps.

_____

9. If he wants to be president, he had better bring about new innovations in Congress.

_____

_____

10. Generally speaking, most of the time it is improper diet that causes gallstones.

_____

_____

11. All of the present clothing styles in our day and age reflect a taste for the bizarre.

_____

_____

12. At 10:00 P.M. at night a strange knock was heard.

_____

_____

13. The consensus of the majority in our class was that we should invite Dr. Boling as our keynote speaker.

_____

_____

14. The story dealt with a cruel murder and a tragic ending that was lamentable.

_____

_____

15. As a usual rule one should lock one's car while shopping.

_____

_____

16. There were three women who decided to volunteer for the job without being forced.

_____

_____

17. Neil Simon writes humorous comedies that really make you laugh.

_____

_____

18. If we don't cooperate together with the major world powers, a nuclear war could annihilate the world.

_____

_____

19. Palestinians and Arabs are very different in various ways.

_____

_____

20. In this day and age it is difficult to find a musician in the entire field of music who gets at people's hearts the way Charles Witt does.

_____

_____

Self-Grading Exercise 16

Revise the following sentences for economy by eliminating redundancies or wasted words. After completing the exercise, turn to the appendix for the answers (there is more than one possible answer for each item).

1. Charles Steinmetz was a man who pioneered in the field of electrical engineering.

_____

_____

2. Long-distance runners training for the Olympics run many miles a day, and they cover as many as 20 miles.

_____

_____

3. Each and every person who stood in line received a ticket.

_____

_____

4. Students today demonstrate poor writing skills for one simple reason: The reason is that they are never required to write.

_____

_____

5. My favorite poet is Emily Dickinson among all the women poets that I like best.

_____

_____

6. In the next chapter that follows we will look at and examine a theory held by Charles Darwin dealing with evolution.

_____

_____

7. In this modern world of today, it is difficult to keep up with the most recent and up-to-date advances in science.

_____

_____

8. Made of solid oak material and a rich brown in color, the table has lasted for over a hundred years of time.

_____

_____

9. One of John's most serious faults is the fact that he continuously apologizes for his errors.

_____

_____

10. The method they most often used to grade objective tests was that of using a Scantron machine.

_____

_____

11. One of the most exciting events of the trip was attending a secret burial ceremony, never performed publicly.

_____

_____

12. Nevertheless, most reasonable judges are rational and do not judge defendants on the basis of feelings or emotions.

_____

_____

13. The pilot was in a terrible dilemma because a crosswind was blowing at right angles to his aircraft's line of flight.

_____

_____

14. All of the children who were observed by media reporters were tall in height.

_____

_____

15. The income from traffic fines is an important source of revenue for New York City.

_____

_____

The impact of an essay is lessened when its sentences are childishly short and loosely strung together. Here is an example:

> The newspaper recently contained an article. The article was about a man named Lewis Stafford. The man had passed some bogus checks. He was put in jail.

This passage would ring with more authority if its sentences were combined by subordinating the lesser ideas to the greater:

> The newspaper recently contained an article about Lewis Stafford, a man put in jail for passing bogus checks.

Subordination is the art of grammatical ranking. Faced with expressing a series of   *sub*
ideas in a single sentence, the writer arranges them in clauses and phrases that mirror their relative importance. In the above example, for instance, the main clause reports on the newspaper article about Lewis Stafford and the subordinate clause mentions his jailing for passing bogus checks. The writer has therefore chosen to emphasize the article in the newspaper over the jailing for bad checks. If desired, the reverse emphasis could have been achieved with another subordinate construction:

> Lewis Stafford was put in jail for passing bogus checks, an event recently reported in the newspaper.

The ranking of one event over another through subordination depends entirely on which event the writer deems more important and wishes to emphasize.

Subordination is achieved by combining short sentences into a single long sentence. This is done by turning main clauses into either phrases or dependent clauses:

1. Subordination by phrase. For a definition of *phrase,* see pages 572–73. The following are phrases:

singing in the rain

left alone with his friend

with its lovely rose garden

to lower his taxes

Note how pairs of sentences can be combined by turning one of the sentences into a phrase:

No subordination	The man left. He sang in the rain.
Subordination	The man left, singing in the rain.
No subordination	He was left alone with his friend. He confided his secret to his friend.
Subordination	Left alone with his friend, he confided his secret.
No subordination	Hoover Library stands as a monument to our city. It has a lovely rose garden.
Subordination	Hoover Library, with its lovely rose garden, stands as a monument to our city.
No subordination	He voted for Proposition 13. He did it to lower his taxes.
Subordination	To lower his taxes, he voted for Proposition 13.

2. Subordination by dependent clause. For a definition of *dependent clause,* see pages 572–73. The following are dependent clauses:

although he was confronted with many alternatives

who have lived in the Orient

if the price of gasoline continues to rise

Notice how pairs of sentences can be combined by turning one of the sentences into a dependent clause:

No subordination	He was confronted with many alternatives. He refused to make a choice.
Subordination	Although he was confronted with many alternatives, he refused to make a choice.
No subordination	Many people have lived in the Orient. They never learned to like Oriental food.
Subordination	Many people who have lived in the Orient never learned to like Oriental food.
No subordination	The price of gasoline continues to rise. He will probably sell his car.
Subordination	If the price of gasoline continues to rise, he will probably sell his car.

Choosing the Right Subordinator

The word that introduces a dependent clause is called a *subordinator.* Your choice of subordinator will depend on the relationship you wish to establish among ideas. The following list serves to classify the various subordinators according to their logical relationship to the main clause:

Condition	If
	Provided that

In case
Assuming that
Unless
Whether or not
Because   Cause/reason
Since
Considering that
When   Time
Whenever
As long as
While
Before
After
Until, till
As soon as
Although   Extent/degree
Inasmuch as
Insofar as
To the extent that
Where   Place
Wherever
Who   Noun substitute
That
Which
What
Whoever
Whom
Whomever
Whichever
Whatever

See also subordinating conjunctions, page 583.

Suppose you wish to combine the following two sentences:

He promised to pay the rent.
She needed the money.

Several options will be open to you, among them the following:

	because she needed the money.
	STRESSES CAUSE
	as long as she needed the money.
	STRESSES TIME
He promised to pay the rent	*insofar as* she needed the money.
	STRESSES DEGREE
	in case she needed the money.
	STRESSES CONDITION
	to whoever needed the money.
	SUBSTITUTES A PRONOUN FOR A NOUN

Your choice of subordinator must depend on the logic by which you wish to link the two sentences.

Exercises

Combine the sentences in each set below into a single sentence, using either dependent clauses or phrases. Try different subordinators and different combinations to see what logical effect is created.

1. a. The doctor was taking the patient's temperature.
   b. Suddenly a rock came crashing through the window.
2. a. In mid-July he was inspecting the dig.
   b. He was alerted by someone.
   c. Someone was moving along the northern edge of the plateau.
3. a. It was a bright day in May.
   b. The drums exploded.
   c. Two priests from the temple appeared.
4. a. The crowd groaned with disappointment.
   b. They had hoped to see a glamorous young girl.
5. a. Others planned the forthcoming battle.
   b. He remained alone in the shaded grove.
   c. He was meditating and praying to his god.
   d. He needed guidance from his god.
6. a. Members of the city council can ill afford to vote themselves additional fringe benefits.
   b. Their constituents mistrust them.
7. a. Alif was entirely wrong.
   b. He guessed that she was in love with Abdul.

    c. In fact, she was merely bedazzled by his brilliant lyrics.
    d. They reminded her of starry nights in Egypt.

8. a. The fraternity members all over campus carried banners.
    b. They marched back and forth tirelessly.
    c. Their signs called for an end to building nuclear reactors.

9. a. Something occurred to Madeline.
    b. Perhaps she could improve the situation.
    c. She could create an atmosphere of goodwill.

10. a. Give out these sample tubes of toothpaste.
    b. Give one to whoever asks for one.

11. a. Phil Brown regularly attends church.
    b. There he loves to hear the old hymns.
    c. He also loves to hear a rousing sermon.
    d. These make him feel purged.
    e. They give him a new lease on life.

12. a. The specific notes had faded from his memory.
    b. Yet a certain melody remained.
    c. It haunted him for the rest of his life.

13. a. Such facts cannot be ignored.
    b. We want to preserve the wilderness.

14. a. Those of us who are prisoners must face the grim truth.
    b. This truth is that even our wives and lovers will leave us.
    c. We have shared the most tender and intimate moments with them.

15. a. The scientific establishment now believes that the earth was formed 10 to 15 billion years ago.
    b. It was formed after an explosion, or "big bang."
    c. This explosion set the universe in motion.

Self-Grading Exercise 17

Combine the sentences in each set below into a single sentence, using either dependent clauses or phrases. Try different subordinators to see what logical effect is created. After completing the exercise, turn to the appendix for the answers (there is more than one possible answer for each item).

1. a. The medieval structure collapsed.
    b. Then the beginning of the modern mode of production started.

2. a. Quite a few years ago a stranger came in and bought our small valley.
    b. This was where the Sempervirens redwoods grew.
    c. At the time I was living in a little town.
    d. The little town was on the West Coast.

3. a. Writing skills can be improved.
   b. But English teachers will have to assign more writing than they now do.

4. a. We began to realize something.
   b. Resources in America are not limitless.
   c. We had thought they were.

5. a. We are an exuberant people.
   b. We are also careless and destructive.
   c. We make powerful weapons, such as the atomic bomb.
   d. We then use them to prove that they exist.

6. a. Uncountable buffalo were killed.
   b. The buffalo were stripped of their hides.
   c. They were left to rot.
   d. Thus a permanent food supply was destroyed.

7. a. He was a teacher.
   b. In that capacity he considered objections by students carefully.
   c. To him it was as if these objections had been made by colleagues.

8. a. Its roof was half torn away by wind.
   b. Its walls were blackened by fire.
   c. Its stone floors were covered with mud.
   d. This hotel looked like the ruins of a Gothic castle.

9. a. I was seventeen and extremely shy.
   b. My third-grade teacher came to visit us.

10. a. Television newscasters are victims of the rating game.
    b. They are hired and fired on the basis of how entertaining they make the news.
    c. The rating game is controlled by anti-intellectual viewers.

11. a. All four of my grandparents were unknown to one another.
    b. But they all arrived in America from the same county in Slovakia.
    c. They had experienced a severe famine.
    d. The famine was due to a potato crop failure.

12. a. Most people believed the earth was roughly six thousand years old.
    b. This idea was based on information in the Bible.
    c. It was accepted until the beginning of the nineteenth century.
    d. At that time geologists and naturalists began to suspect something.
    e. What they suspected was that the earth must have existed for a much longer period of time.

13. a. He drove along the highway like a haunted man.
    b. He was stopped by the police.

14. a. The early Incas did not have the wheel.
    b. Their architectural achievements were spectacular.

15. a. Goethe influenced Thomas Mann.
    b. We can surmise that Mann's *Dr. Faustus* is similar to Goethe's *Faust*.
    c. Both works deal with the theme of the demonic.

Punctuation errors occur with the omission or misuse of one of the following marks: period (.), comma (,), semicolon (;), colon (:), dash (—), question mark (?), exclamation point (!), apostrophe ('), parentheses (()), quotation marks ("..."), italics (underlining), and hyphen (-). The function of punctuation marks is to separate words and phrases within a sentence according to their meanings.

Frequently, meaning may be misinterpreted unless a punctuation mark is provided. Consider the following:

> After we had finished the essays were read out loud.

The sentence must be reread with a pause inserted after *finished:*

> After we had finished, the essays were read out loud.

The key to effective punctuation is to learn what each punctuation mark means and where it must be used.

The Period (.)

Periods are used after declarative or mildly imperative sentences, indirect questions, and abbreviations. (See also run-together sentences, page 588.) Use ellipses—three spaced periods (...)—to indicate omissions from quoted material.

We followed Mr. Smith upstairs to the conductor's room.	Declarative
Visit Old Amsterdam while you are in Holland.	Imperative
The child asked if it was all right to pick an apple.	Indirect question
Since we had so little money, we stayed at the Y.M.C.A.	Abbreviation
(good men) Now is the time for all ... to come to the aid of their country.	Ellipses

Current usage permits the omission of the period after these and other abbreviations: TV, CIA, FBI, UN, NBC, USN. If in doubt whether to omit the period after an abbreviation, consult a dictionary.

The Comma (,)

The comma is used and misused more than any other punctuation mark. (See also comma splice, page 587.) A writer of factual prose must learn to master the comma. Although it is sometimes useful to equate commas with pauses, it is safer to follow the simple rules given below.

1. Use commas to set off phrases or clauses that interrupt the flow of a sentence or that are not essential to the meaning of a sentence. In this use, the commas sometimes function as the equivalent of parentheses:
   a. Tatyana Grosman, as her first name suggests, is Russian by birth.
   b. Mrs. Jones, although charming in every way, held doggedly to her point.
   c. My father, who is a banker, lives in New York.

2. Use a comma after a long introductory phrase or clause:
   a. Near the grove at the top of his block, someone was having a party.
   b. Because I meant my remark as a compliment, I was surprised when my boss became angry.

3. Use a comma to separate the main clause from a long clause or phrase that follows it, if the two are separated by a pause or break:
   a. Certainly no one has tried harder than Jane, although many of her ideas have proved to be disastrous when they have been put into practice.
   b. He awakened something new in me, a devotion I didn't know I was capable of.

4. Use a comma to separate long independent clauses joined by *and, but, or, for, yet, nor:*
   a. The tunnel beside the house was very dark, but after school George used it as his imaginary fortress.
   b. If he uses three or four cans of balls, then that's it, and I don't want him to come to me begging for more.

5. Use commas to separate items in a series:
   a. I felt tired, cold, and discouraged.
   b. He raised his head, closed his eyes, and let out a deep moan.
   An adjective that is essential to a noun is not set off from other adjectives with a comma:
   My aunt is giving away some unusual white elephants, including a gigantic Chinese screen, several old Tiffany lamps, and a cracked ironstone platter.

6. Use a comma after words of address:
   a. Sir, that is not what I meant.
   b. Do you recall that night, Linda?

7. Use a comma to set off yes and no:
   a. Yes, the flight leaves at midnight.
   b. No, the letter has not arrived yet.

8. Use commas to set off dates and places:
   a. Miami, Florida, is humid in the summer.
   b. November 19, 1929, is my birthday.
   c. They live on 41 Parkwood Drive, Sacramento, California.

9. Use a comma to introduce quotations:
   a. Patrick Henry said, "Give me liberty or give me death!"
   b. The thief retorted, "You don't need the money."

10. Use commas to set off titles and degrees from preceding names:
    a. John Lawson, Jr., now runs the bank.
    b. Henry Knittle, M.D.
    c. Mark Hamilton, Ph.D.

The Semicolon (;)

The semicolon has three basic uses.

1. The semicolon is used to connect independent clauses so closely connected in meaning that they do not need to be separate sentences:
   a. He was a wonderful chap; we all loved him dearly.
   b. Loraine left all her money to her stepson; in this respect, she showed considerable generosity.

2. A semicolon may be used to connect independent clauses when the second clause begins with a conjunctive adverb (for a list of conjunctive adverbs, see page 582):
   a. Joe was not a candidate; nevertheless, the gang chose him as their captain.
   b. Following her to the kitchen, I found that she had made two sandwiches; however, I was not hungry, so I did not eat.
   If the conjunctive adverb is not the first word in the second clause, the punctuation is as follows:
      The fever had subsided; my mother felt, nevertheless, that a doctor should be called.

3. The semicolon is used to separate phrases or clauses in a series when commas appear within any one of those phrases or clauses:
   a. Her estate was divided as follows: Books, diaries, and notebooks went to her agent; jewelry, furs, and clothes went to her sister; and everything else went to charity.
   b. For three days we followed a strict diet: eggs, grapefruit, and coffee on the first day; lamb chops, toast, and tomatoes on the second day; and fruit with cottage cheese on the third day.

The Colon (:)

Do not confuse the colon with the semicolon. Colons are used in the following cases:

1. Use a colon when you introduce lengthy material or lists.
   a. The following quotation from Robert Frost will support my view:
   b. Here is a list of all the camping equipment necessary to climb Mt. Wilson:
   c. Literature can be divided into four types: short story, drama, poetry, and novel.

2. Use a colon after the salutation of a formal letter, between title and subtitle of a literary work, between chapter and verse of the Bible, and between hours and minutes in time:
   a. Dear Ms. Landeen:
   b. The Ethnic Cult: New Fashion Trends
   c. I Corinthians 3:16
   d. 10:30 A.M.

The Dash (—)

On the typewriter, the dash is made by two hyphens without spacing before, between, or after. In handwriting, the dash is an unbroken line the length of two hyphens.

1. Use the dash to indicate a sudden break in thought.
   a. The clerk's illiteracy, his lack of judgment, his poor writing skills—all added up until the company fired him.
   b. The secret of the recipe is—oh, but I promised not to tell.
2. Use dashes to set off parenthetical material that needs to be emphasized:
   a. Every house in the neighborhood—from Kenneth Road to Russel Drive—was solicited.
   b. She stood there—tall, proud, and unrelenting—daring her accusers to speak.

The Question Mark (?)

Use a question mark after a direct question. Do not use it when the question is indirect.

Direct	He asked her, "Have you had lunch?"
Indirect	He asked her if she had had lunch.
Direct	Who am I? Where am I going? Why am I here?

Do not follow a question mark with a comma or a period:

Wrong	"When will you leave?," he asked.
Correct	"When will you leave?" he asked.

The Exclamation Point (!)

Exclamation points should be used only to express surprise, disbelief, anger, or other strong emotions:

1. What an adorable baby!
2. What a rat! He couldn't have been that evil!
3. "Jinxed, by God!"

The Apostrophe (')

The apostrophe is used to show possession: "John's book" rather than "the book of John." It is also used to form contractions (can't, don't) and certain plurals.

1. Use an apostrophe to indicate possession. Note that if the plural of a noun ends with an *s* or *z* sound, only the apostrophe is added in the possessive:
   a. the attitude of the student
      the student's attitude
   b. the party of the girls
      the girls' party
   c. the home of the children
      the children's home
   Possessive pronouns do not require the apostrophe: "the book is theirs" *not* "the book is their's."
   For *inanimate* objects, *of* is preferable to the apostrophe: "The arm *of* the chair" *not* "the chair's arm."

2. Use an apostrophe to indicate an omission or abbreviation:
   a. He can't (cannot) make it.
   b. It's (it is) a perfect day.
   c. He graduated in '08.
   Caution: Place the apostrophe exactly where the omission occurs: isn't, doesn't—*not* is'nt, doe'snt.

3. Use an apostrophe to form the plural of letters, symbols, and words used as words:
   a. The English often do not pronounce their *h*'s, and they place *r*'s at the end of certain words.
   b. Instead of writing *and*'s, you can write &'s.

4. An apostrophe is *not* needed for plurals of figures:
   a. Rock groups flourished during the 1960s.
   b. The temperature was in the 90s.

Parentheses [()]

Parentheses always come in pairs. Use parentheses to enclose figures, illustrations, or incidental material:

1. To make good tennis volleys, you must follow three rules: (1) Use a punching motion with your racket, (2) volley off your front leg, and (3) get your body sideways to the flight of the oncoming ball.
2. The big stars of Hollywood's glamor days (Greta Garbo, Clark Gable, Marilyn Monroe) exuded an aura that was bigger than life.
3. Emily Dickinson (often called "the Belle of Amherst") lived a secluded life.

Quotation Marks (" ")

Quotation marks always come in pairs, with the final set indicating the end of the quotation. The most common use of quotation marks is to indicate the exact spoken or written words of another person. There are several other uses of quotation marks as well.

1. Use quotation marks to enclose the words of someone else:
   a. Montesquieu has said: "The first motive which ought to impel us to study is the desire to augment the excellence of our nature, and to render an intelligent being yet more intelligent."
   b. With characteristic bluntness she turned to him and asked, "Are you as old as you look?"

   If the passage being quoted is longer than five lines, indent it but do not use quotation marks:

   The *Los Angeles Times* indicated that actress Estelle Winwood was old but still remarkably spry:

   > She plays bridge for six hours a night, smokes four packs of cigarettes a day, and at 93 Estelle Winwood is the oldest active member on the rolls of the Screen Actors' Guild.
   >
   > Although she professes to be through with acting, her close friends don't believe her. Only recently she joined the distinguished company of Columbia Pictures' "Murder by Death," Neil Simon's spoof of mystery films. And she held her own with the likes of Alec Guinness, Peter Sellers, Maggie Smith, Peter Falk, David Niven, and Nancy Walker.

2. A quotation within a quotation is enclosed by single quotation marks:

   > According to Jefferson's biographer, "The celebrated equanimity of his temper, crystallized in his pronouncement 'Peace is our passion,' extended to his private as well as his public life; his daughter Martha described how he lost his temper in her presence only two times in his life."
   >
   > Fawn M. Brodie, *Thomas Jefferson*

3. Use quotation marks for titles of songs, paintings, and short literary works (essays, articles, short stories, or poems):
   a. My favorite Beatles song is "Eleanor Rigby."   SONG
   b. "The Guest" is a story written by Camus.   SHORT STORY
   c. The "Mona Lisa" by DaVinci hangs in the Louvre museum.   PAINTING

4. Use quotation marks for words used in a special way—for instance, to show irony or to indicate that a word is slang:
   a. They killed her out of "mercy."   THE AUTHOR WANTS THE READER TO KNOW THAT IT WAS NOT GENUINE MERCY.
   b. My mother used to refer to the woman down the street as a "floozy."   SLANG

When using other marks of punctuation with quoted words, follow the proper conventions.

1. Place a period or comma within quotation marks, unless material that is not quoted follows.
   a. "Very well," he said, "let's go to the bank."
   b. "The qualities that make a political leader were less obvious in Lenin than in Gladstone" (p. 451).

2. Place a colon or semicolon outside quotation marks.
   a. He reassured me, "You're a fine boy"; yet, I didn't believe him.
   b. I remember only the following words from Michael Novak's essay "White Ethnic": "Growing up in America has been an assault upon my sense of worthiness."

3. Place a question mark or exclamation point inside quotation marks when they apply to quoted matter, but outside when they do not.
   a. "Who are the eminent?" he asked bitterly.   THE QUOTED MATTER IS ITSELF A QUESTION.
   b. What do you mean when you describe him as "eminent"?   THE ENTIRE SENTENCE IS A QUESTION; THE QUOTED MATTER IS NOT.
   c. In the movie everyone chants, "I'm mad as hell and I won't take it anymore!"   THE QUOTED MATTER IS ITSELF AN EXCLAMATION.
   d. For heaven's sake, stop calling me "Big Boy"!   THE ENTIRE SENTENCE IS AN EXCLAMATION.

Italics (Underlining)

In longhand or typewritten material, italics are indicated by underlining; in print, italicized words are slanted.

1. Use italics for titles of books, magazines, newspapers, movies, plays, and other long works:
   a. Most college students are required to read *Great Expectations* or *Oliver Twist*.
   b. *Harper's Bazaar* is a magazine about fashions.
   c. Although I live in California, I subscribe to the *Wall Street Journal* because it is an excellent newspaper.
   d. Mozart's *Magic Flute* is a long opera.

2. Use italics for foreign words:
   a. Everyone uses the word *détente*.
   b. I found her dress *très chic*.
   c. He gave an *apologia pro vita sua*.

3. Use italics for words, letters, and figures spoken of as such:
   a. Often the word *fortuitous* is misused.
   b. In the word *knight* only *n*, *i*, and *t* are actually pronounced.
   c. In the Bible, the number *7* represents perfection.

The Hyphen (-)

1. Use a hyphen for a syllable break at the end of a line:
   a. sac-ri-fi-cial
   b. nu-tri-tious
   c. lib-er-al

   If in doubt about where to break a word, check with the dictionary.

2. Use a hyphen in some compound words:
   a. brother-in-law
   b. hanky-panky
   c. self-determination
   d. vice-president
   e. two-thirds

3. Use a hyphen in compound modifiers:
   a. well-known movie
   b. blond-haired, blue-eyed baby
   c. low-grade infection

4. The hyphen is omitted when the first word of the compound modifier is an adverb ending in *ly* or an adjective ending in *ish,* or when the compound modifier follows the noun.
   a. a deceptively sweet person
   b. a plainly good meal
   c. a bluish green material
   d. is well known

Exercises

Insert commas where they are needed. If the sentence is correct, write C in the space provided.

1. Professor Grover, as all of his students agree, is one of the most exciting history teachers on campus. _____

2. Madam, I beg to differ with you; that is my purse. _____

3. We were asked to check with Mr. Weaver, our head custodian. _____

4. Because the water was murky, cold, and swift we did not go swimming. _____

5. In denouncing the hypocritical, Truman encouraged honest dealings. _____

6. Let's not give up until everyone agrees with us. *C* _____

7. Because they belong to the neighborhood, they should pay for part of the damage. _____

8. Address your letter to Mrs. Margerie Freedman, 320 N. Lincoln Blvd., Reading, Massachusetts.   _____

9. So many memories are connected with the home of my grandparents, a big red brick mansion surrounded by a white picket fence.   _____

10. Twice the doctor asked, "Have you ever had laryngitis before?"   _____

11. Relaxed and happy, Jim ignored the people who were angered by his decision.   _____

12. July 4, 1776, is an important date for patriotic Americans.   _____

13. Glistening like a diamond in the sun, the lake beckoned us.   _____

14. Readers of the *Times*, however, were not all equally impressed with the editorial on abortions.   _____

15. All together, some ten thousand people filled out the questionnaire.   _____

16. From the mountains, from the prairies, and from numerous villages came the good news.   _C_____

17. "My most exquisite lady," he said gallantly, "you deserve the Taj Mahal."   _____

18. One of her sisters lives in Paris; the other, in London.   _C_____

19. Pat Moynihan, who was once the U.S. ambassador to the United Nations, is a popular lecturer.   _____

20. Well, Mary, are you satisfied with the effect of your crass remark?   _____

21. The laboratory technician has finished the gold tooth, hasn't he?   _____

22. Anyone who feels that this is a bad law should write to his congressman.   _C_____

23. Outside, a spectacular rainbow arched across the deep blue sky.   _____

24. We walk down this street unafraid, not even thinking of danger.   _C_____

25. Now, his grandparents live in a condominium in Florida where they have no yard.   _____

Punctuate the following sentences so that they read easily and clearly.

1. Shakespeare wrote many plays including the famous Hamlet

2. Listen he said if you want we can go to a movie any movie

3. The word renaissance has several pronunciations

4. We can have the party at Johns cabin or the Fieldings apartment

5. Its overtaxed heart failing the race horse collapsed before everyones eyes

6. The most tragic poem I can imagine is Keats Ode to Melancholy

7. Get off my lawn you swine

8. The big bands of the 40s still sell millions of records

9. Last years flowers have wilted they have withered and died

10. As far as the committee is concerned you have lost the grant nevertheless you are to take the exam one more time

11. Just as the situation appeared hopeless a surprising thing happened A number of leading American artists became interested in making lithographic prints

12. Then in the summer of 1976 the counterrevolutionary army took over

13. Do you know the difference between the verbs compose and comprise

14. Wonderful Here comes the beer Cheers

15. He entitled his paper June Wayne Profile of a California Artist

16. He lived a stones throw from Twin Lakes

17. This is what Bertrand Russell says Science from the dawn of history and probably longer has been intimately associated with war

18. Bertrand Russell has said that Science has been intimately associated with war *(Refer to item 17.)*

19. He received his PhD at 9 am on Sunday June 6

20. My friend asked me Did you read Bill Shirleys article Worlds First Bionic Swim Team published in the sports section of the Los Angeles Times

21. The rule is that you must sign up two days in advance. See Section 25 paragraph 2

22. Dear Sir this is in answer to your letter of May 13

23. A slight tinge of embarrassment or was it pleasure crept across his face

24. The first day we studied later in the week however we relaxed

25. The babies carriages were broken

Self-Grading Exercise 18

Insert commas where they are needed. If the sentence is correct, write C in the space provided. After completing the exercise, turn to the appendix for the correct answers.

1. His daughter a leader among the women had spared her father and set him afloat on the sea in a hollow chest. _____

2. As for me already old age is my companion. _____

3. He spoke slowly believing in his heart that he was telling the truth. _____

4. Great dangers lay ahead and some of the soldiers paid with their lives for drinking so heavily. _____

5. Gently he answered "I have come to my home to recover the ancient honor of my house." _____

6. These fierce women steadfastly refused to surrender to the foreign invaders. _____

7. They scorned them terrorized them and robbed them. _____

8. He insisted that he had been saved by the woman in white who had brought him to Venice an exotic city. _____

9. On November 19 1929 a star bright and luminous shot across the sky. _____

10. Let the taxpayers who reside in the county pay for a new road sign at the intersection of Broadway and Main Street. _____

11. The football players however did not care to linger in such a gloomy narrow place. _____

12. Acheron the river of woe pours into Cocytus the river of lamentation.

13. Sir please accept my sincere apologies for the inconvenience this has caused you. _____

14. Because hell is merely an invention of guilty minds why believe in it? _____

15. David Cotton Jr. is doing some important research in the field of high-risk pregnancies. _____

16. On his way to ask his adviser a question about a calculus course Robert arrived at an automatic gate where he blew out a tire causing his Fiat to skid into another car. _____

17. He felt himself degraded by this servile attitude and vowed revenge. _____

18. They told him "God's daylight is sweet to the old." _____

19. Yes Chicago Illinois can be windy and freezing cold in the winter. _____

20. Above some perfume bottles filled with exotic bath oils decorated the wall shelves. _____

Self-Grading Exercise 19

In the sentences below insert all needed marks of punctuation, including italics. Be careful to place quotation marks in proper relation to other marks of punctuation. After completing the exercise, turn to the appendix for the correct answers.

1. According to Mythology a book by Edith Hamilton the Greeks unlike the Egyptians made their gods in their own image

2. Is this an exaggerated view It hardly seems so nevertheless many opponents of the measure dismiss it as unmenschlich

3. The search for a way to stop this vicious cycle has taxed the best minds among the following groups city council members educators and urban planners

4. Let me pose this question Could you love passionately if you knew you would never die

5. Who interrupted me by saying Thats enough for today

6. Dear Mr. Forsythe This is in reply to your request of May 16 1988

7. From now on please cross your t s and dot your i s

8. This is how we propose to assign the various duties The men will scrub the floors ceilings and walls the women will cook mend and garden the children will run errands clean up the yard and pick vegetables

9. But what happens when the national organizations themselves the schools the unions the federal government become victims of a technological culture

10. With his fifth grade education he wrote a marvelous poem entitled Languid Tears

11. The New Yorker is read mostly by people with keen literary interests

12. Students often find it difficult to distinguish between the words imply and infer in fact most people confuse their meanings

13. We currently reside at 451 Bellefontaine Drive Pasadena California

14. One of the delegates was a vegetarian the other was restricted to kosher foods

15. He yelled angrily Get out of my yard

16. Vans boats and campers are not allowed see Regulation #13

17. Have you heard the question asked What can the police department do against the pitiless onslaught of criminal violence

18. This my friends is how I think we can help the world in a time of tyranny by fighting for freedom

19. The age was an age of éclaircissement and self determination

20. You have arrived at your resting place she murmured softly seek no further

21. Inside the antique armoire dominated the room

22. Picture if you please an open space where twenty acrobats stand each locking hands with two different partners then imagine ten acrobats standing on the shoulders of these twenty.

cap *Capitalization errors* result when accepted conventions of capitalizing are not followed. Commonly capitalized are words at the beginning of a sentence and the pronoun *I*. Students tend to ignore rules of capitalization. The most important rules are given here.

1. Capitalize all proper names. The following belong to the group of proper names:
   a. specific persons, places, and things but not their general classes (Jefferson, Grand Junction, Eiffel Tower, Harvard University, and Hyde

Park are capitalized, but people, cities, towers, universities, and parks are not)

   b. organizations and institutions (Rotary Club, Pentagon)

   c. historical periods and events (Middle Ages, World War II)

   d. members of national, political, racial, and religious groups (Mason, Republican, African American, Methodist)

   e. special dates on the calendar (Veterans Day), days (Wednesday), months (July)

   f. religions (Islam, Christianity, Judaism, Methodism) but *not* ideologies (communism, socialism, atheism)

   g. *Freshman, sophomore, junior,* and *senior* are not capitalized unless associated with a specific event ("the Junior Prom will take place next Saturday.")

2. In the titles of literary works, capitalize all words except articles, conjunctions, and prepositions: *All the King's Men,* "The Case Against Welfare in Louisville." Conjunctions and prepositions of five letters or more are capitalized: "The Man Without a Country."

3. Capitalize titles associated with proper names: Mrs. Johnson, Ms. Mary Hanley, Judge Garcia, James R. Griedley, M.D., Henry Hadley, Jr.

4. Titles of relatives are capitalized only when they are not preceded by an article, when they are followed by a name, or in direct address:
   a. I gave the keys to Grandmother.
   b. My Grandmother Sitwell
   c. Could you help me, Grandmother?
   d. I was deeply influenced by my grandmother.

5. Unless a title is official, it is not capitalized:
   a. Peter Ferraro, President of the Valley National Bank
   b. Peter Ferraro is president of a bank.
   c. We shall appeal to the President (the top executive of a nation).

6. Capitalize specific courses offered in school, but not general subjects unless they contain a proper name:
   a. I enrolled in Biology 120.
   b. I am taking biology.
   c. I failed Intermediate French.

Avoid needless capitals. For instance, the seasons (spring, summer, autumn, winter) are not capitalized unless they are personified, as in poetry ("Where are the songs of Spring?"). *North, south, east,* and *west* are not capitalized unless they refer to special regions ("He is the fastest gun in the West").

Note that abbreviations are capitalized or not capitalized according to the unabbreviated version: m.p.h. (miles per hour), M.P. (Member of Parliament), GPO (Government Printing Office), Cong. (Congress), pseud. (pseudonym).

Exercises

In the following sentences, underline the letters that should be capitalized or made lower case. If the sentence is correct, write *C* in the space at the right.

1. Our memorial day picnic was canceled because of rain. _____
2. The headline read: "U.S. agent Fired in Investigation of Missing Ammunition." _____
3. Any mayor of a city as large as Chicago should be on good terms with the President of the United States. _____
4. The democrats will doubtless hold their convention at the cow palace in san francisco. _____
5. The tennis courts at Nibley park are always busy. _____
6. If you have to take a psychology course, take psychology 101 from Dr. Pearson, a graduate of harvard. _____
7. There is something elegant about the name "Tyrone Kelly, III, esq." _____
8. Until easter of 1949, they lived in a big white georgian home. _____
9. During the second world war, switzerland remained neutral. _____
10. I intend to exchange my taurus for a toyota. _____
11. Socrates, the famous Greek philosopher, used Dialogue as a teaching method. _____
12. Some Socialists have joined the Republican Party. _____
13. She said, "the ticket entitles you to spend a night at the Holiday inn in Las Vegas." _____
14. The bible was not fully canonized until the council of Trent. _____

Write a brief sentence in which you use correctly each of the following words:

1. street_____
2. Street_____
3. Democratic_____
4. democratic_____
5. academy_____
6. Academy_____
7. biology_____
8. Biology_____
9. memorial_____

10. Memorial_____

11. father_____

12. Father_____

13. senior_____

14. Senior_____

15. against_____

16. Against_____

17. company_____

18. Company_____

Self-Grading Exercise 20

In the following sentences underline the letters that should be capitalized or made lower case. If the sentence is correct, write C in the space at the right. After completing the exercise, turn to the appendix for the correct answers.

1. Balloting at both the democratic and republican conventions is by states.   _____

2. He had taken many history courses, but none fascinated him more than introduction to western civilization.   _____

3. Delta Delta Delta, the most active sorority, invited speakers from such organizations as daughters of the American revolution, national organization of Women, and the Sierra club.   _____

4. The subject of the lecture was "The Treasures Of The Nile."   _____

5. John Stuart Mill understood Calculus and could read greek when he was a child.   _____

6. Exodus is the second book of the pentateuch.   _____

7. One of his dreams was to see the Taj Mahal.   _____

8. The war of the Triple Alliance was fought between Paraguay on one side and an Alliance of Argentina, brazil, and Uruguay on the other.   _____

9. That is the best photograph ever taken of uncle Charlie.   _____

10. As a capable and tough City attorney, he took action against one of Hollywood's swingers clubs, a place called Socrates' retreat.   _____

11. John toyed with two ideas: joining the peace corps or working without pay for Cesar Chávez' United farm workers of America.   _____

12. Ex-Assemblyman Waldie never ran for Office after the Summer of 1974.   _____

13. Today he is Chairman of the Federal Mine Safety and Health Review Commission. _____

14. The residents of Mammoth Lakes, a mountain resort, are proud of the view of the minarets, a ragged mountain range, seen from highway 395 as one approaches the resort. _____

15. One of my favorite books is a novel entitled *in the heart of a fool.* _____

16. Some women have romantic ideas about returning to feudalism, with knights in shining armor and ladies adhering to the manners of the Middle Ages. _____

17. One of the highest mountain systems in the world is the Hindu Kush, extending 500 miles from north Pakistan into northeast Afghanistan. _____

18. William S. Levey, S.J., is the vice-president of an important men's club. _____

19. I failed Organic Chemistry 101, but I passed french. _____

20. A traditional American holiday is Thanksgiving day. _____

sp *Misspelling* occurs when a word is written differently from the way it is listed in the dictionary (*recieve* instead of *receive*) or when the wrong word is used (*loose* instead of *lose*). The following list* of most commonly misspelled words will help the weak speller. Letters in italics are those that cause the most difficulty. For help in selecting the correct word, refer to the Glossary of Word Choice (pages 614–20).

Commonly Misspelled Words

1. acco*mm*odate	16. cons*cious*	31. experience	46. occurrence
2. achie*v*ement	17. contro*v*ersy	32. explan*a*tion	47. opinion
3. acquire	18. contro*v*ersial	33. fascinate	48. oppo*rt*unity
4. al*l* right	19. de*f*initely	34. h*ei*ght	49. *pai*d
5. among	20. de*f*inition	35. interest	50. particu*lar*
6. app*ar*ent	21. define	36. *its* (*it's*)	51. *per*formance
7. arg*u*ment	22. describe	37. *led*	52. person*al*
8. arg*ui*ng	23. de*s*cription	38. lose	53. person*nel*
9. bel*ief*	24. disa*st*rous	39. losing	54. possession
10. bel*ie*ve	25. *eff*ect	40. marr*ia*ge	55. pos*si*ble
11. bene*fi*cial	26. emba*rrass*	41. mere	56. practi*cal*
12. bene*fi*ted	27. envir*on*ment	42. necessary	57. prec*ede*
13. category	28. exaggerate	43. *occa*sion	58. pre*j*udice
14. co*m*ing	29. *ex*istence	44. occurred	59. prep*are*
15. compar*a*tive	30. *ex*istent	45. occurring	60. prevalent

*From Thomas Clark Pollock, "Spelling Report," *College English,* XVI (November, 1954), 102–09.

61. principal	71. quiet	81. shining	91. there
62. principle	72. receive	82. similar	92. they're
63. privilege	73. receiving	83. studying	93. thorough
64. probably	74. recommend	84. succeed	94. to (too, two)
65. proceed	75. referring	85. succession	95. transferred
66. procedure	76. repetition	86. surprise	96. unnecessary
67. professor	77. rhythm	87. technique	97. Villain
68. profession	78. sense	88. than	98. woman
69. prominent	79. separate	89. then	99. write
70. pursue	80. separation	90. their	100. writing

Exercises

1. Some of the commonly misspelled words may not appear on either list supplied in this handbook section. If not, compile your own list of troublesome words. First, write the word correctly. Then, note the particular difficulty with it:

   bridle   I always spell it bri*dal,* as if it came from *bride.*

   perspiration   I must be sure to pronounce it *per,* not *pre.*

2. Using the dictionary as a guide, study the list of 100 words until you know (1) what each word means, (2) how it is pronounced, and (3) how it is spelled. Study the words in groups of 20.

3. From each group of three, choose the misspelled word and write it correctly in the space provided. Check answers in the dictionary.

   a. existance, describe, personal _____

   b. paid, particular, oportunity _____

   c. benificial, apparent, experience _____

   d. controversy, concious, occurred _____

   e. preformance, similar, succeed _____

   f. probably, marriage, predjudice _____

   g. profession, persue, separate _____

   h. catagory, paid, disastrous _____

   i. effect, disasterous, mere _____

   j. preceed, proceed, procedure _____

   k. embarrass, exaggerate, envirement _____

   l. prevailent, probably, existent _____

   m. coming, heighth, professor _____

   n. define, fascinate, posession _____

   o. repetition, quiet, recieve _____

Self-Grading Exercise 21

Identify the misspelled word of each sentence and spell it correctly in the space provided. After completing the exercise, turn to the appendix for the correct answers.

1. After making an appointment with the manager of the firm, he demanded to see his personal file.   _____

2. When lovers are seperated for long periods of time, their ardor cools.   _____

3. While under the water, he was conscience of the fact that life is fleeting and evanescent.   _____

4. Without exageration, he sounded like a genius.   _____

5. To him she was a shinning star, a brilliant meteor from heaven.   _____

6. Every man on board admitted that it was a most unusual occurrance.   _____

7. Sons often feel pressured to enter the same proffessions pursued by their fathers.   _____

8. They accused him of being predjudice and reactionary.   _____

9. One of the serious concerns of the younger generation is a clean enviroment.   _____

10. The mystery novel ends without a clear explenation of how the murder took place.   _____

11. The heighth of the building was out of proportion to its width.   _____

12. The room was to small for two people.   _____

13. The hero was wearing light apparel whereas the villian was wearing black.   _____

14. One man or women with good typing skills could get that manuscript finished in no time.   _____

15. They wore similar clothes, but their facial characteristics were very different.   _____

16. According to the committee, it was quite alright for the men to smoke.   _____

17. They were lead to believe that he was a victim of his own enthusiasm.   _____

18. I did not care whether or not I received the money back; it was simply a matter of principal.   _____

19. Because of blustering winds she kept loosing her hat.   _____

20. Just sit quietly and listen to the rythm of your heartbeats.   _____

APPENDIX:

Answers to Self-Grading Exercises

The answer keys that follow correspond in number to the self-grading exercises found in Part V, "English Usage."

Self-Grading Exercise 1

1. Libraries contain the wisdom of civilization.
2. In the district of Wymar, burglars were ransacking the stores.
3. In Hemingway's novels matadors are highly respected.
4. A clear conscience is the best sleeping pill.
5. The silver-gray vest suited his taciturn personality.
6. Most middle-class homes in the Southwest are built with air conditioning.
7. The outdoor markets in Europe attract numerous tourists.
8. Noise pollution in towns and cities blots out the sounds and silences of the outdoor world.
9. A cup of good tea or coffee must be brought to me early each morning.
10. I wish to describe two kinds of tours available.

Self-Grading Exercise 2

1. Television | has contributed to the decline of reading skills.
2. Incensed by their rudeness, the senator | left.
3. Michelangelo's work | continues to attract admirers all over the world.
4. Wars | go on endlessly.
5. Divorce | affects children most of all.
6. Professional tennis | has become big business in the United States.
7. Most people | insist on paying their bills on time.
8. Within five weeks one hundred polio victims | had been claimed.
9. Spain | is no longer a strong world power.
10. Many areas of Saudi Arabia | have experienced droughts.

Self-Grading Exercise 3

1. I	6. I	11. I	16. I
2. I	7. P	12. I	17. D
3. P	8. I	13. P	18. P
4. I	9. D	14. I	19. I
5. D	10. D	15. D	20. P

Self-Grading Exercise 4

1. We asked him if he would be willing to do it alone.
2. Are you usually alert to the problems of older people?
3. Sound the alarm! Then run for your life!
4. I am as angry as a cornered cat.
5. Do you mean to tell me that all of the money simply disappeared?
6. They inquired as to whether or not we would accompany the performers.
7. Heavens! What a way to get attention!
8. Go straight down the aisle and interrupt his conversation.
9. Would you be so kind as to direct me to the British Museum?
10. Whew! What a terrible odor!

Self-Grading Exercise 5

1. A	6. C	11. B	16. B
2. B	7. A	12. A	17. A
3. C	8. D	13. B	18. C
4. D	9. D	14. D	19. A
5. C	10. A	15. A	20. C

Self-Grading Exercise 6

1. noun	8. preposition
2. verb	9. adjective
3. adjective	10. verb
4. preposition	11. pronoun
5. adverb	12. adverb
6. verb	13. noun (verbal)
7. coordinating conjunction	14. pronoun

15. noun
16. coordinating conjunction
17. conjunctive adverb
18. article
19. adverb
20. adjective
21. preposition
22. verb
23. subordinating conjunction
24. verb
25. subordinating conjunction (relative pronoun)
26. verb
27. preposition
28. noun
29. adverb
30. verb
31. article
32. preposition
33. noun
34. adverb (subordinating conjunction)
35. pronoun
36. verb
37. noun
38. verb
39. verb
40. adverb

Self-Grading Exercise 7

1. Frag	6. C	11. CS	16. CS
2. C	7. Frag	12. CS	17. C
3. CS	8. C	13. C	18. C
4. Frag	9. C	14. C	19. RT
5. RT	10. Frag	15. Frag	20. CS

Self-Grading Exercise 8

1. makes	6. C	11. are	16. is
2. are	7. is	12. C	17. watches
3. has	8. are	13. Do	18. C
4. C	9. require	14. C	19. sit
5. causes	10. C	15. is	20. appeals

Self-Grading Exercise 9

1. him	6. he and I	11. you or me	16. her
2. whoever	7. my	12. whomever	17. We
3. who	8. its	13. whom	18. whoever
4. he or she	9. Their	14. whom	19. I
5. me	10. whom	15. her	20. Whom

Self-Grading Exercise 10

1. As they listened to the music, Sir Peregrine remarked about the success of the races while his wife dreamed about love.   B

2. A person must accept the fact that he or she can't always win.   A

3. All secretaries who worked in the office were asked to give their opinions and to say how they felt.   A

4. The airline attendants wondered why so many passengers were standing in the aisle and who had given them permission to leave their seats.   D

5. If I were wealthy and if I were living in Zaire, I'd tell Mobutu a thing or two.   C

6. He pored over all of his notes and checked out many library books.   E

7. Mrs. Olson walks into strangers' kitchens and tells them how to make coffee.   E

8. The professor informed us that the test would be given and asked if we were ready.   B

9. First the insane man quoted lines from Richard Lovelace; then he recited a passage from the "Song of Solomon."   B

10. "Raise the property tax—and impose rent control!" he yelled with fervor.   C

11. When you buy a foreign car, you have to expect poor service.   A

12. The matter suddenly came to a crisis, but just as suddenly it was resolved.   F

13. It is essential that he bring the document with him and that he be here by noon.   C

14. We fear the unknown whereas we often welcome the known.   E

15. Our constitution protects our right to pursue happiness; however, it does not guarantee that we shall find this happiness, no matter how diligently we pursue it.   F

16. The tenant claims that he paid the rent and asked me to convey this fact to the landlord.   D

17. The skylark gracefully lifts itself into the sky, lets out a joyful warble, and disappears into a cloud.   B

18. The sea breeze was blowing harder and felt colder.   B

19. As one walked into the slaughterhouse, one could
    see hundreds of carcasses hanging on hooks.   A

20. Because most of the children loved to go swimming,
    the group went to the beach.   B

Self-Grading Exercise 11

1. We are now expected to drive less, use public transportation, and conserve heating fuel. Saving energy is a realistic goal.

2. Some diet experts say that a tablespoon of vinegar in some sugar and oil will reduce the appetite.

3. The newspaper said that a rebirth of great art is taking place in China.

4. When Byron was on the Continent, he carried on a lively correspondence with Shelley.

5. The world was expecting Golda Meir's death.

6. My brother does not make full use of his enormous talent.

7. During lunch John always sat alone while the other students sat together chatting away. This isolation of his didn't last long, however.

8. Mahatma Gandhi wanted only the sparsest of furniture in his room.

9. In an interview with a group of millionaires, the master of ceremonies told the audience that the millionaires he interviewed were very articulate.

10. Melissa invited Ruth to travel to Spain with her because she thought Ruth was interested in Spanish history.

11. A psychologist has no right discussing his patients' personal problems with his friends because the patients could be embarrassed if their identities were discovered.

12. The passerby wondered about the significance of the young boy's dashing out of the store and running down the street.

13. On our flight across the Atlantic the weather was beautiful.

14. Despite its dark and rough water, the Blue Grotto of Capri was a splendid sight.

15. My friend John loves to watch basketball for hours on end, but his wife doesn't approve of his doing so.

Self-Grading Exercise 12

1. As he bowed to the audience, his violin fell to the floor.

2. Filled with terror, the tiny kitten sat shivering in the corner.

3. As I watched them from behind a bush, camera in hand, the bears seemed like harmless pets.

4. What the teacher needs is a neatly typed list of students.

5. Students who speak French fluently will not need to pass the three conversation examinations.

6. During World War II the Nazis gave Jewish prisoners only cabbage to eat, nothing else.

7. Instead of asking for forgiveness, she offered a piece of chocolate cake as her sign of repentance.

8. Even when confronted with the full truth, they ignored the facts.

9. Hearing the bell ring, the boxer triumphantly flung his glove to the ground.

10. Out of breath and revealing a look of anxiety, the lover ran up the stairs.

11. The day drew to a close with anguished prayer that God would spare the infant.

12. We enjoy not only music, but also painting and sculpture.

13. The law was enacted immediately after Congress adjourned.

14. Scorched by the sizzling heat, we thought jumping into the river made a great deal of sense.

15. At a Neiman-Marcus store, we tried on some Givenchy pants that cost $150.

Self-Grading Exercise 13

1. He wanted to marry her because she was bright, pleasant, and unselfish.

2. Her boss fired her because her letters were sloppy, ungrammatical, and poorly typed.

3. The handbook revealed two ways in which the unity of a paragraph could be broken: (1) one could stray from the topic sentence, (2) one could obscure the central thought with excessive details.

4. By exercising daily, by eating proper food, and by avoiding stress, he can regain his health.

5. This simple man did not doubt that after death there was a paradise for good people and a hell for bad people.

6. Most of them were either athletic or strong.

7. Handing out oil coupons seemed both intelligent and necessary.

8. She insisted that he must leave and never return.

9. The man is either an idealist or a fool.

10. Today pocket calculators are inexpensive, durable, and easily obtained.

11. The Byronic hero was a man who felt alienated from mainstream society, who withdrew into haughty superiority, who loved passionately, and who felt an element of self-pity.

12. This is the case not only with policemen but also with firemen.

13. Here is what you will need to know: how to open a bank account, how to judge a contract, and how to sell equipment.

14. He climbed Mount Whitney not because he wanted to test his endurance, but because he was arrogant.

15. To err is human; to forgive is divine.

Self-Grading Exercise 14

1. After noticing that the watch and the bedspread were gone, they immediately (suspicioned, <u>suspected</u>) his stepdaughter.

2. Dorothy insisted on keeping her (personnel, <u>personal</u>) opinions hidden from her students.

3. The hiring committee preferred communicating by telephone because they believed in (<u>oral</u>, verbal) interviews.

4. I was always told that (this type, <u>this type of</u>) novel was cheap and aimed at the sensation seekers.

5. (Sit, <u>set</u>) the flower pot in front of the brick wall, where it will look lovely.

6. The (amount, <u>number</u>) of registered students varies from semester to semester.

7. In the upper left-hand corner of his (<u>stationery</u>, stationary) one could clearly discern three modest initials.

8. Earl Warren was considered a Supreme Court justice of immense (<u>stature</u>, statue, statute).

9. The team that climbed Mt. Whitney included (quite a number, <u>a rather large number</u>) of women.

10. Twenty years and six children later, the marriage was finally (<u>over</u>, over with).

11. Day after day his fiancee waited (<u>for</u>, on) him to return from the war.

12. Thank you for the (complement, <u>compliment</u>)—how kind!

13. (Your, <u>you're</u>) either for us or against us.

14. He never returned the suitcase (like, <u>as</u>) he was asked to do.

15. We (<u>can hardly</u>, can't hardly) distinguish one twin from the other.

16. The (farther, <u>further</u>) he delved into St. Paul's theology, the more fascinated he became.

17. When the real estate agent had received a firm bid, he (appraised, <u>apprised</u>) his clients of the fact.

18. He could never be (<u>persuaded</u>, convinced) to travel overseas on an airplane.

19. The (<u>site</u>, cite) for the international hotel was near the center of town.

20. While he was in Vietnam, all of his mail was (censured, <u>censored</u>).

Self-Grading Exercise 15

1. To add to our depression, a period of *driving snow* set in.
2. Vicky *beamed with pride* as she walked off the stage with her gold medal.
3. I liked *going to luxurious restaurants, visiting excellent museums, and attending the ballet* in the city.
4. His extreme selfishness *left him isolated and friendless.*
5. He chewed his food noisily, he talked with his mouth full, and he wiped his lips with his hand; in short, his manners were *disgustingly boorish.*
6. For six days and nights, he *battled* with fever and death.
7. A delicate sea shell is a *miraculous piece of sculpture.*
8. All of the fun at Joe's birthday party was ruined because the children *dropped ice cream on the carpet, left fingerprints on the windows, and broke a chair.*
9. The Mohave Desert of California and the Sinai Desert of Egypt *both experience extreme temperatures and searing winds.*
10. Every large city *suffers from overcrowded conditions, traffic congestion, and lack of green spaces.*
11. She was a hopeless, desiccated old lady *hobbling across* the street with her cane, her *stooped form* serving as a symbol of her despair.
12. In 1925 a terrible dust storm *swept* across the Midwest, *ripping chimneys off roofs, seeping through closed windows, and ruining entire vegetable crops.*
13. Many of the old Tin Pan Alley songs reveal poignantly *the poverty of the unemployed, the despair of the old, and the cold arrogance of the rich.*
14. We tried various cleaning solutions, but the kitchen floor remained *streaked with grime.*
15. People who throw *trash* out of their car windows while they drive along our highways reveal a disgusting kind of vulgarity.

Self-Grading Exercise 16

1. Charles Steinmetz was a pioneer in electrical engineering.
2. Long-distance runners training for the Olympics run as many as 20 miles a day.
3. Each person in line received a ticket.
4. Students today demonstrate poor writing skills for one simple reason: They are never required to write.
5. My favorite female poet is Emily Dickinson.
6. In the following chapter we will examine Charles Darwin's theory of evolution.

7. It is difficult to keep up with today's scientific advances.

8. Made of solid brown oak, the table has lasted for over a hundred years.

9. One of John's most serious faults is continuously apologizing for his errors.

10. Most often they graded the objective tests with a Scantron machine.

11. One of the most exciting events of the trip was attending a secret burial ceremony.

12. Nevertheless, most judges are rational and do not judge defendants emotionally.

13. The pilot was in a terrible dilemma because he was flying into a crosswind.

14. All of the children observed by reporters were tall.

15. Traffic fines are an important source of revenue in New York City.

Self-Grading Exercise 17

1. When the medieval structure collapsed, the beginning of the modern mode of production started.

2. Quite a few years ago, while I was living in a little town on the West Coast, a stranger came in and bought our valley, where the Sempervirens redwoods grew.

3. If writing skills are to be improved, English teachers will have to assign more writing than they now do.

4. We began to realize that resources in America are not limitless as we had thought.

5. Although we are exuberant people, we are also destructive and careless, making powerful weapons, such as the atomic bomb, which we then use to prove that they exist.

6. Uncountable buffalo were killed, stripped of their hides, and left to rot, thus destroying a permanent food supply.

7. As a teacher he considered objections by students carefully, as if these objections had been made by colleagues.

8. Its roof half torn away by wind, its walls blackened by fire, and its stone floors covered with mud, this hotel looked like the ruins of a Gothic castle.

9. I was seventeen and extremely shy when my third-grade teacher came to visit us.

10. Hired and fired on the basis of how entertaining they make the news, television newscasters are victims of a rating game controlled by anti-intellectual viewers.

11. Although unknown to one another, all four of my grandparents arrived in America from the same county in Slovakia, where they had experienced a severe famine resulting from a potato crop failure.

12. Based on information in the Bible, most people believed the earth was roughly six thousand years old until the beginning of the nineteenth century, when geologists and naturalists began to suspect that the earth must have existed for a much longer period of time.

13. Driving along the highway like a haunted man, he was stopped by the police.

14. Considering that the early Incas did not have the wheel, their architectural accomplishments were spectacular.

15. Assuming that Goethe influenced Thomas Mann, we can surmise that Mann's *Dr. Faustus* is similar to Goethe's *Faust*, both of which deal with the theme of the demonic.

Self-Grading Exercise 18

1. His daughter, a leader among the women, had spared her father and set him afloat on the sea in a hollow chest. _____

2. As for me, already old age is my companion. _____

3. He spoke slowly, believing in his heart that he was telling the truth. _____

4. Great dangers lay ahead, and some of the soldiers paid with their lives for drinking so heavily. _____

5. Gently he answered, "I have come to my home to recover the ancient honor of my house." _____

6. These fierce women steadfastly refused to surrender to the foreign invaders. ___C___

7. They scorned them, terrorized them, and robbed them. _____

8. He insisted that he had been saved by the woman in white, who had brought him to Venice, an exotic city. _____

9. On November 19, 1929, a star, bright and luminous, shot across the sky. _____

10. Let the taxpayers who reside in the county pay for a new road sign at the intersection of Broadway and Main Street. ___C___

11. The football players, however, did not care to linger in such a gloomy, narrow place. _____

12. Acheron, the river of woe, pours into Cocytus, the river of lamentation. _____

13. Sir, please accept my sincere apologies for the inconvenience this has caused you. _____

14. Because hell is merely an invention of guilty minds, why believe in it? _____

15. David Cotton, Jr., is doing some important research in the field of high-risk pregnancies. _____

16. On his way to ask his adviser a question about a calculus course, Robert arrived at the automatic gate, where he blew out a tire, causing his Fiat to skid into another car. _____

17. He felt himself degraded by this servile attitude and vowed revenge. ___C___

18. They told him, "God's daylight is sweet to the old." _____

19. Yes, Chicago, Illinois, can be windy and freezing cold in the winter. _____

20. Above, some perfume bottles filled with exotic bath oils decorated the wall shelves. _____

Self-Grading Exercise 19

1. According to *Mythology,* a book by Edith Hamilton, the Greeks, unlike the Egyptians, made their gods in their own image.

2. Is this an exaggerated view? It hardly seems so; nevertheless, many opponents of the measure dismiss it as *unmenschlich.*

3. The search for a way to stop this vicious cycle has taxed the best minds among the following groups: city council members, educators, and urban planners.

4. Let me pose this question: Could you love passionately if you knew you would never die?

5. Who interrupted me by saying, "That's enough for today"?

6. Dear Mr. Forsythe: This is in reply to your request of May 16, 1988.

7. From now on, please cross your *t*'s and dot your *i*'s.

8. This is how we propose to assign the various duties: The men will scrub the floors, ceilings, and walls; the women will cook, mend, and garden; the children will run errands, clean up the yard, and pick vegetables.

9. But what happens when the national organizations themselves—the schools, the unions, the federal government—become victims of a technological culture?

10. With his fifth-grade education he wrote a marvelous poem entitled "Languid Tears."

11. *The New Yorker* is read mostly by people with keen literary interests.

12. Students often find it difficult to distinguish between the words *imply* and *infer;* in fact, most people confuse their meanings.

13. We currently reside at 451 Bellefontaine Drive, Pasadena, California.

14. One of the delegates was a vegetarian; the other was restricted to kosher foods.

15. He yelled angrily, "Get out of my yard!"

16. Vans, boats, and campers are not allowed (see Regulation #13).

17. Have you heard the question asked, "What can the police department do against the pitiless onslaught of criminal violence"?

18. This, my friends, is how I think we can help the world in a time of tyranny: by fighting for freedom.

19. The age was an age of *éclaircissement* and self-determination.

20. "You have arrived at your resting place," she murmured softly. "Seek no further."

21. Inside, the antique armoire dominated the room.

22. Picture, if you please, an open space where twenty acrobats stand, each locking hands with two different partners; then imagine ten acrobats standing on the shoulders of these twenty.

Self-Grading Exercise 20

1. Balloting at both the democratic and republican conventions is by states.   _____

2. He had taken many history courses, but none fascinated him more than introduction to western civilization.   _____

3. Delta Delta Delta, the most active sorority, invited speakers from such organizations as daughters of the American revolution, national organizaton of Women, and the Sierra club.   _____

4. The subject of the lecture was "The Treasures Of The Nile."   _____

5. John Stuart Mill understood Calculus and could read greek when he was a child.   _____

6. Exodus is the second book of the pentateuch.   _____

7. One of his dreams was to see the Taj Mahal.   C

8. The war of the Triple Alliance was fought between Paraguay on one side and an Alliance of Argentina, brazil, and Uruguay on the other.   _____

9. That is the best photograph ever taken of uncle Charlie.   _____

10. As a capable and tough City attorney, he took action against one of Hollywood's swingers clubs, a place called Socrates' retreat.   _____

11. John toyed with two ideas: joining the peace corps or working without pay for Cesar Chávez' United farm workers of America.   _____

12. Ex-Assemblyman Waldie never ran for <u>O</u>ffice after the <u>S</u>ummer of 1974. _____

13. Today he is Chairman of the Federal Mine Safety and Health Review Commission. ___C___

14. The residents of Mammoth Lakes, a mountain resort, are proud of the view of the <u>m</u>inarets, a ragged mountain range, seen from <u>h</u>ighway 395 as one approaches the resort. _____

15. One of my favorite books is a novel entitled *in the <u>h</u>eart of a <u>f</u>ool.* _____

16. Some women have romantic ideas about returning to feudalism, with knights in shining armor and ladies adhering to the manners of the Middle Ages. ___C___

17. One of the highest mountain systems in the world is Hindu Kush, extending 500 miles from <u>n</u>orth Pakistan into <u>n</u>ortheast Afghanistan. _____

18. William S. Levey, S.J., is the vice-president of an important men's club. ___C___

19. I failed Organic Chemistry 101, but I passed <u>f</u>rench. _____

20. A traditional American holiday is Thanksgiving <u>d</u>ay.

Self-Grading Exercise 21

1. personnel	6. occurrence	11. height	16. all right
2. separated	7. profession	12. too	17. led
3. conscious	8. prejudiced	13. villain	18. principle
4. exaggeration	9. environment	14. woman	19. losing
5. shining	10. explanation	15. similar	20. rhythm

Acknowledgments

THE CODE By Richard T. Gill. Reprinted by permission; © 1957, 1985, The New Yorker Magazine, Inc.

RICHARD CORY From *The Children of the Night* by Edwin Arlington Robinson (New York: Charles Scribner's Sons, 1897).

IT'S OVER, DEBBIE From *The Journal of the American Medical Association,* Jan. 8, 1988, v. 259, p. 272. Copyright 1988, American Medical Association.

MAROONED IN ALASKA Reprinted with the permission of Macmillan Publishing Company from *O Rugged Land of Gold* by Martha Martin. Copyright 1952, 1953 by Macmillan Publishing Company, renewed © 1980, 1981 by Christina H. Niemi.

THE LIMPING MAN OF MAKIN-MEANG From *A Pattern of Islands* by Arthur Grimble. Reprinted by permission; © 1952, Penguin Books Ltd.

THE DISCUS THROWER By Richard Selzer. *Harper's Magazine,* 1977.

COATS Reprinted by permission; © 1993 Jane Kenyon. Originally in *The New Yorker.*

COME ON IN From *The Journey Home: Some Words in Defense of the American West* by Edward Abbey. Copyright © 1977 by Edward Abbey. Reprinted by permission of the publisher, Dutton, an imprint of New American Library, a division of Penguin Books USA, Inc.

THE MONSTER From *Of Men and Music* by Deems Taylor. Reprinted by permission of Curtis Brown, Ltd. Copyright © 1937, 1965 by Deems Taylor.

PICKETT'S CHARGE AT THE BATTLE OF GETTYSBURG By Private John W. Haley, 117th Maine Regiment. From *The Rebel Yell and The Yankee Hurrah,* edited by Ruth L. Silliker. Reprinted by permission of the publisher, Down East Books, Camden, Maine.

THE ODORS OF HOMECOMING From PASSIONS AND IMPRESSIONS by Pablo Neruda, translated by Margaret Sayers Peden. Translation copyright © 1983 by Farrar, Straus & Giroux, Inc. Reprinted by permission of Farrar, Straus & Giroux, Inc.

WE'RE POOR From *Homecoming: An Autobiography* by Floyd Dell. Copyright 1933, © 1961 by Floyd Dell. Reprintd by permission of Henry Holt and Company, Inc.

LATE RISING By Jacques Prevert. Translated by Selden Rodman. From *One Hundred Modern Poems,* published by New American Library. Reprinted by permission of Selden Rodman.

Index